ASIAN HISTORICAL DICTIONARIES
Edited by Jon Woronoff

1. *Vietnam,* by William J. Duiker. 1989
2. *Bangladesh,* by Craig Baxter and Syedur Rahman. 1989
3. *Pakistan,* by Shahid Javed Burki. 1991
4. *Jordan,* by Peter Gubser. 1991
5. *Afghanistan,* by Ludwig W. Adamec. 1991

Historical Dictionary
of
AFGHANISTAN

by
Ludwig W. Adamec

Asian Historical Dictionaries, No. 5

The Scarecrow Press, Inc.
Metuchen, N.J., & London
1991

British Library Cataloguing-in-Publication data available

Library of Congress Cataloging-in-Publication Data

Adamec, Ludwig W.
    Historical dictionary of Afghanistan / by Ludwig W. Adamec
       p.   cm. -- (Asian historical dictionaries ; no. 5)
    Includes bibliographical references.
    ISBN 0-8108-2491-4 (acid-free paper)
    1. Afghanistan--History--Dictionaries. I. Title. II. Series.
DS356.A27 1991
958.1'003--dc20
                                                  91-31544

To Rahella

CONTENTS

EDITOR'S FOREWORD

Most Americans are only familiar with the recent, tragic period of Afghan history since it has been embroiled in great power struggles and underwent a long and painful war. But there is much more to Afghanistan than that. As this book shows, it is heir to a tradition of 3,500 years, replete with great kingdoms and celebrated leaders. It would be extremely useful for Americans, and others, who want to understand the recent past to take a look further back, to see where Afghanistan is coming from and get an inkling of where it may be going.

Thanks to numerous entries on the various periods, prominent figures and important events, this Afghanistan Historical Dictionary points the way. It makes the transition from one period to another easier with a comprehensive chronology. And it directs those who want to know more toward further literature on subjects that interest them. Even for the recent period, which we think we know best, it helps refresh our memory of "who is who" and what they did. I am therefore certain that this new volume will be particularly welcome.

It was written by Ludwig W. Adamec, professor of Near Eastern Studies at the University of Arizona in Tucson. He has considerable familiarity with Afghanistan, having visited it frequently and written on it extensively. Among others, he has produced works on Afghanistan's diplomatic history and foreign affairs, an historical gazetteer, a biographical dictionary, and a Who is Who. This has stood him in good stead for this book, which combines many of these facets and others.

Jon Woronoff
Series Editor

ACKNOWLEDGMENTS

It is my pleasant duty to express my thanks for the advice I have received from three well-known Afghan personalities. They saw portions of early typescripts and took the time to suggest a number of additions and changes. They are, Professor Rawan Farhadi, one-time deputy foreign minister for political affairs; Mr. Sayyid Qasem Reshtia, diplomat, cabinet member, and author of numerous historical works; and Ustad Abdur Rahman Pazhwak, a scholar and diplomat who was president of the 21st General Assembly of the United Nations. Dr. David Katz, an American diplomat and Afghanistan expert, read the entire manuscript and gave me the benefit of his advice. I had to produce a "camera-ready" copy of this book which involved greater expertise in computer technology than I could at times muster, and I was therefore fortunate to be able to draw on the superior computer skills of Dr. Katz when I was faced with some problem. Last, but not least, I owe thanks to my wife Rahella, who helped with numerous tasks, including the canvassing of materials in Persian and Pashto. Of course, any faults of omission or commission are solely my own.

Ludwig W. Adamec
Professor of Near Eastern Studies
The University of Arizona, Tucson

ABBREVIATIONS AND ACRONYMS

A.	Arabic
Af.	Afghani (monetary unit)
AIG	Afghan Interim Government
AGSA	Afghanistan Security Service
ASDP	Afghan Social Democratic Party, also called Afghan Millat
D.	Dari, the Farsi of Afghanistan
DRA	Democratic Republic of Afghanistan, later ROA
Harakat	*Harakat-i Inqilab-i Islami* of Muhammadi
Hizb (H)	*Hizb-i Islami* of Hekmatyar
Hizb (K)	*Hizb-i Islami* of Khales
Ittihad	*Ittihad-i Islami Barayi Azadi-yi Afghanistan* of Sayyaf
Jabha	*Jabha-yi Milli Najat-i Afghanistan* of Mujaddidi
Jam'iat	*Jam'iat-i Islami* of Rabbani
KAM	Workers' Information Service
KHAD	State Information Service
Khalq	Faction of the PDPA and its newspaper
MAHAZ	*Mahaz-i Milli* of Pir Gilani
Nasr	*Sazman-i Nasr* of Shaikh Mir Husain Sadeqi
NFF	National Fatherland Front
NFROA	National Front of the Republic of Afghanistan, formerly NFF
NIFA	English Acronym for *Mahaz*
NWFP	North-West Frontier Province of India, now Pakistan
P.	Pashto
Parcham	Faction of the PDPA and its newspaper
PDPA	Peoples Democratic Party of Afghanistan, now Watan Party
Q.v.	*Quod vide* (which see)
R.	Rupee (monetary unit)
ROA	Republic of Afghanistan, formerly DRA
SAZA	*Sazman-i Inqilab-i Zahmatkeshan-i Afghanistan*, Organization of the Revolutionary Toilers of Afghanistan
SCDH	Supreme Council for the Defense of the Homeland
Shu'la	*Shu'la-yi Javid*, name of a newspaper and party
T.	Turkic
WAD	Ministry of State Security, formerly KHAD

USER'S NOTES

Alphabetization and Spellings. Names beginning with "Abdul" (A. 'abd-al, meaning, servant or slave), followed by one of the names of Allah (God), as for example Abdul Ahad (Servant of the One) or Abdul Hakim (Servant of the Wise), form a unit and should not be taken as first and last names. Abdul Hakim will therefore be found under "A" not "H." Similarly, the name Ghulam (A. slave) and its complement, as for example Ghulam Muhammad, is found under "G" not "M." Compounds with Allah, like Fazlullah (Fazl Allah), Nurullah (Nur Allah), Habibullah (Habib Allah), will be found in alphabetical order under its compound version. Although not forming a construct, Afghan practice considers names beginning with Muhammad, as for example, Muhammad Daud, Muhammad Afzal, etc., one unit; therefore the names will be found be under "M."

The arrangement of entries in alphabetical order treats headings as if they were one word, disregarding punctuation marks; for example, Afghani is preceded by Afghan Hound and followed by Afghan Interim Government. Muhammadi is preceded by Muhammad Hashim and followed by Muhammad Ishaq, and Tanai, Lt. Gen. Shahnawaz is preceded by Tanai Coup.

Names of individuals are spelled in a modified form of transliteration, even if the person described has his own idiosyncratic spelling; for example, Cher Ali, or Scher Ali are spelled Shir Ali; Kayeum and Kayum are spelled Qayyum, and Abaucy is Abbasi. Variant spellings of names are cross listed. Titles and honorifics are not included in the entry headings.

Statistics. Population statistics are estimates for the pre-war (1979) period, unless otherwise indicated. Estimates of the Afghan population vary from 13 to 15.5 million; this includes about 2 million nomads. Measurements are throughout in the British, rather than the metric, system.

Nomenclature. Afghan rulers of the Sadozai branch of the Durranis (1747-1818) held the title "Shah," king; but the succeeding Barakzai rulers were known as "amirs," which means chief, prince, commander, as well as king. Amanullah assumed the title Shah in 1926; in order to avoid referring pedantically to Amanullah's title at a particular time, I have employed the appellation of "king" throughout.

Scope. The purpose of this volume is to provide a concise reference work on Afghanistan, including entries on major historical events, important places, leading personalities - past and present - and significant aspects of culture, religion, and economy. The focus is on the political history of contemporary Afghanistan. The reader who desires more extensive biographical information may refer to the biographical dictionaries by this author (1975 and 1987). Geographical and tribal information beyond the scope of this work can be found in the Gazetteers compiled by this author (1972-85, also see Bibliography). Although not definitive in scope, this work should provide a good introduction for the study of Afghanistan and a basis for more extensive study or research.

INTRODUCTION

Afghanistan, the "Land of the Afghans," began as a political entity in 1747 when Ahmad Shah (q.v., 1747-73) was crowned king of a tribal confederation; it is an ancient land with a glorious history of kingdoms dating back some 3,500 years. As part of the nation-building process, Afghan historians in the twentieth century popularized the idea of an organic link existing between modern Afghanistan and its ancient roots. They see a continuum from Ariana (q.v., 1,500 B.C.) of the Indo-Iranians, centered around Balkh, city of Zoroaster (q.v.), in northern Afghanistan to the Buddhist kingdom of the Kushanids (q.v., about 50-250 A.D.) with its capital in Peshawar and Bagram. Intermittently Afghanistan was peripheral to empires as a satrapy of the Achaemenid empire in the sixth century B.C., of Alexander the Great in the fourth century B.C., and the Maurian kingdom of Ashoka (q.v.) a century later.

Afghanistan's Islamic roots began with the Muslim Arab invasion in the 7th century A.D., but it was not until the tenth century that Islam was firmly established and not until the end of the nineteenth century that the last vestiges of pre-Islamic communities disappeared. The first indigenous Islamic state was the Ghaznawid empire (q.v., 977-1186), named after its capital Ghazni, a town in eastern Afghanistan. It was destroyed by the Ghorids (q.v., 1150-1217) whose capital was Ghor, a town in central Afghanistan. The domains of both empires included large portions of northern India. The Mongols wreaked destruction in the thirteenth century, as did Timur-i Lang (q.v.), almost two centuries later. Timur's descendants rebuilt Herat and made it a great cultural center. By the sixteenth century Afghanistan was again peripheral to powerful neighbors.

Almost simultaneously three empires emerged in the early sixteenth century: the Safavid rulers of Iran (1501-1786) who controlled portions of western Afghanistan; the Moghul rulers of India (1526-1858) who made Kabul their capital in 1504, until Babur (q.v., 1526-1530) and his successors established themselves in Delhi and Agra; and the Shaibanid Uzbaks (q.v., 1500-98) who founded a kingdom which extended from the plains north of the Hindu Kush (q.v.) far into Transoxania.

Modern Afghanistan was born as a result of revolt against foreign occupation. Mir Wais (q.v.), founder of the short-lived Hotaki dynasty (q.v., 1709-38), rose in rebellion against Gorgin Khan, the Safavid governor of Kandahar; he defeated the avenging Safvid armies and, encouraged by his

1

success, raided far into Iran. The Abdali (later Durrani) tribes liberated Herat, and Afghan tribes flocked to the banner of Mahmud, son of Mir Wais (1716-25), who beseiged Isfahan in the battle of Gulnabad (q.v.) in 1722 and ended the rule of the Safavid kings. The Hotaki Ghilzais were soldiers, not empire builders. They could not hold on to their conquests, and Nadir Shah Afshar (q.v., 1736-47) reunited Iran under his short-lived dynasty, which included Afghanistan and northern India.

Ahmad Shah commanded an Afghan contingent of Nadir Shah's army and, at the sudden death of the latter, was able to intercept a convoy of booty destined for Iran. This gave him the means to augment his forces and consolidate his power. Following the example of previous guardians of the "gateway to India," he led nine invasions into the Indian subcontinent and made himself the undisputed ruler of an empire to which Afghans refer as the "historical" Afghanistan. The boundaries of this state were the Amu Daria (q.v.) in the north, the Indus river in the east, the Indian Ocean in the south, and the present Iranian provinces of Khorasan and Sistan in the west. Ahmad Shah ruled a heterogeneous population which in addition to the dominant Pashtun element forming the core of his armies included a largely sedentary population of Dari/Farsi speakers, Turkic, and Baluch minorities, and a multitude of ethnic and sectarian groups.

The Afghan heartland is a mountain fastness, surrounded by deserts in the north, west, and south, with cultivation supported by five major river systems, dependent on melting snow from the mountains for irrigation. Subsistence agriculture, small-scale mining, and a handicraft industry for domestic consumption did not provide sufficient surplus wealth to support a lavish court. The ruling Durranis and allied tribes depended on a system of military feudalism which allocated agricultural lands to the chiefs in exchange for military service, corresponding to the size of their fiefs (*tiyul*). An alternative was territorial conquest. The Afghans saw it their manifest destiny to rule the fertile Panjab plains if not all of northern India.

A policy of conquest had definite advantages: it brought prosperity to the Pashtun tribes and kept them united. Ahmad Shah was not an absolute ruler; he was a *primus inter pares* who had to contend with the ambitions of the *khans*, the chiefs of the major tribes. It was for this reason that he also recruited a force of non-Pashtun *qizilbash* (q.v.) soldiers. When Timur (q.v.), one of Ahmad Shah's six sons, succeeded to the Afghan throne in 1773, he transferred the capital from Kandahar to Kabul, where he was more secure from the intrigues of the Kandahar chiefs. Described as "more a scholar than a soldier," Timur Shah faced revolt in the periphery of the empire. Shah Zaman (q.v.), one of Timur's twenty-three sons, ascended the throne in 1793, amid internecine warfare which led to the eventual demise of the Sadozai dynasty. Britain extended her control in India, and the emergence of the Sikh empire of Ranjit Singh (q.v., 1780-1839) in the Panjab definitely ended Afghan aspirations of eastward expansion.

At the beginning of the nineteenth century, Afghanistan became directly involved in European empire politics. In addition to Russia and Britain, France emerged as a contender in the "Great Game" for imperial conquest.

The first contact between a British envoy, Mountstuart Elphinstone (q.v.), and an Afghan ruler (Shah Shuja, q.v., 1803-10 and 1839) took place at Peshawar in February 1809 and led to an alliance against a Franco-Persian invasion which, however, never materialized. The next, more fateful encounter, was the first of three Anglo-Afghan wars (q.v., 1839-42).

In 1600 the British East India Company obtained a charter for exploration and commerce in Bengal, India, and a century-and-a-half later, the company was the *de facto* ruler of Bengal. Its Board of Control appointed a governor-general as executive who conducted the government for the Company until 1858, when the crown ended the charter and appointed a viceroy, subject to the control of the London government. At the same time Britain continued its territorial conquests and started to worry about how to protect its new acquisitions from Afghan attacks or from Russian expansionism, which had reached Persia's borders in the Caucasus.

When Dost Muhammad (q.v., 1835-39 and 1842-63), first of the Barakzai amirs, ascended the Kabul throne in 1835, Persia occupied Khorasan with Russian support and beseiged Herat, while Ranjit Singh conquered Multan, Kashmir, Derajat, and Peshawar. Fearing an Afghan alliance with Russia, Lord Auckland, governor-general of the East India Company, decided to restore Shah Shuja (q.v.) to the Afghan throne. The British invasion, though initially successful, resulted in a disastrous defeat in the first Anglo-Afghan war. The British government refrained for almost 40 years from conducting a "forward" policy at its northwestern frontier. However, Russian advances in Central Asia continued and voices in London and Delhi demanded a new policy and consolidation of a "scientific" frontier for the defense of India. In 1877 the Queen of England was proclaimed empress of India and a year later, British-Indian armies again invaded Afghanistan. Amir Shir Ali (q.v., 1863-79), who had negotiated with a Russian envoy at Kabul, was forced to seek refuge in northern Afghanistan where he died shortly afterwards. He was succeeded by his son Muhammad Yaqub (q.v.) who signed the Treaty of Gandamak (q.v., 1879) and permitted a permanent British mission to be established in Kabul. Insurrection and the massacre of the British envoy and his staff led to the demise of Yaqub Khan and recognition in 1880 of Abdur Rahman Khan as the next Afghan ruler.

With Amir Abdur Rahman (q.v., 1880-1901), the traditional system of rule came to an end. The "Iron Amir" no longer appointed princes as governors of major provinces, a practice which had led to much strife in the past. He ended the local autonomy of Uzbak khans in the north, Hazaras in the center, and the Kafirs in the east of Afghanistan. Abdur Rahman reconquered the country and expelled or killed any of the notables who could pose a threat to his power. He claimed both the highest secular and spiritual powers and limited the influence of the *ulama* (q.v., religious establishment) and the tribes. His reign marked the beginning of centralized rule and the bureaucratization of the government. His regular army gradually replaced feudal and irregular levies, ending the system of military feudalism. An alliance with Britain protected Afghanistan from unprovoked Russian aggression and provided the funds and weapons to eliminate all domestic challenges to his power. In exchange, the Afghan ruler agreed to conduct his relations with neighboring states through the medium of the British government. Abdur Rahman formulated a foreign policy which served Afghanistan well, until King Amanullah (q.v., 1919-29) in the third Anglo-Afghan war (q.v., 1919) ended the country's dependence on Britain. A window to the West, which gradually had begun to open when Amir Habibullah (q.v., 1901-19) received a German mission during World War I, was thrown wide open under King Amanullah. Afghanistan established diplomatic relations with major European and Asian countries.

A contemporary of Kemal Ataturk of Turkey and Reza Shah of Iran, Amanullah ushered in Western reforms and first introduced the institutions of constitutional government. A short period of reaction under Habibullah Kalakani (q.v., 1929) did not end the process of modernization, most visible in the expansion of education during the reigns of Nadir Shah (q.v., 1929-33) and his son Zahir Shah (q.v., 1933-73).

The fact that the experiment with democracy in the 1960s ended in failure, war, and foreign intervention should not be surprising. The socioeconomic conditions which favor a trend to a stable, if not democratic, government still did not exist. Muhammad Daud (q.v.) felt that strong leadership was required; he revolted against his cousin, the king, and established a republican form of government, taking direct command of the affairs of the state. He was toppled from power in 1978 by his Marxist supporters who thought they had a cure for the socioeconomic ills of the country. Feeling secure about receiving Soviet support, the Marxist government initiated unpalatable innovations which resulted in armed resistance and civil war. It evolved into a war of liberation, after the Soviets intervened in support of the Kabul government.

During almost 250 years of its existence, Afghanistan has evolved from empire to state and may be on its way to becoming a nation. It has progressed from rule by a Pashtun warrior caste, followed by civil war, to a more cohesive system established by Amir Abdur Rahman and continued until the 1970s. It was only as a result of the present war in Afghanistan that bureaucratic urban control has given way to autonomy of the countryside. Its inaccessible terrain and the existence of two imperialist neighbors have defined Afghanistan's "natural" borders, and three wars against Britain and one against the Soviet Union have welded a heterogeneous population together.

The departure of Soviet troops from Afghanistan in February 1989 raised hopes that peace would be quickly restored and a popularly elected government could promptly begin the arduous task of political and economic reconstruction. The war has resulted in the emergence of new elites and the politicization of rural Afghanistan; but sectarian and ethnic strife has continued as has interference by foreign powers. The "Afghanistan Crisis," which once attracted the attention of the world, has disappeared from the headlines of the international press and is now seen by many as merely the last confrontation of the cold war era. The devolution of the Soviet empire, the war in Iraq and its aftermath, starvation and catastrophies in Africa and

Asia, and the needs of the developing states in eastern Europe make it unlikely that Afghanistan will again be the center of international attention. Afghans are increasingly left to resolve their political and economic problems as best as they can. An optimistic view of the future would hold that the willingness to compromise will prevail and that peace and a measure of prosperity can be achieved by a government which enjoys the support of the majority of its people.

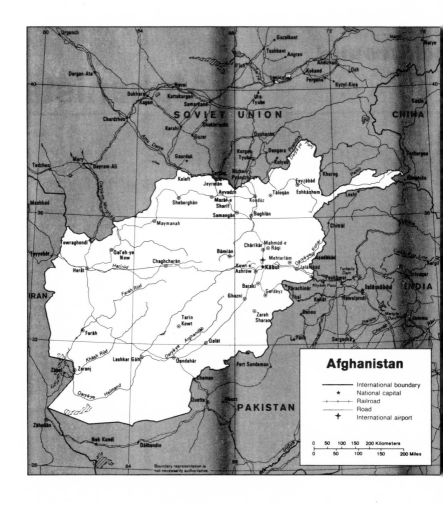

Afghanistan

— International boundary
★ National capital
╫ Railroad
— Road
✈ International airport

| 0 | 50 | 100 | 150 | 200 Kilometers |
| 0 | | 50 | 100 | 150 | 200 Miles |

Boundary representation is
not necessarily authoritative.

ABDALI. The original name of the Durrani, the royal Pashtun tribe, located in the Kandahar area. They claim descent from Tarin and his youngest son Bar Tarin, or Abdal, hence their name Abdali. In 1747 Pir Sabir Shah, a sufi shaikh, proclaimed Ahmad Khan of the Abdali tribe king, *"Badshah, Durr-i Dauran"* (King, the Pearl of the Age), which Ahmad Shah later changed to *Durr-i Durran* (Pearl of Pearls). His Abdali tribe became henceforth known as the Durrani. See AHMAD SHAH and DURRANI.

ABDUL AHAD, GENERAL See **MALIKYAR, ABDUL AHAD.**

ABDUL GHAFUR, MIR See **RAHIM, MIR ABDUL GHAFUR.**

ABDUL GHANI. An Indian Muslim, born in 1864 and educated in Gujrat, Panjab. He went to England in 1885 where he met Sardar Nasrullah, son of Amir Abdur Rahman, and obtained a scholarship for study in England from the amir. In 1890 he came to Kabul to serve as private secretary to Amir Abdur Rahman. Subsequently he served for three years as principal of the Islamia College at Lahore, but returned to Afghanistan under Amir Habibullah and was appointed chief medical officer, director of public instruction in Afghanistan, and principal of Habibia school. He was a champion of political and social reform and attracted a circle of "Young Afghans" who formed a secret organization called *sirr-i milli* (Secret of the Nation). In 1909 he and a number of his followers were arrested for having plotted against the life of Amir Habibullah. He was freed when King Amanullah ascended the throne and was appointed a member of the Afghan delegation to the peace conference at Rawalpindi in August 1919. He subsequently returned to India and wrote about Afghanistan and Central Asia. He died in 1945. See SIRR-I MILLI.

ABDUL HADI DAWAI See **DAWAI, ABDUL HADI.**

ABDUL HAQ (ABD AL-HAQQ). A mujahedin commander affiliated with the *hizb-i Islami* (Islamic Party) of Yunus Khales (q.v.) who had been active in the Kabul area. He is an Ahmadzai Pashtun, born about 1958 near Jalalabad, and as a student was affiliated with the Islamic Youth (*jawanan-i musulman*) which opposed the reformist regime of President

7

Muhammad Daud. He was imprisoned in 1975 and freed in 1978, after the Saur Revolt. He was based in the Shiwaki area, south of Kabul, and was responsible for organizing guerrilla attacks on government posts within Kabul. In 1987 he suffered a crippling injury to his foot which prevented him from more than occasional forays into Afghanistan from his headquarters in Peshawar. Also see ISLAMIST MOVEMENT.

ABDULILLAH, SAYYID. Minister of finance (1973), second deputy prime minister (1975), and vice president (1977); he was close to President Daud and was said to have been groomed to be his successor as president of the republic. Born about 1945 and educated in Kabul, he began his career in the ministry of interior and subsequently was director of the foreign exchange department at the Pashtanai-Tejarati Bank. He was killed in the palace together with President Daud and members of his family on April 28, 1978.

ABDUL KARIM. A Ghilzai mulla, the son of Din Muhammad, the famous mulla Mushk-i- Alam (q.v.). Amir Abdur Rahman gave him the title "Khan-i-Ulum" (Chief of [religious] Sciences), but he became disaffected when the amir ended the virtual autonomy enjoyed by the Ghilzai tribes and imposed taxes on hitherto exempt lands. He was one of the leaders of the Ghilzai Rebellion of 1886-87, which was suppressed only with great difficulty. It was the last of three uprising of this tribe in the 19th century. Also see GHILZAI.

ABDUL KHALIQ. Son of a Hazara servant of Ghulam Nabi Charkhi (executed by King Nadir), who avenged the killing of his master by assassinating Nadir Shah a year later on November 8, 1933. He was a student at Najat (Amani) high school and attended a graduation ceremony in the palace garden where the assassination took place. He was handed over to the King's bodyguard for execution. A number of relatives, students, and teachers of Najat and Istiqlal schools were executed in December 1933. This was the last bloodletting in the struggle for power between supporters of King Amanullah and the new royal family. Also see MUHAMMAD AZIM, WALI MUHAMMAD, and GHULAM NABI CHARKHI.

ABDULLAH, SAYYID WAHID (ABD ALLAH). Deputy minister of foreign affairs, 1973-77, and acting foreign minister under President Daud until the Saur Revolt. He entered the Afghan foreign service and was assigned to Afghan embassies in Tehran, Ankara, and London. He was executed in May, 1978, after a short confinement in prison.

ABDUL MAJID. President of Kabul University (1947), minister of health (1948-51), education (1951-56), justice (1973), and without a portfolio (1977) in the last year of President Daud's government. He served as ambassador at Tokyo (1956-63), Washington (1963-67), and London (1967-69). He was born in 1914 and educated in the United States. A supporter of Prime Minister Daud in 1965, he was imprisoned (or under house arrest) in the early Marxist period and left Afghanistan in 1984 for the United States, where he died in 1988.

ABDUL QADIR, MAJ. GEN. A Parchami member of the PDPA. Commander of the Air Defense Forces in 1973, when he supported Muhammad Daud in his coup against Zaher Shah. Actively participated in the Saur Revolt and was head of the Revolutionary Council until a civilian government was formed under Nur Muhammad Taraki. He became minister of defense for three months in May 1978, but in August he was sentenced to death (commuted to 15 years) for plotting against the Khalqi regime. Freed when Babrak Karmal came to power, he was restored to his party positions and served as minister of defense (September 1982-85). In November 1985 he resigned from the Politburo for "reasons of health" and in November 1986 was appointed ambassador to Warsaw. Recalled two years later and elected a lowly member of parliament, he is said to have moved to Bulgaria in 1989. Born 1944 of a Tajik family in Herat province, he went to military school and attended pilot training and staff college in the Soviet Union.

ABDUL QUDDUS. A nephew of Amir Dost Muhammad (q.v.) and general who lived with Amir Abdur Rahman (q.v.) in exile in Bukhara and Samarkand. On their return, he assisted the Amir in extending his power over Afghanistan. He captured Herat from Ayyub Khan, son of Amir Shir Ali (q.v.), in 1881 and subsequently the Hazarajat. Amir Habibullah gave him the title *Itimad-ud-Daula* (Confidence of the State) and appointed him prime minister, in which position he was confirmed by King Amanullah. In the third Anglo-Afghan war Abdul Quddus commanded the Kandahar front. A British officer characterized him as "A Tory of the most crusted type in politics, and an apostle of Afghanistan for the Afghans." His descendants who were prominent in Afghan government adopted his title, Etemadi, as their family name. See ETEMADI.

ABDUL RAHIM. A Safi general from Kuh Daman, north of Kabul, who from the age of 16 served in various military units and rose from the ranks to become general. At the outbreak of the civil war in 1928 he espoused the cause of Habibullah Kalakani (q.v.). He captured Maimana and Herat for Habibullah and became governor of Herat. Having a powerful base in Herat, the Afghan king was unable to remove him from his post until 1934. In June 1936 he was appointed minister of public works and subsequently served as deputy prime minister from 1938 to 1940. He was imprisoned in the 1940s on suspicion of plotting against the government of Prime Minister Hashim. Abdur Rahim is the maternal uncle and father-in-law of Khalilullah Khalili (q.v.).

ABDUL RAHMAN, AMIR (ABDUR RAHMAN, 1880-1901). Amir of Afghanistan the oldest son of Amir Muhammad Afzal Khan (q.v.) who assumed the Kabul throne at the end of the second Anglo-Afghan war. He fought his uncle Amir Shir Ali (q.v.) in 1864 and was forced to flee to the court of the Amir of Bukhara. Returned to Afghanistan in 1866, he defeated Amir Shir Ali and recognized his father, Afzal Khan, as the new king. Three years later Amir Shir Ali regained the throne and Abdur Rahman was forced into exile, spending some ten years in Bukhara, Tashkent, and Samarkand. After the death of Amir Shir Ali in February 1879, Abdur Rahman Khan returned to Afghanistan and on his way south gathered a large army. The British occupation force feared a repetition of the debacle of the first Anglo-Afghan war and, on July 22, 1880, grudgingly recognized Abdur Rahman as "Amir of Kabul and its Dependencies," in spite of the fact that he had come with Russian support. In September 1881 the amir took possession of Kandahar, defeating the forces of Ayub Khan (q.v.), son of Amir Shir Ali. Herat was taken in August, and Abdur Rahman was undisputed ruler of Afghanistan.

Abdur Rahman concluded an agreement with the British government, by which Britain guaranteed him protection from unprovoked Russian aggression, provided he permitted Britain to conduct his foreign relations. He obtained a subsidy in money and materiel to strengthen the defenses of his country. Abdur Rahman considered this treaty an alliance between equals and, having protected his northern borders, he kept the British at arms length, never allowing them to gain any influence in the country under the aegis of their common defense. He formulated a "buffer-state policy" which aimed at playing off Afghanistan's imperialist neighbors against each other. This policy served Afghanistan well until the end of World War II, when changed conditions required new approaches in the conduct of Afghan foreign policy. Afghanistan's northern and eastern boundaries were demarcated during the Amir's tenure, including the Durand Line (1893), which he accepted under "duress" in the Durand Agreement (q.v.). He built the Bagh-i Jahan Noma in Khulm, the Salam Khana castle in Mazar-i Sharif, and in Kabul the Masji-i Idgah, the Arg, the Shahrara tower, and the Bagh-i Bala castle. Abdur Rahman died in 1901 and was buried in Bustan Saray in Kabul.

The amir was an impressive personality, being "of middle height, inclined to be fat, and of sound and masculine face and features. He wore a full beard...was hard-working...in State affairs he consulted none.... He had a curious Afghan humour, and a peculiar fascinating attitude towards all his servants, who dreaded him, yet loved him." He had five wives and two concubines. Of his five sons Habibullah and Nasrullah succeeded to the throne; the latter was amir only for three days.

ABDUL WAKIL. Member of the Parcham faction of the PDPA and minister of foreign affairs since 1986. Born in 1947 in Bagrami district and educated at Habibia Shool and Kabul University, where he obtained a degree in economics. A member of the PDPA since 1965, he was repeatedly arrested for his political activities. After the Saur Revolt he served as general secretary in the ministry of foreign affairs for two months and was then sent as ambassador to London in July 1978. Purged by the Khalqi regime, he remained abroad until the return of the Parchamis to power. Babrak Karmal (his cousin) appointed him finance minister in 1980 and ambassador to Hanoi in 1984, and Dr. Najibullah appointed him as ambassador in Prague in 1986, before he assumed the position of foreign minister. Said to be Pashtun.

ABDUL WALI. Commander-in-chief of the Central Forces until 1973. Imprisoned as a result of the coup by his cousin Muhammad Daud in 1973. Born in 1924, the son of Marshal Shah Wali ([q.v.] and cousin of ex-King Zahir). Educated in France and England where he attended Sandhurst as well as the Command and General Staff College at Camberley. He is married to Princess Bilqis, daughter of the former King Muhammad Zaher, and has been living in Italy since 1976, where he acts as a spokesman for the former king.

ABDUL ZAHIR. Minister of health (1956 and 1964), president of Parliament (1961- 64), he became prime minister in 1971. Born in 1909 in Laghman and educated in the United States where he received the M.D. degree from Columbia University in 1944. Served as ambassador in Pakistan, Italy, and India. He died on October 21, 1982.

ABI. Irrigated land in Afghanistan (from D. *ab*, water), as distinct from *lalmi* land which is dependent on "dry-farming" agriculture. Only about 12 percent of Afghanistan's area of 245,000 square miles is cultivable land.

AB-I ISTADA (lat. 32-32' N, long. 67-57' E). "Standing Water," a brackish lake of some 17 miles in length, located astride the border of Ghazni and Paktika provinces, about 65 miles south-southwest of Ghazni and 44 miles northeast of Kalat-i-Ghilzai. It is a shallow lake and reaches a depth of 12 feet only at its center. The banks of the lake are encrusted with salt and its major feeder is the Ghazni river. The lake is at an altitude of more than 7,000 feet and the surrounding land is barren with few permanent settlements. In spite of the desolate surroundings the lake is populated by multitudes of flamingoes and other birds.

AB-I WAKHAN (lat. 37-0' N, long. 72-40' E). A river which rises southwest of the Wakhjir Pass in the eastern Wakhan Corridor and runs in a westerly direction as far as the small town of Ishkashem when its name changes to Ab-i-Panj (or Panja) which forms part of the northeastern boundary with the Soviet Union. See WAKHAN.

ABU HANIFA (AL-NU'MAN B. THABIT B. ZUTA). A legal scholar and founder of the Hanafite school, one of the four orthodox schools (*madhhab*) of Islamic jurisprudence. His grandfather is said to have been taken prisoner in Kabul and transported to Kufa, an early Arab town on the Euphrates river in present Iraq, where Abu Hanifa was born. He studied at Kufa and gradually gained influence as an authority on legal questions, founding a rationalist school which became named after him. Afghanistan adheres to the Hanafite interpretation of Islamic law which is the largest in number of adherents and the most liberal of the four schools and permits a certain amount of personal reasoning and free judgment in arriving at legal decisions. Abu Hanifa died in 767 A.D.

ACHAKZAI. An important subtribe of the Durranis, located in an area east of Kandahar. The eponymic ancestor of the Achakzai was Achak Khan, a grandson of Barak Khan. Smaller communities of Achakzai are also found in Herat and Farah as well as in Chaman, Pakistan. See Durrani.

ADMINISTRATIVE DIVISIONS. Since the time Timur Shah (q.v., 1773-93) made it his capital, Kabul has been the center of the kingdom, and princes ruled more or less autonomously in the provinces. Major provinces headed by princes included Kandahar, Herat, Afghan Turkestan, and Qataghan and Badakhshan. Amir Abdur Rahman (q.v., 1880-1901) was recognized by Britain as "Amir of Kabul and its Dependencies," and he saw to it that Herat, Afghan Turkestan, the Hazarajat, Nuristan, and Badakhshan were part of his realm. Under Nadir Shah (q.v., 1929-33) Afghanistan was divided into five major and four minor provinces.
As a result of the Constitution of 1964, Afghanistan was divided into 26 provinces (*wilayat,*) each with a provincial center (*markaz*) which is graded according to importance into first, second, or third grade; Kabul, Ghazni, Gardez, Jalalabad, Mazar-i-Sharif, Herat, and Kandahar are first grade administrative centers. They are headed by a governor, *wali*, who is the executive officer, responsible to the ministry of interior in Kabul. In addition, each province has representatives of various departments at the administrative center who report directly to Kabul. There were also a number of subprovinces, *loy woluswali*, which have since been absorbed into provinces. Each province is subdivided into districts, *woluswali*, with an administrator called *woluswal*, who is responsible to his supervising governor and may himself be in charge of one or more subdistricts, *alaqadari*. The administrator of a subdistrict, *alaqadar*, resides in a major village and is responsible to all his supervising administrators. Districts are divided into four grades, depending on population. Not counting Sar-i-Pul, a Hazara province recently established, the 26 provinces were in the 1970s divided into six subprovinces, 175 districts, and 118 subdistricts. Villages and rural subdivisions or *qarya*, are headed by a village headman (*qaryadar, malik,* or *arbab*) who acts as a link between the rural population and the district chief. Cities are divided into wards, or *nahiya*. The table below provides population statistics for Afghan provinces:

Province	Area	Population	Wols.	Alaq.	Center
Badakhshan	48,176	484,000	5	7	Faizabad
Badghis	21,854	247,000	4	1	Qala-i-Nau
Baglan	17,165	486,000	5	4	Baghlan

Balkh	11,833	570,000	7	3	Mazar-i Sharif
Bamian	17,411	285,000	4	2	Bamian
Farah	58,834	356,000	8	2	Farah
Fariab	22,274	547,000	7	5	Maimana
Ghazni	32,797	701,000	10	12	Ghazni
Ghor	38,658	341,000	5	1	Chagh-charan
Helmand	61,816	570,000	8	4	Lashkargah
Herat	50,245	685,000	11	1	Herat
Jozjan	25,548	642,000	5	6	Shiberghan
Kabul	4,583	1,372,000	8	4	Kabul
Kandahar	49,430	699,000	11	4	Kandahar
Kunduz	7,926	575,000	5	1	Kunduz
Laghman	7,227	387,000	4	1	Mehterlam
Logar	4,409	424,000	3	3	Pul-i-Alam
Maidan (1)	9,699	310,000	4	4	Kota-i Ashro
Nangarhar (2)	18,636	786,000	17	14	Jalalabad
Nimruz	41,347	112,000	3	1	Zaranj
Oruzgan	28,756	483,000	8	-	Tirinkot
Paktia (3)	17,772	706,000	11	21	Gardez
Parwan	5,911	418,000			Charikar
Kapisa	5,358	366,000			Mahmud Raqi
Samangan	16,640	275,000	3	2	Aibak
Takhar	12,325	528,000	6	5	Taloqan
Zabul	17,298	181,000	5	3	Qalat
(1) Also called Wardak. (2) Including Kunar. (3) Including Paktika.					

(Groetzbach, 1990)

In the 1960's the Afghan government estimated the Afghan population at about 16 million and yearly added 2.6 percent to this number, until in the 1970s a demographic survey by a team from New York University arrived at a much lower fugure (10,020,600). Hamidullah Amin and Gordon B. Schilz in their *A Geography of Afghanistan.* (Omaha, 1976) give an agricultural population of 10,839,870 and 2,500,000 nomads for a total of 13,339,870. The government of Hafizullah Amin claimed a population of 15.5 million; Goetzbach's estimate (1990) agrees with this figure.

AFGHAN. A citizen of Afghanistan. Until the early twentieth century only Pashto-speakers were referred to as Afghans, whereas other citizens of Afghanistan were called by their ethnic designations (i.e., Nuristani or Hazara). In the process of nation-building, the term gained acceptance as a designation for all citizen of Afghanistan.

AFGHAN ACADEMY (PASHTO TOLANA). Founded in 1937 as a national umbrella organization for research in the social sciences and humanities. It was fashioned initially by combining the Literary Society (*anjoman-i adabi*) of Kabul, founded in 1930, with the Pashto Society (*anjoman-i Pashto*) of Kandahar, founded in 1931. The Literary Society promoted research in the social sciences and humanities and conducted cultural and scientific relations with foreign countries. In 1932 it began publishing the *Kabul Yearbook* (q.v.) which appeared without interruption until 1981. The Pashto Society was to promote Pashto language and literature with the objective of making it the official language of Afghanistan to replace Dari from its preeminent position as the language of the court, the government, and education. The Pashto Society office was moved to Kabul in 1935 and two years later the two societies were merged into one institution, the Pashto Tolana. It was headed by Salahuddin Saljuqi with Sardar Muhammad Naim (q.v.), a brother of President Daud, as the honorary president. The Academy was under the administrative control of the department of press. It subsequently included the institutes of social sciences, natural sciences, and languages and literature, the international center for Pashto studies, and a number of general directorates for press, encyclopedia and dictionary production. It finally came under the direction of the ministry of education and was headed by leading scholars and writers, such as Abdur Rahman Pazhwak, 1941-?; Abdur Rauf Benawa, 1946-51; Siddiqullah Rishtin, 1951-56; Gul Pacha Ulfat, 1956-?; and Siddiq Ruhi, 1973-79. After the Saur Revolt the Afghan Academy was renamed the Academy of Sciences. Sulaiman Layeq was appointed president in 1980, and in 1986 it included, in addition to three vice presidents, also eight academicians, 32 candidate academicians, and 22 members who are in charge of various journals and research institutes.

AFGHAN CONSTITUTIONAL DEVELOPMENT See CONSTITUTIONAL DEVELOPMENT.

AFGHAN DYNASTIES See SADOZAI and MUHAMMADZAI.

AFGHAN ENCYCLOPEDIA SOCIETY (ARIANA DA'ERAT AL- MA'AREF). An organization within the Pashto Tolana (Afghan Academy, q.v.) whose principal task was the production of an encyclopedia in Dari and Pashto, published by the Afghan Government Press. The project was started in 1941 under the sponsorship of Sardar Muhammad Naim (q.v.); Mia Husain Mujaddidi, a subsequent finance minister, was its first director. The Dari version comprises six volumes: the first volume was published in 1948 and the last in 1970. The project was overly ambitious, the first five volumes (A-F) each numbering one thousand pages and the sixth covering subjects for the rest of the alphabet in 371 pages. Insufficient funding was given as the reason for ending this monumental project. Leading Afghan scholars contributed articles for this work which was patterned in scope after major Western encyclopedias.

AFGHAN FOREIGN RELATIONS. Afghanistan's relations with her neighbors were always influenced by the fact that the territory inhabited by the Afghans was the "gateway" to the Indian subcontinent. The power that controlled the tribes and the passes leading south and east would not encounter any great physical obstacles in the conquest of the subcontinent and its fabulous riches. Mahmud of Ghazni (q.v., 988-1030), Tamerlane (q.v., Timur-i Lang, 1370-1405), and Nadir Shah Afshar (q.v., 1736-47) crossed the Afghan passes for the propagation of Islam, for glory, and for booty. It is therefore not surprising that Ahmad Shah Durrani (q.v., 1747-73), the founder of the state of Afghanistan, saw it his manifest destiny to create an empire which included a large portion of northern India. He invaded India eight times and defeated the powerful Mahratta confederation at the Battle of Panipat, north of Delhi, in 1761. But by the turn of the century, the gradual northwest expansion of British influence resulted in a confrontation between Britain and Afghanistan which was to continue into the twentieth century. Afghanistan's foreign relations can be divided into five major periods: First, the expansionist period, which lasted from 1747 to 1800; second, the period of foreign conflict, from 1800 to 1880, which involved Afghanistan in hostilities with Persia and the rising Sikh nation in the Punjab as well as with Britain and Russia; third, the period of defensive isolationism and "buffer-state" politics, initiated by Amir Abdur Rahman (1880-1901) and continued by Amir Habibullah (1901-1919) until his death; fourth, the period of defensive neutralism which opened Afghanistan to foreign influences and lasted until after World War II when Britain's departure from India ushered in a new era of peaceful coexistence which, nevertheless, ended with the Marxist coup in 1978 and the Soviet intervention. The final, fifth period, was one of close cooperation with the Soviet Union.

During the expansionist period Afghan rulers conquered territories north of the Hindu Kush and east of the Indus river, but internecine fighting among the Durrani *sardars* (princes and chiefs) and the emergence of new players in the "Great Game" in Central Asia made the Afghan empire a short-lived enterprise. When in 1798 Zaman Shah (q.v.) invited the Marquess Wellesley, governor of Bengal (1798- 1805), to join him in a campaign against the Mahratta confederacy of northwestern India, Wellesley sought Persian assistance "to keep Zaman Shah in perpetual check." The period of foreign conflict saw the emergence of the Sikh nation under Ranjit Singh (q.v.) and the loss of the Punjab to the Afghans. Britain saw the appearance of a French mission in Tehran in 1807 a threat to India, and the Russian territorial gains in the Caucasus were feared to lead to an increase in Russian influence in Persia. Therefore, in 1908 the British governor-general, Lord Minto, sent Mountstuart Elphinstone (q.v.) to Peshawar to conclude a treaty of friendship and common defense against Franco-Persian attacks. Shah Shuja (q.v.), who had ascended the Kabul throne, obligated himself, in exchange for military support, to prohibit Frenchmen from entering his realm. This treaty as well as others concluded between Britain and Fath Ali Shah, the ruler of Persia, were "inoperative" almost as soon as they were ratified. Shah Shuja was ousted in 1810 and, after an interval of internecine fighting, the Muhammadzai branch of the Durranis replaced the Sadozai rulers.

Dost Muhammad (q.v.), a capable ruler, succeeded to the throne in 1826. He wanted British friendship, but also wanted to regain Peshawar from Ranjit Singh whose forces had conquered Multan in 1810, Kashmir in 1819, and Peshawar in 1823. But Lord Auckland, governor- general of British India (1836-42), favored a forward policy; he concluded the Tripartite Agreement of July 1838 (q.v.) with Ranjit Singh and Shah Shuja to restore the Shah to the Kabul throne. Dost Muhammad's negotiations with a purported Russian envoy and the amir's hostility to the Sikh ruler were the *casus belli*, and the Simla Manifesto of 1838 (q.v.), issued by the British government, constituted the declaration of war. The "Army of the Indus," as it was proudly called in India, invaded Afghanistan in what came to be known as the first Anglo- Afghan war (q.v.). Once installed on the Kabul throne, Shah Shuja was unable to consolidate his power even with British support. The British forces were forced to negotiate an ignominious retreat which resulted in the virtual annihilation of the "Army of the Indus" See ANGLO-AFGHAN WARS.

This extraordinary setback for Britain led to the restoration of Dost Muhammad to the throne (1842-63). Like Shah Shuja he had been in Indian exile and his return to Kabul began the rule of the Muhammadzai (q.v.) dynasty, a collatoral branch of the Sadozai, which lasted until 1973. The British-Indian government resigned itself to a period of "masterly inactivity" which left Afghanistan to revert to civil war following the succession of Amir Shir Ali in 1863. But the search for a "scientific" frontier and the desire to fill a "power vacuum" in Afghanistan led to a return to a forward policy. Baluchistan came under British control in 1879 and the Indian government had to decide where its boundary with Afghanistan should be: the crest of the Hindu Kush, the Amu Daria, or the tribal belt of the northwestern frontier? Lacking any direct control over Afghanistan, Britain wanted envoys stationed at Herat and Kabul who could guard Indian interests in those vital areas. Amir Shir Ali was willing to forge an alliance with Britain, but he wanted protection from Russian aggression, a subsidy in weapons and funds, and British recognition of his son, Abdullah Jan, as his successor. When he could not obtain a clear commitment from Britain, he listened to the overtures of General Kaufmann, the Russian governor general of Turkestan province, and permitted a mission under General Stolietov to proceed to Kabul. The Russians promised "that if any foreign enemy attacks Afghanistan and the Amir is unable to drive him out ... The Russian Government will repel the enemy either by means of advice or by such other means as it may seem proper."

The British government now insisted that the Amir receive a mission, headed by General Neville Chamberlain with an escort of 1000 men. Shir Ali asked for a postponement of the mission, but the mission proceeded in spite of the wishes of the amir. When it was stopped at the Afghan frontier, Britain presented an ultimatum and on January 8, 1879, British troops occupied Kandahar in the start of the Second Anglo-Afghan war (q.v.). The promised Russian support was in the form of "advice," namely that the amir should make his peace with the British. Shir Ali felt betrayed; he was forced to flee and died two months later near Mazar-i Sharif.

His son Yaqub Khan (q.v.) succeeded to the throne at the cost of ceding territory to British India in the Treaty of Gandamak (See GANDAMAK, TREATY OF) and permitting Sir Louis Cavagnari to come to Kabul to head a permanent British mission. History repeated itself when the members of this British mission were also massacred in Kabul. General Roberts (q.v.), son of Sir Abraham Roberts (q.v.), the commander of Shah Shuja's forces during the first Anglo-Afghan war, occupied Kabul. In the meantime other contenders for the Kabul throne came to the fore. Ayub Khan, another son of Shir Ali, wiped out General Burrows' forces in the Battle of Maiwand (1880, q.v.), and Abdur Rahman Khan, a grandson of Amir Dost Muhammad, entered Afghanistan after twelve years in Central Asian exile. To avoid disaster and to extricate their forces from Afghanistan, the British found it advisable to recognize Abdur Rahman as amir of "Kabul and its Dependencies."

Amir Abdur Rahman (q.v., 1880-1901) was quick to eliminate all rivals to his power. He united the country, initiated domestic reforms, and formulated a foreign policy which served Afghanistan well until World War I. He fashioned a cautious alliance with Britain which obligated Britain to defend Afghanistan from unprovoked Russian aggression and strengthened his power with aid in money and arms. Abdur Rahman agreed to conduct his relations with foreign powers through the intermediary of the British government. Having protected himself from the danger in the north, the Amir formulated a policy which was to prevent Britain from gaining influence within his domains under the aegis of their common defense. This policy rested on the following triad: militant assertion of independence, defensive isolationism, and a balancing of the pressures by the two imperialist neighbors.

The "Iron Amir" considered his agreement with Britain an alliance between equals in which the two partners contributed to their common defense. He would not accept Afghanistan's status as a British protectorate. He permitted the establishment in Kabul of a British agency, headed by an Indian Muslim whose sphere of activity was strictly limited, but refused to accept British civilian or military advisers and declined an offer of British help in extending the Indian rail system into Afghanistan. Although in 1893 he accepted under "duress" the Durand Line (q.v.) which cut large portions of Pashtun territory from the Afghan state, he did not assist in the complete demarcation of the border and continued to lay claim to the free "unadministered" tribal belt which constituted a kind of buffer between the two states. When Britain made punitive expeditions into this area, the Afghan ruler supported the tribes with shipments of arms and granted fugitives from India shelter in his domains.

Amir Abdur Rahman was on a state visit in India in 1885 when Russian troops moved into the Panjdeh oasis (See PANJDEH INCIDENT). The fact that Britain did not assist him against Russian aggression convinced him that he could only rely on himself.

Amir Habibullah (q.v., 1901-19) continued the policy of his father. He resisted British demands for modifications of the agreements concluded with Amir Abdur Rahman and succeeded in 1905 in obtaining a treaty which confirmed all the existing provisions (See ANGLO-AFGHAN TREATY OF 1905). Two years later, Amir Habibullah visited India for talks with the Governor General, Lord Minto, unaware of the fact that at the same time Russia and Britain had concluded the Anglo-Russian Convention of 1907 (q.v.). The Amir never permitted Russia the commercial privileges expected under the Convention and made sure that the imperialistic neighbors would not solve the "Afghanistan Question" at the cost of his independence. The situation was drastically changed during World War I when both the Central Powers and the Allies vied for the support of the Afghan ruler. The Hentig-Niedermayer expedition (q.v., August 1915-May 1916) was able to conclude a treaty with the Amir, but could not provide any tangible support in funds and weapons (See GERMAN-AFGHAN RELATIONS). Therefore Habibullah remained neutral, hoping to win rich rewards and complete independence for his country; when these expectations were not realized he paid for the failure of his policy with his life. Amir Habibullah was assassinated on the night of February 19-20 at Kalla Gush in Laghman province. Amanullah Khan ascended the throne over the rival claims of his uncle, Nasrullah Khan (q.v.), and his brother, Enayatullah Khan (q.v.).

King Amanullah (1919-29, he adopted the title of king in 1926) demanded a new treaty from British India which would recognize Afghanistan's absolute independence. When the Indian government was reluctant to comply, he started military action which resulted in the third Anglo-Afghan war of 1919. With India in semi-revolt and British forces demobilized after the European war, the British government did not find this an opportune time to wage war and agreed to a peace treaty at Rawalpindi (August 8, 1919, q.v.). It took another three months of negotiations at Mussoorie (Mussoorie Conference, April 17 - July 18, 1920, q.v.) and almost one year of talks at Kabul (Kabul Conference, Jan. 1, 1921 - Dec. 2, 1921. See KABUL TREATY of 1921.) before normal, neighborly relations were established. By that time Amanullah had established diplomatic relations with the Soviet Union, Turkey, Persia, and Italy and had modified Abdul Rahman's policy to end the isolation of his country. A contemporary of Reza Shah of Iran and Kemal Ataturk of the young Turkish republic, Amanullah initiated such drastic social reforms that he was ousted by a wave of reaction after a ten-year period of tenuous rule. Next followed the chaotic ten-months rule of a "lowly" Tajik Habibullah Kalakani (Jan. 18 - Nov. 3, 1929 q.v.), called "The Son of a Water Carrier" (Bacha-e Saqqau) by his friends and "Amir Habibullah Ghazi, Servant of the Religion of the Messenger of God" (*Khadem-i Din Rasul Allah*), by his followers after his coronation.

The new dynasty of Nadir Shah (1929-33, q.v.) and Zaher Shah (1933- 73, q.v.) continued Afghanistan's traditional policy of foreign relations but now tried to enlist Germany as a "third power" in obtaining the technical and political support which the Afghan rulers did not dare to accept from their neighbors (See GERMAN-AFGHAN RELATIONS). Economic and cultural collaboration between Afghanistan and Germany was greatly expanded and Germans were soon the largest European community in the country. But the deterioration of the political situation in Europe and the outbreak of World War II ended any possibility that the economic cooperation might evolve into political collaboration. Afghanistan remained neutral during the war.

The end of the war created an entirely new situation: the Soviet Union, although severely battered, acquired nuclear technology and emerged as a superpower, and Britain, in spite of her victory, was forced to relinquish her hold on India in 1947. During the short reign of King Amanullah, Afghanistan's border with the Soviet Union was open to commercial relations and regular air service to Tashkent existed, but his successors maintained a closed border policy. Keeping Afghanistan's border to the north closed was seen in Moscow as inconsistent with friendly "neighborly" relations. Soviet demands for a "normalization" of relations could not be ignored, but it was hoped in Kabul that the United States would fill the vacuum left by the British and serve as a balancing force against the Soviet Union (See UNITED STATES-AFGHAN RELATIONS).

The United States formally recognized Afghanistan in August 1934, but did not have an accredited representative in Kabul until 1942 when it appeared possible that the German advance into the Caucasus might make it impossible to maintain a link to the Soviet Union through western Iran. In spite of its status as an independent state, Washington considered Afghanistan within the British sphere of influence and not very important in terms of international trade. With the onset of the cold war during the Truman administration and the policy of containment of Communism under John Foster Dulles, secretary of state under President Eisenhower, the Afghan government might have entered into an alliance with the United States if it could have been given explicit guaranties of protection from Soviet attack.

The United States government had never been willing to give that kind of guarantee; a possible Soviet advance was to be stopped at the Khaibar Pass, not north of the Hindu Kush. The Baghdad Pact (subsequently renamed in 1959 Central Treaty Organization, CENTO) united in 1955 Turkey, Iraq, Iran, and Pakistan with Britain as the representative of the West and the United States as the sponsor and "paymaster." The alliance inherited the legacy of regional disputes between Middle Eastern neighbors and upset the balance of power.

A turning point occurred in December 1955, when Nikita Khrushchev and Nikolai Bulganin came to Kabul. The Soviets supported Afghanistan in the "Pashtunistan" dispute (q.v.) and offered massive aid, which the United States was unwilling to match. The government of Prime Minister

Daud (q.v.), in spite of its misgivings, turned to the Soviet Union for the weapons it could not obtain from the West.

The weapons arrived with Soviet advisers and experts and thousands of Afghans went to the Soviet Union for military training. Graduates from Afghan institutes of higher education won fellowships to foreign universities, including the USSR, and there emerged a growing cadre of military officers, students, and technocrats with leftist and republican, if not pro-Russian, sympathies. When Sardar Muhammad Daud on July 17, 1973, staged a coup against his cousin, the king, he counted the Left (and Parchamis, q.v.) among his supporters. Five years later a Marxist coup ended the "aristocratic" republic and established the Democratic Republic of Afghanistan. Its alliance with the Soviet Union and the subsequent war, which Soviet intervention in 1979 turned into a war of liberation, resulted in the eventual Soviet withdrawal in 1989 and a "simmering" civil war with no end in sight.

AFGHAN HOUND. A hunting dog, called *tazi* (P. swift, running) in Afghanistan, is greatly valued for its speed and keen eyesight. It is longlegged, has floppy ears, and a silky coat, measures about 24 - 28 inches tall and weighs 50-60 pounds. It is a much-desired and fashionable pet in Afghanistan and abroad.

AFGHANI (AF.). Name of the Afghan monetary unit which replaced the Afghan *ropia* in 1925-26. Initially the Afghani was a silver coin subdivided into 100 *puls*, or two *qrans*, and 25, 10 and 5 puls of nickel coins, but inflation has since eliminated the use of any change smaller than one Afghani. Paper money was first issued by King Amanullah in 1919, but the notes were withdrawn a year later, because traders refused to accept them. New bank notes were prepared shortly before the fall of King Amanullah and issued by Amir Habibullah (Kalakani), again with little success.

In November 1935, notes printed in Switzerland in denominations of 5, 10, 20, 50, and 100 Afghanis were issued by the Bank-i Milli (q.v.) and continued in circulation since then. In December 1958 coins of 2 and 5 Afghanis were put in circulation, and notes issued by the governments of Zahir Shah, President Daud, and the PDPA are currently in circulation. In 1991 the US dollar was traded in the bazar at 1,000 Afghanis. Banknotes of the monarchy often fetched a somewhat higher course. Also see BANKING and DA AFGHANISTAN BANK.

AFGHAN INTERIM GOVERNMENT See ISLAMIC ALLIANCE FOR THE LIBERATION OF AFGHANISTAN and MUJAHEDIN.

AFGHANI, SAYYID JAMALUDDIN. Born in 1838. "Father of the Pan-Islamic movement," Islamic modernist, and political propagandist who advocated unity of the Islamic world and selective borrowing from the West for the purpose of stemming the tide of Western imperialism. He was the adviser of Muslim rulers in many parts of the Islamic world

and a political activist in Iran, Afghanistan, India, Egypt, and the Ottoman empire.
Frequently opposed by the ulama (Muslim clergy, q.v.) and suspected as an intrigant by the temporal powers, he was often on the run. When one of his followers assassinated the Persian ruler Nasruddin Shah (1848-96), Afghani was placed under house arrest by the Ottoman Sultan Abdul Hamid. He died in Istanbul in 1897. Afghans revere his memory and believe him to be a descendant of a family of Sayyids from Asadabad in the Kunar province of Afghanistan (see Muhammad Amin Khugiani's *Hayat-i Sayyid Jamal ud-Din Afghan* - The Life of Sayyid Jamaluddin Afghan), but Iranian and Western scholars accept the fact that he was born in Asadabad, Iran (see Iraj Afshar and Asghar Mahdavi's *Majmu'e-h-yi Asnad va Madarek-i Chap-Nashodeh dar bara-yeh Sayyid Jamal ud-Din Mashur be Afghani* [Collection of unpublished documents about Sayyid Jamal ud-Din known as Afghani] and Nikki R. Keddie's, *Sayyid Jamal-ud-Din al-Afghani, a Biography*).
This writer found a news report from Kabul from the year 1866, which calls Afghani a "Constantinople Syud, or Syud Rumi" (Anatolia was called Rum after the eastern "Roman" empire) and claims that he has come to Kabul "for some political object," and that he "is often admitted at 10 or 11 o'clock at night to secret audiences with the Ameer (Muhammad Azam Khan)." He is described as follows: "Pale complexion, open forehead, azure eyes, has a goat-beard, with some red hairs in it, moustache small, slender make, head shaved, age about 35 years. Is dressed like a Nogai [?], drinks tea constantly, and smokes in the Persian style. Is well versed in geography and history, speaks Arabic and Turkey [sic] fluently, talks Persian like an Irani [Persian]. Apparently follows no particular religion. His style of living resembles more that of a European than of a Mussulman." Abdul Hai Habibi (q.v.), in a book called *Nasab wa Zad-gah-i Sayyid Jamal al-Din Afghani* (Genealogy and Birthplace of Jamaluddin Afghani), says that according to Kunar shari'a tribunal records, Sayyid Safdar was the father of Afghani from his first wife. Safdar went on the Hajj and on his return also took an Iranian wife, claiming that this accounts for the Iranian "connection."

AFGHANISTAN. A quarterly journal published by the Afghan Historical Society since 1946 with articles in English and French. It is an important source on Afghan history and culture.

AFGHANISTAN BANK See **BANKING** and **DA AFGHANISTAN BANK.**

AFGHANISTAN, THE LAND AND THE PEOPLE. See under the headings of provinces and under ADMINISTRATION, ETHNIC GROUPS, and GEOGRAPHY.

AFGHAN MILLAT (Afghan Nation). An Afghan weekly newspaper, the organ of the Afghan Social Democratic Party (ASDP - Da Afghanistan Tolanpal Woluswak Gund), first published on April 5, 1966, by Ghulam

M. Farhad with his brother Qudratullah Haddad and Habibullah Rafi'i
as editors. Because of its political activism the newspaper was frequently
closed. The newspaper is still published at irregular intervals in Pakistan
under the editorship of Eng. Inam Wak.

The ASDP was established during a meeting of the 62-member founding
congress on March 8, 1966, at the residence of Qiyamuddin Khadem
(q.v.). Ghulam Muhammad Farhad (q.v., one-time mayor of Kabul) was
elected chairman and held the position until his death in 1984. During
his tenure *Afghan Millat*, the popular name of the party, was more
nationalist than socialist.   It advocated the restoration of "Greater
Afghanistan," including the territory of the North-West Frontier Province
and Baluchistan, which now constitute the western provinces of Pakistan.
Because of its irredentist policy, the party contributed to the friction existing between Afghanistan and Pakistan. The party did not support
President Daud, even though it agreed with him on the "Pashtunistan"
question and the attempt to make Pashto the national language.   In
October 1979, the Amin government accused the party of attempting a
coup and arrested a number of its members in Kabul.

In the late-1960s, Feda Muhammad Fedai seceded and formed his own
party, called *Millat*, and after the death of Ghulam Muhammad Farhad
in 1984, Dr. Muhammad Amin Wakman (q.v.), who resides in the United
States, was elected chairman of *Afghan Millat* at a congress in Peshawar,
Pakistan, on March 8-9, 1990. It was attended by 390 (out of 500)
delegates who also elected a 29-member supreme council and chose Stana
Gul Sherzad as its secretary general. Anwar al-Haq, Qudratullah Haddad,
and Yaqin Yusufzai are members of the secretariate. Shams al-Duha
Shams from Kunar province and a number of his supporters did not
participate in the elections.

The party opposed the Tanai-Hekmatyar alliance against the Najibullah
regime (See TANAI, SHAHNAWAZ) and called on its members and
sympathizers to continue the struggle to capture political power. The
party now emphasizes social democratic policies and, although largely
Pashtun in membership, tries to broaden its base to become a national
party. The ASDP had a small mujahedin force in the field which was
severely mauled by Hekmatyar's (q.v.) forces. The Pakistani government
did not give the Afghan Millat official recognition and material support,
because of its irredentism. Three of its activists were assassinated by
unknown gunmen in Peshawar, including Dr. Sadat Shigawal and in
September 1991, Taj Muhammad Khan.

AFGHAN SECURITY SERVICE. After the Saur Revolt, the Taraki
government established a security service, named AGSA (*Da Afghanistan
da Gatay da Satanay Edara* - Afghanistan Security Service Department),
which was headed by Asadullah Sarwari (q.v.) from May 1978 till August
1979. The service was renamed KAM (*Da Kargarano Istikhbarati Mu'asa-
sa* - Workers' Security Institution) at the accession to power of Hafizullah
Amin who appointed Sarwari's (q.v) nephew, Aziz Ahmad Akbari (August
- September 1979) and subsequently his own nephew, Dr. Asadullah Amin

as its head. Akbari was sent on diplomatic assignment to Baghdad and Asadullah Amin was assassinated shortly before the overthrow of Hafizullah Amin by Soviet troops.

Within a week of their assumption of power on December 27, 1979, the Parchami regime purged the security service of Khalq supporters and renamed it KHAD (*Khedamat-i Ettela'at-i Daulati* - State Information Service). It was headed by Dr. Najibullah before he succeeded to the position of general secretary of the PDPA in 1986 and president of Afghanistan. Najibullah upgraded KHAD to ministerial status, therefore its new acronym WAD (*Wizarat-i Amniat-i Daulati* - Ministry of State Security). WAD was subsequently headed by General Ghulam Faruq Yaqubi (q.v.). The organization is said to control from 15 to 30 thousand operatives, organized on the KGB model, with its own military units, including a national guard. Former Afghan prisoners have accused WAD and its predecessors of torture, intimidation, and assassination.

AFGHAN WOLUS (Afghan Nation). An Afghan weekly newspaper published in 1969 by Qiamuddin Khadem (q.v.), a poet and one-time vice president of the Pashto Academy. The short-lived paper favored a nationalist, pro-Pashtunistan policy. Its editors were Mozafer Sadeq and Abdul Qayyum Adramzai.

AFGHAN YEARBOOK. An almanac, or yearbook, published since 1932/1311 by the Afghan Literary Society. It was entitled *Salnama-yi Majalla-yi Kabul* (Kabul Magazine Yearbook), until 1940 when it was renamed *Da Kabul Kalanai* (Kabul Almanac), and finally *Da Afghanistan Kalanai* (Afghanistan Almanac). Each volume carries a general introduction, including an article on the royal family or subsequent rulers, followed by a section with detailed information on members of all branches of government and the diplomatic community and a record of activities during a particular year. Much space was devoted to aspects of Afghan culture and society as well as to international news. The almanac was richly illustrated, including photos of leading members of the Afghan government and, after elections, of all members of parliament. It is a unique source for research on Afghanistan. Initially it was written in Dari (Farsi) but gradually became a bilingual Dari/Pashto publication. Abridged versions of the yearbook have also appeared in English since 1966. After the Saur Revolt (1978) only two English language volumes appeared, one published by the Khalqis in 1979, the other by the Parchami regime in 1981.

AFKAR-E NAU (New Ideas). An weekly newspaper published by one Nurullah Nurzad in 1971 under the editorship of Zia Haidar. The paper supported middle-class, law- and-order causes and an "Islamic" policy.

AFRIDI. A Pashto-speaking tribe which is located in the area of the Khaibar Pass, just beyond the Afghan border. Herodotus, the Greek historian, mentions the "Aprytae," the tribe of Osman who called himself "God's

Creature" (*afrideh-ye khoda*), whom some Afghan scholars consider the eponymic ancestor of the Afridis. For centuries, the Afridis saw themselves as the "guardians" of the gate to India, and invaders since ancient times have found it preferable to pay for passage rather than fight their way through the Khaibar. At times Afridis entered the services of Afghan rulers, primarily as bodyguards and tribal militias, and in conflicts between Afghanistan and British India they sided with the Afghans. The tribe is divided into seven sections as follows: Kaki Khel, Malik Din, Kambar, Kamr, Lakha Khel, Aka Khel, and the Sipahs. In the 1960s the Afridis were said to be able to muster an armed force of 50,000 men. A British officer described them as "wiry, shaven-headed, full-bearded, Pashto-speaking hillmen of uncertain origin" (Ridgway, 1910).

AGSA See AFGHAN SECURITY SERVICE.

AHMAD SHAH. Member of the *Ittihad-i Islami* of Sayyaf (q.v.) and, in 1988, prime minister of an interim cabinet founded by the *ittihad-i Islami-yi Mujahedin-i Afghanistan* (q.v.), an umbrella group of the seven mujahedin parties headquartered in Peshawar, Pakistan. Born in 1943 in a village in the Bagrami district of Kabul and educated at Ibn Sina School, Kabul Polytechic Institute, and Kabul University, where he obtained an engineering degree in 1958 and started work with the department of agriculture and irrigation. He came to the United States in 1972 and obtained an M.A.degree in engineering from Colorado State University in 1974. In 1975 he started a teaching career at King Faisal University in Saudi Arabia, but came to Peshawar after the Soviet intervention in Afghanistan. He joined the Sayyaf group and became president (*ra'is*) of the committee for education and later the committee for finance. He is married to an American woman.

AHMAD SHAH, ABDALI DURRANI. King of Afghanistan, 1747-73, and founder of the Sadozai dynasty of the Abdali (Durrani) tribe. Born in 1722 in Herat the son of Muhammad Zaman Khan, who was governor of Herat. After capturing Kandahar, Nadir Shah of Iran (1736-47, q.v.) exiled Ahmad Khan to Mazandaran in northern Iran and subsequently appointed him governor of that province. At the death of Nadir Shah, Ahmad Khan was commander of an Afghan contingent of the Persian army at Kandahar. He was able to capture a caravan with booty from India and thus gained the means to win the support he needed to be elected King (Shah) of Afghanistan in October 1747 by an assembly of Pashtun chiefs. The Pashtun tribesmen rallied to his banner, and Ahmad Shah led them on nine campaigns into India in search of booty and territorial conquest. He added Kashmir, Sind, and the Western Punjab to his domains and founded an empire which extended from eastern Persia to northern India and from the Amu Daria (q.v.) to the Indian Ocean. Ahmad Shah appointed his son Timur (See TIMUR SHAH) as his successor and died of a natural death two months later on April 14, 1772. He was buried in Kandahar, which had become the capital of Afghanistan until Timur Shah (1773-93) moved the capital to Kabul. Sir Percy Sykes in his *History of Afghanistan* called Ahmad Shah "a monarch whose high descent and warlike qualities made him peculiarly acceptable to his aristocratic and virile Chiefs, as well as to his warlike subjects in general. In short, he possessed all the qualities that enabled him successfully to found the kingdom of Afghanistan." Also see ABDALI.

AHMADULLAH. Minister of public works under Prime Minister Etemadi in 1965 and minister of interior in the Maiwandwal cabinet, 1967. He was born in 1925 of a Kharoti (Ghilzai Pashtun, q.v.) tribal family and is said to be a cousin of Hafizullah Amin (q.v.), the Khalqi leader who was assassinated at the time of the Soviet intervention in Afghanistan. Ahmadullah was educated in Afghanistan and the United States and served as governor of Jozjan (1964) and Kunduz (1965) before his ministerial appointments. He was president of the Ghori Cement Factory until 1973, and subsequently emigrated to the United States.

AHMADZAI. A section of the Sulaiman Khel division of the Ghilzai tribe. They are settled in a "triangle" formed by a line drawn from Kabul to Jalalabad and Gardez. They are generally wealthy and often employed as traders, while some held high positions in the Afghan government and have intermarried with the Durranis. Amir Abdur Rahman settled a number of Ahmadzai families in northern Afghanistan to weaken their power and serve as Pashtun colonists among the Turkic population. Only a small number of Ahmadzai is nomadic.

AHMADZAI, LT. GEN. SHAHPUR. Born about 1925 in Surkhab, Logar, of an Ahmadzai Ghilzai family. Head of the Kabul Military Academy, 1973-77, and Chief of General Staff, 1978. Arrested in July 1978 for "plotting" against the Khalqi regime and executed on August 18, 1978.

AIBAK, Now SAMANGAN (lat. 36-16' N, long. 68-1' E). A town, also called Haibak, located at an altitude of 3,000 feet, which is the capital of Samangan province and in 1964 renamed Samangan. The town is famous for its pre-Islamic archaeological sites. Most important is *Takht-i Rustam* (the Throne of Rustam), a large stupa hewn into solid rock, which is unique for its size, type, and construction. Nearby, at Dara-ye Gaz is a complex of ten Buddhist temples, called by the Chinese pilgrim Hsuan-Tsang (7th century A.D.) "Kie Tehe." The town has about 8,000 inhabitants and is located on the main route from Kabul to Mazar-i Sharif. It has a small bazar, a park in the center of town, and a mosque and administrative center. It was for centuries a major commercial center. Little is known how the present war has affected the town. Also see SAMANGAN.

AI KHANUM (Moon Lady, lat. 37-8' N, long. 69-27' E). A small town at the confluence of the Kokcha and Amu rivers. In November 1964 French archaeologists, headed by Daniel Schlumberger and Paul Bernard, discovered at Ai Khanum the site of a large Greek town (2nd to 1st century B.C.) with an abundance of Greek architecture, ceramics, and inscriptions.

AIMAQ. The name of an ethnic group of some 800,000 sunni Muslims who speak Dari (Afghan Persian) with some Turkic admixture. The word either means "nomad" (in Turkic) or "administrative district" (in Mongol). They are also called Chahar Aimaq and include three groups: the Jamshidis, Firuzkuhis, and Taimanis and the sunni Hazaras of Qala-i Nau (See HAZARA). They were at times independent or allied with a Durrani prince ruling in Herat. Amir Abdur Rahman (q.v.) severely curbed the power of their chiefs and put them under the control of the governor of Herat. The tribes are semi-nomadic and dwell in conical felt yurts. They raise sheep and cattle and are concentrated primarily in Herat, Ghor, and Badghis provinces.

AKBAR, SARDAR MUHAMMAD (Called GHAZI). The ambitious son of Amir Dost Muhammad (1826-38 and 1842-63) who was a major figure in the defeat of the British in the first Anglo-Afghan war (1839-42). He was the premier of the Afghan chiefs with whom the British force of occupation sought to negotiate safe passage from Kabul to India. During negotiations with Sir William Macnaghten (q.v.), he killed the British envoy "in a fit of passion." He saved the lives of British women and children as well as a number of officers whom he had taken into "protective" custody during the arduous retreat. Few others survived the massacre of the British expeditionary force of some 16,000 troops and camp followers. Akbar wanted to regain territory lost in the Punjab; but his father, Amir Dost Muhammad, who had been restored to the throne in 1942, favored a policy of accommodation with Britain. In 1845 Akbar rebelled but he died at the age of 29 of poisoning before he could pose a serious challenge to his father. He is equally revered by all Afghans and called Ghazi (Victor against Infidels), and a residential area of Kabul and a major hospital have been named Wazir Akbar Khan after him.

AKHUND. A religious instructor (Persian, Dari, and Pashto); A descendant of an Akhund is called Akhundzada.

AKRAM, MUHAMMAD. Cultural attaché in Moscow (1962-63), minister of education (1969), and ambassador to Cairo (March-Sept. 1973) and Paris (1975-79). He was born 1916 in Kabul and educated in Kabul and France. A leading educator and diplomat in exile in Paris where he is president of the Centre de Recherches et d'Etudes Documentaires sur l'Afghanistan (CEREDAF), a research and documentation center which collects materials on Afghanistan and publishes occasional monographs. His mother tongue is Dari.

ALAQADARI. Smallest administrative division, a subdistrict of a province (*welayat*) in Afghanistan. It is headed by an *alaqadar*, an administrator appointed by the Kabul government or the governor of a province. He is responsible to a *woleswal*, head of a district, or the *wali*, governor of a province. See ADMINISTRATIVE DIVISIONS.

ALAWI, SAYYID MUHAMMAD NASIM. Minister of communications in Prime Minister Khaliqyar's new government, announced on May 27, 1990. Born in Kabul province in 1935, he was educated at Istiqlal Lycée in Kabul and in France, where he received an engineering degree in communication. He served as director of statistics, vice president of the planning department of the ministry of communications, and eventually as president of the department of telephone and telegraph. In 1983 he was appointed deputy minister of communications. He is not a member of the PDPA.

ALI AHMAD. Known as "Wali" (Governor) of Kabul under King Amanullah and proclaimed "king" by Afghan tribes in Nangarhar after the abdication of Amanullah in January 1919. Born in 1883, the son of Loinab Khushdil Khan, he was educated in India and served as chamberlain, *shahghasi mulki*, of Amir Habibullah (q.v.). He was president of the Afghan Peace Delegation at Rawalpindi in 1919 and successful as a commander in the Mangal (q.v.) uprising (1924) and the Shinwari (q.v.) rebellion (1928). He fought Habibullah Kalakani (q.v.) and was defeated; brought to Kabul in chains he defiantly kissed the cannon by which he was executed in July 1929.

ALIM See ULAMA.

ALI MUHAMMAD. Minister of Court, 1963-73, and minister in Rome, 1927, and London, 1933-39. Began his career as an educator, inspector of schools, and served as minister of commerce, 1928; education, 1929; foreign affairs, 1939-52; and deputy prime minister, 1953-63. A Tajik, he was opposed to the Pashtunistan (q.v.) policy of Prime Minister Daud (q.v.). He died in December 1977 in Kabul.

ALLAH. The only God, the Transcendent, Omniscient, Omnipotent, Creator, and Judge of the universe. Afghans, like all Muslims, adhere to a strict monotheism, one God (A.,Allah and P. Khoda), and recognize Muhammad as his prophet. Idolatry is a sin, and there are no partners to Allah. The Islamic Holy Book, the Qor'an, is the word of Allah, revealed to the world through the medium of Muhammad. Moses and Jesus are among the prophets recognized by Islam, but Muhammad is the last. Allah is merciful and compassionate. He will reward or punish men and women on the Last Day. Also see ISLAM.

ALLAH NAWAZ (NAWWAZ). An Indian from Multan (now Pakistan) who came to Afghanistan in 1915 and held high positions. He was assistant editor of the *Ittehad-i Mashraqi* (The Eastern Union), first published in 1920 in Jalalabad, and minister of court in 1929. In 1933 he was appointed minister of public works. He served as Afghan minister in Berlin, 1935-45, and subsequently remained in Germany.

AL-NASR See NASR.

AMAN-I AFGHAN (Afghan Peace). A weekly newspaper founded on April 12, 1919 (22. Hammal 1298) as the semiofficial organ of the Amanullah era (1919-29). Its motto was to "discuss every kind of scientific and political question and things of interest to the Government and the Nation." The newspaper, named after King Amanullah (*aman Allah* - peace, or protection of God) continued the journalistic tradition began by the *Seraj al-Akhbar* (q.v.). In order to provide economic support, government officials and courtiers were expected to subscribe. During the first year of its existence there were frequent changes of editors, beginning with Abdul Hadi Dawai (q.v.) who was succeeded by Muhammad Ismail, Faiz Muhammad, and subsequently by Ghulam Nabi (who was assassinated during the Kalakani regime in 1929). The newspaper was printed on excellent paper and was handsomely illustrated and represents one of the most important examples of early twentieth century Afghan journalism.

AMANULLAH, KING (AMAN ALLAH, called GHAZI). King of Afghanistan, 1919-29. Born in 1892, the son of Amir Habibullah and Sarwar Sultanah, the Ulya Hazrat - queen. When Amir Habibullah was assassinated in Jalalabad in February 1919, Amanullah Khan was governor of Kabul and in possession of the arsenal and the treasury. He was crowned in Kabul over the prior claims of his uncle Nasrullah, whom he denounced as a usurper and an accomplice in the murder of his father. King Amanullah (he assumed the title of king in 1926) was an ardent reformer and contemporary of like-minded rulers, Muhammad Reza in Iran and Kemal Ataturk in Turkey. He demanded a revision of the Anglo-Afghan agreements concluded by Amir Abdur Rahman which left Britain in charge of Afghanistan's foreign relations in exchange for protection from unprovoked Russian aggression and a subsidy in money and military materiel (See AFGHAN FOREIGN RELATIONS). British reluctance to accept a change in the *status quo* led to Afghan armed attacks, culminating in the start of the third Anglo-Afghan war (q.v.) on May 3, 1919. Britain was war-weary and in no condition to wage war on the Indian frontier and, after lengthy negotiations in Rawalpindi, Mussoorie, and Kabul, peace was restored, leaving Afghanistan free and independent from British control (See ANGLO-AFGHAN WARS, ANGLO-AFGHAN TREATY, and AFGHAN FOREIGN RELATIONS). King Amanullah became a national hero and turned his attention to reforming and modernizing his country. He established diplomatic and commercial relations with major European and Asian states, founded schools in which French, German, and English were the major languages of education, and promulgated a constitution which guaranteed the personal freedom and equal rights of all Afghans.

He built a new capital, named Darulaman (Dar al-Aman - Abode of Peace), which included a monumental parliament and other government buildings as well as villas of prominent Afghans. Social reforms included a new dress code which permitted women in Kabul to go unveiled and encouraged officials to wear Western dress. Modernization proved costly for Afghanistan and was resented by the traditional elements of Afghan society. The Khost rebellion (q.v.), a tribal revolt in 1924, was suppressed and Amanullah felt secure enough to travel to Europe in December 1927. Upon his return he faced increasing opposition and, in 1928, an uprising of Shinwari tribesmen, followed by attacks of the Kohdamani and Kuhistani forces of Habibullah Kalakani (q.v.), forced the reformer king into exile. After an unsuccessful attempt at regaining the throne, he crossed the Indian border on May 23, and settled in Italy and Switzerland until his death on April 26, 1960. He was buried in Jalalabad at the side of the tomb of Amir Habibullah.

AMIN, HAFIZULLAH. Born 1929 in Paghman, Kabul province. President of the Democratic Republic of Afghanistan from September 1979 until his assassination on December 27, 1979. He was of the Kharoti (Ghilzai Pashtun) tribe whose family came to Paghman in the 19th century. Educated in Afghanistan and the United States, where he was known as a Pashtun nationalist, he became a teacher and later principal of Ibn Sina and Teachers Training schools in Kabul. His conversion to Marxism is said to have occurred in 1964. He was elected to the 13th session of parliament (1969) as a representative from Paghman. During the republican period (1973-78) he successfully recruited followers in the army in competition with Parchami efforts. After the Saur Revolt he was appointed vice premier and minister of foreign affairs. In April 1979 he became prime minister and, after he ousted Nur Muhammad Taraki, he became president on September 16, 1979. He was at odds with Alexandr Puzanov (q.v.), the Soviet ambassador to Kabul, and successfully demanded his recall. Some observers called him the Afghan "Tito" because of his independence and nationalistic inclinations. He was accused of responsibility in the assassination of thousands. Soviet special forces attacked him and his bodyguard in Darulaman, assassinating him on December 27, 1979. He was replaced by Babrak Karmal of the Parchami faction of the PDPA.

AMIR. Commander, also nobleman, prince, ruler, chief (from A. *amara*, to command). Caliph Omar (634-44) first assumed the title Amir al-Mu'minin (Commander of the Believers). In Afghanistan the Sadozai rulers carried the title "king" (Shah), but the Muhammadzai rulers from 1826 assumed the title "amir" until Amanullah Khan adopted the title of king in 1926. Among some mujahedin groups an "amir" is a commander with civil and military powers.

AMU DARIA (lat. 34-40' N, long. 59-1' E, **DARYA**). A river, called Oxus by the ancient Greeks, which forms for about 280 miles the boundary between the Soviet Union and Afghanistan. Its easternmost sources are the Ab-e Wakhan and the Ab-i Pamir, which rise in the Little Pamir mountains and run into the Ab-e Panj near the village of Qal'a-ye Panjeh. It is fed by the Kukcha and further west the Kunduz rivers, at which point it is called the Amu Daria. It then flows in a northwesterly direction to run into the Aral Sea. It is navigable only in parts although its length from the farthest source to the mouth of the Aral Sea extends some 1,500 miles. A bridge near Hairatan, completed in 1982, links the Afghan highway from Mazar-i-Sharif with the Soviet rail terminal at Termez.

ANAS, MOHAMMAD. Minister of education (1964-65), and minister without portfolio (1966). Born in 1915, a Muhammadzai, he was educated in Afghanistan and Turkey and began his career in the ministry of education. He served as president of Kabul University (1941-63), ambassador to India (1963-64), and was appointed governor of Kandahar in 1970. During the reign of President Daud he was head of the president's auditing department. A bachelor, he died in Kabul in 1983.

ANDKHUI (lat. 36-56' N, long. 65-8' E). A town in Fariab province with about 15,000 inhabitants located some 45 miles northwest of Shiberghan in Fariab province. In Timurid times (late 15th century) and again from the 17th to the 19th centuries Andkhui was an important commercial center. It shared the fate of Maimana and Balkh in being part of Uzbak khanates under Afghan or Bukharan suzereignty until Amir Abdur Rahman (q.v.) took direct control of Afghan Turkestan in the 1880s. It now has a mixed, but largely Uzbak population, and is a market place for Turkoman rugs, qaraqul skins, sheep, and cattle. Among its important shrines is the tomb of Baba Wali (a sufi pir) which is widely known as a place of pilgrimage. Industrial development, limited to the establishment of a tannery which employs 250 workers, has been difficult due to a scarcity of water.

ANGAR, FAIZ MUHAMMAD. A Kandahar businessman and member of the *Wish Zalmayan* (q.v., P. Awakening Youth), a Pashtun political club. He published the Persian/Pashto biweekly, *Angar* (1951), which was critical of the Afghan government and therefore banned after a few months of existence. Nur Muhammad Taraki (q.v.) claimed to have contributed an article, "What Do We Want?" which was censored and led to the demise of the paper. Angar died in the 1970's in Kandahar.

ANGLO-AFGHAN TREATY OF 1905. Renewal in form of a treaty of agreements signed between Amir Abdur Rahman and Sir Lepel Griffin, chief political officer in Afghanistan, in June and July 1880. At the death of Amir Abdur Rahman on October 3, 1901, the British Indian government insisted that the agreements with the amir were personal and therefore subject to renegotiation with his successor. The government of

India sought modifications and concessions including a more "liberal commercial policy" on the part of Afghanistan, delimitation of the Mohmand border (between Afghanistan and India), and noninterference of Afghanistan in the politics of the transborder (Indian) tribes. Britain exerted great pressure, stopping subsidy payments and prohibiting Afghan imports of arms, but Amir Habibullah did not yield. He invited Louis W. Dane of the Indian foreign department to Kabul and, after three months of negotiations, the "Independent King of Afghanistan and its Dependencies" and Louis W. Dane, "Foreign Secretary of the Mighty Government of India" signed the treaty at Kabul on March 21, 1905. For Amir Habibullah this was a great victory: none of the British objectives was won, the arrears in subsidy were paid, and Britain affirmed that it would not interfere in the internal affairs of Afghanistan. This treaty remained in force until repudiated by Amir Amanullah in 1919.

ANGLO-AFGHAN TREATY OF 1919. Peace treaty between the British and the Afghan governments after the third Anglo-Afghan war (q.v.). It was negotiated at Rawalpindi and signed on August 8, 1919, by A.H. Grant, foreign secretary of the government of India, and Ali Ahmad Khan (q.v.), commissary for home affairs. The treaty made a return to the "old friendship" between the two states contingent on negotiations started after a six-month waiting period. In the meantime Britain would not permit Afghanistan to import arms and ammunition through India, the payment of a subsidy would be ended, and the arrears in payments would be confiscated. Finally, undefined portions of the Khaibar were to be demarcated by a British commission and Afghanistan was to accept the Indo-Afghan frontier as marked. An annexure stated that "the said Treaty and this letter leave Afghanistan officially free and independent in its internal and external affairs." British hopes that a contrite Amir would again conclude an exclusive alliance were soon seen to be unrealistic. Amir Amanullah sent a mission to the Soviet Union, Europe, and the United States and acted on his right to establish diplomatic relations with foreign powers. The Pashtun tribes on the Indian side of the frontier were made to believe that the treaty represented only a cease-fire after which war was to be resumed if Britain did not agree to various Afghan demands. Indeed it was only after a fruitless, three-month conference at Mussoorie (q.v.) (April 17 - July 18, 1920) and the Kabul Conference (q.v.) (Jan. 20 - Dec. 2, 1921) that normal neighborly relations between Britain and Afghanistan were established.

ANGLO-AFGHAN TREATY OF 1921. Also called "Treaty of Kabul" because it was negotiated and signed at Kabul by Henry R. C. Dobbs, the British envoy, and Mahmud Tarzi, chief of the Afghan delegation, after arduous, eleven-month negotiations. The treaty restored "friendly and commercial relations" between the two governments after the third Anglo-Afghan war and negotiations at the Mussoorie Conference (q. v.) and Rawalpindi (q. v.). The negotiations proceeded in four phases: During the first session, January 20 to April 9, 1921, the Afghan Amir unsuccessfully demanded territorial concessions, while Britain wanted the exclusion of Russian consular offices from southeastern Afghanistan. In the second phase, from April 9 to mid-July, 1921, Britain asked Afghanistan to break the newly established diplomatic relations with Russia in exchange for a subsidy of 4 million rupees and weapons, as well as guarantees from unprovoked Russian aggression. When in the third stage, from mid-July to September 18, the British foreign office informed the Italian government that it was about to conclude an agreement which would, "admit the superior and predominant political influence of Britain" in Afghanistan, the Afghans refused to accept an "alliance." An exclusive treaty was impossible after Afghanistan announced ratification of the Russo-Afghan treaty of 1921 (q.v.). In the fourth and final stage of negotiations, from September 18 to December 8, 1921, the British mission twice made preparations to return to India, when finally an agreement was signed at Kabul on November 22, 1921. Ratifications were exchanged on February 6, 1922.

In the treaty both governments "mutually certify and respect each with regard to the other all rights of internal and external independence." Afghanistan reaffirmed its acceptance of the boundary west of the Khaibar, subject to minor "re-alignment." Legations were to be opened in London and Kabul, consulates established in various Indian and Afghan towns, and Afghanistan was permitted to import arms and munitions through India. No customs duties were to be charged for goods in transit to Afghanistan and each party agreed to inform the other of major military operations in the frontier belt. Representatives of both states were to meet in the near future to discuss conclusion of a trade convention, which was signed in June 1923.

ANGLO-AFGHAN WARS. *First Anglo-Afghan War (1839-42)*: In the nineteenth century, European rivalry for commerce and empire quickly extended into the Middle East. In 1798 the Napoleonic invasion of Egypt temporarily established a French foothold in this strategic area which Britain feared as an important step in a move against India. Russia moved into Central Asia and by the end of the 19th century the Czar's influence extended to the Amu Daria. Britain was moving into the Punjab in search of a "scientific" frontier to make sure that her possesions in India were safe.

In Kabul internecine warfare led to the ouster of Shah Shuja (q.v.), the last of the Sadozai rulers, and Dost Muhammad (q.v.), first of the Muhammadzai rulers, ascended the throne. He wanted an alliance with India and hoped to regain Peshawar which had been lost to the emerging Sikh nation under Ranjit Singh (q.v.). Lord Auckland, the British governor-general of India, chose an alliance with the Sikh ruler instead and decided to restore Shah Shuja to the Afghan throne. The presence of a purported Russian agent at Kabul (See VITKEVICH) and Dost Muhammad's hostility to the Sikh ruler were the reasons for the declaration of war (See SIMLA MANIFESTO). A tripartite treaty was signed in July 1838 between Shah Shuja, Ranjit Singh, and Lord

Auckland, and the "Army of the Indus" invaded Afghanistan. The invaders met with little resistance, Shah Shuja was put on the Kabul throne and Dost Muhammad was forced into Indian exile. But it was soon apparent that the Sadozai ruler needed British protection to maintain himself in power and the army became a force of occupation. The families of British officers came to Kabul and thousands of Indian camp-followers engaged in the lucrative business of importing from India the necessities of colonial life. But all was not well. In November 1841 a mob stormed the British mission and killed all its members, including Alexander Burnes (q.v.), its head. Muhammad Akbar (q.v.), a son of Dost Muhammad, together with a number of chiefs now rallied his forces and increasingly threatened the occupiers. The British were forced to negotiate a retreat from which only few of the 16,000 troops and camp-followers survived. Britain felt it necessary to have its martial reputation restored and in 1842 sent in General George Pollock, who wreaked vengeance on Kabul, laying torch to the covered bazar and permitting plunder which destroyed much of the rest of the city. The British forces left and Amir Dost Muhammad returned in 1843 to rule Afghanistan until he died a natural death twenty years later. He is buried in Gazar-Gah cemetary in Herat.

Second Anglo-Afghan War (1878-79): The "Signal Catastrophe" of the previous war inclined the British to pursue a policy of "masterly inactivity" which was to leave Afghanistan to the Afghans. But a generation later the advocates of a "forward policy" to counter Russian moves in Central Asia succeeded in being heard.

Amir Shir Ali (q.v., 1863-79), a son of Amir Dost Muhammad, had ascended the Afghan throne after eliminating a number of rivals. He gained British recognition in 1869 and was invited to meet Lord Mayo in Ambala, India. Shir Ali was worried about Russian advances in Central Asia and wanted British guarantees from Russian aggression and recognition of his son, Abdullah Jan, as crown prince and his successor; but the viceroy was willing to give only presents of 600,000 rupees and a few pieces of artillery, and no guarantees from Russian attack. Disappointed, he was receptive when General Kaufmann, the Russian governor-general at Tashkent, made overtures, promising what Britain was not willing to give. General Stolietoff arrived in Kabul on July 22, 1878, with the charge to draft a treaty of alliance with the Afghan ruler. Britain was now alarmed, and sent General Neville Chamberlain to lead a British military mission to Kabul. Arrangements had been made with the independent tribes on the frontier for the mission's escort of one thousand troops, but when the British reached the border, they were prevented from entering Afghan territory. To avoid a "loss of face" with the tribes, the Indian government issued an ultimatum and dispatched an army under General F. Roberts (q.v.) which entered Kabul on July 24, 1879. Shir Ali fled north in the hope of receiving Russian support. No help was forthcoming and the amir died of natural causes in Mazar-i-Sharif on February 21, 1879.

Britain recognized his son Yaqub Khan (q.v.) as the Afghan ruler (Abdullah Jan had preceded his father in death) at the cost of his signing the Treaty of Gandomak (q. v.) on May 26, 1879. Louis Cavagnari was established as British envoy at Kabul, and history repeated itself when after only six weeks in Kabul, mutinous troops whose pay was in arrears stormed the British mission and assassinated the envoy and his staff. The incident encouraged attacks on British positions which grew, in spite of British attempts at pacification, and culminated in the rout of General Burrows at the Battle of Maiwand (July 27, 1879). Fearing a repetition of the "Signal Catastrophe," the British-Indian government recognized Abdur Rahman (q. v.) as "amir of Kabul and its dependencies," and thus facilitated an orderly exit from Afghanistan. Also see SHIR ALI, ABDUL RAHMAN, and YAQUB KHAN.

Third Anglo-Afghan War (1919): A short war between Afghanistan and British Indian forces which lasted from May 4 until adoption of a ceasefire on June 3, 1919. Amir Amanullah (1919-29 q.v.) had ascended the throne in February 1919, after the assassination of his father, Amir Habibullah. He was an ardent nationalist and reformer and was said to have been a member of the "war party" at the Afghan court, which favored an attack on India during World War I. Afghanistan had remained neutral in the "holy war" against Britain, and Amir Habibullah expected a generous financial reward and British recognition of Afghanistan's complete independence. But once the European conflict was ended, Britain showed no intention of freeing the country from its control. Amir Amanullah therefore declared Afghanistan independent. He demanded a treaty which would end Afghanistan's political dependence on Britain and establish normal, neighborly relations between the two states.

Lord Chelmsford, the viceroy of India, however, suggested that no new treaty was required, despite the fact that previously India had held that the agreements with Afghan rulers were personal and therefore subject to renegotiation with each new ruler. He merely acknowledged Amanullah's election as amir "by the populace of Kabul and its surrounding," implying that he was not in complete control of his country. The subsidy paid to previous Afghan rulers was halted, and when Amanullah sent his new envoy to India he was asked "what amir" he represented.

To emphasize his demands, Amanullah sent three of his generals to the border: Saleh Muhammad, the commander-in-chief, arrived at Dakka, the border town, on May 3; Abdul Quddus, the prime minister (*sadr-i a'zam*) moved to the area of Qalat-i Ghilzai (q.v.) on May 5; and a day later Muhammad Nader, the former commander-in-chief (and subsequent king of Afghanistan), moved to Khost (q.v.) with a tribal *lashkar* (army) of several thousand men in addition to his regular forces. Hostilities began on May 4, 1919, when Afghan troops cut the water supply to Landi Kotal on the Indian side of the border, and Britain retaliated by closing the Khaibar pass. The Afghans wanted to make a concerted effort involving the frontier tribes and the people of Peshawar, but a Peshawar revolt was prevented when British forces cut the supplies of water, electricity, and food to the city. Saleh Muhammad's forces became prematurely engaged and had to give ground. It was primarily on the Waziristan front (See WAZIRI) that the Afghans were able to break through the British defenses and capture the British base at Thal. The entire Northwest Frontier was in ferment and Indian tribesmen were ready to rally to support the Afghans. Therefore the Indian government felt it advisable to make overtures to Amanullah, who agreed to a ceasefire on June 3, 1919. Long negotiations followed at Rawalpindi (q.v.), Mussoorie (q.v.), and Kabul until normal, neighborly relations between Afghanistan and Britain were established. (Also see AFGHAN FOREIGN RELATIONS and ANGLO-AFGHAN TREATIES.)

ANGLO-RUSSIAN CONVENTION. An agreement between Great Britain and Russia concluded on August 31st, 1907, which was to "ensure perfect security on their respective frontiers in Central Asia and to maintain in these regions a solid and lasting peace." It divided Iran into spheres of influence between the two powers, permitted Russia to have direct relations of a nonpolitical nature with local Afghan officials in northern Afghanistan, and provided for equal access to "commercial opportunity." Tibet was to be under Chinese sovereignty but the British were free to deal with Tibetans in commercial matters while Russian Buddhists could deal with the Dalai Lama on religious matters. Although Britain was to continue its treaty obligation of 1905 to protect Afghanistan from unprovoked Russian aggression, and Russia declared Afghanistan outside her sphere of influence, Amir Habibullah (q.v.) saw this agreement as an attempt of solving the "Afghanistan Question" over his head. Amir Habibullah was on a state visit of India in January 1907 when Britain and Russia negotiated the treaty, but he was not informed of the Convention until September 10, 1907. He was shocked and felt betrayed by the British and, when he was requested to agree to the Convention, he took a year with his reply, refusing to ratify the agreement. Russia never obtained the expected commercial and political benefits, and the Bolshevik government repudiated the Convention in 1918 in an attempt to win the goodwill of its Asian neighbors. As far as Afghanistan was concerned the Convention was a "dead letter" from the beginning.

ANIS, GHULAM MUHAYUDDIN. A supporter of King Amanullah and, in 1927, founder of a private newspaper, named after him *Anis*. During the civil war period (1929), he temporarily edited *Habib al-Islam* ("Beloved of Islam.") the newspaper of Amir Habibullah (Kalakani). In 1931, the paper, *Anis*, came under government control and, with the exception of the republican period (1973-75) has existed as a national, daily newspaper to the present. A Tajik, Anis was born in Herat and educated in Egypt. Arrested after Nadir Shah ascended the throne, he remained in prison until his death in 1938. He is the author of *Crisis and Salvation* (*Buhran wa Nejat*) which describes Nadir's defeat of Habibullah Kalakani.

ANJOMAN-I ADABI (Literary Society). A literary circle founded by Nadir Shah in 1930. Early members included Qari Abdullah (q.v.), the poet laureate; Ghulam Muhammad Ghobar (q.v.); Sarwar Joya (q.v.); Muhammad Karim Nazihi; Sarwar Goya and others. They edited and published the periodical "Kabul" and from 1932 the *Salnamah, Kabul Annual*. The Literary Society and the Historical Society later became part of the Afghan Academy (q.v.).

ANSARI, KHWAJA ABDULLAH (1006-1089). Also called "Pir-i Herat" (Sufi Master of Herat). A much celebrated sufi poet and philosopher who was born in Herat and spent most of his life in that city. A "mystic of love," he became a "mystic of *tauhid* (Unity)." He wrote both in Arabic and Persian. His Arabic collection is said to contain more than 6,000 couplets, and his Persian poetry is said to amount to about 14,000 verses. His tomb is in Gazargah, near Herat, amid remains from the Timurid period.

AQCHA (lat. 36-56' N, long. 66-11' E). A town with about 10,000 inhabitants in Jozjan province. It is on the road from Shiberghan to Mazar-e Sharif, about 30 miles from the former and 42 miles from the latter. It was an Uzbak Khanate until annexed by Amir Dost Muhammad. The population is still largely Uzbak. Major enterprises include a carpet industry, tanneries, and the production of vegetable oil. Aqcha is known for its bazar of silver jewelry.

ARAB. There are some 4,000 Arabs living in four villages in Jozjan and Balkh provinces who still speak Arabic (Farhadi - but Barfield in *The Central Asian Arabs of Afghanistan*, has not found any). In addition, there are about 100,000 others scattered all over northern Afghanistan and Herat province who no longer speak Arabic. They are sunni Muslims and claim to be the descendants of the Muslim Arab conquerors of Khorasan (q.v.). More likely, they are the descendants of Arabs from Damascus who in the 15th century were settled in Samarkand by Timur-i Lang (q.v.).

ARG Or **ARK**. A citadel within a walled city, traditionally the residence of a ruler. After the Bala Hisar (q.v.) was destroyed by British forces in 1879, Amir Abdur Rahman built the new Arg, located in the center of Kabul. It took five years to build and housed in addition to the Amir and his court the major government buildings as well. It was surrounded by a moat and a fifty foot wall. Later additions and modification radically changed the original plan when modern buildings replaced the early residences. In the *Salam Khana* (Audience Hall) the affairs of government were conducted. The *Del Kusha* (Heart's Delight) Palace was added by Amir Habibullah and the *Gul Khana* Palace was built to be the royal office of King Amanullah. After the coup by Muhammad Daud in July 1973, the president's office was established in the Arg. During the Khalqi period (1978-79) Nur Muhammad Taraki (q.v.) moved in and the Arg was renamed the "House of the People" (*Khana-yi Khalq*). In December 1979, Hafizullah Amin left the Arg and established himself in the Tapa

Taj Beg Palace in Darulaman, where he was assassinated purportedly by Soviet troops.

ARGHANDAB (lat. 31-27' N, long. 64-23' E). A major Afghan river which has its source in the Kuh-e Safi (mountain) northwest of Ghazni. It flows in a southwesterly direction north of Kandahar city and, after a course of about 350 miles runs into the Helmand river. Only the upper part of the stream is perennial. In June 1950, Morrison Knudsen, an American engineering firm, began construction of the 145-foot high Arghandab Dam located about 18 miles above Kandahar city; it was finished in 1952 and greatly increased the land under irrigation in the Kandahar basin. There are also two districts (*woleswali*) named Arghandab -- one in Kandahar province with an area of 214 square miles and a population of 43,000, and the other in Zabul province with an area of 808 square miles and a population of 18,000 (estimates are for 1978).

ARGHANDIWAL, MUHAMMAD ANWAR. Deputy prime minister of social and cultural affairs, 1991, and member of the national salvation society, a non-partisan organization which wants to achieve a political solution to the war in Afghanistan. A Pashtun, he was born in 1930 in Kabul and educated in Kabul, Turkey, England and the United States. From 1971 to 1973 he served as minister of justice and attorney general and as governor of Kunduz from 1973-78. He is not a member of the PDPA.

ARGHASTAN (lat. 31-23' N, long. 65-46' E). A river which is part of the Helmand-Arghandab system. It is a continuation of the Lori river and runs in a west-southwesterly direction into the Dori, about 25 miles south of Kandahar, and into the Helmand river south of Lashkar Gah. Arghastan is also the name of a district (*woleswali*) with an area of 1,663 square miles and 166 villages, including Arghastan village, the administrative center.

ARIAN, ABDUL RASHID (ARYAN). A member of the Khalqi faction of the PDPA since 1964 and member of the Khalqi central committee since 1977. After the Saur Revolt he was deputy minister of information and culture (April to October 1978) and ambassador at Islamabad (1978-80). In 1980, Babrak Karmal appointed him deputy prime minister (1980-81), minister of justice (1980-81, as well as president of the high judiciary council and attorney general). In 1981 he lost his ministerial positions but was elected vice president of the revolutionary council (1981-88) and to the senate in 1988. Born in 1941 in Kandahar of a Pashtun family, he worked as a typesetter and later as journalist with the daily *Tulu-yi Afghan*. He was expelled from the party for his complicity in the attempted Tanai coup of March 1990. See TANAI.

ARIANA (ARYANA). Name of the first territory of the Arians, as mentioned in the Avesta, around 1,500 B.C. Afghan historians point with pride to the illustrious roots of the Afghan state, suggesting a direct link between the ancient Arians and the modern Afghans. The name *Ariana* is frequently prefixed to other names to draw attention to Afghanistan's ancient history (for example, Ariana Afghan Airlines (q.v.), and *Ariana*, the name of a monthly journal published since 1942 by the Afghan Historical Society.

ARIANA AFGHAN AIRLINES. The Afghan airline which was started on a small scale in 1955 by Peter Baldwin, an American businessman. At first flights connected major Afghan towns and transported pilgrims to Saudi Arabia and ran charters to Beirut and Tehran. Baldwin owned 49% of the stock and in 1957 sold out to Pan American Airways for $400,000. Subsequently PAN AM played a key role in operating the Airline, maintaining regular service on three routes: Kabul-Tehran-Beirut-Istanbul-Frankfurt-London; Kabul-Tashkent-Moscow; and Kabul-Delhi. During the Republican period (1973-78) the company acquired a DC 10, a wide-body aircraft which was delivered after the Saur Revolt and operated for a number of years. The company eventually lost landing rights in Western Europe but provided regular services to East Bloc countries. It was subsequently merged with the domestic air service and called Bakhtar Afghan Airlines. In 1988 the company again adopted the former name. In the 1980s the company acquired several Antonov AN-26 turboprops for domestic routes and two Turpolev TU-154s for international flights. Also see AVIATION IN AFGHANISTAN.

ASOKA (269-32 B.C.). Indian ruler over an empire that extended from southern India into Afghanistan. Tired of the bloodshed he had wreaked, he repented and dedicated himself to propagating Buddhism. He set up rock edicts (Pillars of Morality) throughout his empire, several of which were found in the area of Kandahar and Laghman. His edicts advocated humanity in government and the abandonment of aggressive wars and constitute the "oldest surviving Indian written documents of any historical significance." (Basham, *The Wonder that was India*.)

ATAN. A Pashtun tribal dance performed on festive occasions and as a physical exercise in the army. It is performed to the ever-faster rhythm of drums, the tribesmen's long hair whipping in unison, and is often continued to exhaustion. In some respects it resembles the dance of the "whirling dervishes" of the Ottoman empire. Although Pashtun in origin, it has also been adopted by other ethnic groups as the Afghan national dance.

'ATA-UL-HAQ ('ATA AL-HAQQ). Foreign minister in the short-lived government of Amir Habibullah (Kalakani), 1919. He was arrested with Habibullah and jailed until 1938. Born about 1885, a Sahibzada of Charikar district, he lived in India until age 16, then joined the Afghan army and became colonel in 1914. During the reign of King Amanullah he spent two years in Moscow in charge of Afghan students. Ata-ul-Haq is the father of Walah, the editor of the newspaper *Caravan*.

AVIATION IN AFGHANISTAN. Aviation in Afghanistan began in 1921
when King Amanullah acquired a British fighter plane. Additional planes
were purchased or acquired as gifts from Britain and the Soviet Union;
the latter donated a number of aircaft on condition that they be operated
and serviced by Soviet nationals. By the end of the 1920s, Afghanistan's
air force consisted of 22 machines (Bristol Fighters, D.H. 9s, Caprioni
Scouts, and a Junker Monoplane) operated by some 25 officers, three of
them Afghans, four Germans and the rest Russians. Young Afghans were
sent to Italy, the Soviet Union, India, and other countries for training as
pilots and aircraft mechanics. The air service was largely devoted to
transporting the mail, foreign diplomats, and members of the Afghan
government. In 1926, average flying times were: Kabul to Kandahar - 3
hours; Kabul to Jalalabad - 50 minutes; Kabul to Termez (on the Soviet
side of the Amu Daria) - 2 hours and 40 minutes; and Jalalabad to
Kandahar - 3 1/2 hours. The flight from Kabul to Moscow took five days,
crossing the Hindu Kush at 5,000 meters. Although half the fleet was out
of operation, control of the airspace proved important in suppressing the
Khost Rebellion (q.v.) and other tribal revolts. After the ouster of King
Amanullah, Nadir Shah did not renew the Soviet concession, but Soviet
planes continued at an irregular schedule to transport diplomatic
personnel to the Soviet Union. In 1937 the Lufthansa Airline established
regular air service from Berlin to Kabul, but this was discontinued as a
result of the outbreat of World War II. For post-war air service, see
ARIANA AFGHAN AIRLINES.

AVIENNA See **IBN SINA'**.

AYUB KHAN, MUHAMMAD (AYYUB). Son of Amir Shir Ali (q.v.) and
brother of Amir Yaqub Khan (q.v.). Victor in the Battle of Maiwand,
July 27, 1880, where he defeated the British Brigadier General Burrows
(See MAIWAND, BATTLE OF). He proclaimed himself king (Amir) in
1880 and marched against Kandahar, but was routed by the forces of
Amir Abdur Rahman. He was forced to seek exile in India, where he remained until his death in 1914.

AZAN (ADHAN). The call to prayer, five times a day, by the *muezzin* from
the door of a mosque or a minaret of a large mosque. The muezzin
chants with some repetitions the following formula: Allah is most great.
I testify that there is no god but Allah. I testify that Muhammad is the
apostle of Allah. Come to prayer. Come to salvation. "Allah is most
great. There is no god but Allah." At the morning prayer the words
"prayer is better than sleep" are added. The shias add the words "come
to the best work!" And also "I testify that Ali is the *wali* [protected
friend] of God."

AZHAR, ABDUL SAMAD. A member of the Parcham faction of the PDPA
who was appointed ambassador to Belgrade in 1989 and defected in 1990.
A Pashtun from Laghman province (q.v.), who was trained as a police

officer in Kabul and Egypt. A member of President Daud's investigation team of the Maiwandwal "affair" in 1973 (See MAIWANDWAL), he is believed to have been the assassin of the former prime minister. He was arrested in May 1979 by the Khalqi goverment of Hafizullah Amin (q.v.) and held until January 1980. The Karmal government appointed him commander of police (Tsarandoy) in January 1980 and alternate member of the central committee; he became a full member in 1986. He served as ambassador at Cuba, 1983-86, and Delhi, 1986-89.

AZIMI, GEN. MUHAMMAD NABI. Member of the Parcham faction of the PDPA and minister of defense, 1984-86. He served as commander of Kabul garrison and of the Eastern Front in 1989 and is a member of the central council of the Watan party. He was awarded the order of "Ghazi King Amanullah" in May 1991. He took part in the 1973 and 1978 coups. In March 1983 he was wounded in a skirmish with mujahedin forces. His mother tongue is Dari.

AZIZ, ABDUL HAI. Minister of planning in 1963 and an active participant in the constitutionalist movement. He was born in 1914, a Muhammadzai, and educated at Istiqlal high school in Kabul and in France and England. He started his career in 1939 with the Afghan National Bank at Kabul and, after a career as teacher and dean of the faculty of law of Kabul University and adviser to various ministries, he returned as acting president (1960-62) of the bank. In 1951 he became assistant editor of *Watan* (Homeland), a liberal, biweekly newspaper and was imprisoned for a year as a result of his journalistic activities. He died in Paris in 1963.

AZIZ, ABDUL HUSAIN. First Afghan minister at Washington (1943) and first representative at the United Nations (1946). A Muhammadzai, born in 1896 in Iran and, after finishing his education in Tehran and Kabul, he joined the Afghan foreign service and was appointed consul-general to Delhi in 1918. He was Afghan minister at Rome (1930-32), and ambassador at Moscow (1933-38), and at New Delhi in 1954. He returned to Kabul and became minister of public works in 1938 and minister of communications in 1940. He served a short term as minister of education in 1949. Died in 1960.

AZIZI, HAYATULLAH. Minister of rural development (May 1990). Born in 1940 in Mazar-i Sharif and educated at Bakhtar Lycée in Mazar and in engineering in London, England; he embarked on a career of teaching and government work in a cotton ginning factory in Mazar-i Sharif. In 1973 he began work in the Afghan Industrial Development Bank and was promoted its president in 1985. He is not a member of the PDPA.

B

BABA JAN, LT. GEN. ABDUL WAHED. Member of the Parcham faction of the PDPA and chief of general staff of the armed forces, Jan. 1980 - Jan. 1984, and for a short time caretaker at the ministry of national defense. He was elected an alternate member of the PDPA central committee and served as head of the Kabul military academy and as ambassador to Berlin (1985-88). He was educated in military schools in Kabul, Turkey, and the USSR. He is the recipient of the "Order of the Golden Star."

BABUR, ZAHIR AL-DIN MUHAMMAD (1483-1530). Founder of the Moghul empire, the "greatest soldier of his age," and a talented writer and great poet (Sykes, 1940). He was a Barlas Turk who descended on his mother's side from Genghis Khan and on the male side from Tamerlane (Timur-i Lang). He was ousted from his native Ferghana, the Turkic lands north of the Amu Daria, and when he could not retake his homeland he settled in Kabul in 1504. Probing expeditions into India led to territorial conquests which became the foundation of the Moghul empire. He loved Kabul and wrote fondly about the town and wanted to be buried in the Bagh-i Babur, a garden he himself had planted on the western slope of Sher Darwaza mountain. He died in Agra on December 26, 1530, and his body was transported to Kabul where his rather modest tomb is still located.

BACHA-I SAQQAU See HABIBULLAH KALAKANI.

BACTRIA. Name of an ancient kingdom north of the Hindukush and south of the Oxus with the capital at Bactra, near the present Balkh. Bactria was part of the Achaemenid empire, first conquered by Cyrus the Great (559-30 B.C.), it later became a Greek colony of Alexander (331 B.C.) and his successors. Excavations have revealed numerous examples of Greek sculpture, architecture, and inscriptions from the 3rd to 1st centuries B.C. The area came under Turkish control in the sixth century and was invaded by the Muslim Arabs a century later. Afghan nationalists seek the historical roots of the present state of Afghanistan in this ancient kingdom. Also see BALKH and ARIANA.

BADAKHSHAN (lat. 36-45' N, long. 72-0' E). A province in northeastern Afghanistan, comprising an area of 15,786 square miles and a population of about 484,000. The province includes the Wakhan Corridor (q.v.) a narrow valley which extends to the Chinese border and separates the Soviet Union from the Indo- Pakistan subcontinent. The province is divided into five districts (*woleswali*) and seven subdistricts (*alaqadari*) with Faizabad as the administrative capital. The province is mountainous with a number of high valleys and peaks reaching a height of 16,000 feet. It is rich in mineral resources including silver, copper, lead, precious stones, and virtually all the lapis lazuli mined in Afghanistan. Famed for its Marco Polo sheep, ibex, and snow leopards, Badakhshan was beginning to develop into an important hunting preserve for wealthy foreigners before the war in Afghanistan interrupted further development. The yak is still used in the Wakhan as a beast of burden. The population is Tajik with Uzbak communities in the west and Wakhis and Qirghiz in the Wakhan Corridor (most of the latter have fled as a result of Soviet occupation). Much of Badakhshan was ruled by autonomous khans until in 1850 Dost Muhammad (q.v.) took it under the direct control of the Kabul government. By the time of Amir Abdur Rahman, it had become an integral part of the Afghan state. In 1893 a mission under Sir Mortimer Durand demarcated Afghanistan's northern border and allocated the Wakhan Corridor to Afghanistan. Amir Abdur Rahman was reluctant to accept this "arm that could easily be cut by an enemy," but agreed to accept the Wakhan as a buffer between the Russian and British empires when Britain offered to increase his subsidy by 650,000 Indian rupees for his cost of the administration and defense. A large part of Badakhshan appears presently under mujahedin control with the *jam'iat-i Islami* of Burhanuddin Rabbani as the major resistance force.

BADAKHSHI, TAHIR. With Babrak Karmal and Nur M. Taraki, one of the founders of the PDPA, and member of the central committee in 1965. In 1967 he sided with Parcham in the factional dispute, but left the party to found the *Setam-i Milli* ("National Oppression" - a Marxist, anti-Pashtun faction) about 1968. He was born in Faizabad, Badakhshan, and educated in Kabul at Habibia High School, and at the faculty of economics of Kabul University. Married to Jamila, a sister of Sultan Ali Keshtmand. He was imprisoned in Pul-i Charkhi jail, summer 1978, and executed during the rule of Hafizullah Amin on September 17, 1979.

BADAL. An aspect of the Pashtun tribal code of honor which requires retaliation for insults and the shedding of blood. It serves as a deterrent to reckless lawlessness but often results in long periods of hostilities between individuals, groups, and entire tribes and causes great suffering for all. Afghan governments have tried to extend Kabul's jurisdiction into the tribal area, without being able to eliminate the practice. Also see PASHTUNWALI.

BADALZAI See BARECHI.

BADEZAI See ACHAKZAI.

BADGHIS (lat. 35-0' N, long. 63-45' E). Badghis is a province in northwestern Afghanistan which was part of Herat province prior to 1964. The province has an area of 8,438 square miles and an estimated populatio of 47,000. Major districts include Jowand, Ghormach, Qades, Murghab, Qal'a-i Nau, and Kushk-i Kohna. The province borders on the Soviet Union in the north and on Herat in the west. Badghis is a country of beautiful grassy hills but virtually without trees or even bushes in spite of an abundance of good water near the hills. The climate is, as in most parts of Afghanistan, cold in the winter and hot in summer. Barley and wheat are the major crops and pistachio nuts are harvested in considerable quantities. The area was densely populated until it was devastated by Mongol invaders (13th and 15th centuries) and again by the Safavids under Shah Abbas II (1642-66). Subsequently it was inhabited only by nomadic tribes because of the danger of Turkoman raids from the north. The present population includes Pashtuns, Jamshidis, Hazaras, and small communities of other ethnic groups.

BADINZAI See **ACHAKZAI**.

BAGH-I BALA. A garden in Kabul, near the present Intercontinental Hotel, where Amir Abdur Rahman's palace is located. After his death, the garden and building were closed and fell into neglect. Because of its strategic location on top of a hill overlooking the city, Habibubullah Kalakani (q.v.) used it as a command post in 1929 during the civil war. In the 1970s the palace was restored and turned into a fashionable restaurant.

BAGHLAN (lat. 36-11' N, long. 68-44' E). A province in northeastern Afghanistan with an area of 6,627 square miles and a population of about 486,000. Baghlan is also the name of the administrative capital of the province, counting about 39,000 inhabitants. The province includes the northern slopes of the Hindu Kush range which are crossed by the Rabatak, Barabi, Khawak, and Salang passes. The northern part is largely agricultural with irrigation from the Baghlan, Qara Batur, Chunghar, and Mar Khana rivers. Sugar beets and cotton are the major crops and pomegranates, grapes, and pistachio nuts are important items of export. Qaraqul sheep (see QARAQUL) are raised in the northern part of the province. Sugar production, started in 1940 with Czech assistance, has become the most important industry. Coal is extracted in the Karkar valley near Pul-i Khumri (q.v.). A silk industry was started in 1951. Not much is known about the effect of the war on the area.

BAGHLANI, MUHAMMAD BASHIR. Minister of justice and attorney general, Oct. l983. Minister of Justice and chief prosecutor (P. *loya tsaranwal*), 1985. He was a member of Dr. Najibullah's 1986 constitution drafting commission. Born in 1940 in Takhar province and educated in the legal profession, serving as an advocate for 12 years. A head of the "Organization of Revolutionary Toilers of Afghanistan" (*Sazman-i Inqilab-i Zahmatkeshan-i Afghanistan* [SAZA]), but is not a member of the PDPA. It has been reported that he recently left SAZA.

BAGRAM (BEGRAM) (lat. 34-58' N, long. 69-17' E). Site of an ancient city with an abundance of Buddhist, Graeco-Roman, and Phoenician artifacts. According to some sources, it is the site of *Alexandria ad Caucasum* (Alexandria by the Caucasus, built by Alexander the Great in 330-329 B.C.) which flourished for centuries until it was destroyed by the hordes of Genghis Khan in the 13th century. The town is north of Kabul near the confluence of the Panjshir and Ghorband rivers, about five miles west of Charikar. Bagram is now a small town, the center of the *woleswali* (district) of the same name in Parwan province, and the location of an air base built with Soviet assistance in the 1950s. Soviet troops landed there in December 1979 and held Bagram as a base for the protection of Kabul and the Salang pass.

BAHER, ABDUL GHAFUR. Minister of Islamic affairs under Babrak Karmal (1985) and member of the Islamic consultative council of Dr. Najibullah (1988) and again minister in 1989. In 1990 he was appointed ambassador to Jakarta. He has been a candidate academician of the Academy of Science since 1986. Born in 1932 in Alishing, Laghman province, of an Akhundzada (q.v.) family. He was educated at Abu Hanifa Madrasa, the college of theology, Kabul University, and Al-Azhar University in Egypt. He was elected to the 12th Parliament (Nov. 1965) as a representative of Alishing and accompanied Prime Minister Maiwandwal on an official visit to Moscow, 1966. He was appointed president of the theology department of the ministry of education in 1980. He is not a member of the PDPA.

BAHES, BAHRUDDIN (Also BAES). A native of Darwaz, Badakhshan, educated in Islamic studies and law at Kabul University. He became an opponent of the Daud government and the subsequent Marxist regime. Said to have been a sympathizer of *Setam-i Milli* (q.v.) and possibly also a member of SAMA (See KALAKANI, ABDUL MAJID). He was arrested after the Saur Revolt in 1978 and was secretly executed during the Taraki period. According to unconfirmed reports the kidnappers of the American Ambassador Adolph Dubs wanted to gain Bahes' freedom in exchange for Dubs.

BAHSUD Or BEHSUD See HAZARA.

BAIANZAI See ACHAKZAI.

BAIHAQI, ABU'L FAZL (995-1077). Secretary to the the Ghaznawid (q.v.) court and historian of the dynasty. Of his monumental work, the 30-volume *Mujalladat*, the extant portion covers the period of Mas'ud (1030-41), called *Tarikh-i Mas'ud* (History of Masud) also called *History of Baihaqi*, and *Tarikh- Naseri*. Baihaqi was born in 995 in Baihaq, the present Sabzawar in Farah province of Afghanistan.

BAIQARA, SULTAN HUSAIN (1469-1506). Timurid ruler at Herat and great sponsor of the arts. At his court were gathered Kamaluddin Behzad (q.v.), the master calligrapher and miniature painter; Abdur Rahman Jami (q.v.), mystic, scholar and one of the great classical Persian poets; and others. Sultan Husain's Wazir Amir Shir Ali Nawa'i was a great statesman who wrote poetry in Turkish.

BAKHTAR AFGHAN AIRLINE See **ARIANA AFGHAN AIRLINE** and **AVIATION IN AFGHANISTAN**.

BALA HESAR (CITADEL). A citadel within a walled town on top of a ridge or hill, serving as the residence of Afghan rulers in Kabul or governors in provincial towns. The Bala Hesar of Kabul is a huge complex built southwest of the ancient wall on Sher Darwaza mountain. Until the 19th century its high stone walls surrounded a strong citadel which was the residence of the Kabul ruler and his court. Babur Shah (q.v.) and Timur-i Lang (q.v.) are said to have resided in it. High military and civilian officials were quartered within the outer walls. The six- century-old fortress was destroyed on order of the British General Roberts in 1978-79 and lay in ruins until Nadir Shah (q.v.) started the process of reconstruction. It has served as a military college and garrison since 1939.

BALKH (lat. 36-46' N, long. 66-54' E). A province in north-central Afghanistan with an area of about 4,633 square miles and a population of about 570,000. The administrative capital of the province is Mazar-i Sharif (q.v.) with about 103,000 inhabitants in 1978, and the location of a shrine Afghans believe to be the burial place of the Caliph Ali. The town of Balkh, located on the Balkhab river about 14 miles west of Mazar-i Sharif, derives its name from the ancient city of Bactra amidst the ruins of which it is located. According to local tradition Balkh was founded by Balkh ibn Balakh ibn Saman ibn Salam ibn Ham ibn Nuh (Noah). Zoroastrian tradition holds that it was the birthplace of Zoroaster (q.v.) and was built by the Arian ruler Bakhdi (or Keiomarz?) who founded the Pishdadian dynasty. The city was captured by Alexander the Great (320s B.C.) and became the capital of the Greek satrapi of Bactria. In the 2nd century B.C. Bactria was invaded by Turkic nomads who renamed the area Tukharestan. Subsequently the Kushans (See KUSHANID KINGDOM) ruled over the area to be followed by other dynasties. The ancestor of the famous Barmakid family of Abbasid waziers (781-803), Barmak (priest), was a native of Balkh. Genghiz Khan (1206-26) destroyed the city, but it was rebuilt during the Timurid period (15th century). In 1480 the tomb of the Caliph Ali was believed to be discovered where Mazar-i Sharif is now located and Balkh lost its significance. Because of its antiquity, the town is known as "Mother of Cities." Also see BACTRIA.

BALKHI, JALALUDDIN RUMI (1207-73). Known as Jalaluddin Rumi (from A. *Rum*, Asia Minor), where he spent the greater part of his life. He is acclaimed as the most eminent sufi poet in Persian, famous for his mystical *mathnawis* (a poetic form in rhyming distichs) which "rank among the great poems of all time" (E. G. Brown). Jalaluddin was the founder of the *maulawiyya* order of "whirling dervishes," whose dance was part of their ritual. He was born in 1207 in Balkh and is therefore claimed as a native son by the Afghans and called by the appellation Balkhi (the one from Balkh).

BALKHI, RABI'A. Famous poetess in Dari and a contemporary of Rudaki (the first great poet in Persian after the advent of Islam, d. 940 A.D.) was born in Balkh in the tenth century and therefore called Balkhi by Afghans. Some of her ghazals are extant. Legend has it that she fell in love with a Turkish slave, named Baktash, and had to pay for this illicit love with her life.

BALKHI, SAYYID MUHAMMAD ISMAIL. Founder of the Islamic Center at Jamal Mina, Kabul, and a major spokesman of the *shi'a* community. He was born in Balkh and educated in theology at *shi'a* madrasas and came to Kabul in 1948. He came to be known as a liberal *shi'a* preacher and his Friday sermons in the Takia Khana-yi Umumi, their spiritual center in Chandawol, were said to have been popular with *shi'a* youth. Arrested for involvement in an assassination attempt on Shah Mahmud (q.v.) in 1950, he was jailed until 1964. He died in Kabul in 1968.

BALUCH. One of Afghanistan's ethnic minorities located primarily in Nimruz and scattered in small numbers over Helmand, Farah, Herat, Fariab, Jozjan, Kunduz, and Badakhshan provinces. Their numbers are estimated in the 1970s at between 100,000 and 200,000. Virtually all are sunnis and speakers of the Baluchi language (except for the Dari- speaking Qataghan Baluch). The Baluch are no longer organized into specific tribes and are largely sedentary; their "heartland" lies in the Baluchistan provinces of Iran and Pakistan, where they are said to number about 5 million. Small numbers also exist in the Soviet Union. Since the mid-1970s some 2,500 Baluch guerrillas, fighting for autonomy in Pakistan, have found shelter in southern Afghanistan. After the Saur Revolt, the Taraki government issued Decree No. 4 for the "evolution of literature, education and publication in mother tongues of tribes and nationalities" and declared Baluchi a "national" language whose use was permitted on Afghan media. The Brahui (q.v.) who speak a Dravidian language have now largely assimilated with the Baluch.

BAMIAN (lat. 34-50' N, long. 67-50' E). A province in central Afghanistan with an area of about 6,757 square miles and a population of about 285,000 and a town of the same name which is the administrative center of the province. The town lies at an altitude of about 8,200 feet above sea level, about 205 miles by road north of Kabul. Bamian is part of the Hazarajat, the mountainous country of central Afghanistan which is inhabited primarily by Hazaras (q.v.). The province is famous for its two Buddha statues, respectively 120 and 175 feet in height, dating from the fifth and third centuries A.D. The statues are hewn into solid rock and overlaid with stucco, and, although they have suffered from the ravages of time and destruction by man, some of the stucco works and wall paintings are still preserved. The walls of the 300-feet high cliffs are honeycombed with caves which served as living quarters of Buddhist monks and are still inhabited today. The sculptures and paintings are "an eclectic hybrid mixing Indian, Central Asian, Iranian, and classical European art styles and ideas."

BAND-I AMIR (lat. 34-50' N, long. 67-12' E). A series of five clear, blue lakes on the north side of the Kuh-i Baba (q.v.) in Bamian province. The lakes are formed by the flow of water over a succession of natural dams, running from the higher to the next one below. According to local tradition the dams were the creation of Caliph Ali, and the word "Amir" (Commander) refers to the Caliph, not to any Afghan ruler.

Band-i Amir is also the name of a river which rises in the Band-i Amir lakes and runs through the Yakowlang valley in a southwesterly direction until it turns northeast, at which point it is known as the Balkhab; finally it turns north and dissipates in the Turkestan plains. The country on its upper course, especially the Yakowlang valley, is inhabited by Dai Zangi Hazaras (See HAZARA).

BAND-I BABA (lat. 34-37' N, long. 62-40' E). A range of hills north of the Harirud (q.v.) valley, called by the Turkomans Barkhudung Dagh and known in European sources as the Paropamisus. The Koh-i Baba forks into three branches: the Band-e Turkoman in the north, the Band-i Baian in the south, and the central range of the Band-i Baba which extends east and rises to a height of some 5,000 feet above the Herat valley.

BAND-I TURKESTAN (lat. 35-30' N, long. 64-0' E). The northern branch of the Koh-i Baba mountain range which runs in a northwestern direction, circling the basin of the upper Murghab river and dividing it from Band-i Amir river. It extends from an area about 45 miles southwest of Maimana (q.v.) and runs for about 125 miles in a generally east-west direction, its northern slopes giving rise to the Sar-i Pul, Maimana, and Kaisar rivers. The highest peak in the range is the Zangilak which reaches an altitude of about 11,600 feet.

BANK-I MILLI See **BANKING**.

BANKING. Until the early 1930s there were no banks in Afghanistan and the banking business was conducted by private individuals and moneylenders. In addition to the Afghan *ropia*, minted in Kabul, silver and gold coins from neighboring countries were also in circulation. It was at times necessary to send caravans of gold and silver bullion to the interior of the country to meet the demand for financial transactions, a risky practice in times of unrest. In 1932 Abdul Majid Zabuli (q.v.), a pioneering Afghan enterpreneur, founded a stock company (Shirkat-i Ashami-yi Afghanistan) which was chartered as a commercial bank in 1934. Incorporated with a capital of 35 million Afghanis (£745,500), it was authorized to issue banknotes, import sugar and petroleum products, transact all government purchases and sales, and had sole option on the exploitation of all mines, and the establishment of all industrial institutions in Afghanistan. It became a vital factor in the process of industrialization of Afghanistan and the establishment of a textile industry in the Kunduz and Pul-i Khumri (q.v.) areas. Its monopoly was ended in 1938 with the establishment of the Da Afghanistan Bank which performed the functions of a central bank. Its task was to issue currency notes and control the exchange rate of the currency. In 1955 the Afghan Commercial Bank (Pashtanai Tejarati Bank) was established as a joint-stock company for the purpose of developing the commerce of the country. A bank of construction and mortgages existed since 1948 to assist the construction of low-cost houses for government employees as well as hotels and various public buildings. All banks were nationalized during the Daud regime, a policy which was continued after the Saur Revolt of 1978. In the 1990s the Bank-i Milli had seven branches in Kabul and ten in the provinces, as well as offices in London, New York, Hamburg, and Karachi. The war in Afghanistan and the occupation of rural areas by mujahedin forces has severely restricted banking activities. Also see AFGHANI and DA AFGHANISTAN BANK.

BARAKATULLAH, MAULAWI. An Indian revolutionary and "prime minister" in 1919 in the "Provisional Government of India in Exile" in which Mahendra Pratap (q.v.) was president, and Maulana Obaidullah (q.v.) home minister. He met Sardar Nasrullah (q.v.) in England during the latter's visit in 1895 and became a newswriter (political reporter) for him thereafter, and in 1915 he came to Kabul as a member of the Hentig-Niedermayer expedition (q.v.). Subsequently he represented Mahmud Tarzi (q.v.) as editor of the *Seraj al-Akhbar* (q.v.) while Tarzi was in Europe. In 1927 Barakatullah accompanied Mahendra Pratap to the United States and died shortly thereafter in San Francisco.

BARAKI. A tribe of Tajiks (q.v.), intermarried with Ghilzais (q.v.), and settled in the Logar and Butkhak areas, south and east of Kabul, by Sultan Mahmud of Ghazni (q.v.) in the 11th century. The Barakis accompanied the Ghaznawid ruler on his invasions of India and were rewarded for their services with a perpetual grant of the lands of Kaniguram in Waziristan. They are divided into the Barakis of Rajan who speak Persian and the Barakis of Barak who speak an idiom of their own.

BARAKZAI. An important section of the Zirak branch of the Durrani (q.v.) to which the Barakzai/Muhammadzai ruling family belongs. In numbers, economic and political strength they were the paramount tribe of Afghanistan. Their heartland is in the area south of Kandahar, the valley of the Arghastan river, the banks of the Helmand, and the plains bounded by the Helmand river. They were soldiers in the service of Nadir Shah (q.v.), founder of the short-lived Afsharid dynasty in Iran, and were settled on land conquered from the Ghilzai (q.v.). They continued to hold *jagirs*, fiefs, in exchange for their military services to Ahmad Shah Durrani (q.v.). When Paianda Khan (q.v.), leader of the Barakzais, was assassinated, the Barakzais chiefs under Dost Muhammad (q.v.) ousted and replaced the Sadozai dynasty. The Barakzai continued to possess large areas of agricultural land and extensive flocks in the area between Herat and Kandahar.

BARECHI. A tribe of Afghans inhabiting the Shorawak region, south of Kandahar. They are divided into the Mandozai, Zakozai, Badalzai, and Shirani, the first three of whom are said to descend from Barech, son of Sharaf-ud-Din and grandson of Saraban, the son of Qais, the putative ancestor of all the Pashtuns. The Barechis are cultivators irrigating their lands from the Lora, which is the lifeline of the Shorawak valley. They are also known as camel breeders and export their wool to Kandahar. They have been described as peaceful and "fine men ... and excellent swordsmen." They intermarry with their Brahui neighbors and, like them, are of the sunni school of Islam.

BAREQ-SHAFI'I, MUHAMMAD HASAN. A leading Afghan poet, writer, and high-ranking member of the PDPA. He is a Pashtun, born in 1932 in Kabul and educated at Ghazi high school and the theological college in Kabul. He was editor of a number of newspapers and journals, including *Nendari* (Theater), *Zhuandun* (Life), *Pashtun Zhagh*, (Pashtun Voice) and director of *Paiyam-i Imruz* (q.v., Message of the Day). Member of the Parchami faction of the PDPA from the beginning, he became editor of *Khalq* (q.v.) in 1966. After the Saur Revolt he became minister of information and culture in 1978, and minister of transport in 1979. During the Khalqi period he was forced to denounce Babrak Karmal and, after the latter succeeded to power, Bareq-Shafi'i was demoted to the status of alternate member of the central committee. He was appointed first vice president of the central council of the National Fatherland Front (q.v.) in 1982 and subsequently became governor of Herat province. In 1985 he was appointed second secretary of the Afghan embassy in Libya, and in May 1987 he was appointed editor-in-chief of *Haqiqat-i Inqilab-i Saur* (The True Saur Revolution), the party organ during the presidency of Babrak Karmal, and of *Payam*, its successor, in 1989. He was chairman of the union of journalists, but is presently unemployed. His daughter is married to Nur Ahmad Nur (q.v.).

BARITS, NUR AHMAD. Minister of higher and vocational education (1988) and minister without portfolio (1990). Born in 1928 in Kandahar (a brother of Faiz Muhammad Angar, q.v.) and educated at Habibia School (q.v.) and the faculty of medicine of Kabul University, he was a physician at Aliabad hospital and teacher at Kabul University. In 1987 he was appointed chairman of the physicians union and president of the United Nations Association of Afghanistan. He is not a member of the PDPA.

BARYALAI, MAHMUD. Appointed by Dr. Najibullah as first deputy prime minister in May 1990, and member of the executive board of the central council of the *hizb-i watan*. Born in 1944 in Kabul and educated at Habibia School, Kabul University, and the Soviet Union, he is a half-brother of Babrak Karmal and son-in-law of Anahita Ratebzad (q.v.). A charter member of the PDPA, he was imprisoned in 1965-66 for his political activities. Went to the Soviet Union and received an M.A. degree in political economics. After the Saur Revolt he was appointed Afghan ambassador to Pakistan in July 1978 and recalled and purged in October by the Khalqi regime but did not return to Kabul. After the ouster of Hafizullah Amin, he became head of the international relations department of the PDPA. In 1980 he also became editor of the party organ, *Haqiqat-i Inqilab-i Saur*. He was expelled from the party in July 1991, shortly before the return of Babrak Karmal to Afghanistan.

BASHGAL Or **LANDAI SIND** (Short River, lat. 35-20' N, long. 71-32' E). A river which rises in the southern slopes of the Hindu Kush near the Mandal pass (15,300 feet) in Kunar province and, running in a south-southwesterly direction, debouches into the Kunar river. The river is also known by its Pashto name, Landai Sind, and the name Arnawai. The Bashgal valley of Nuristan is inhabited by the Katir, Madugal, Kashtan, and Kam people. They were converted to Islam in 1897.

BASMACHIS. An irregular force, called Basmachis (T. bandits) by the Soviet government, which fought the Bolshevik army in the mountains of Tajikistan and Ferghana in Soviet Central Asia from 1919 until the 1930s. Their leaders included Muhammad Amin Beg, Ibrahim Beg (q.v.), and Enver Pasha (q.v.), the minister of war and leader of the Ottoman war government who was forced to flee the country after the war. For a time the Basmachis enjoyed a measure of support from King Amanullah, who was not averse to becoming the king of a Central Asian confederation. When the Bolshevik government succeded in consolidating its power in Central Asia, Ibrahim Beg was forced to use Afghanistan as a sanctuary. After a hot pursuit into Afghan territory by the Red Army, Sardar Shah Mahmud (q.v.) expelled Ibrahim Beg, who was captured by Soviet forces and executed in April 1931. See IBRAHIM BEG and SOVIET-AFGHAN RELATIONS.

BAZAR. A traditional marketplace varying in size from a few temporary stalls in a village lane with a minimum of goods for a rural population to a major market place in a large town. The bazar is often adjacent to the mosque and in towns and cities it was frequently covered. Shops are usually segregated according to crafts and the types of goods sold. The bazar is usually in the old town, whereas Western-type shops exist in the "new town" (D., *Shahr-i Nau*).

BEHESHTI, SAYYID ALI. President of the Revolutionary Council of the Islamic Union of Afghanistan (*Shura-yi Inqelabi-yi Ittefaq-i Islami-yi Afghanistan* which until 1982 controlled large portions of the Hazarajat. He is a native of Bamian and was educated in Saudi Arabia and Iraq, where he was a contemporary of Ayatollah Khomeini. He opened a madrasa in Waras to spread his revivalist ideas among Hazaras and was speaker in the Takkia Khana at Kabul until the Saur Revolt. In September 1979 he was elected president of the Shura by a council of elders and *Mirs*. Formed a traditional Islamic resistance group, commanded by Sayyid Muhammad Hasan "Jagran" (Major), with headquarters in Waras in Ghor province and became a major force in the Hazarajat until the Shura lost ground to the Islamist forces of *Nasr*. The Shura recruited its fighters from the Hazara peasantry, officered by sayyids (q.v.). Beheshti appointed governors and mayors of towns, disarmed the population and created a state apparatus along traditional lines. Torn by factional fighting and pressed by radical Islamists, his domains were greatly reduced.

BEHZAD, KAMALUDDIN (1450(60?)-1535). Master calligrapher and miniature painter who founded the Herati school of miniature painting. He was a protege of Shir Ali Nawa'i, Sultan Husain Baiqara's prime minister. After the Safavid ruler Shah Ismail captured Herat in 1510, he took Behzad to Tabriz where he became director of the royal library and continued the tradition. Behzad died at age 100 in Tabriz. Also see HERAT.

BENAWA, ABDUL RAUF. A writer, Pashtun activist and diplomat. He was born in 1913 in Kandahar and educated in that city. Published the newspaper *Tulu-i Afghan* (Afghan Sunrise), a number of articles, and a book entitled *Pashtana Likwal* (Writers of Pashto). He became president of the Pashto Academy (see Afghan Academy) and later director of Radio Kabul. Served as press attaché in New Delhi (1954-55) and Cairo (1964-66) and became minister of information and culture in 1967. He was ambassador to Libya, 1980- 84, and came for medical treatment to the United States where he died in 1984.

BIRUNI, ABU RAYHAN AL- (973-1048). Chronicler, astrologer, and scholar at the court of Mahmud of Ghazni (q.v.) who accompanied the Ghaznawid ruler on his campaigns to India where he studied Sanskrit and Indian philosophy. Born about 973 A.D. near Khiva, he was first at the court of the Khwarizm Shahs in Transcaspia, and was called to the court of Mahmud of Ghazni. He was a prolific scholar, said to have 180 works to his name and as tradition has it, his works have "exceeded a camel-load."

BISMIL, MUHAMMAD ANWAR. Poet and director of the Afghan Literary Society (See Afghan Academy) in the early 1930s. Born in 1908 in Kabul and educated at Habibia high school, he was imprisoned in 1932 for membership in the secret "Young Afghan Society" (*Jawanan-i Afghanistan*), a reformist social and political movement. In the 1960s he was appointed a member of the senate. Mother tongue Dari.

BITAB, SUFI ABDUL HAQ. Poet Laureate (*Malik al-Shu'ara*) of Afghanistan who attained the status of master (*Khalifa*) of the Naqshbandi (q.v.) sufi fraternity. He was born in 1892 in Qasab Kocha (Butcher's street) in Kabul city and educated under the supervision of his uncle Mulla Abdul Ghafur, after which he embarked on a career of teaching at Habibia High School and Kabul University. He was awarded the title of "poet laureate" in 1951, but was also respected as a commentator of *Hadith*, and author of numerous publications in a variety of fields. He died in 1958.

BOST See LASHKARGAH.

BRAHUI. A small ethnic community who speak a Dravidian language and are located in the southern parts of Nimruz and Kandahar provinces. They are tenant farmers and hired herders and number about 20,000 (although numbers as high as 200,000 are given). Most Brahui also speak Pashto and Baluchi and consider themselves akin to the Baluch. The majority of Brahui live in the Pakistan province of Baluchistan, where they are divided into two major branches: the Sarawan tribe, claimed to be of Afghan descent, in the area north of Kalat and the Jhalawan to the south. The leading, but by no means largest, section among the Sarawan is the Raisani whose chief is the sardar of all the Sarawan. Among the Jhalawan the Muhammad Hasanis, or Mamasanis, are the most numerous. They are sunni muslims of the Hanafi school.

BRESHNA, ABDUL GHAFUR. Most prominent of Afghan painters as well as an expert musician, composer, and playwright. Succeeded Ghulam Muhammad Maimanagi (q.v.) as director of the Kabul School of Fine Arts in 1933, and later became president of all Afghan fine arts schools. He wrote plays for Radio Kabul and was a master cartoonist for the *Anis* newspaper. Composed the national anthem of the Republic of Afghanistan, established in 1973 by Muhammad Daud (q.v.). Born in 1907 of a Muhammadzai family, he was educated at Habibia school and in Germany. He died on January 4, 1974.

BURNES, ALEXANDER (1805-41). A captain in the Indian Army who was sent by Lord Auckland, governor general of the the British East India Company, to the court of Amir Dost Muhammad in September 1837 for the purpose of concluding an alliance with Britain and establishing peace between the Afghan ruler and Ranjit Singh (q.v.) who had captured Kashmir and occupied Peshawar. Burnes was well received at Kabul and it appeared that an agreement with the Amir was possible; but in spite of Burnes' recommendations Lord Auckland was not willing to make any promises. He recommended that Dost Muhammad waive his claims on Peshawar and make peace with the Sikh ruler. The Afghan amir's correspondence with Russia and the presence of a purported Russian emissary at Kabul, named Vitkevich (q.v.), was India's reason for starting the first Anglo-Afghan war (q.v.). Burnes returned to Kabul with the invading forces to serve as deputy and presumed successor of Sir William Macnaghten (q.v.), the envoy and minister of the British government at Kabul. A revolt in Kabul resulted in the assassination of Sir Alexander (he had been knighted shortly before) on November 2, 1841, and the British debacle in the war (See ANGLO-AFGHAN RELATIONS, ANGLO-AFGHAN WARS, and SIR WILLIAM MACNAGHTEN).

BUZKASHI. An Afghan national game originating in Central Asia and played primarily by Uzbaks, Turkoman, and Tajiks of northern Afghanistan. Buzkashi means "goat-pulling" and is played on horseback by two opposing teams who use the carcass of a calf (a goat was used in former days) as their object of competition. The purpose is to lift up the carcass from the center of a circle, carry it around a point some distance away, and put it again in its original place. All this has to be done on horseback and the *chapandaz*, expert player, must try to keep possession of the headless carcass. Cash prizes are given to the player who scores a goal and to the winning team. Champion teams used to perform each year on major holidays and the king's birthday in Kabul. The tradition of Buzkashi has been continued even in Pakistan exile.

-C-

CALENDAR. Afghanistan reckons time according to the Islamic era which begins with the emigration (*hijra*) of the Prophet Muhammad from Mecca to Medina in 622 A.D.

Afghans use two dates, one for Islamic festivities based on the Arabic lunar (*qamari*) year, the other for administrative purposes based on the solar (*shamsi*) year. The lunar year is eleven days shorter than the solar calender and the months do not correspond to the seasons. One of King Amanullah's lasting innovations was the introduction of the solar calendar. The Afghan solar year begins on March 21, which is *nauruz*, New Year's day, and in 1990 corresponds to the solar year 1369, or the lunar year 1410. Newspapers in Afghanistan usually carry all three dates. The months are named after the signs of the Zodiac as follows:

Dari	Pashto	Zodiac	English
Hammal	Wray	Aries (Ram)	March 21
Saur	Ghwayai	Taurus (Bull)	April 21
Jauza	Gargholai	Gemini (Twins)	May 22
Saratan	Chungash	Cancer (Crab)	June 22
Asad	Zmarai	Leo (Lion)	July 23
Sonbola	Wazhay	Virgo (Virgin)	August 23
Mizan	Talàh	Libra (Scales)	September 23
Aqrab	Larum	Scorpio (Scorpion)	October 23
Qaus	Lindah	Sagittarius (Archer)	November 22
Jadi	Merghumai	Capricornus (Goat)	December 22
Dalw	Salwagah	Aquarius (Water Carrier)	January 21
Hut	Kab	Pisces (Fish)	February 20

The first six months have 31 days, the next five months have 30 days each, and the last (Hut) has 29 days and 30 days in a leap year. The week ends on Friday, *Jum'a*, which is the day of rest. The four seasons are spring - *bahar*, summer - *tabestan*, fall - *khazan*, and winter - *zemestan*.

According to one author (Poladi, 1989) the Chagatai, twelve-year cycle still exists in the Hazarajat (q.v.). The years are named after animals as follows:

Mush	Mouse	Baqar	Ox
Palang	Leopard	Khargush	Rabbit
Nahang	Dragon *	Mar	Snake
Faras	Hare *	Gusfand	Sheep
Shadi	Ape	Murgh	Hen
Kalb	Dog	Khuk	Pig

Winter season, lasting much longer than in most parts of Afghanistan, is divided into eleven *Toghal* (countings).   * Translation dubious, LWA.

CALIPHATE.   The word is derived from the Arabic *khalifa*, meaning successor, and was adopted as a title by the leader of the Muslim community after the death of the Prophet Muhammad. The office was first held by the companions of the Prophet, the four Rightly Guided Caliphs (632-750), then by the Abbasids (750-1258) until the Mongol conquest of Baghdad. The rise of military rulers, sultans, ended the importance of the caliphate until Ottoman rulers claimed both the sultanate and the caliphate in an effort to legitimize their rule over the entire Islamic world. Afghanistan and India recognized the legitimacy of the Ottoman claim, but were unable to heed the caliph's call for war (*jehad*) against the Allies in World War I. After the defeat of the Ottoman empire, Mustafa Kemal Ataturk, the founder of modern Turkey, abolished the office of the caliphate in March 1924.

CAMPBELL. A British mercenary who fought in the army of Ranjit Singh (q.v.) and during the third Anglo-Afghan war (q.v.) in the service of Shah Shuja. He was captured by forces of Dost Muhammad and became military adviser and artillery instructor in the Afghan army. He eventually converted to Islam, assuming the name Shir Muhammad Khan, and rose to the rank of general and commander-in-chief of the Turkestan army at Balkh. He died in Mazar-i Sharif in 1866.

CAVAGNARI, SIR LOUIS. Signatory for the British government of the Treaty of Gandamak (q.v., 1979) with Amir Yaqub Khan (q.v.). He was appointed British envoy to the amir's court at Kabul after the conclusion of the second Anglo-Afghan war. He arrived in Kabul in July 1879, but on September 3, mutinous soldiers and a Kabuli mob attacked the British residence and killed Cavagnari and his staff. The British government feared a debacle similar to the first Anglo-Afghan war and extricated its forces from Afghanistan by recognizing Abdur Rahman Khan (q.v.) as the new amir. It was not until 1922 that a British envoy was again appointed to Kabul. Also see ANGLO-AFGHAN WARS.

CHADARI. Chadari (D. *tent*) is a tentlike garment, or veil, worn by women in Afghanistan. It consists of a headpiece with an embroidered eye patch through which a woman can see without revealing her face. The headpiece is attached to a pleated cloak which envelops the entire body. This garment was obligatory for all except nomad and peasant women at work. In the final year of his reign King Amanullah (q.v) encouraged women to discard the veil and many did, but the civil war of 1929 brought an end to this innovation. It was not until 1959 that Prime Minister Daud again permitted women to appear in public without the veil and by the late 1970s women of all walks of life had abandoned the chadari and participated in the economic life of the country.

CHAGHCHARAN (lat. 34-31' N, long. 65-15' E). A small town built near a fort (qasr) in the early 1960s as the administrative center of Ghor province. It is located on the Hari Rud at an altitude of about 7,000 feet which is the cause of its severely cold winters. Agriculture, facilitated by irrigation from the Hari Rud and Murghab rivers, and livestock breeding are the major occupations of the inhabitants who are primarily Taimanis. Chaghcharan was the heartland of the Ghorid sultanate which flourished in the 11th to 13th centuries and ruled over an empire that extended from eastern Iran to Delhi in India and from Marv south to the Persian Gulf. Also see GHOR and GHORID DYNASTY.

CHAHAR AIMAQ See **AIMAQ**.

CHAIKHANA. Is the institution of the "tea house," a traditional resting place where travelers stop to eat, listen to bazar gossip, and find shelter for the night. *Chai khana* (D. *chai* = tea, *khana* = house) exist in every village and along roads leading to towns, but motorized travel on major highways has greatly reduced the traveler's need for the service offered by the tea house.

CHAKHANSUR (lat. 31-10' N, long. 62-4' E). A small town located amid the ruins of the ancient capital of Sistan and an administrative district in Nimruz (until 1968 Chakhansur) province in the extreme southwest of Afghanistan. The district lies on a high plateau which is seasonally irrigated by the Khashrud and bordered by desert. The inhabitants of the area are in order of numerical strength: Baluch, Brahui, Tajik or Farsivan, and Pashtuns - most of them sunni Muslims.

CHAMKANI Or **TSAMKANI** (lat. 33-48' N, long. 69-49' E). A district in the north of Paktia province with an area of 102 square miles. The area is inhabited by people who claim to be Sulaiman Khel Ghilzais and subsequently adopted the name of the district as their tribal designation, Chamkani and Chakmani. In Pashto the pronunciation is Tsamkani. Haji Muhammad Chamkani, a member of this tribe, was appointed vice president and adviser to President Najibullah and chairman of the nationalities and tribal council, established in May 1988.

CHANDAWOL See **QIZILBASH.**

CHAPAN. A traditional coat for men popular among the Turkic population of northern Afghanistan, but worn also by other Afghans. It is a long, buttonless caftan with knee-length sleeves which in warm weather is worn open with a sleeve rakishly thrown over a shoulder. In cold weather fur-lined or quilted chapans are worn, tied around the waist with a cummerbund. It comes in various colors, often striped, and is fashioned of cotton or silk.

CHAPANDAZ. A "master" horseman in the Buzkashi competition. See **BUZKASHI.**

CHARIKAR (lat. 35-1' N, long. 69-11 E). A town with about 22,500 inhabitants located at the mouth of the Ghorband about 40 miles north of Kabul, and an administrative district with an area of 73 square miles in Parwan province. At the turn of the century the town was inhabited by Tajiks, Uzbaks, Qizilbashes, Hazaras and some Hindus (all of the latter traders and shopkeepers). The position of Charikar is of great importance as the roads over the Hindu Kush unite in its neighborhood. In 1839 Charikar was a major British military outpost, which was virtually wiped out by Kuhistani forces who had joined in the general uprising against the British occupation forces.

CHARKHI. A family from Charkh, a village and administrative district in Logar province. Prominent members of this family were three brothers: Ghulam Siddiq, Ghulam Nabi, and Ghulam Jilani (the sons of Amir Abdur Rahman's famous General Ghulam Haidar, q.v.). They were supporters of King Amanullah and hostile to the new dynasty established by Muhammad Nadir. For information on the above persons, see under the individual names.

CHEHEL ZINA. An archaeological site on the western outskirts of Kandahar. Chehel Zina (D. forty steps), refers to steps hewn into solid rock, leading up to a vaulted chamber with inscriptions, describing the conquests of the Moghul Emperor Babur (1483-1530) and subsequent rulers.

CHISHT (lat. 34-21' N, long. 63-44' E). A village and subdistrict in Herat province about 26 miles east of Obeh. It is called Chisht-i Sharif because of the location of sufi shrines in the village. It is inhabited by a section of Taimanis who claim descent from the ancient inhabitants of Ghor and assumed the name Chishtis. It is the birthplace of Muin ud-Din Muhammad (b. 1142), founder of the Chishti sufi fraternity and much revered in India. Abu Ishaq, also reputed to be a founder of the Chishti, came from Asia Minor and settled in Chisht. There are a number of other sufi saints who bore the name (*nisba*) Chishti. Members of the local community proclaimed a "Sufi Republic" in early the 1980s.

CLIMATE AND TOPOGRAPHY. The climate in Afghanistan varies with a particular geographic zone. Subarctic conditions exist in the northeast and Hindu Kush mountains, semiarid steppe climate in low lying areas, and mild, moist weather in the areas bordering Pakistan. The estimated annual rainfall is between 11 and 15 inches.

About 83 percent of the *Wakhan-Pamir* area lies at an altitude above 10,000 feet and another 17 percent at an altitude of between 6,000 and 10,000. Therefore, perpetual snow covers mountains above 12,000 feet and most passes are seasonally closed. The yak and bactrian camel are utilized in the transportation of people and goods.

Similar climatic conditions exists in the *Central Mountains* including most of central and eastern Hazarajat, and the Hindu Kush ranges extending from the Shibar Pass through the Koh-i Baba in the west, which is crossed by the Salang tunnel at an altitude of about 11,000 feet. A limited amount of agriculture exists in the valleys and nomads seasonally graze their livestock on the foothills.

The *Eastern Mountains* include four major valleys: Kabul, Kuhistan/Panjshir, the Ghorband, and Nuristan, the latter being the most inaccessible. Temperatures reach lows of one degree Fahrenheit, and winter lasts from December until March. Summer temperatures depend on altitude.

In the southwest, stony deserts extend to the Iranian border, and the Registan, "Country of Sand," extends south of the Helmand river and eastward as far as Shorawak, forming an almost impregnable boundary with Pakistan. On the edges of the Registan the desert gradually changes into a hilly landscape of sandhills thickly sprinkled with bushes and vegetation and grass after rains, where Baluch and Brahui nomads seasonally graze their flock. The major agricultural areas are confined to the valleys watered by the Amu Daria and the "Turkestan" plains, the Hari Rud/Murghab system in the northwest, the Helmand/Arghandab system, and the Kabul river system. The melting snow feeds the dry riverbeds in spring and provides much of the water for irrigation.

CONSTITUTIONAL DEVELOPMENT. Until the late 19th century Afghanistan was governed by a tribal aristocracy, first under the Sadozai and later under the Barakzai branch of the Durranis. Power was decentralized and members of the royal clan ruled autonomously in the provinces, accepting the suzerainty of the King, or Amir, in the capital city.

Although various administrative departments had already existed since the time of Ahmad Shah (q.v.), the king headed all departments and made the influential officers share in the responsibilites of decisions. As his sign of sovereignty his name was mentioned in the Friday sermon (*khutba*) and coins (silver and copper) were struck in his name. The courts were in the hands of the clergy, *ulama*, but the death penalty had to be approved by the King or a governor. Ahmad Shah forbade the mutilation of limbs and he drafted a code which was, however, not enacted. Little was changed until the time of Amir Shir Ali, who was the first Afghan ruler to establish an advisory council to serve as a consultative body.

Amir Abdur Rahman, who increasingly centralized all powers in his hand, took the first steps to institutionalize a consultative body. He relied on advice from a council which was composed of three groups: the *sardars* members of the royal clan; loyal tribal chiefs; and the *ulama*. The "Iron Amir" claimed all temporal and spiritual powers (*imarat* and *imamate*) and there existed no restraint on his arbitrary rule, except the obligation to conform in his actions to the rules of Islamic law (q.v.). Amir Habibullah, Abdur Rahman's son, continued the tradition of his father. The first written document detailing the prerogatives of the ruler and the rights of the ruled was the Afghan constitution (*nizam-nama- yi tashkilat-i asasiya-yi Afghanistan*) promulgated by King Amanullah in October 1923. It consisted of 73 articles which enumerated the rights and prerogatives of the King, presented a "bill of rights" of Afghan citizens, and outlined the duties of ministers and government officials. It authorized the establishment of an advisory committee and provincial councils, half of whose members were to be elected by the people, and established a supreme court (*divan-i ali*). Financial affairs and the activities of provincial departments were defined.

King Amanullah was the chief executive, commander-in-chief, and last court of appeals. He appointed the ministers and presided over cabinet meetings, unless he delegated this task to the prime minister. He was the "defender of the faith," had the sole right to issue currency and have his name invoked in the Friday sermons (*khutba*) during noon prayers. His power was absolute, but he established the institutions which could have evolved in representative government and a constitutional monarchy. The constitution promised civil rights to all, abolished slavery, granted non-Muslims religious freedom (but missionary activity was forbidden), and declared the homes of citizens immune from forcible entry. A number of later statutory enactments (*nizam-nama*) further defined the powers and composition of parliament, which was housed in a new building just completed in Darulaman (q.v.). Social reforms, such as the emancipation of woman and free compulsory education, were decreed. King Amanullah's constitution was never completely implemented and his reforms were abandoned in a wave of reaction under a coalition of forces led by Habibullah Kalakani (q.v.). Amir Habibullah (Kalakani) abrogated all constitutional reforms and attempted to rule in the tradition of Amir Abdur Rahman.

A new attempt at constitutional government was made in October 1931 by Nadir Shah (1929-33). His fundamental law (*usul-i asasi-yi daulat- i Afghanistan*) was similar to Amanullah's constitution. It included 16 sections with 110 articles which outlined general principles, enumerated the rights of the king, the rights of the people, and the duties of a national council (*shura-yi milli*) and provincial advisory committees. Like his predecessor, Nadir Shah enjoyed emergency and veto powers. Non-Muslims had equal rights and were not required to pay a poll tax or be obligated to wear a distinctive type of dress. No legislation was to be contrary to Islamic law, but a distinction was made between civil and religious courts. Torture and confiscation of property were prohibited and publications, including newspapers, and free commercial activity were permitted. As a concession to the religious establishment, two members of the Mujaddidi family held the position of minister of justice until 1935. The important position of prime minister was held by members of the royal family until 1963.

A new, liberal era began with the promulgation of the 1964 constitution (October 1, 1964 - *qanun-i asasi-yi Afghanistan*) which limited the participation of members of the royal family in government. Members of the royal family could serve in the foreign service, be advisers (*mushawer*), and hold low-level positions in government departments, but not the positions of prime minister, supreme court justice, and membership in parliament. This was directed against Sardar Muhammad Daud (q.v.), the king's cousin, a strong prime minister (1953-63) whose Pashtunistan policy (q.v.) had been a disaster in foreign relations. While Zahir Shah (q.v., 1933-73) continued to hold supreme powers, he permitted an unprecedented degree of democratic government. His constitution, the result of a constitutional drafting committee, included a preamble and eleven titles, comprising 128 articles. Primogeniture was introduced with a provision that "the Throne shall pass to his [Zahir's] eldest son." Freedom of thought, possession of property, unarmed assembly, and education were guaranteed. Afghan citizens were given the right to a free press and to form political parties, subject to the provisions of certain ordinances provided that no actions were in violation of traditional norms and Islamic law. The provision on formation of political parties was never ratified by the king.

From the time of King Amanullah, constitutional development represents a process of modernization and the gradual introduction of concepts of the division of powers and individual rights. It also brought into being a process where the symbols of democratic government were beginning to gain concrete reality. But socioeconomic factors prevented the rapid implementation of political reforms. Universal education, envisioned by the constitution, remained an aim rather than a reality, and Afghanistan has remained largely illiterate. The introduction of secular schools, in addition to the traditional mosque/madrasa system, produced two essentially hostile elites. Afghanistan is still predominantly agricultural, and a great division exists between the urban and rural population. Sectarian and ethnic differences have prevented the forging of a heterogeneous population into a nation. When Sardar Muhammad Daud staged his coup in 1973, the experiment with democracy came to a halt.

Daud wanted one-party government and "democracy based on social justice." His constitution (*qanun-i asasi-yi daulat-i jumhuri-yi Afghanistan*), promulgated on February 14, 1977, aimed at the "exercise of power" by the majority, the "farmers, workers, and enlightened people and the youth." In 13 chapters and 136 articles, the republican government presented its aspirations. It called for the "elimination of exploitation in all its forms," nationalized the mineral resources of the state, large industries, communications, banks, and "important food procurement establishments." Land reforms were to be carried out and cooperatives were to be encouraged. Women were to enjoy equal rights and obligations and every Afghan 18 years or older was to have the right to vote. President Daud enjoyed absolute powers: he could convene and dismiss the national assembly (*milli jirgah*), whose members were nominated by his party (See NATIONAL REVOLUTIONARY PARTY), and could veto any law. He felt he had to be strong to fight the evils of "hunger, ignorance, and disease;" but his one-man rule proved to be fatal. His leftist supporters in the army did not permit Daud's shift to the right, and before he could eliminate them from positions of power they staged the Saur Revolt of April 27, 1978.

The new regime wanted to establish a government of workers and peasants, with the PDPA as a vanguard to implement its revolutionary objectives. Decrees demanded the emancipation of women, land reforms, and the introduction of far-reaching social changes. But the provisions of the "Fundamental Principles of the Democratic Republic of Afghanistan" could never be implemented. Armed resistance rose within a few months which turned into a war of liberation after the Soviet intervention.

The government of Dr. Najibullah has virtually eliminated the trappings of Marxist government in its Constitution of 1987, and the Afghan Interim Government of the seven mujahedin groups in Peshawar has published the outlines of a constitution which favors the establishment of an Islamic state. The traditional groups, represented by Sayyid Ahmad Gailani, Sebghatullah Mujaddidi, and Muhammad Nabi Muhammadi, favor the establishment of a democratic Islamic government, not excluding the possibility of a constitutional monarchy; whereas the Islamist groups headed by Gulbudin Hekmatyar, Abdul Rasul Sayyaf, Yunus Khales, and Burhanuddin Rabbani tend with some variations to favor an "Islamic state" on a more authoritarian model. They would limit the sphere of activity of women in public life and tend to limit manifestations of westernization. The shi'a groups appear to favor a federated state in which the interests of the minorities are protected. Some, like the *Pasdaran* (q.v., Guardians) and perhaps *Nasr* (q.v., Victory) look to Iran as a model of the Islamic state, whereas the *Shura* (Council) appears to prefer a traditional political system. The Shi'as claim to constitute a fifth of the Afghan population and want this to be reflected in parliamentary representation. As long as their claimed popular strength is not reflected in an Afghan interim government, they have refused their participation. The war in Afghanistan has politicized a large part of the hitherto quiescent population and the prospects are for greater grassroots participation in the political life of Afghanistan. Also see ISLAMIC LAW.

CONVENTION OF 1907 See **ANGLO-RUSSIAN CONVENTION**.

COURTS See **LAW.**

CURRENCY See **AFGHANI.**

CUSTOMARY LAW See **LAW.**

-D-

DA AFGHANISTAN BANK. Afghanistan's central and major commercial bank, founded by the government in 1939, as a result of the success of the Bank-i Milli (q.v.). It has sole rights to issue currency and control of foreign exchange. The bank has branches in major Afghan towns and its impact and operations are confined largely to urban areas. Subsequently a number of specialized banks were established, but all banks were nationalized with the establishment of President Daud's republican government. In the 1980s the Da Afghanistan Bank is governed by a supreme council and its director holds cabinet rank. The formal banking system is still poorly developed in Afghanistan and its functions are augmented by the informal money bazar. Therefore, the traditional system of moneylending has survived all regimes and foreign exchange dealings have remained a major activities of the bazar. Also see BANKING.

DAI KUNDI HAZARAS See **HAZARA.**

DAI ZANGI HAZARAS See **HAZARA.**

DAILY PRAYERS See **ISLAM.**

DANESH, MUHAMMAD ISMAIL. Member of the Khalq faction of the PDPA and minister of mines and industries under Taraki, Amin, and Karmal (1978-85). Born in Kabul in 1939 and educated at Habibia School and in the United States and the Soviet Union, he embarked on a career with the ministry of mines and industries. His longevity in office was ascribed to his Qizlbash (q.v.) background and "inoffensive manner." He served as ambassador to Libya (1985-87) and remained a member of the central committee until he was dismissed in 1989.

DANE, SIR LOUIS W. Head of a British mission to Kabul (January 1 to December 2, 1921) which negotiated the Treaty of Kabul. See ANGLO-AFGHAN TREATY OF 1921, AFGHAN FOREIGN RELATIONS and ANGLO-AFGHAN WARS.

DARI. The name of the Farsi spoken in Afghanistan and with Pashto one of the two "official" languages. The name derives from *darbar*, royal court, because it was the language of the Central Asian and Moghul Indian courts. Other etymologies suggested are *darra*, valley, or the language of Darius (522-486 B.C.), the Achaemenid emperor. Afghan scholars claim Dari was the language of Khorasan in which some of the oldest Persian poetry was written. In its written form Dari differs very little from the Farsi of Iran, except that it employs a greater amount of Arabic vocabulary and some archaic words no longer used in Farsi. Of the spoken Dari variants the Herati comes closest to Farsi followed by the educated Kabuli idiom. Hazaragi, spoken by the Hazara, and Tajiki are other major Farsi dialects. All are mutually intelligible. Afghan governments have attempted to make Pashto the national language and have expended considerable resources to Pashtunize Afghan society, but Dari is still the major language of higher education and serves as a "lingua franca" for all linguistic groups.

DARIS, GHULAM MUHYIUDDIN. Minister of justice in Prime Minister Khaliqyar's government of May 27, 1990. He was born in 1932 in Panjshir district and educated in Kabul with a degree in law. He embarked on a career of teaching at the faculty of law and political science of Kabul University and was subsequently dean of the faculty of *fiqh* at the Islamic University. He is not a member of the PDPA.

DARULAMAN (DAR AL-AMAN) (lat. 34-28' N, long. 69-0' E). The administrative capital of Afghanistan under King Amanullah who, in the early 1920s, constructed a number of government buildings, including a monumental parliament and a municipality building. Members of the court and high government officials built villas in the new capital, and a narrow-gauged railroad led to the center of Kabul some six miles away. It is a monument to Amanullah's ten-year reign and ceased being the capital after his downfall. The town was renamed Darulhabib (Abode of Habib) after Habibullah Kalakani and Darulfunun (Abode of the Arts) in 1930, until in 1947 it was again given its original name. The Municipality building was subsequently converted into the famous Kabul Museum (q.v.), which houses valuable archaeological and ethnographic collections from the Hellenistic, Graeco-Buddhist, and Ghaznavid periods. Train service was ended, and the major administrative offices were again located in the old city. The parliament building was gutted by fire in 1969 and restored to house the ministry of defense. It was again severely damaged as a result of the Tanai coup of March 1990 (q.v.).

DAR UL-ISLAM (DAR AL-ISLAM). The "Abode of Islam," or a country in which the ordinances of Islam are established and which is under the rule of a Muslim sovereign. The *Shari'a*, Islamic law, prevails in this area, and non-Muslims are subject to their own religious and customary laws, but without the possibility of full citizenship. Hindus and Jews of Afghan citizenship enjoyed equal rights, but at certain times had to pay a special poll tax and were exempt from military service. In 1920 the Indian *Hijrat* (or *Khilafat*) movement led to a mass emigration of Muslims from British

India, the *dar ul-harb*, to Afghanistan, the *dar ul-Islam* (See HIJRAT MOVEMENT).

DAR UL-MU'ALLEMIN (DAR AL-MU'ALLEMIN). A teachers training college founded in 1914 at Kabul. Initially students entered the school for three years of study after completing six years of primary education. During King Amanullah it was upgraded and students were required to complete nine grades of education before being admitted. The college was established to train the teachers for the newly-established secular school system. Eventually teachers training colleges were also established in the major provincial centers.

DARWAZ (lat. 38-26' N, long. 70-47' E). The name of an administrative center in the district of the same name in northern Badakhshan province. It was part of an independent khanate (headed by a khan, chief) on both sides of the Amu Daria, but became part of Afghanistan as a result of the settlement of the Russo-Afghan boundary in 1895, when Darwaz became Afghan territory and Shighnan, situated across the Amu Daria was ceded to Russia.

DASHT-I MARGO (lat. 30-45' N, long. 63-10' E). A large desert lying between the Helmand and Khash rivers about 150 miles in length and some 85 miles in width. It is a plateau, about 2,000 feet above sea level, windswept and barren, visited by Baluch herdsmen who alone know the paths leading to occasional water holes. It formed a natural boundary between Afghanistan and British India.

DAUD MUHAMMAD, See **MUHAMMAD DAUD.**

DAWAI, ABDUL HADI (PARESHAN). A Kakar Pashtun, famous poet, diplomat, and government official who published under the pen name Pareshan (worried). He was elected senator and became president of the senate from 1966 to 1973. Born in 1894 in Kabul, he was a graduate of the first class of Habibia High School in 1912. In the same year he became assistant editor of the famous *Seraj al-Akhbar* (q.v.) and in 1920 of the *Aman-i Afghan* (q.v.). He entered the foreign service, participating in the Rawalpindi and Mussoorie peace conferences. He was appointed Afghan minister in London in 1922, served as minister of commerce from 1925 until his resignation in 1928, and as Afghan minister in Berlin from December 1929-31. From 1933 until 1946 he was imprisoned as an Amanullah supporter. In 1950 he was elected to parliament and became speaker of the House. He served as secretary of King Muhammad Zahir and tutor of the crown prince. He was appointed ambassador to Cairo (1952-1954), and to Jakarta (1954-58). He retired from political life and died in 1982 in Kabul.

DEHGAN. A small tribe settled in the Kunar valley who speak the Laghmani or Kohistani language. The tribe is divided into the Dumeh, Chaguni,

Kuli, Buzurg, Debazai, and Malikzai sections, the last four of which are found chiefly in the Kunar and Safi valleys.

DEOBAND. A town near Delhi, India, and the location of an Islamic university (*madrasa*) founded in 1867. It is a strictly orthodox institution whose members have traditionally supported pan-Islamic, anti-British, and fundamentalist causes. Graduates of Deoband readily found teaching positions in Afghanistan where a madrasa of international reputation did not exist. Amir Abdur Rahman and King Amanullah at times forbade Deobandis from teaching in Afghanistan. Yunus Khales, Amir of the Islamist Hizb, is a graduate of Deoband.

DHIMMI Or ZIMMI. Also called *ahl al-dhimma*, "people of the covenant or obligation," are non-Muslim monotheists who under Islamic law enjoy freedom of life, liberty, and property provided they are loyal citizens. The dhimmis include Christians, Jews, and in Afghanistan, Hindus even though they are not considered monotheists. At various times a special tax (*jizya*) was levied on adult male *dhimmis* and Hindus were obligated to wear a dress distinctive from Muslims, but were exempt from serving in the armed forces. Each community was culturally autonomous. As part of the nation-building process in the twentieth century, King Amanullah proclaimed all Afghans equal and abolished the separate legal status of *dhimmis*.

DIN. Din (A.) for religion. *Din-i Islam*, the religion of Islam. See ISLAM.

DIN MUHAMMAD, MASHK-I ALAM (1790-1886). Considered a national hero by Afghans because of his implacable hostility to the British. A frontier mulla whose grandfather came from India and settled among the Andar Ghilzai near Ghazni. He studied with various ulama and was given the name Mashk-i Alam, "Scent (or Musk) of the World," by one of his teachers because of his excellent mind. He was a militant mulla who opened a madrasa for the training of mullas and gained considerable influence among the Ghilzais (q.v.). He received an allowance from Amir Shir Ali and preached *jihad* against the British during the second Anglo-Afghan war. When Amir Abdur Rahman tried to restrict his activity he incited the Mangal and Ghilzais to rebellion. After his death in 1886, his son, Mulla Abdul Karim, led a Ghilzai uprising against Amir Abdur Rahman which was suppressed only with great difficulty.

DOBBS, SIR HENRY. British envoy and chief of the British mission to Kabul which negotiated the Anglo-Afghan Treaty of 1921 and established "neighborly" relations after the end of the third Anglo-Afghan war. Before that he also headed the British contingent at the Mussoorie conference (April 17-July 18, 1920) which failed to normalize Anglo-Afghan relations. He first came to Afghanistan in 1903, when as a political officer he directed a small British contingent whose task was to restore or repair boundary pillars at the Russo-Afghan border. See ANGLO-AFGHAN WARS and AFGHAN FOREIGN RELATIONS.

DORAH PASS (lat. 36-0' N, long. 71-15' E.). A pass over the eastern Hindu Kush range, lying at an elevation of 14,800 feet and crossed by a route leading from Zebak to Chitral in Pakistan. It is located in Zibak district of Badakhshan province and is so named because two roads (D., *do rah*) converge from it to Zebak and to Nuristan.

DORI RIVER (lat. 31-29 N, long. 65-12' E) . A river formed by the junction of the Kadanai and Kushebai streams south of Shah Pasand and the Lora stream which originates in Pakistan. It is replenished by the Arghastan, Tarnak, and Arghandab rivers and numerous streams and finally runs into the Helmand.

DOST MUHAMMAD, AMIR (1826-38 and 1842-63). Afghan ruler, known as the "Great Amir" (*Amir-i Kabir*), who was ousted by the British in the first Anglo-Afghan war, but was able to regain the Afghan throne after four years in Indian exile. He was born in 1792 in Kandahar, the son of Painda Khan (q.v.), who was killed by Zaman Shah (q.v.) when Dost Muhammad was only eight years old. He became acting governor of Ghazni and, after the death of Muhammad Azam (q.v.) in 1824, established himself as ruler of Kabul. He next defeated his rival, Shah Shuja (q.v.), at Kandahar and gradually extended his control over the rest of Afghanistan. He defeated the Sikhs at the Battle of Jamrud (1837) and assumed the title Amir-ul-Mu'minin (Commander of the Faithful). The British-Indian government turned against him when Dost Muhammad made overtures to Russia and Persia and permitted a Russian agent to come to Kabul. Dost Muhammad wanted to regain territory captured by Ranjit Singh (q.v.) and was willing to ally himself with the British, but the British government decided to support the Sikh ruler and restore Shah Shuja to the Afghan throne. A British army invaded Afghanistan and sacked Kabul on July 23, 1839. On November 2, 1940, after a few skirmishes, Dost Muhammad gave up; he surrendered to the British who took him as a hostage to India. However, the British occupation of Afghanistan became increasingly tenuous as their lines of communication were disrupted and tribal forces slowly expelled garrisons from outlying areas. Eventually, the army in Kabul was forced to negotiate an ignominious retreat in which most of the British army was eliminated (see ANGLO AFGHAN WARS). Facing a situation of chaos in Afghanistan, the Indian government permitted Dost Muhammad to return and regain his throne. But it took a number of years to consolidate his power: he took Kandahar in 1855 and Herat in 1863. Dost Muhammad died a few days after he entered Herat. Of his 27 sons, Muhammad Afzal and Muhammad Azam, ruled for short periods, followed by Shir Ali (See individual entries).

DOST, MUHAMMAD ANWAR. Minister of light industries and foodstuffs in Prime Minister Khaliqyar's government of May 27, 1990. He was born in 1940 in Kandahar province and educated at Mir Wais Nika Lycée at Kandahar, in Kabul and Germany. He embarked on a career of teaching at the faculty of economics of Kabul University where in 1988 he was appointed dean. He is not a member of the PDPA. Mother tongue Pashto.

DOST, SHAH MUHAMMAD. A diplomat and member of the PDPA, who became deputy foreign minister in 1978 and foreign minister in 1980 under the Babrak Karmal. He served as U.N. ambassador in New York from 1987 to 1988, and as minister without portfolio after 1988. He was born in 1929 and educated in Kabul. He served in various positions under the Maiwandwal and Etemadi governments, and was appointed to the Afghan embassy in Washington as second secretary in 1958, first secretary in Islamabad in 1970, and consul in Peshawar in 1972. He is said to be a member of the Parchami faction of the PDPA. Mother tongue Dari.

DOSTUM, LT. GEN. ABDUL RASHID. Commander of the Jozjani "Dostum Militia" comprising some 20,000 regular and militia soldiers, most of them Uzbak, and entrusted with guarding Jozjan, Fariab, and Sar-i-Pol provinces for the Kabul government. He was awarded the distinction of "Hero of the Republic of Afghanistan" and is a member of the central council of the Watan (formerly PDPA) party. Born in 1954 in Khwaja Dokoh, Jozjan province, of an Uzbak family, he worked for the Oil and Gas Exploration Enterprise of Shiberghan and in 1980 went to the USSR for training. He then joined the ministry of state security and became commander of Unit 374 in Jozjan province. His forces served in various parts of the country and, it is said, that one thousand of his soldiers were captured in the mujahedin conquest of Khost.

DRA. Acronym for the Democratic Republic of Afghanistan which has been changed under President Najibullah to Republic of Afghanistan (ROA).

DURAND AGREEMENT. An agreement signed on November 12, 1893, at Kabul by Sir Henry Mortimer Durand and Amir Abdur Rahman which defined the boundary between Afghanistan and British India, subsequently called "Durand Line." This boundary was drawn without regard to the ethnic composition of the population and severed a large portion of Pashto-speaking Afghans from their brothers in Afghanistan. Amir Abdur Rahman accepted under "duress" a line running from "Chitral and Baroghil Pass up to Peshawar, and thence up to Koh-i Malik Siyah in this way that Wakhan, Kafiristan, Asmar, Mohmand of Lalpura, and one portion of Waziristan" came under his rule. He renounced his claims for "the railway station of New Chaman, Chagai, the rest of Waziri, Biland Khel, Kurram, Afridi, Bajaur, Swat, Buner, Dir, Chilas and Chitral." The Durand Line was never completely demarcated because of the hostility of the tribes and the tribes on the Indian side of the border never came under the direct administration of the Indian, or subsequently Pakistani, governments. Abdur Rahman obtained an increase in subsidy of 6,000,000 rupees and a letter with the assurance that Britain would continue to protect Afghanistan from unprovoked Russian aggression, provided that the Amir "followed unreservedly the advice of the British Government" in regard to his external relations. The Afghan government subsequently claimed that the agreement was forced on Afghanistan in the form of an ultimatum. After the death of Amir Abdur Rahman, Britain insisted that the treaties with the late ruler were personal, rather than dynastic and therefore subject to renegotiation, but they excluded the Durand Agreement as not subject to this provision. Article 5 of the treaty of peace concluded at Rawalpindi (q.v.) on August 8, 1919, stated that "The Afghan Government accept the Indo- Afghan frontier accepted by the late Amir [Habibullah]," and the Treaty of Kabul (q.v.) carried a similar provision. When the state of Pakistan was created in 1947, the Afghan government demanded the right of the Pashtuns to decide whether they wanted an independent Pashtunistan, union with Afghanistan, or union with Pakistan. The Kabul government did not accept a plebiscite which allowed only a choice for union with Pakistan or India, and in 1979 the Afghan parliament repudiated the Durand Agreement. The "Pashtunistan question" has remained an issue between Afghanistan and Pakistan and has prevented the establishment of cordial relations between the two Muslim countries. Also see AFGHAN FOREIGN RELATIONS and PASHTUNISTAN.

DURAND, SIR MORTIMER. Foreign secretary of the government of India who came to Kabul in September 1893 for the purpose of negotiating an agreement defining the Indo-Afghan boundary, subsequently called the Durand Line. (See DURAND AGREEMENT.)

DURRANI DYNASTY (1747-1973). The Durrani dynasty was founded in 1747 by Ahmad Shah "Durr-i Durran" (q.v.) who ruled Afghanistan until 1978. Ahmad Shah was a direct descendant of Sado, an Abdali chief at the court of the Savafid ruler Shah Abbas the Great (1588-1629). The Durrani are divided into the Sadozai branch (a section of the Popalzai tribe) and the Muhammadzai (a section of the Barakzai tribe). The succession from Ahmad Shah to Muhammad Zahir (Muhammad Daud established a republican government) is as follows:

Sadozai Branch	
Ahmad Shah	1747
Timur Shah	1773
Shah Zaman	1793
Shah Mahmud	1799
Shah Shuja	1803
Shah Mahmud	1810-18
Civil War	

Barakzai Branch		
Dost Muhammad		1835
First Anglo-Afghan War		
Shah Shuja (Sadozai)		1839
Dost Muhammad		1839
Shir Ali		1863
Civil War		
Muhammad Afzal		1866
Muhammad Azam		1867
Shir Ali		1870
Second Anglo-Afghan War		
Yaqub Khan		1879
Abdur Rahman		1880
Habibullah Khan		1901
Nasrullah Khan		1919
Amanullah Khan (King)		1919
Third Anglo Afghan War		
Enayatullah Khan	Jan.	1929

Muhammad Nadir		1929
Muhammad Zahir		1933-73

DURRANI TRIBE. Since 1747 the royal Afghan tribe, originally named Abdali, until Ahmad Shah (q.v.), founder of modern Afghanistan (1747), assumed the title "Durr-i Durran" and his tribe the name Durrani (See ABDALI and DURRANI DYNASTY). The Durranis originated in the mountains of Toba, or Ghor, and in 1876 numbered about 500,000 which are divided into the Zirak and Panjpai divisions.

The Zirak branch includes the following sections:

The Barakzai, Achakzai (probably an offshoot of the Barakzai), Popalzai, and Alikozai,

The Panjpai branch includes the following sections:

The Nurzai, Alizai, and Ishaqzai.

The Khugiani and the Maku have no subdivision.

The Durrani predominate in the Kandahar and Farah provinces and in the Sabzawar district of Herat. They received their lands from Nadir Shah, Afshar, as military fiefs on condition of service in his army. Each of the great clans of the Durranis is headed by a sardar and subdivisions are headed by khans chosen from the major families. The Durranis are largely sedentary and engage in agriculture and stock breeding. Their houses are built of adobe brick, surrounded by high walls, commanded by the fort of the Khan which also includes rooms for occasional guests. The herders live in black tents and seasonally move to the uplands in the north and south of Kandahar.

DUTANI Or DOTANI. A tribe of *powindahs*, nomad merchants who used to travel seasonally between India and Afghanistan, selling silk, carpets and hashish (*chars*). They are also called Lohani and are now settled on the Indian side of the border. See POWINDAH.

-E-

ECONOMY. Afghanistan's economy resembles that of other less-developed countries in the sense that agriculture is the largest sector and that the government controlled mining and certain industries, including electric power stations and airlines. After 1977, it took control of all major industries and banking. At that time about 40% of cultivable land was owned by large landowners who made up only two percent of the agricultural population, whereas 80% of farmers each owned less than 11 acres (*Area Handbook for Afghanistan*). About 90% of the population is engaged in agriculture and animal husbandry. In the prewar years about 85% of Afghan agricultural exports consisted of fresh and dried fruit. Qaraqul skins and the Afghan carpet industry (which comprises more than 50% of the handicraft industries) were other important hard currency earners. The Soviet Union was the major trading partner and the only market for Afghan natural gas.

Prime Minister Muhammad Daud (1953-63) began a program of development and modernization. Two five-year plans (1956-61 and 1962-67) were to provide the infrastructure of communications while the third (1967- 72), initiated by a subsequent government, aimed at agricultural self-sufficiency. About $1.2 billion in foreign aid was expended by the early 1970s, of which the Soviet Union provided 50% and the United States 40%.

Prewar figures given by *The Afghan Statistical Yearbook* (July 1976) show the following values in US dollars of Afghan exports in 1975:

Qaraqul skins	$10 million
Fresh fruit	$27 million
Dried fruit	$50 million
Carpets and kelims	$17 million
Natural gas	$41 million

Exports in barter-trade with neighboring countries:

Soviet Union	$81 million
India	$29 million
Pakistan	$33 million

Exports and imports with major trading partners:

	Exports	Imports
United States	$10 mil.	5 mil.
United Kingdom	$15 mil.	8 mil.
Germany	$21 mil	10 mil.
Japan	----	60 mil.

(The numbers are rounded off.)

President Daud projected a seven-year plan (1976-83) which emphasized industrial development over the agricultural sector and nationalized large industries, mines, and banks. Aid from the Gulf countries (the Shah of Iran had promised $2 billion) permitted a survey for construction of a railroad, which was to link Iran with the Indian subcontinent. A sudden fall in the price of oil and the downfall of the Iranian and Afghan rulers in the late 1970s ended these ambitious plans.

Afghanistan still cannot produce most manufactured goods and processed raw materials. One of the first measures of the Marxist regime was to decree land reforms and to abolish the traditional bazar system of agricultural financing, without providing alternate sources of funds. Since it soon lost control over much of the countryside, the Kabul government never could implement its reforms; nevertheless, in 1983, the Kabul government claimed that it had redistributed about one-fourth of cultivable land. The war in Afghanistan has wreaked enormous damage which cannot be assessed at this time. An agricultural survey conducted under the auspices of the Swedish Committee for Afghanistan examined the decline in agricultural production in Afghanistan between 1978 and 1987 and gave the following statistics:

	Percent growers	Av.area jeribs	Av.yield seers/jerib	Production per farmer
Irrigated wheat	7	-23	-26	-45
Rainfed wheat	-22	-33	-29	-52
Maize	-14	-9	-27	-49
Rice	-14	-20	-19	-40
Barley	-14	-21	-18	-35
Alfalfa	-11	-5	-16	-54
Clover	-25	-5	+3	-58
Bean	-20	-22	-21	-50
Mung Bean	-44	-26	-12	-51
Cotton	-43	-23	-29	-58
Linseed	-8	+30	-39	-14
Melon	-0	-31	-37	-69
Potato	-0	-5	-28	-47
Sesame	-20	-51	-19	-70
Sugar beet	-60	-63	-60	-85
Grape	-4	-3	-21	-36

(Decline in percentages. One hundred *jerib* is twenty hectares, and one *seer* is 7,066 grams.)

The process of economic rehabilitation, pending the restoration of peace in Afghanistan will be a slow and difficult one.

EDUCATION

The modern system of education in Afghanistan dates from the early twentieth century, although attempts at educational reforms were first made under Amir Shir Ali (q.v., 1863-79). In 1868 he opened two schools, a military school, located in the Sherpur district of Kabul and a civil, or royal, school in the Bala Hesar (q.v.). Both schools were directed by Qazi Abdul Qadir, Shir Ali's secretary of the army and publisher of the *Shams al-Nahar* (q.v.). Education was free and food and lodging were provided for the students. The schools were for princes and the sons of notables and the system was adapted from Muslim India and the Ottoman empire. Because of the second Anglo-Afghan war, the experiment was not continued.

Amir Abdur Rahman (q.v., 1880-1901) claimed, with some exaggeration, that he could fill only three clerical positions after advertising all over Afghanistan for 30 positions of literate Afghans. This prompted him to open "various schools for the education of members of my family, my personal attendants, and page boys; for prisoners of war; for the army, and for the children of my officials and other subjects." (Sultan Mahomed Khan, 1900).

The traditional system of education in Afghanistan was the domain of the *ulama* (q.v., clergy). It consisted of elementary schools, *maktab*, usually attached to a mosque, where mullas would teach reading, writing and arithmetic, recitation of the Koran (Qur'an, q.v.), and the Islamic duties and prohibitions. There was no uniformity in curriculum and often students would confine their activities to recitation and memorization of the Koran. The well-to-do would hire tutors for their children.

The secondary system of education was the *madrasa* in which the *mudares* (teacher), or *alem* (pl. *ulama*), would teach Persian and Arabic literature, poetry, calligraphy, and the Islamic sciences of *tafsir* (exegesis), *ulum-i Illahi* (Islamic theology), *fiqh* (jurisprudence), and *akhlaqiat* (ethics) as well as the "foreign" sciences of logic, philosophy, medicine, mathematics, astronomy, and astrology. The *madrasa* trained the *kazi* (judges), *mufti* (legal experts), and *ulama*, doctors of Islamic sciences (See ISLAMIC LAW). Most *madrasa* were not state institutions, but private enterprises of individual Islamic scholars who would certify completion of a student's course of study. In the late 19th century the most important college of this type was the *Madrasa-yi Shahi* (royal college) at Kabul.

A modern system of education evolved from the time of Amir Habib-ullah. He founded Habibia School in 1904, first as a *madrasa*, which later adopted the curriculum of British-Indian secular schools. He appointed his son, Sardar Enayatullah as his head of education and allocated an annual budget of 100,000 rupees. Conditions were spartan: the teacher sat on a chair and the students on mats on the floor. In winter open charcoal braziers provided some warmth. In addition to a few Afghan teachers, Indian Muslims were contracted, including the principal, Dr. Abdul Ghani (q.v.).

A school for the children of notables, *maktab-i malikzadaha*, was founded next and eventually developed into the Royal Military College, *madrasa-yi harbi-yi sirajiya*. Its principal was a Turkish officer, Mahmud Sami, who operated under the direction of Sardar Enayatullah, another son of Amir Habibullah. The curriculum included Islamic and military sciences as well as gymnastics and drill.

In 1907 an Office of Textbooks (*dar al-ta'lif*) was founded to produce texts for the new secular schools. In 1914 a Teachers Training School (*dar al-mu'allemin*) was founded and a year later the primary school system was expanded. Education and textbooks were provided free of charge and students received a small stipend for living expenses. Primary schools (*ebteda'iya*) included four years of religious education, reading and writing, arithmetic, and geography. Graduates could then enter the military school, continue at Habibia school, or end their education to become lower-level civil servants. Middle schools (*rushdiya*) conducted a three-year program in Persian and Arabic literature and a foreign language. Graduates were preparing for government jobs or continued their education in the next cycle of higher education, (*e'dadiya*). Education at this level was in English.

King Amanullah (q.v.) further expanded the system of education by founding primary schools in major towns and district centers and, in 1922, the French-language *Amania* School (subsequently renamed by Nadir Shah *Istiqlal* [q.v.] - Independence) with a French curriculum and several French teachers. *Amani* School (renamed *Najat* [q.v.] by Nadir Shah, and again *Amani* since the Marxist regime) was founded in 1923 as a German-language school. The top graduates from these schools were sent abroad for higher education. A ministry of education was established in 1919 and Sardar Abdur Rahman was appointed as the first minister. Schools were next opened also in the provinces. The *Ghazi* School (Victor - named after Amanullah's title) was founded in 1927 and administrative schools, the *maktab-i hukkam* and *maktab-i usul-i daftari*, were opened to train accountants and administrators.

During the reign of Zahir Shah (q.v., 1933-73) the Afghan system of education was further expanded and extended to the provinces. Kabul University was formally established on a separate campus in 1947, but before that the faculty of medicine was founded in 1932, followed by the faculty of law and political science in 1938. Faculties of science and letters were added in 1942 and 1943. In the 1950s theology, agriculture, and economics departments were founded, and in the 1960s home economics, education, engineering, pharmacy, and a polytechnic institute were established. Some departments were affiliated with foreign universities, mostly German, French, and American. The Soviet Union built and directed the operations of the Polytechnic Institute from 1967, and the teachers college of Columbia University reorganized the faculty of education. By 1950, expenditures on education amounted to forty percent of the Afghan budget.

Women's education was first sponsored under King Amanullah with the establishment in 1921 of a school in the building of the present Zarghuna high school in Kabul. Afghan and some foreign ladies taught the same curriculum as the boys' schools, as well as cooking, sewing, child care and readings of the biographies of famous women of the world. Coeducation began in 1928 for the first and second grades at Istiqlal school at Kabul, and some female students were sent to Turkey to continue their education. Coeducation and girls' schools were discontinued for several years after the ouster of King Amanullah. In 1931, under Nadir Shah (q.v.) women were permitted to take courses at Masturat Hospital in

Kabul, and girls' schools were reopened in 1939 - two high schools in 1947, and a women's faculty of education in 1948. Coeducation was resumed again in the early 1960s at Kabul University. A Women's Institute (*mu'asasa-yi niswan*) was started in 1946 in Kabul under the sponsorship of Queen Humaira, wife of Zahir Shah, which gave classes in handicrafts and became the largest supplier of needlework of various types.

In 1936-37 the Afghan government decided to replace Dari with Pashto as the language of instruction in public schools, but in 1946 this policy was abandoned in favor of Dari/Pashto bilingualism. Pashto- speaking provinces and a few "tribal" schools, like Rahman Baba at Kabul, used Pashto. In 1963 Nangarhar University was founded in Jalalabad in which Pashto was the language of instruction, and seven professional and technical schools have existed since 1964 that also use Pashto for instruction.

By 1970 secondary schools existed in every province except Zabul, and vocational and teachers training schools, as well as commercial, agricultural, and technical schools existed in Kabul and a number of provincial towns. The existence of a dual system of education, the traditional system under the ulama and the newly-established secular system, created two elites who competed for government positions. The graduates of the secular system tended to benefit from the process of national development and had little difficulty in finding employment. The state eventually also integrated the madrasa system in the faculty of theology of Kabul University, but an independent, private system of madrasas continued to exist. Thus the ulema had lost its monopoly of education and felt threatened in its position of leadership.

The Marxist government emphasized adult education and literacy programs and printed texts in the newly recognized "national languages" of Baluch, Turkmani, Uzbak, and Nuristani (Kati) as well as in Dari and Pashto. Universities were established in Balkh and Herat, and primary education was permitted in regional languages. The Afghan ministry of education is responsible for curriculum and educational policy at all levels. War and destruction have closed virtually all provincial schools, except for a few *maktab*, operated by mujahedin groups and local communities. In Marxist controlled areas, purges of faculty, the drafting of graduates, and changes in curriculum to conform to Soviet models have led to a drastic reduction of students.

The "new education policy" initiated by President Najibullah has dispensed with most of the Marxist innovations.

Education will be one priority in the effort of reconstruction once peace has been restored. Also see KABUL UNIVERSITY and schools under individual entries.

EJAZI, MEHR MUHAMMAD. Minister of public health in Prime Minister Khaliqyar's government of May 1990. He was born in 1934 in Kabul province and educated at Istiqlal school and the faculty of medicine of Kabul University, after which he went for specialized studies to France.

He began as physician at various hospitals and was appointed dean of the faculty of medicine of Kabul University in 1982, and served as president of the Kabul Medical Institute (1983-88). In 1989 he was appointed minister of higher and vocational education. He is not a member of the PDPA.

ELPHINSTONE, MOUNTSTUART (1779-1859). Envoy of the British East India Company to the court of Shah Shuja in 1808-9 who negotiated an alliance of "eternal friendship" with the Afghan ruler and called for joint action in case of Franco-Persian aggression. He left Delhi on October 13, 1808, with an escort of 400 Anglo-Indian troops and reached Peshawar on February 25, 1809, where he presented Britain's proposals to the Afghan ruler. This was the first contact between a British official and an Afghan ruler. Elphinstone used the opportunity to learn as much as he could about the "Forbidden Kingdom," and later published a book on Afghanistan, entitled *An Account of the Kingdom of Caubul* (1815), which is one of the first comprehensive accounts on Afghan society. He was rewarded for his services with the appointment as governor of Bombay. See AFGHAN FOREIGN RELATIONS, ANGLO-AFGHAN WARS, and SHAH SHUJA UL-MULK.

ELPHINSTONE, MAJOR GENERAL WILLIAM. Commander of the British army in Afghanistan in 1841 and the person held responsible by British historians for the debacle in the first Anglo-Afghan war. Gen. Elphinstone was in his sixties and infirm when he accepted the army command. He did not take "decisive" action when Alexander Burnes (q.v.), the assistant to the British envoy at Kabul, was assassinated with the members of his mission. He quartered his troops in the vulnerable cantonment, which was commanded from the nearby hills, instead of moving them to the protection of the Bala Hisar (q.v.) fortress. Surrounded by Afghan tribal armies, the British had to negotiate a retreat which turned into a rout in which most of the 16,000 troops and camp-followers died of the freezing cold weather or were otherwise killed. Elphinstone did not survive the disaster; on April 23, 1842, he died in captivity of exhaustion and various maladies. See ANGLO-AFGHAN WARS, AFGHAN-FOREIGN RELATIONS, and AKBAR, SARDAR MUHAMMAD.

ENAYATULLAH, SARDAR. King of Afghanistan, after King Amanullah's abdication on January 14, 1929, and forced to abdicate three days later, when Habibullah Kalakani (q.v.) ascended the throne. He was born on October 20, 1888, the eldest son of Amir Habibullah. His father gave him the title "Supporter of the State" (*muin al-sultanat*) and appointed him "Marshal," *sardar-i salar*, in 1905, and minister of education in 1916. He and Sardar Nasrullah (q.v.) were on friendly terms with the members of the Hentig-Niedermayer expedition (q.v.) in Kabul. At that time he was believed to be in favor of Afghan intervention in the war against Britain. He married a daughter of Sardar Mahmud Tarzi, editor of the *Seraj al-Akhbar* (q.v.) and later foreign minister. After the assassination of Amir Habibullah in Nangarhar province, Sardar Nasrullah went through the form of offering him the throne in the presence of Nadir Khan (q.v.) and other prominent officials. He, however, declined and recognized Nasrullah as the king. But the army revolted and Sardar Amanullah, who was in Kabul, won recognition as the new king. Enayatullah Khan was in virtual retirement during the reign of his brother. On December 14, 1928, when King Amanullah was forced to resign, he appointed Enayatullah Khan his successor; three days later Enayatullah was forced to surrender to Habibullah Kalakani. On January 18, 1929, he and his immediate family were evacuated to Peshawar, India, in an aircraft of the British air force. He lived in Tehran as a guest of the Iranian king until his death on August 12, 1946.

ENGERT, CORNELIUS VAN. First American minister plenipotentiary resident at Kabul (1942-43). American diplomats in Tehran or Delhi were accredited to the Kabul government until 1942 when a permanent legation was established. Van Engert was Austrian by birth. See UNITED STATES-AFGHAN RELATIONS.

ENVER (ANWAR) PASHA. Minister of war and, with Jemal Pasha (c.v.) and Talat Pasha, member of the ruling triumvirate in the Ottoman war government (1913-18). Senteced to death in 1919, he escaped to Germany after the war and from there to the Soviet Union. He failed to gain Soviet support in replacing Kemal Ataturk as the head of the Turkish government and moved to Central Asia. He apparently intended to seek a safe haven in Afghanistan, where Jemal Pasha had already preceded him and was active as an adviser to King Amanullah. He was arrested by Basmachi (q.v.) counterrevolutionaries, but convinced them of his sympathies and became one of their leaders. He fought on their side against the Red Army until he was killed in a skirmish on August 4, 1922.

ERSHAD-UL-NISWAN (IRSHAD AL-NISWAN). Women's weekly magazine first published in Afghanistan in March 1921 by Asma Samia, known as "Bibi Arabi," the wife of Mahmud Tarzi. Editor-in-chief was Ruhafza, known as "Munshia," (secretary), wife of Muhammad Zaman Khan and sister of Habibullah Tarzi. The magazine carried domestic and foreign news of interest to women as well as advice on cooking, needlework, and touched on problems facing women in society. It was discontinued after the fall of King Amanullah.

ESHAQ See **ISHAQ.**

ESMATI, MAS'UMA (WARDAK). Minister of education in Prime Minister Khaliqyar's government of May 1990 and appointed president of the Afghan Women's Council in 1987. A Pashtun, she was born in 1930 in Kabul province and educated in Kabul and at the National College of Education, Evanston, Illinois, where she got an M.A. degree in education

She became an instructor at Malalai Lycée in 1948 and principal of Zarghuna Lycée in 1958, and was elected to parliament in 1969. In 1980 she was appointed to the social science center of the Academy of Sciences. She claims not to be a member of the PDPA.

ETEHAD See **ITTIHAD.**

ETEMADI, NUR AHMAD (I'TIMADI). A diplomat and government official who served as ambassador to Karachi (1964), prime minister and minister of foreign affairs from 1967 to 1971, and subsequently as ambassador to Rome (1971), Moscow (1973), and Islamabad (1976-78). President Daud summoned him to Kabul for consultation on April 24, 1978, three days before the Saur Revolt. He was imprisoned by the Taraki government and secretly executed in August 1979 (Rumors persist that he is alive and held somewhere in the Soviet Union). He was born in 1921 in Kandahar and educated at Kabul. He was a grandson of Abdul Quddus (q.v., Etemad ud-Daula).

ETEMADI, SALEHA FARUQ. Appointed minister of social affairs in Prime Minister Khaliqyar's government of May 1990. Born in 1929 of a Sayyid family and educated in Kabul, she began her career as a teacher in 1949, advancing to the position of vice principal at Malalai School. She became president of the Women's Association in 1962 and editor of *Mermun* (Woman) magazine. In 1963 she was appointed lecturer at the faculty of literature of Kabul University. She is not a member of the PDPA.

ETEMADI, SARWAR GOYA. Scholar, historian, and bibliographer who played an important role in cultural relations with Iran. Born in 1909 and privately educated, he became an adviser to the ministry of education. He published documents on the Timurid period of Herat.

ETEMAD UD-DAULA (I'TIMAD AL-DAULA) See **ABDUL QUDDUS.**

ETHNIC GROUPS. The Afghan population is heterogeneous with numerous ethnic groups, speaking various dialects or mutually unintelligible languages. The largest ethnic group are the Pashtuns followed by the Tajiks, Uzbaks, and Hazara. Orywal (1986) lists the following ethnic groups in Afghanistan:

Pashtun	Tajik	Uzbak
Hazara	Turkoman	Aimaq
Taimani	Tahiri	Baluch
Mauri	Brahui	Arab
Qirghiz	Moghol	Gujar
Qipchaq	Eshkashimi	Munjani
Rushani	Sanglichi	Shighnani
Vakhi	Farsi/Farsiwan	Qarliq
Nuristani	Pashai	Firuzkuhi

Jamshidi	Timuri	Zuri
Maliki	Mishmast	Jat
Jalali	Ghorbat	Pikragh
Shadibaz	Vangavala	Qazaq
Qizilbash	Tatar	Parachi
Tirahi	Gavarbati	Ormuri
Shaikh Muhammadi	Jogi	Kutana
Jews (Yahudi)	Sikh	Hindu

Estimated population figures in millions (Groetzbach, 1990) are:

Pashtun	6
Tajik & Farsiwan	4
Uzbak	1.3*
Hazara	1.1
Aimaq	.5
Turkoman	.4
Baluch & Brahui	.16
Arab	.1
Nuristani	.1
Pashai	.1
Tatar	.06
Qizilbash	.04
Hindu & Sikh	.03
Qirghiz & Moghol	.11

* According to Hazara claims, they number as many as two million people in Afghanistan and another two million in Iran and Pakistan.

Virtually all Jews have left Afghanistan in the 1970s (of some 600 families, only six individuals remain in Kabul).
The introduction of state-sponsored education dictated the use of Dari as the language of instruction. Dari has been the language of royal courts since Ghaznavid times (q.v.) and was widely used also by the Turkic rulers of Central Asia and the Moghuls of India.
Since the early twentieth century Afghan governments have promoted Pashto as the national language, but any attempts to replace Dari in education have failed. One of the first decrees (No. 4) issued by the Marxist government was to recognize and permit the use of Turkmani, Uzbaki, Baluchi, and Nuristani as "national languages" to ensure the "essential conditions for evolution of the literature, education, and publication in mother tongues of the tribes and nationalities resident in Afghanistan." It ordered the respective ministries to start broadcasting on radio and television and publication of newspapers in these languages. This was an adoption of the Soviet nationalities policy and was seen by some as an attempt of divide and rule. For information on major ethnic groups, see individual entries.

-F-

FAIZABAD (lat. 37-6' N, long. 70-34' E). Capital of Badakhshan, with about 12,000 inhabitants, the central commercial market of the province, situated on the Kokcha river at an altitude of 3,300 feet. Until the late 17th century the town was called Jauz Gun, or Jauzun, because of the abundance of nuts (*jauz*) in the area. The name of the town was changed to Faizabad (abode of divine bounty, blessing, and charity), when in 1691 Mir Yar Beg brought what was believed to be the Blessed Robe (*khirqa-yi mubarak*) of the Prophet Muhammad to the town. (Ahmad Shah Durrani [q.v.] later brought the *khirqa* to Kandahar where it still is today.) In 1821 Murad Beg, the ruler of Kunduz, destroyed the town, but a few years later it again reached a population of 8,000. Many mosques and historical shrines now exist in the area. In 1937 Faizabad became the terminal of a road, connected to the northern highway between Baghlan and Kunduz, which was later extended east toward the Wakhan Corridor (q.v.). The natives speak a number of Badakhshi languages in addition to Dari.

FAIZANI, MAULAWI. An early Islamist activist from Herat, and comrade of Abdur Rasul Sayyaf (q.v.) and Ghulam Muhammad Niazi (q.v.), who had been a militant anti-Communist since the 1960s. He was arrested in 1975 together with Abdul Rasul Sayyaf (q.v.) and Ghulam Muhammad Niazi (q.v.) and was assassinated in 1978 by the Khalqi government in Pul-i Charkhi prison. See ISLAMIST MOVEMENT IN AFGHANISTAN.

FAIZ MUHAMMAD, AL-HAJJ MULLA. Court historian under Amir Habibullah and author of the three-volume *Seraj al-Tawarikh* (Torch of Histories), a valuable historical text in Dari. He was born in 1861, the son of Muhammad Sa'id, a Hazara, and studied Islamic sciences in India and Iran. In 1893 he entered the services of Sardar Habibullah, son of Amir Abdur Rahman, and began work on his monumental three-volume history. A fourth volume is said to exist in manuscript form, extant in the National Archives of Afghanistan in Kabul. Faiz Muhammad died in 1931, purportedly from the complications of a severe beating by Habibullah Kalakani (q.v.), who had sent him to bring a document of submission from the Hazarajat.

FAIZ MUHAMMAD, ZIKRIA (ZAKARIA). Diplomat and high government official, as well as a poet and writer with the pen name "Faizi Kabuli." Born in 1892 and educated at Habibia School (q.v.), he entered the foreign service in 1921. He accompanied the Afghan mission under Muhammad Wali (q.v.) to Europe and the United States to conclude agreements for establishing diplomatic relations. He became King

Amanullah's minister of education in 1925, and subsequently served as a member of Habibullah Kalakani's "Council for the Maintenance of Order." Appointed foreign minister by Nadir Shah in 1929, he served until 1938, and as ambassador to Turkey (1938-48), Great Britain (1948-50), and Saudi Arabia (1955-60). He retired in 1960 and lived in the United States where he died in 1979. He is buried in Peshawar.

FAMILY. Although great variations exist between and even within groups, the family among most Afghan ethnic groups is patrilineal, patrilocal and characterized by a low incidence of polygyny, a low divorce rate, and a high birth rate. The extended family is the major economic and social unit. Marriages are arranged by the families of the prospective groom and bride (or an intermediary) and a bride price is paid by the family of the groom. Cousin marriages are often preferred. Afghan rulers since Amir Abdur Rahman (q.v.) have tried to limit the bride price (*mahr*) and costly festivities and have forbidden such practices as "child marriage" (contracted long in advance), but these customs still prevail, except among the urban upper classes. While in theory divorce is easy for men (a man can divorce his wife simply by saying "I divorce thee" three times), economic factors and the fact that marriages are often concluded within the clan or are alliances between families make it difficult to divorce. The same factors limit polygyny, inspite of the fact that Islamic law permits a man to have four wives.

The extended family consists of the patriarch, his wife (or wives) and his married sons. Authority descends in the male line and the Islamic law of inheritance (which allocated a set portion to women) is often ignored in favor of the male members. Afghan law requires the registration of marriages, but this is enforced only in the larger urban areas. The Marxist regime of Nur Muhammad Taraki tried to limit the bride price to a token amount of 300 afghanis (then six dollars), demanded freedom of choice of the partners, and set a minimum age for marriage at 16 for women and 18 for men. Like previous Afghan rulers, the Marxist government was not able to enforce its marriage laws and eventually rescinded them as well as other unpopular innovations.

FAQIR OF IPI, HAJI MIRZA ALI KHAN. A frontier mulla residing with the Waziri tribe on the Indian side of the Durand Line. He was an implacable foe of the British who incited the tribes to wage *jihad* against India. He collaborated with the Axis powers during World War II and was in touch with their legations in Kabul. The Germans gave him the code name "Feuerfresser" (fire- eater) and supported his efforts by paying him a regular subsidy. The Faqir's activities compelled Britain to keep large forces on the Frontier which could have been deployed elsewhere. At one time an army of 40,000 troops was searching for him; he always found shelter among the Waziris (q.v.) and often was forced to hide in a cave. After the creation of Pakistan, the Faqir demanded independence for Pashtunistan (q.v.); he was elected "president" of Pashtunistan by a

tribal council and continued his fight against the new state. He received
financial support from the Afghan government until his death in 1960.

FARAH (lat. 32-22' N, long. 62-7' E). A province in western Afghanistan
with an area of 21,666 square miles; it is the second largest Afghan
province, with a population of about 356,000. The province is divided
into the districts of Farah, Anardara, Bala Boluk, Purchaman, Bakwa,
Shindand, Kala-i-Kah, Gulistan, Khak-i-Safid, and Farsi. The capital of
the province is the town of Farah with about 18,800 inhabitants. The
province is traversed by the Farah Rud, the Khash Rud, and the Harut
Rud (rivers); major mountain ranges include the Khak-i-Safid, Siyah Kuh,
Malmand, Kuh-i- Afghan, and the Reg-i-Rawan. The economy of the
province depends primarily on agriculture and livestock breeding; barley,
cotton, and wheat are the major crops and livestock includes sheep,
Qaraqul sheep, as well as goats, cattle, camels, and donkeys. An
important junction in Indo-Persian trade in the 17th century, Farah was
destroyed in 1837 and remained a small walled town until the early
twentieth century when a new town was gradually developed, with a
population of about 6,000 in 1934. The town gradually declined when the
new Kandahar-Herat highway, completed in 1965, bypassed the town. In
1972 floods destroyed much of the town and the provincial administration
moved for two years to Farah Rud (q.v.). The population is largely
Pashtun, but Tajik and other ethnic communities are also represented in
Farah.

FARAH RUD (lat. 31-29' N, long. 61-24' E). A river which rises in Ghor
province and flows in a southwesterly direction and runs into the
Hamun-i-Saberi, a shallow, brackish lake in Nimruz province, which
extends across the Iranian border.

FARANGI Or FRANGI. The Dari word is a curruption of "Franks" or French,
a name originally applied throughout the Middle East to Italians and
Frenchmen, but which was later extended to designate all European
Christians.

FARHAD, GHULAM MUHAMMAD. Afghan nationalist and founder of the
Afghan Social Democrat party (*jami'yat-i susyal demukrat*), popularly
called *Afghan Millat* (q.v., Afghan Nation). Educated in Kabul and
Germany, where he obtained an engineering degree, he was president of
the Afghan Electric Company (1939-66), and mayor of Kabul (1948-54).
He built the *Jada-yi Maiwand* (Maiwand Street), the first major avenue
through the old town of Kabul, relocating displaced residents, and
changed the traffic from the British Indian system to right-hand driving,
which was subsequently adopted throughout Afghanistan. He demanded
the restoration of "Greater Afghanistan" with the inclusion of Pakistan's
North-West Frontier Province and Baluchistan. Publisher of *Afghan
Millat*, 1966- 67 (q.v.), a weekly newspaper, which subsequently became
the name also of the party. He was pro-German and accused of giving

preference to German technology and experts in the allocation of various developmental contracts. In 1968 he was elected to parliament but resigned his seat in 1970. In 1978 he was arrested by the Khalqi regime and his party was accused of attempting a coup, but was freed in 1980 in the general amnesty of Babrak Karmal (q.v.). He died in 1984 in Kabul. He was a Pashtun and an ardent supporter of the Pashtunistan (q.v.) cause. Also see AFGHAN MILLAT.

FARHADI, ABDUL GHAFUR RAWAN. Afghan diplomat and scholar who became director general for political affairs in the foreign ministry in 1964, served as secretary to the cabinet (1966-71), and as deputy minister for political affairs (1970-73). Born in 1929 in Kabul, he was educated at Istiqlal high school and in France where he obtained the Ph.D. degree in Indo-Iranian philology in 1955. He entered service in the foreign ministry in 1955, and was appointed first secretary at the Afghan embassy in Karachi (1958), counselor at Washington, D.C. (1962), and ambassador at Paris (1973), but was recalled by the republican government of Muhammad Daud. He was arrested during the Khalqi regime, freed in 1980, and employed as an adviser of the ministry of foreign affairs until he left for France and the United States. His mother tongue is Dari.

FARHANG, MIR MUHAMMAD SIDDIQ. Deputy minister of planning (1964-65), member of the Constitutional Drafting Committee (1964), and member of parliament. Born in 1915, the son of Sayyid Habib (and brother of Sayyid Qasim Reshtia [q.v.]), he was educated at Istiqlal (q.v.) Lycée and took a position with the Bank-i-Milli at Kabul. Was appointed member of the Kabul city council and deputy mayor (1949). Editor of *Watan* (Homeland), a liberal biweekly newspaper, 1951-52. Imprisoned twice, he took service with the ministry of mines and industries until 1965, when he became a deputy of parliament and chairman of the legislation committee. He served as ambassador to Belgrade, 1972-73, and as adviser to the prime ministry in 1980. He left Afghanistan in 1981 and resided in the United States where he published a two-volume history, in Dari, entitled *Afghanistan in the last five Centuries* (1988 and 1990). He died in April 1990. His mother tongue was Dari.

FARIAB (lat. 36-0' N, long. 65-0' E). A province in north-central Afghanistan with an area of 8,226 square miles and a population of about 547,000. The province borders on the Soviet Union in the north and northwest, on Badghis province in the south and Jozjan in the east. The capital of the province is the town of Maimana (q.v.) with about 38,000 inhabitants. Fariab is famous for horsebreeding and its *buzkashi* (q.v.) games. Melons, nuts, cereals and cotton are the major agricultural products. Qaraqul sheep are bred for the export of skins and carpet weaving is an important industry. Also see MAIMANA.

FARSIWAN. An ethnic group of some 600,000 Farsi-speaking Shi'a Muslims living near the Iranian border, in Herat, Kandahar, Ghazni and scattered over southern and western Afghan towns. They are of Mediterranean stock and are mostly engaged in agriculture. Pashto-speakers refer to all Dari-speakers as Farsiwan.

FATEH KHAN (FATH). Oldest son of Painda Khan (q.v., head of the Muhammadzai branch of the Barakzai tribe), born in 1777 in Kandahar. He was a skillful politician and soldier and helped Shah Mahmud (q.v., 1799-1803 and 1810-18) gain the Afghan throne, capturing Farah and Kandahar, from the forces of Zaman Shah (q.v.). He was given the position of grand wazir and established law and order and conducted the government for Mahmud with great skill. When Shah Shuja (q.v., 1803-10 and 1839) succeeded to the Kabul throne, Fateh Khan was again appointed grand wazir, but Fateh Khan remained loyal to Mahmud and helped to restore him to power. Fateh Khan consolidated Afghan control over Kashmir and established order in Herat. Kamran, son of Shah Mahmud, was jealous of Fateh Khan's power and had him blinded and, in 1818, killed. The Barakzai chiefs revolted and the ensuing conflict led to the overthrow of the Sadozai dynasty and the assumption of power by the Barakzai/Muhammadzai branch of the Durranis.

FATWA. A formal legal opinion by a *mufti*, or sunni canon lawyer, in answer to a question by a judge or private individual. Laws in Afghanistan had to conform to Islamic law, as certified by the *fatwa* of a council of *ulama*. See ISLAMIC LAW.

FAZL AHMAD, MUJADDIDI See **MUJADDIDI.**

FAZL OMAR See **MUJADDIDI.**

FIKRI, ABDUL RAUF SALJUQI See **SALJUQI.**

FIQH. The science of law, or jurisprudence, in Islamic law. See ISLAMIC LAW.

FIRDAUSI, ABU'L QASEM MANSUR (934?-1020?). Author of the great national epic, the *Shahnama* (Book of Kings), which contains all the legends and history of Persia and ancient Afghanistan known to him. A native of Khorasan (q.v.), he spent twenty-five years on the *Shahnama* and presented it to Mahmud of Ghazni (988-1030), at whose court he had completed the work. His work is the most voluminous collection of early Persian poetry and therefore an important source for linguistics and literary studies.

FIRST ANGLO-AFGHAN WAR See **ANGLO-AFGHAN WARS.**

FIRUZ KUH (lat. 34-30' N, long. 63-30' E). A mountain range, also called Safid Kuh (White Mountain), extending in a westerly direction from the area of Chaghcharan into eastern Herat province.

FIRUZKUHI. One of the sunni Chahar Aimaq tribes (See AIMAQ), located in eastern Badghis and northern Ghor povinces. They number about 100,000 and are Farsi speakers. Their name, according to one version, comes from Firuz Kuh, a mountain near Semnan in Iran, where they lived until the 14th century, when Timur-i Lang (q.v.) transferred them to Herat from where they subsquently migrated further east. According to another version their name derives from an eponymic ancestor, Firuz, who was one of the sons (or slaves?) of Sanzar (progenitor also of Taiman the eponymic ancestor of the Taimanis-q.v.). The descendants of Firuz were at first small chiefs under Taimani Khans until they took over most of the Taimani territory southeast of Herat. Major subdivisions are the the Mahmudis, including the Zai Murad and the Zai Hakim clans and the Darazis, all of which are subdivided into a number of sections.

FIVE YEAR PLANS See **ECONOMY.**

FLAG. Afghanistan's first national flag was the Abdali (q.v.) banner, depicting a cluster of wheat, a sword, and stars on a background of red and green. Important chiefs and princes had their own flags. Amir Shir Ali's (q.v.) standard was triangular in shape, red and green, with Koranic inscriptions. Abdur Rahman (q.v.) preferred a black banner (Abu Muslim's Abbasid standard) on which was drawn in white a *mihrab* (prayer niche), *minbar* (pulpit), a sword, and a gun. Amir Habibullah's (q.v.) "national flag" (*bayraq-i daulati*) was similar except that it omitted the sword and gun. King Amanullah (q.v.) introduced the tricolor flag in 1928 with broad horizontal stripes of black, red, and green and an emblem showing the rising sun over snow- capped mountains clothed in wheat. The name Allah was inscribed in the upper left corner.
Nadir Shah (q.v.) continued the tricolor, but with vertical stripes, and an emblem depicting a mosque with pulpit and mihrab (See MOSQUE). The mosque was flanked by two banners and the emblem was framed by a wreath of wheat. A scroll carried the inscription "Afghanistan" above which was the date 1348 (lunar year, corresponding to 1929), the year in which he assumed the throne. The emblem was in the red center portion of the flag.
President Daud designed the republican flag in May 1974 retaining the tricolor in horizontal lines. An emblem in the upper left corner consisted of a stylized eagle, *mihrab* and *minbar*, surrounded by a wreath and a scroll with the inscription *Da Afghanistan Jumhuriat* (Republic of Afghanistan) and the date 26th of Saratan (July 17, 1973), the day he staged his coup. Black was on the top, followed by red, each one-fourth of the width of the flag, the lower half was green.
In Ocober 1978 the Taraki regime introduced the red flag with an emblem in gold in the right hand corner. It consisted of the traditional wreath with the name Khalq (People) in the center, a five- cornered star above it, and a scroll with the Pashto inscription *Da Afghanistan Da Demukratik Jumhuriat* (Democratic Rebublic of Afghanistan). It carried

the date of the Saur Revolt, 7 Saur 1357 (April 27, 1978). The Khalqi flag strongly resembled the USSR flag and those of the Soviet Republics and therefore aroused the ire of many Afghans. When Babrak Karmal replaced Hafizullah Amin he restored the tricolor, but kept the red flag as the banner of the party.

FOREIGN RELATIONS See **AFGHAN FOREIGN RELATIONS.**

FOREIGN TRADE See **ECONOMY.**

FORWARD POLICY See **AFGHAN FOREIGN RELATIONS.**

-G-

GAHIZ MINHAJUDDIN (MINHAJJ AL-DIN). Member of the Islamist, anti-Communist, movement and publisher of the *Jarida-yi Gahis* (Newspaper of Gahiz [Dawn in Pashto]). He was born in 1922 of a Pashtun family in Koh Daman and educated at the teachers training high school in Kabul, becoming a teacher at Ghazi high school. His newspaper carried articles on Islamic topics and political attacks at the emerging Marxist movements. He is said to have been killed in 1971 by Communist agents who had entered his home as "visitors."

GAILANI, SAYYID AHMAD (AFANDI SAHIB, GILANI). Descendant of the Muslim Pir Baba Abdul Qadir Gailani (1077-1166) and hereditary head of the Qaderia sufi fraternity. He succeeded to his position upon the death of his older brother, Sayyid Ali, in 1964. Born in 1932 in Kabul, the son of Sayyid Hasan Gailani, he was educated at Abu Hanifa College and the faculty of theology of Kabul University. He left Afghanistan after the Saur Revolt (q.v.) and founded the National Islamic Front (NIFA - *Mahaz-i Milli-yi Islami-yi Afghanistan*) in Peshawar. His movement is part of the seven-member Alliance which in 1989 formed the "Afghan Interim Government." Although Sayyid Gailani did not want any position in the interim government, he later accepted the post of supreme justice (*Qadhi al-Qudhat*). Gailani is married to Adela (daughter of Sardar Abdul Baqi and Aziza - a daughter of Amir Habibullah) and has three daughters and two sons: Fatima, Mariam, Hamed, Muhammad, and Zahra. Also see MAHAZ.

GAILANI, SAYYID ALI (GILANI). Born in 1923 in Kabul, the son of Sayyid Hasan Gailani (q.v.) and leader of the Qadiria religious brotherhood. He died in 1964 and was succeeded by his younger brother Sayyid Ahmad Gailani. His son Ishaq Gailani is affiliated with Jabha (q.v.).

GAILANI, SAYYID HASAN (GILANI). Born about 1862 in Baghdad. Sayyid Hasan Gailani is the son of Sayyid Ali Gailani, the son of Sayyid Salman

Gailani, descendant of al-Imam Hasan, son of Caliph Ali, son of Abu Taleb. Member of the family of the Naqib al-Ashraf of Baghdad, Sayyid Hasan Gailani came to Afghanistan in 1905. He was welcomed warmly by the king and the *qadirites* of Afghanistan. Amir Habibullah paid him an allowance of Rs. 3,500 per month, and built him a winter residence at Chaharbagh, near Jalalabad. Thus he became known as the Naqib Sahib of Charharbagh, as well as the Pir Naqib of Baghdad, the place where his ancestor's tomb is located. His reasons for leaving Baghdad and coming to Afghanistan were: primarily a disagreement with his older brother, Sayyid Abdur Rahman Gailani, who was the oldest in the family and was Naqib al-Ashraf of Baghdad. He wanted to get married in spite of the wishes of his brother, and Sayyid Hasan Gailani -- wherever he would have gone -- would have been sent back, because of the influence of his brother. So he went to Afghanistan, which was not a part of the Ottoman Empire. Furthermore, Afghanistan is a Hanafite Islamic country which has many Qaderi followers. Those Afghans who were visiting the Mausoleum of Shaikh Abdul Qadir Gailani in Baghdad had told Sayyid Hasan Gailani about "the Afghan's firm beliefs, their purity of soul and character," and had also familiarized him with their language. And his faithful companion Mahmud Tokhi (an Afghan subject) had told Gailani about the goodwill of the Afghans toward him. Therefore, he decided to make a journey to Afghanistan. "The faith of the people and the insistence of the King induced him to accept Afghan citizenship and to stay in Afghanistan." Sayyid Hasan was respected by the Afghans who took him as an example of the Qaderia life. He was treated with the utmost respect by Amir Habibullah Khan and Sardar Nasrullah Khan. He issued a farman in support of King Nadir Shah in 1931. Sayyid Hasan Gailani had a daughter, Fatima, from his first wife and two sons, Sayyid Ali Gailani and Sayyid Ahmad Gailani, from his fourth wife. In 1941 he died of a brain hemorrage and was buried in his Chaharbagh garden in Jalalabad.

GANDAMAK (lat. 34-18' N, long. 70-2' E). A village on the Gandamak stream, a tributary of the Surkhab, about 29 miles southwest of Jalalabad. The area was the scene of a number of battles between British and Afghan forces including the massacre of the last remnants of the British army in 1842. It was also the scene of a treaty concluded between Major Louis Cavagnari (q.v.) and Amir Yaqub Khan (q.v.), signed on May 2, 1879. See GANDAMAK, TREATY OF.

GANDAMAK, TREATY OF. A treaty concluded between the British government and Amir Yaqub Khan (q.v.), signed by the amir and Major Louis Cavagnari (q.v) on May 2, 1879, and ratified by Lord Lytton, viceroy of India on May 30, 1879.
The treaty was to establish "eternal peace and friendship" between the two countries upon conclusion of the second Anglo-Afghan war (Article 1). It provided for an amnesty for Afghan collaborators with the British occupation forces (Article 2), and obligated the amir to "conduct his relations with Foreign States, in accordance with the advice and wishes

of the British Government." In exchange Britain would support the amir "against any foreign aggression with money, arms, or troops" (Article 3). A British representative was to be stationed at Kabul "with a suitable escort in a place of residence appropriate to his rank and dignity" and an Afghan agent was to be at the court of the viceroy of India (Article 4). A separate commercial agreement was to be signed (Article 7), and a telegraph line from Kurram to Kabul was to be constructed (Article 8). The Khaibar and Michni passes were to be controlled by Britain (Article 9), Kandahar and Jalalabad was to be "restored" to the amir with the exception of Kurram, Pishin, and Sibi which were to be under British control, but were not "considered as permanently severed from the limits of the Afghan kingdom." Afghan historians consider the treaty a sell out to Britain and a treasonable act by Amir Yaqub Khan (q.v.)

GANDHARA. A state in the Peshawar valley with its capital at Taxila (or Charsada?), which flourished from the late-first to the mid-fifth century A.D. It is famous for the fusion of Hellenistic and Buddhist civilization and art styles. The Kabul museum holds numerous specimens of that art. See KABUL MUSEUM.

GARDEZ (lat. 33-37' N, long. 69-7' E). Gardez is a town with about 20,000 inhabitants and a district in Paktia province, located at an altitude of 7,620 feet. The town is inhabited largely by Ghilzai Pashtuns and some Dari-speakers and is, at the time of this writing, still controlled by the Kabul government. Most of the surrounding villages have been destroyed and the inhabitants have fled to Pakistan. It is a strategically important town because it controls the route north over the Altamur pass (9,600 feet) to Kabul. It is an ancient town, with a strong citadel and fortress, which for a short time was the seat of the Kushanid (q.v.) rulers of Kabul. It was a center of Buddhist culture and, in the early Islamic period, a base of the Kharijite (*Khawarij* - The Seceders) sect of Islam.

GARMSIR. A low-lying, hot country (*garm* = warm), in contra-distinction to *sardsir* (*sard* = cold), a cold place, and therefore summer habitation in high grounds. Nomads would seasonally move from one to the other. Garmsir (or Garmsel) is also the name of a district in Helmand province.

GAZAR-GAH (lat. 34-22' N, long. 62-14' E). The name of a range of low hills to the north of Herat and the location of the tomb of Khwaja Abdullah Ansari (q.v.), a celebrated eleventh-century philosopher and sufi poet. The shrine is the residence of the Mir of Gazargah, a man widely revered as the guardian of Ansari's mausoleum.

GENEVA ACCORDS. The result of "proximity" talks between Afghanistan and Pakistan in Geneva, initiated on June 16, 1982, by Diego Cordovez under the auspices of the United Nations and concluded on April 14, 1988. The Accords consisted of four documents and an annex; three

between the Republic of Afghanistan and the Islamic Republic of
Pakistan; one between the Soviet Union and the United States, promising
to "refrain from any form of interference and intervention;" and an annex
with a memorandum of understanding, assisting the UN in the implementation of the agreements. The United States and the Soviet Union
were the guarantors of the accords. The talks aimed at ending the
"external interference" in the war in Afghanistan with a view to
establishing peace. The accords resulted in the withdrawal of Soviet
troops in mid-February 1989, but failed to end foreign interference or to
bring the warring parties closer to peace. One reason for the failure was
that the mujahedin were not a party to the accords, another was that
Washington, and virtually everyone else, expected the Marxist government
to disintegrate promptly. When the Soviets departed, they left a
considerable amount of war materiel and promised to supply more under
the treaty of friendship of December 1978. The United States was
obligated to cease military support of the mujahedin. The result was a
haggling over "symmetry" and "negative symmetry" of arms supplies, not
part of the formal agreements. Eventually the Soviets and the U.S.
informally agreed on "positive symmetry," that is to say, they reserved
themselves the right to send arms in response to shipments by the other.
The result was that both powers continued to support their "clients" and
Pakistan continued to permit the passage of weapons through its territory.
The war continued and the superpower guarantees of non-interference in
the internal affairs of Afghanistan were ignored.

GEOGRAPHY. Afghanistan is a mountainous, land-locked state of some
251,000 square miles, which is approximately the area of Texas, and has
a population of about 15.5 million (estimate based on demographic
research under the auspices of the Afghan Central Statistics Office).
The climate in Afghanistan varies in accordance with the particular geographic zone: subarctic conditions in the northeast and Hindu Kush
mountains (with peaks at 14,000 to 17,000 feet), a semiarid steppe climate
in low lying areas, and mild, moist weather in the southeast bordering
Pakistan. The estimated annual rainfall is between 11 and 15 inches with
great variations -- more on the southeastern slopes of mountains exposed
to the monsoon rains and much less in the southwestern deserts.
About 83 percent of the *Wakhan-Pamir* area lies at an altitude above
10,000 feet and another 17 percent at an altitude of between 6,000 and
10,000 feet. Therefore, snow covers mountains above 16,000 feet and
most passes are seasonally closed. The yak and bactrian camel are
utilized in the transportation of man and goods.
A similar climate exists in the *Central Mountains* including most of central
and eastern Hazarajat, and the Hindu Kush ranges, extending from the
Shibar Pass (q.v.) through the Koh-e Baba (q.v.) in the west, which is
crossed by the Salang (q.v.) tunnel at an altitude of about 11,000 feet. A
limited amount of agriculture exists in the valleys and nomads seasonally
graze their livestock on the foothills.

The *Eastern Mountains* include four major regions: Kabul, Kohistan/-Panjshir, the Ghorband, and Nuristan, the latter being the most inaccessible. Snow exists at altitudes between 10,000 and 12,000 feet. Temperatures reach lows of one degree Fahrenheit, and winter lasts from December till March. Summer temperatures depend on altitude. In the southwest, stony deserts extend to the Iranian border, and the Registan, "Country of Sand," extends south of the Helmand river and eastward as far as Shorawak, forming a natural boundary with Pakistan. On the edges of the Registan the desert gradually changes into a hilly landscape of sandhills thickly sprinkled with bushes and vegetation and grass after rains. Baluch and Brahui nomads seasonally graze their flock in this areas. The major agricultural areas are confined to the valleys watered by the Amu Daria and the northern plains, the Hari Rud/Murghab system in the northwest, the Helmand/Arghandab system, and the Kabul river system. The melting snow feeds the dry riverbeds in spring and provides much of the water for irrigation (for specific rivers, see independent entries).

GERMAN-AFGHAN RELATIONS. German-Afghan relations date from the time of World War I when the Hentig-Niedermayer Expedition (q.v.) in August 1915 first established official contact with an Afghan ruler (the claim by one Afghan writer that a secret German mission was sent to the court of Amir Shir Ali (q.v.) cannot be substantiated on the basis of British or German archival sources). The first German known to reside in Kabul was Gottlieb Fleischer, an employee of Krupp Steelworks of Essen, Germany, who was contracted by Amir Abdur Rahman in 1898 to start manufacture of ammunitions and arms in the newly constructed factory (*mashin-khana*) at Kabul (he was killed in November 1904 near the border while traveling to India). Afghanistan existed in self-imposed isolation and the British-Indian government refused to permit passage to Afghanistan to other than their own nationals. It was not until World War I that Germans again appeared in Kabul. A number of Austrian and German prisoners of war, held in Russian Central Asia, escaped and made their way to Kabul, where they were "interned" but enjoyed freedom of movement and contributed their skills to various public works projects. The first official contact was the Hentig-Niedermayer mission (q.v.) which included also Turkish and Indian members and was charged with establishing diplomatic relations between the Central Powers and Afghanistan. The Germans hoped that Amir Habibullah would heed the Caliph's call to holy war and, together with the Pashtun Frontier tribes, attack India. The mission caused considerable anxiety in India, but although Amir Habibullah wanted to rid himself of British control, he was not to be drawn into a conflict whose outcome seemed at best dubious (See AFGHAN FOREIGN RELATIONS). Nevertheless, the mission was not a complete failure as it forced Britain to maintain troops on its northwest frontier which could have been used in the European theater of war. Habibullah appeared to be willing to act, but demanded assistance in funds and arms which only a victorious Germany could have

provided. When it became apparent that no such victory was in sight, he
informed Britain that he would remain neutral in the war in exchange for
a financial reward and British recognition of Afghanistan's independence
(See HABIBULLAH, AMIR).

Germany rendered Afghanistan a potentially important service by insisting
on Russian recognition of Afghan independence in Article VII of the
Treaty of Brest-Litovsk (March 3. 1918), which ended Russian participation in World War I.

German influence became solidly established during the reign of King
Amanullah (q.v., 1919-29). The "Reformer King" won the independence
of his country in a short, undeclared war (See ANGLO-AFGHAN
WARS) and quickly established relations with the major powers of the
world.

In 1923 Fritz Grobba, the German minister plenipotentiary, joined the
diplomatic representatives of the Soviet Union, Persia, Britain, Turkey,
and Italy in Kabul, and it was soon clear that there existed a community
of interest between Germany and Afghanistan. King Amanullah needed
Western expertise for his modernization projects and felt that nationals
from states other than his powerful neighbors should be engaged. The
United States was reluctant to move into an area which it considered
within the British sphere of influence (See UNITED STATES-AFGHAN
RELATIONS); Italy was willing to assist, but the execution of an Italian
who killed an Afghan policeman, soured relations between the two countries. France was seen as a colonial power which had acquired large
portions of the Ottoman empire, whose ruling sultan/caliph Afghans had
recognized as the spiritual head of the Islamic world. Germany had been
an ally of the Ottomans and offered Afghanistan industrial hardware and
skilled technicians at competitive rates. A consortium of German
enterprises formed the Deutsch- Afghanische Companie (DACOM) which
established an office in Kabul. In 1923, King Amanullah founded the
German-language high school, *Amani* (called *Najat* under Nadir Shah),
in addition to French and English-language secondary schools, and
German influence was growing. By 1926 the German colony was second
only to the Russians and soon became the largest of all foreign groups.
Relations developed to the extent that major incidents which might have
had a serious impact on German-Afghan relations were resolved
amicably. In November 1926, a German national killed an Afghan nomad
and in June 1933 an Afghan student, and supporter of the deposed King
Amanullah, shot Sardar Muhammad Aziz, a half brother of Nadir Shah
and his minister at Berlin. In September 1933, Muhammad Azim, a
teacher at the German high school wanted to provoke an international
incident by shooting the British minister at Kabul (he killed an
Englishman, an Afghan, and an Indian employee instead). The last two
incidents were seen as the manifestation of a power struggle between the
followers of King Amanullah and the new ruling family, and there existed
some worries in Kabul that Germany was supporting the ex-King. These
incidents had no lasting effect on German-Afghan relations.

In October 1936 the two countries agreed in a "confidential protocol" on the delivery 15 million marks of war materiel on credit to be repaid in half with Afghan products. By that time Germany had become an important economic and political factor in Kabul and the way seemed clear for even closer cooperation. In 1937 Lufthansa Airline established regular service from Berlin to Kabul with the intention of eventually extending service to China. And in summer 1939, shortly before the outbreak of World War II, a German commercial delegation arrived in Kabul to expand German-Afghan trade; but the political situation precluded any desire of the Kabul government to tie itself even closer to Nazi Germany. German annexation of Austria in March 1938 and the annexation of Czechoslovakia a year later, and above all the conclusion of a nonaggression pact between Germany and the Soviet Union in August 1939, made it appear likely that Europe would be engulfed in war. Germany could no longer be a "third force" in Afghanistan's attempt to balance the influences of her powerful neighbors.

At the outbreak of World War II, Zahir Shah proclaimed Afghanistan's neutrality and was determined to stay out of the war. For Germany Afghanistan's strategic location gained a priority over commercial consideration. The German foreign ministry and its political counterpart, the *Aussenpolitische Amt*, toyed with the idea of supporting a pro-Amanullah coup to establish an allied government in Kabul. It sent Peter Kleist, a German diplomat, and Ghulam Siddiq (q.v.), a former Afghan ambassador and supporter of King Amanullah, to Moscow to query Vyacheslav Molotov, the Soviet foreign minister, whether the Soviets would support such a move. The Soviets were noncommittal and nothing came of the project. When Germany invaded the Soviet Union in June 1941, Afghanistan's neighbors were allied for the second time since the Anglo-Russian Convention of 1907 (q.v.) and they were soon to take a common stand in Kabul: in separate diplomatic notes of October 9 and 11, 1941, the Soviet Union and Britain demanded the evacuation of all Axis nationals from Afghanistan. Prime Minister Muhammad Hashim (q.v.) was forced to comply, even though the Afghan government considered it an infringement of its sovereign rights. A *Loya Jirga* (q.v.), national council, convened on November 5 and 6, approved the decision after the Axis nationals had left for India and traveled under a promise of free passage to a neutral country. Axis diplomats were permitted to stay and their contacts with Pashtun tribes on the Indian side of the border did not achieve any tangible results. In spite of sympathies for the enemy of Afghanistan's traditional enemies, there was no question of armed cooperation with Germany.

After its defeat in World War II, the German "phoenix" rose from its ashes again, and soon German expertise again found a ready demand in Kabul. Although Germany was unable for a while to deliver industrial products, her nationals would again be a major factor in Afghanistan's development projects. A dam and hydroelectric power station at Sarobi became one of the first major German projects after the war. American funds and German contractors built the new campus of Kabul University. German teachers served in the faculties of science and economics of Kabul University and by the 1970s, German economic aid ranked third after Soviet and American assistance.

Najat school became a model institution, rivalling the French-supported *Istiqlal*, and the English-language schools in Kabul. The *Deutsche Entwicklungsdienst* (German Development Service), a volunteer organization, brought Germans with attractive skills to Afghanistan. The Goethe Institute for the promotion of German language and culture was opened in Kabul and a consortium of German universities offered Afghans opportunities to study in Germany. East Germany, not recognized by the Afghans, eventually also appeared on the scene, vying with its Western "brothers" to win friends and influence people. West German influence lasted long after the Soviet intervention in Afghanistan, although East Germans gradually replaced Germans from the West. Because of its long and fruitful association with Afghanistan, her nationals have enjoyed a good reputation in Kabul and may well continue to have an important cultural and economic role in Afghanistan.

GHAFFAR KHAN, See **KHAN ABDUL GHAFFAR KHAN.**

GHAUS, ABDUL SAMAD. Director of the UN affairs department and under President Daud, director-general of political affairs in the ministry of foreign affairs in 1974. He served as deputy minister of foreign affairs from June 1977 until the Saur Revolt in April 1978. Imprisoned in 1978, he was freed in 1980 and went to he United States in 1981. He was born in 1928 in Rome, attended Istiqlal High School and continued his studies in Switzerland, and started his career in the ministry of foreign affairs in 1956. He published a book on Afghanistan, entitled *The Fall of Afghanistan: An Insider's Account* (1988), which describes President Daud's negotiations with various heads of state, including Leonid Brezhnev of the Soviet Union.

GHAUSUDDIN, GEN. Commander of Afghan forces at the time of the Panjdeh Incident (q.v.) in March 1885. He confronted Col. Alikhanov, commander of the Russian forces, but was defeated by the superior power of the Russians. He was a native of Logar and the ancestor of the Ghausi clan.

GHAZI. A veteran in holy war (*ghazw*) and a title given to a victorious commander. Mahmud of Ghazni (q.v.), King Amanullah (q.v.), Habibullah Kalakani (q.v.), Nadir Shah (q.v.) and others claimed this title. The sons of Sardar Shah Mahmud (q.v.) adopted his title as a family name.

GHAZI COLLEGE. Founded at Kabul in 1928 by King Amanullah. It received its name from the king's title *Ghazi*, "Victor" in the third Anglo-Afghan war. Like Habibia school, it is a 12-grade English-language preparatory school, most of whose graduates continued their higher education at Kabul or abroad.

GHAZI, SHAH MAHMUD. War minister and commander-in-chief from 1929 until 1946, when he became prime minister until 1953. Born in 1886, the youngest son of Muhammad Yusuf, he embarked on a military career. He served as military commander and governor in various provinces and was appointed deputy interior minister in 1928. Assisted his brother Nadir Khan in defeating Habibullah Kalakani (q.v.) and served Nadir Shah and his successor Zahir Shah as prime minister until 1953, when he resigned in favor of Sardar Muhammad Daud (q.v.). He allowed substantial freedom of speech and of the press, but reverted to more authoritarian measures when the political liberalization led to increasing attacks on his government. He died in December 1959.

GHAZNAVID DYNASTY (977-1186). A dynasty of Turkic origin founded by Nasir al-Daula Sebuktegin (977- 97) with its administrative capital in the city of Ghazni. During the reign of Sultan Mahmud Ghazni (q.v. 998-1030) the Ghaznavid empire extended from the Tigris to the Ganges river and from the Indian Ocean to the Amu Daria. The city of Ghazni experienced a period of enormous wealth, most of it amassed by Mahmud during some seventeen campaigns into the Indian subcontinent. He attracted some 400 scholars and poets to his capital, including Abu'l Qasim Firdausi (q.v.) and Abu Rayhan al-Biruni (q.v.). Although the dynasty counted nineteen rulers over a period of two centuries, the empire began to disintegrate after Mahmud's death. Under Mahmud's son, Mas'ud, the Seljuks took possession of Khorasan and during the reign of Bahram Shah (1117-57) Ghazni was sacked by 'Ala-ud-Din of Ghor. Ogadai, son of Genghis Khan, seized the city in 1221 and it became part of the Ilkhanid empire. See MAHMUD OF GHAZNI.

GHAZNI (lat. 33-33' N, long. 68-26' E). The name of a province and town in eastern Afghanistan. The town has about 30,000 inhabitants and is located at an elevation of some 7,000 feet on the road from Kabul to Kandahar, about 80 miles southeast of Kabul. The old town on the left bank of the river is walled and guarded by a citadel which is garrisoned by Afghan army units. Ghazni derives its fame from the fact that it was the capital of the Ghaznavid dynasty (see above). It is strategically located and was the scene of severe fighting between Afghan and British forces during the first two Afghan wars. A British garrison stationed in the town during the first Anglo-Afghan war was wiped out in December 1841. The population of the town is largely Tajik with some Ghilzais, Durranis, Hazaras, and a few Hindu shopkeepers. The province of Ghazni covers an area of 12,663 square miles and has a population of about 700,000. The state is subdivided into 24 districts and is inhabited by Tajiks in the north, Ghilzais in the center and south, and Hazaras in the west. There are also some Durrani Pashtuns. It is a major agricultural and industrial center, famous for its sheepskin coats (pustin), and a trading center for corn, fruit, madder, sheep's wool, and camel-hair cloth. There is also a river with this name which was said to have been channeled from a dam built by Sultan Mahmud from three streams: the Gardan-i-Masjid, Barikao, and the Shimiltu. The river passes the town and, growing increasingly brackish, runs into the Ab-i-Istada (q.v.).

GHIASI, BURHANUDDIN. Member of the Parcham faction of the PDPA who served as minister of higher and professional education, 1983-87; and minister of commerce, 1989-90. He was executive secretary of the Democratic Youth Organization of Afghanistan and is a member of the central council of the Hizb-i-Watan. At present he does not hold any office.

GHILZAI. A major Pashto-speaking tribe inhabiting an area roughly bounded by Kalat-i-Ghilzai in the south, the Gul Kuh range in the west, the Sulaiman range in the east, and the Kabul river on the north. The Ghilzai call themselves Ghaljai (pl. Ghalji) and count themselves the descendants of Ghalzoe, son of Shah Husain, said to have been a Tajik or Turk, and of Bibi Mato who descended from Shaikh Baitan (the second son of Qais - progenitor of the Afghan nationality). The origin of the name Ghilzai comes either from "Ghal Zoe" (thief's son), "Khilji" the Turkic word for swordsman, or the name of Khilji Turks who came into the area in the tenth century.
From Ghalzoe the tribe divided into the Turan and Burhan (Ibrahim) divisions; see Appendix.
The Sulaiman Khel are the most important of all and the Ali Khel are the most important of the Burhan. For details on the major subdivisions see the individual headings. In the 19th century they were said to number about 100,000 families with 30,000 to 50,000 fighters. They were largely nomadic and called *Powindas* (q.p.) in India and often travelled far into India, making a living as merchant nomads.
The Hotaki Ghilzais achieved their fame in Afghan history as the liberators of Kandahar from Safavid control and the leading tribe in the invasion of Iran and the destruction of the Persian empire in 1722. Mir Wais (q.v.), a descentant of Malakhi, a leading chief at Kandahar, was taken by the Safavid governor to Isfahan, but was later permitted to return. He raised a revolt against the Kandahar governor and ruled over the province for some years (1709-15). His son Mahmud raised an army and invaded Persia, defeating the Safavid armies at the battle of Gulnabad in 1722. However, Mahmud was unable to hold on to his conquest. Nadir Khan, founder of the short-lived Afsharite dynasty, reunited the Persian empire and in turn invaded Afghan lands. After the death of Nadir Shah (q.v.), the Ghilzai were weakened to such an extent that they could not prevent the emergence of the Durrani dynasty (q.v.). The Ghilzai fought the British when they invaded Afghanistan and subsequently became the major rivals of the Durranis (q.v.). They revolted repeatedly against Muhammadzai rule and were suppressed only with difficulty in 1801, 1883, 1886, and 1937. Urban Ghilzai have since

intermarried with Muhammadzai. The Ghilzai are well represented in the Marxist leadership (Taraki, Najibullah, Hafizullah Amin, Watanjar, Layeq, Rafi'i and many others) but also among the resistance (Hekmatyar and Sayyaf), which prompted one expert to remark that for the first time power has passed from the Durrani to the Ghilzai. See ABDUL KARIM, HOTAKIS, and POWINDAH.

GHOBAR, MIR GHULAM MUHAMMAD. A historian, writer, and poet who was widely known for his critical analyses of Afghan history in his book *Afghanistan dar Masir-e Tarikh*, (Afghanistan in the Path of History) published in 1967. Born in 1897 in Kabul of a Sayyid family, he entered the services of King Amanullah. He was editor of *Sitare-yi-Afghan*, 1919-20; chief of police, 1920-21; and served as secretary at the Afghan embassies in Paris, 1926, and Berlin, 1930. In the final days of King Amanullah he participated in the Paghman Loe Jirga. He became a prominent member of the Afghan literary society, 1931-32, and the historical society, 1943-48, and a literary adviser to the department of press, 1948. Imprisoned in 1933-35 and again 1952-56, he served intermittently as representative of Kabul in parliament in 1948, and again in 1949-51. He was a founding Member of the *Watan* party and editor of *Watan* (Homeland), its newspaper in 1951. He died at age 81 on February 5, 1978, in Germany.

GHOFRAN, MUHAMMAD. Minister of agriculture in Prime Minister Khaliqyar's cabinet of May 1990. He was born in 1933 in Nangarhar province and educated at the Kabul Agricultural Lycée and the University of California. He started his career in the ministry of agriculture and rose to be general director of the forestry department. He was first appointed minister of agriculture in 1988. He is not a member of the PDPA.

GHOR (GHUR) (lat. 34-0' N, long. 65-0' E). A west-central province of Afghanistan with an area of 13,808 square miles and a population of about 341,000. The capital of the province is the town of Chaghcharan. The province is mountainous with some wheat and barley cultivation in the valleys of the Farah, Harirud, and Murghab valleys. Major mountain ranges include the Firuzkoh (Safidkoh), Siyahkoh, and Band-i Bayan. The population is primarily of Taimani (Chahar Aimaq) origin. Also see GHORID DYNASTY.

GHORBANDI, ABDUL QUDDUS. Said to have been a Parchami who joined the Khalqi faction of the PDPA and was appointed minister of commerce during the Khalqi period (May 1978-December 1979). He was jailed in December 1979 when Babrak Karmal assumed power in Kabul and freed only after Dr. Najibullah replaced Karmal in 1986. Ghorbandi became a member of the PDPA central committee in 1986 and first deputy chairman of the NFF, subsequently a member of the National Front of the Republic of Afghanistan. At present he is an alternate member of the central council of the executive body of the Watan (PDPA) party. He was born in 1933 in Ghorband and educated at Kabul Technical School and in the United States. Began his career as a civil servant with the Afghan Air Authority, 1955.

GHORID DYNASTY (1150-1217). The Ghorid dynasty derived its name from Ghor, its capital near the present Qala-i-Ghor (Taiwara). At the height of their power, the Ghorids ruled over an area from eastern Iran to Bengal in India. In the early 11th century, Ghor was conquered by Mahmud of Ghazni (q.v.) and forced to pay tribute to the Ghaznavids (q.v.), but in 1151 the Ghorid Ala ud-Din in turn sacked and destroyed Ghazni. In 1176 the Ghorids, under Ghias ud-Din, took Herat, in 1198 Balkh, in 1200 Nishapur, Merv, Sarakhs, and Tus and moved far into India. The empire quickly disintegrated after the death of Ghias ud-Din in 1202, and subsequent invasions by the hordes of Genghis Khan and Tamerlane ended the brief glory of Ghor. In 1958 a French archaeologist discovered a minaret from the time of Ghias ud-Din.

GHULAM HAIDAR CHARKHI. Commander-in-chief of the Afghan army in the second Anglo-Afghan war and an implacable foe of the British. When General Roberts proclaimed a general amnesty on December 20, 1880, he was one of four Afghan sardars excluded. He served Amir Abdur Rahman, subduing the tribes in the Eastern province, and in 1882 was again appointed commander-in-chief. In 1888, the Amir gave him the title of Wazir. He died in 1898.

GHULAM JILANI CHARKHI. Major general of Amir Habibullah who led successful campaigns against rebellious tribes. He was born in 1886, the son of Ghulam Haidar. In 1912, he was appointed superintendant of the military college in Kabul. He served King Amanullah as governor and commander of troops in various provinces and was appointed minister at Ankara in 1925. Recalled to Kandahar by King Amanullah in April 1929, he was unable to defeat the forces of Habibullah Kalakani (q.v.) and fled to India with the King and accompanied him to Rome. He returned to Afghanistan in August 1930, but was arrested and executed in 1933.

GHULAM NABI CHARKHI. A general in the service of Amir Habibullah. A native of Charkh and son of Ghulam Haidar. King Amanullah appointed him minister to Moscow, 1922-24, and later deputy minister of foreign affairs. He continued to direct pacification campaigns and served in the Logar valley during the Mangal Rebellion, 1924-25. Toward the end of King Amanullah's reign he served short assignments as minister at Paris and Moscow. In 1929 he led an army officered by Afghan cadets who had been studying in Turkey in an attempt to return Amanullah to power. But he was unable to defeat the forces of Habibullah Kalakani and was forced to withdraw to the Soviet Union. In 1932 he returned to Afghanistan under a pardon, but was executed because of "subversive activities" against Nadir Shah.

GHULAM SIDDIQ CHARKHI. A diplomat and high government official of King Amanullah who with his brothers, Ghulam Jilani and Ghulam Nabi, was a foe of the Yahya Khel dynasty. Born in 1894, the son of Ghulam Haidar, he entered the service of King Amanullah. Was second counsellor to the Afghan mission of Muhammad Wali Khan (q.v.), which visited European capitals and the United States for the purpose of establishing diplomatic relations after the end of the third Anglo-Afghan war. He was Afghan minister at Berlin, 1922-26, first private secretary to King Amanullah and minister of court, 1927, and foreign minister in 1928. Left Afghanistan with King Amanullah and served shortly as minister in Berlin, but was dismissed as a supporter of the deposed king. He married a sister of Queen Suraya and remained in Berlin until the end of World War II. He died in 1962 and is buried in Afghanistan.

GHURID See **GHORID DYNASTY**.

GILANI, See GAILANI.

GIRISHK (lat. 31-48' N, long. 64-34' E). A town on the Helmand river in Helmand (formerly Girishk) province. It lies on the road from Kandahar to Herat, about 78 miles from Kandahar. The town, located at a strategic position and protected by a strong citadel and high walls, was destroyed by Nadir Shah, Afshar (q.v.), and rebuilt by Sardar Kohan Dil. In 1839 it was captured by General Sale, but beseiged during the entire war, and finally abandoned by the British. A British officer visited Girishk in 1879 and described the town as "a fort with half a dozen small villages scattered round it, and a bazar outside the gate." He said the fort was almost useless, but the position of great strategic importance. Reconstruction of the area was begun in 1937, and the Helmand project produced some growth; but in 1957 the state capital was transferred from Girishk to Lashkargah (Bost) and the town lost some of its earlier importance.

GOD-I-ZIRREH (GOWD or **GAUD)** (lat. 30-5' N, long. 61-45' E). A large depression in southwestern Afghanistan, extending close to the Iran/Pakistan border. About once every decade water from the Hamun-i-Helmand overflows and runs down the Shelag channel creating a shallow lake. The water has a high salt content and when dry the God-i-Zirreh is covered with a thick deposit of salt.

GOLDSMID AWARD. Was the result of the Sistan boundary arbitration in 1872 made by Sir Frederic Goldsmid in which the boundary between Iran and Afghanistan was drawn. Persian forces had occupied portions of Sistan claimed by Afghanistan and the British government offered its good offices to resolve the dispute. Gen. Goldsmid made the following award: "That Sistan proper, by which is meant the tract of country which the Hamun on three of its sides and the Helmand on the fourth cause to resemble an island, should be included by a special boundary line within the limits of Persia; that Persia should not possess land in the right of the

Helmand...." It was also stipulated that no works should be carried out to interfere with the supply of water from the Helmand. Neither Iran nor Afghanistan was satisfied with the award and the question of the distribution of the Helmand waters remained a potential conflict. It was not until 1973 that the Helmand Water Treaty was concluded and ratified by the Afghan government in 1977.

GORCHAKOFF See **GRANVILLE GORCHAKOFF AGREEMENT.**

GRANVILLE-GORCHAKOFF AGREEMENT. An Anglo-Russian agreement concluded in 1873 in an exchange of letters between the foreign ministers, Lord Granville and Prince Gorchakoff, which stipulated that "Badakhshan with its dependent district of Wakhan from Sar-i-Kul on the east to the junction of the Kokcha River with the Oxus (or Panja) forming the northern boundary of this Afghan Province throughout its entire length." Further west, however, the border was not clearly defined which eventually enabled Russia to annex Panjdeh. Russia agreed that Afghanistan was outside its sphere of influence and, except for the territorial changes of Shignan (q.v.) and Roshan (q.v.) and the Panjdeh (q.v.) oasis, the Afghan border has remained as it is today.

GULABZOI, MAJ. GEN. SAYYID MUHAMMAD. A member of the Khalqi faction of the PDPA who was "aide de camp" to President Taraki and minister of communications (1978-79). Babrak Karmal appointed him minister of interior in 1980 and Dr. Najibullah confirmed him in this position in June 1988. But in November 1988 he was appointed ambassador to the Soviet Union and in March 1990 he was dismissed from the party for his involvement in the Tanai coup (q.v.). Born in 1945 in Paktia province of a Pashtun family, he attended Nadir Shahkot school, a military academy and an air force college in the Soviet Union. He became a military officer and participated in the 1973 coup against Zahir Shah. Said to have been a nationalist and member of Afghan Millat before becoming a communist.

GULBAHAR (lat. 35-9' N, long. 69-17' E). A town on the west bank of the Panjshir river and the site of an important industrial center. In 1960 a textile industry was established with German financial assistance which eventually employed some 5,000 people. A new town was built apart from the old village to house the employees of the new industrial enterprise.

GULDAD, PROF. Member of the Khalq faction of the PDPA who was appointed director of the Nangarhar Valley Development Authorty (1978-79) and served as minister of higher and vocational education (1980-82) and deputy prime minister (June 1981 until June 1988). He is a Pashtun, educated in Kabul and India, and was employed with the Nangahar Valley Authority (a Soviet development project).

GULNABAD, BATTLE OF. An important victory of Afghan forces under Mahmud, son of the Ghilzai chief Mir Wais, which marked the end of the Safavid empire of Iran. On March 8, 1722, Mahmud met and decisively defeated a superior Iranian army and then beseiged Isfahan for six months before taking the capital of the empire. The Ghilzais proved to be better soldiers than empire-builders; they were forced to yield power to Nadir Shah Afshar (q.v.) and withdrew to their Afghan homeland where they were superseded by the Durranis. Also see NADIR SHAH, AFSHAR; MIR WAIS, and GHILZAI.

GUMAL (GOMAL) (lat. 31-56' N, long. 70-22' E). A river in southeastern Afghanistan which rises in the Sulaiman range and runs into the Zhob.

-H-

HABIB, ASADULLAH. A poet and writer who joined the PDPA and was president of the writers' union in 1980 and rector of Kabul University, 1982-88. In 1986 he was elected a candidate academician of the Academy of Sciences (See AFGHAN ACADEMY) and member of the central committee of the PDPA. He was born in 1941 in Maimana of an Uzbak family and educated in Maimana, Kabul, the United States, and the Soviet Union, where he obtained the Ph.D. degree.

HABIBI, ABDUL HAI. Educator, historian, and representative of Kandahar in parliament. Self educated, he started as a teacher and became editor of the Pashto daily *Tulu-yi Afghan* (Afghan Sunrise) in 1931. He was a Pashtun nationalist and a member of *Wish Zalmayan* (q.v., Awakened Youth). In 1940 he was appointed president of the Pashto Academy (q.v.) and in 1941 dean of the faculty of literature of Kabul University. He was forced to live in exile because of his opposition to the government of Shah Mahmud (q.v.) and published *Azad Afghanistan* (Free Afghanistan), a political journal, in Pakistan in which he advocated the replacement of the monarchy by a republic. In 1961 he was permitted to return to Afghanistan and became professor in the faculty of letters of Kabul University. He was appointed president of the Afghan Historical Society in 1966, and published a number of books on Afghan history as well as a purported Pashto record of early poetry, the *Pata Khazana* (Hidden Treasure). An adviser to the ministry of information and culture during the Daud and Marxist periods, and a member of the Academy of Sciences, he refused to join the "Fatherland Front." Shortly before he died in Kabul in 1984, he published a book on the constitutionalist movement in Afghanistan (*junbesh-i mashrutiyat dar Afghanistan*) which described the movement as nationalist, rather than socialist.

HABIBIA, SCHOOL (or COLLEGE). A preparatory school of higher education, established in 1904 and named after its founder Amir

Habibullah. It started as a madrasa (Islamic school of higher education), but was gradually transformed into a school with British-Indian curriculum. The language of instruction is English and the most successful students could win scholarships for study abroad. The school eventually adopted a modified American curriculum. Also see EDUCATION.

HABIB UL-ISLAM (HABIB AL-ISLAM). A weekly newspaper published during the short-lived reign of Habibullah Kalakani (q.v.) to legitimize the government of the "outlaw turned king" and to propagate a return to "orthodox" Islamic principles. It was founded in January 1929 (17. of Ramadhan 1348/9) and edited by Ghulam Muhyi ud-Din (succeeded by Sayyid Muhammad Husain and Burhanuddin Kushkaki). See HABIBULLAH KALAKANI.

HABIBULLAH, AMIR (1901-19). Amir of Afghanistan who kept his state neutral in World War I, but wanted to end Britain's quasi-protectorate over his country. He was born in Samarkand on April 21, 1871, the son of Amir Abdur Rahman and an Uzbak lady from Badakhshan. During his father's life he took an active part in the administration, and was generally popular. He succeeded to the throne on October 3, 1901 and assumed the title of *Seraj al-Millat wa'd-Din* (Torch of the Nation and Religion). He increased the pay of the army, permitted exiles to return, including many sardars (nobles) and their families, released prisoners and also promised reforms.

The British government was not satsified with some of the provisions of the agreements concluded with Amir Abdur Rahman, and therefore wanted to force certain changes before it recognized the new amir. London maintained that the agreements were with the *person* of the amir, not the State of Afghanistan, and therefore had to be renegotiated with his successor. In spite of severe pressures, Habibullah did not yield. In December 1904, he finally agreed to meet in Kabul with Louis W. Dane, foreign secretary of the government of India (India was ruled by a viceroy who was responsible to the British government in London). The result was a complete victory for Habibullah when Britain was forced to renew the agreements concluded with Amir Abdur Rahman in the form of a treaty (March 1905), which recognized Habibullah's title as "Independent King of the State of Afghanistan and its Dependencies."

Amir Habibullah showed great interest in Western technology, and he embarked on a process of modernization. He imported automobiles and built roads, founded Habibia School in 1904, the first modern school in Afghanistan, and brought electricity to Kabul. In January 1907 Amir Habibullah travelled to India and was cordially received by the Viceroy, Lord Minto. A crisis in relations with British India occurred when Habibullah learned that Afghanistan's powerful neighbors had concluded the Anglo-Russian Convention of 1907 (q.v.). This agreement divided Afghanistan (and Iran) into spheres of influence with provisions for "equality of commercial opportunity" in Afghanistan for Russian and British traders and the appointment of commercial agents in Kabul. The

Amir was invited to ratify the agreement, but he refused and the Convention was never implemented.

The outbreak of World War I posed another crisis in foreign relations: in spite of warnings not to do so from the viceroy of India, Amir Habibullah received a German mission at Kabul. He met with members of the Hentig-Niedermayer expedition (q.v., which also included a Turk and several Indians) and initialed the draft of a secret treaty of friendship and military assistance with Germany to provide for the eventuality of an Allied defeat. Germany could not deliver and Britain promised a handsome reward for Afghan neutrality; therefore, a realistic appraisal of the situation prompted the Afghan ruler to stay out of the war.

Britain showed herself miserly and, once the crisis was over, she wanted to reestablish its exclusive control over Afghanistan. The "war party" at his court felt that the Amir had failed to take advantage of a unique opportunity of winning independence from Britain and his enemies conspired to depose him. He was assassinated on February 20, 1919, while he was on a hunting trip at Kala Gosh in Laghman.

Amir Habibullah was about 5 feet 4 inches in height, very powerfully built. He had a speech impediment, a slight stammer which he was, however, able to control. He was the father of Sardar Amanullah (q.v.) who succeeded him to the throne.

HABIBULLAH KALAKANI, AMIR. A Tajik of humble origins who was a leader of the anti-reformist reaction which swept King Amanullah from power and him to the throne. He was known as "Bacha-i-Saqqao" son of a water carrier - the occupation of his father, Aminullah, a Tajik from the village of Kalakan in the Kohdaman district (north of Kabul). With the support of a loose coalition of Kohistani forces, he took advantage of a tribal revolt by Shinwari, Sulaiman Khel, and other Pashtun tribes in the east to capture Kabul and have himself proclaimed Amir Habibullah, Ghazi (Victor). Following the custom of Afghan rulers, Habibullah adopted the title "Servant of the Religion of the Messenger of God," (Khadem-i Din-i Rasulullah) and set about to consolidate his power.

Two factors militated against his royal aspirations: he was of Tajik, rather than the dominant Pashtun ethnic background; and he was known as a brigand, albeit of a Robin Hood nature, as seen from the perspective of his Kohistani brothers.

British archival sources provide the following composite regarding Habibullah's antecedents:

Born about 1890 at Kalakan village near Sarai Khwaja in Kohdaman, the son of Aminullah, a water carrier (saqqao). Said to have held various menial positions, including work as a servant of an Afghan official (Muhammad Wali, q.v.) until he joined Jemal Pasha's [a head of the Ottoman war government] regiment (the *Qita Namuna*) in Kabul, 1919. Deserted with his rifle because of sympathy with the Mangals [q.v.] in the rebellion of 1924. Later fled to Peshawar where he worked for some time as a tea seller, after which he went to Parachinar, where he was sentenced to eleven months' imprisonment for house breaking. After the Mangal revolt he became a highwayman and "showed considerable generosity to the poor, but was merciless to Afghan officials and wealthy travellers." (Adamec, 1974.)

Habibullah was a natural leader and charismatic personality, but his assumption of the throne was challenged from the beginning. A British officer reported from Peshawar that "Bacha-i-Saqao's accession has come as a profound shock to the tribes on both sides of the Durand Line." Even the Shinwaris whose revolt started the civil war were not willing to submit to the new king. The fact that Habibullah had found some 750,000 British pounds at the conquest of the Arg (royal palace) nevertheless permitted him to pay his troops and win some tribal support.

The *Habib al-Islam* (q.v., Habib [=his name] of Islam) depicted Habibullah as a pious Muslim, a brave fighter, and a wise ruler. He issued a proclamation that all sectors of Afghan society had recognized his rule, including the Shinwaris, Khugianis, Ghilzais, and Amanullah's own Durranis.

Attempts by forces loyal to King Amanullah were unable to recapture the throne, but Muhammad Nadir (q.v.) and his brothers succeeded. Shah Wali Khan (q.v.), brother of Nadir and brother-in-law of King Amanullah, captured the Arg in October 1929, and Habibullah was forced to surrender. On November 1, Habibullah, his brother Hamidullah, and Sayyid Husain together with nine leaders of their turbulent regime were executed. Habibullah's purported autobiography *My Life: From Brigand to King*, (London, 1936) describes his career as bandit and king and a recent book in Persian, entitled *A Hero from Khorasan*, by Khalilullah Khalili (q.v.), also a Kohistani and poet laureate, depicts him as a *mujahed*, a holy warrier, against an infidel king. Khalili's maternal uncle was Abdul Rahim (q.v.), the general who contributed to Kalakani's conquests and served as his governor at Herat.

HABIBURRAHMAN (HABIB AL-RAHMAN). One of the four leaders of the Organization of Muslim Youth (*Sazman-i Jawanan-i Musulman*), called *Ikhwanis* by their opponents, who was secretary of the council (*Shura*) until 1975 when he was replaced by Gulbudin Hekmatyar. He recruited Ahmad Shah Mas'ud (q.v.), the present Jamiat commander, as his deputy. He was arrested in 1973? and executed during the Khalqi regime (1979?). See ISLAMIST MOVEMENT IN AFGHANISTAN.

HADDA. A village in the Chapriar (Chaparhar) district about 6 miles south of Jalalabad, inhabited largely by Mohmands. In the fourth century Hadda was a great center of Buddhism and the location of numerous shrines. The name Hadda means "bone" and refers to the belief that Buddha's head was enshrined there. The village is famous for the archaeological excavations nearby which yielded an abundance of stupas, Buddhas, and various statuary. The village is also known for the "Hadda Mulla," one Najm-ud-Din, who preached jehad against the British and was a leader of numerous hostile actions against British India. At present there is an important madrasa in this village, called *Najm al-Madares* (Star of Madrasas). The stupas discovered at Hadda were partially destroyed in military operations and looted during the present war.

HAFIZ. Title of honor given to one who has memorized the Koran in its entirety.

HAIBAK See AIBAK.

HAJ Properly spelled **HAJJ**.
See **HAJJ**.

HAJIGAK (lat. 34-40' N, long. 68-6' E). A village located near the pass of the same name in Bamian province (According to some sources the name comes from the Hazara *aja-gak*, meaning "dear [or little] mother"). Foreign experts from a number of countries have found high grade iron ore in the area, with estimated reserves amounting to almost two billion tons. The area is inaccessible and the development of infrastructure and construction of a furnace complex, planned under President Daud's seven-year plan (1976-83), was never begun.

HAJJ. Pilgrimage to Mecca. A legal obligation of every adult Muslim of either sex to travel at least once in a lifetime to Mecca, provided the person is economically able to do so. Thousand of Afghans perform this obligation each year and special Ariana Airline flights are chartered for this purpose.

HAJJI. Title of honor of a person who has performed the pilgrimage to Mecca.

HAJJI MIRZA ALI KHAN See FAQIR OF IPI.

HAKIM. A wise man, philosopher, doctor, practitioner of traditional "Greek medicine," *tebb-i yunani* (pronounced hakeem). A governor of a sub-province, commander (pronounced haakem).

HAKIM, MUHAMMAD See MUHAMMAD·HAKIM.

HAMED, ABDUL SAMAD. Legal expert and high government official, presently living in exile in Germany. He was born in 1929 in Jalalabad of a Pashtun family and educated in Kabul and in Switzerland. He began his carrier as profeesor of law and political science at Kabul University and was elected president of the university in 1964. A member of the drafting committee of the constitution and of the Loya Jirga, 1964. President of Kabul University and minister of planning, 1965 and 1967-69. Served as president of the national economic high council, 1967-69 and 1971-72, and as deputy prime minister and minister for tribal affairs from 1971 to 1972. Was imprisoned during the Khalqi regime

(January 1979 to January 1980) and left Afghanistan in 1980, working for mujahedin causes in Germany.

HAMUN. A term used for a shallow depression or morass, usually of high salt content in southern and western Afghanistan. The hamuns are seasonally filled with water and become shallow lakes. The Hamun-i Sabari in Nimruz province extends into Iran and the Hamun-i-Lora in Kandahar province extends across the border into Baluchistan province of Pakistan. The God-i-Zirreh (q.v.) another large hamun in Nimruz province, is located near the Pakistani border.

HAQANI, MAULAWI JALALUDDIN (JALAL AL-DIN HAQQANI). Deputy chief of Hizb/Khales who joined Yunus Khales after the break with Hekmatyar's faction in 1979. Born in 1930, a Jadran (Zadran) from Paktia province, he was educated at a private madrasa and finished his studies at Peshawar. He became a major commander who had the support of his own Jadran tribe and has, since 1979, held large areas of Urgun in Paktia province under his administration. Except for occasional visits to Peshawar, he has remained in Paktia province. Haqani was one of a number of commanders whose forces captured Khost (q.v.) in March 1991. He is said to have since formed his own party.

HARAKAT-I INQILAB-I ISLAMI. The Islamic Revolutionary Movement, Harakat, is one of the earliest mujahedin movements, which arose from the merger of Islamist factions of the 1960s, represented in the Jam'iat, Hizb-i Islami, and others. It was headed by Muhammad Nabi Muhammadi (q.v.). In the early 1980s it was the largest mujahedin movement, but lost some of its influence when the Islamists under Rabbani and Hekmatyar seceded and formed their own parties. Harakat is based on a network of clergy and madrasa students with some Pashtun tribal support in the south. Among its commanders are Sayyid Murtaza (Logar), Muhammad Shah (Farah), Shafiullah (Kuh-i Safi), and Qari Taj Muhammad (Ghazni). The movement is traditional in outlook and is counted among the moderate forces represented in the Mahaz of Gilani and Jabha of Mujaddidi. Also see MUHAMMAD NABI MUHAM-MADI.

HARAKAT-I ISLAMI. A shi'a mujahedin group headed by Muhammad Asef Muhsini which is not a member of the Shi'a Unity Party, *hizb-i wahdat.* For further details see MUHSINI, AYATOLLAH MUHAMMAD ASEF.

HARI RUD (lat. 37-24' N, long. 60-38' E). A river in western Afghanistan which is formed by the confluence of the Sar-i-Jangal and Lal streams. It runs in a westerly direction past the city of Herat and then turns north, forming the boundary between Iran and Afghanistan, and crosses into the Soviet Union at Zulfiqar and dissipates in the desert.

HARUT RUD (lat. 31-35' N, long. 61-18' E). A river, also called Adraskan in its northern portion, which rises southeast of Herat and runs in a southwestern direction, eventually turning south and running into the Hamun-i-Sabari.

HASHIM KHAN, MUHAMMAD. Prime minister of Afghanistan from 1929 to 1946 and de facto regent of the young king. Born in 1886, the son of Sardar Yusuf Khan (and half-uncle of ex-King Zaher), he was described as "austere and tough in his dealings with the people." He underwent military training and became commander of Amir Habibullah's body guard. He served as governor of the Eastern Province and officiated as minister of war in 1922. He served as minister in Moscow, 1924-26, and there acquired a considerable dislike of the Soviet government. He took a fatherly attitude to the young king and was the de facto ruler during his tenure. He was never married and seemed to groom his nephews Muhammad Daud and Muhammad Na'im as his successors. He died on October 26, 1953.

HASHT-NAFARI. A system of recruitment imposed on the frontier tribes by which they were to provide one able-bodied man out of eight (D., *hasht* -eight, *nafar*-persons). Amir Abdur Rahman introduced this system in 1896; similar to previous feudal levies, the notables and chiefs of tribes had to make the selection and provide the enlistee with all his needs. The tribes were willing to perform military service, but wanted to do so only during emergencies; therefore, there were occasional revolts, protesting the hasht-nafari recruitment during peacetime.

HATEF, ABDUR RAHIM. Vice president of the Republic of Afghanistan (1988), deputy chairman of the supreme council for the defense of the homeland (SCDH), and chairman of the national front (NFROA formerly NFF). Born in 1926 in Kandahar of a Pashtun family and educated at Habibia School and Kabul University, he taught for a number of years at Kandahar schools and subsequently went into business. He was elected a representative of Kandahar in parliament in 1965. He is said to be wealthy and not a member of the PDPA.

HAYATULLAH KHAN. Born in 1888, the second son of Amir Habibullah Khan. He served as governor of Kataghan (now Kunduz province) in 1905, and after the death of his father became minister of education (1923) and minister of justice (1925). Although a brother of King Amanullah and a minister, he did not take a very active part in public life. Arrested in January 1929 by Habibullah Kalakani and accused of planning a coup, he was executed on October 17, 1929.

HAZARA. Hazaras are a people with predominantly Mongoloid features, mostly *imami* shi'a (q.v.). Small numbers are Isma'ilis (q.v.), and those in the Darra-yi Hazara in Panjshir are sunnis. Their number has been estimated at about one million, but Hazaras claim a population of about two million and up to two million more in neighboring countries. All the Hazaras were originally sunni Muslims until the 16th century when they were converted to shi'ism under the Safavid dynasty of Iran (1501-1786). Their heartland is the Hazarajat (q.v.), but they are also found in the major cities of Afghanistan where many are employed as day laborers or seasonal workers. They speak a Farsi dialect, called Hazaragi, which also includes some Turkic and Mongol vocabulary (A dictionary of the Hazara dialect, *Qamus-i Lahja-yi Dari-yi Hazaragi*, by Ali Akbar Shahrestani, published in Kabul in 1982, lists some 1200 words, which according to Dr. Ravan Farhadi are 90% of eastern Turkic origin, rather than Mongol).

The Hazara are no longer organized along tribal lines and are largely sedentary. They are divided into a number of groups (See Genealogies in Appendix.).

Kala Nau Hazaras (formerly also Dai Zangi and Dai Kundi) are mostly sunnis and inhabit an area of about 2,300 square miles. They claim descent from the hordes of Genghiz Khan who settled in Kala Nau (now Badghis province) and were moved into the area under the Persian ruler Nadir Shah, Afshar (q.v.). Their first chief was Mir Kush Sultan whose son, Aghai Sultan, was the founder of Kala Nau. The tribe was involved in the struggle for control of Herat province, collaborating with the rulers of Herat. Yar Muhammad (q.v.), Shah Kamran's (q.v.) wazir, destroyed the power of the Hazaras in 1847. When in 1856 the Persians beseiged and took Herat, they removed the tribe to Khorasan. Most of them returned 14 years later, but about 2,000 families remained in the Isfarayin area, south of Bujnurd in present Iran. They supported the governor of Herat against Amir Dost Muhammad (q.v.) and were in constant conflict with the Jamshidis (q.v.) and Firuzkuhis (q.v.).

The Dai Mirdad Hazaras inhabit the area of Dara-i-Suf (now Samangan province) and at the turn of the century amounted to about 1,000 families. They resemble Pashtuns more than Hazaras and dress like Tajiks or Uzbaks.

The Dai Kundi and Dai Zangi are two different groups, but have been closely connected regarding to location and administration.

The Ghazni (q.v.) Hazaras comprise the Jaghatu, Muhammad Khwaja, and the Chahar Dasta Hazaras.

Since the founding of modern Afghanistan in 1747, the Hazaras came increasingly under the juristiction of the Kabul government, paying taxes, but living under the independent or autonomous control of their Mirs (chiefs). Yazdan Bakhsh (q.v.) was undisputed chief of the Hazaras in the mid-19th century but was eventually assassinated. Amir Abdur Rahman fought the Hazaras piecemeal and, his general Sardar Abdul Quddus (q.v.) completed the conquest of the Hazarajat in a war which lasted from 1890 to 1893. The war caused considerable destruction in the Hazarajat, annexation of territory by Pashtun tribes, and the flight and enslavement of many. Amir Habibullah proclaimed an amnesty and asked the Hazara refugees to return to Afghanistan; but many remained in India and a large community now exists in Quetta, Pakistan. King Amanullah abolished slavery and won Hazara support in his fight with Habibullah Kalakani (q.v.) in 1929.

Since 1979 the Hazarajat has enjoyed virtual independence, at first under an elected Shura (council) headed by Sayyid Ali Beheshti (q.v.), who took over all the functions of the pre-war Afghan government. He levied taxes, recruited men into his mujahedin forces, and set up his own bureaucratic establishment. But his authority was soon challenged by a combined force of Nasr and Pasdaran Islamists (q.v.) who conquered most of the Hazarajat. In spring 1988, the Kabul government created the Hazara province of Sar-i-Pul by adding the districts of Shulgara, Charkent, and Keshendeh from Balkh province, combining it with the districts of Sar-i-Pul, Balkhab, Sozma Kala, and Kohestanat from Jozjan province. This appears to have been a political move to appeal to Hazara nationalism. For Hazara calendar, see CALENDAR.

HAZARAJAT (lat. 33-45' N, long. 66-0' E). The name of a mountainous area in central Afghanistan in which the Hazara people predominate. Its heartland includes Ghor, Oruzgan, and Bamian provinces, and portions of the adjoining provinces.

The Hazarajat is dominated by the Koh-i Baba (q.v.) range and its branches whose peaks are at altitudes from 9,000 to 16,500 feet. The mountain ranges are crossed by passes at altitudes of from 8,000 to some 10,000 feet. Few roads for motorized transportation exist, and the modern highway from Kabul to Herat skirts the Hazarajat. The central route from Kabul to Bamian and east to Chaghcharan can be taken with great difficulty by four-wheel vehicles during the few summer months.

Because of the high alttitude, the climate of the Hazarajat is characterized by long and cold winters, lasting from late September to April. Heavy snowfall from December until spring provides the reservoir which feed the major rivers which take their origin in the Hazarajat and irrigate the rest of the country. July and August are hot and dry. The area is rich in mineral deposits, most of which are too inaccessible to be profitably mined. For people and history, see HAZARA.

HAZRAT OF SHOR BAZAR. A title given the head of the family of Sirhind spiritual leaders who adopted the family name of Mujaddidi. They were among the most important and influential religious leaders in Afghanistan in the years following King Amanullah's accession. Their residence was in the area of Shor Bazar in Kabul, hence the head's designation "Excellency" (*Hazrat*) of Shor Bazar. For members of the family, see MUJADDIDI.

HEKMATYAR, GULBUDDIN. Amir (chief) of the *Hizb-i Islami-yi Afghanistan* (q.v., Islamic Party of Afghanistan), one of the seven mujahedin groups headquartered in Peshawar. His party is radical Islamist and fights for the establishment of an Islamic republic, to be governed according to the dictates of Islamic law. Born in 1947 in Baghlan, a Kharoti Ghilzai Pashtun, Hekmatyar attended the faculty of engineering at Kabul University for two years and became involved in campus politics. He became a member of the "Muslim Youth" movement in 1970 and joined Eng. Habiburrahman (q.v.), Mawlawi Habiburrahman (q.v.), and others on its excecutive council (*shura*). He was imprisoned in Dehmazang jail in Kabul, 1972-73, and, after the Daud coup of 1973, fled to Pakistan. In 1975 he became a leader of the *Jam'iat-i Islami*, the forerunner of the *Hizb-i Islami*, and began armed attacks from bases in Pakistan with clandestine support from the Bhutto government. Elected amir of Hizb in December, 1978, he was able to win Pakistani support and forge a dedicated group of commanders who became a major force in the war against the Soviet and Kabul forces. His party is the most ideological and radical of the Islamist groups and his influence is said to be due to the fact that he has enjoyed greater foreign support than the other mujahedin groups. He surprised friends and foes alike when he allied himself with Gen. Shahnawaz Tanai (q.v.), a radical Khalqi, in a coup against the Kabul government of Dr. Najibullah. In August 1989 Hekmatyar left the Afghan Interim Government (see ISLAMIC ALLIANCE FOR THE LIBERATION OF AFGHANISTAN), but pressed by some of his own commanders, has tried to reconcile with the AIG. His party has been engaged in internecine warfare with commanders of other mujahedin groups and his alliance with Tanai has been seen as an opportunistic disregard of ideology and an attempt to achieve power as the future ruler of Afghanistan. Also see HIZB-I ISLAMI-YI AFGHANISTAN (HEKMATYAR).

HELMAND (lat. 31-0' N, long. 64-0' E). A province in southwestern Afghanistan with a population of about 570,000 and an area of 23,058 square miles the largest of Afghan provinces. The capital of the province (Girishk until 1957) is Lashkargah (q.v., Bost) with about 21,600 inhabitants. The population is largely Pashtun with some Hazara in the north and Baluch in the south. The economy of the province is based primarily on agriculture: barley, cotton, and wheat and a great variety of fruit. Livestock raised include sheep, goats, cattle, camels, horses, and donkeys.
The province is irrigated by the Helmand river which also provides hydroelectric power. The river rises near the Unai pass and with its five tributaries -- the Kaj Rud, Tirin, Arghandab, Tarnak, and Arghastan -- drains all of southwestern Afghanistan. After running in a southwestern direction as far as Khwaja Ali, the Helmand runs due west to Band-i-Kamal Khan and then north to the Lash Juwain hamuns. The river formed part of the border with Iran, and when it changed channels the Goldsmid boundary arbitration (q.v.) was again called into question. Also see LASHKARGAH and HELMAND VALLEY AUTHORITY.

HELMAND VALLEY AUTHORITY. An Afghan organization which was created to oversee an irrigation and electrification project in the Helmand valley. It was fashioned after the American Tennessee Valley Authority to implement work in conjunction with the Morrison-Knudsen Afghanistan construction company of Boise, Idaho. From 1946 to 1959 the American firm built the Arghandab and Kajakai dams and a network of canals to bring additional land in the Helmand valley under cultivation. The project soon drained the hard-currency resources of the country to the extent that the Afghan government was forced to apply for loans to the US Import- Export Bank (21 million in 1951 and 18 million in 1953) and for Point Four assistance (an assistance program which pre-dates USAID). When the project was finished in 1959 some 100 million dollars (40% of the state budget) had been expended for rather modest gains. The failure by the Afghan government to conduct adequate soil studies was responsible for waterlogging in some areas and excessive salination in others. Cultural factors, such as the inclinations and interests of the people in the area, were ignored and many of the 1300 nomad and peasant families settled in the Nad-i-Ali area eventually left their lands. When high expectations turned into disappointment Americans prestige suffered. Remedial measures where eventually taken with American financial support.

HENTIG-NIEDERMAYER EXPEDITION. An expedition conceived in August 1914 by the German general staff for the purpose of "revolutionizing India, inducing Afghanistan to attack India, and securing Iran as a bridge from the Ottoman empire to Afghanistan." The leading members were Werner Otto von Hentig, a young German diplomat who had served in Iran, and Oskar von Niedermayer (q.v.), a captain in the German army. They were accompanied by Kazim Bey (q.v.), a Turkish officer, Maulawi Barakatullah (q.v.) and Mahendra Pratap (q.v.), two Indian revolutionaries, and a number of Afridi Pashtuns who had been taken from a prisoner of war camp. Hentig carried an unsigned letter purported to be from the German Kaiser and a message from von Bethmann-Hollweg, the chancellor, for Amir Habibullah. He was to establish diplomatic relations and conclude a treaty of friendship or, if possible an alliance, with Afghanistan. Niedermayer was to discuss matters of a military nature and the Indians were to appeal to Amir Habibullah (q.v.) for support in the fight against the British in India. Kazim Bey was to convey special messages from the Sultan-Caliph and the leaders of the Ottoman war government. The expedition crossed Iran and entered Afghanistan in August 1915 and five weeks later reached Kabul.

Amir Habibullah was well aware of the power of Britain and, although his heart and ultimate loyalty was with the Ottoman sultan-caliph, he was not willing to rush into a risky adventure. He initialled the draft of a treaty which was so extravagant in its demands, that only a victorious Germany could have provided the financial and military support requested. The expedition disbanded in May 1916 and Hentig returned to Germany by way of the Wakhan Corridor to China and from there to the United States. Niedermayer went through Russian Central Asia to Iran and the Ottoman empire. The expedition was the first diplomatic contact with Germany and marked the beginning of the end of the British monopoly over the conduct of Afghan foreign relations. In 1970, von Hentig visited Afghanistan as guest of Zahir Shah. Hentig published a book, entitled *Mein Leben eine Dienstreise*. Also see NIEDERMAYER.

HERAT (lat. 34-20' N, long. 62-12' E). Herat is a province in northwestern Afghanistan with an area of 16,107 square miles and a population about 685,000. The capital of the province is Herat with about 140,000 inhabitants, the third largest city in Afghanistan.

The economy of Herat is based primarily on agriculture, the planting of cotton, rice, and wheat. Pistachios are an important item of export. Also important is livestock breeding, including the Karakul sheep. Local industries produce cement, edible oil, and textiles. Home industries produce carpets, silk materials, pustins (fur jackets and coats), and products of camel-hair.

The province is drained by the Murghab, Harirud, Farah Rud, and Adraskan rivers which permit extensive irrigation. Kariz (q.v.), subterranean water channels, are also widely used to bring water from the foothills to villages and fields.

The city of Herat, located at an altitude of 2,600 feet, is the major commercial center of western Afghanistan. The old town was surrounded by a wall built in 1885 and mostly destroyed in the 1950s. It is crossed by two streets which divide the old town into four districts, named the Bazar-i-Kushk in the east, the Bazar-i-Iraq in the west, the Bazar-i-Malik in the north, and the Bazar-i-Kandahar in the south. The new town, *shahr-i nau*, was largely constructed in the period after World War II and has been considerably expanded since.

Herat is of great strategic importance and therefore has been the site of fortified towns since antiquity. It is an ancient city, first mentioned in the Avesta (the holy book of Zoroastrianism) as *Hairava*, which Afghan historians conjecture to be derived from Aria, or Ariana, the first "Afghan" kingdom flourishing about 1,500 B.C. The town was on the route of the Achaemenid armies of Cyrus and Darius and two centuries later of Alexander the Great, who in 330 B.C. built *Alexandria Ariorum* on the site of Herat. In the 11th century Herat became a famous urban center in Islamic Khorasan (q.v.) where scholars like Khwaja Abdullah Ansari (q.v.) and others flourished. The city had been destroyed numerous times by Turkomans in the 12th century, and a century later by the hordes of Genghis Khan, when only a handful of the population survived a general massacre. In the 14th century Timur-i-Lang's (q.v.) forces devastated the city. Rebuilt by Timur's son Shah Rukh, the city experienced a period of glory. Again in the early sixteenth century, Sultan Husain Mirza Baiqara (q.v.) made Herat "the most renowned center of literature, culture, and art in all Central and Western Asia." The city and its vicinity has numerous archaeological remains. The principal buildings are the Jumma Masjid, built under the Ghorids (q.v.) in about 1200 A.D., which measured 465 feet in length by 275 feet width and had 408 cupolas, 130 windows, 444 pillars, 1300 arches and six entrances. Minarets of the Timurid theological colleges, the Mosalla, and the shrine of the Sufi poet

Abdullah Ansari are located near the city. The tomb of Amir Dost Muhammad (q.v.) is located nearby. A building of more recent date is the Arg-i-Nau, the citadel.

In 1509 the city came under Safavid rule until in about 1715 the Abdalis (q.v.) took control of the city. In 1730 it was captured by Nadir Shah Afshar (q.v.) and in 1750 by Ahmad Shah Durrani (q.v.). Next Herat was ruled by various princes whose internecine fighting invited Persian attack. In December 1837, the Safavid ruler, Muhammad Shah, beseiged the city, but the endurance of the Heratis and British intervention in the Persian Gulf forced him to give up after a nine-month long effort. Amir Abdur Rahman (q.v.) ended Herat's semi-independence. About 70 years ago the city was still confined to the walled town and had about 20,000 inhabitants. King Amanullah (q.v.) began the construction of the new town, *shahr-i nau*, in 1925 which quickly grew in population to about 73,000 by 1970 and 140,000 ten years later. The present war in Afghanistan has lead to considerable destruction, which began with a popular revolt against the Kabul government in March 1979. The city remains under government control, but portions of the countryside are in the control of the mujahedin.

HEZB See HIZB.

HIJRAT MOVEMENT. "Emigration Movement," also called *Khilafat* movement (of 1920), which originated in the North-West Frontier Province of India in protest of the destruction of the Ottoman empire by Britain and her allies. Indian Muslims recognized the Ottoman claims to the caliphate and spiritual leadership of the (sunni) Islamic world. Muhammad Ali and other leaders of the movement proclaimed it the "Islamic duty" of Indian Muslims "to abandon a country ruled by a sacrilegious government," the *dar al-harb* (Abode of War) and migrate to the *dar al- salam* (Abode of Peace - Islamic state). Encouraged by King Amanullah, who had just won the independence of his country, some 18,000 Muslims came to Afghanistan. The Afghan King hoped to attract professional and skilled manpower, but most of the immigrants (*muhajerun*) were unskilled and poor and could not adapt to the new environment. Some Pashtuns from Peshawar were settled in the area of Kunduz and some Sindhis in the area of Balkh, and a few went on to the Soviet Union and Europe, but most of the *muhajerun* eventually returned to India.

HINDKI (HINDUS). The name of Hindus living in Afghanistan who speak a Panjabi dialect (except for those in Kandahar who speak Sindhi and Riasti) and number about 15,000. They are scattered all over Afghanistan, but are primarily in Kabul, Kandahar, Kunduz, Nangarhar, and Paktia provinces, where they are occupied in trade. They once transacted most of the banking business in the country. As non-Muslims they were at times subjected to the *jizya*, poll tax, and were restricted in their religious observances to the privacy of their homes. Since the days of Amir Habibullah, the Hindkis have gradually gained full citizen status. One Hindki, Naranjan Das (q.v.), received the title of civil colonel in 1906 and was appointed chief revenue officer and finally civil brigadier under King Amanullah. This gained the Afghan ruler a positive image in India. There are also about 7,000 Sikhs (q.v.) in Afghanistan, all of them Panjabi-speakers.

HINDU KUSH. The major mountain massif which originates in the southwestern corner of the Pamirs and with its extension, the Kuh-i-Baba, runs the entire length of central Afghanistan, constituting a formidable barrier to north-south communication. Its general elevation is between 14,500 and 17,000 feet, with numerous peaks over 20,000 feet high. Several passes leading across the massif lie at altitudes above 12,000 feet. The name Hindu Kush is of uncertain origin and is not used generally by Afghans, who have local names for the range in their area. In the West the name has been interpreted as "Killer of Hindus;" but the name may be derived, according to some sources, from Hindu Kuh, marking the most northern extent of pre-Muslim Hindu control.

The range is divided into three major sections: the eastern from the Pamirs to the Dorah pass; the central from the Dorah to the Khawak pass; and the western from the Khawak pass to the termination of the range near the Shibar pass.

During the winter months, the mountain range seals off northern Afghanistan from the rest of the country and the rugged terrain has allowed small, non-martial populations to survive in remote, economically marginal valleys. Poor lines of communication fostered a measure of autonomy and extensive linguistic and cultural diversity. The construction of the Salang (q.v.) tunnel and an all-weather road in 1964 has contributed to the strengthening of central control over the northern part of the state. In the present war in Afghanistan, the Salang highway has become an important artery for supplying the Kabul government with Soviet materiel, and therefore has been a frequent object of attacks by mujahedin forces, especially those of Commander Mas'ud (q.v.).

HISTORICAL SOCIETY OF AFGHAN (ANJOMAN-I TARIKH-I AFGHAN-ISTAN). Founded in 1941 at the suggestion of Zahir Shah for the purpose of research and study of Afghanistan's historical heritage. It was part of the Afghan Literary Society since 1933 and under the administrative control of the department of press and later the ministry of education and developed into a research and translation institute. It produced numerous publications, including the journals *Aryana* (1942) and *Afghanistan* (1945). Ahmad Ali Kohzad (q.v.) held the position of president of the Historical Society for many years. At present it is part of the Afghan Academy of Sciences. See AFGHAN ACADEMY.

HIZB. The word *hizb* (from Arabic) means "party" and is used in the name of various parties and movements, as for example, *Hizb-i Demukrat-i*

Khalqi-yi Afghanistan, People's Democratic Party of Afghanistan (PDPA). For parties see individual entries.

HIZB-I INQILAB-I MILLI. Party of President Daud; see NATIONAL REVOLUTIONARY PARTY.

HIZB-I ISLAMI (HEKMATYAR). The larger of two Islamist mujahedin movements with the same name, headed by Gulbuddin Hekmatyar. It has its origin in the "Muslim Youth" movement of the 1960s (See ISLAMIST MOVEMENT OF AFGHANISTAN) which opposed the secularization of Afghan society and the emergence of Marxist groups on the campus of Kabul University. The movement was forced underground during the republican government of President Daud (1973-78). Hekmatyar fled to Pakistan and from there carried out raids into Afghanistan. Isolated raids developed into modern guerrilla warfare after the Saur Revolt in April 1978. The party adopted from the Muslim Brotherhood (or Leninist model?) such features as centralized command structure, secrecy of membership, organization in cells, infiltration of government and social institutions, and the concept of the party as an Islamist "vanguard" in Afghan society.

Being Islamist rather than nationalist, the party enjoyed considerable support from the Pakistan government and from like-minded groups in Pakistan and the Gulf. Specifics regarding the type of government desired by the Hizb are not clear. Hekmatyar has at times rejected such traditional Afghan bodies as the Loya Jirga (q.v., national council), because its decisions may be subject to manipulation by his opponents. He accepts a *shura*, council of Islamic legal experts (*ahl-i hal wa-aqd*), which is to advice the *amir*, leader of the community of Muslims (*umma*). The amir is elected by a council (*shura*) which delegates considerable powers to its leader. How the *shura* is to be chosen is not clear. The people swear *bay'a*, loyalty, to the chosen amir and, by definition, are bound in obedience to him. The incumbent may nominate his successor. The Hizb favors the establishment of an Islamic state in which the *shari'a* (q.v., Islamic law) prevails and Islamic obligations are enforced. The participation of women in public life is to be restricted; the consumption of alcohol prohibited; and innovations adopted from the West eliminated.

HIZB-I ISLAMI (KHALES). An Islamist party headed by the mujahedin leader Yunus Khales (q.v.) which in 1979 split from the more radical group headed by Gulbuddin Hekmatyar. It is represented primarily in Pashtun regions, especially in Nangarhar, Kabul (Commander Abdul Haq, q.v.) and Paktia (Commander Jalaluddin Haqani, q.v.) provinces. His group enjoys some tribal support, especially among Khales' own Khugiani and the Jadran (q.v.) tribes. Ideologically, the party of Khales differs little from the other Islamist groups (See Hizb-i Islami [Hekmatyar]), but, unlike Hekmatyar's group, favors cooperation with all mujahedin parties. Also see ISLAMIST MOVEMENT.

HIZBULLAH (HIZB ALLAH). The "Party of Allah," headed by one Shaikh Ali Wusuqi, is a small shi'a group of mujahedin in Herat and a few scattered areas with ties to the Iranian Pasdaran (Guardians of the Revolution). In 1990 the Kabul government gave permission for the formation of political parties, one of which carries the name Hizbullah. It is headed by Shaikh Yusufi of Ghazni, but no details are known regarding the program or members of this shi'a group.

HOTAKIS Or OHTAKS. A main division of the Ghilzai tribe located in the Kushkrud and Tarnak valleys. The Hotakis numbered about 7,000 families at the turn of the century. The Hotaki Ghilzais made their mark in Afghan history when they liberated Kandahar from Persian control and then proceeded to invade Iran, thus ending the reign of the Safavid dynasty (See GHILZAI). Hotaki rulers include the following:

Mir Wais Khan	in Kandahar	1709-15
Mir Abdul Aziz	in Kandahar	1715-16
Mir Mahmud	in Persia	1716-25
Mir Ashraf	in Persia	1725-30
Mir Husain	in Kandahar	1730-38

HUDUD AL-'ALAM. Title of a tenth-century anonymous Persian geography which is one of the first sources mentioning the name Afghanistan.

HUMAIRA, QUEEN. Wife of ex-King Muhammad Zahir and daughter of Ahmad Shah by his first wife Zarin. She encouraged the emancipation of women and accompanied the king on many trips abroad. She now lives in Italy with her husband.

HUSAIN KHAN. Ruler of Maimana. See MAIMANA.

-I-

IBN SINA', ABU ALI (AVICENNA). The great philosopher-physician, "Prince of Physicians," known as Avicenna in the West, was born near Bukhara (now Soviet Central Asia) in 980 A.D. and died in Hamadan (or Isfahan?), Iran, in 1037. He wrote in Arabic and Persian and continued the traditions of Aristotle in philosophy and Hippocrates and Galen in medicine and was dominant in both fields. His *Kitab al-Qanun fi Tibb*, Book of Medicine, and *Kitab al-Shifa*, Book of Healing, were valued in Europe until the 17th century. Afghans claim him as a native son because his father was a native of Balkh. A hospital and a high school in Kabul are named after him.

IBRAHIM BEG. An Uzbak Basmachi (q.v.) leader who fought the Bolshevik government in Central Asia, at times using Afghan territory as a safe haven. He visited Kabul in 1926 and was entertained as a state guest by King Amanullah, who was not averse to the idea of becoming ruler of a Central Asian confederation of Muslim states. In May 1929 Ibrahim Beg supported Habibullah Kalakani (q.v.), and fought King Amanullah's general, Ghulam Nabi Charkhi (q.v.), taking a prominent part in the capture of Mazar-i-Sharif. In 1930, after repeated representations by the Soviet Union, the government of Nadir Shah took steps to prevent Ibrahim Beg from raiding across the border, with the consequence that he started raiding in Afghanistan as well. Therefore, he was finally driven from Afghan territory and captured by Soviet troops. The battles between Afghan troops and Ibrahim Beg's supporters is called by Afghans *Jang-i Laqay* (War of the Laqai - name of Ibrahim's Uzbak tribe). He was executed in April 1931. Also see BASMACHIS.

IJAZI See EJAZI, MEHR MUHAMMAD.

IJMA'. Consensus or agreement of the Islamic community, and subsequently of the *ulama*, is one pillar of Islamic law. See ISLAMIC LAW.

IJTIHAD. Independent analysis or interpretation by a qualified scholar (*mujtahid*) of a legal or theological issue. Muslim modernist support the legality of *ijtihad*, but traditionalist maintain the the "Gate of *Ijtihad*" was closed after the passing of the founders of the great law schools. Ijtihad is still practiced in Shi'a Islam. See ISLAMIC LAW.

IKHWAN AL-MUSLIMIN, See MUSLIM BROTHERHOOD.

IMAMI SHI'AS See SHI'A and ITHNA ASHARIYA.

INAYATULLAH KHAN see EHANAYATULLAH.

ISHAK See ISHAQ.

ISHAQ KHAN, MUHAMMAD See MUHAMMAD ISHAQ .

ISHAQZAI. A section of the Durrani tribe (see DURRANI). The majority of the Ishaqzai inhabit the Pusht-i Rud area, where they amounted to about 7,000 families at the turn of the century. Smaller groups of Ishaqzai are established near Sar-i Pol in Jozjan province.

ISLAH (RECONSTRUCTION). A national Dari newspaper, first published in 1923 under the editorship of Muhammad Bashir in Khanabad, Badakhshan, when Nadir Khan, the subsequent king, visited the province. In 1929 Nadir Khan founded another Dari/Pashto newspaper with this name as part of his campaign against Habibullah Kalakani (q.v.). It continued as a daily Kabul newspaper until 1973, when Sardar Muhammad Daud took power and proclaimed the republic. Among the first editors were Burhanuddin Kushkaki (q.v.), Abdur Rahman Pazhwak (q.v.), and Qiamuddin Khadem (q.v.).

ISLAM. A monotheistic religion which continues the prophetic Judeo-Christian tradition and recognizes Muhammad as the last of the prophets. It is the religion of virtually all Afghans. The word Islam (A.) means submission, the obligation to "submit" to the commands of Allah, the omniscient and omnipotent God. Islam can be summarized under a code of rituals called the "Five Pillars of Islam," as follows:

1. *Shahadat*, the profession of faith. A Muslim says: "I testify that there is no god but Allah and I testify that Muhammad is the Messenger of Allah." Anyone who sincerely testifies to that fact is a Muslim.

2. *Salat*, prayer, which is to be performed five times a day, facing the *qibla*, prayer direction, the location of the *Ka'ba*, a cube-like building, in Mecca (built by Abraham, according to the Qor'an). Prayers include recitation of the Arabic text accompanied by rhythmical bowings, *rak'ah*, and can be performed in public or private. A ritual washing, *wudhu*, is required before prayer. If there is a congregation, one person is the leader, *imam*, and the rest perform their prayers in unison. The muezzin, *mu'adhdhin*, sounds the *azan*, call to prayer, often from top of a minaret. The Friday sermon, *khutbah*, may have political significance because the name of the ruler is invoked, indicating the political loyalty of the congregation.

3. *Zakat*, almsgiving, is the requirement to give either a percentage of one's wealth or of one's yearly income to the poor. This obligation is not uniformly enforced in the Islamic world.

4. *Sawm*, fasting (*ruza* in Dari), is enjoined during the Muslim month of Ramazan (*ramadhan*), "the month during which the Koran was sent down." From sunrise to sundown the believer is to abstain from food or drink, which poses considerable hardship when Ramazan occurs during the long, hot, summer months. Children, the ill, pregnant mothers, travelers, and soldiers in war are exempt, but those prevented must make up this obligation at a later time.

5. *Hajj*, pilgrimage, is a legal obligation of every adult Muslim of either sex to travel at least once in a lifetime to Mecca, provided he/she is economically able to do so. Thousands of Afghans now travel yearly in special flights to Saudi Arabia, and one who has performed pilgrimage carries the honorific title of "hajji."

Minor differences exist in the performance of these obligations within the four orthodox sunni schools. In Afghanistan the Hanifi school, named after Abu Hanifa (q.v., d. 767) is the prevalent one; it is the most liberal in the interpretation of Islamic law, Shari'a.

In addition to acts of devotion and rituals (*ibadat*), Islam also involves a creed of beliefs (*i'tiqad*): Muslims believe in one God, Allah, who is the Creator, Supreme Power, Judge, and Avenger, but is also the Compassionate and Merciful One.   Angels are Allah's messengers and, like humans, His creatures and servants.   They record men's actions and bear witness against them on the Day of Judgment.   The Angel Gabriel is God's chief messenger.   There are also *jinn* spirits, who are good or evil like men.   The fallen or evil jinn are called *shaitans*, devils, whose leader is the Shaitan or Iblis (Satan).   He is given "authority over those who should be seduced by him."   God sends his prophets to bring his message. The major messengers include Adam, Noah, Abraham, Moses and Jesus, but Muhammad is the last of the prophets and the Koran is the last message, superceding the Torah of Moses, the Zabur (Psalms) of David, and the Injil (Gospel) of Jesus.   Muslims believe in a Day of Judgment, when the good will enter Paradise and the evil will be condemned to eternal hellfire.   Personal responsibility before God is important in Islam and there is no belief in atonement.

Jihad (q.v.), "Striving in the Way of God," is not one of the Five Pillars of Islam. Jihad is a war in defense of Islam, securing immediate salvation and heaven to the fallen martyr; but jihad is any effort in a good cause. Also see SHI'ISM.

ISLAMIC ALLIANCE FOR THE LIBERATION OF AFGHANISTAN.   A loose coalition founded on January 27, 1980, by five mujahedin groups with headquarters in Pakistan.   It was headed by Abdul Rasul Sayyaf, who at that time did not have a force of his own.   The sixth group, Hekmatyar's Hezb, did not participate because it was not given preeminent status. The Alliance was formed for the purpose of gaining recognition as a government in exile and to secure support from the Islamic Foreign Ministers Conference, held in Islamabad in May 1980.   The Alliance disintegrated in December of the same year.   In early 1981, the Pakistan government announced that it would henceforth recognize only six groups (later seven) and that all refugees in the country must register as members of one of these groups.   Refugee aid as well as mujahedin support would be channelled through these groups.   Thus in 1985 the Alliance reconstituted itself under the label of *Islamic Unity of Afghan Mujahedin* with the moderates in the "Unity of Three" (Gilani, Mujaddidi, and Muhammadi) and the radicals organized in the "Unity of Seven" of whom only four (Rabbani, Hekmatyar, Sayyaf, and Khales) represented viable groups.   While the moderates were reasonably united, the radicals were constantly at odds, especially the groups headed by Rabbani and Hekmatyar.   In May 1983, the Alliance elected Sayyaf chairman for a term of two years, but when, in 1985, he attempted to remain in this position the Alliance members objected.

Subsequently a chairman of the Alliance served on a rotational basis for three months. There was otherwise little coordination between the groups. Upon becoming spokesman in February 1988, Pir Sayyid Ahmad Gilani announced the formation of an Afghan Interim Government (AIG). Eng. Ahmad Shah, an American-educated Afghan and member of Sayyaf's party, was chosen as prime minister, and the cabinet included the following:

Dr. Zabihullah Mujaddidi (Jabha)   deputy prime minister
Maulawi Muhammad Shah Fazli (Harakat)   deputy prime minister
Haji Din Muhammad (Hizb Khales) defense
Sayyid Nurullah Ahmad (Jamiat) interior
Qazi Najiyullah (Hizb Hikmatyar) foreign affairs
Muhammad Ismail Siddiqi (Harakat) finance
Faruq Azam (Mahaz) rehabilitation and reconstruction
Maulana Mir Hamza (Jamiat) education
Mutiullah Muti (Hizb Khales) agriculture and livestock
Din Muhammad Gran (Mahaz) scientific research
Ali Ansari (Hizb Hikmatyar) justice
Yasser (Ittihad Sayyaf) publicity and Islamic guidance
Abdul Aziz Faruq (independent) planning
Wasiq Wayezzada (Jabha) health

Elections were to be held among the mujahedin and refugees within three months. The government was short-lived: it did not hold a valid election as planned, because of disagreement regarding representation in a 520 man assembly (*shura*). Each of the seven groups was to delegate sixty members. Twenty "good Muslims" (Afghans under Marxist control, but not supporters of the regime) from Kabul were to be included, and sixty seats were allocated to the Shi'a groups in Iran. The shi'a groups wanted 120 seats and refused to participate; Sebghatullah Mujaddidi's offer of 100 seats and seven of 28 ministerial positions was not acceptable to some Peshawar groups.

On February 20, 1989, the *shura* (at Madinatul Hajjaj, a town near Rawalpindi), elected an Afghan Interim Government (AIG), naming Sibghatullah Mujaddidi president and Abdul Rasul Sayyaf prime minister. The first meeting of the new cabinet was held on March 10, 1989, in the village of Shiwa in Khost province of southeastern Afghanistan. Leaders of the alliance held major portfolios:

Maulawi Muhammad Nabi Muhammadi	defense
Muhammad Shah Fazli (Harakat)	scientific research
Maulawi Islamuddin (Harakat)	agriculture
Gulbuddin Hekmatyar	foreign affairs
Ali Ansari (Hizb Hekmatyar)	frontier affairs
Qazi Najibullah (Hizb Hekmatyar)	justice
Yunus Khales	interior
Haji Dean Muhammad (Hizb Khales)	national security
Maulawi Abdur Razzaq (Hizb Khales)	religious affairs
Burhanuddin Rabbani	reconstruction
Najibullah Lafra'i (Jamiat)	Islamic guidance
Ishan Jan (Jamiat)	mining and industries
Ahmad Shah (Ittihad)	communications
Sayyid Nadir Khurram (Jabha)	health

Additional portfolios were reserved for Iran-based mujahedin and representatives from Kabul. In May 1989, Pir Sayyid Ahmad Gailani challenged the legitimacy of the government, and in August of the same year Gulbuddin Hekmatyar again withdrew.

Disagreement as to the type of a future Afghan government and ethnic and sectarian divisions have prevented the AIG from becoming a viable institution. Gulbuddin Hekmatyar took independent action in disregard of the cost to Afghan unity. On July 9, 1990, Sayyid Jamal, one of his commanders in Takhar province, ambushed and killed a number of commanders, most of them from Jam'iat; the deed was eventually avenged. This was only one in a long series of incidents in which Hekmatyar's Hezb was the culprit. Such actions led credence to the suspicion that Hekmatyar does not want unity, but intends to gain sole control of the Afghan government.

ISLAMIC LAW. Islamic law (*shari'a*, A. from *shar'* = the path) is God-given and a prescription for the believer to the right life in this world and for salvation in the world to come. During the lifetime of the Prophet Muhammad, he transmitted Allah's commands. These were eventually collected in the book of readings or recitations, the Koran (Qur'an). The Koran was the basis of law for all Muslims, although various sects and schools differed in its intepretation. When no conclusive guidance was found in the Koran, the *sunna*, practice of the Prophet and his companions, was consulted. Four schools of law eventually developed in sunni Islam, named after early legal scholars: the *Malikite*, named after Malik ibn Anas (d. 795); the *Shafi'ite*, named after ibn. Idris al-Shafi'i (d.819); the *Hanbalite*, named after Ahmad ibn Hanbal (d. 855); and the *Hanifite*, named after Abu Hanifa (d.767). The Hanifite school has the largest number of adherents and is the dominant one in Afghanistan. In addition to the Koran, it recognizes the *sunna*, *ijma* (consensus of the Muslim community), and *qiyas* (reasoning by analogy) as a basis of jurisprudence. Legal reasoning is called *ijtihad*, the struggle, or effort, in arriving at a legal decision. By the tenth century Muslim jurists decided by consensus that Islamic law was complete and that independent interpretation, *ijtihad*, was no longer permissible. Henceforth, Muslims were to follow, or imitate (*taqlid*), God's law. Islamic modernists want to reopen the "Gate of Ijtihad," to permit a reinterpretation of Islamic law in order to meet new, modern requirements. Judges (*qadis*) in shari'a courts are to apply the law, subject to consultation with legal experts (*muftis*) who issue legal decisions (*fatwas*). A jurist (*faqih*) is trained at an Islamic college (*madrasa*) to serve as lawyer, teacher, judge, and mufti. Punishments include the penalties for major offenses prescribed in the Qur'an (*hadd*, pl. *hudud*), discretionary and variable punishments (*ta'zir*), and retaliation (*qisas*).

Although the shari'a has been the law of Afghanistan, there has always existed a dichotomy of "God's law" and the "King's law." During the time of Ahmad Shah (q.v., 1747-73) there were central and provincial courts whose administration was in the hands of the *qadis*, all of whom were appointed by the ruler on the recommendation of the court *imam*. The death penalty could not be exacted without the king, or governor's, approval. Ahmad Shah forbade mutilation of limbs and drafted a legal code, which was, however, not enacted. Tribal courts existed in the

Pashtun frontier areas where cases were decided by council, (jirga). Timur Shah first appointed a minister of justice, *amir-i dar al-qaza* and a chief justice, *qazi al-quzat*, to whom all courts were subordinated. All legal functionaries were appointed by Kabul. Amir Abdur Rahman established a court of appeals with twelve members, headed by the *khan-i ulum* (chief of [religious] sciences). Under Amir Habibullah there existed courts headed by his sons Nasrullah Khan and Enayatullah Khan, the *shari'at*, and the *kotwali*, police court. Appeals against decisions of governors and high officials were made to the Amir. The Ottoman codification of Hanafi law (*majalla*) was translated into Dari (*siraj al-ahkam*).

The sphere of the "king's law," was considerably expanded during the period of King Amanullah (q.v., 1919-29). He drafted the first constitution in 1923 and initiated judicial reforms, *nizam-namah*, which aimed at reducing the influence of the *ulama* (clergy), and a guide for judges in civil and criminal law was produced (*tamasuk al-quzzat*). The introduction of administrative courts for civil servants, commercial courts, and reconciliation courts took over many functions of the Shari'a courts. A number of statutes restricted the powers of the *qazis*, judges. These innovations were abolished after the fall of King Amanullah, but were resumed as a result of Nadir Shah's constitution of 1931. The *usul-namah*, a code of statutory legislation, replaced the *nizam-namah*. It was more conservative in nature and merely supplementary to Islamic law. A hierarchy of primary and appellate courts existed with the court of cassation (*tamyiz*) at the highest level. The mufti played a role only on the primary level.

The constitution of 1964 (*qanun-i asasi*) established an independent judiciary with the supreme court as the highest official organ. In March 1967 the office of public prosecutor was established, and the offices of minister of justice and attorney general were combined. Penal and civil codes were enacted, and criminal procedure was divided into "customary law" (Islamic law) and statutory law (*qanun*). The supreme court was temporarily replaced with a high judicial council, after Muhammad Daud established a republican form of government. The gap between statutory law and the sharia widened. The sovereignty of God was gradually replaced by sovereignty of the nation or the people.

President Daud's constitution of 1977 centralized the legal establishment and the vestiges of separation of powers were abolished, as the minister of justice took over the functions of the chief justice. The *Milli Jirga* (National Council) replaced parliament, and the Revolutionary Council was the highest authority in the state. The Marxist government set up a higher council of the judiciary which was responsible to the revolutionary council. Revolutionary and extraordinary courts existed for some time which were responsible for the executions of many. In spite of the trend toward secularization of law, the lower courts in the provinces and small towns have continued to operate in the traditional manner. The *shari'a* has remained dominant in matters of family law, inheritance, property, and contracts. Also see CONSTITUTIONAL DEVELOPMENT.

ISLAMIC UNITY OF AFGHAN MUJAHEDIN See **ISLAMIC ALLIANCE FOR THE LIBERATION OF AFGHANISTAN.**

ISLAMIST MOVEMENT. The movement was born in large measure as a reaction to the process of Westernization in Afghanistan and the growth of secular, liberal ideologies among Afghan youth. The movement owes much of its organization and ideology to the influence of the Muslim Brotherhood (q.v.) of Egypt (*Al-Ikhwan Al-Muslimun*), and its adherents were therefore dubbed *Ikhwanis* by their opponents. The party originated in religious, intellectual circles in the late 1950s and had as its chief ideologues and mentors Dr. Ghulam Muhammad Niazi (q.v.), Burhanuddin Rabbani (q.v.), Dr. Sayyid Musa Tawana (q.v.), and others who had studied at al-Azhar University in Egypt and taught at the faculty of theology of Kabul University. They soon gathered a circle of like-minded students, who organized themselves in 1970 in the Islamic Youth (*Jawanan-i Muslimin*) movement. At first they went through a process of ideological development when members studied the works of Islamic thinkers Hasan al-Banna' (1906-49), the "Supreme Guide" of the Ikhwanis; Sayyid Qutb, executed in Cairo in 1966; and Abu'l Ala Maududi (died 1979), founder of the Pakistani *Jama'at-i Islami* (q.v.) and author of religio-political treatises. The movement took a political turn during the premiership of Sardar Daud (1953-63) and the subsequent liberal period. Islamist students staged demonstrations, protesting government policies and such international issues as Zionism and the war in Vietnam. By 1970 Islamists won a majority in student elections, a fact which alarmed the Marxists and their supporters. In 1971 the movement began to formally organize at a meeting in Kabul at the house of Professor Rabbani (q.v.). A leadership council was formed of which Rabbani was the chairman, Abdul Rasul Sayyaf his deputy, and Engineer Habibur Rahman (q.v.) was secretary. Council members were assigned responsibility for financial, cultural, and political tasks. Some leaders, like Niazi, refrained from open participation, others, like Hekmatyar, were jailed. The organization selected the name *Jam'iat-i Islami* (Islamic Society) but the student faction, operating quite openly, was known as the *Jawanan Musulman*, (Muslim Youth), and popularly called Ikhwanis. Other Islamist individuals and circles, not affiliated with the Jam'iat were Minhajuddin Gahiz, who in 1968 published his newspaper *Jarida Gahiz*, (Dawn); *Khuddam al-Quran* (Servants of the Koran) founded by the Mujaddidi family; and the *Jam'iat-i Ulama-i Muhammadi* (Society of Muslim Ulama) founded by Sebghatullah Mujaddidi (q.v.).

After the coup of Muhammad Daud (July 17, 1973), the movement was forced to go underground. Rabbani raised the question of armed struggle, and weapons were collected; but before any action could begin, the government police arrested many of the members, including Ghulam Muhammad Niazi. Rabbani and Hekmatyar fled to Pakistan where they sought help from the Pakistan government and the Islamist *Jama'at-i Islami*. In 1975, Hekmatyar staged sporadic raids into Afghanistan and when the attacks failed, the differences between Rabbani and Hekmayar became public.

After the Saur Revolt of April 1978 an attempt at reconciliation was made. Each party nominated seven members to a 21-member reconciliation committee including the mediators. The *Jam'iat* members voted for Rabbani to be president of the party, and Hekmatyar's party voted for Qazi Muhammad Amin as deputy president. The mediators voted for Maulawi Fayez who became the compromise president. But the Islamists were divided on ethnic and ideological lines. The largely Tajik supporters of Rabbani favored preparation rather than precipitous armed activity. Hekmatyar aspired to leadership of the Islamists and advocated immediate armed struggle. In April 1978 Maulawi Nabi Muhammadi was chosen as a compromise leader, but the movement broke up over the distribution of funds provided by foreign donors. Hekmatyar organized the *Hezb-i Islami*, and the traditionalist Muhammadi founded his own *Harakat-i Inqilab-i Islami* party. Rabbani worked with Mujaddidi and his *Jabha-yi Najat-i Milli-yi Afghanistan* (National Liberation Front), and continued to lead his own Jam'iat. Yunus Khales had formed his own Hizb in 1979.

The Islamists were puritanical moralists who perceived moral laxity, lack of respect for traditional values, and an infatuation with Western secular culture among the Afghan youth and were determined to impose the laws of Islam on the social and political life of the state. They were not fundamentalist, but reformist and supported a political activism first seen in the great Pan-Islamist, Jamaluddin Afghani (q.v.). They were critical of the fundamentalist views of the *ulama* and were themselves the object of criticism of the clergy. They went underground and organized in cells, and were accused of resorting to political assassinations and were themselves the objects of assassinations. They rejected aspects of both Communism and democracy although they copied from both. For additional information, see individual party entries and ISLAMIC ALLIANCE FOR THE LIBERATION OF AFGHANISTAN, TAWANA, and MUSLIM BROTHERHOOD.

ISMA'IL KHAN See MUHAMMAD ISMA'IL.

ISMA'ILIS (ISMA'ILIYA). A Shi'a Islamic sect which originated when the Shi'a Imam Isma'il (son of Ja'far al-Sadeq) died in 765 A.D. and was thought by his followers to be the final, Seventh, Imam, destined to return on the Day of Judgment. The present leader of the Isma'ili community is Karim, Agha Khan IV, who administers to some 300,000 people residing in Africa, Syria, Iran, Tajikistan, India, and Pakistan, as well as in northeastern Afghanistan. Isma'ilis pay a tax which goes to the support of the community. The Isma'ilis believe in an esoteric interpretation of the Koran with stages of initiation, depending on the comprehension of the believer. The head of the Isma'ili community in Afghanistan was Nadir Shah Kayani, known as Sayyid-i Kayan. As a small sectarian community, the Isma'ilis refused to cooperate with the sunni mujahedin groups operating in their territory. Also see SHI'ISM and SAYYID-I KAYAN.

ISTALIF (lat. 34-50' N, long. 69-0'). A small town in the Koh Daman area, located about 20 miles north-northwest of Kabul, which is famous for its scenic beauty and blue colored pottery. The village is "built on the side of the hills in the form of a pyramid, the houses rising one above the other by terraces, and the whole being crowned by the magnificent chinars which denote the shrine of Hazrat Eshan, whilst far below in a deep glen rushes a foaming yet clear brook...(Gazetteer, 6)." The name, Istalif, has been linked to the Greek *istafel*, grapes, which are grown there in great abundance.

Istalif was captured and destroyed by British troops in the first Anglo-Afghan war. During the present war it has been held by mujahedin groups and is said to have suffered considerable destruction.

ISTIQLAL LYCEE. An academic high school in Kabul with a French curriculum, founded by King Amanullah in 1922, hence its name *Amania*. After the accession of Nadir Shah it was renamed *Istiqlal* (Independence) Lycée. It began with five French and twelve Afghan teachers, and in 1926 had 33 teachers and 350 students. Subsequently it was greatly expanded and became one of the prestigious preparatory schools in the country. Also see EDUCATION.

ITHNA 'ASHARIYA (Twelver). A Shi'a sect believing that the Twelfth (A. *ithna 'ashariya*) Imam, Muhammad al-Mahdi, is the last imam (leader of the shi'a community) who went into occultation to return at the end of time "to announce the last judgment and to fill the earth with justice." In the early 16th century the Safavid rulers of Iran made Twelver Shi'ism the state religion and forcefully converted much of its sunni population. In Afghanistan most of the Hazara, the Qizilbash (q.v.) and about half of the population of Herat belong to this sect. The Twelvers are also called *Imami shi'as* and constitute a religious minority in Afghanistan. Also see SHI'A.

ITIMADI See ETEMADI.

ITTIHAD-I ISLAMI BARAYI AZADI-YI AFGHANISTAN. "Islamic Union for the Liberation of Afghanistan," founded by Abd al- Rab Rasul Sayyaf (q.v.), after he served as chairman of the Islamic Alliance (q.v.), 1980-81. It is a small Islamist group which favors the establishment of an Islamic state in Afghanistan. Sayyaf has been able to gain considerable financial support from the Arab Gulf states which helped him to found his own organization. It is part of the loose federation of the Islamic Unity of the Afghan Mujahedin. See SAYYAF, ABDUL RASUL; ISLAMIC ALLIANCE FOR THE LIBERATION OF AFGHANISTAN, and ISLAMIST MOVEMENT IN AFGHANISTAN.

-J-

JABAL-US-SIRAJ (JABAL AL-SIRAJ) (lat. 35-1' N, long. 69-14' E). A town and administrative district in Parwan province which has become a center of Afghanistan's textile industry. Built by Amir Habibullah in 1906, the town got its name from the Amir's title *Seraj al-Millat wa'l Din* (Torch of the Nation and Religion). It included a fortress and Arg (palace) and a cantonment, housing some 12,000 men. Between 1910 and 1913 a hydroelectric plant was constructed by a Scottish engineer, James Miller, to provide electricity for Kabul. For a long time this was the only plant of its type in Afghanistan. Subsequently the industrial base was further expanded with the construction of a textile mill in the 1930s and a cement factory in the early 1960s.

JABBAR KHEL. A section of the Ghilzai tribe occupying the area of Hisarak-i Ghilzai in Nangarhar province, between the Siah Koh range and the Surkhab river, and scattered over the greater part of Laghman province.

JABHA-YI MILLI NAJAT-I AFGHANISTAN. National Liberation Front, one of the seven mujahedin groups headquartered in Pakistan, founded by Sebghatullah Mujaddidi in 1978. It advocates the overthrow of the Marxist regime in Kabul and the establishment of a traditional Islamic state with a parliamentary democracy. The *Jabha* is ideologically close to the moderate groups of Gailani and Muhammadi and cooperates with them. Also see MUJADDIDI, SEBGHATULLAH.

JADRAN (DZADRAN or ZADRAN). A tribe related to the Khostwal Pashtuns, inhabiting the eastern slope of the Sulaiman range in Paktia province. They are excellent fighters, and entered the war against the Kabul government in 1979. Under the command of Jalaluddin Haqani (q.v.), they have been able to expel government troops from the area of Urgun. The Jadran are loosely affiliated with the party of Yunus Khales (q.v.). Also see HAQQANI and KHALES, YUNUS.

JAGIR. A feudal, military fiefdom, such as granted by Ahmad Shah Durrani to chiefs of his tribe. It was an allotment of land which was tax-free but required its holder to provide a number of troops and arms corresponding to the size of the *jagir* (also called *tiyul* and A. *iqta'*).

JAGRAN, SAYYID MUHAMMAD HASAN (JAGLAN). Jagran (major) is the title under which Sayyid Hasan, the 50-year old commander of the Hazara front in Behsud, Ghazni province, is known. Successful in various military engagements against government forces, he reportedly has administered his area autonomously since 1980. He is affiliated with the *shura-yi ittifaq-i Islami* of Sayyid Ali Beheshti which is the only shi'a mujahedin movement attending the consultative council of commanders in Rawalpindi, Pakistan, in February 1989. Jagran has fought Nasr (q.v.) and Pasdaran (q.v.) and does not enjoy good relations with the other shi'a groups. Also see BEHESHTI, SAYYID ALI and SHI'A MUJAHEDIN GROUPS.

JAJI. A tribe in Paktia province, estimated to number about 5,000 families. They are sunnis and have engaged in occasional bloodfeuds with the neighboring shi'a Turis (q.v.). They have a reputation as good fighters. They supported the Sulaiman Khel in ousting King Amanullah (q.v), and sided with Nadir Shah (q.v.) against Habibullah Kalakani (q.v.). After 1930 many Jaji chiefs came to Kabul and, encouraged by Shah Mahmud Ghazi (q.v.), established themselves in the trucking business. In the present war in Afghanistan the Jajis eventually allied themselves with the Mahaz of Gailani (q.v.).

JALALABAD (lat. 36-46' N, long. 65-52' E). The capital of Nangarhar province which had an estimated 54,000 inhabitants in the 1970s, reportedly increased by 1988, as a result of the influx of internal refugees, to about 200,000. When the mujahedin besieged the city in March 1989, this number was again considerably reduced. The population is largely Pashtun of Khugiani, Shinwari, Tirahi (Tira'i), Mohmand, and Ghilzai tribal background, in addition to Sikhs, Hindus, and some Tajiks and Sayyids. It has the largest community of Sikh and Hindu merchants (about 4,000) of any Afghan city. Situated at an altitude of 1950 feet in a fertile valley watered by the Kabul and Kunar rivers some 90 miles east of Kabul, Jalalabad lies on the trade route to the Indo-Pakistani subcontinent. Invaders passed through the Jalalabad valley, including Alexander the Great (330 B.C.), Babur Shah (1504) and the British who occupied the town in two Anglo-Afghan wars.

Babur Shah, the founder of the Moghul empire of India, first planted beautiful gardens in the area and in 1560 A.D. his grandson Jalaluddin Akbar founded the town, hence its name Jalalabad. In the 19th century it was a walled town with about 2,000 inhabitants which swelled during the winter to some 20,000.

Because of its beauty and mild climate it was the winter capital of Afghan kings. Amir Habibullah was assassinated in the vicinity of the town on February 20, 1919, during one of his visits. He and his son Amanullah are buried in the city. A dam on the Kabul river and a hydroelectric power station at Darunta north of Jalalabad have made possible the irrigation of additional land, providing the city with electricity. Mechanized farms produced large quantities of citrus fruits and olives, wheat, and alfalfa. The area is famous for its orchards and gardens. Virtually all the citrus fruit in Afghanistan comes from there. The civil war caused considerable destruction in 1929 and the present war has forced many to flee the town and surrounding area. In March 1989, mujahedin forces attacked the city but were unable to take it.

JALALLAR, MUHAMMAD KHAN. Minister of finance (1971-72) and commerce (1974-78) and reappointed as minister of commerce by the government of Babrak Karmal in 1980. He continued in his post until January 1989. Born in 1936 in Andkhoi of a family which immigrated from Tajikistan to Afghanistan around 1930. Educated in Kabul and after graduation in 1958 began service in the ministry of planning. Jalallar's participation in various governments served to maintain the loyalty of the Uzbak community and to promote their economic interest. He accompanied President Daud on his official visit to Egypt, 1977, and reportedly passed information to the Soviets about Daud's discussions with President Sadat. Served as economic adviser in the prime ministry during the Khalqi period. Although he did not become a member of the PDPA, Jalallar was elected a member of the Revolutionary Council. He was dismissed from government in January 1989 and is said to have gone to Canada.

JAM (lat. 34-21' N, long. 64-30' E). A village in Ghor province west of Chaghcharan. Located near the village stands a 190-foot high minaret which was discovered by the governor of Herat and examined by a French archaeologist in 1958. The minaret was constructed in the 12th century under the Ghorid ruler Ghias ud-Din and is located in a desolated area. The geometric design of the brickwork can still be recognized and kufic inscriptions from the Qur'an give the *sura* (verse) of Mary, mother of Jesus.

JAMA'AT-I-ISLAMI. Name of a Pakistani political organization founded by Maulana Abu'l- Ala Maududi (1903-79) in 1940 which advocates the establishment of an Islamic state patterned after the early Islamic community. Olivier Roy (1986) characterized the Jama'at as an elite religio-political society, similar to the Opus Dei. It is pan-Islamic in nature and looks at the Muslim community as one nation (*umma*) and rejects nationalism and ethnic separatism as contrary to the concept of Islamic brotherhood. The Jama'at opposed the creation of Pakistan and favors union with Afghanistan as a first step in reestablishing the Islamic Umma. Zia-ul-Haq, the Pakistani president, tried to implement some of Maududi's ideas. The Jama'at has strongly supported the forces of Gulbuddin Hekmatyar and other Islamist mujahedin groups in Afghanistan, in preference to the nationalist and traditionalist groups.

JAMALUDDIN AFGHANI See AFGHANI, JAMALUDDIN.

JAM'IAT-I ISLAMI-YI AFGHANISTAN. Islamic Society of Afghanistan, headed since 1971 by Prof. Burhanuddin Rabbani (q.v.) and since 1978 a mujahedin force to fight the Marxist government in Kabul. It is one of the seven *mujahedin* groups accorded recognition by Pakistan and headquartered in Peshawar, and is largely non-Pashtun in membership. Affiliated commanders control areas in northeastern, northern, and western Afghanistan. They include Ahmad Shah Mas'ud (q.v.), in the

Panjshir valley, and Isma'il Khan (q.v.) who operates in Herat province. The party is Islamist (See ISLAMIST MOVEMENT IN AFGHAN- ISTAN) in orientation and favors the establishment of an Islamic state. Although most Afghan males smoke, the party outlawed smoking as sinful and subject to punishment. In spite of their common ideological origin, the *Jam'iat* has been in a virtual state of war with Gulbuddin Hekmatyar's Hizb. On July 9, 1989, a group of mostly Jam'iat commanders returning from a strategy meeting with Commander Mas'ud in Takhar province were attacked and killed, some of them after they were captured alive. In October 1990, Commander Mas'ud came to Peshawar and approved a reconciliation between Jam'iat and Hizb. Internecine warfare has considerably limited military action against the Kabul regime.

JAM'IAT-I-'ULAMA'. A consultative body of *ulama* (scholars of Islamic sciences) founded by Nadir Shah in 1931 to judge the constitutionality of laws. For a time this council had considerable powers as all new laws had to be submitted to it; but its powers waned after Muhammad Daud became prime minister in 1953 and it became a rubber-stamp legitimizing body of Afghan governments. It published a journal called *Al-Falah* (Sal- vation). After the Saur Revolt, remaining members of the council issued *fatwas* (legal decisions [q.v.]) which recognized Nur Muhammad Taraki as the legitimate ruler of Afghanistan and authorized "jihad" against the "Ikhwanis," Islamist mujahedin groups.

JAMILURRAHMAN, MAULAWI HUSAIN (JAMIL AL-RAHMAN). Amir of the *Jama'at-i Da'wa*, an Islamic rivivalist movement whose members call themselves *Salafis* and are popularly called "Wahhabis." He captured most of Kunar province and proclaimed an "Islamic Amirate," which he ruled for a time to the exclusion of other mujahedin groups. Born in 1933 in Pech district of Kunar province of a Safi (q.v.) family, he received a traditional education. In the early 1970s he became a member *Jam'iat-i Islami* (q.v.) and took part in armed attacks against the goverment of President Daud. After the Saur Revolt he joined the *Hizb-i Islami* of Hekmatyar (q.v.) and was until 1982 his amir in Kunar province. Eventually he broke with Hekmatyar and ousted other mujahedin groups from his area. He issued decrees allowing only bearded men to enter his territory and prohibited the consumption of tobacco in all its forms.

In February 1991 he announced his cabinet which included among others the following portfolios:

Defense	Maulawi Rahmatullah
Interior	Haji Rozi
Foreign Affairs	Mur Muhd. Majidi
Justice	Maulawi Ihsan
Information	Shurish
Finance	Rahman Gul
Education	Qari Din Muhammad

On April 20, 1991, an explosion at his Asadabad headquarters so decimated the ranks of his followers (including numerous Pakistanis and

Arabs) that Hekmatyar's forces, supported by commanders of other groups, were able to capture Asadabad and expel most of the "Wahhabis" from Kunar province. Muhammad Husain, alias Jamilurrahman, was assassinated by an Egyptian in Pakistan. One Maulawi Sami'ullah succeeded as leader of the remnant of the party. Also see KUNAR.

JAMI, MULLA NURU'D-DIN ABDUR RAHMAN. The last great poet of classical Persian, scholar, and mystic who was born in Jam (now Khorasan province of Iran) in 1414 (which was then under the political control of Herat) and died in Herat in 1492. Afghans consider Jami a native son because he lived in Herat at the court of Sultan Baiqara (q.v.) where he enjoyed the friendship and support of the wazir Ali-Shir Nawa'i (1469-1506). Afghan historians therefore call him Abdur Rahman *Harawi*, the Herati. See HERAT and BAIQARA, SULTAN HUSAIN.

JAMSHIDI. One of the Chahar Aimaq communities, variously estimated to number from 40 to 80 thousand people, concentrated in western Badghis and in smaller groups in Herat province, northwestern Badghis, and southern Fariab provinces. They trace their name to Jamshid, their purported eponymic ancestor and call themselves Kayanis, claiming descent from the legendary pre- Islamic Kayan kings of Sistan. According to some sources their name is a corruption of *jam-shoda*, which means "collected together." A member of the Jamshidi clan was put in charge of the district of Badghis by Shah Abbas (1642-68), and Khushi Khan, contemporary of Nadir Shah Afshar (q.v.), was the first chief of the Jamshidi tribe. The Jamshidis are Hanafi sunnis and speak Dari.

JAT. Gypsy-like groups of sunni itinerants who call themselved *Ghorbat* (travelers) and make a living as musicians, dancers, fortune-tellers and therefore are considered to be of low status. Their women engage in door-to-door selling of small bazar items. They belong to six different ethnic groups and speak various dialects, some of Iranian and others of Indian origin. Their number has been estimated as from 9 to 12 thousand, who are scattered all over the country.

JIHAD. Jihad, holy war (A., literally "great effort," but generally "holy war"), is the obligation to fight against "unbelievers" until they accept Islam or submit to Islamic rule. Monotheists with a sacred book, like Christians and Jews, are not forced to convert and enjoy the status of protected subjects (*dhimmis*, q.v.). A Muslim who dies in *jihad* is a martyr, *shahid*, and is assured of Paradise. Technically Muslims constitute one community, *umma*, and war between them is forbidden; therefore an enemy is proclaimed sinful or apostate before he can be legally fought. Although the PDPA in Afghanistan has not officially adopted the atheism of Marxist ideology, it has been accused by the mujahedin (fighters in *Jihad*) as apostate and therefore subject to be eliminated. On the other hand, the council of Afghan clergy (*jami'at-i ulama*) in 1978 issued a *fetwa*, legal decision, legitimizing the Kabul government and proclaiming

"Jihad" against the Islamist mujahedin. During Jihad, all tribal hostilities must temporarily stop. Muslim modernists quote a Koranic passage that says: "Fight in the Way of God against those who fight against you, but do not commit aggression...", maintaining that the obligation of jihad was binding only for the early Islamic period and that Jihad also means fighting political and social war and inwardly waging war against the carnal soul - a kind of moral imperative.

JIRGA. A tribal council, which has legislative and juridical authority in the name of the tribal community. Although the Afghan government claims exclusive jurisdiction, it permits Pashtun tribes in the border areas to resolve internal disputes in their traditional manner. Jirgas can be composed of chiefs and notables or of all adult male members of a tribe. A chief, or respected greybeard, leads the discussion, and votes are weighed rather than counted. The decision of a jirga is binding on all members of the tribe. Jirgas also resolve intratribal disputes, often with the mediation of a respected member of the *ulama* (clergy) or *pirs* (leaders of mystical orders).

In times of national emergency Afghan rulers have convened a *Loya Jirga* (q.v.), Great Council, which includes representatives from all parts of the country. Its decisions thus become an expressions of the "national will." See LOYA JIRGA.

JIZYA. A tax levied on monotheistic non-Muslims who are possessors of a scripture, the *ahl al-kitab*, or Peoples of the Book (such as Christians and Jews). Only adult males of sound mind and body and financial means were to be so taxed. In exchange, they enjoyed freedom of life, liberty, and property, and were not drafted into the military. In Afghanistan this tax was levied largely on Indians. Afghan constitutions since the time of King Amanullah declared all Afghan citizens equal and abolished the jizya. Also see DHIMMIS.

JOYA, MUHAMMAD SARWAR. A poet, writer, and social critic who was a supporter of King Amanullah's reforms and opposed to the regime of Nadir Shah. Founded the Danesh printing press in Herat, and served as editor of the daily newspaper *Ittefaq-i-Islam* (Consensus of Islam) in Herat, 1928-30, the daily *Anis* (q.v.) and the biweekly *Watan* (q.v.). Was jailed repeatedly and died in prison in 1961.

JOZJAN (JOWZJAN) (lat. 36-30' N, long. 66-0' E). A province in north-central Afghanistan with an area of 10,126 square miles and an estimated population of about 642,000. The administrative capital of the province is Shiberghan with some 19,000 inhabitants. The province is rich in mineral resources; oil and natural gas have been discovered at Khwaja Gugirdak and Jarquduq, near Shiberghan, and reserves of natural gas have been estimated at 500 trillion cubic feet. A pipeline transporting natural gas to the Soviet Union was completed in 1968, and except for a limited amount of local use in the production of fertilizer, all is delivered to the Soviet Union at a cost much below the world market.

JUDICIARY See ISLAMIC LAW.

JUM'A. The day of "general assembly," Friday, and the Islamic sabbath, when Muslims attend religious services, preferably in a major mosque, often referred to as the *Jum'a* (or Friday) Mosque. A sermon, *khutba*, is read on Fridays in the name of the ruler. After the sermon, those in attendance often discuss matters of importance to the community and to the congregation. The *khutba* has political significance because it indicates the loyalty of the congregation. It is a sign of rebellion if the ruler's name is omitted or if it is replaced by another name. In the civil war of 1929, the governor of Herat had the *khutba* read in the name of the "Islamic King" to avoid making a choice between King Amanullah and Habibullah Kalakani.

JUMHURIAT **(Republic)** (A daily newspaper which temporarily replaced Anis (q.v.) and Islah, after President Daud proclaimed the Republic in 1973. It was the official organ of the republican government and ceased to exist after the Marxist coup of 1978.

-K-

KABUL (lat. 34-31' N, long. 69-12' E). The capital and largest city in Afghanistan, situated at an altitude of almost 6,000 feet above sea level, and a province with an area of 1,822 square miles and a population of 1,372,000. In 1978 the city had some 500,000 inhabitants, but this number has, according to UN estimates, increased to about one million and a half as a result of the influx of refugees from the war-ravaged areas. Kabul is strategically located in a valley surrounded by high mountains at the crossroads of north-south and east-west trade routes. Therefore it has been the site of towns since antiquity, called Kubha in the Rigveda (about 1,500 B.C.) and Kabura by Ptolemy (second century A.D.). Muslim Arabs under Abdur Rahman Samurah captured Kabul in the middle of the 7th century A.D., but it took the Islamic invaders another 200 years before the Hindu rulers of Kabul were finally ousted. Kabul continued to be disputed, resulting in much destruction until Islam was definitely established under the Saffarids (9th century A.D.). The city was part of the Ghaznavid empire to suffer again from Genghiz Khan's hordes (13th century A.D.). Kabul became the capital of a province of the Moghul empire, whose founder, Babur Shah (q.v.), is buried on the eastern slope of the Sher Darwaza mountain. In 1775-76 Timur Shah made Kabul his capital, and Afghan Amirs ruled henceforth from that city. In the 19th century Kabul endured British occupation during the two Anglo-Afghan wars and the destruction of its covered Bazar as a punitive measure. The city includes the old town, between the northern slope of the Sher Darwaza mountain and Kabul river, and a new town (shahr-i nau) began in 1935. A large wall, twenty feet high and twelve feet thick, parts of which archaeologists believe to date from the 5th century A.D., still stands. It extends to the Bala Hisar, the citadel, an imposing fortress which was destroyed by the British in 1878 and rebuilt to serve as a garrison and military college in 1939. Afghan Amirs resided in the Bala Hisar until in 1888 Amir Abdur Rahman constructed the Arg (q.v.), a citadel and walled palace, in the center of town. At the beginning of this century Amir Habibullah further modernized the town, providing electricity for the Arg and eventually also for other parts of the town. In the 1920s the city had 60,000 inhabitants. King Amanullah constructed his own capital in Darulaman, about six miles from the center of town, with several government buildings and an imposing parliament building. Members of the royal court and high government officials built their villas in the new capital, but after his fall from power the center of government moved back into town.

The city grew rapidly after World War II with the addition of new quarters. Karta-yi Chahar (Fourth District) was developed in 1942, followed by Khairkhana in the northwest, Nur Muhammad Shah Mina east of the old town, Nadir Shah Mina to the northeast, Wazir Akbar Khan east of Shahr-i Nau, and Khushhal Khan Mina. In 1953 the Jada-yi Maiwand (Maiwand Street), was drawn through the old city followed by paved avenues, villas, highrise buildings, and prefabricated apartment complexes which have replaced much of the old town. The streets were paved with Soviet assistance and a grain silo and bakery were constructed. A network of paved roads connects Kabul via the Salang Pass tunnel to the north, via the Tang-i Gharu (Gharu Gorge) to Pakistan, via Kandahar and Herat to Iran. Hydroelectric power stations in Sarobi (1957), Mahipar, and Naghlu (1966) provided electricity for the city. Soviet-style city planning and the construction of pre-fabricated apartment complexes have given parts of the town the appearance of a Soviet Central Asian town. Since the late 18th century Kabul has been the seat of political power and to be recognized as ruler of Afghanistan, one had to be in possession of the town. Kabul is still the preeminent city in Afghanistan and the seat of a government which exerts a tenuous control over the major towns and arteries of transportation. The city is now under siege and subject to destructive missile attacks.

KABUL MUSEUM

An important repository of archaeological and ethnographic collections of the Hellenistic, Graeco-Buddhist, Ghaznavid, and subsequent periods. Its main collection, workshop, and offices are housed in the former municipality building, constructed under King Amanullah in Darulaman. The museum is unique in scope, housing among others some 20,000 artifacts of the Gandharan school, about 40,000 coins, and priceless manuscripts. During the regime of Hafizullah Amin some, or most, of the contents were removed, but later returned to the museum. As of 1989, some of the most valuable items have been on display in a small building in the Arg (q.v.), and portions of the ethnographic materials have been relocated to a separate museum. It was feared that as a result of the war in Afghanistan some of the treasures may be lost, but the Kabul government claims that all the contents have been preserved.

KABUL RIVER (lat. 33-55' N, long. 72-14' E). A river which rises on the eastern slopes of the Sanglakh range near the Unai pass, about 45 miles west of Kabul. It flows in an easterly direction, past Kabul, and through the Tang-i Gharu to Dargai, Jalalabad, and then on to Dakka where it enters Pakistan territory and finally runs into the Indus at Attock after a course of about 350 miles. It is the only Afghan river system which flows into an ocean. Major tributaries in Afghanistan include the Panjshir, Logar, Surkhab, Laghman, and Kunar rivers. Much of the upper part of the river is used for irrigation; therefore, it is almost dry during the summer months. It becomes a sizable river only after the confluence, east of Kabul, of its four major tributaries.

KABUL TIMES, THE. An English language, daily newspaper published under the auspices of the ministry of information and culture in Kabul since 1962. Before that time diplomats and foreign residents depended on newsletters in various languages, published by embassies and the ministry of information and culture. The ministry subsidizes the paper and provides the physical plant, but at times permitted the paper a measure of autonomy. After the Saur Revolt (April 1978) it became a mouthpiece of the Marxist government. President Nur Muhammad Taraki changed the name of the paper to *The Kabul New Times* to reflect the new ideology in Kabul. In the process of discarding ideological trappings, the Parchami regime restored the paper's former title.

KABUL TREATY OF 1921 See ANGLO-AFGHAN TREATY OF 1921.

KABUL UNIVERSITY. Kabul University is the major educational institution in Afghanistan. It was founded in 1932 with the establishment of the school of medicine with French and Turkish professors. Faculties of law and political science (1938), natural sciences (1941), economics (1957), home economics (1962), education (1962) engineering (1963), and pharmacy (1963) were eventually added. The University was inaugurated officially in 1946, when a president was appointed by the ministry of education and an academic senate was formed. In 1965, a university law was passed which provided for autonomous governance under an elected president.
A new campus was constructed with American financial assistance in 1964, and two years later the Soviet-directed Polytechnic Institute was education. The departments of agriculture, education, and engineering

were affiliated with American universities; law and political science enjoyed French support, and a consortium of German institutions was affiliated with the faculties of science and economics; the faculty of theology established links with al-Azhar University of Egypt. Outstanding graduates of Kabul University often won fellowships to continue their studies at affiliated institutions. In the 1960s, Kabul University became a center of political discourse and a training ground for cadres of the entire political spectrum. About half the student body lived in dormitories on campus. The leadership of the Islamist, Marxist, and nationalist parties emerged from its campus, where they would hone their oratorial skills and engage in verbal and often physical violence. Therefore, the Afghan government in 1968 banned political activities on campus.

After the Saur Revolt, the curriculum of Kabul University was changed to conform to Soviet models and Russian became a favored foreign language. Because of the need for manpower in the present war, graduates have at times been recruited directly from campus. Therefore, the student body has been greatly reduced in numbers (from 8,500 in 1976) and, in 1990, is said to be composed seventy percent of women. Of 800 teachers in the 1970s only 350 remained in the late 1980s. Politics has interfered in admissions and academic policies. Nevertheless, the university campus has continued to be a volatile center of student protest. President Najibullah proclaimed a "new educational policy" in 1990 which dispensed with much of the Marxist innovations. Also see EDUCATION and POLYTECHNIC INSTITUTE, KABUL.

KAFIR. Arabic, for an "unbeliever" or "infidel," a name popularly given to non-Muslims, but technically referring only to polytheist and "worshippers of idols," who do not have a "Book," or scripture. In Afghanistan Kafirs were the inhabitants of Kafiristan (q.v.) who remained pagans until they were converted to Islam in 1896. Kafirs are destined for hell, whereas "Peoples of the Book" (*ahl al-kitab*), such as Christians and Jews, are monotheists and not condemned to eternal hellfire. Also see DHIMMI.

KAFIRISTAN (lat. 35-30' N, long. 70-45' E). "The Land of the Infidels," was an area in eastern Afghanistan now called Nuristan (q.v.), the "Land of Light," meaning the light of the Islamic religion which was brought into the area by conquest in 1896. Kafirs and now Nuristanis are generally divided into two categories: free men who can own pasture for their animals and former slaves and craftsmen who did not own goats, sheep or cattle. These lower classes served as shepherds or craftsmen, making all the tools and structures in the communities.

There were no chiefs as such, but free men who demonstrated superior capabilities and generosity could gain leadership status and a corresponding influence in community affairs. Because the Kafirs inhabited valleys with dense forests, their material culture varied significantly from neighboring peoples. Kafirs sat on chairs and stools, unlike neighboring peoples who sat on knotted carpets. Their idols, houses, furniture, and other implements are carved from wood with intricate patterns. There existed little or no ceremony in marriage, as long as the bride price was paid and men could divorce their women at will. Polygamy was practiced. There is a considerable incidence of blond or red hair and blue or light eye color, which gave rise to legends that they were the descendants of the armies of Alexander the Great. Physical anthropologists speculate that Kafirs were contemporaries of the Arian migrations who moved south into India. The Kafirs had a reputation as excellent fighters, and their mountainous, forested country had given them a refuge from their Islamic neighbors. When the Durand Line (q.v.) included the larger part of Kafiristan within Afghan territory, Amir Abdur Rahman lost little time in taking control. He ordered his army to invade the country from all directions and within forty days controlled much of the area, although it took years to stamp out all resistance. Some Kafirs were deported to the Kuhdaman area, and others converted when offered gifts and protection from their traditional enemies. In 1906, Amir Habibullah changed the name of the country to Nuristan, and today all Nuristanis are Muslims. Also see NURISTAN.

KAJAKAI DAM (lat. 32-22' N, long. 65-11' E). A dam built as part of the Helmand valley irrigation and electrification project by the Idaho-based Morrison-Knudsen Company. The dam is 300 feet high, 887 feet long, and stores a reservoir which is 32 miles long and has a capacity of 1,495,000 acre-feet of water. It was completed in April 1953. Also see HELMAND VALLEY AUTHORITY.

KAKAR. A Pashtun tribe, which claims descent from Kak or Kakar. It is loosely organized into four divisions, all located across the Afghan border in Pakistan, south and southeast of Kandahar: the Sanzar Khel, located in the Zhob valley as well as in Pishin and Loralai; the Sanatia, who live primarily in the Quetta-Pishin district; the Targhara, in Pishin district; and the Sarghara, also in Pishin. The Kakars were merchant nomads (see POWINDAH) and traveled seasonally far into India.

KALA-I-NAO HAZARA See HAZARA.

KALAKANI, ABDUL MAJID. A poet and writer and one of the founders of the Marxist *Sho'la-yi Javid* (Eternal Flame) party, idealized by some as the "Afghan Che Guevara." He was born in 1939 at Kalakan in Kuhdaman district (north of Kabul). A biography, published by his organization, states that in 1945 his father and grandfather were hanged, but does not give any details. He went with members of his family into exile in Kandahar. After the Marxist takeover, he was one of the founders of the "Organization for the Liberation of the Afghan People," (*SAMA - Sazman-i Azadibakhsh-i Mardum-i Afghanistan*). SAMA was an underground movement whose aim was the formation of a working-class party, a united front with like-minded groups, and the creation of a "people's army." In 1980 it claimed to muster an armed force of about

8,000 men, officered by deserters from the Afghan army. It opposed the Pashtun-dominated PDPA. On February 27, 1980 Kalakani was arrested and executed on June 8. His brother Abdul Qayyum Rahbar (born in 1942 and educated at al-Azhar) succeeded to the leadership of SAMA, but was killed by unknown assailants on January 27, 1990 in Peshawar. A number of other members of this family have been assassinated since the beginning of the war. According to recent declarations, SAMA advocates the establishment of a "national democratic" government with universal suffrage, the protection of human rights and freedom of worship. It favors a federated state and the protection of minorities and denies that it is a Maoist party. It split and appears to be now a party of exiles.

KALAKANI, AMIR HABIBULLAH See HABIBULLAH.

KALANTAR. The term for an official during the reign of Amir Abdur Rahman who was to preserve law and order in urban areas. He was (similar to the official known as *muhtasib*) responsible for dealing with minor offenses and had powers of arresting an offender. He was also in charge of producing lists of names of all males age sixteen to twenty-eight in his district for the purpose of establishing a pool of possible recruits for the police force. The *kalantar* was chosen by the community, unlike the *muhtasib*, who was chosen by a *qazi*. Also see MUHTASIB.

KAM. Workers Intelligence Institute (*Da Kargarano Istikhbarati Mu'assasa*) of Pres. Hafizullah Amin which succeeded AGSA (q.v.), the security service of President Nur Muhammad Taraki, with minor changes in personnel. It was headed by Aziz Ahmad Akbari for two months (August-September 1979) and then by Hafizullah's nephew, Dr. Asadullah Amin who was killed with Hafizullah Amin on December 27, 1979. Akbari is the nephew of Asadullah Sarwari (q.v.) and joined him in virtual exile as first secretary at the Afghan embassy at Ulan Bator, Mongolia. For further details also see KHAD and AFGHAN SECURITY SERVICE.

KAMRAN, PRINCE. The son of Mahmud Shah (1800-1803 and 1809-18 [q.v.]) and "King of Herat" after the death of his father in 1830. During the wars of succession, following the ouster of Shah Zaman (q.v.), Kamran supported his father, who became Afghan king in 1800. Kamran recovered Peshwar for his father and was appointed governor of Kandahar. When his father was defeated by Shah Shuja (q.v.) in 1803, Kamran was driven from the city by Qaisar, son of Zaman Shah, and forced to seek safety in Herat. During the second reign of Shah Mahmud he established himself in Herat where Fateh (Fath) Khan, the oldest son of Paianda Khan (q.v.) was wazir. Kamran was ambitious and resented the power of the wazir; therefore, he had him blinded and subsequently killed. This started a struggle for power between the Sadozai and Muhammadzai branches of the Durrani clan, resulting in the fall the Sadozai dynasty. In 1818 Dost Muhammad (q.v.) captured the Kabul throne and in 1819, Shah Mahmud proclaimed himself king at Herat and made Kamran his wazir. Shah Mahmud died in 1829 under mysterious circumstances and was succeeded by Kamran. Kamran had the reputation of being a cruel and power-hungry man; he eventually ignored the conduct of the affairs of state and delegated much authority to his wazir, Yar Muhammad Alekozai (q.v.). Trying to reassert his power, he made preparations to rid himself of the wazir, but was captured and killed in 1842, after ruling Herat for twelve years - the last of the Sadozai rulers.

KANDAHAR (QANDAHAR, lat. 31-35' N, long. 64-45' E). A province in south-central Afghanistan with an area of 19,062 square miles and a population of 699,000. The province borders on Pakistan in the south, Helmand province in the west, Oruzgan in the north, and Zabul in the east. Kandahar is the second largest town in Afghanistan, lying at an elevation of 3,050 feet and comprising an area of 15 square miles; in the late 1970s, it had about 178,000 inhabitants. Its strategic location has made it a desirable spot for settlements since ancient times. It was the capital of Afghanistan from 1747-1775, when Timur Shah (q.v.) established his capital at Kabul. It is one of the major Pashtun cities and is inhabited mostly by Durranis, but also has a Hazara population and Afghans of other ethnic groups. The old, walled town, of which only traces remain, was built by Timur Shah. The mausoleum of Ahmad Shah (q.v.), founder of modern Afghanistan, is one of the major architectural features, as is the mosque of the *Khirqa Sharif,* where the cloak of the Prophet Muhammad is believed to be kept under lock and key. In the garden of the citadel overlooking the town is the shrine of Baba Wali which is frequently visited by pilgrims. On the same hill and carved into the rock are the "Forty Steps," *Chel Zina,* leading to a niche with 16th-century inscriptions from the days of the Moghol rulers Babur and Akbar Shah.

The city was part of the Achaemenid empire of Darius I (521-485 B.C.). It was rebuilt by Alexander the Great in 329 B.C., hence the name Kandahar, a corruption of "Iskander," the Eastern name for Alexander. Muslim Arabs conquered Kandahar in the seventh century. Thereafter Kandahar formed part of various Islamic kingdoms. In the 16th century the city was disputed between the rulers of the Safavid and Moghol empires until Mir Wais (q.v.), a Ghilzai chief of Kandahar, revolted against Safavid control and began the process which led to the establishment of Afghanistan in 1747. British forces occupied the city in two Anglo-Afghan wars and suffered one of their severest defeats nearby at the Battle of Maiwand (July 27, 1880) when Sardar Muhammad Ayub (q.v.) wiped out a British Brigade under General Burrows.

Kandahar is surrounded by fertile land, covered with orchards and famous for its grapes and pomegranates. The city is connected by a paved highway with Kabul, Herat, and Chaman, which lies on the Pakistan border. It has a major airport which the Afghan government had planned as a link in international travel. Its location made Kandahar an important trade and commercial center and key route to Iran and south into

Pakistan where a train link connects it with Karachi. Kandahar is dominated by Durranis who are rivals of the Ghilzai (q.v.) and tended to support ex-King Muhammad Zahir. When Russian troops evacuated the city, the Kabul government installed Nur-ul-Haq Ulumi, a Durrani, as governor. At present there appears to be a stalemate in the war, Kabul forces and mujahedin troops occupy different sections of town and have largely reduced their activities to defensive operations.

KAPISA (lat. 34-45' N, long. 69-30' E). A province created in 1964 with its capital at Mahmud Raqi and subsequently merged with Parwan province. It is named after the ancient town of Kapisa, located at the present Bagram, which was said to have been founded by Alexander the Great (fourth century B.C.) and the summer capital of Kanishka, the ruler of the Kushanid kingdom (second century A.D.). The city was destroyed in the 8th century.
The province is watered by the Nijrab, Panjshir, and Tagab rivers. It is known for an abundance of mulberries and pomegranates. Major industries include the Gulbahar textile mills and cement production in Jabal-us-Siraj. For further details see PARWAN.

KARAKUL See QARAQUL.

KARIZ Or QANAT. An underground water channel used widely in southern and western Afghanistan for the purpose of irrigation in areas where electricity and pumps are not available. Well-like shafts are drawn to the water table as much as 50 feet deep and connected by a channel which conducts water to fields some distance away. The channels are kept in working condition by dredging, a dangerous and difficult job, since a channel may collapse and bury the person working in it. As a result of the war in Afghanistan many kariz have fallen into disuse or have been destroyed and formerly irrigated land has been lost.

KARMAL, BABRAK. President and secretary general of the PDPA from January 1980 until May 1986, when Dr. Najibullah took over control of the Afghan government. Born in 1929 in Kabul, the son of Major General Muhammad Husain (one-time governor of Paktia province and probably a Ghilzai Pashtun). He adopted the pen name Karmal (friend of labor) in about 1954. A founding member of the PDPA, he was a student activist at Kabul University and known as a communist. Jailed from 1953 to 1956, he then worked in departments of the ministries of education and planning. In 1965 and 1969 he was elected to parliament as representative of Kabul. He was a member of the central committee and subsequently secretary of the central committee of the PDPA. As a result of a dispute with Nur Muhammad Taraki over leadership of the party in 1965, he led the Parcham faction until it reunited with the Khalqis in 1977 and became a member of the secretariat and the politburo. In 1978 he was imprisoned after the funeral of Mir

Akbar Khaibar (q.v.), but liberated as a result of the Saur Revolt. He was then elected vice-chairman of the revolutionary council and deputy prime minister of Afghanistan. In July 1978, the Khalqi regime purged the Parchami leadership, appointing Karmal Afghan ambassador to Czechoslovakia. In August, 1978, he was accused of plotting against the Khalqi government and stripped of party membership and all his positions. Restored to power with Soviet assistance, he succeeded Hafizullah Amin on Dec. 27, 1979. Karmal was described as an idealist, rather than a revolutionary. He was an eloquent orator in Dari and with Anahita Ratebzad (q.v.), an expert propagandist and the best known of the Marxist leadership. Having been restored to power with Soviet support, he was unable to consolidate his power and, in 1986, he was replaced by Dr. Najibullah. He left Afghanistan for Moscow, but returned to Kabul in June 1991 and does not hold any office.

KAWIANI, NAJMUDDIN AKHBAR. Member of the Parcham faction of the PDPA and member of the politburo since 1987. He served as secretary of the central committee of the PDPA from 1986 and head of the international affairs department and the organizational department from 1987. He was born in 1948 in Kabul province of Panjshiri parents and educated with an engineering degree. He did not hold any positions before the Saur Revolt. He is married to Jamila Palwasha, a member of the PDPA central committee. He was jailed with other Parchamis under Hafizullah Amin. After the founding of the Watan party, he became one of four vice presidents of its executive body.

KAZI Or KADHI See QAZI.

KAZIM BEY, CAPT. Delegated by Enver Pasha, the Ottoman minister of war, to accompany the Hentig-Niedermayer Expedition (q.v.) to Afghanistan for the purpose of winning Afghan support in World War I. When the group disbanded in May 1916, Kazim Bey remained in Herat until the end of the war and then proceeded to Russian Central Asia. Together with Barakatullah (q.v.), a Muslim-Indian member of the Hentig expedition, he conducted Pan-Islamic propaganda in Russian Turkestan. In September 1919 he accompanied the Afghan mission of Muhammad Wali (q.v.) to Moscow before he returned to Turkey.

KESHTMAND, SULTAN ALI. Member of the Parcham faction of the PDPA and at one time second in command in the goverment of Babrak Karmal. Born in 1935 in Kabul province of a Hazara family and educated in economics at Kabul University, he took a position in the ministry of mines and industries. He was elected to the PDPA central committee at its founding congress, siding with Babrak Karmal in his disputed with Nur Muhammad Taraki. After the Saur Revolt he was purged with other leading Parchamis and sentenced to death, but his sentence was commuted to 15 years imprisonment. At the return to Karmal he became a member of the politburo and a year later was appointed prime minister

(1981-88). Since 1988 he has held the position of secretary of the central committee and chairman of the executive committee of the council of ministers. In May 1990 he was appointed first vice president of the Republic of Afghanistan, the highest ranking Hazara in the PDPA. He was ousted from his position on February 28, 1991, and went to Moscow until July 1991. As a private individual he now attacks Pashtun chauvinism and demands equal representation in government for Afghan shi'as.

KHAD Now WAD. The State Information Service (*Khedamat-i Ittila'at-i Daulati*) of Babrak Karmal which evolved with some replacements in leadership out of AGSA (q.v.), established by Nur Muhammad Taraki, and KAM (q.v.) of Hafizullah Amin. It was headed by Dr. Najibullah before he succeeded to the position of general secretary of the PDPA and president of Afghanistan. Najibullah upgraded KHAD to ministerial status hence its new acronym WAD (*Wezarat-i Amniat-i Daulati*). General Ghulam Faruq Yaqubi (q.v.) succeeded Najibullah. The organization is reputed to control thousand operatives and informers, as well as the National Guard and other fighting units. They are the best trained and disciplined forces and are well paid and provisioned and a major source of Dr. Najibullah's power. WAD is now Parchami controlled and a balancing factor to the Khalqi strength in the military, which WAD has effectively penetrated. Its task appears to be similar to that of the KGB: (1) detecting and eradicating domestic political opposition; (2) subverting armed resistance; (3) penetrating opposition groups abroad; and (4) providing military intelligence to the armed forces. It is said to have been set up with the assistance of Soviet and East German intelligence officers. Also see KAM, AGSA, and AFGHAN SECURITY SERVICE.

KHADEM, QIAMUDDIN. A poet and writer who was vice-president of the Pashto Academy (q.v., 1941) and in 1943 director of the Pashto encyclopaedia project (see AFGHAN ENCYCLOPAEDIA SOCIETY). He served as editor of the *Ittihad-i- Mashriqi* (1942), *Tulu-ye Afghan* (1950), *Kabul Majalla* (1951), *Islah* (1953), *Zeri* (1955), *Haywad* (1963), and as publisher of *Afghan Wolus* (1969). He was born in 1907 in Kama, Nangarhar Province, and educated under the supervision of his father. He began his career as a teacher, but then turned to journalism. A founding member of *Afghan Millat* (q.v.). He was appointed a senator in 1965 and died in 1979.

KHAIBAR, MIR AKBAR. Chief Parchami party ideologue whose assassination sparked the Saur Revolt of 27th April 1978. Born in 1925 in Logar province, he attended Kabul Military School and became instructor in the Police Academy. Arrested in 1950 as a leftist agitator, he met Babrak Karmal in prison and became his ally and a founding member of the Democratic Peoples Party of Afghanistan. He was called "Ustad," Master, by his Parchami comrades and was for a time editor of *Parcham*, the party newspaper. His major activity was to recruit army officers for his party. He was assassinated on April 17, 1978, a day after he visited the air force base at Bagram, according to Parchami claims, by *Khalqis*, his communist rivals. The Marxists blamed the Daud government for the assassination and staged mass demonstrations in Kabul which led to the arrest of some party leaders. A few days later, members of the armed forces started the Saur coup which brought a Marxist government to power.

KHAIBAR PASS (lat. 34-1' N, long. 71-10' E). A historic pass leading through a gorge and barren hills from the Afghan border to Peshawar, Pakistan. It starts about ten miles from Peshawar, at Ali Masjid village, narrows to about 200 yards, and reaches its highest point at 3,518 feet. Eventually the pass widens and ends at Torkham, the Afghan frontier post. The population within the area of the pass is largely Afridi (q.v.). A narrow-gauge railroad, built by the British in the late 19th century, connects the pass with the Peshawar rail terminal. Britain gained control of the pass in the Treaty of Gandamak (q.v.) and this Afghan "gateway to India" is now on the Pakistani side of the Durand Line. Landi Kotal, located a few miles within the pass, is one of the smugglers' markets of the Frontier where one can buy foreign-made goods found only in the tribal area of Pakistan. The capture of Torkham by mujahedin troops and the seige of Jalalabad have severely curbed this lucrative trade, but will probably never end it.

KHALES, MUHAMMAD YUNUS. Leader (Amir) of the Hezb-iIslami (q.v.), one of two groups with the same name headquartered in Pakistan. Born in 1919 in Gandamak, Khugiani, and educated in Islamic law and theology. He is a radical Islamist and fervent anti-Communist and in the 1960's contributed articles to the conservative *Gahiz* newspaper. After the Daud coup in 1973 he was forced to flee to Pakistan, because he had made many enemies among Daud's supporters.

A member with Hekmatyar (q.v.) of Hezb-i-Islami, he seceded and formed his own group with the same name which fought the Kabul government in the Khugiani area. He often accompanies Jalaluddin Haqani (q.v.), his deputy, on raids inside Afghanistan. Other commanders of his include Abdul Haq in the Kabul area, Amin Wardak in Wardak, Abdul Ghani Barech in Nimruz, Haji Qadir in Nangarhar, Maulawi Baqi Ahmad in Farah, and Mullah Malang in Kandahar. Khales is opposed to universal suffrage, the emancipation of women, and has opposed Shi'a participation in the Afghan Interim Government, although he was a strong supporter of the AIG. In May 1991 he resigned from his position as interior minister of the AIG. Also see ISLAMIC ALLIANCE FOR THE LIBERATION OF AFGHANISTAN, ISLAMIST MOVEMENT, and HEKMATYAR.

KHALIFA See CALIPHATE .

KHALILI, KHALILULLAH. Afghan "Poet Laureate" whose collected works (diwan) have been published in three parts in 1960, 1975, and 1984. He was born in Kabul the son of Muhammad Husain Khan (financial secretary of Amirs Abdur Rahman and Habibullah). His father was executed in the early Amanullah period and Khalili moved with members of his family to Kohistan (q.v., now in Parwan province) until the rise of Habibullah Kalakani (q.v.) in 1929. He held various offices under the Tajik king, but then lived as a refugee in Tashkent and later with his uncle Abdul Rahim Khan (q.v.) in Herat. At Herat he wrote his first work, "History of Herat," which attracted wide acclaim. In 1944 Khalili and members of his family were imprisoned as supporters of the Safi revolt. After a period of exile in Kandahar, Khalili became lecturer at Kabul University (1948), and secretary of the Shah Mahmud cabinet (1949). In 1951 he became minister of press and information and chief adviser for press and information to King Zahir (1953). In 1965 he was elected a member of parliament from Jabal Seraj and founded the centrist *Wahdat-i-Milli* (National Unity) party. He was appointed Afghan ambassador to Saudi Arabia and Iraq from 1969-78. In 1985 he left Afghanistan and died in Pakistan two years later. He published a historical biography of Habibullah Kalakani (q.v.), called *A Hero from Khorasan*, in which he depicts the Tajik king as a noble mujahed and sensitive man. See HABIBULLAH KALAKANI.

KHALILULLAH, Lt. GEN. Minister of transport in Dr. Najibullah's government of May 1990, and member of the Parchami faction of the PDPA. He was born in 1944 in Shiwaki, Laghman, and educated at Ghazi school and at the military schools of Kabul. He was chief of staff of the 88th Corps and played an important role in the coups of 1973 and 1978. Arrested during the Khalqi period (July 1978 - December 1979), he was freed when the Parchamis returned to power and became commander of the Central Forces and the Kabul garrison. Appointed deputy minister of defense, he was removed from this post after a conflict with the minister of defense (General Abdul Qadir) and appointed governor of Herat and commander of the Western Zone. He is married to a Russian woman.

KHALIQYAR, FAZL HAQ. Appointed prime minister in May 1990, after serving as governor of Herat province and minister without portfolio (1988-90). He was born in 1930 in Herat and educated with a B.S. degree in economics from Kabul University. He served in various Afghan ministries and, after the Saur Revolt, was appointed adviser to the Finance ministry (1978- 79), deputy minister of finance (1985), and minister of state for financial and economic affairs (1985-87). He is not a member of the PDPA.

KHALIS See KHALES.

KHALQ. Meaning "people," is the name of a weekly newspaper first published on April 11, 1966 (and banned on May 23), by Nur Muhammad Taraki and edited by Bareq-Shafi'i (q.v.). The name of the paper was subsequently given to the Taraki/Amin faction of the PDPA, in distinction to the Parchamis (q.v., also named after their party organ) headed by Babrak Karmal. The newspaper was banned by the Afghan government six weeks after its first appearance. Also see PEOPLES DEMOCRATIC PARTY OF AFGHANISTAN and KHALQI (PARTY).

KHALQ (PARTY). One faction of the PDPA headed by Nur Muhammad Taraki (April 1978 to September 1979) and Hafizullah Amin (September to December 1979), popularly named so after its newspaper, *Khalq*. The party split into two major factions in 1965. Khalq continued under the leadership of Taraki until 1977 when it reunited with the Parcham faction, led by Babrak Karmal. Together they staged the Saur Revolt (April 27, 1978), but Taraki's faction captured the government and purged the leadership of Parcham. In December 1979 Karmal returned to power with Soviet support and Parcham has become the dominant faction of the PDPA. At the time of this writing only two of six party members in Dr. Najibullah's government (May 1990) are Khalqis: Muhammad A. Watanjar (q.v.) and Raz Muhammad Paktin (q.v.). The factions have never stopped fighting for supremacy, the latest manifestation of which was the attempted coup by the Khalqi minister of defense, Shahnawaz Tanai (q.v.). As a result of this a number of prominent Khalqis were expelled from the party, including Sayyid Muhammad Gulabzoi (q.v.), Niaz Muhammad Mohmand (q.v.), Gen. Nazar Muhammad (q.v.), Saleh Muhammad Zeari (Ziri) (q.v.), Asadullah Sarwari (q.v.) and others. For information on the PDPA, see PEOPLES DEMOCRATIC PARTY OF AFGHANISTAN.

KHAN. Title of tribal chiefs, landed proprietors, and heads of communities. Feudal khans were given honorary military ranks in exchange for providing levies for the Afghan army in case of national emergency. The title was also used in designating the tribe of the ruling family, *khan khel*, and in positions like *khan-i ulum*, chief justice. Now Khan is used like mister when placed after the name of a person.

KHAN, KHAN ABDUL GHAFFAR. Pashtun nationalist, acclaimed as the "Frontier Gandhi," because he advocated nonviolent means for gaining independence from Britain for the Frontier Afghans. He was born in 1890 in Utmanzai village in the North-West Frontier Province (NWFP) of India and educated in village schools and in high schools in Peshawar. He founded various organizations, including the *Khuda-i Khidmatgaran* (Servants of God), also called "Red-Shirts" (q.v.), and attracted many followers in the NWFP and Afghanistan. He was imprisoned many times by the British Indian and Pakistan governments and was always an honored guest at Kabul, where the Pashtunistan (q.v.) issue was strongly supported. King Amanullah gave him the title "Fakhr-i Afghan" (Pride of the Afghans) and he lived intermittently in Kabul as guest of the royal, republican, and Marxist governments. He died in Peshawar in the late 1980s and is buried in Jalalabad.

KHASHRUD (lat. 31-11' N, long. 62-1' E). A river which rises in the Siahband range, runs in a southwesterly direction past Dilaram and the village of Khash. From there it continues to Chakhansur in Nimruz province, circles Zaranj, and after a course of about 250 miles dissipates in the Hamun (q.v.) on the Iranian side of the border.

KHATAK, KHUSHHAL KHAN (1613-89). A famous Afghan warrior poet and tribal chief of the Khatak tribe who called on the Afghans to fight the Moghuls then occupying their land. He admonished Afghans to forsake their anarchistic tendencies and unite to regain the strength and glory they once possessed. But he was pessimistic, saying "The day the Pashtuns unite, old Khushhal will arise from the grave." Khushhal Khan was born near Peshawar, the son of Shahbaz Khan, a chief of the Khatak tribe. By appointment of the Moghul emperor, Shah Jehan, Khushhal succeeded his father in 1641, but Aurangzeb, Shah Jehan's successor, kept him a prisoner in the Gwaliar fortress in Delhi. After Khushhal was permitted to return to Peshawar he incited the Pashtuns to revolt. His grave carries the inscription: "I have taken up the sword to defend the pride of the Afghan, I am Khushhal Khattak, the honorable man of the age." The Khatak tribe of Khushhal Khan now lives in the area of Kohat, Peshawar, and Mardan in the North-West Frontier Province of Pakistan and numbers between 100,000 and 160,000 people.

KHILAFAT MOVEMENT See HIJRAT MOVEMENT.

KHORASAN. The word means the East or "Land of the Rising Sun," which is the name of a province in northeastern Iran and the historical name of an area which roughly corresponds to eastern Iran and Afghanistan at the time of Ahmad Shah (q.v., 1747-73). It was part of the Achaemenid and Sasanian empires, then conquered by the Muslim Arabs in A.D. 651- 52. Abu Muslim raised the "Black Banner" of the house of Abbas and with his Khorasanian army defeated the Umayyads, bringing the Abbasid Caliphs to power. Khorasan was virtually independent under the Tahirid, Saffarid, and Samanid dynasties (821-999), and part of Ghaznavid, Seljuk, and Khwarizm empires. The Mongols controlled the area and the Safavids fought the Uzbaks over Khorasan, before it became the heartland or Ahmad Shah's empire. Khorasan was called the "creadle of classical Persian culture."

KHOST (lat. 33-22' N, long. 69-52' E). A town and district (woleswali - see ADMINISTRATIVE DIVISIONS)) in Paktia province, which has seen severe fighting in the present war in Afghanistan because it lies astride of the supply line of the mujahedin forces. The town was commonly called "Little Moscow" because of the fact that many of the Marxist leadership are native to this area and therefore enjoyed the support of the population. Located only about 18 miles from the Pakistan border, the town had been besieged since 1986, when the land route was cut. After a concerted attack by a coalition of mujahedin groups, which started on March 14, the town was finally captured on March 31, 1991. The Kabul government declared a day of mourning and claimed that the mujahedin had armed support from Pakistan and violated the sanctity of the month of Ramazan to stage their attack. The mujahedin leadership, among whom Maulawi Jalaluddin Haqani had a prominent role, denied that they had Pakistani support. The number of refugees in Pakistan has been augmented by some 2,000 supporters of the Kabul regime who felt no longer safe in the area.

In addition to a limited amount of agriculture and livestock breeding, Khost supports a timber industry. It is one of the few wooded areas in Afghanistan and timber is smuggled to Pakistan where it fetches a good price. Because of the present war, government prohibitions of timber export to Pakistan are ignored and deforestation is resulting in irreparable harm.

KHOST REBELLION. A rebellion led by the Mangal (q.v.) tribe which seriously threatened the rule of King Amanullah. The revolt started in March 1924 in response to the king's reforms. The Mangals under Abdullah Khan and Mulla-i-Lang (the Lame Mulla) were able to establish a base in Khost and were about to advance on Kabul. At the same time Abdul Karim, son by a slave girl of ex-Amir Yaqub Khan (q.v.), escaped from British-Indian exile and joined the rebels. In April 1924, the rebels were beaten but not yet defeated. Sulaiman Khel and Ali Khel tribes (see GHILZAI) joined the revolt. In August, King Amanullah dramatically proclaimed holy war against them. But it was not until January 1925 that the rebels were defeated. Abdullah Khan and the Mulla-i-Lang were captured and executed together with 53 prisoners. The citizens of Kabul were treated to a victory parade, headed by Muhammad Wali Khan (q.v), which carried the booty, followed by almost 2,000 prisoners, including women and children, organized according to tribal affiliation. The prisoners were, in the words of the German representative in Kabul, "wild men with sullen, taciturn faces who did not take the least notice of the amir." The revolt slowed down the amir's process of reform until 1928, when King Amanullah again forced the process of Westernization.

KHUGIANI. A Durrani tribe settled primarily in the Jalalabad area, but also in Laghman and Kandahar. It is divided into three major clans: The Wazir, Kharbun, and Sherzad. They are neighbors of the Shinwaris (q.v.) and Ghilzais (q.v.). In 1928 they joined the Shinwaris and other tribes in a revolt which led to the ouster of King Amanullah. In the present war, the Khugianis make up the majority of the mujahedin forces of the Hizb of Yunus Khales.

KHULM See **TASHQURGHAN**.

KHURD KABUL (lat. 34-23' N, long. 69-23' E). A pass on the route between Kabul and Jalalabad where Ghilzai forces annihilated some 3,000 members of the British expeditionary force on January 8, 1842. See ANGLO-AFGHAN WARS.

KHURRAM, ALI AHMAD. Minister of Planning from 1974 until his assassination on November 17, 1977. According to an article by Zalmai Popal, an official in the ministry of planning, Ali Ahmad Khurram fell victim to President Daud's change of policy. Daud wanted to broaden economic ties with the West and discontinue "excessive reliance" on Soviet support in the process of developing the country. Arab and Iranian funds were expected to become available, and Khurram had instructions to speedily complete projects started with Soviet technical and financial assistance and not accept any new ones. The assassin, one Muhammad Marjan, is said to have had Khalqi connections but claimed to have acted "in the name of the Islamic Revolution." He was sentenced to imprisonment for life but was later freed in a general amnesty. Khurram was born in 1931 in Kabul and educated at Kabul University and in the United States, and began work in the ministry of planning in 1956.

KHUTBA. Friday sermon delivered at a congregational mosque. It has political significance because the Khateb (preacher) traditionally invokes the name of the recognized ruler. When Afghanistan was in rebellion against King Amanullah, preachers in disputed areas read the sermon "in the name of the Islamic king," to avoid indicating their loyalty. Also see ISLAM and MOSQUE.

KHYBER See **KHAIBAR**.

KIRGHIZ See **QIRGHIZ**.

KISHTMAND See **KESHTMAND**.

KIZILBASH See **QIZILBASH**.

KOH-I BABA (lat. 34-41' N, long. 67-30' E) . A mountain range extending from east to west across the center of Afghanistan and forming part of the Hindu Kush mountain massif. The range includes peaks rising over 16,000 feet and difficult passes reaching altitudes of 12,000 and 13,000 feet. North of the Koh-i- Baba the Turkestan plateau extends to the Amu Daria (q.v.).

KOH-I NUR. A diamond measured at 191 carats (subsequently cut in London to 108 carats) which was part of Nadir Shah Afshar's (q.v.) booty from the Moghul treasure of Delhi. After Nadir's assassination in 1747, the Koh-i-Nur (Mountain of Light) came into the possession of Ahmad Shah (q.v.), founder of the Durrani empire, who passed it on to his sons. As a result of internecine fighting between Afghan princes, Shah Shuja was forced to flee and seek the hospitality of the Sikh ruler Ranjit Singh (q.v.). The latter, took possession of the precious stone in 1813. When in 1849 the British defeated their erstwhile ally they took the Koh-i Nur from the Sikhs. The viceroy of India subsequently presented it to Queen Victoria and it has since been worn in the crowns of British queens (superstition has it that it brings misfortune if worn by men).

KOHISTAN (lat. 35-1' N, long. 69-18' E). A district in Parwan province north of Kabul. It includes the valleys of Tagao, Nijrao, Panjshir, Ghorband, and Charikar as well as collateral valleys. The population is largely Tajik and sunni Muslim. Habibullah Kalakani (q.v.), Afghan king for nine months, was a native of this district.

KUCHI. Kuchi (T.) literally means a person who migrates. In Afghanistan the term is applied to all nomads. In India the term Powindah is used for Kuchi. Also see POWINDAH.

KUNAR (lat. 35-15' N, long. 71-0' E). A province in northeastern Afghanistan with an area of 3,742 square miles and a population of about 250,000, which is composed principally of Nuristanis in the north and west and Pashtuns in the south and east. The two ethnic groups have long been at odds because of infringement by the Pashtuns on Nuristani land. The province is traversed by the Kunar river, which is fed by the Pech, Waigal, and Chitral streams, and runs in a southwesterly direction into the Kabul river near Jalalabad. It provides irrigation for corn, rice, and wheat cultivation, largely on a subsistence level. Kunar and Paktia provinces are the major forested areas in Afghanistan. The province borders on Pakistan in the east, Nangarhar province in the south, Laghman in the west, and Badakhshan in the north. The administrative center of the province is Asadabad, (near Chegha Sarai) which Afghans believe to be the birth place of Sayyid Jamaluddin Afghani (q.v.). In the 1970s Kunar province was absorbed into Nangarhar province, with Asadabad the administrative center of the sub-province (Loya Wolewali); but in 1977 it was again designated a province. After the withdrawal of Soviet forces in 1988, the Kabul government created Nuristan (q.v.) province from portions of Kunar and Laghman provinces. The remainder of Kunar was once again consolidated into Nangarhar province.

The mujahedin revolt began in 1978 in Kunar province. Within a year government bases were captured. Virtually all mujahedin groups operate in the province, but in Asadabad the "Wahhabi Republic" (or *Salafia -* Islamic revival movement) headed by Maulawi Jamilur Rahman and

Hekmatyar's Hizb are the major contenders. Based on Saudi and Kuwaiti support, Jamilur Rahman (q.v.) was able to win a large following, which has adopted the alien Hanbali school as its religious authority. Radical Islamist volunteers from Arab countries have provided both military and financial support to the "Wahhabis" forces. Daulat (State), another "Wahhabi" group headed by one Maulawi Afzal, has some strength in the areas of Kamdesh and Bargamatal. The "Wahhabis" have been accused of killing their prisoners and enslaving women, and have therefore come under criticism from other mujahedin groups. The Iraqi invasion of Kuwait has led to a cut in funds and greatly limited the activities of Jamilurrahman's forces. In February 1991 he announced his cabinet (See JAMILURRAHMAN) and proclaimed his area an "Islamic Amirate." The amirate was severely weakened as a result of an explosion of an ammunition store in their Asadabad headquarters, and in late August a combined force of Afghan mujahedin expelled the "Wahhabis" from Kunar province.

KUNDUZ (QONDUZ) (lat. 36-45' N, long. 68-51' E). A province in northern Afghanistan with an area of 2,876 square miles and an estimated population of 575,000. The province borders on the Soviet Union in the north, Takhar province in the east, Baghlan in the south, and Samangan in the west. The administrative capital of the state is the town of Kunduz with about 53,000 inhabitants. Kunduz river, called Surkhab at its source in the Koh-i-Baba range, meanders through Kunduz province and runs in a northwesterly direction into the Amu Daria. Afghanistan's cotton industry began in Kunduz in the 1940s. An industrial complex, the Spin Zar Company, grows and gins cotton and produces edible oil and soap. Sericulture was started at about the same time, and silk weavers produce colorful fabrics for local use and export. Uzbak garments, like the long-sleeved *Japan* (caftans), soft-soled boots, and embroidered caps, constitute an important home industry. The population is largely Uzbak, but Pashtuns and Persian-speakers as well as other ethnic communities can also be found.

KUSHANID KINGDOM. A kingdom which flourished during the first two centuries A.D. and included parts of the Indus valley, eastern Afghanistan, and Central Asia north to the Aral Sea. It was founded by Kajula Kadphises (40-78 A.D.) and enjoyed its cultural greatness under his successor Kanishka (d. 123 or 173 A.D.), whose capitals were located at Peshawar and Kapisa (now the site of Bagram, q.v.) as well as in Mathura, south of Delhi. The empire brought about a cultural renaissance and the spread of Buddhism into China. A hundred temples were built in Kapisa supporting some 6,000 monks. Gandharan art, representing a fusion of Hellenistic and Buddhist civilizations and art forms, testify to the splendor of the Kushanid court. The kingdom was destroyed by Hephtalite invaders in the 5th century.

KUSHANI, MAHBUBULLAH. Deputy prime minister in Prime Minister Khaliqyar's new cabinet, announced on May 27, 1990. Born in 1944 in Faizabad, Badakhshan, and educated at Habibia School in Kabul and at the University of Moscow, he worked in the department of water and power in Kabul and in the ministry of planning from 1980-87. He served as deputy chairman of the council of ministers and as president of the state committee for planning. He was first appointed deputy prime minister in 1987 and also served as first secretary of the central committee of SAZA, the Organization of Revolutionary Toilers of Afghanistan (*sazman-i zahmatkeshan-i kargari-yi afghanistan*) since 1985.

KUSHKAKI, BURHANUDDIN. Educator, journalist, and scholar of Islamic law, born in 1894 in Kushkak, Nangarhar province. He served as editor or director of many important Afghan newspapers, including *Ittihad-i Mashriqi* (Eastern Union) in Jalalabad, and *Aman-i Afghan* (q.v., Afghan Peace), *Habibul Islam* (q.v., Friend of Islam), and *Islah* (q.v., Reconstruction) in Kabul. He is the author of *Rahnama-yi Qataghan wa Badakhshan* (Guide to Qataghan and Badakhshan) and translated the Koran into Pashto. He died in 1953.

KUSHKAKI, SABAHUDDIN. Minister of information and culture, 1972-73, and member of the Cultural Council of the Afghan Resistance in Islamabad, Pakistan. Born in 1933, the son of Burhanuddin (above) and educated in Kabul and the United States, he embarked on a career in journalism. He served as editor of *Islah* (q.v., Reconstruction), news editor of Radio Afghanistan, 1960, and publisher of *Carawan*, 1968. He was jailed during the Khalqi period (May 1978-January 1980) and moved to Islamabad after Babrak Karmal's amnesty in 1980. He is engaged in cultural services for the Afghan resistance.

-L-

LAGHMAN (lat. 35-0' N, long. long. 70-15' E). A province in eastern Afghanistan which comprises an area of 2,790 square miles and a population of about 387,000. Laghman borders on Kapisa in the west, Badakhshan in the north, Kunar in the east, Nangarhar on the south, and Kabul province in the southwest. The administrative center is the village of Mehterlam.

According to local mythology, Laghman got its name from Lamech, father of Noah, whose ark is supposed to have landed on Kund mountain, which forms part of the Kafiristan mountain range. From Lamech the name changed to Lamakan and Laghman. Lamech was supposed to have taken the country from the Kafirs, but was killed in the battle. Sultan Mahumd of Ghazni, inspired by a dream, went to Mehtarlam and built a tomb over the presumed grave of Lamech.

Originally occupied by Kafirs, the area was subsequently taken over by Jabbar Khel and Abu Bakar Khel Ghilzais.

LALMI. Land cultivated without the benefit of irrigation.

LANGUAGE GROUPS. Three languages predominate in Afghanistan -- Pashto, Dari (or Farsi), and Turki (including Uzbak, Turkoman, and Qirghiz). No reliable statistics exist, but Pashto is said to be the language of about six to six and one-half million Afghans. Pashto-speakers are the dominant group and were until recently the only ones called Afghans, whereas the others were known by their ethnic appellation (Tajik, Baluch, etc.). The Pashtuns predominate in the south of Afghanistan and in the cities of Kandahar and Jalalabad, although they can be found in smaller communities in most parts of the country.
Second in numbers are the speakers of Dari and its dialects, including Hazaragi, spoken by the Hazara. They number about 5 million and predominate in the center, northwest, and northeast of Afghanistan as well as in urban areas. Dari is still the predominant language in education, although the Afghan government has made a great effort to make Pashto the national language. The Afghan constitution of 1964 recognized both Pashto and Dari as official languages of Afghanistan. Turkic languages include Uzbak, with one million speakers the largest of this group of languages, followed by Turkoman, Moghol, and Qirghiz, spoken by about 150 thousand people. The Baluch, Brahui, and Nuristani languages are spoken by fewer than 500,000. Although there exist groups of Arab descent, none of them presently speaks Arabic or an Arabic dialect. Indian languages are spoken by small groups, including Hindu and Sikh citizens of Afghanistan. Most Afghans are bilingual and most newspapers carry articles in both Pashto and Dari. Only since the Saur Revolt has an effort been made to cultivate other minority languages. The "homogenizing" effort at creating an Afghan nation out of many nationalities gave way to a policy of cultural autonomy when the Marxist government recognized Uzbak, Turkmani, Baluchi, Pashai, and one Nuristani dialect as "national languages." Newspapers have appeared in these languages and radio and television have offered programs in minority languages. Also see ETHNIC GROUPS.

LASH JUWAIN (lat. 31-43' N, long. 61-37' E). A small town and administrative district in the southwestern corner of Farah province. The name is a combination of Lash, a fort on the Farah river, and Juwain, the surrounding plain, and is also written Lash-o-Juwain or Lash-i-Juwain. The country surrounding the town is scattered with ruins testifying to a prosperous past which ended with Mongol invasions. The land is fertile and in the 1970s supported an agricultural population of some 15,000.

LASHKARGAH (lat. 31-35' N, long. 64-21' E). Capital of Helmand province with about 21,600 inhabitants in the 1970s and also the site of an ancient town built by Sultan Mahmud of Ghazni in the tenth century. It is located on the Helmand river, a few miles south of the main road linking Kandahar and Herat. The Ghurids sacked the town in 1150 A.D., but rebuilt it in new splendor. It was irreparably destroyed by the hordes of Genghiz Khan (1226). Because of its strategic location, Afghan rulers constructed a number of forts on the site. A visitor to the area at the turn of the century observed the fortified plateau "covered thickly with the remains of towers, forts, and palatial buildings, which exhibit traces of great architectural skill, and afford evidence of the existence at one time on this site of a large and important city, fortified with unusual skill and strength, and inhabited by a people who combined a knowledge of military art with considerable taste and culture" (Gazetteer 2).

The town was called Lashkari Bazar by the local population as well as Kala-i Bist or Bost. Also see HELMAND.

LAW See ISLAMIC LAW.

LAWRENCE, COLONEL T.E. The Englishman of "Lawrence of Arabia" fame is suspected by many Afghans to have been a link in a conspiracy to topple King Amanullah from his throne. The Afghan government learned from reports in the London *Sunday Express* of September 13, 1928, that Lawrence was on the Afghan border on a "secret" mission. He was indeed there under the alias of "Shaw." The *Aman-i Afghan* (q.v.) of December 12, 1928, commented that it was certain that the man who had "gathered the miserable Arabs in a revolt against the Turks" was up to mischief in Afghanistan. But the paper debunked his effectiveness on the Afghan Frontier, for after all "he is only an Englishman." The London *Daily News* of December 5, 1929, reported that Lawrence was in India, busily learning Pashto and "inferred he intends to move into Afghanistan." Much of the non-British press was convinced that this was a conspiracy in support of Habibullah Kalakani (q.v.). No sources have been found in British archives to support this conspiratorial theory, and the British government denied all charges. In a letter to Edward Marsh, dated June 10, 1927, Lawrence reported: "... do you know that I nearly went there [Kabul], last week? The British Attaché at Kabul is entitled to an airman clerk, and the Depot would have put my name forward, if I had been a bit nippier on a typewriter." Lawrence spent eighteen months in India, most of this time in Karachi, but a short time also in Miranshah (across the border from Paktia province) as well as one weekend in Peshawar. After the British minister at Kabul, Sir Francis Humphrys, frantically appealed to London, Lawrence was finally sent back to Britain.

LAYEQ, SULAIMAN. An acclaimed poet and writer in Pashto and Dari who was a founding member of the PDPA, member of the politburo, the party secretariat and president of the Afghan Academy of Sciences (q.v.). He is the author of the Marxist national anthem. Born on October 7, 1930 of the Sulaiman Khel (q.v.) tribe, he studied Islamic sciences but was expelled from school because of his leftist activism. He was employed with *Haiwad* newspaper and Radio Kabul and in 1968 became publisher and editor of the Marxist newspaper *Parcham*. After the Saur Revolt he became minister of radio and television, but was purged by the Khalqi regime and imprisoned. After the Parchami faction of the PDPA came to power, Layeq was appointed president of the Academy of Sciences (April 1980) and minister of frontier affairs (1981). In the Najibullah government he has remained a member of the politburo and the secretariat of the central committee and became first vice president of the Watan party.

LOGAR (lat. 33-50' N, long. 69-0' E). A province south of Kabul with an area of 1,702 square miles and a population estimated in the late 1970s at 424,000 (in 1989 about 176,000 of whom were refugees in Pakistan). The province is bounded in the west by Wardak province, in the north by Kabul, in the east by Nangarhar, in the south by Paktia, and in the southwest by Ghazni province. The administrative center is the town of Pul-i Alam, located about 50 kilometers south of Kabul. The population is largely Pashtun of the Ahmadzai tribe and some Tajik in the Khoshi area. In 1979, about 80 percent of the population were farmers and the area was called the "granary of Kabul." Fruit, specifically grapes and apples, and vegetables were the major cash crops. This is supplemented with animal husbandry and trading. The present war has caused considerable damage to the economy of the province.

LOHANI Or LOWANA. Nomadic tribes, also called Powindas, who conducted cross-border trade with India. They are Ghilzai Pashtuns, and claim descent from Ibrahim, second son of Ghalzoe, whose mother called him "Loeday," meaning he is the "greater son." They are now located in the NWFP of Pakistan in the area of Kohat, Bannu, and Peshawar. The 16th-century Afghan Lodi dynasty of India is named after the Lohanis. Also see POWINDAH.

LOINAB, See ALI AHMAD.

LOYA JIRGA. Great (or national) council, it is the highest organ of state power which Afghan rulers convened to decide matters of national importance. It was first held by Mir Wais (q.v., 1709-15), the Hotaki Ghilzai chief who revolted against the Persian occupation of Kandahar. Ahmad Shah's assumption of the throne was legitimized by a Loya Jirga of tribal chiefs, as were the constitutions of King Amanullah (1923) and Zahir Shah (1964). When in October 1941 the Allies forced the Afghan government to expel all Axis nationals, the Loya Jirga reluctantly gave its approval, but insisted that they be given free passage through Allied territory.

Amir Abdur Rahman's Loya Jirga was composed of *sardars*, the heads of the royal families; important *khans*; and high religious leders. The 1964 Loya Jirga was composed of 455 members representing the following sectors:

Elected members   176

National assembly	176
Appointed by the King	34
Senate members	19
Cabinet members	14
Supreme court members	5
Constitutional committee	7
Constitutional advisory commission	24

(Dupree, 1973)

Some jirgas were easily manipulated and no more than rubber stamps of the decisions of the Afghan ruler, but at times jirgas defied the monarch. A jirga convened by King Amanullah in Paghman in August 1928 forced the king to compromise and rescind some of his reforms. In the present war both the mujahedin and the Kabul government have convened Loya Jirgas in support of their cause. However, the validity of the jirgas was disputed because they were not representative of the Afghan population and, in the case of the mujahedin, were convened outside Afghan territory.

-M-

MACNAGHTEN, SIR WILLIAM. British chief secretary to the Indian government, appointed envoy and minister to the court of Shah Shuja (q.v.), after the occupation of Kabul on August 7, 1839, in the first Anglo-Afghan war (q.v.). With the benefit of hindsight, historians gave him a good measure of the blame for the British debacle which also cost Sir William his life. Soon after the invasion it became apparent that Shah Shuja would not be able to maintain himself on the throne without the protection of a British garrison. Therefore Macnaghten was prepared for an indefinite occupation of Afghanistan. He became the power behind an insecure throne, paying subsidies to tribal chiefs and directing the affairs of the country to safeguard British imperial interests. Deceived by the apparent quiescence of the Afghan chiefs, he permitted the families of British officers to come to Kabul to join a colony of some 4,500 soldiers and 11,500 camp-followers. All seemed well and, as a reward for his services, Macnaghten was to receive the much coveted governorship of Bombay; Alexander Burnes (q.v.) was to succeed him in Kabul. But Afghan forces began to harass the British lines of communication and, eventually, a mob in Kabul attacked Burnes' residence and killed the members of the mission. Realizing the danger of his situation, Macnaghten concluded a treaty with the dominant tribal chiefs which provided for the withdrawal of the British army to India. But he had still not given up hope. Trying a divide-and-rule tactic, the envoy bribed some of the sardars after contracting with Sardar Muhammad Akbar (q.v.), the ambitious son of Amir Dost Muhammad. When the latter discovered the duplicity, he killed Macnaghten in a "fit of rage." Only a few survived the retreat of the "Army of the Indus" (See ANGLO-AFGHAN WARS, SIMLA MANIFESTO, and AFGHAN FOREIGN RELATIONS).

MADRASA. A school of higher education in Islamic sciences usually attached to a principal mosque. In Afghanistan, as elsewhere in the Islamic world, education was the domain of the Islamic clergy. Mullas (q.v.) taught the basics, reading and recitation of the Koran. The *ulema*, doctors of Islamic sciences, trained the judges (*qazis*), *muftis* (q.v.), and other members of the religious establishment. In the 15th century, Timurid rulers (see TIMUR-I LANG) established famous madrasas in Herat, some of which continued as major centers of education until the early 19th century, but invasions and civil wars led to a general decline of the educational system. After Amir Abdur Rahman ascended the throne in 1880, he founded the Royal Madrasa at Kabul which became the foremost institution of its type. When Amir Habibullah founded Habibia School in 1904 as a secular school, he established a dual system of education which has continued to this day. Also see EDUCATION.

MAHAZ-I MILLI-YI AFGHANISTAN. The National Islamic Front of Afghanistan (NIFA) was founded in 1979 in Peshawar as an armed resistance movement by Sayyid Ahmad Gailani (q.v.). It is a liberal, nationalist, Islamic party and, according to its manifesto, advocates both the protection of the national sovereignty and territorial integrity of Afghanistan and the establishment of an interim government which would draft a national and Islamic constitution with the separation of executive, legislative, and judicial powers. It demands an elected and free government which would guarantee such fundamental rights as free speech, freedom of movement, the protection of private property, and social justice, including medical care and education for all Afghans. Until establishment of a democratically elected government in Afghanistan, NIFA aims to strengthen the unity and solidarity of the mujahedin movements and its Afghan Interim Government (AIG), to prepare the draft of a national-Islamic constitution and its eventual implementation. In its foreign relations, NIFA wants good relations with its neighbors and supports the principles of the Charter of the United Nations, the Declaration of Human Rights, and the Islamic Organization Conference. NIFA favors a policy of nonalignment, respect for the rights of all nations, and condemns expansionistic and hegemonistic policies. It is part of a loose coalition of traditional, or moderate, mujahedin groups. Also see GAILANI, SAYYID AHMAD.

MAHMUDI, ABDUR RAHIM. Founder and publisher of *Shu'la-yi Javid* (q.v., Eternal Flame), a leftist weekly newspaper in Pashto and Dari, which was banned after nine issues in July 1969 because it advocated armed struggle to achieve power. In the 1970s his brothers founded the New Democratic Organization of Afghanistan (*Sazman-i Demokratik-i Navin-i Afghanistan*, commonly called the *Shu'la-yi Javid* party after the name of its newspaper. He was imprisoned from 1969 to 1972 and went underground in 1973 when Muhammad Daud proclaimed the republic. Several members of his family were killed during the Khalqi period and he was forced to flee abroad. He now resides in Germany.

MAHMUDI, ABDUR RAHMAN. Founder of *Nida-yi Khalq* (q.v., Voice of the People), a biweekly Dari/ Pashto language newspaper in 1951 which was banned after 29 issues. Born in 1909 and educated in Kabul, Mahmudi was one of the first graduates of the faculty of medicine of Kabul University. Elected to parliament in 1949, he was later jailed for ten years; he died a few months after he was freed in 1963. His brothers, Hadi and Rahim (see above), founded the *Shu'la-yi Javid* (q.v.) party.

MAHMUD OF GHAZNI (998-1030). Son of Sebuktigin and creator of the Ghaznavid empire (q.v.) which had its capital at Ghazni (q.v.), southwest of Kabul, and controlled an empire extending from eastern Iran to the Indus river and from the Amu Daria to the Persian Gulf. Muslims see him as the epitome of the Ghazi warrior, the "Breaker of Idols," as he called himself, and Hindus remember him as the plunderer of Hindustan. He lavished the treasures he amassed in India on a court that was famous for its wealth and splendor and for being a center of intellectual life where poets like Firdausi (q.v.), author of the *Shahnama*, (Book of Kings), the historian Baihaqi (q.v., d. 1077), the philosopher al-Farabi (d. 950) and the scholar Biruni (q.v., 973-1048) flourished. The British historian, Sir Percy Sykes, called Mahmud "a great general who carefully thought out the plan of each campaign that he engaged in," who was not a fanatic and "whose encouragement of literature and science and art was as remarkable as his genius for war and for government." Mahmud's tomb was spared Ghorid (q.v.) destruction and can still be seen in the outskirts of Ghazni. See GHAZNAVID DYNASTY and GHORID DYNASTY.

MAHMUD PACHA, SAYYID. Also called Babu Jan, a spiritual leader to whom Amir Shir Ali (q.v.) gave some territory in the Kunar valley as endowment. In 1868 Mahmud Pacha revolted against Azam Khan (q.v., 1867-69) who was then nominally Amir. On the return of Amir Shir Ali to power Mahmud Pacha was appointed a member of the newly-formed advisory council at Kabul, but for a time was deprived of his chiefship. Amir Abdur Rahman (q.v.) confirmed him in his position, but gradually deprived him of his independence and forced him to remit revenues to Kabul. He revolted against the amir but was forced to accept exile in India. His descendants, called the Sayyids of Kunar, have held important positions in 20th century Afghanistan. Afghan historians claim that the great pan-Islamist, Sayyid Jamaluddin Afghani, is a descendant of the Kunari sayyids. See AFGHANI, JAMALUDDIN.

MAHMUD SHAH (1800-03 and 1809-18). One of the twenty-three sons of Timur Shah (q.v.) who was engaged in an internecine struggle for power. He was governor of Herat, and from this base successfully fought his brother Zaman Shah (q.v.) for the Kabul throne. He became Afghan king in 1800, but did not show great interest in the conduct of state affairs and delegated much authority to his Barakzai ministers Fath Khan and Shir Muhammad. However, internecine warfare continued and, in 1803, Shah Shuja, the seventh son of Timur Shah, captured Kabul and made Mahmud his prisoner. Mahmud managed to escape and, with the help of Fath Khan, moved against Kandahar in 1809 and subsequently on Kabul, regaining the throne in 1813, where he ruled until 1818 when he was again driven from Kabul. He fled to Herat where he enjoyed all the "honors of sovereignty" while his son Kamran held all real power. Mahmud was poisoned by his ambitious son Kamran (q.v.) in 1829.

MAHSUD. A Pashtun tribe in Waziristan in the North-West Frontier Province of Pakistan counting about 70,000 members. *The British Handbook of the Indian Army* describes them as "democratic," permitting any tribesman the opportunity to rise to the position of chief "if he distinguishes himself in bravery or wisdom," and says approvingly that their "physique and stamina are good, and they are highly spoken of as soldiers." The Mahsuds have frequently been involved in border wars and supported the forces of Nadir Khan (q.v.) in the third Anglo- Afghan war (q.v.) and on his conquest of Kabul in 1929.

MAIDAN (NOW WARDAK) (lat. 34-15' N, long. 68-0' E). A province in east-central Afghanistan which is now called Wardak. See WARDAK.

MAIMANA (lat. 35-55' N, long. 64-47' E). A town in northern Afghanistan with about 38,000 inhabitants, mostly Uzbaks, and the capital of Fariab province. Maimana was at one time the capital of a semi-independent *khanate* (chiefship, from *khan*, chief) and a dependency of the ruler of Kabul.
When the Persian ruler Nadir Shah died in 1747, a soldier of fortune and comrade-in-arms of Ahmad Shah, the first Afghan king, was appointed *wali*, governor, of Maimana and Balkh on the condition that he provide a certain number troops upon request. He was an Uzbak named Haji Khan and upon his death his fiefdom was passed on to his son Jan Khan. But Timur Shah (q.v.) reduced the size of the fiefdom by taking Balkh and Akcha under the direct control of Kabul. Jan Khan's son fought over the succession and one son, Ahmad Khan, was able to rule from 1798 to 1810. Because of his misrule, he was assassinated by the people of Maimana and replaced by his nephew Allah Yar Khan who ruled until his death in 1826. Nizrab Khan, the oldest son of Ahmad Khan, succeeded but was involved in numerous wars and was eventually poisoned in 1845. Wazir Yar Muhammad (q.v.), ruler of Herat, made war against Maimana in 1846 and kept the province under the control of Herat. The *khans* of Maimana tried to stay in power by playing off one force against another, including the Shah of Iran and the Amir of Bukhara, but in 1861 they had to resubmit to control by Herat, and in the 1880s, Amir Abdur Rahman took direct control of the *khanate*.

Maimana was said to have had from 15 to 18 thousand inhabitants in 1845, but its population was greatly reduced as a result of protracted warfare and had no more than about 16 to 17 thousand inhabitants in 1973. More recently, the town and surrounding districts have greatly increased in population as a result of industrial development and internal migration. The town now has a modern grid system of streets with bungalow-style housing. Little is known of recent developments or of the social and economic impact of the present war in Afghanistan upon this town.

MAIMANAGI, GHULAM MUHAMMAD MUSAWWER. Founder and director of the Kabul School of Fine Arts. Born in 1873 in Maimana province, he moved to Kabul when he was eight years old and studied painting and techniques of enameling. After advanced study in Berlin he embarked on a career of teaching, training an entire generation of Afghan artists. He died at the age of 62 in Kabul. The Kabul Institute of Fine Arts was named after him.

MAIWAND, BATTLE OF. A battle during the second Anglo-Afghan war in which Sardar Muhammad Ayyub (q.v.) defeated the British general Burrows near the village of Maiwand, northwest of Kandahar, on July 17, 1880, wiping out the 66th British regiment to a man. Legend has it that Malalai, a tribal maiden, used her veil as a banner to incite the Afghan forces to heroic deeds. The defeat at Maiwand was a factor in convincing the British occupation forces that Afghanistan could not be held at a tolerable cost, leading to the recognition of Sardar Abdur Rahman (q.v.) as the new king.

MAIWANDWAL, MUHAMMAD HASHIM. Prime Minister (1965-67) and founder of the Progressive Democratic Movement (*jam'iat-i dimukrat-i mutaraqi*), whose program he announced on Radio Afghanistan in August 1966. It recognized Zahir Shah (q.v.) as the "personification of national unity" and advocated a program of action "in accordance with the principles of Islam, constitutional monarchy, nationalism, democracy and socialism" and aimed at reforms in the "economic, social, cultural, civic, moral and spiritual spheres" of Afghan national life. He published the weekly Persian/Pashto newspaper *Musawat* in January, 1967, to propagate his ideas. He resigned in 1967 because of ill health. Born in 1919 and educated at Habibia (q.v.) high school in Kabul, he embarked on a career as editor of *Itifaq-i Islam* (Agreement of Islam, 1942-45) in Herat and subsequently as editor of the daily newspaper *Anis* (q.v.). President of the press department, 1951. He served as deputy minister of foreign affairs in 1955 and as ambassador to Britain (1956), Pakistan (1957-58), the United States (1958-63), and again Pakistan (1963). He was imprisoned when Muhammad Daud took power in 1973 and was killed in jail, reputedly under torture. The government announced that he had committed suicide, but sentenced him posthumously to death in December 1973.

MAJLIS. Originally the name of a tribal council (from A. *jalasa*, to sit with someone) in pre-Islamic Arabia which conducted the affairs of a tribe. Thus, the name was used for a parliament or similar representative body. In Afghanistan the term was used for the senate (*majlis-i ayan*); the Pashtu equivalent of *majlis* is the *jirga*. See JIRGA and LOYA JIRGA.

MAJRUH, SAYYID BAHA'UDDIN. Professor of philosophy and sociology at Kabul University and president of the Afghan Historical Society (1972) who fled Afghanistan after the Saur Revolt and founded the Afghan Information Centre in Peshawar. He published the *Monthly Bulletin*, which is an independent newsletter reporting on the events in the Afghan war. He was assassinated in Peshawar in February 1988 by unknown assailants who did not share his moderate views. Born in 1928 in Kunar province, the son of Sayyid Shamsuddin (q.v.), he was educated at Istiqlal high school and studied in Britain, Germany, and France where he obtained the Ph.D degree. He was the author of numerous publications, including *Azhdaha-yi Khudi* (Dragon of Selfishness) which was translated from Dari into French and published under the title *Voyageur de Minuit*.

MAJRUH, SAYYID SHAMSUDDIN. Born in 1910, the son of Sayyid Hazrat Shah. He became a member of parliament in 1935, and inspector in the Afghan National Bank in 1939. In 1950 he was appointed president of the department of tribes, and minister of justice in 1963, and in 1966 ambassador to Cairo. In 1989 he protested the influence of the Pakistan government. He has been living in the United State since 1990.

MALIK. A "big man" or "petty chief" among the Pashtuns who possesses influence rather than power. He is a leader in war and an agent in dealings with representatives of the government. The term is synonymous to *arbab* in the west, and *beg* and *mir* in the north of Afghanistan. In non-Pashtun areas, a malik is elected from among local landowners and acts as middleman in the collection of taxes and other services demanded by the central government.

MALIKYAR, ABDUL AHAD. A general and civil and military commander in various provinces from 1930 to 1951, when he became minister of interior (1951-53). Known as Abdul Ahad Khan, before the family adopted the name Malikyar (assistant, or friend, of the king), he was born in Ghazni in 1902, the son of Brigadier Abdul Ahmad. After attending Habibia School and military college in Kabul and Turkey, he embarked on a career in the armed services and advanced quickly to officer with the general staff. He fought Habibullah Kalakani (q.v.) and became aide-de-camp to Nadir Shah. He died in 1956.

MALIKYAR, ABDULLAH. Minister of finance (1958), deputy prime minister (1963) and subsequently Afghan ambassador in London (1964), Washington (1966-76), and Tehran (1976). Born in 1908 in Kabul, the son of Brig. Abdul Ahmad of Ghazni, he was educated in Kabul and

Tehran. He became governor of Herat in 1944 (and again in 1949) and served as minister of commerce (1957). In 1952 he was president of the Helmand development project. He has been living in the United States since 1980.

MANGAL. A Pashtun tribe which inhabits parts of the Kurram valley and Zurmat in Paktia (q.v.) province. The Mangals have always been jealous of their independence and fought Afghan rulers and British alike. In 1924 they were the major force behind the Khost rebellion which seriously threatened the government of King Amanullah. In the present war they have supported the mujahedin. See KHOST REBELLION.

MANGAL, MUHAMMAD SARWAR. Member of the Parchami faction of the PDPA and appointed deputy prime minister in 1988 and again in the new cabinet of May 1990. Born in 1945 in Paktia province, he obtained degrees in economics from Kabul University and an institution in the Soviet Union. In 1978 he was appointed deputy minister of public works but shortly thereafter was purged from the government with other Parchamis and imprisoned until the end of the Khalqi period. He became deputy minister of higher and vocational education in 1980, and minister (1982-83). Served as president of the state planning committee, 1983-86, and as ambassador to Budapest, 1986-88, and Belgrade, 1990.

MANGAL REVOLT See KHOST REBELLION.

MAQSUDI, ABDUL HUSAIN. Founder and leader of the *ittihad-i mujahidin-i Islami* (Union of Islamic Fighters), a Hazara group which operates outside the Hazarajat and has headquarters in Quetta, Pakistan. Born in 1933 in Ghazni province and educated privately, he represented Nawor in Parliament (1965-73). In 1979 he founded his mujahedin group and is said to have played an important role in coordinating the flow of supplies from Pakistan to the Hazarajat.

MARGO, DASHT-I (lat. 30-45' N, long. 63-10' E). An extensive, almost waterless desert lying between the Helmand and Khash rivers, extending from eastern Nimruz province to western Helmand province. The highway from Kandahar to Herat passes to the north of it. The desert was frequented by Baluch herders during certain times of the year but it was impassable for anyone who did not know the scant sources of water.

MASJID See MOSQUE.

MAS'UD, AHMAD SHAH (MASSOUD). One of the most successful and most publicized, active mujahedin leaders in the Panjshir valley of Parwan province, north of Kabul. He withstood numerous Russian invasions into his territory; but in 1983 concluded a temporary truce with Soviet forces, which was described as a tactical measure since it did not prevent him from carrying out attacks elsewhere. He organized a supervisory council and is one of few commanders who sought to set up a civil administration, instill discipline in his troops, and use modern military principles of tactical warfare. He is a member of the *Jam'iat-i Islami-yi Afghanistan* (q.v.), headed by Professor Burhanuddin Rabbani (q.v.), which is largely of non-Pashtun background. After the withdrawal of the Soviet troops from Afghanistan he was able to extend his territorial control, establishing his headquarters at Taluqan. His group was involved in bloody clashes with Gulbuddin Hekmatyar's *Hizb-i Islami* (q.v.) which resulted in considerable casualties on both sides. In October 1990 Mas'ud participated in a meeting of mujahedin commanders from many parts of Afghanistan to coordinate their efforts and subsequently came to Pakistan where he and Hekmatyar appeared to have reconciled their differences. Because of his successes, Mas'ud is called "The Lion of Panjshir" by his admirers. Born in 1956, he was educated at Istiqlal High School and the Military Academy, where he graduated in 1973. He was a member of the radical Islamist movement. See ISLAMIST MOVEMENT.

MAULAWI (MAWLAWI). A graduate from a *madrasa*, college of Islamic studies; also an *alim* (pl. *ulama*, q.v.), doctor of Islamic sciences.

MAZAR-I SHARIF (lat. 36-42' N, long. 67-6' E). Capital of Balkh (q.v.) province with an estimated population of 70,000 and at one time also the name of a province which included the present Jozjan, Balkh, and Samangan provinces. Mazar-i Sharif, located about 13 miles east of Balkh village, is named "The Noble Tomb" according to a local claim that the Caliph Ali (656-61) is buried in the city (Najaf in present Iraq is generally accepted as the burial place). According to that claim, Ali's body was placed on the back of a white camel which was permitted to wander about. It was decided to bury the caliph on the spot where the camel eventually halted. Two cupolas were constructed over the tomb by Sultan Ali Mirza in the early fifteenth century. Subsequently a great mosque and shrine was built in its location and Mazar-i-Sharif became an important place of pilgrimage. As the town grew it eventually superseded Balkh in importance and became the capital of the province. (McChesney, 1991, quotes the twelfth-century *Tuhfat al-Albab*, describing the discovery of Caliph Ali's grave as the result of a dream by the citizens of the village of al-Khayr, the site of Mazar-i Sharif. The tomb was rediscovered in the fifteenth century, and Abdur Rahman Jami and Abdul Ghafur Lari, a student of the Herati poet Jami, claim that the fifth Shi'a imam, Muhammad Baqir, "charged Abu Muslim with the task of transporting the body of Ali to Khurasan to protect it from desecration by the Umayyads.").

In the late 19th century the town had some 20,000 inhabitants and by the 1930s it had become the major commercial center in northern Afghanistan. In the 1970s the new part of the town was built according to principles of modern town planning, with avenues intersecting at right angles and with construction of modern shops rather than the traditional bazar. The town is an important commercial center and famous for its

Qaraqul skins, carpets, and melons and is developing into a major industrial town for fertilizer and textile production. Because of its proximity to the Soviet border and its flat terrain, the area can be easily defended from mujahedin attacks and has become a stronghold of the Marxist regime. It lies about 270 miles northwest of Kabul on the paved road which connects the capital with northern Afghanistan.

MAZDURYAR (MAZDOORYAR). Member of the Khalq faction of the PDPA, and minister of interior (1979), frontier affairs (1979), transportation (1980-88), and civil aviation (1989-90). In August 1990 he was appointed ambassador to Budapest. Born in 1945 in Ghulaman, Tarinkot, a Pashtun who graduated from the Kabul military academy in 1964. He participated in both the 1973 and 1978 coups, and became commander of the central garrison and the 4th armored division. According to some reports, he was fired for plotting to assassinate Hafizullah Amin (q.v.) and took refuge in the Soviet embassy in Kabul.

MELMASTIA See PASHTUNWALI.

MESHRANO JIRGAH. Pashto name for the Upper House (or House of Notables) of the bicameral parliament established by the 1931 and 1964 constitutions. According to the 1931 constitution, its members were appointed by the king; in accordance with the 1964 constitution a third of the members were appointed and the rest were elected. Its minimum membership was 20, but was subsequently increased. The Upper House was also called by the Dari name, *majlis-i a'yan* which also means House of Notables.

MIHRAB See MOSQUE.

MILLER, JAMES. A Scottish engineer engaged by Amir Habibullah during his Indian tour in 1907. He set up a furniture factory and, having accomplished this, built a clock tower in the garden of the Dilkusha (Arg, q.v.) palace. Subsequently he was employed on various irrigation schemes and built the Darunta bridge over the Kabul river northwest of Jalalabad.

MINBAR See MOSQUE.

MIR KHWAJA JAN. A Kohistani, belonging to the Sahibzada family of religious leaders. He was exiled to India by Amir Abdur Rahman (q.v.), but Amir Habibullah (q.v.) permitted him to return to Kabul. He served on the amir's advisory council, and later on the staff of the amir's son, Sardar Enayatullah. He had three sons who became important members of Amir Habibullah Kalakani's (q.v.) government: Ata-ul-Haqq, his foreign minister; Shir Jan, minister of court; and Muhammad Siddiq, who commanded the Gardez forces and fought General Nadir Khan in 1929. Mir Khwaja Jan died in 1971. See HABIBULLAH KALAKANI.

MIR SAYYID JAN PACHA. Known also as the "Badshah (ruler) of Islampur" in Kunar province, where he had his home. A sayyid (descendant of the Prophet Muhammad), pupil and successor of the Hadda Mulla, whose tradition of militant hostility to the British government in India he continued. Probably the most powerful mulla in Afghanistan in 1913. He operated a mosque and a *langar*, or charitable kitchen, at Hadda (q.v.), six miles south of Jalalabad, which was built for his predecessor by Amir Abdur Rahman. Said to have received Rs. 12,000 per annum from Amir Habibullah. Crowned Sardar Nasrullah Khan (q.v.) in 1919, but later submitted to King Amanullah.

MIR WAIS KHAN HOTAKI (1709-15). A Ghilzai Pashtun (q.v.) and founder of the short-lived Hotaki dynasty (1709-38). Leader of the Afghan tribal revolt against Persian domination which led to the foundation of modern Afghanistan. He was a Ghilzai chief who lived as a hostage at the court of the Safavid ruler in Isfahan while Kandahar was ruled by Gorgin Khan, a Georgian governor. Mir Wais got permission to go on a pilgrimage to Mecca where he obtained a *fatwa* (legal decision, q.v.) authorizing revolt against the *shi'a* domination of western Afghanistan (which is largely *sunni*, q.v.). Upon his return to Kandahar he used the *fatwa* to win the support of tribal chieftains and, in 1709, staged a successful revolt against Gorgin Khan's troops. Mir Wais and his Afghan forces defeated all attempts by the Safavid armies to recapture Kandahar, and laid the basis for the Afghan invasion of Persia and the defeat of the Safavids at Gulnabad in 1722. Also see HOTAKI and GHILZAI.

MISAQ, ABDUL KARIM. A writer and Khalqi minister of finance (May 1978 to December 1979) who was imprisoned in December 1979 when the Parchami faction came to power. In August 1989 he reemerged in public life when he was appointed mayor of Kabul. A Hazara, born in 1937 in Jaghatu district, Ghazni province, he was self-educated and held various positions in the ministry of interior as well as a job as a mechanic. He is a longtime member of the Khalqi faction of the PDPA, but continued to be a member of Dr. Najibullah's central committee. He is reported to have been jailed and defected in 1990 and lives in Germany.

MOGHOLS (MONGOLS). A small ethnic group southeast of Herat who speak Dari with a small amount of Mongolian vocabulary and claim to be the descendants of 13th century Mongolian soldiers who intermarried with local people. They belong to the sunni school of Islam and numbered about 800 families at the turn of the century. In recent years they were estimated at from one to five thousand persons.

MOHMAND. A powerful tribe of eastern Pashtun origin which migrated from the area north of Kandahar to the Peshawar area. Their territory was dissected by the Durand Line in 1893 (see DURAND AGREEMENT), but they continued to be factor in the politics of both states. In the early twentieth century they were estimated to comprise

some 40,000 families and could raise 18,000 fighters. They supported
Prince Kamran (q.v.) in the early 19th century and joined the Shinwaris
(q.v.) in their revolt against King Amanullah in November 1928. In 1930
the Haji of Turangzai, a tribal mulla, led them against British forces on
the frontier. The Mohmand area was always autonomous and the British-Indian, as well as the Pakistan government, controlled the Mohmand
Agency indirectly by means of an agent who acted as the representative
of the government. In September 1935, they staged a major uprising
against the British government and during the present war, the
Mohmands have generally remained neutral.

MOHMAND, FAZLURRAHIM. Minister of agriculture and land reform
(1980-82) and of agriculture (1983). Born in 1944 in Jalalabad and
educated in Kabul, India, and the United States, he embarked on a career
in the ministry of agriculture. In 1973 President Daud appointed him
deputy minister of agriculture and irrigation. He was a member of the
revolutionary council (1980-88) and president of the Central Statistical
Office.

MOHMAND, NIAZ MUHAMMAD. Member of the Parchami faction of the
PDPA and full member of the politburo since 1981, and deputy of the
international affairs department of the central committee until 1990. He
was ousted from the party as a supporter of the Tanai coup (q.v.). A
Pashtun, born in Darra Isakhel on the Pakistani side of the border, he
was educated at Khushhal Khan Lycée in Kabul and in the Soviet Union,
where he earned a Ph.D. degree in economics.

MOSQUE (MASJID). A mosque or Islamic place of worship where Muslims
assemble for prayer, especially on Fridays when communal prayers are
obligatory and the traditional sermon (*khutba*) is delivered. Masjids vary
in size from one-room buildings to monumental structures, but all mosques have a prayer niche (*mihrab*) which indicates the direction of the
Ka'ba (q.v.), the Islamic shrine in Mecca. Before prayer Muslims must
perform a ceremonial washing, *wudhu'*, and enter the prayer room without
their shoes. Prayer includes repeated bowings (*ruku'*) whereby one
touches the ground with the forehead. Prayers are usually performed in
unison with one person leading in prayer. Larger mosques have a pulpit,
minbar, and minarets from which the "crier," *muezzin*, gives the call to
prayer. Cathedral mosques usually have a large courtyard with fountains,
high minarets, and buildings for schools and colleges.
On special holidays Afghan kings attend prayers at the Idgah Mosque in
Kabul and high government officials attend prayers in provincial capitals.
The Friday sermon is read in the name of the ruler and, therefore, has
political significance (see ISLAM and KHUTBA). Until the government
took over these functions, mosques were centers of education, public
welfare, and social or political gatherings. Mosques are supported by the
state or local communities, as well as by pious endowments administered
by the *ulama* (q.v., the doctors of Islamic sciences). Also see ISLAM.

MUFTI. A canon lawyer of reputation who gives a formal, legal opinion, *fatwa*, in answer to a question submitted to him either by a judge or a private individual. All laws passed by Afghan legislatures are required to be in conformance with Islamic law and it is (or was) the duty of a high member of the *ulama* or a council of the *ulama* (*jam'iat-i ulama*, q.v.) to pass on the constitutionality of laws. The 1957 law on the administration of justice by shari'a relegated the function of the *mufti* to primary courts, but the constitution of 1964 dispensed with the services of a *mufti*, and established a supreme court. Also see ISLAM and ISLAMIC LAW.

MUHAMMAD AFZAL, AMIR (1866-67). Eldest son of Amir Dost Muhammad (q.v.) who served as governor of northern Afghanistan in the 1850s. He fought his half brother, Shir Ali, for the throne and was proclaimed Amir in 1866. He died a year later in Kabul of cholera and was succeeded by his brother Muhammad Azam (q.v.). Muhammad Afzal was the father of the subsequent Amir Abdur Rahman (q.v.).

MUHAMMAD ASGHAR. President of Kabul University (1954-60), deputy minister of interior (1960-62) and minister of justice (1967-69). Born in 1914 in Kabul and educated in Kabul and the United States, he became a university professor and dean of the faculty of law. In October 1989 he became president of a 15-member "National Salvation Society" of former high officials who were not affiliated with the PDPA and demanded an end to the bloodshed and a political solution to the war in Afghanistan.

MUHAMMAD AZAM, AMIR (1867). Son of Amir Dost Muhammad Khan who succeeded his brother Muhammad Afzal to the Kabul throne in 1867, but was defeated by his half brother Shir Ali and forced to flee to Iran, where he died in October 1869 on his way to Tehran.

MUHAMMAD AZIM. A teacher at the German-language Amani (later Najat) high school in Kabul who entered the British legation in Kabul on September 6, 1933 with the intention of assassinating the minister, Sir Richard Maconachie. He wanted to precipitate war between Britain and Afghanistan. Instead of killing the minister he shot an English mechanic, and two employees of the legation. This act was seen as a continuation of the struggle between the followers of King Amanullah (q.v.) and Nadir Shah (q.v.). Muhammad Azim was executed on September 13, as were six prominent prisoners and high officials of King Amanullah, including Muhammad Wali (q.v.) and Ghulam Jilani Charkhi (q.v.).

MUHAMMAD AZIZ. Half-brother of Nadir Shah (q.v.) and father of President Daud (q.v., 1973-75). He was born in 1877, the son of Sardar Muhammad Yusuf, and entered service as assistant private secretary of Amir Habibullah (q.v.) and supervisor of Afghan students in France in the 1920s. Nadir Shah appointed him ambassador to Moscow in 1929 and in 1933 to Berlin where he was assassinated on June 6, 1933 by one Sayyid

Kemal, apparently in retaliation for the killing of Ghulam Jilani Charkhi (q.v.).

MUHAMMAD DAUD, SARDAR. President of the Republic of Afghanistan from July 1973 until his assassination in April 1978 as a result of the Saur Revolt. Born in 1909 in Kabul, the son of Sardar Muhammad Aziz (q.v.), and educated in Kabul and France. He embarked on a military career and was governor and general officer commanding of the Eastern Province (1934), Kandahar (1935), and commander of Central Forces (1939-47) stationed in Kabul and minister of defense in 1946. A minister of interior (1949-50) and prime minister (1953-63), he encouraged social reforms and in 1959 permitted women to abandon the veil, thus contributing to their emancipation and participation in the economic life of Afghanistan. He initiated two five-year plans (1956-61 and 1962-67) and a seven-year plan in 1976, and relied for military and development aid on the Soviet Union. He demanded the independence of Pashtunistan (q.v.), the North-West Frontier Province of Pakistan, which led to repeated crises with Pakistan and ended with his resignation in 1963. Ten years later Muhammad Daud staged a coup against his cousin, King Zahir, and in July 1973 proclaimed Afghanistan a republic. Whether he just wanted power or felt that the political liberalization during the democratic decade (1963-73) had failed to remedy the social and economic problems of Afghanistan is not clear. He relied on the support of leftists to consolidate his power, crushed the emerging Islamist movement, and in 1975 established his own "National Revolutionary Party" (q.v.) as an umbrella organization for all political movements. Thus he wanted to limit the power of the left and create a left-of-center movement loyal to himself. Toward the end of his rule he attempted to purge his leftist supporters from positions of power and sought to reduce Soviet influence in Afghanistan. Financial support from Iran and the Arab Gulf states was to enable him to repay Soviet loans and improve his relations with the West. He and members of his family were assassinated on April 27, 1978, as a result of the Saur Revolt which brought Marxist parties to power in Kabul.

MUHAMMAD HAKIM. Appointed minister of finance in Prime Minister Khaliqyar's government of May 1990. Born in 1934 and educated at Kabul and in Switzerland, he began work in the foreign relations department of Kabul University. He was appointed adviser to the ministry of finance in 1971, and in 1972 he became president of Da Afghanistan Bank. He also was president of Hotel Enterprises and in 1986 was appointed president of the Chambers of Commerce and Industries. He is not a member of the PDPA.

MUHAMMAD HASANI Or MAMASANI. A Brahui tribe located in the area of Shorawak. See BRAHUI.

MUHAMMAD HASHIM, SARDAR. Prime minister of Afghanistan (1929-46), said to have been a good administrator but austere and harsh in his dealing with the Afghan people. He groomed his nephew, Muhammad Daud, for the position of prime minister. Born in 1886, the son of Sardar Yusuf Khan, he embarked on a military career and commanded Amir Habibullah's bodyguard. He became King Amanullah's governor of the Eastern Province (1919) and served as Afghan minister in Moscow (1924-26) before joining his half-brother Muhammad Nadir (q.v.) in France. When in December 1929, Nadir Khan ascended the throne, Muhammad Hashim became his prime minister and ruled with a strong hand until his retirement in 1946. He died on October 26, 1953.

MUHAMMADI, MAULAWI MUHAMMAD NABI. Leader of the *harakat-i inqilab-i Islami* (Islamic Revolutionary Movement), a traditional Islamic mujahedin group headquartered in Pakistan. He was born in 1921 in Logar, the son of Haji Abdul Wahhab, and educated in *madrasas* (religious colleges) in Logar province. In the 1950s he was one of the first members of the religious establishment who agitated against "Communist influence" in the Afghan educational system. Elected to Parliament in 1964 as a representative of Logar province. After the Marxist coup, he fled to Pakistan and utilized a network of *maulawis* (graduates of madrasas) to organize armed resistance against Kabul. In the early 1980s his Harakat was the largest of mujahedin groups, but it lost members to the more radical Islamist parties of Sayyaf (q.v.) and Rabbani. It has Pashtun support in Kandahar, Ghazni, Logar, Kabul, and Baghlan provinces. Also see HARAKAT-I INQILAB-I ISLAM.

MUHAMMAD ISHAQ (ESHAQ). Since 1982, political officer of Jam'iat and frequent contributor to its fortnightly *AFGHANews*. Born in 1952 in Panjshir and a graduate of the faculty of engineering of Kabul University, he became a member of the *Jawanan-i Musulman* (see ISLAMIST MOVEMENT). He cooperated in 1975 with Commander Mas'ud (q.v.) in raids against military posts of the Daud government, and after the Saur Revolt joined Mas'ud in armed attack against the Kabul government.

MUHAMMAD ISHAQ. Son of Amir Muhammad Azim Khan (q.v.) and cousin of Amir Abdur Rahman (q.v.) who in June 1888 had himself proclaimed amir and unsuccessfully fought Abdur Rahman for the throne. Born about 1851 of an Armenian mother, he was at age 18 in command of Abdur Rahman Khan's forces in Afghan Turkestan. He was defeated by Amir Shir Ali (q.v.) and lived with Abdur Rahman in exile at Samarkand. In 1879 he returned with Abdur Rahman Khan to Afghanistan. When the latter assumed the Kabul throne, he appointed Muhammad Ishaq governor of Turkestan, as the northern provinces were then called. Ishaq Khan was ambitious; he demanded autonomy amounting to virtual independence, subject to token allegiance to the Kabul throne. He next extended his control over Herat province and when Amir Abdur Rahman was ill in 1888, proclaimed himself amir. Amir

Abdur Rahman quickly recovered and raised an army under General Ghulam Haidar (q.v.) which decisively defeated the amir's rebellious cousin on September 19, 1888. Ishaq Khan was forced to flee to Russian Turkestan where he died shortly thereafter.

MUHAMMAD ISMA'IL. Mujahedin commander affiliated with the *Jam'iat-i Islami* (q.v.) who operates in the Herat area as the "Amir" of Herat, Badghis, Ghor, and Farah provinces with civil and military powers. He is said to have built a good military organization and is a good administrator. He was born in 1946 in Shindand (now Farah province), the son of Muhammad Aslam. After completing his elementary education in Shindand, he continued his education at Kabul Military School and the Military Academy. He was a second lieutenant in the 17th Division stationed in Herat when he defected and participated in the uprising of March 1979. When the uprising was suppressed, he fled to Iran and made his way to Pakistan, where he joined the forces of the mujahedin leader Burhanuddin Rabbani (q.v.). In 1987 he was said to have received stinger missiles which have helped him to secure control of much of Herat province. Most recently he has lost some ground to Kabul troops.

MUHAMMAD NADIR SHAH. King of Afghanistan, 1929-33. Born in 1883, the son of Sardar Muhammad Yusuf Khan, he embarked on a military career. Appointed a brigadier in 1906, he was promoted to lieutenent general, *naib salar*, for his services in suppressing the Mangal revolt in December 1912. Appointed general, *sipah salar*, 1914. He and other members of the Afghan court had accompanied Amir Habibullah to Jalalabad, the winter capital, and when the amir was assassinated in his sleep, he was arrested. Amir Amanullah exonerated him of any involvement and sent him to command the troops in Khost province. During the third Anglo-Afghan war, Nadir Khan led an army across the Afghan border into Waziristan and invested the British base at Thal. This threatened to cause a general uprising among the "British" Afghans and was one of the factors forcing Britain to accept Afghan independence (See ANGLO- AFGHAN WARS). Amir Amanullah appointed him minister of war in 1919, in which post he served until 1924, when he was appointed Afghan minister at Paris. He resigned two years later because of illness (or because he disagreed with King Amanullah's policies). Nevertheless, he remained in France where he was joined by his half-brother Muhammad Hashim Khan and his brother Shah Wali Khan. After the abdication of King Amanullah in January 1929, Nadir left France for India and established himself at the Afghan frontier. He collected tribal support, including Waziri tribal forces from the Indian side of the border, and, after initial setbacks, defeated Habibullah Kalakani (q.v.) and captured Kabul on October 13, 1929. Nadir Khan was proclaimed king two days later. He made great efforts to reorganize the country and reopen schools and founded the faculty of medicine in 1932 which ten years later merged with a number of faculties to become Kabul University. He drafted a new constitution (1931) which provided for a bicameral parliament, the national council (*shura-i-milli*), the senate (*majlis-i-a'yan*), and an advisory council (*jami'at al-ulama*, q.v.). He fought those who aimed at restoring King Amanullah to the throne and executed Ghulam Nabi, one of his chief opponents, in 1932. He was assassinated in 1933 by a Hazara student who was an adopted son of Ghulam Nabi (q.v.).

MUHAMMAD NAIM. Minister of foreign affairs and deputy prime minister (1953-63) and foreign policy adviser of President Daud (1973-78). Born in 1912, the son of Muhammad Aziz (q.v.) and brother of Muhammad Daud (q.v.), he embarked on a diplomatic career and served as Afghan minister in Rome (1932), London (1946-47), and the United States (1948-50). He was assassinated together with President Daud and members of their family as a result of the Saur Revolt of April 27, 1978.

MUHAMMAD NAZAR See NAZAR MUHAMMAD.

MUHAMMAD OMAR. Chief of general staff (1932) and minister of defense in Shah Mahmud's government (1948). Subsequently he served as Afghan ambassador in Paris (1949-55), Tehran (1955-57), and Delhi (1958-64). Born in 1898 of a Yusufzai Pashtun family, called Abawi, he underwent military training and quickly advanced in rank. He was in charge of military and diplomatic missions abroad and served for a time as military attaché in Berlin. He retired and died in Kabul in 1964.

MUHAMMAD RAFI'I, COL. GENERAL. Member of the Parchami faction of the PDPA who was minister of public works in the first Khalqi cabinet (May to August 1978), and was purged with other Parchamis and arrested and sentenced to twenty years for plotting against the Taraki government. Appointed minister of defense by the Karmal government (1980-82) and again (1986-88), he has been a member of the politburo since 1981. In 1988 he was one of four vice-presidents of the Najibullah government. Born in 1946 of a Kharoti Ghilzai (q.v.) family of Paghman, he was educated at the Kabul Military Academy and the Academy of General Staff in the Soviet Union. When he became a member of the PDPA in 1973, he was the highest ranking party member in the Afghan army.

MUHAMMAD YUSUF. Afghan prime minister in 1963, succeeding Sardar Muhammad Daud as the first commoner in this position. He served during the process of drafting and ratification of the Constitution of 1964. The newly elected, bicameral parliament was soon bogged down in recriminations and political infighting. When the lower house, *wolesi jirgah* (P., People's Council), decided to hold closed meetings, demonstrations, largely by students, led to police repression in which three persons were killed and a number of others wounded. Thereupon Dr. Yusuf resigned. The *Sewwum-i Aqrab* (the third of Aqrab, corresponding to October 25, 1965), was subsequently a day of protest and demonstrations by the Left. Born in 1917 in Kabul, Muhammad Yusuf was educated at

Najat school (q.v.) and in Germany, where he received the Ph.D. degree in physics. He became a professor at Kabul University and deputy minister of education in 1949. He held the position of minister of mines and industry for ten years (1953-63), before his appointment as prime minister. After his resignation he served as Afghan ambassador to Bonn (1966-73) and Moscow in 1973, but was recalled after the Daud coup. He presently lives in Germany and continues to be active in Afghan politics.

MUHAMMAD ZAHIR SHAH See **ZAHIR SHAH.**

MUHAMMADZAI. The Muhammadzai (a branch of the Barakzai of the Durrani tribe) are the descendants of Sardar Painda Khan (q.v.). They captured the Kabul throne in 1826 under Amir Dost Muhammad (q.v.)and continued in power (with the exception of the nine-month rule of the Tajik, Habibullah Kalakani) until the Marxist coup in 1978 deposed President Daud. For Muhammadzai rulers, see individual entries. Also see genealogy in Appendix.

MUHSINI, AYATOLLAH MUHAMMAD ASEF. A Hazara, born in 1935 in Kandahar province and educated in the shi'a universities in Iraq. He is called Ayatollah by his supporters. Upon his return to Afghanistan he founded a cultural organization called "Dawn of Science" (*sobh-i danesh*) which became the nucleus of the rural-based mujahedin group, *harakat-i Islami-yi Afghanistan* (Islamic Movement of Afghanistan). In 1980 he was elected chairman of the "Afghan Shi'a Alliance," a mujahedin umbrella group headquartered in Iran, but subsequently he left the alliance and moved to Quetta. His group once rivalled Nasr (q.v.) in importance and collaborated with Nasr in expelling the Shura (q.v.) of Ayatollah Beheshti from most of the Hazarajat. In June 1990, the shi'a groups announced formation of a new organization, called "Unity Party" (*hizb-i wahdat*), but Muhsini has presented a number of conditions for his joining the coalition. Some of his commanders, including Sayyid Hadi Behsudi, Abdul Ali Mazari, and Sayyid Ibrahim Shah Husaini, are said to be cooperating with the *hizb-i wahdat*. Muhsini is known as a moderate who does not receive any support from Iran.

MUHTASIB. An overseer of public morality, common in Afghanistan before local police forces were established. He was to discourage sinful behavior, encourage attendance at prayers, check measures and weights in the bazars, and ascertain that foodstuffs were not adulterated. He was appointed by a qazi (judge) and paid from the public treasury and was empowered to administer whippings for minor offenses. With the establishment of regular police forces in towns, in the early 1920s, the position of *muhtasib* began to disappear. Also see KALANTAR.

MUJADDIDI. The name of a family of religious leaders who are the descendants of the sufi reformer Shaikh Ahmad Sirhindi (purported to be born in Kabul province in 1564 and buried in Sirhind, India, 1624), called *Mujaddid Alf-I Thani*, (Renewer of the Second Millenium). Qayyum Jan Agha (descendant in seven generations of the Shaikh) came to Afghanistan in the early 19th century and founded a *madrasa* (Islamic college) and *khanqa* (sufi center) in the Shor Bazar area of Kabul and his successor therefore assumed the title Hazrat Saheb of Shor Bazar. Succession went from Qayyum Jan Agha to Fazl Muhammad (*Shams al-Mashayekh* - the Sun of Shaikhs, who assumed this title in 1925); then to Fazl Omar (*Nur al-Mashayekh* - the Light of Shaikhs); and finally to Muhammad Ibrahim (*Zia al-Mashayekh* - the Light of Shaikhs, who assumed the title in 1956). Members of the family also established themselves in Herat (the Hazrat Saheb of Jaghatan), and other towns in Afghanistan. They are leaders of the Naqshbandia (q.v.) sufi order in southern Afghanistan and have long played an important political role. They preached *jihad* (holy war) against Britain, opposed the secular reforms instituted by King Amanullah and Muhammad Daud, and encouraged tribal revolts to restore their concept of Islamic orthodoxy. Some members held government positions and some lived in exile. In January 1979, Muhammad Ibrahim and some 96 male members of the Mujaddidi family were arrested and executed by the Khalqi regime.

MUJADDIDI, SEBGHATULLAH. Elected president in February 1989 of an "Afghan Interim Government" made up of members of the seven-party alliance of mujahedin headquartered in Pakistan (See MUJAHEDIN). He founded and leads the National Liberation Front of Afghanistan (*jabha-yi milli najat-i Afghanistan*, q.v.) which has been conducting armed attacks on Soviet and Afghan government forces since about 1980. Born in 1925 in Kabul, the son of Muhammad Masum, he was educated in Kabul and at al-Azhar University in Egypt and subsequently taught Islamic studies at high schools and colleges in Kabul. He publicly denounced "unbelievers" and communists and was imprisoned (1959-64) for involvement in a purported plot to assassinate the Soviet premier, Nikita Khrushchev. When he was freed, he traveled abroad for two years, and upon his return founded the *jam'iat-i ulama-i Muhammadi* (1972, Organization of Muslim Clergy). He was again politically active and participated in anti-reformist demonstrations in Kabul in the 1970s and was forced to flee abroad in order to escape arrest. He was head of the Islamic Center in Copenhagen, Denmark (1974-78); and after the Saur Revolt he went to Pakistan where he has led the armed resistance of the National Liberation Front. His supporters are primarily Pashtun members of the Naqshbandi sufi order in Paktia and Kunar provinces. In spite of his radical background, he is counted among the moderate groups who do not rule out the establishment of a constitutional monarchy.

MUJAHEDIN (MUJAHEDUN). Fighters in holy war, *jihad*, (q.v., A., sing. *mujahed* pl. *mujahedun, mujahedin*). Afghan resistance fighters adopted this designation to indicate that they are waging a lawful war against an "infidel" government (according to Islamic law, a *jihad* can be fought only against non-Muslims). The mujahedin are organized in a tenuous alliance of seven sunni groups stationed in Peshawar, including the moderate leaders Muhammad Nabi Muhammadi, Sebghatullah Mujaddidi, and Sayyid Ahmad Gailani; and the Islamist radicals Burhanuddin Rabbani, Muhammad Yunus Khales, Gulbuddin Hekmatyar, and Abdul Rasul Sayyaf (see individual entries). In 1989, these groups formed an Afghan Interim Government (AIG) with Sebghatullah Mujaddidi (q.v.) as the president. In 1989 a *shi'a* alliance of eight groups (most of them small or inactive) in Iran united in an umbrella organization called *hizb-i wahdat* (Unity Party) which has, however, refused to join the AIG of the sunni groups because of what they considered was insufficient representation. Refugees in Pakistan and commanders in the field were required to be affiliated with one of the seven groups if they wanted to receive outside assistance. The Pakistani government recognized only six (later seven) groups which prevented the proliferation of parties. The Pakistani military Inter Service Intelligence (ISI) has taken an active part in planning and executing attacks and favored Islamist (rather than nationalist) groups, especially Hekmatyar's *Hizb-i Islami*, in the supply of funds and war materials. Many of the commanders do not necessarily share the ideology of their leader and some have switched "allegiance," when it helped in obtaining supplies. Mujahedin are also grouped according to regional, tribal, and ethnic origin; the Jam'iat of Rabbani, largely non-Pashtun in ethnic composition, is active in northern Afghanistan. Although Rabani is Islamist (See ISLAMIST MOVEMENT IN AFGHANISTAN), the Jam'iat has increasingly come in conflict with its ideological brother, the Hizb of Gulbuddin Hekmatyar. Ideological purity (never precisely defined) has also suffered as a result of the "tactical alliance" in March 1990 between Shahnavaz Tanai (q.v.), a Khalqi hardliner, and Hekmatyar, one of the most vocal radical Islamists. Also see JIHAD and individual entries for mujahedin groups.

MUJTABA KHAN. In charge of a school of accounting in Kabul, the *Maktab-i Usul-i Daftari*, opened by Amir Amanullah in 1919. It had 100 students who were trained to be tax collectors. Mujtaba Khan was active in the financial administration and held the positions of financial secretary (*mustaufi*) of Kabul, 1920-24; deputy finance minister, 1929 (under Kalakani) and 1932; and inspector general of the tribunal at the prime ministry, 1945. He became a member of the senate in 1952. He died in the late 1950s. His descendants have adopted the family name Mustamandi.

MULLA. A preacher and spiritual adviser as well as a teacher in elementary mosque schools (*maktab*-see EDUCATION). There is no clergy in sunni Islam, no need for an intermediary between God and man, no ordination, or strict hierarchy, and educational preparation ranges from informal study to rigorous training at a faculty of theology or well- known Islamic university. A mulla performs such religious activities as recitation of the *adhan* (call to prayer) in the ear of the newborn and presides at marriage and burial ceremonies. He is paid for his services by donations from his parish and often needs to supplement his income by pursuing a trade or agricultural work. Mullas vary considerably in educational background from the barely literate to those with some *madrasa* education. They never have held political power on a national scale, but some had great influence on a grass-roots level. They sometimes mediate in tribal disputes (not being members of the tribe) and have been active in mobilizing the masses against a foreign invader or an "infidel" ruler. Famous mullas include Mashk-i Alam (See DIN MUHAMMAD) who proclaimed *jihad* against the British in the second Anglo-Afghan war and subsequently led Mangal (q.v.) and Ghilzai (q.v.) forces against Amir Abdur Rahman; as well as Mulla-i-Lang (the Lame Mullah) who led a tribal army against King Amanullah (See KHOST REBELLION). Amir Abdur Rahman first tried to keep mullas under state control by requiring tests for certification and made attempts at improving the quality of religious education in Afghanistan. Since the time of King Amanullah (1920s) the Afghan government established state-sponsored *madrasas*, and in 1951 a faculty of theology affiliated with Al-Azhar University in Cairo, but the informal, private system of religious education has continued to exist to this day. Most mullas are either self-described or recognized by others as such. For the higher religious functionaries, see ULAMA.

MUNJANI. A small ethnic group of Isma'ili Muslims living in twelve villages in the Munjan valley of Badakhshan province. They are engaged in agriculture and speak Munjani (a northeastern Iranian language of the Pamir group) as well as Farsi.

MURGHAB (lat. 38-18' N, long. 61-12' E). A river formed by the confluence of the Chiras and Wajan streams, rising in the eastern ranges of the Band-i-Baba (q.v.) and Band-i- Turkestan (q.v.) mountains. It flows in a westerly direction and turns northwest about eleven miles below Bala Murghab in Badghis province, where it receives the waters of the Karawal Khana. It then crosses into the Soviet Union and, running in a northerly direction, dissipates in the plains of Merv. The river is some 500 miles in length, about half of its course is in Afghanistan.

MURSHID. Master, or head, of a mystic order.

MUSAHEBAN. A family also called Yahya Khel, because its members descended from Muhammad Yahya (and Muhammad Yusuf) who were companions, *musaheb*, of Amir Habibullah. Prominent members of the family were Muhammad Nadir, the Afghan king (1929-33), and his brothers and half-brothers Muhammad Aziz, Muhammad Hashim, Shah Wali, and Shah Mahmud, who held high positions in Zahir Shah's government. They were exiled in India until 1901 when Amir Habibullah permitted them to return to Afghanistan.

MUSA SHAFIQ, See **SHAFIQ, MUHAMMAD MUSA.**

MUSHK-I-ALAM, See **DIN MUHAMMAD, (MASHK).**

MUSLIM BROTHERHOOD. The Society of Muslim Brethren (*Jam'iat-i Ikhwan al-Muslimin*), founded in 1929 in Isma'iliyya, Egypt, by Hasan al-Banna (1906-49), was a religio-political organization which eventually spread to other parts of the Islamic world. Al-Banna, as ascetic and charismatic teacher, was the "Supreme Guide", *murshid al-'amm*, who advocated social and economic reforms, expulsion of the British from Egypt, and establishment of an Islamic state. The movement is Pan-Islamic in outlook and aims at imposing Islamic law on all aspects of the social and political life of the Muslim nation (*umma*). As a political party it was never very successful, but it was able to mobilize considerable support among the masses of the lower urban and rural classes. The Ikhwan was accused of political assassinations and, Hasan al-Banna was himself assassinated in 1949 (reputedly by government agents). The Ikhwan is presently represented in the Egyptian parliament and other, more radical groups, have taken over the Islamist cause.

A number of founders of the Islamist movement (q.v., Rabbani, Sayyaf, Niazi) in Afghanistan became members or sympathizers of the Ikhwanis while residing in Egypt for study and upon returning to Afghanistan, contributed to the spread of the movement's ideology. They were the teachers of young intellectuals recruited from Afghan government schools who formed the nucleus of the Islamist movement. The Islamists are popularly called "Ikhwanis" in Afghanistan. See **ISLAMIST MOVEMENT.**

MUSSOORIE CONFERENCE. A conference at Mussoorie, north of Delhi in India (April 17-July 18, 1920), which was to restore "friendly" relations between the governments of Afghanistan and British-India after the third Anglo-Afghan war. It was a sequel to the peace treaty at Rawalpindi (August 8, 1919, see **AFGHAN FOREIGN RELATIONS** and **ANGLO-AFGHAN WARS**), and pitted the Afghan foreign minister, Mahmud Tarzi, against the foreign secretary to the government of India, Sir Henry Dobbs, in a fruitless attempt to conclude a treaty of friendship between the two states. A British *aide-memoire* provided for some economic assistance but postponed the establishment of normal, neighborly relations for another conference at Kabul (January 1-December 2, 1921). Also see **ANGLO-AFGHAN TREATY** of 1921.

-N-

NADIM, ABDUL GHAFUR. Dari poet and traditional scholar. Born about 1880 at Kabul, the son of Rajab Ali Khan. Although he died at 37, he wrote some 3,500 verses, consisting mainly of odes and other lyrical poetry. His poems are still greatly appreciated. He taught Dari literature at Habibia High School (q.v.) for several years and in 1915 published the first modern Dari grammar, entitled *Sarf-i-Nadim* (the Grammar of Nadim). He also published a newspaper called *Inkesar*. He died in 1918 in Kabul.

NADIRI, SAYYID SHAH NASIR See SAYYID-I KAYAN.

NADIR SHAH. King of Afghanistan (1929-33). See MUHAMMAD NADIR SHAH.

NADIR SHAH, AFSHAR. Ruler of Iran (1736-47) and founder of the short-lived Afsharid dynasty (1736-95). Born in 1688 as Nadir Quli in northern Khurasan (q.v.) the son of Imam Quli of a clan affiliated with the Afshar tribe, he started life as a raider for booty and became one of the last great nomadic conquerors of Asia. He ended the Ghilzai dream of ruling an empire after Mahmud, son of Mir Wais (q.v.), captured Isfahan in 1722. Nadir defeated the Afghans and drove them out of Iran. He attacked Herat and invaded India, where he defeated the Moghul army at Karnal, near Delhi, in 1739. Rather than fighting the Afghan tribes he enlisted them into his army, making Ahmad Khan Abdali (the subsequent Ahmad Shah, q.v.) one of his military commanders. He moved the Abdali tribe from Herat to their original home in the Kandahar area and settled them on Ghilzai lands. This led to the ascendancy of the Abdalis (Durrani) over the Ghilzais and contributed to the long-standing rivalry between these two Pashtun tribes. Nadir Shah also settled Jewish and Armenian traders from Iran in Afghan towns to encourage trade with India. Ruling over a heterogeneous population he wanted to unite his subjects by proclaiming shi'ism the fifth (Jafarite) orthodox school of sunni Islam. The shi'a clergy objected to this. Nadir became increasingly tyrannical and was eventually killed by one of his own tribesmen. Some of Nadir's Qizilbash (q.v.) soldiers settled in Afghanistan where their descendants had successful careers in the army, government, the trades, and crafts. At the time of Nadir Shah's death, Ahmad Khan, Abdali, was able to fill the political vacuum and become the first Durrani ruler of Afghanistan.

NAGHLU (lat. 34-38' N, long. 69-43' E). A village in the southern part of Laghman province on the left bank of the Kabul river, opposite Sarobi. It is the site of a 350-foot high dam for irrigation and generation of electricity. The project was financed by the Soviet Union, started in January 1960 and completed in 1968.

NAIM MUHAMMAD, See MUHAMMAD NAIM.

NAJAT SCHOOL (NEJAT). A comprehensive elementary and secondary school founded in Kabul by King Amanullah in 1923. The school had a German curriculum and German was the language of education. Many of the graduates were sent by the Afghan government to German-speaking countries for higher education. The school was first named Amani after King Amanullah (Aman Allah), but was renamed Najat (also spelled Nejat - Liberation) School after Nadir Shah (q.v.) defeated Habibullah Kalakani in 1929 and ascended the throne. The school was renamed Amani by the Marxist regime in the 1980s as part of its effort to establish links between it and the progressive policies of King Amanullah. Also see EDUCATION.

NAJIBULLAH. President of the Republic of Afghanistan and general secretary of the PDPA since May 1986. Born in 1947 in Kabul of an Ahmadzai (Ghilzai Pashtun) family (his father was Afghan trade agent in Peshawar), he was educated at Habibia high school and Kabul University, graduating from the College of Medicine in 1975. He became a member of the Parcham faction of the PDPA in 1965, and was repeatedly arrested for his political activities. After the Saur Revolt he was appointed Afghan ambassador in Tehran (July-October 1978), in a move to get leading Parchamis out of the country, but was quickly dismissed with other Parchamis by the Taraki government, when they were suspected of plotting a coup. He remained abroad and returned to Kabul with Babrak Karmal (q.v.) after the ouster of Hafizullah Amin in the final days of December 1979. He next held the position of general president of KHAD (1980-86) and in 1986 replaced Babrak Karmal as secretary general of the PDPA. He purged the central committee and brought in new members and reorganized government in 1988 and 1990. In March 1990, he successfully withstood a Khalqi coup, headed by Shahnawaz Tanai (q.v.), his defense minister. He has downplayed Marxist ideology and annulled most of the early "reforms." He has refused to step down (as demanded by the mujahedin) but indicated his willingness to permit national elections and accept the results. He is married to a Muhammadzai. Also see PEOPLES DEMOCRATIC PARTY OF AFGHANISTAN.

NANAWATI. Nanawati (mediation or protection) is a vital element of the Pashtun code, *pashtunwali*. It is the obligation to afford protection or asylum to anyone in need or assist in mediation to help the weaker in a feud who seeks peace with someone he has injured. See PASHTUN-WALI.

NANGARHAR (lat. 34-45' N, long. 70-50' E). A province in eastern Afghanistan which comprises an area of 7,195 square miles and a population of about 740,000 of which almost 400,000 are settled in refugee camps in Pakistan. The capital of the province is Jalalabad with a peacetime population of about 56,000 (presently increased to 200,000). The population is largely Pashtun of the Khugiani, Mohmand, Shinwari, and Tirahi tribes, but other major ethnic groups are also represented in Jalalabad.

Local tradition associates the name, Nangarhar, with "*nuh*" - nine, and "*nahar*" - river, or, according to another version, with the Sanskrit "nau vihara" - meaning "nine monasteries." The Nangarhar area was a flourishing center of Buddhism until the 5th century. Because of its mild climate, Jalalabad was the winter capital of Afghan kings, after they were established in Kabul. The eastern part of the province is well irrigated, producing two or three crops a year. Wheat, corn, and some rice are the major crops, and Soviet- developed mechanized state farms produce olive and citrus fruits, much of which were formerly exported to the Soviet Union. Timber is cut on the upper slopes of the Safid Kuh (q.v.) and smuggled to Pakistan where it fetches a better price. The Darunta Dam on the Kabul river provides hydroelectric power and makes possible large irrigation projects. In March 1989 a mujahedin assault on Jalalabad failed to dislodge the forces of the Kabul regime. This demonstrated the fact that the mujahedin are as yet unable to switch from guerrilla-type warfare to conventional war, which has led to a lull in large-scale military operations. Also see JALALABAD.

NAQIB OF BAGHDAD. Title of Sayyid Abdur Rahman, in the late 19th century, Naqib al- Ashraf (Representative of the Sayyids) and custodian of the Baghdad Shrine of the sufi saint Abdul Qadir Gailani (1077-1166 A.D.), founder of the Qadiriyya sufi fraternity (q.v.). He was in contact with Amir Habibullah through his brother Sayyid Hasan Gailani, a man of great importance and influence in Afghanistan. He was often visited by Afghans going on Haj via the Hijaz railway. He was the brother of Sayyid Hasan Gailani who came to Afghanistan in 1905 and the uncle of Sayyid Ahmad Gailani, head of Mahaz. See GAILANI.

NAQSHBANDI (NAQSHBANDIYYA). A sufi fraternity named after its founder, Muhammad ibn Muhammad Baha' al-Din al-Bukhari Naqshband (1317-89 A.D.), which has many devotees in Afghanistan. The Hazrat Sahib of Shor Bazar (q.v.) of the Mujaddidi family (q.v.) is the leader of the Kandahar and eastern branches of the order by virtue of his descent from the Naqshbandi reformer Shaikh Ahmad Sirhindi. Among the mujahedin forces of Sebghatullah Mujaddidi (q.v.) are many devotees of the Naqshbandi order, whereas northern (non-Pashtun) Naqshbandis are affiliated with the Jam'iat of Rabbani (q.v.).

NARANJAN DAS. An Afghan Hindu who held high offices during the reigns of Amir Habibullah and King Amanullah. Born in Kabul about 1853, he was accountant-general (a kind of finance minister) at Kabul and was granted the rank of civil (not military) colonel in 1906. He was a member of the Afghan delegations to the peace conference at Rawalpindi in 1919 (See ANGLO-AFGHAN TREATY OF 1919) and the Mussoorie conference in 1920 (q.v.). His participation in the Afghan delegation had an excellent propaganda effect among the Hindu population of India, who saw King Amanullah as a potential ally in their struggle for independence.

NASIR Or NASAR. One of the wealthiest and strongest of the Kuchi (q.v.) Pashtun tribes which dwells in black tents and formerly traveled into the Indian subcontinent in the winter. They have a reputation of being democratic and not dominated by their chiefs. They have long feuded with the Waziris (q.v.), who attacked the Nasir when they passed through their territory. At such time the Nasir stopped all feuds and united in obedience under a chief. Amir Abdur Rahman wanted to settle the tribe in Herat province; they refused and agreed to pay taxes to continue their nomadic way of life. For further details, see POWINDAH.

NASR, SAZMAN-I. "Victory Organization," a Hazara mujahedin party, founded by Shaikh Mir Husain Sadeqi (q.v.), after the Saur Revolt. It recruited its followers from Hazaras living in Iran and obtained some material support from Iran. It eventually succeeded in becoming a major force in the Hazarajat and allied with the Pasdaran (q.v.) in expelling the traditionalist Shura (headed by Beheshti, q.v.) from much of the area. It is radical Islamist in outlook and is said to govern with the assistance of Islamic *komites*, ideological committees. Also see SADEQI, HOJJAT AL-ISLAM MIR HUSAIN.

NASRULLAH KHAN, SARDAR. Second son of Amir Abdur Rahman and viceroy, *na'eb al-saltana*, in charge of most of the government administration while his brother Amir Habibullah was amir. He was commander-in-chief of the army and president of the amir's advisory council. He was conservative in outlook, a sponsor and supporter of the religious establishment, and a militant foe of the British. When Amir Habibullah was assassinated in February 1919, Nasrullah Khan was proclaimed king in Peshawar, but the army supported Amanullah Khan who was in control of the Kabul palace and the treasury. Nasrullah was arrested and died while in confinement. He is buried in Qol-i Chakan in Kabul.

NATIONAL FATHERLAND FRONT (NFF). A national umbrella organization (*jabha-yi milli-yi pader-watan*) established by Babrak Karmal (q.v.) in 1980 to "unite all progressive forces." Dr. Saleh Muhammad Zirai (Zeary) was appointed chairman, and the PDPA was the vanguard or "guiding force" in an organization that included all unions, guilds, women's and professional organizations. The NFF was said to have had 55,000 members in 1984, but it never succeeded in mobilizing the masses under party control. (Similar "national front" governments, set up in East-bloc countries, remained under Communist party control.) In 1987 the Afghan government renamed the organization the National Front of the Republic of Afghanistan (NFROA), headed by Abdul Rahim Hatef (q.v.).

NATIONAL ISLAMIC FRONT (NIFA). Name of the *Mahaz-i Milli-yi Islami-yi Afghanistan*, one of seven resistance organizations permitted by Pakistan to operate after the Saur Revolt. It is headed by Pir Sayyid

Ahmad Gailani. For details, see MAHAZ-I MILLI-YI AFGHANISTAN and GAILANI, SAYYID AHMAD.

NATIONAL LIBERATION FRONT OF AFGHANISTAN. Name of the *Jabha-yi Milli Najat-yi Afghanistan*, one of seven resistance organizations sanctioned by Pakistan after the Saur Revolt. It is headed by Prof. Sebghatullah Mujaddidi. See JABHA-YI MILLI NAJAT-I AFGHAN-ISTAN and MUJADDIDI, SEBGHATULLAH.

NATIONAL RESCUE FRONT. A short-lived mujahedin organization founded in June 1978 by Burhanuddin Rabbani. It was a forerunner of the Jam'iat. See JAM'IAT-ISLAMI and ISLAMIC ALLIANCE FOR THE LIBERATION OF AFGHANISTAN.

NATIONAL REVOLUTIONARY PARTY. *Hizb-i Inqilab-i Milli*, name of a party founded in 1975 by President Muhammad Daud to support his republican regime. It was headed by a central council which included Dr. Abdul Majid (q.v.), Gen. Ghulam Haidar Rasuli (the minister of defense, q.v.), Sayyid Abdulillah (minister of finance, q.v.), and Prof. Abdul Qayyum. Only one political party was to be permitted and the NRP was to be an umbrella organization for "all progressive forces." It represented an attempt by Muhammad Daud to limit the influence of his erstwhile Communist supporters and gain grassroots support.

NATIONAL SALVATION SOCIETY See MUHAMMAD ASGHAR.

NAURUZ. New Year (D., *nau* - new, *ruz* - day), the first day of the Afghan and Iranian solar calendar, coinciding with the vernal equinox on March 21 (1. *Hamal*). Nauruz is an important holiday, going back to pre- Islamic times, which is celebrated throughout Afghanistan and Iran. See CALENDAR.

NAZAR MUHAMMAD, LT. GEN. Khalqi member of the PDPA who was chief of staff of the armed forces and minister of defense in 1984-86. He joined Defense Minister Shahnawaz Tanai in a plot against the Najibullah regime and was ousted from all his positions on March 8, 1990. He is a Durrani Pashtun, born in 1935 in Herat province, and educated at the Afghan Military Academy and at the USSR General Staff Academy. He joined the PDPA in 1974 and in March 1979 was appointed by the Taraki regime a member of the "Homeland High Defense Council" which was organized as a result of the increasing mujahedin threat. His air force background was important in the execution of the Saur Revolt. He was arrested as a result of his support of the Tanai coup (q.v.).

NEJAT SCHOOL See NAJAT SCHOOL.

NEW DEMOCRATIC PARTY. *Jam'iat-i Demukrati-yi Nawin*, official name of the *Shu'la-yi Javid* (q.v.).

NEWSPAPERS See PRESS.

NIAZI, ABDUR RAHMAN (NIYAZI ABD AL-RAHMAN). One of the leaders of the Islamist youth movement. See ISLAMIST MOVEMENT.

NIAZI, GHULAM MUHAMMAD. One of the founders of the *sazman-i jawanan-i musulman* (Organization of Muslim Youth) which was affiliated with the *jama'at-i islami* (Islamic Society) in Pakistan and formed the nucleus of the subsequent Islamist movement (See ISLAMIST MOVEMENT). He was born in Katawaz, Ghazni province, and educated at Abu Hanifa Theological School in Kabul and at al-Azhar University at Cairo, where he was exposed to the teachings of the *Ikhwan al-Muslimin* (Muslim Brotherhood, q.v.). He returned to Afghanistan and became teacher and later dean at the faculty of theology of Kabul University. The mujahedin leaders Burhanuddin Rabbani and Abdul Rasul Sayyaf were his students and Rabbani succeeded him in 1972 as amir (leader) of the youth movement. Niazi was arrested in 1974 and executed during the Khalqi regime in 1978.

NIDA-I-KHALQ. A biweekly Persian/Pashto newspaper with a circulation of about 1500. It was published by Dr. Abdur Rahman Mahmudi (q.v.) and edited by Wali Ahmad Ata'i and represented the views of *Khalq*, a liberal group (unrelated to the Khalqi faction of the PDPA). Its first edition appeared on September 15, 1971 (*du shanba*, 12. *hamal* 1330 q.) and ceased publication in January 1972.

NIEDERMAYER, OSKAR VON. A German officer from Bavaria and in 1915-16 co-leader, with Werner Otto von Hentig, of an expedition to Afghanistan for the purpose of winning Amir Habibullah's support for military action against British India during the first World War. The expedition did not achieve its objectives (see HENTIG-NIEDERMAYER EXPEDITION). After the defeat of Germany, Niedermayer was in the Soviet Union under provisions of the secret Treaty of Rapollo of 1922, where he and other German military officers participated in the modernization of the Red Army. At the end of World War II, Niedermayer was arrested by Soviet forces in eastern Europe and died in Moscow's Lubjanka prison in about 1945.

NIFA. The English-language acronym for the National Islamic Front of Afghanistan, the mujahedin party of Pir Sayyid Ahmad Gailani. For details see MAHAZ-I MILLI-YI AFGHANISTAN and GAILANI, SAYYID AHMAD.

NIGHT LETTERS. Clandestine leaflets attacking Afghan rulers and government officials, which have been a potent propaganda tool. Night letters, protesting the secular policies of Afghan governments, were hand-written or copied and distributed by Islamist groups since the 1960s. President Daud was the target of such hostile leaflets, as were Russian soldiers and the Marxist government after 1978. They are distributed at night, hence the name, *shabnama* (D., *shab* night, *nama* letter).

NIKZAD, FAQIR MUHAMMAD. Minister of construction in Prime Minister Khaliqyar's government, announced on May 27, 1990. Born in 1936 in Kabul province. He has a Ph.D. degree in engineering and began his career in the ministry of public works. In early 1980 he was president of the Banai construction unit, and in 1985 president of construction in the ministry of planning. Beginning in 1989 he served as president of the Kabul city and housing construction department. He is not a member of the PDPA.

NIMRUZ (lat. 30-30' N, long. 62-00' E). A province in southwestern Afghanistan with an area of 20,980 square miles and a population of 112,000. The capital of the province is Zaranj, a small town built in the 1960s. The province was called Chakhansur until 1968 and is part of ancient Sistan. Although the second largest in area, it is the smallest province in population. The economy is based primarily on agriculture in the Helmand valley and animal husbandry. Baluch nomads graze their herds in the deserts. A strong wind prevails for about 120 days and is harvested by countless windmills. Nimruz is watered by the Helmand, Khashrud, and Farah rivers which dissipate in the hamuns (q.v.) east of Zaranj.

A multitude of *tepe*, mounds, indicating ancient settlements, as well as mud brick and baked brick ruins can be found throughout the province, testifying to a flourishing civilization before its destruction as a result of Mongol invasions. Also see CHAKHANSUR.

NIZAMNAMA. A code of regulations enacted in the 1920s by King Amanullah which embody his reforms, such as the Constitution of 1923 (*nizam-nama-yi asasi* - basic law). Nizamnama included regulations as to the organization of the state and the payment of taxes, as well as rules concerning engagements and marriages, and the establishment of schools for women. Traditional elements strongly opposed these innovations, which they considered contrary to Islamic law, and with tribal support succeeded in ousting King Amanullah. Also see ISLAMIC LAW.

NOMADS See POWINDAHS.

NORTH-WEST FRONTIER PROVINCE (NWFP). The North-West Frontier Province of India (now Pakistan) which is inhabited largely by Pashtuns, the same ethnic group which is politically dominant in Afghanistan. Because of the inaccessibility of the Frontier area and the martial reputation of its people, the British and Pakistani governments found it preferable to rule the area indirectly, leaving it politically and culturally autonomous under their tribal chiefs. The province had been part of Afghanistan since 1747, but gradually came under British control as

Britain was searching for the "scientific frontier" in the defense of India. In 1893 Sir Mortimer Durand, foreign secretary of the government of India, drew a boundary line, subsequently called Durand Line (q.v.) in disregard of ethnic and cultural considerations, which Amir Abdur Rahman accepted under "duress." The 1893 agreement has been reconfirmed in subsequent Anglo-Afghan treaties. When the state of Pakistan came into existence, the Afghan government wanted the Pashtuns of the NWFP to be given the choice of reunion with Afghanistan or independence in addition to the option of union with Pakistan or India. These choices were not given and a minority of Pashtuns of the NWFP opted for union with Pakistan. The "Pashtunistan Question" subsequently had a deleterious effect on Afghan-Pakistani relations. According to recent reports, some Pashtun nationalists of the NWFP demanded the right to call their province by its ethnic designation Pakhtunkhwa, Land of the Pashtuns. See PASHTUNISTAN and DURAN AGREEMENT.

NUR, NUR AHMAD. Member of the Parcham faction of the PDPA who was appointed permanent Afghan representative at the United Nations in New York in August 1989, after serving shortly as ambassador to Warsaw. He was appointed minister of interior after the Saur Revolt, but assigned as ambassador to Washington in August 1978. He was then purged with other leaders of the Parcham faction on suspicion of plotting a coup. He lived in eastern Europe until Babrak Karmal came to power in December 1979. Born in 1937 in Panjwa'i, Kandahar, the son of Abdul Sattar, a prominent landlord, he was educated at Habibia High School and Kabul University. He embarked on a career in the foreign ministry, but resigned in 1965 to run for parliamentary election as a representative of Panjway district. Once a close friend of Babrak Karmal and an early member of the PDPA, he did not regain any portfolio in the Najibullah cabinet, but has been a member of the politburo and the central committee since June 1981. In April 1988, he was appointed Afghan ambassador to Warsaw, and in January 1991 as ambassador to Havana.

NURISTAN (lat. 34-57' N, long. 70-24' E). A district (since November 1990 a province) in Laghman province which comprises an area of 1,404 square miles and is part of the ancient Kafiristan. See KAFIRISTAN.
The Nuristanis are sunni Muslims, estimated at numbering 90 to 100 thousand. They predominate in Kunar and Laghman provinces and speak several languages and dialects of languages which have intrigued historical linguists, since they have elements of both Indian and Iranian languages. This suggests that these languages (and populations) became isolated at a time when Indo-Iranian populations had not differentiated. Their country was called by Afghans "Kafiristan" (Land of Unbelievers) until 1895/6 when Amir Abdur Rahman conquered it and converted the Kafirs to Islam. Henceforth the country was called Nuristan (Land of Light - meaning the enlightenment of Islam). The Nuristanis and their neighboring Safi Pashtuns were among the first people to rise in October 1978 in rebellion against the PDPA regime. After attempts to pacify

Nuristan failed, the area has remained largely autonomous and is an important base for mujahedin operations. As part of its nationalities policy, the Kabul government has elevated Kati (not a lingua franca for all Nuristani communities) to the status of a "national" language and permitted the publication of radio broadcasts and newspapers in that language. Also see KUNAR and LAGHMAN.

NURISTANI, ABDUL QADIR. Commandant general of the police and gendarmerie, 1973-75, and minister of interior, 1975-78. He participated in the Daud coup in 1973 and was responsible for the arrest of Marxist leaders. He was loyal to President Daud and remained with him in the palace when Daud and his family were killed by Marxists who stormed the palace on April 27,1978.

NURZAI. A large and prosperous tribe of Durranis located primarily in the Rabat and Kadanai districts of Kandahar province and in Farah and Herat provinces. In the early 1930s they were estimated to number about 30,000 fighting men. They are largely cultivators and live in mud-brick villages as well as in the traditional black tents.

NURZAI, DR. ABDUL QAYYUM. Deputy prime minister in Prime Minister Khaliqyar's government of May 1990. Born in 1942 in Farah province, he graduated from the Teachers Training College in Kabul and Kabul University and embarked on a career of teaching. Appointed deputy minister of education in April 1978, and shortly thereafter deputy minister of information and culture. In March 1979 he became editor-in-chief of *Khalq*, the newspaper of the PDPA-faction commonly called *Khalq*. He subsequently held no ministerial positions, but became editor-in-chief of *Dehqan*, the organ of the central committee. He is a member of the Khalqi faction of the PDPA.

NWFP See NORTH-WEST FRONTIER PROVINCE.

-O-

OBAIDULLAH, MAULAVI. An Indian Nationalist and revolutionary, exiled to Kabul in 1915. He was an associate of Mahendra Pratap (q.v.) and with him established the "Free Government of India" in exile with himself as "Home Secretary." He was a Sikh who had converted to Islam and was educated at the Deoband Islamic School in India and subsequently was prominent in the "Wahhabi" (fundamentalist, anti-British) movement. He fled India in February 1915 and arrived in Kabul, October 1915, where he was a leader of the "Pan-Islamic Party" of Muslim Indians in Kabul. He eventually returned to India where he founded a political party in the 1940s, known as "Jamna Narbada Sind Sagar Party," (an all-India party, including the Jamna, Narbada, and Sind rivers and the ocean washing India's shores) and died shortly thereafter.

OBEH (lat. 34-22' N, long. 63-10' E). A small town and administrative district in eastern Herat province which lies on the Hari Rud (q.v.). The inhabitants are primarily Qipchak (Turks) as well as some Taimanis, Ghilzais, and Sayyids (see individual entries). About 26 miles east of Obeh is the village of Chisht, the birthplace of Muinuddin Muhammad (b. 1142), founder of the Chishti sufi fraternity and one of the great sufi masters of India.

OFUQ, MUHAMMAD ZAHIR. Head of the "Revolutionary Society of Afghan Toilers," a small leftist group, which in July 1986 joined the PDPA. Ofuq was a founding member of the PDPA and an alternate member of the central committee. He was pro-Khalqi but subsequently left the party and formed his own group. In 1986 he was appointed first vice president and scientific secretary of the Academy of Science. He is reported to have been arrested in 1991.

ORAKZAI. Pashtun tribe located at the Pakistani side of the Afghan border which is divided into seven clans: the Sultanzai, Bahramzai, Ismailzai, Massuzai, Alizai (or Sturi Khel), Lashkarzai, and Daulatzai. There are various traditions as to its origin: According to one, they are the descendants of a Persian prince, Sikander Shah, who was exiled (i.e., "Wrukzai") in the Kohat area a thousand years ago; another tradition claims its origin from Abdul Aziz a descendant of Warak, one of three brothers, who came from Afghanistan to the Orakzai hills. Western scholars speculate that they are of Indian stock with some infusion of Turkic blood, and are now reckoned to be Ghurghusht Pashtuns (Ridgeway, 1910).

ORMURI. A group of perhaps 300 families who speak Ormuri one of a number of almost extinct eastern Iranian languages. They are sunni Muslims and also speak Pashto and Dari and are located primarily in the Logar valley as well as in Peshawar and Waziristan on the Pakistani side of the border.

ORUZGAN (lat. 33-15' N, long. 66-0' E). A province in central Afghanistan with an area of 11,169 square miles and about 483,000 inhabitants and also the name of a village and its surrounding district. The population is largely Hazara with some Pashtuns and other ethnic communities in the south. The administrative center of the province is Tirinkot. The province is part of the Hazarajat (q.v.) and in the late 19th century was incorporated into Kandahar province. In 1964 Oruzgan became a province and elected representatives to the Afghan parliament.

It is a mountainous area, easily accessible only from the south, through valleys at altitudes at of 3,000 to 7,600 feet. It is traversed by the Helmand river and its tributaries. The province is largely agricultural with the cultivation of cereal grains. Major handicrafts include the production of woven carpets, called *gelim*.

OXUS. Greek name of the Amu Daria (q.v.) which is still used in the West. See AMU DARIA.

-P-

PAGHMAN (lat. 34-36' N, long. 68-57' E). A foothill town about 12 miles northwest of Kabul, where King Amanullah built a modern town, including a royal palace. Members of the upper class also built beautiful villas. A triumphal arch (*taq-i zafar*) was built in honor of the martyrs in the Anglo-Afghan wars. An open-air theater was constructed for the entertainment of Kabuli citizens who would visit the town on weekends during the hot summer months.

The town is at an altitude of about 8,000 feet on the eastern slope of the Paghman range. A reservoir and water line from the area supplies Kabul with potable water. Although it is near Kabul, it is surrounded by woods and high mountains and has been a shelter for mujahedin groups. Much of the town is destroyed. Paghman is the birthplace of several prominent political leaders, including the Khalqi President Hafizullah Amin (q.v.) and the radical Islamist mujahedin leader Abdul Rasul Sayyaf (q.v.).

PAIGIR, See PEIGIR.

PAINDA KHAN (PAYANDA). Chief of the Muhammadzai section of the Durranis (q.v.) and ancestor of the families of both King Amanullah and ex-King Zahir Shah. He was the son of Haji Jamal Khan (lived 1719-1805) who helped Ahmad Shah (q.v.) gain the throne in 1747. Painda Khan backed Zaman Shah (q.v.) in his struggle for the throne against other sons of Timur Shah (q.v.), but subsequently plotted against him and was executed at the direction of Zaman Shah. Painda Khan's sons avenged this deed and thus contributed to the downfall of the Sadozai dynasty. His son, Dost Muhammad (q.v., 1826-38 and 1842-63), became the founder of the Muhammadzai dynasty (q.v.).

PAKHTUN. Another form of Pashtun, as pronounced in the eastern Pashtun dialect. See PASHTUN.

PAKTIA (lat. 33-35' N, long. 69-35' E). A province in eastern Afghanistan comprising an area of almost 3,860 square miles and a population of about 484,000. The capital of the province is Gardez with a pre-1978 population of about 10,000. Until the early 1970s Paktia also included Paktika province and southeastern parts of Ghazni provinces. The province is largely mountainous, but well-watered and cultivated, and shares an almost 125 miles long border with Pakistan. The population is largely Ghilzai Pashtun (q.v.), but in the south and west are found Jadran and in the east Jaji, Mangal, Tani, and Waziri tribes (for tribes, see individual entries).

The economy depends largely on agriculture with wheat, maize, barley, and rice being the principal crops. Landholdings are generally small, and animal husbandry and illegal timber cutting supplement agricultural activities.

Paktia is an area of strategic importance for the mujahedin because it has a common border with Pakistan and lies on the route to Kabul. There has been considerable fighting in the area because many of the PDPA leadership are Ghilzais from Paktia, where the Kabul government also enjoyed some support. A mujahedin offensive finally led to the capture of Khost on March 31, 1991 (see KHOST). According to UN estimates a large portion of the population lives as refugees in Pakistan, more than from any other province.

PAKTIKA (lat. 32-25' N, long. 68-45' E). Paktika province was created during the time of President Daud (1973- 78) from the southeastern districts of Paktia and Ghazni provinces. It comprises an area of about 7,336 square miles and has an estimated population of about 245,000. The provincial capital is Sharan and the population is largely Ghilzai of the Sulaiman Khel, Kharoti, and Jadran tribes, but also includes Tajiks and Waziri Pashtuns. About 31 percent of the population have settled as refugees in Pakistan.

Paktika has suffered greatly from the war, and the destruction of the ancient system of irrigation in the Katawaz plain has greatly reduced the amount of cultivated land. Unrestricted cutting of timber has denuded formerly forested areas. As of 1990 the province was in mujahedin control.

PAKTIN, RAZ MUHAMMAD. Khalq member of the PDPA who was appointed minister of interior in Prime Minister Khaliqyar's government of May 1990, in the aftermath of the Tanai coup (q.v.). Born in 1938 in Zurmat, Paktia province, he was educated at the Kabul Teachers College and in the Soviet Union, where he obtained the Ph.D. degree in engineering. He joined the party in 1966 and after the Saur Revolt was appointed ambassador to the Soviet Union (1978-79), deputy minister of water and power (1979), and minister of water and power (1982-88).

PAMIRS (lat. 38-0' N, long. 73-0' E). A mountain range running in a north-south direction, dividing the Oxus basin from the plains of Kashgar, Sinkiang province of China. There are a series of valleys forming plateaus at altitudes of from 11,000 to 13,000 feet. Located in the Wakhan Corridor, which extends to the Chinese border, the plateaus were inhabited by Qirghiz (q.v.) hunters and herders, most of whom fled to Pakistan and emigrated to Turkey.

PANJA. The name given to the Wakhan (q.v.) branch of the Amu Daria. See AMU DARIA.

PANJDEH INCIDENT. A military encounter in 1885 in which a Russian force under General Alikhanov annexed the Panjdeh district north of Herat province (now part of the Turkmen Soviet Republic). The military action pitted superior Russian troops against about 500 defending Afghan soldiers headed by the Afghan General Ghausuddin (q.v.). Afghan rulers claimed the area by virtue of the fact that the Turkomans of Panjdeh had been their occasional tributaries, but the Russians insisted that they were part of the Turkoman nation of Khiva and Merv, which Russia had annexed in 1881 and 1884. An Anglo-Russian commission was to meet and resolve the dispute, but military action began on March 30, 1885, before Sir Peter Lumsden, a British Indian general, and his Russian counterpart had arrived on the scene. Amir Abdur Rahman learned of the incident while he was on a state visit in Rawalpindi, India, and accepted the fait accompli at the urging of Lord Dufferin, the viceroy of India. The fact that Britain did not come to Afghanistan's defense, as she was obligated to do in case of unprovoked Russian aggression, confirmed the Afghan ruler in his belief that he could not rely on British promises of support.

PANJSHIR (lat. 34-38' N, long. 69-42' E). An administrative district in northern Parwan (now Kapisa) province with an area of about 273 square miles and an agricultural population of about 30,000. The district is traversed by the Panjshir river which rises on the southern slopes of the Hindu Kush in the vicinity of the Khawak pass.

According to local tradition, the valley was called *Kach Kan* until the Ghaznavid period (q.v.) when Sultan Mahmud was building the "Sultan Dam." He recruited people from all over the country, but only five men came from the valley who claimed that no more were needed. And indeed, they performed extraordinary labor, so that the Sultan called them the "five lions." The Panjshiris call them "panj piran-i panjshir," (the five saints of Panjshir) and built a mausoleum for them.

The population is largely Tajik which have been converted to sunni Islam as late as the 16th century. The area was often independent or autonomous and, although the Panjshiris acknowledged the Afghan amir as their ruler, they rarely paid taxes to the Kabul government. It has only been since the time of Amir Abdur Rahman that the Kabul government asserted its sovereignty over the area. The Panjshir valley is quite inaccessible; therefore, in the present war the Soviet and Kabul forces have never succeeded in bringing it under full government control. Its location, impinging on the strategic Salang road which connects Kabul with the northern provinces, made the Panjshir valley an ideal base for mujahedin activity. Ahmad Shah Mas'ud (q.v.), called "The Lion of Panjshir" by his admirers, was able to withstand numerous Soviet incursions, and has not been evicted from the valley, making him one of the most successful mujahedin commanders.

PANJSHIRI, DASTAGIR. A founding member of the PDPA of the Khalqi faction, who became minister of education (May - August 1978) and minister of public works (October - December 1978). He was born in 1933 in the Panjshir district and educated in Kabul. He held various positions with the ministry of information and culture and was jailed for his political activities from 1969 to 1972. In 1973 he tried unsuccessfully to form his own "workers" party *junbesh-i kargari*, (Workers Movement). He was a member of the politburo (1980-85), but did not hold any ministerial position in the Parcham governments and was expelled from the PDPA in March 1990 together with a number of Khalqis involved in the Tanai Plot (q.v.).

PARCHAM. A weekly newspaper founded in March 1968 by the Parcham (Banner) faction of the PDPA. It was published by Sulaiman Layeq (q.v.) and edited by him and Mir Akbar Khaibar (q.v.), the faction's major ideologist. It carried articles in Pashto and Dari and was openly critical of the Afghan government and was therefore closed in July 1969. One faction of the PDPA which supported Babrak Karmal in opposition to Nur Muhammad Taraki was subsequently named Parcham after this newspaper. See PEOPLES DEMOCRATIC PARTY OF AFGHANISTAN.

PAROPAMISUS (lat. 34-30' N, long. 63-30' E). Name given by Western writers to the Safid Kuh and Band-i-Baba, the range bounding on the Hari Rud (q.v.) valley on the north. See BAND- I-BABA.

PARSIWAN See FARSIWAN.

PARWAN (lat. 35-15' N, long. 69-30' E). A province located north of Kabul with an area of 2,282 square miles and a population of about 418,000. Parwan now includes also the former province of Kapisa (created in 1964 and subsequently made a sub-province, *loya wolewali*). The capital of Parwan is Charikar, a town with 22,500 inhabitants, located at the mouth of the Ghorband valley about 49 miles north of Kabul. The province is famous for its grapes, some of which are dried and exported as raisins. The first cement plant in Afghanistan was started at Jabal-us-Siraj (q.v.) and a hydro- electric power plant provided electricity for Kabul. Subsequently a textile industry was developed at Gulbahar (q.v.). The province is of great strategic importance as it is crossed by the Salang (q.v.) highway which leads from Kabul north over the Hindu Kush (q.v.).

PASDARAN-I JIHAD-I ISLAM. A radical Islamist shi'a group, inspired and supported by the Iranian *pasdaran* (Guardians of the Iranian Revolution) which established itself in the Hazarajat in 1983. Akbari, one of its leaders, collaborated with Sadeqi of Nasr (q.v.) and by 1984 succeeded in the expulsion of the Shura (q.v.) commanded by Sayyid Ali Beheshti (q.v.) from most of the Hazarajat. The pasdaran were recruited with Iranian support from Hazaras resident in Iran and local militants in the

Hazarajat who seceded from the Shura. They are led by young members of the ulama, educated in Iran, and follow the "line" of Ayatollah Khomeini, professing hostility to the Soviet Union and the United States ("neither East nor West") and look to Iran as a model for an Islamic state. The pasdaran seem to be moving away from close cooperation with their Iranian brothers. Also see NASR and SADEQI.

PASHAI. A collective term for a Dardic language of an ethnic community of about 100,000 sunni Muslims located primarily in Laghman and Kapisa provinces. In 1981 the Kabul regime declared Pashai one of Afghanistan's national languages and began broadcasting in that language on Radio Kabul.

PASHTO Or PAKHTO. Pashto is the language of the largest Afghan ethnic group and of about an equal number of people in parts of Baluchistan and the North West Frontier Province (q.v.) of Pakistan. Until the early twentieth century in Afghanistan, only the Pashto-speakers were called Afghans, while the rest of the population was called by their ethnic or tribal designation.

Pashto is an Indo-Iranian language related to Dari, but the two languages are not mutually intelligible. Two main dialects are spoken, the "hard" or "Peshawari," called "Pakhto," and the "soft," or "Kandahari," called "Pashto." The former is also called the "northern" or "eastern" dialect, the latter the "southern" or "western." The earliest Pashto book is the *History of the Yusufzai* (1417), by Shaikh Mali, a Yusufzai chief. There is a considerable amount of native literature, consisting mainly of tribal and national histories and love poems. Most important of these are the Divan (Collection) of Khushhal Khan Khatak (1644-90); the *Makhzan-i Afghani* (Afghan Treasure), by Akhund Darwaza, a Tajik; the *Tarikh-i Murassa*, (History of Jewels) by Afzal Khan, Khatak, a grandson of Khushhal Khan (15th-16th c).

In Afghanistan, as in Central Asia and parts of India, Persian (or Dari) was the language of the royal court, but since the early twentieth century Afghan governments have promoted Pashto as the national language. In 1923 a literary group, *Da Pashto Maraka*, was formed for this purpose, followed by the Pashto Academy (see AFGHAN ACADEMY), which conducted research in Pashto literature and culture. But Dari remains the language of education in the greater part of Afghanistan and virtually all educated Afghans speak and understand it. Many urban Pashtuns use Dari as their first language and some Pashtun nomads are now Dari-speakers. The Constitution of 1964 declared both Pashto and Dari official languages.

PASHTO TOLANA See AFGHAN ACADEMY.

PASHTUN(S). Also called Pakhtuns (and Pathans in India), have been the politically dominant group in Afghanistan, with a population estimated at from 6 to 7 million concentrated largely in the west, south, and east, but also scattered throughout Afghanistan. Another 7 million Pashtuns live in Pakistan across the Durand Line. Except for the Turis (q.v.) and a few groups in Pakistan, all Pashtuns are sunni Muslims, and most were converted to Islam by the 10th century A.D. The Pashtuns are excellent soldiers and many an invader of India chose to enlist them in his armies rather than force his way through their territory. Tribal society is organized along family, clan, sectional, and tribal lines. The tribe, *qabila*, or clan, *qaum*, (from the Arabic *qama* - "those who rise together in war") are named after their eponymic ancestor and carry the suffix "zai," as in Muhammadzai, the "sons of Muhammad;" the clan or a group living in the same locality is called, *khel*, like in Yahya Khel; and a kinship group is called the *kor*, or *kahol*. Alien affiliated groups, like *hamsaya*, (dwellers under the same shade) are often attached to a tribe and enjoy its protection. Each section has its own chief, or "malik," and the most powerful clan often provides the chief of the tribe. Although the tribal system has undergone changes, traditionally, chiefs have to be successful leaders and exemplify Pashtun values; that is they have to be generous and brave. They are not absolute rulers of their fellow tribesmen. Each clan decides matters of its welfare by council, the *jirga* (q.v.). Jirgas also arbitrate disputes.

The Pashtuns living in the inaccessible areas on both sides of the Durand Line (q.v.) adhere to their traditional code of behavior, the *Pashtunwali*, which guides the jirgas in resolving disputes. The principal pillars of this code are *nanawati*, mediation or protection; *badal*, retaliation; and *mailmastia*, hospitality (See PASHTUNWALI). Urban Pashtuns still have a direct or emotional link to their tribes. The frontier Afghans are politically autonomous along the tribal belt on both sides of the Durand Line, but the rest have come increasingly under the control of the central governments.

Their dress consists of long shirts and wide pants which are gathered and tied around the waist. A turban (*lungi*) is wound in various styles over a skull cap and open sandals (*chaplis*) are worn, regardles of the severity of the weather. A shawl of wool or cotton is wrapped around the body for protection from the cold. Frontier tribesmen also carry daggers and guns, which are usually manufactured in village workshops. Women wear long shirts, trousers, and a kerchief and adorn themselves with coins stitched to their shirts, as well as bracelets, necklaces, and earrings. Their long hair is usually kept in a braid. A Pashtun tribal dance, the *atan*, is performed by men; it has been adopted with some changes as the Afghan national dance (See ATAN).

About two million Pashtuns are still partially nomadic, most of them Ghilzai Pashtuns (called Kuchis in Afghanistan and Powindahs in India) who used to migrate each year far into British-India (also see POWINDAHS). Afghanistan's relations with Pakistan since 1947 and the present war in Afghanistan have ended most of the seasonal transborder migrations, and many nomads from the frontier belt have remained in Pakistan.

Because secular education was largely in Dari, the Afghan government opened tribal boarding schools in Kabul and subsequently in the southern and eastern provinces where Pashto is the language of education. Some of these schools prepared students for higher eduction in Kabul, Jalalabad, and Kandahar provinces. Many opted for military careers, and Pashto-speakers were drawn into the political mainstream of Kabul politics. Also see TRIBES, PASHTUNS.

PASHTUNISTAN. "Land of the Afghans" (or Pashtuns), the name given by Afghan nationalists to the North-West Frontier Province and parts of Baluchistan in present Pakistan. It was part of Afghanistan when the state was founded in 1747, but soon came under the control of the Sikh ruler Ranjit Singh (q.v.) and subsequently the British-Indian government. Direct rule of the area was difficult because it is mountainous and difficult of access; therefore the Pashtun tribes were allowed a considerable measure of autonomy. The British government cut the area from Afghanistan in 1893, drawing a border without regard to ethnic and cultural boundaries. Amir Abdur Rahman (q.v., 1880-1901) had scarcely consolidated his power and felt he had to accept "under duress" the Durand Line as his border (See DURAND AGREEMENT). In 1901, the British-Indian government created the North-West Frontier Province, but left the tribal lands outside of the directly administered areas. Five Tribal Agencies (Malakand, Khaibar, Kurram, North Waziristan, and South Waziristan) were set up with autonomous khans (chiefs), governed by tribal councils. A British agent protected the interests of the government. Tribesmen were engaged as militia to keep order in their own areas, and if a tribe conducted raids into the low lands, punitive campaigns were organized.

In 1947, when India was to be divided on the basis of a plebiscite, the Afghan government and Pashtun nationalists demanded that the Pashtuns be given an option to vote, if not for union with Afghanistan, then for the creation of an independent "Pashtunistan." This option was not given and, as a result of a boycott by members of the Frontier Congress, a Muslim party allied with the Hindu Congress party, 68 percent of a low-voter turnout agreed to union with Pakistan. Afghanistan protested the procedure and cast the only vote against Pakistan's admission to the United Nations. Afghanistan's relations with Pakistan were subsequently plagued by the "Pashtunistan Question." The Afghan government supported the Pashtun nationalists. Pakistan retaliated by closing the border at times. This issue seems now to be dormant, if not dead; but just in case, the Pakistani government tended to support Islamist mujahedin groups, like Gulbuddin Hekmatyar's *hizb-i Islami* (q.v.), to the exclusion of nationalist groups. Pashtun nationalists have protested the fact that the NWFP is the only province in Pakistan not named after its inhabitants, and demanded the adoption of the name *Pakhtunkhwa* (P. for Pashtunistan). Also see AFGHAN FOREIGN RELATIONS and DURAND AGREEMENT.

PASHTUNWALI. Name of the Pashtun traditional code of behavior which can be summarized under the terms of *nanawati*, mediation or protection; *badal*, retaliation; and *melmastia*, hospitality.

Nanawati is the obligation to give protection to anyone seeking asylum even at the risk of the protector's life, and to mediate for the weaker party in disputes in which he seeks peace with someone he has injured. It is, therefore, a means of ending a feud. *Badal* must be exacted for personal insults, damage to property, or blood feuds. *Badal* is exacted for the murder of a member of one's family or *hamsaya* (client); and for violation of safe conduct (*badragga*). Feuds may involve entire tribes and last for years until a jirga of elders, or mullas, succeeds in mediating a solution. *Khunbaha*, blood-money, has to be paid for murder, except in the case when an even number of feuding individuals were killed. Each injury has a price: at the turn of the century 180 to 300 rupees had to be paid for a life; the loss of an eye, ear, arm or leg carried a certain value (the British government in India codified tribal law, including the amounts of money to be paid). Anthropologist disagree as to the major cause of feuding, whether it is in defense of female honor, competition for land, or retaliation for personal insult.

Mailmastia is considered a sacred duty and every village has a guest house or uses its mosque as a shelter for visitors. A guest's person and property is protected, and a Pashtun is proud to "offer the guest or stranger what he can not even afford for himself."

In a sense, each Afghan tribe constitutes a nation and no one may enter a tribe's territory without the permission of a tribe and the assurance of safe conduct *badragga*. A traveler pays for an armed escort which will convey him through the territory of a tribe and hand him over to a *badragga* of the neighboring tribe.

Violation of the Pashtun code will bring dishonor and shame not just to an individual but to the entire tribe or the community. The process of "detribalization," sedentarization, and Islamization has led to a weakening of the of the practice of *Pashtunwali*.

PASHTO TOLANA See AFGHAN ACADEMY.

PAYAM. Organ of the Watan party (formerly PDPA) which succeeded the *Haqiqat-i Saur Inqilab*, the former party ogan. *Payam* is under the editorship of Bareq-Shafi'i (q.v.).

PAYAM-I IMRUZ. "Message of Today," a weekly newspaer published in Dari by Ghulam Nabi Khater and edited by Abdul Rauf Turkmani and Muhammad Tahir Muhsini. It was first published on February 9, 1966, and ceased publication on May 25 when the editors resigned. It was an opposition paper which demanded justice, equality, national unity, and the eradication of social vices. It favored the expansion of education and agricultural and industrial development.

PAZHWAK, ABDUR RAHMAN. A poet, scholar, and writer in Pashto and Dari who served as president of the 21st General Assembly of the United Nations in 1966, and as ambassador to Bonn (1972), New Delhi (1973), and London (1976-78). Born in 1919 in Ghazni and educated in Nangarhar and at Habibia School in Kabul, he started a career as journalist. He was editor of *Islah* (q.v., 1939), director general of the Pashto Academy, 1941, and was appointed press attaché at the Afghan embassy in Washington in 1948 and London, 1946 and 1951. In 1955 he was appointed general director of political affairs in the ministry of foreign affairs. In 1958 he became Afghan ambassador to the United Nations. During the Taraki regime he was under house arrest and left Afghanistan for medical treatment in 1982. He applied for political asylum to the United Nations and went to the United States, but has moved to Peshawar in April 1991.

PAZHWAK, NE'MATULLAH. Appointed one of five deputy prime ministers in Prime Minister Khaliqyar's government of May 1990. Born in 1928 in Nangarhar province and educated in Kabul and the United States, he took a position in the ministry of education and became head of the Teachers Training and Habibia schools. He was appointed governor of Bamian, 1970, and Kabul 1971, and served as minister of interior in Musa Shafiq's government (q.v., 1972-73) and minister of education under President Daud (1973). After the Saur Revolt he was appointed minister without portfolio (1980). Because he is not a member of the PDPA and was prominent in pre-1978 governments, his participation in Parchami governments lent an element of legitimacy to the regime.

PEIGIR, SAYYID AKRAM (PAIGIR). Minister without portfolio in Prime Minister Khaliqyar's government of May 1990, and member of the central council of the executive body of Watan party. Born in Jozjan province of a Turkoman family and, after receiving a B.A. degree, taught in a Jozjan province school. In 1977 he was appointed mayor of Shiberghan, where he served until the Saur Revolt. A member of the Parcham faction of the PDPA, he became president of the liaison and documents department of the central committee (1979). In 1987 he was appointed minister of state for direct cooperative affairs, and in 1988 minister of repatriate affairs.

PEOPLES DEMOCRATIC PARTY OF AFGHANISTAN (PDPA). Afghan Marxist party (since June 1990 called *Hizb-i Watan*, Fatherland Party) was founded in 1965 and succeeded to power on April 27, 1978, in a coup, called the Saur Revolution (named after "Saur," the month of the revolt). The party was officially founded on January 1, 1965, at a meeting of about 30 persons in Nur Muhammad Taraki's (q.v.) house in Karte Char, Kabul. Taraki was chosen general secretary of the party and Babrak Karmal deputy secretary and secretary of a central committee, whose membership consisted of Taraki, Karmal, Ghulam Dastagir Panjshiri, Dr. Saleh Muhammad Zirai, Shahrullah(?) Shahpar, Sultan Ali Keshtmand, and Taher Badakhshi. Alternate members were Dr. Shah Wali, Karim Misaq,

Dr. Muhammad Taher, and Abdul Wahhab Safi (See individual entries). The party drafted a manifesto which stated that it was a workers' party. It declared Afghanistan a feudal society which should be transformed into a socialist state. It claimed its intention of obtaining power by democratic means.

From the beginning there was rivalry between the two leading personalities, Karmal being urbane and known from his activities on the campus of Kabul University and as a member of parliament. He attracted followers among the Kabul intelligentsia, students, and government officials, and some military officers of various ethnic backgrounds. Taraki, on the other hand, was more successful among the Pashtuns, military officers, and students and teachers of schools in which tribal Pashtuns predominated. The PDPA published a newspaper, called *Khalq* (Masses), first appearing on April 11, 1966. Only six issues appeared until it was banned on the recommendation of parliament for being "anti-Islamic" and opposed to the new constitution. Taraki was the publisher and Muhammad Hasan Bareq-Shafi'i (q.v.) the editor. By 1967 the party split into two entities, subsequently called *Khalq* and *Parcham*, after their respective newspapers. *Parcham* (Banner) was founded in 1968, published by Sulaiman Layeq (q.v.) and edited by him and Mir Akbar Khaibar (q.v.). Having been successful in winning a parliamentary seat, Babrak Karmal was willing to cooperate with Afghan governments, while the Khalqis remained aloof. Personality differences rather than ideological disputes were the cause of factional strife which has continued. In 1977 the two factions reunited in a tenuous coalition with the help of Soviet and Indian Communist Party mediation.

The Saur Revolt was precipitated when the Parcham ideologue, Mir Akbar Khaibar (q.v.), was assassinated, according to some sources by Khalqis who resented his recruiting efforts in the army. The Marxists, however, accused the government of the deed and the party followed up with a funeral procession which turned into a public demonstration of a crowd of about 15,000 against the Daud government. The government reacted with arrests of the leadership, but three days later, on April 27, 1978, Marxist officers in the armed forces staged their successful coup. The Democratic Republic of Afghanistan was proclaimed and in early May the formation of a government was announced with Nur Muhammad Taraki as president and premier and Babrak Karmal as deputy premier. The majority of cabinet members were Khalqis (see Chronology). By July the Khalqis had purged members of the Parcham faction, including Babrak Karmal. Leading Parchamis were given diplomatic assignments abroad and a purported Parcham coup in August was suppressed. Abdul Qadir, minister of defense, Sultan Ali Keshtmand, minister of planning, and Muhammad Rafi, minister of public works (see individual entries), were arrested. On September 22 the Parcham ambassadors were dismissed and stayed abroad until their return with Soviet support.

Once in power, the leaders of the PDPA avoided calling themselves Marxists, but party members used the appellation *rafiq*, "comrade," and the banner of the Democratic Republic was patterned after that of an

East-bloc state (See Flag). A number of decrees issued by the Khalq revolutionary council established Taraki as the "great leader" (No. 1), set up a government with Taraki as president of the revolutionary council and Karmal as vice president (No. 2), and abrogated the Daud constitution (No. 3). Subsequent decrees elevated the status of Uzbaki, Turkmani, Baluchi, and Nuristani languages to the status of "national languages," to be promoted in the Afghan media (No. 4); deprived members of the royal family of their citizenship (No. 5), cancelled mortgages (No. 6), gave equal rights to women (No. 7), and ordered land reforms (No. 8). Former government officials and political opponents were arrested and thousands were assassinated.

Unlike some foreign observers, Afghans had little doubt about the Marxist character of the PDPA. During its brief existence, the newspaper *Khalq* had called for class struggle and extolled the achievements of the Great October Socialist Revolution, attacking the "feudal" conditions in Afghanistan. *Parcham* voiced similar sentiments and caused quite a sensation when its editor Bareq-Shafi'i used the title *dorud* (praise) for "the great Lenin" in a poem. This term was customarily used as an appellation of the king or the Prophet Muhammad.

Khalqi supremacy did, however, not end strife in the PDPA. Hafizullah Amin had become vice premier and minister of foreign affairs and on July 8, 1978, was elected secretary of the secretariat of the central committee. By that time it became apparent that he was the dominant personality in the party. He became prime minister and minister of foreign affairs in April 1979, and president on September 16, 1979. Barely a month later, on October 9, Taraki was assassinated. A split occurred in the Khalqi faction between the "Red Khalqis" of Taraki and the "Black Khalqis" of Amin. A third faction, the followers of a Dr. Zarghun already existed. They were called the "Paktia Khalqis." Increasing guerrilla activity of mujahedin forces may have prevented further strife in the Khalqi camp. Amin was said to have shown a tendency to develop into an "Afghan Tito" and demanded the recall of the Soviet ambassador, Alexandr M. Puzanov (q.v.), who expected Amin to follow his bidding. Puzanov was reported to have been implicated in a plot to assassinate Amin.

Mass arrests and executions, blamed on the Taraki era, were not ended, as was apparent from a list published with about 12,000 names of killed or missing persons. Hafizullah Amin's intelligence service, KAM (q.v.), replaced Taraki's AGSA (q.v.) and new government and party positions were announced. About 5,000 Soviet advisers resided in Afghanistan when, on December 25, 1979, an airlift of Soviet troops began that eventually brought in some 115,000 troops. On December 27, a Parchami coup, reputedly with Soviet armed support replaced Hafizullah Amin with Babrak Karmal.

Karmal announced a government (see Chronology) which included the dreaded head of AGSA, Asadullah Sarwari, as deputy premier and two other Khalqis, Sayyid Muhammad Gulabzoi as minister of interior, and Sherjan Mazduryar as minister of transport. KAM was purged and renamed KHAD, and the Parchami regime promised a new deal and an end to the excesses of the previous governments. Additional Soviet troops arrived in Afghanistan and established bases in various strategic locations. The government proclaimed a general amnesty and opened the doors of the feared Pul-i-Charkhi prison. Early Khalqi decrees of land reform (Nos. 6 and 8) and the emancipation of women (No. 7) were rescinded and the tricolor replaced the red flag. But it was too late to overcome the "sins" of the past. The presence of Soviet forces in Afghanistan quickly transformed a civil war into a war of liberation, and many of those freed from jail augmented the growing forces of the mujahedin. Karmal's lack of success in destroying the mujahedin was the likely reason for his resignation (or ouster) on May 4, 1986, and his replacement by Dr. Najibullah, the one-time head of KHAD.

Ideological devolution continued under Najibullah when the Kabul government initiated a policy of "national reconciliation" and changed the name of the PDPA to *hizb-i watan*, Fatherland Party. The early orthodoxy of adherence to Marxism-Leninism has been gradually replaced by a general, socialist orientation and political liberalization, as the Parchami government attempts to survive in a national front coalition of "progressive" parties. Soviet troops withdrew from Afghanistan on February 15, 1989, but the party is still in command of Kabul and the major urban centers in Afghanistan. In a speech to the Watan Party Congress in July 1990, Dr. Najibullah claimed a party membership of 173,614 of whom 15,924 are women. Although the party would continue to be "revolutionary," it would relinquish its monopoly of power and henceforth adhere to the "traditional principles of democracy." The newspaper *Payam*, edited by Bareq-Shafi'i, is the new party organ. The reduction of military activity in recent months and war-weariness of the Afghan people has raised hopes for a peaceful solution of the war. See Appendix for membership in the central council of the Watan Party.

PIONEERS. *Sazman-i Peshahangan* is a youth movement of the PDPA patterned after the Soviet model. It recruits children between the ages of ten and fifteen who are led by adults. Most of the pioneers are the children of party member. Upon reaching the age of fifteen, the pioneers are enlisted into the Democratic Youth Organization of Afghanistan, and upon reaching the age of twenty-one are recruited into the PDPA (since renamed Fatherland Party). Under Parchami rule the former ideological adherence to socialism and Marxism-Leninism has given way to a socialist-oriented, nationalist stage of political development.

PIR. A religious leader, old man, title given to heads of sufi orders.

POLYTECHNIC INSTITUTE, KABUL. A technical institute for post-secondary education in Kabul, opened in February 1967 with Soviet assistance, and staffed with Soviet and Afghan instructors. It awards degrees in fields of engineering with special emphasis on geology, exploration, and extraction of mineral and natural gas resources. It was one sector of Afghan education where the Soviet Union was dominant and rivalled the American-supported engineering department of Kabul University. Many graduates of the institute went to the Soviet Union for advanced studies. After the Saur Revolt it was given a monopoly in engineering education, while the Kabul University engineering department was closed for reasons of "redundancy." Also see EDUCATION AND KABUL UNIVERSITY.

POPAL, ALI AHMAD. Minister of education (1955-63, 1963-64, 1967-69) and ambassador to Bonn (1964-66), Ankara (1966-67), Karachi (1969-74), Tokyo (1974-77), and the Moscow (1977-78). Born in 1916 and educated at Najat high school and in Germany where he obtained the Ph.D. degree. Retired after the Saur Revolt and still lives in Kabul.

POPALZAI. A main division of the Durranis (q.v.). The Sadozai, a chief branch of the Popalzai, produced the kings of modern Afghanistan from 1747 to the 1830s when the Muhammadzai branch of the Durranis succeeded to power. The Popalzai heartland lies to the north of Kandahar, but colonies of this branch exist also in Multan and Dera Ismael Khan on the Pakistani side of the Durand Line.

POWINDAH Or KUCHI. A term applied in India to Pashtun merchant-nomads who seasonally traveled far into India. There is disagreement as to the etymology of the name: one source derives the word from the Persian *parwinda*, a bale of merchandise, because of their occupation as merchant nomads, more likely from *pawidan*, to wander, or perhaps from the Pashto word *powal*, to graze flocks. In Afghanistan Powindahs are called Kuchis.

The majority of the Powindah are Sulaiman Khel Pashtuns, one of the largest of the Ghilzai tribes. They lead a pastoral way of life, some as nomad shepherds, others as merchants and camelmen, carrying on trade between Afghanistan and India. Individuals who left their families behind at times engaged in day labor, sold clothing, or lent money at interest. They were formerly scattered over northern India and would occasionally travel as far as Burma and Nepal.

In the Frontier Belt they were always heavily armed, but upon entering India deposited their weapons, keeping only their daggers and swords. The Powindahs created an image in India of the Afghan from their appearance in their "storm-stained Afghan clothing, reckless manners, and boisterous voices," tall and haggard but proud and free. Their chiefs, *maliks*, were in charge only during migration and when crossing hostile tribal territory. They are sunni Muslims of the Hanafi school and adhere to a sufi fraternity; but their law is a mixture of tribal code and the *Shari'a* (see ISLAMIC LAW).

After the British left India in 1947 and the creation of Pakistan, the Powindah were gradually limited in their migrations across international borders. As a result of the Pashtunistan dispute (q.v.), Pakistan closed its borders to large-scale migration and the Powindah were forced to redirect their routes of migrations. Afghan governments have tried to settle the nomads, but have had only limited success. The nomads have been able to adapt to new ways by moving into the motorized transport business and former nomads now control much of the transport from Afghanistan to the port of Karachi in Pakistan.

POYA, NADIR ALI. Second in command to Majid Kalakani (q.v.) of SAMA, a leftist, anti- Pashtun movement which fought the Kabul regime after the Soviet intervention. Born in the 1940's in Chimtal village, Mazar-i-Sharif, the son of Brigadier Samad Ali Khan, a Dai Zangi Hazara (q.v.), and educated in Mazar-i Sharif and at the Polytechnic Institute at Kabul. He was a member of *Shu'la-yi Jawid* (q.v.) and was imprisoned in Kabul for two years in the 1960s. He subsequently became a member of SAMA. He was arrested in 1981 and executed in 1982. He had a reputation as a competent debater, organizer, and agitator.

PRATAP, MAHENDRA. Hindu member of the Hentig-Niedermayer Expedition (q.v.) who formed a "Provisional Free India" government in Kabul with Maulawi Obaidullah (q.v.) as "home minister" and Barakatullah (q.v.) as "prime minister and himself as president. He was in touch with Indian revolutionaries and independence movements in India and frequently visited Germany and the Soviet Union to solicit support and political recognition. He eventually returned to India and wrote "My German Mission to High Asia." He later founded the "Great School of Love" a religious, industrial arts school and the Society of the "Servants of the Powerless," a syncretist religion combining aspects of Islam, Christianity, Judaism, and Buddhism.

PRESS AND JOURNALISM. According to undocumented claims, the first impetus for the establishment of journalism in Afghanistan came from the great Pan-Islamist and modernist Jamaluddin Afghani (q.v.), who in the 1860s was said to have published the first newspaper, named *Kabul*. There is no evidence of the existence of a paper called *Kabul*, nor of the fact that Afghani was instrumental in the publication of the *Shams al-Nahar* (The Morning Sun), which was published in the 1870s during the reign of Amir Shir Ali (q.v.). An extant copy of this 16-page paper, published in January or February 1873, carried official announcements, "profitable and necessary information," and reports on events from London, America, Prussia, China, Russia, and Austria, in addition to domestic news from Badakhshan and Kabul. It appeared twice a month and cost 25 rupees a year, which was deducted from the salary of officials; chiefs, courtiers, and notables were invited to make a donation commensurate to their status. The paper ceased publication in the late 1870s as a result of the British invasion in the second Anglo-Afghan war (q.v.).

In 1906, Maulawi Abdur Rauf, head of the Royal Madrasa at Kabul, started a newspaper called *Seraj al-Akhbar-i Afghanistan* (Torch of News of Afghanistan) which appeared, however, only once in January 1906.

Journalism was permanently established by Mahmud Tarzi (q.v.), the "Father of Afghan Journalism," with the publication of the *Seraj al-Akhbar-Afghaniya* (Beacon of Afghan News, 1911-18). Its name derived from Amir Habibullah's title, *"seraj al-millat wa'd-din"* (Beacon of the Nation and Religion). In the first year of its existence the paper was lithographed from a handwritten copy by Muhammad Ja'far Kandahari and edited by Mahmud Tarzi. Subsequent issues were typeset and illustrated and the paper soon became appreciated for its quality and relative independence. It served as a medium of information for a small circle of courtiers, government officials, and literate Kabulis, providing both domestic and foreign news. It adopted a Pan- Islamic, anti-British tone and advocated an Islamic modernist policy of reform. It continued with minor interruptions until 1918. Under King Amanullah (q.v.) the press experienced considerable growth. The weekly *Aman-i Afghan* (1919, Afghan Peace - derived from Amanullah's name) took over the tradition of the *Seraj al-Akhbar* with a reformist and decidedly nationalistic tone. Provincial newspapers appeared for the first time: *Ittihad-i Mashriqi* (1919, The Unity of the East) in Jalalabad, *Ittifaq-i Islam* (1920, The Concord of Islam) in Herat, and the weekly *Tulu-yi Afghan* (1921, The Rise of the Afghan) in Kandahar.

The first national newspaper which survived subsequent regimes was *Anis* (Companion), first published on May 5, 1927. *Islah* (Reform), published in late 1929 by Nadir Khan (the subsequent king), served as his organ to counter attacks in Habibullah Kalakani's *Habib al-Islam* (q.v.).

Beginning in the 1930s numerous journals and magazines appeared in both Pashto and Dari as private individuals and government ministries published their house organs or specialized papers. The press experienced considerable growth with the increasing literacy resulting from the expansion of education after World War II. The *Kabul Times* (q.v.), an English-language daily newspaper, was founded in 1962 under the auspices of the ministry of information and culture, as a semiofficial medium with a measure of editorial autonomy. Article 31 of the Constitution of 1964 permitted freedom of the press, subject to respect for the fundamentals of Islam, the constitutional monarchy, and public morality. New, privately-funded weeklies appeared in 1966: *Payam-i Imruz* (q.v., Message of Today), published by Ghulam Nabi Khater, demanding "justice, equality, national unity," and social and economic reforms; *Khalq* (The People) and *Parcham* (Banner), organs of the Marxist PDPA, published respectively by Nur Muhammad Taraki and Sulaiman Layeq (see individual entries); *Mardum* (People), an anti-Marxist paper published by Sayyid Moqadas Negah; Wahdat (Unity), published and edited by Maulana Khasta; *Afghan Millat* (The Afghan Nation) organ of the Afghan Social Democrats, a Pashtun nationalist paper, published by Ghulam Muhammad Farhad; and *Musawat* (Equality) published by Abdul Shukur Reshad, organ of the Progessive Democratic Party founded by Muhammad Hashim Maiwandwal (q.v.). Most papers were banned soon after their first appearance on the grounds that they offended Islamic sentiments or constitutional provisions, or on such technicalities as lacking an editor. Private newspapers were replete with *ad hominem* attacks and appealed only to small circles of the Kabul public. Therefore they were not economically viable. A publisher had to obtain a license from the ministry of information and culture and deposit from 10 to 15 thousand Afghanis as a security bond. *Khalq* and *Parcham* had the largest circulation of private newspapers, no doubt because they were secretly subsidized and espoused a Marxist line.

The relatively free press in Afghanistan ended in the period of President Daud and the founding of *Jumhuriat* (1973, Republic) as the official organ. No independent papers were tolerated. After the Saur Revolt *The Kabul Times* was transformed for a few years into *The Kabul New Times*, *Anis*, and *Haywad* and continued under new editorship. The new party organ was the *Da Saur Inqilab*, renamed *Haqiqat-i-Saur Inqilab* under the Parchami regime (now called *Payam* of the Watan party). The contents of Kabuli newspapers was reproduced virtually unchanged in the provincial press, which now also included newspapers in Baluchi, Uzbak, Turkmani, Pashai, and Nuristani. The Kabul government censors the press, but since Najibullah became president the press has discarded a great deal of the Marxist rhetoric and appeals to the war-weary masses to win acceptance for the continuation of the regime. (See individual entries for names of newspapers and persons in this article.)

PROGRESSIVE DEMOCRATIC PARTY (PDP). Founded by Prime Minister Maiwandwal (q.v.) as a social democratic movement in support of parlimentary democracy and the principles of the 1965 constitution. Its organ was *Musawat* (Equality), a weekly which first appeared on June 24, 1966, with articles in Dari and Pashto. It was published by Abdul Shakur Reshad and Muhammad Sharif Ayyubi and edited by Muhammad Rahim Elham and Abdul Ghani Maiwandi. Also see MAIWANDWAL.

PROVINCES See **ADMINISTRATIVE DIVISIONS.**

PUL-I-CHARKHI (lat. 34-33' N, long. 69-21' E). A village on the Kabul river east of Kabul which is the site of a modern prison, built in the time of President Daud and heavily utilized since. The prison, built from a West German design, had a capacity of 5,000 prisoners but during the Khalqi period it was said to have housed more than twice that amount. The prison has special wings for political prisoners, foreigners, and women. During the early years following the Saur Revolt, large numbers of prisoners at Pul-i Charkhi were executed. In 1979, the Amin government produced a list of approximately 10,000 Afghans who had been killed. When Babrak Karmal came to power in 1980 he disassociated himself from the Khalqi executions and amnestied most of the prisoners.

PUL-I-KHUMRI (lat. 35-56' N, long. 68-43' E). An industrial town named after a bridge over the Surkhab/Kunduz river on the main highway from Kabul north to Baghlan and Kunduz. In 1938 the textile company *Nasaji* began construction of an electric power plant and a textile industry as well as a small town. At first the town only housed the industrial workers and staff, but it gradually grew with the addition of other industries engaged in the production of cement, briquettes, and mining nearby. In 1973 the town had about 20,000 inhabitants, mostly Tajik and Pashtuns, but also about 20 percent Hazaras. According to local tradition, the name Khumri comes from the name of Khumari, a young lady who lived in the area about four hundred years ago, and had a bridge built to facilitate trade across the river.

PURDAH See CHADARI.

PUSHTU See PASHTO.

PUZANOV, ALEXANDR. Soviet ambassador accredited to Kabul in 1972, the final year of Zahir Shah, and an important figure during the republican and early Marxist periods. He was an active politician in Kabul and was therefore dubbed the "little czar." He may have been instrumental in helping to reunite the two factions of the PDPA in 1977 and was quoted saying that the Saur Revolt "came as a complete surprise to me." One expert describes him as "an alcoholic seventy-two-year-old castoff from Kremlin political struggles... [who] was trout fishing in the Hindu Kush" (Bradsher, 1983) when the Saur Revolt occurred. He supported Nur Muhammad Taraki against Hafizullah Amin and was credited with having lured Hafizullah Amin into an ambush. The "palace shoot-out" of September 14, 1979, misfired and Amin demanded the recall of Puzanov; he left Kabul on November 19, 1979.

-Q-

QADHI See QAZI.

QADIRI (QADIRIYYA). A sufi order named after Shaikh Abdul Qadir al-Gailani (1088-1166), an ascetic preacher, acclaimed the most popular saint in the Islamic world. His tomb in Baghdad is a place of pilgrimage, maintained by the *Naqib*, custodian of the shrine, who is his descendant and the hereditary head of the qadiri sufi fraternity. Sayyid Hasan Gailani (q.v.), younger brother of the Naqib al-Ashraf of Baghdad, came to Afghanistan in 1905 and established himself there. Upon the death of his brother, he was asked to return to Baghdad, but he stayed in Afghanistan. He was succeeded in Afghanistan by Sayyid Ali Gailani (q.v.), who was succeeded by Sayyid Ahmad Gailani (q.v.), who is also the head of the National Islamic Front (q.v.) of mujahedin forces. The Qadiri order is strong among the Ghilzai and Wardakis in southern Afghanistan.

QALAT Or **QALAT-I GHILZAI** (lat. 32-7' N, long. 66-54' E). The administrative center of Zabul province located on the road from Kandahar to Ghazni and Kabul, about 87 miles northeast of Kandahar. Its celebrated 18th-century fort was occupied by the British in the second Anglo-Afghan war. In 1973, the town had about 4,000 inhabitants, mostly from the Ghilzai tribe.

QANAT See **KARIZ.**

QANDAHAR See **KANDAHAR.**

QANUN. Statutory laws enacted after the 1965 Constitution.

QARAQUL Or **KARAKUL.** A sheep bred originally in Russian Central Asia and introduced to Afghanistan at the time of World War I. Uzbak breeders began a lucrative industry in Afghanistan which soon became the major hard- currency winner. Qaraqul skins became popular in Europe, and Afghan merchants were able to corner the market until the end of the 1940s, when the Soviet Union and South Africa became major competitors. In the face of increasing competition, the Afghan Qaraqul Institute was founded in 1966 to provide quality control and promote the export of the pelts. The skins come in various colors, most commonly grey and black but also brown and other colors, and are used in Afghanistan primarily to fashion the customary headgear for men, called *kula.*

QARI, ABDULLAH "MALIK AL-SHU'ARA". Proclaimed Afghan poet laureate in 1936. His *Diwan,* collection of poetry, was published in India and Kabul. Born in 1871 in Kabul and self-educated, he became an attendant of Amir Habibullah (q.v.) and tutor to his son Prince Enayatullah (q.v.). He was a teacher at Habibia School and member of the Afghan Literary Society. He died in 1944.

QARLIQ Or **QARLUQ.** A small ethnic community of sunni Turks in Kunduz, Takhar, and Badakhshan provinces. They migrated from the Ghorband valley (now Parwan province) north during the time of Amir Abdur Rahman (1880s). The Qarlik resemble the Uzbak, but speak a different dialect.

QASIM-AFGHAN, USTAD MUHAMMAD. Ustad (Master), the best known singer and musician in Afghanistan in the first half of the 20th century. Born in 1881, the son of Ustad Sattar Kashmiri, he was court singer during the rule of Amir Habibullah and was responsible for creating an Afghan style of music which was akin to the concept of classical Indian music. He trained many Afghan singers. He died in 1957.

QATIL, SARDAR AZIZULLAH. Poet, diplomat and honorary member of the Afghan Literary Society (See AFGHAN ACADEMY). Born in 1892 in Kabul, the son of Sardar Nasrullah, he served in the department of census during the reign of King Amanullah and was subsequently appointed ambassador at Tehran (1930). He died in 1935.

QAZI Or QADHI. A judge with jurisdiction in cases of civil and criminal law. He usually is a graduate of a madrasa (q.v.) or theological college. See ISLAMIC LAW.

QIBLA. Prayer direction, the Ka'ba (q.v.) in the center of the Great Mosque of Mecca, which Muslims face when performing their daily prayers. In mosques and areas reserved for prayer the *qibla* is indicated either by the prayer niche, *mihrab*, or outdoors by a *sutra* (covering). See ISLAM.

QIRGHIZ (KIRGIZ). A community of Turkic sunnis of about three million people in the Qirghiz Soviet Republic of whom a small number lived in eastern Badakhshan province. As as a result of the Soviet intervention in Afghanistan in the 1980s, they fled first to Pakistan; later, most emigrated to Turkey. They visited Afghanistan seasonally in the early 19th century from Russian Central Asia and the Sinkiang province of China and settled in the Afghan Pamirs in Wakhan Corridor (q.v.) during World War I. They lived in yurts and subsisted as herders of sheep, goats and yaks. In the early 1970s the Afghan Qirghiz numbered about 1,900 persons.

QIZILBASH. Meaning "Red Heads" (T.), they are named after the color of pleats in their turbans. They were one of seven Turkic tribes who revered the Safavid ruler Ismail (1499-1524) as both a spiritual and temporal ruler. The Persian ruler Nadir Shah, Afshar (q.v.), stationed a rear guard (*chandawol*) of Qizilbash troops at Kabul on a campaign to India. They are shi'a and were quartered in an area called Chandawol today. Estimated at about 30,000, they no longer to speak their original Turkic dialect and live now mainly in the cities of Herat, Kabul, and Kandahar. As an ethnic and religious minority, the Qizilbash have tended to be politically inactive to avoid discrimination, but have held prominent positions in government service and commerce. They held military positions until the 1860s, the end of Amir Dost Muhammad's reign (q.v., one of his wives was a Qizilbash). Also see NADIR SHAH, AFSHAR.

QOR'AN Or KORAN. The sacred book of Muslims which is a collection of God's revelations through the medium of the Prophet Muhammad. Muslim orthodoxy considers the Qor'an literally the "Word of God." *Qor'an*, means "reading" or "recitation," also called *al-Kitab* "The Book." It is divided into 114 chapters (*suras*), arranged roughly according to length and subdivided into sections (*aya*, pl. *ayat*). Also see ISLAM and ISLAMIC LAW.

QUNDUZ See KUNDUZ.

-R-

RABBANI, BURHANUDDIN. Leader of the *Jam'iat-i Islami-yi Afghanistan* (Islamic Society of Afghanistan), the largely non-Pashtun group of mujahedin headquartered in Peshawar. Born in 1940 in Faizabad, Badakhshan province, and educated in Islamic studies at Kabul University and Al-Azhar University, Cairo, where he received an M.A. degree in 1968. After returning to Afghanistan he taught in the faculty of theology at Kabul University. He became editor of *Majallat-i Shari'at* (Journal of Islamic Law) in 1970, and was a leading member of the Islamist movement (q.v.) since the late 1950s. He organized university students to oppose the secular trend in Afghanistan and to counteract the activities of leftist students on campus. The 15-member high council of the *Jam'iat-i Islami* selected him as its leader in 1971, and in 1974 he fled to Pakistan where he sought the support of the Pakistan government and the *Jama'at-i Islami* (q.v.). In 1975, the Jam'iat carried out raids into Afghanistan and failure of the armed attacks revealed policy disagreements between Rabbani and Hekmatyar (q.v.). Thereupon Hekmatyar founded his *Hizb-i Islami* in 1976. Rabbani continued to lead the Jam'iat after the Saur Revolt. Also see JAM'IAT-I ISLAMI-YI AFGHANISTAN.

RABI'A BALKHI See BALKHI, RABI'A .

RADIO AFGHANISTAN. National Afghan radio station, first called Radio Kabul, with daily medium-wave and short-wave domestic service in Pashto and Dari and, since the Saur Revolt, also in several minority languages. Its foreign broadcast program offers regular services in Arabic, English, Urdu, and Russian. Broadcasting began under King Amanullah in 1925 with the construction of a station in Kabul and was temporarily stopped at the end of his reign in 1929. In 1937 the Marconi company set up transmitters in Kabul, Khanabad, Khost, and Maimana and experimental broadcasts resumed in 1939. A year later broadcasts reached a relatively wide public: 8,000 radio sets were owned by Afghans, most of them in Kabul, and loudspeakers were set up in bazars and public places. In order to justify this innovation, the Afghan government stated its purpose as spreading the message of the Koran, promoting a spirit of nationalism, preserving Afghan culture and folklore, and advancing public education. The system soon expanded throughout the country with the establishment of stations in the provinces.
Radio Afghanistan contributed to the development of Afghan music. In 1964 more than half of the domestic programs consisted of native music. Qor'an and poetry readings were regularly featured and plays were subsequently added. Programming was controlled by the government and no private radio or television stations were permitted. In 1977 television was established in Kabul to give a new dimension to the cultural and political objectives of the Afghan government.

RAHIM, MIR ABDUL GHAFUR. Appointed minister of water and power in Prime Minister Khaliqyar's government of May 1990. Born in 1947 in Kabul and educated at Habibia high school and abroad (probably in the Soviet Union) with an M.A. degree in engineering, he embarked on a career in the ministry of water and power. He served intermittently as president of the planning department of the ministry of irrigation and water sources in 1973, 1976, 1977, and 1981. In 1985 he was appointed deputy minister of construction affairs. He is not a member of the PDPA.

RAHMAN See ABDUL RAHMAN and HABIBURRAHMAN.

RAHMAN BABA. Contemporary of the 17th century Pashto poet Khushhal Khan, Khatak, and mystical poet in the Pashto language. Afghans call him the "Pashtun Hafiz" in reference to the great Persian poet. A school in Kabul, originally intended to teach tribal students in Pashto, is named after him.

RAHMAN QUL, HAJI. Chief of the Pamir Qirghiz (q.v.). He fled from Sinkiang province, China, after the Communist takeover in 1949 and settled with about 2,000 followers in the Wakhan Corridor (q.v.). After the Saur Revolt he fled to Pakistan with most of his followers, then settled with them in eastern Anatolia, Turkey. Also see QIRGHIZ.

RAMAZAN (RAMADHAN). Name of the ninth month of the Islamic (lunar) calendar and "the month in which the Qor'an was sent down" during which Muslims are enjoined to observe complete abstinence from food or drink during daylight hours. See ISLAM.

RANJIT SINGH. King (1780-1839) of the newly-emerged Sikh nation, a religio-political entity, who in 1820 controlled most of the northern Punjab, Kashmir, and Peshawar. He captured Lahore from its Afghan garrison in 1798, compelling Shah Zaman (q.v.) to appoint the Sikh chief as governor of the Punjab. Ranjit Singh quickly annexed Kashmir and Peshawar in spite of efforts by Dost Muhammad (q.v.) to regain these territories. Dost Muhammad sought an alliance with Britain to recover Peshawar. Lord Auckland, governor general of India, sided with the Sikh ruler and concluded an alliance with Ranjit Singh and Shah Shuja for the purpose of restoring the latter to the Afghan throne (See SIMLA MANIFESTO, SIKH, and ANGLO-AFGHAN WARS). Ranjit Singh did not provide any troops and therefore did not share the British disaster. Ranjit Singh died in 1839 and his empire was soon annexed by his former British allies. Also see KOH-I-NUR.

RASULI, MAJ. GEN. GHULAM HAIDAR. A supporter of Muhammad Daud (q.v.) who was appointed chief of central forces in 1973, chief of general staff in 1975, and minister of defense in 1977. He was killed as a result of the Saur Revolt in 1978. Born in 1919 in Rustaq of a Kandahar

Muhammadzai family, he received a military education in Afghanistan and India.

RATEBZAD, ANAHITA. Member of the Parcham faction of the PDPA and highest ranking woman in the party. President Taraki appointed her minister of social affairs and tourism, but removed her two months later and sent her as Afghan ambassador to Belgrade. Accused of plotting against the Khalq regime, she was purged with other Parchamis and stayed abroad until Babrak Karmal succeeded to power. In the first Parcham government she served as minister of education (1980-81) and was elected to the PDPA politburo. At the same time she was caretaker of the ministries of information and culture, higher and vocational education, and public health. But in 1981 she gave up all these positions and became a member of the presidium of the revolutionary council (1981-88). In 1991 she lives in Kabul, but does not hold any official positions.

Born in 1931 in Guldara, Kabul province, and educated at Kabul Malalai school, Chicago School of Nursing, and Kabul University where she obtained the M.D. degree in 1963 as the first woman doctor in Afghanistan. In 1965 she was one of three successful PDPA candidates for parliament, and in the same year founded the PDPA-controlled Democratic Women's Organization. She has been a member of the PDPA central committee since 1976.

RAWALPINDI PEACE CONFERENCE See ANGLO-AFGHAN PEACE TREATY OF 1919.

RED SHIRTS. A Pashtun independence movement, also called *khuda-i khidmatgaran* (The Servants of God), founded in 1921 by Khan Abdul Ghaffar Khan (q.v.) in the NWFP of India. The movement was organized in cells and had members in most villages on the tribal belt. It was allied with the Indian Congress party of Mahatma Ghandi and accepted his policy of peaceful resistance. Membership adhered to seven basic tenets: (1) admission open to all adults, (2) rejection of the Indian caste system, (3) wearing of national dress, (4) readiness to serve the people, (5) dedication of one's life to the interests of the people, (6) recognition of all members as brothers, and (7) obedience to the orders of the party.

The British government suspected them of being a Communist front because of their red uniforms and insistence not only on national autonomy but also on "freeing the oppressed, feeding the poor, and clothing the naked." Khan Abdul Ghaffar Khan and his supporters were frequently arrested and the movement remained localized until 1947 when it espoused the cause of a "Free Pashtunistan." Also see KHAN, KHAN ABDUL GHAFFAR and PASHTUNISTAN.

REGISTAN (lat. 31-0' N, long. 65-0' E). "The Country of Sand," a vast expanse of ridges and hillocks of loose red sand which covers the southern parts of Kandahar, Helmand, and Nimruz provinces. This desert is sprinkled with bushes and vegetation, including alluvial soil in the hollows which is cultivated by Baluch and Brahui nomads. It has formed a natural boundary with India (now Pakistan) and has been an obstacle to penetration by conventional military forces.

RELIGION See ISLAM.

REPUBLIC OF AFGHANISTAN. New name of the Democratic Republic of Afghanistan. See PEOPLES DEMOCRATIC PARTY OF AFGHANISTAN.

RESHTIA, SAYYID QASIM. Writer, historian, and diplomat. Born in 1913 and educated in Kabul, he embarked on a career in government service. He was editor of *Salnama*, (Kabul Almanac) and of *Kabul Magazine*, 1934-38. In 1948 he was appointed president of the department of press (with cabinet rank), reappointed in 1957, and minister of press in 1963. He served as ambassador in Prague (1960), Cairo (1962), and Tokyo (1970). He was vice president of the committee for drafting of the constitution, 1963, and minister of finance in 1964. He is the author of numerous publications on Afghan history.

ROBERTS, GEN. SIR ABRAHAM. Commander of Shah Shuja's "Army of the Indus" in the first Anglo- Afghan war (1838-42). He escaped the British debacle when he was recalled by Lord Auckland, governor general of India, who disliked Roberts' criticism of his policy. His son (below) was a British general in the second Anglo-Afghan war. Also see ANGLO-AFGHAN WARS.

ROBERTS, GEN. SIR FREDERICK. British general in the second Anglo-Afghan war (1878-80) and son of Sir Abraham (above). He invaded Afghanistan through the Kurram valley and reached Kabul on October 12, 1879, where he was the *de facto* ruler after the abdication of Yaqub Khan (q.v.). He was a legendary figure, called "Bobs" by his fellow generals and famous, or infamous, for ordering executions of Afghans. General MacGregor said of him: "Bobs is a cruel blood-thirsty little brute, he has shot some 6 men already in cold blood. I have saved three men from his clutches already" (Trousdale, 1985). Although Sir Frederick was able to defeat Ayyub Khan (q.v.) near Kandahar on September 1, 1880, the Indian government agreed to withdraw from Afghanistan in April 1881 to avoid a repetition of the disaster of the first Anglo-Afghan war. Sir Frederick died in 1914. See ANGLO-AFGHAN WARS.

ROSHAN (lat. 37-56' N, long. 71-35' E). A district in northern Badakhshan province on the left bank of the Panja, or upper Amu Daria, with an area of 1,413 square miles and an agricultural population of about 6,500. The Granville-Gorchakoff Agreement (q.v.) of 1873 between Russia and Britain defined the Amu Daria as the northern boundary of Afghanistan; it was not known at the time that Shignan and Roshan included territory on both sides of the Amu Daria. In 1893 Sir Henry Durand (See DURAND AGREEMENT) succeeded in forging a compromise in which Afghanistan gained territory on the Afghan side for land lost across the river, thereby reducing the original size of Roshan. The climate of Roshan is moderate in spite of the fact that the valley lies at an elevation of 6,000 feet. There are said to be considerable deposits of iron and copper in the area. Some mines are operated by the population, which consists largely of Ghilzai Pashtuns, Tajiks, and Ismailis (q.v.) including Roshanis, Sanglichis, Wakhis, and Shignanis.

RUIGAR, ABDUL BASHIR. Minister of information and culture in June 1988 and reappointed in 1990. Born in 1946 in Kabul and educated in Kabul with an engineering degree, he was employed with the ministry of water and power and in this capacity directed a number of projects. He was elected a member of the presidium of the artists union in 1986 and became editor-in-chief of the *Majala-yi Honar* (Art Magazine) in 1990. He is a member of the PDPA.

-S-

SAADABAD PACT. A treaty of friendly relations and cooperation between Afghanistan, Iran, Iraq, and Turkey concluded in 1937 and renewed in 1943. The treaty, also dubbed the "Oriental Entente," was a gesture of solidarity rather than being of political importance. One Afghan diplomat commented on the nature of the agreement, posing the rhetorical question: "what do you get when you add zeros." Nevertheless, the Soviet government supected some kind of British plot in view of the fact that Iraq was still not emancipated from British control and could be seen as a *de facto* member. When Britain and the Soviet Union occupied Iran in World War II, none of the signatories of the pact protested.

SADEQI, HOJJAT AL-ISLAM MIR HUSAIN. One of the founders of *Sazman-i Nasr* (Victory Organization), a Hazara movement which follows the line of Ayatollah Khomeini, but appears to be not under Iranian political control. The movement was publicly proclaimed by Sadeqi and three other ulama (Shafaq and Abdul Ali Mazari) in 1980 in Meshed and now controls most of the Hazarajat. A Hazara, Sadeqi was born in the early 1930s in Nili in the Turkman Valley and studied Shi'ite theology in Kabul under Shaikh Muhammad Amin Afshar, and in Najaf, Iraq. A book, entitled *Sayyid Gera'i*, was published under his name, which questioned the political control of the *Sadat* (non-Hazara sayyids) of Hazara society. He is said to have advocated armed struggle against Pashtuns as well as against Soviet forces and broke with Beheshti who supports the unity of the Afghan state. He fled to Iran in 1974 where he became active in the Islamist movement.

SADO. Eponymic ancestor of the Sadozai dynasty which ruled Afghanistan from 1747-1818. His place of birth is not known, but from the poetry he wrote Afghan historians assume that he belonged to the Mohmand tribe. He lived in Qal'a Bahadur near Peshawar and is buried in Hazar Khana, Peshawar. The line from Sado to Ahmad Shah (q.v.) extends over five generations. Also see DURRANI DYNASTY and DURRANI TRIBE.

SADOZAI. A subdivision of the Popalzai branch of the Durrani Pashtun tribe which furnished the Afghan rulers from 1747 until 1818 and included the following kings:

Ahmad Shah	1747 - 1773
Timur Shah	1773 - 1793
Shah Zaman	1793 - 1799
Shah Mahmud	1799 - 1803
Shah Shuja	1803 - 1810 and 1839
Shah Mahmud	1800 - 1803 and 1810 - 1818

For information on Sado, see above entry; for Sadozai rulers, see individual entries.

SAFI Or QANDARI. A tribe located northeast of Jalalabad which is of Nuristani origin, and speaks a Kohistani dialect in addition to Pashto (some scholars count them as Pashtuns). They claim to be the descendants of the original Gandharis and among the last to convert to Islam when they adopted the name Safi as well as Qandari. They are divided into three sections -- the Gurbuz, Masud, and the Wader. At the turn of the century they numbered about 3,000 fighting men. The Safis revolted in 1947-49 and as a result were forcefully moved to areas in northern Afghanistan.

SAFI, ABDUL WAHHAB. President of the judges' tribunal of the supreme court, 1987, and chairman of the constitution council in 1988. A member of the 1965 central committee of the PDPA, he was appointed president of the legislative department of the ministry of justice, 1978; deputy minister of judicial affairs in Sept. 1979; and minister of justice and attorney general, 1981-83. He is a Pashtun from Kunar province.

SAFID KUH Or SPIN GHAR (lat. 33-58' N, long. 70-25' E). The "White Mountain," a high range on the Pakistan side of the border, forming part of the Sulaiman mountain system (q.v.) which separates the basin of the Kabul river from Kurram. Its highest point is the Sikaram Peak at a height of 15,620 feet. The Paiwar Kotal (Pass) is about 5 miles from the peak. Another range with this name is in the eastern part of the

Koh-i Baba (q.v.) which runs south of the Harirud valley into the vicinity of Herat.

SAFI, SAMIULLAH. A mujahedin leader operating in the Pich (Paich) valley. Born in 1940 in Murchel, Dara-i-Pich, Kunar province, the son of Sultan Muhammad Khan. Graduated from Kabul Teachers College, 1963, and received a degree in journalism from Kabul University, 1967. A member of the Wolesi Jirga of Dara-i-Pich, 1969-73, and editor, *Irfan*, magazine, 1976.

SAFI, WADIR. Appointed minister of civil aviation in 1991 and member of President Najibullah's Loya Jirga in 1990. He was born in 1948 in Kabul, the son of Ghulam Hasan Safi (onetime ambassador to Jakarta, Prague, and Budapest) and educated at Ghazi high school, Kabul and Prague with a Ph.D. degree in law and literature. He embarked on a career of teaching at Kabul University in 1977, and served as dean of the faculty of law, 1987-91.

SAILANI, MUHAMMAD SIDDIQ. Minister of Islamic affairs and religious trusts in Prime Minister Khaliqyar's government of May 1990. Born in 1936 in Logar province and educated in Kabul, he started a teaching career at Najat school in 1959 and became principal of Abu Hanifa Madrasa in 1970. He served in various positions in the ministries of education and justice and in 1978 was appointed president of research in the ministry of justice. He became rector of the Islamic University in 1988 and acting minister of justice a year later. He is not a member of the PDPA.

SAKHRA, LT. GEN. MUHAMMAD AREF. Member of the central council of Watan party and first deputy minister of WAD, 1987-90. He served as president of the political affairs department of WAD until his appointment as ambassador to Prague in August 1990. Born in 1953 in the village of Bayan, Parwan province, of a Tajik family, he was educated in Parwan and at Kabul University in physics and mathematics. He worked as a teacher in Parwan until the Saur Revolt, when he became director of education of Parwan. He went underground during the Khalqi period and began his career in KHAD (later WAD) in 1980.

SALAH, ABDUL SAMAD. Minister of mines and industries in Prime Minister Khaliqyar's government of May 1990. Born in 1935 in Kabul province and educated at Najat School and in West Germany, where he graduated with an engineering degree in 1957. He was employed in various departments of the ministry of mines and industries and became president of the geological survey department in 1984. In 1985 he became acting head of the Petroleum Enterprise Institute, but then was without work until his appointment as minister of mines. He is not a member of the PDPA.

SALANG (lat. 35-22' N, long. 69-4' E). A village and district in Parwan province near the famous Salang pass (altitude 13,350 feet) and Salang tunnel which opened in 1964. The 1.7 mile long tunnel as well as a modern highway was constructed with Soviet assistance under an agreement signed in 1956. It is an all- weather route over the Hindu Kush from Kabul to northern Afghanistan. Since the Soviet intervention in Afghanistan, this route has become vital as a line of supplies for the Kabul government. Therefore, the tunnel, located at an altitude of 11,100 feet, has been a major target of attacks by the mujahedin forces.

SALE, LADY FLORENTIA. Wife of Brigadier Sir Robert Sale, commander of the garrison at Jalalabad during the first Anglo-Afghan war (q.v., 1838-42). Lady Sale was a hostage with other British women and some of their officer husbands and thus escaped the general massacre of the British forces. She recorded her experience in a book, entitled *A Journal of the Disasters in Afghanistan, 1841-2* which is an important source on the British misadventure. See ANGLO-AFGHAN WARS.

SALIM, ABDUL SAMAD. Appointed deputy prime minister for economic affairs in 1991. Born in 1924 and educated in Kabul and the United States, he embarked on a career in the ministry of mines and industries in 1954. He became deputy director of the department of geology in 1958, deputy minister of mines in 1960, and minister in 1967. He was appointed dean of the faculty of geology of Kabul University in 1986, and vice president of the Academy of sciences in 1988.

SALJUQI, FIKRI ABDUL RAUF. Poet, historian, and expert on the Herati school of miniature and Persian calligraphy. Born in 1900 in Herat. He is a cousin of Salahuddin below.

SALJUQI, USTAD SALAHUDDIN. A philosopher, writer, and poet in Persian and Arabic, appointed president of the department of press (1953) and ambassador to Cairo (1955-62). Born in 1895 in Herat, the son of Sirajuddin Mufti, he received a traditional education and became a teacher of Persian and Arabic at Habibia and Istiqlal schools. Appointed director of the Herat newspaper *Ittifaq-i-Islam* (Consensus of Islam, 1923) and *Sarwat* (Wealth, Kabul, 1925), he became secretary to King Amanullah (1926). He served as consul general in Bombay (1931) and Delhi (1935). Participated in the Ariana encyclopedia project and was a member of the Pashto Academy. He died in the late 1960s.

SAMA See KALAKANI, ABDUL MAJID.

SAMADI, ABDUL HAQ. Reputedly a Khalqi member of the PDPA who became chief of military intelligence in 1978, governor of Parwan in 1979, and Afghan ambassador to East Germany, December 1979. He was born in 1941 in Balkh province and educated at military colleges in Kabul and the Soviet Union. Director, Air Defense, 1973, and a supporter of the

Daud coup. Promoted to lieutenant colonel and served as director of studies and research in the ministry of defense, 1975. He has since retired.

SAMANGAN (lat. 36-15' N, long. 67-40' E). A province in north-central Afghanistan with an area of 6,425 square miles and a population of 275,000. The administrative center of the province is Aibak with about 8,000 inhabitants, which is an important archaeological site. The province is rich in mineral resources and is famous for its fruits, especially melons. The population is largely Uzbak who breed horses for the famous "Buzkashi" (q.v.) games. Also see AIBAK and TASHQURGHAN.

SANA'I, HAKIM (1081-1150). A scholar, philosopher, physician, and mystical poet who wrote the first mystical epic in Persian. He is acclaimed as one of three great mystical poets in Persian. He was born and died in Ghazni in present Afghanistan.

SARABI, See SORABI.

SARANDOY (TSARANDOY). The name of the Afghan Boy Scouts organization begun in 1932 and headed by the Afghan Crown Prince Muhammad Zahir (the subsequent king) and later by his son Ahmad Shah.
President Daud organized a gendarmerie force called Sarandoy of some 20,000 men, which the Khalqi government continued and Babrak Karmal in 1981 reorganized into a defense force of six brigades, 20 battalions of 6,000 men and various support units. The Sarandoy forces are stationed in major urban areas held by the Kabul government. Important commanders in 1988 include Maj. Gen. Nadir Ali, Lt. Col. Qurban Sherzad, and the commanders of Kabul - Lt. Gen. Saifullah and of Herat - Lt. Gen. Ghulam Mustafa, the "Hero of the Republic of Afghanistan." The Sarandoy is under the direction of the ministry of interior and was a Khalqi stronghold under Col. Gen. Gulabzoy (q.v.) and his successors. In 1990, its academy was headed by Brig. Muhammad Kabir Katawazi. It used to rival the power of Parcham-dominated KHAD (q.v.) until the Tanay (q.v.) coup of March 1990.

SARBILAND, ABDUL MAJID. Member of the Parchami faction of the PDPA and minister of information and culture, Jan. 1980-82. Also member of the central committee and revolutionary council. A deputy chairman of the council of ministers, 1981-86, and ambassador to Havana in 1986 and Managua, Nicaragua, 1988. He is said to have moved to the United States.

SARDAR. Title of the heads of Durrani clans, meaning leader, general or prince. The title was awarded by the king also to commoners but subsequently was reserved for members of the Afghan royal family.

SAR-I KOL Or **ZOR QUL** (lat. 37-25' N, long. 73-42' E). A lake, called Lake Victoria by the British, located at the head of the Pamir branch of the Amu Daria. It is 12 miles long and 1-1/2 to 2-1/2 miles wide and lies at an altitude of 13,390 feet.

SAR-I PUL (lat. 36-13' N, long. 65-55' E). A town and a district in Jozjan province which is the nucleus of a new province formed by the Marxist government in April 1988. The town is located at an altitude of 2,155 feet and lies on the river of the same name. During the reign of Ahmad Shah Durrani, Sar-i-Pul was a dependency of Maimana. It became independent in 1810, but was annexed by the Kabul government in 1875. A village with about 950 families in 1885, the town counted 12 to 16 thousand inhabitants in 1973, who are mostly Uzbacks and Tajiks. A new town on the northwest edge was started in 1963. A shrine, the Ziarat-i Hazrat-i Yahya, is a well-known place of pilgrimage which attracts many visitors, especially during *nau ruz*, New Year (March 21). The discovery of natural gas and oil nearby has led to the construction of buildings and workshops. An oil refinery was planned, but never constructed.

SARWARI, ASADULLAH. Member of the Khalq faction of the PDPA and head of AGSA (q.v.), the security service of Nur Muhammad Taraki. He was replaced by Hafizullah Amin's nephew, Asadullah Amin in October 1979. When Babrak Karmal succeeded to power in the last days of December 1979, Sarwari was appointed vice president and deputy prime minister; but he was soon afterward appointed ambassador to Ulan Bator, Mongolia (1980- 86). He was stripped of membership in the Politburo in 1981, and expelled from the central committee in July 1986. Dr. Najibullah appointed him ambassador to Berlin until 1988, and to Aden, South Yemen, in 1989. He came to Delhi, India, at the time Shahnawaz Tanai (q.v.), the commander-in-chief, attempted a coup against the Najibullah regime. Born about 1930 in Ghazni and educated in Afghanistan, he went to the Soviet Union to be trained as a helicopter pilot. He participated in the Daud Coup in 1973, and after the Saur Revolt became first deputy prime minister and vice president of the Revolutionary Council. He is reported to have been arrested in India and the Afghan government has requested his extradition.

SAUR REVOLUTION See **PEOPLES DEMOCRATIC PARTY OF AFGHANISTAN.**

SAYYAF, ABDUL RASUL (ABD AL-RABB AL-RASUL). Leader of the *Ittihad-i Islami Barayi Azadi-yi Afghanistan* (q.v., Islamic Union for the Liberation of Afghanistan), a radical Islamist movement which aims at the establishment of an Islamic State in Afghanistan (See ISLAMIST MOVEMENT). He was born in 1946 in Paghman and educated in Paghman and at Abu Hanifa Theological school, and at the faculty of theology of Kabul University. He went to Egypt and obtained an M.A. degree at Al-Azhar University. He was a member of the Islamist movement and in 1971 deputy of Burhanuddin Rabbani. In 1974, when he was about to leave for the United States for legal training, he was arrested at Kabul International Airport by intelligence officers and spent more than 5 years in prison. Freed by the Parcham regime in 1980, he went to Peshawar and joined the mujahedin as spokeman of the Alliance. Elected for a period of two years, he wanted to continue in this position but was forced to step down. He then formed his own group, the Ittihad. He is an eloquent speaker in Arabic and has been able to receive financial support from Arabic Gulf states. He is ideologically close to the groups headed by Hekmatyar and Khales, but was accused of having allied himself with Arab "Wahhabi" mujahedin groups. Also see ISLAMIST MOVEMENT IN AFGHANISTAN, ISLAMIC ALLIANCE FOR THE LIBERATION OF AFGHANISTAN, and ITTIHAD BARAYE AZADI-YI AFGHANISTAN.

SAYYID (SAIYID). Sayyid (pl. Sadat) means prince, lord, chief, or mister in Arabic and is applied as a title for the descendants of the Prophet Muhammad. In Afghanistan the name is also applied to healers and holy men. Communities of Sayyids exist in Kunar province and the Hazarajat, where they constitute a hereditary clergy.

SAYYID ABDULILLAH See ABDULILLAH, SAYYID.

SAYYID HUSAIN. A Tajik of Charikar and minister of war in the government of Amir Habibullah (Kalakani). He was born about 1895, the son of a wealthy landowner, who "quickly squandered" his inheritance and "never had any profession but highway robbery." As minister of war he made himself unpopular with his extortions and cruelty. He was executed together with Habibullah on November 1, 1929. Also see HABIBULLAH KALAKANI (AMIR).

SAYYID-I KAYAN. Sayyid Nadir Shah Husain, commonly called Sayyid-i Kayan, was elected head of the Ismaili community in Afghanistan by the Agha Khan and served for 45 years until his death in the 1960s at age 83. He was a scholar and writer who published a number of works on religious, literary, and historical topics. Before his death, he appointed his son Sayyid Shah Nasir Naderi as his successor.

Sayyid Shah Nasir Nadiri was born in 1933 in Darra-yi Kayan in Baghlan province. He was educated under the supervision of his father and studied privately and Islamic sciences and literature with such teachers as Maulawi Khan Muhammad Khasta, Maulawi Qurbat (from Bukhara), Sayyid Daud Khatat, and Sayyid Muhammad Ibrahim Alamshahi. He declined to take work in the government administration and instead founded the Shirkat-i Sahami of Dushi in Baghlan province. He was elected to parliament in 1965, and in 1968 became vice president of the *wolesi jirga*. Six months after the republican coup of 1973, Sayyid Nadiri and his four brothers were imprisoned. While in prison, Sayyid Nadiri wrote a book, entitled *Khaterat-i Zendan* (Memories from Prison), and poems which were published in Afghan newspapers. Freed after two years, Sayyid Nadiri and his brothers were again jailed after the Saur Revolt. He was in Pol-i Charkhi prison until Babrak Karmal proclaimed an amnesty in 1980. Sayyid Shah Nasir Nadiri left Afghanistan in 1981 and now lives in England. His brothers Sayyid Nuruddin Raunaq, Sayyid Abdul Qadir, and Sayyid Gauhar Khan are missing and presumed dead. Raunaq was a noted Afghan poet. Sayyid Mansur is acting head of the community. Other brothers of Sayyid Shah Nasir Nadiri are Muhammad Sa'di Nadiri and Maj. Gen. Sayyid Jafar Nadiri who are in Afghanistan, the former is deputy chairman of the Hazara nationality central committee, and the latter is governor of Baghlan province.

SAZA See BAGHLANI.

SAZMAN-I NASR See NASR, SAZMAN-I and SADEQI, HOJJAT AL-ISLAM MIR HUSAIN.

SCHOOLS See EDUCATION.

SECOND ANGLO-AFGHAN WAR See ANGLO-AFGHAN WARS.

SEPAH-I PASDARAN See PASDARAN.

SERAJ AL-AKHBAR AFGHANIYA. A biweekly newspaper, published during the reign of Amir Habibullah from 1911 to 1918. It was edited by Mahmud Tarzi (q.v.) and propagated pan-Islamic and modernist ideas. One of the staff member was Abdul Hadi Dawai (q.v.) who became president of the Afghan senate, 1966-73. During the first year of its existence the paper was lithographed but subsequent editions were handsomely typeset and illustrated, occasionally with political cartoons. Although circulation was small (1,600 copies), the paper had a regular readership as far distant as Russian Central Asia, Iran, the Ottoman empire, India, and even Japan. To make the paper economically feasible, Mahmud Tarzi requested courtiers and government and military officials to subscribe. The newspaper was independent, but Amir Habibullah occasionally censored an issue when the British-Indian government protested its hostile attitude. The paper ceased publication in December 1918, two months before the assassination of Amir Habibullah. Also see PRESS AND JOURNALISM.

SERAJ AL-MILLAT WA'D DIN. "Torch of the Nation and Religion," the title adopted by Amir Habibullah upon being sworn in as Amir in 1901. His descendants subsequently adopted Seraj as a family name.

SETAM-I MILLI See BADAKHSHI, TAHIR.

SEWWUM-I-AQRAB. The Afghan date of a series of demonstrations (the 3th of Aqrab 1344, corresponding to October 25, 1965), when students under leftist leadership protested the secret session of parliament, which was to decide on a vote of confidence for the government of Prime Minister Muhammad Yusuf. Troops responding to stone-throwing students opened fire and killed three and wounded several others. As a result of the demonstrations the prime minister resigned and the "Sewwum-i-Aqrab" subsequently became a rallying cry of the Afghan left.   Also see MUHAMMAD YUSUF.

SHAFIQ, MUHAMMAD MUSA. Afghan foreign minister 1971 and prime minister from October 1972 until the coup of Sardar Muhammad Daud in July 1973. Arrested by the Daud government 1973-76 and, later under house arrest until the Saur Revolt, when he was executed during the Taraki regime. Born in 1930 in Kabul, he attended Koran school and the Islamic College (Dar al- Ulum-i Sharia) in Kabul, Al-Azhar in Cairo, Egypt, and studied Islamic and comparative law at Columbia University. He opened the first private law firm in Kabul in 1961, and had a major role in drafting the Constitution of 1964. Served as Afghan ambassador to Cairo from 1968 to 1971.

SHAHBAZ, MUHYIUDDIN. Minister of statistics in Prime Minister Khaliqyar's government of May 1990, and minister of planning, 1991. Born in Kabul in 1947 and educated in Kabul and the United States with a degree in economics, he became an employee of the power company in Kabul. In 1980 he was appointed vice president of the central statistics office and in 1985 he became president. He is not a member of the PDPA.

SHAHIDI, NAZIR AHMAD. Appointed minister of statistics in 1991. Born in 1946 in Logar province and educated at Kabul University and Bonn University, where he received the Ph.D. degree in economics. Served as deputy dean of the faculty of economics, 1986-89, and subsequently as dean. He is not a member of the PDPA.

SHAH MAHMUD, GHAZI See GHAZI, SHAH MAHMUD.

SHAHNAMA See FIRDAUSI.

SHAH SHUJA-UL-MULK (1803-10 and 1839). Born about 1792, the seventh son of Timur Shah, he became governor of Peshawar in 1801 during the reign of his full brother Zaman Shah. In 1803 he captured Kabul, imprisoned Mahmud (q.v.), and proclaimed himself king. He accepted a British mission in 1809 under Mountstuart Elphinstone (q.v.) and concluded a treaty of alliance which states in Article 2:

> If the French and Persians in pursuance of their confederacy should advance towards the King of Cabool's country in a hostile manner, the British State, endeavouring heartily to repel them, shall hold

themselves liable to afford the expenses necessary for the above-mentioned service to the extent of their ability.

This treaty was to prevent a Franco-Persian invasion of India which never occurred.

Two years later Mahmud, who had managed to escape, captured Kabul and forced Shah Shuja to flee to Bukhara and later to India where he remained as an exile for almost 30 years. En route to India he had to pass through the territory of the Sikh ruler Ranjit Singh (q.v.) who took from him the Kuh-i-Nur (q.v.), a prized diamond which is now part of the British crown jewels. The internecine fighting between the Sadozai princes brought Dost Muhammad to power and marked the end of the Sadozai dynasty. In 1839 Britain invaded Afghanistan and restored Shah Shuja to the throne in a campaign which became known as the first Anglo-Afghan war (q.v.). The Sadozai ruler was not able to govern without British protection and was assassinated a few months after the British army was forced to a disastrous retreat. See ANGLO- AFGHAN WARS.

SHAH WALI. A Khalqi member of the PDPA who was appointed minister without portfolio in Prime Minister Khaliqyar's government of May 1990. Born in 1939 and educated in Kabul, he obtained a medical degree and served as surgeon in various hospitals. He joined the PDPA in 1965 and, after the Saur Revolt, became minister of health (May 1978) and deputy prime minister (March 1979). Under Hafizullah Amin he was appointed minister of planning (October 1979) and minister of foreign affairs. He was imprisoned after the Parchami faction came to power in December 1979 and remained jailed for a number of years.

SHAH WALI, MARSHAL. Conqueror of Kabul from the forces of Habibullah Kalakani (q.v.) in October 1929. He was born in 1885, the son of Sardar Muhammad Yusuf Khan and brother of Nadir Shah (q.v.). He headed Amir Habibullah's bodyguard, and commanded King Amanullah's forces during the Khost Rebellion (q.v.) of 1924-25. He left for France in 1926 and remained there with Nadir Khan until they started their campaign against the Tajik king. Nadir Shah appointed him minister in London in 1930 and Paris 1932; Zahir Shah assigned him as ambassador to Karachi in 1947 and London 1949. During the later reign of Zahir Shah, he was an advisers to the king. He carried the title of Marshal. President Daud placed him under house arrest. He died in Rome in 1976.

SHAHR-I-BARBAR. The remains of an ancient city on a hill between the Firuzbahar and Band-i Amir streams in Bamian province. It is said to have been the capital of a kingdom comprising the Hazarajat (q.v.) and inhabited by a people called Barbar, probably the ancestors of the Hazaras who were also known as Barbari.

SHAH ZAMAN (1793-99). Born in 1772, one of 23 sons of Timur Shah (q.v.), and his successor to the throne in 1793. During most of his reign he was engaged in intermittent warfare with his brothers Mahmud and Humayun. He wanted to win the British for a concerted war against the Mahratta confederacy in India. Instead the British concluded an alliance with Persia to keep the Afghans out of India (See AFGHAN FOREIGN RELATIONS). Shah Zaman appointed Ranjit Singh governor of Lahore, in spite of the fact that he had previously revolted. He abolished the hereditary posts established by Ahmad Shah Durrani and carried out bloody executions which antagonized many Afghans. While he was in the Panjab, Mahmud captured the Kabul throne. Shah Zaman was blinded and imprisoned but eventually escaped and lived in Indian exile until his death in 1844.

SHAIKH ALI HAZARAS See HAZARAS.

SHAMS AL-NAHAR. The "Sun of the Day" was the first Afghan newspaper published during the reign of Amir Shir Ali (q.v.) at Kabul from 1873 to 1877. An extant copy in possession of this writer (dated the 15th *zi 'l-hijja* 1290, corresponding to February/March 1873) shows a masthead consisting of an emblem enscribed *Shams al-Nahar Kabul*, positioned between two lions who hold a dragon with one paw and a sword in the other. Around it are four couplets which state: "The work I have begun with your support, you, my Lord, complete with excellence." The price of a copy was ten annas, in cash or deducted from the creditors account (salary?). Notables, courtiers, chiefs, and government officials paid "according to their glorious ranks and names."   The 16-page paper featured public announcements, international and domestic news, and a weather report. Human interest stories discuss the manner of solving paternity suits in China and Kafir religious practices, as told by a recent convert to Islam. Only the name of the printer, one Mirza Abdul Ali, was given. Also see PRESS AND JOURNALISM.

SHAMSI CALENDAR. The solar (*shams*, Ar. sun), year calendar introduced in Afghanistan under King Amanullah. See CALENDAR.

SHAMS, MUHAMMAD ANWAR.   Minister of higher and vocational education in Prime Minister Khaliqyar's government of May 1990. Born in 1944 in Herat province and educated in Kabul and the Soviet Union with a Ph.D. degree in physics from Moscow University. In 1970 he became assistant at the Kabul Polytechnic Institute, lecturer in 1977, and rector in 1989. He is not a member of the PDPA.

SHARI'A, See ISLAMIC LAW.

SHARQ, HASAN. Minister of refugee repatriation (1987), deputy prime minister (1987- 88), and prime minister (1988-89).   Born in 1925 in Anardara, Farah province, he was educated at military school and Kabul University, where he obtained a medical degree. A supporter of Prime Minister Daud, he headed the prime minister's secretariat (1953-63) and was unemployed after the resignation of Daud (1963-73). In 1973, President Daud appointed him first deputy prime minister. Served as ambassador to Tokyo (1977-78) and Delhi (1980-86). At present he does not hold any office.

SHI'A Or SHI'ISM. A Muslim sect which derives its name from *shi'at Ali*, the party of Ali, and holds that leadership of the Islamic community should be by dynastic succession from *Imam* Ali (cousin and son-in-law of the Prophet Muhammad) and his descendants. Their view conflicts with the *sunni* principle, that Muhammad's successor, *khalifa* (caliph), should be elected. *Shi'as* divide into three major sects according to which of their *imams* is believed to be the "Expected One," who will return on judgment day: the fifth, seventh, or twelfth. In Afghanistan the small Qizilbash (q.v.) and Farsiwan communities, and most of the Hazara population are "Twelver" (*Ithna 'ashariyya*, or *imami*) shi'as, the same sect which predominates in Iran. There are also small groups of *Isma'ilis*, (q.v.) or "Seveners," who live in northeastern Afghanistan.

The Twelvers believe their *imam* is infallible and that their theologians, the *mujtahids*, may legislate in the absence of the imam. In addition to Mecca and Medina, their holy places are Najaf and Karbala in Iraq, as well as Mashshad and Qum in Iran. They accept the practice of temporary marriages, *mut'a* (called *sigha* in Dari), and *taqqiya*, prudent denial of their religion if in danger of persecution. They believe in an esoteric interpretation of the Koran, but like the *sunnis* accept the "Five Pillars of Islam" (See ISLAM) with only minor exceptions. In Afghanistan the *shi'as* constitute about 15 percent of the Afghan population and, in addition to being a sectarian minority, also are an ethnic minority. None of the ruling Pashtun groups is *shi'a* and the resistance fighting the Kabul government is divided into two loose alliances, *sunni* and largely Pashtun groups in Peshawar and *shi'a* groups in Iran and the Hazarajat. The *shi'as* refused to participate in the Afghan Interim Government in Peshawar because they did not receive the representation they claim due to their numerical strength. Their most active mujahedin groups are Nasr (q.v.), Shura (q.v.), *Harakat-i Islami* (q.v.), and Pasdaran (q.v.). The Isma'ilis in northeastern Afghanistan have found it in their interest not to cooperate with the mujahedin.

Among the Marxist groups the *shi'as* were represented primarily in the Sh'ola-yi Jawid and numerous small groups, collectively labeled as Maoist. The highest-ranking *shi'a* in the Kabul government is Sultan Ali Keshtmand (q.v.), a Hazara. Also see ISLAM and SHI'A MUJAHEDIN GROUPS.

SHI'A MUJAHEDIN GROUPS. The people of the Hazarajat, home to a large part of the Afghan *shi'a* population, revolted in February 1979 and by the end of the year had liberated their area from Marxist control. The Revolutionary Council of Islamic Unity of Afghanistan (*shura-yi inqilab-i ittifaq-i islami- yi Afghanistan*) established a government headed by Sayyid Ali Beheshti (q.v.) with its administrative center at Waras in Bamian province. It set up administrative offices, formed a defense force drafted from the local population, and collected taxes to defray the costs of running a state. Until about 1983, the Shura was the dominant movement; but radical-Islamist parties, headed by young intellectuals emerged, which challenged the authority of the traditional Shura. The *Sazman-i Nasr* (q.v., Organization for Victory), headed by Mir Husain Sadeqi; the *Pasdaran* (q.v., Guardians), modelled after the Iranian *Sepah-i Pasdaran* and following the "line" of Ayatollah Khomeini, gained strength and conquered much of the Hazarajat from the Shura. Smaller groups controlling enclaves in the Hazarajat are the *ittihad-i mujahedin-i Islami* (Union of Islamic Fighters), led by Abdul Husain Maqsudi and the *harakat-i Islami* (Islamic Movement) of Muhammad Asef Muhsini (q.v.), headquartered in Quetta. Numerous groups, like *ra'd* (Thunder), headed by Shaikhzada Khaza'i, and *hizbullah* (The Party of God) of Shaikh Ali Wusuki, and others, Islamist or Marxist, published their manifestos but never succeeded in winning popular support. Unifying efforts were not successful. In 1987 they founded the Council of Islamic Alliance which the Shura joined a year later. And during a meeting of commanders in Bamian on June 16, 1990, creation of the Party of Islamic Unity of Afghanistan (*hizb-i wahdat-i Islami-yi Afghanistan*) was announced. Abdul Ali Mazari was appointed its spokesman and one Mustafa Kazimi became a leading member of the central council. Muhsini has not as yet joined *Wahdat*. Major divisions exist between the traditional and Islamist groups and a multitude of notables and khans, sayyids (q.v.), and the new elite of Islamist intellectuals who are competing for leadership. Wahdat issued a declaration supporting the independence of an indivisible Afghanistan, demanding freedom for all nationalities and sects, and security and social justice for all. It supports women's rights, including the right to vote.

SHIBERGHAN (lat. 36-41' N, long. 65-45' E). The capital of Jozjan province, located some 80 miles west of Mazar-i Sharif. In 1970 the town was estimated to have 15,000 inhabitants. Afghan historians link the name to Asaburgan, a properous 9th-century town which was destroyed as a result of Turco-Mongolian invasions. The town was surrounded by a wall and the seat of an independent Uzbak khan (chief) until it was annexed in 1859 by Amir Dost Muhammad. In the late 1930s the Afghan government began construction of a new town and further expansion resulted from the discovery of natural gas in the vicinity and the construction of a pipeline and complex of buildings for the needs of the rapidly growing oil industry. A World Bank study estimates that the fields at Yatimdagh, Khwaja Gugerdak, Jarquduq, and Khwaja Burhan, northeast and southeast of Shiberghan contain a combined reserve of natural gas amounting to 140 billions of cubic meters. In the 1970s Shiberghan was a modern town with wide open streets and avenues and flat roofed houses, and a thriving handicraft industry in leather and wood. Because of the large Russian personnel involved in the oil industry, Shiberghan was popularly called the "Russian" town (Lashkargah [q.v.] being the "American" town). The

Americans left in the late 1970s and most Russians departed with the Soviet troops in 1989.

SHIGHNAN (lat. 37-27' N, long. 71-27' E). A district in northern Badakhshan which until 1859 was an independent Tajik khanate. It came under the direct administration of the Kabul government in 1883. Britain and Russia in 1873 recognized the Amu Daria as Afghanistan's northern boundary and the limit of Russian influence. But the agreement (See GRANVILLE-GORCHAKOFF AGREEMENT) was concluded in ignorance of the fact that Shighnan extended across the river. The boundary question continued to be an issue until in 1893 Amir Abdur Rahman ceded the portions of Shighnan lying across the river in exchange for Dawaz which was on the Afghan side of the river. The Shighnanis speak a language of their own and are Isma'ili (q.v.) shi'as. Also see ROSHAN.

SHINWARI. The Shinwaris are Pashtuns who migrated in the 16th century into the area of Nangarhar. The tribe is divided into four divisions: the Mandezai, Sangu Khel, Sipah, and Alisher Khel who can muster a fighting force of 12,000 men. The Alisher Khel, on the Pakistani side of the Durand Line, have a reputation as excellent soldiers.
In the early 11th century the Shinwaris accompanied Mahmud of Ghazni (q.v.) on his invasions of India. They fought the British in three Anglo-Afghan wars (q.v.) and in the late 19th century repeatedly rose against Amir Abdur Rahman. The Shinwaris were members of a coalition of tribal forces which caused the downfall of King Amanullah (q.v.). Also see SHINWARI MANIFESTO.

SHINWARI MANIFESTO. A proclamation by the Shinwari leaders Muhammad Alam and Muhammad Afzal, in November 1928, listing their principal grievances against the government of King Amanullah (q.v.) and declaring war against the Afghan king. The manifesto objected to the king's legal and social reforms, such as the framing of legal codes, recommendation of monogamy, the removal of purdah, and the opening of theaters and cinemas in Kabul. They invested Dakka and Jalalabad and tied down Amanullah's forces, enabling Habibullah Kalakani (q.v.) to capture Kabul and install himself on the Kabul throne.

SHIR ALI, AMIR (1863-79). One of Amir Dost Muhammad's 27 sons who became amir of Afghanistan in 1862-3, and spent much of his tenure to meet challenges from his brothers who governed various provinces. By 1869 he had consolidated his power and traveled to Ambala, India, in response to an invitation from the viceroy, Lord Mayo. He was willing to form an alliance with India in exchange for British protection from Russian attacks, assistance in weapons and money, and recognition of the succession of his favorite son Abdullah Jan. But the viceroy merely expressed his pleasure that the civil war among the princes had come to an end and gave the Afghan ruler a present of 600,000 rupees and a few pieces of artillery.

Disappointed in his dealings with Britain, the amir agreed to listen to Russian overtures. Russia sent General Stolietov to Kabul on July 22, 1878, promising what Britain was not willing to grant. Alarmed, the viceroy's government dispatched General Neville Chamberlain who was not permitted to enter Afghanistan. Following an ultimatum, a British army invaded Afghanistan in a campaign known as the second Anglo-Afghan war (q.v.). Shir Ali left his son Yaqub (q.v.) in command at Kabul and went north to seek Russian support, but General Kaufmann, the Russian governor general of Turkestan province, merely advised Shir Ali to make peace with the British. Shir Ali died on February 21, 1879, in Mazar-i-Sharif, and was succeeded in Kabul by his son Yaqub.

Shir Ali was the first to initiate modern reforms: he established an advisory council to assist in the administration of the state, and created an army organized on European lines. He abolished the feudal system of tax-farming, set up a postal system, and published the first Afghan newspaper, the *Shams al-Nahar* (q.v., Sun of the Day).

SHIR (SHER) DARWAZA. A hill on the outskirts of Kabul, overlooking the town and the location of the "noon cannon," which sounds noontime and the end of daylight fasting during month of Ramadhan (See ISLAM).

SHIRKAT-I SAHAMI-YI MILLI See BANK-I MILLI .

SHU'LA-YI JAVID. Name of a weekly Marxist newspaper with articles in Dari and Pashto, published by Dr. Rahim Mahmudi (q.v.). The newspaper was banned in July 1969, three months after its first appearance, because it advocated the violent overthrow of the Afghan government. It was the organ of the New Democratic Party (*Jam'iat-i Demukrati-yi Nawin*), popularly also called *Shu'la-yi Javid* (Eternal Flame), and vied with other leftist groups in organizing strikes and student demonstrations. The party opposed Pashtun nationalism and advocated the right of self-determination of all nationalities and therefore found supporters among ethnic and sectarian minorities. It appeared to be ideologically closer to China than the Soviet Union. Prominent leaders include Dr. Abdul Hadi Mahmudi (q.v.), brother of Rahim, and Professor Akram Yari and Muhammad Osman. After the Saur Revolt the party opposed the Khalqi regime and set up a mujahedin group; but it was soon decimated and most of its members fled abroad or were killed.

SHURA. Council, consultative body, or parliament. Islamic political theory demands that rulers seek council, *shura*. Islamic modernists base their demands for a representative government on this principle.

SHURA-YI INQILAB-I ISLAMI-YI HAZARAJAT. The *shura* led by Ayatolla Beheshti. See BEHESHTI, SAYYID ALI.

SIKH, SIKHISM. A religio-political community which rose in the Panjab, India, in the 15th century, founding a state which reached its height under

Ranjit Singh (q.v.) in the late 18th century. Sikhism began as a syncretist religion, combining Islamic and Hindu beliefs under Nanak, the first guru (sage). Subsequently belief in ten gurus and the Granth Sahib, their sacred book, constituted the creed of the Sikhs. In constant conflict with Indian and Afghan rulers, the Sikhs became increasingly militant and under Ranjit Singh took Multan in 1818, Kashmir 1819, and Peshawar in 1834.

The Sikh nation supported the British invasion of Afghanistan in the first Anglo-Afghan war (q.v.) but did not provide any troops and thus avoided the British debacle. After the death of Ranjit Singh, the British ended Sikh rule when it annexed the Panjab in the "Sikh Wars" of 1845-46 and 1848-49. At the partition of India, the Sikhs opted for the Indian part of the Panjab where Amritsar, their holy city is located. In recent years, however, they have started a campaign of violence with the object of gaining an independent state, *Khalistan*. Indian troops invaded the Sikh temple in Amritsar to disarm militant Sikhs and this intrusion into their holiest shrine only spurred the campaign. In retaliation, a Sikh nationalist assassinated Indira Gandhi and the turbulence in the Panjab now threatens the integrity of the Indian state.

There are about 10,000 Sikhs in Afghanistan who are primarily merchants and live in urban areas of Kabul, Jalalabad, Ghazni, Gardez, and Kandahar, as well as scattered throughout the country. They speak a Panjabi dialect as well as Dari and Pashto and many of them lived in Afghanistan for several generations. Also see RANJIT SINGH.

SIMLA MANIFESTO. A document issued by the governor general of India on October 1, 1838, which declared war on the Afghan Amir Dost Muhammad (q.v.). It accused him of "a sudden and unprovoked attack" on its ally, Ranjit Singh (q.v.), and announced Britain's intention of restoring Shah Shuja (q.v.) to the Afghan throne. The result was the first Anglo- Afghan war (1839-42). See ANGLO-AFGHAN WARS and AFGHAN FOREIGN RELATIONS.

SINGH See RANJIT SINGH.

SIRAJ See SERAJ.

SIRR-I-MILLI. Name of a secret organization which in 1909 plotted a coup against Amir Habibullah and aimed at the establishment of a republican form of government (*mashruta*). Its reputed head was Maulawi Muhammad Sarwar Wasif, a native of Kandahar. Dr. Abdul Ghani, an Indian Muslim who was head of Habibia school, and some of his students were accused of membership in the *sirr-i milli* (Secret of the Nation). The organization wrote increasingly threatening letters to Amir Habibullah, telling him to "mend his ways, or face the consequences." Abdul Ghani was arrested and jailed until 1919, when King Amanullah ascended the throne. Also see ABDUL GHANI.

SOCIETY OF ULEMA See **JAMI'AT-I 'ULAMA**.

SORABI, ABDUL WAHID. Vice president (1988) and deputy prime minister and minister of planning in Prime Minister Khaliqyar's government of May 1990. In May 1991 he replaced Keshtmand in the position of vice president. Born 1926 in Sarab Valley, Ghazni province, of a Hazara family, he was educated at Najat School and in Austria with a Ph.D. in economics. He taught economics at Kabul University and was appointed dean of the faculty of economics in 1960 and 1965-66, and deputy rector of Kabul University in 1963. In 1967 he became minister without portfolio, and minister of planning, 1969-73. Arrested in 1974-75 and unemployed until the Saur Revolt. He became minister of irrigation in 1982, minister without portfolio in 1985, and minister of higher education in November 1987. He is a member of the academy of sciences and deputy chairman of the central committee of Hazara nationality, but claims not to be a member of the PDPA.

SOVIET-AFGHAN RELATIONS. Formal diplomatic relations between Russia and Afghanistan began in June 1919, when the Soviet Union and Afghanistan recognized their respective governments and announced their intention to establish legations in Kabul and Moscow. A ceasefire had just been declared in the third Anglo-Afghan war (q.v.), and King Amanullah wanted to demonstrate Afghanistan's independence by establishing diplomatic relations with European powers. A mission, headed by Muhammad Wali (q.v.), proceeded to Tashkent and Moscow where it was given a rousing welcome. N. N. Nariman, a spokesman of the foreign ministry, announced that "Russian imperialim, striving to enslave and degrade small nationalities, has gone, never to return." Muhammad Wali expressed the hope that "with the assistance of Soviet Russia, we shall succeed in emancipating our Afghanistan and the rest of the East." He presented V. I. Lenin a letter from King Amanullah which was received "with great pleasure." A Bolshevik diplomat, Michael K. Bravin (who subsequently defected and was killed by an Afghan), proceeded to Kabul, to arrange for the arrival of a permanent representative, Z. Suritz, in January 1920. Suritz immediately set about to negotiate the preliminaries for the Treaty of 1921, which recognized the "mutual independence" of both states and bound them not to "enter into any military or political agreement with a third State, which might prejudice one of the Contracting Parties." The Soviet Union agreed to permit free and untaxed transit of Afghan goods, and recognized the independence and freedom of Khiva and Bokhara "in accordance with the wishes of the people." It provided for Soviet technical and financial aid of one million rubles in gold or silver and promised a return of the "frontier districts which belonged to the latter [Afghanistan] in the last century," a reference to the area of Panjdeh (q.v.). Britain had held a monopoly in the supply of arms and war materiel which could only be shipped to Afghanistan by way of India; the treaty now opened a new avenue for materiel purchased in Europe. It helped King Amanullah to crush the Khost Rebellion (q.v.)

mer 1924, with the assistance of several aircraft from the Soviet
and a number of foreign pilots, including several Russians.

ite of the friendly rhetoric, differences existed between the two
tries: King Amanullah wanted Khiva and Bukhara to be free from
Soviet control, possibly associated with Afghanistan in a Central Asian
confederation, but the "Young Khivan and Bukharan" revolted and opted
for membership in the Soviet Union. The Soviet Union saw this as an
expression of the "wishes of the people" and retained the Tsarist
possession of Central Asia. A more serious crisis in Soviet-Afghan
relations occurred in December 1925 when Soviet troops occupied the
island of Darqad (also called Urta Tagai and Yangi Qal'a) on the Amu
Daria. At the turn of the century the course of the Amu Daria had
changed from south of the island to the north and, since the main stream
was designated as the Afghan boundary, Kabul considered the island
Afghan territory. After the Bolshevik Revolution, refugees from the
Soviet Union settled on the island, including some Basmachi (q.v.)
counterrevolutionaries, who made it a base for raids into Soviet Central
Asia. The matter threatened to develop into an international conflict, but
the Soviets apparently wanted good relations with King Amanullah and
evacuated their troops on February 28, 1926. Moscow paid the promised
subsidy only irregularly, and by the mid-1920s the Kabul government had
expanded its diplomatic base to the extent that it did not need to maintain
a special relationship with the Soviet Union.

During the 1929 civil war the Soviet Union had maintained its embassy
in Kabul and immediately recognized the government of Nadir Shah. The
new king sent Muhammad Aziz, his half brother, as ambassador to
Moscow, to indicate the importance of the post, but he was determined
to end Soviet influence in Afghanistan. He renegotiated and signed on
June 24, 1931, the treaty of 1921, with the inclusion of an article calling
for the prohibition in both territories of activities which "might cause
political or military injury" to the other. Nadir Shah was thinking of the
followers of ex-King Amanullah who might attempt a return to power and
the Soviets were concerned about the Basmachi threat. A commercial
treaty had to wait until 1936, and the Afghan government did not renew
a Soviet airline concession and eventually dismissed all Soviet airline
pilots and mechanics. The Afghan government turned increasingly to
Germany for its technological and developmental needs and a special
relationship developed which greatly disturbed Moscow and was accepted
in London only as the lesser of two evils. The outbreak of World War II
and the temporary alliance between Germany and the Soviet Union
resulted in fears in London and Kabul that the Soviets might support a
pro-Amanullah coup. And, indeed, these worries were not unwarranted.
The German foreign ministry considered Zahir Shah (1933-73) pro-British
and toyed with the idea of supporting a coup against the monarch. Count
Schulenberg, the German ambassador in Moscow, queried Vyacheslav
Molotov whether the Soviet Union would permit the transit of Afghan
forces into northern Afghanistan. But Molotov was noncommittal and the
matter was dropped.

On June 22, 1941, Germany attacked the Soviet Union and Moscow joined the Western alliance. The alliance of Britain and the Soviet Union caused considerable anxiety in Kabul because Afghan foreign policy had been based on the premise that its territorial security depended on the continued rivalry between its imperialist neighbors. Concerted Allied action was soon to follow: In October 1941, the Allies presented separate notes to the Afghan government demanding the expulsion of all Axis nationals. Kabul was forced to comply and the Afghan king convened a Loya Jirga (q.v.), Great Council, which gave retroactively its approval after the Axis nationals had left. The Afghan government insisted that they be given safe passage to a neutral country. From that time the Afghan government kept its northern border closed to non-diplomatic travelers, but trade continued between the two countries.

When India became independent in 1947 and the State of Pakistan was created, Afghanistan repudiated the treaties which accepted the Durand Line as international boundary and demanded that the Afghans of the NWFP be given the choice of independence. Afghanistan was the only country voting against the admission of Pakistan to the United Nations. The cold war had begun and the Eisenhower administration sought to contain Moscow's expansionism by sponsoring alliances with states bordering on the Soviet Union. Washington supported creation of the Baghdad Pact (later renamed CENTO), which united Britain, Turkey, Iraq, Iran, and Pakistan in a defensive alliance. This alliance guaranteed international borders and ignored irredentist and nationalist aspirations in the Middle East. As a result, relations between Afghanistan and Pakistan, a Western ally, turned increasingly hostile.

The Afghan government "normalized" its relations with the Soviet Union and in 1946 agreed to accept the *thalweg* (middle) of the Amu Daria as the international boundary. A telegraph link was established with Tashkent in 1947, and in 1950 Afghanistan signed a four-year trade agreement with the USSR. The Soviet government praised Afghanistan's "positive" neutrality and, when in December 1955 Nikita Krushchev and Nikolai Bulganin came to Kabul, the stage was set for major rapprochement. The two countries renewed the Treaty of 1931 for ten years, the Soviet Union granting Afghanistan a $100-million loan at two-percent interest for projects selected by a joint USSR-Afghan committee. The Afghan national airline started flights from Kabul to Tashkent in 1965, which were subsequently extended to Moscow and other European countries. In the same year the Treaty of 1931 was renewed for ten years. The Afghan government wanted to purchase arms from the United States, and when it was unable to obtain what it wanted, Prime Minister Daud turned to the Soviet Union for help. In 1956 the first shipments of East Bloc weapons arrived and the Afghan armed forces began to be Soviet-equipped. Thousands of Soviet advisers came to Afghanistan and thousands of Afghan technicians and military officers went to the Soviet Union for training. The result was a growing cadre of military officers, students, and technocrats with leftist, if not pro-Russian sympathies. When Muhammad Daud staged a coup with leftist support on July 17,

1973, the stage was set for the Saur Revolt which brought a Marxist government to power. The Kabul government accepted Soviet advisers in virtually all its civilian and government branches and concluded a series of treaties which made the Soviet Union the dominant influence in Afghanistan. On December 5, 1978, the Taraki (q.v.) regime concluded a treaty of friendship, similar to one the Soviet Union concluded with Vietnam, which also provided for military assistance and which became the basis for military intervention a year later. Resistance was growing against the Marxist regime, resulting in a civil war which turned into a war of liberation when Soviet troops tried to prop up a faltering regime. The war turned out to be costly to Afghanistan: mujahedin sources claim that as many as one million Afghans have perished, whereas the Kabul government claims that 243,900 soldiers and civilians were killed. After Soviet troops evacuated Afghanistan in February 1989, Moscow announced it had suffered about 13,000 deaths and another 35,500 wounded

SUFISM. Islamic mysticism (A., *tasawwuf*), emerged in the eighth century A.D. and rapidly spread over most of the Islamic world. The generally accepted etymology derives the word Sufism from *suf*, wool, the robes of coarse wool worn by Muslim mystics. Sufism was long in conflict with Islamic orthodoxy, because it sought the personal experience (*ma'rifa*) of union with God, rather than rational knowledge (*'ilm*), the scholasticism of sunni Islam. Al-Ghazzali (d. 1111), the great canonist and theologian, was largely instrumental in reconciling sufism with orthodox Islam.

Sufi orders originated among the urban artisan classes which organized into brotherhoods (*tariqa* - way, path), following a particular spiritual leader or saint (*pir, shaikh*, or *murshid*). Sufi lodges (*khanaqah*) were founded at the residence or tomb of a venerated *pir* and supported with contributions of the disciples (*murid*). Members meet regularly in homes or public places to perform *zikr* (A. remembrance), ecstatic recitations of the names of Allah, or passages of the Koran, accompanied by rhythmical breathing and physical movement.

Sufism has experienced a revival in Turkey after orders were closed in the early 1920s in conformance with the Kemalist policy of secularization. The Hanbali (q.v.) school of Islamic jurisprudence prevalent in Saudi Arabia also does not accept sufism as an orthodox practice.

Famous mystical poets which Afghanistan shares with the Islamic world are Sana'i (q.v.) of Ghazni, who wrote the first mystical epic in Persian in the early 12th century A.D.; Jalaluddin Rumi (q.v.), famous for the *maulawia*, whirling derwishes, who was born in 1207 in Balkh (therefore called Balkhi by Afghans); and Jami (q.v.) born in Jam, Khorasan who died in Herat in 1492. The most important contemporary sufi orders in Afghanistan are the *Qadiri* (q.v.) and *Naqshbandi* (q.v.). The Qadiri order is headed by Pir Sayyid Ahmad Gailani (q.v.) whose ancestor, Abd al-Qadir al-Jilani (d.1166) - "the sultan of saints" founded the order. Gailani's devotees are primarily among the Pashtuns in southern and eastern Afghanistan. The Naqshbandi order originated in Bukhara in the

14th century and is found in parts of northern and southern Afghanistan. The Mujaddidi family is associated with devotees of the Naqshbandi order in southern Afghanistan. Of about 200 orders, 70 are still active in the Islamic world. Also see QADIRI, NAQSHBANDI, GAILANI, AND MUJADDIDI.

SULAIMAN KHEL. A division of the Ghilzai tribe. See GHILZAI and POWINDAH.

SULAIMAN RANGE. The name given by Western geographers to the southern portion of the great watershed between the Helmand and the Indus rivers. The range probably got its name from the Sulaiman Khel Ghilzais (See GHILZAI) through whose territory it passes. Starting from the Shutur Gardan pass (11,200 feet) in Paktia province, it runs in a south-southeasterly direction under the names of Mangal and Jadran hills where its peaks reach altitudes between 11,000 and 12,000 feet. The British-Indian general staff considered the route over the Shutur Gardan the best avenue for an attack on Kabul. There are two ranges with this name -- one which extends along the Afghan border and the other, the eastern range, which runs along the Baluchistan-Punjab border in a generally north-south direction.

SUNNA. The tradition (A., trodden path), the deeds and sayings of the Prophet Muhammad which have become part of Islamic law. See ISLAMIC LAW.

-T-

TAHZIB, NIZAMUDDIN. Member of the Parcham faction of the PDPA, appointed minister of frontier affairs after the Saur Revolt, jailed from August 1978 to December 1979, and chief justice of the supreme court, 1980-89. A Pashtun born in Kunduz in 1935, he was educated at the faculty of theology of Kabul University. In 1990 he was appointed member of the central council of the *Hizb-i Watan* (PDPA) and also serves as a senator.

TAIMANI. One of the Chahar Aimaq tribes (See AIMAQ) which numbers about 180,000 Farsi-speaking sunni Muslims. They are the most numerous of the Chahar Aimaq and occupy the hilly country southeast of Herat between the district of Sabzawar (also called Shindand) in Farah province on the west and the Hazarajat on the east. Their country is virtually barren of trees and bushes except for the upper course of the Farah Rud. The Taimanis are of Turco-Mongol origin.

TAIMURI (TIMURI). Also called Aimaq-i Digar (the other Aimaq) as distinguished from the Chahar Aimaq (q.v.). They are sunnis, number about 30,000, and inhabit the area of northwestern Herat, Farah, and southern Fariab provinces. They claim Arab descent and derive their name from Sayyid Timur, Kurkhan, of Tirmiz in Bukhara. The Taimuris participated on various sides in the civil wars of the Sadozai princes, as a result of which a part of the tribe was compelled to move to Khorasan, Persia. In 1893 there were about 12,000 Taimuris each in the Khorasan province of Iran and western Afghanistan.

TAJIK. A name, generally applied to Farsi/Dari speakers whose number has been estimated at about 4 to 5 million people. The term comes from the Persian "*tazi*" (running) or "*taj*," (crown?) meaning "Arab," but the Turks applied it to non-Turks and eventually only to Farsi- speakers. They are largely sunni Muslims, except for the "mountain Tajiks" who are Ismailis (See Shi'a) and inhabit various areas of Badakhshan province.
The Tajik are the ancient population of Khorasan (q.v.) and Sistan (q.v.) who were sedentary and made a living as traders. They were also located in northern Afghanistan and predominated in Balkh and Bukhara, until they moved south as a result of Timurid invasions. Now they are scattered all over the country, but are concentrated in communities in western, northern, and northeastern Afghanistan. They are mainly agricultural, except in the towns where many are artisans or engage in commercial activities. They have been engaged as clerks and predominate in the government administration. As a community, the Tajik are relatively better educated and more modernized. Conscious of a great cultural tradition, the elite of the Tajiks have been the "men of the pen," whereas the Pashtuns have been the "men of the sword" of Afghanistan.

TAKHAR (lat. 36-30' N, long. 69-30' E). A province in northeastern Afghanistan with an area of 6,770 square miles and a population estimated at 528,000. The province borders on the Soviet Union in the north, Badakhshan province in the east, Parwan/Kapisa in the south, and Baghlan and Kunduz in the west. Since 1963 the administrative center of the province has been Taloqan, a town of about 20,000 inhabitants. Major agricultural products of the province include cotton, corn, and wheat; local industries include gold and silver mining and carpet production. Takhar provides two-thirds of the salt used in Afghanistan.

TAMERLANE See TIMUR-I-LANG.

TANAI Or TANI. A section of the Khostwal Pashtun tribe. They inhabit the southwest corner of the Khost valley.

TANAI COUP See TANAI.

TANAI, LT. GEN. SHAHNAWAZ. Member of the Khalq faction of the PDPA, chief of general staff since 1986, and minister of defense from 1988 to 1990. A Pashtun born in Paktia province of the small Tani tribe (q.v.). A captain-major until the Saur Revolt, he was considered a rising star in the PDPA, when on March 6, 1990, Tanai and several Khalqi officers staged a coup from the Bagram air force base. They attacked the presidential palace and key government facilities in Kabul, but were unable to topple the government. Gulbuddin Hekmatyar, leader of the Islamist and most radical of mujahedin groups, gave the coup his support. This alliance of hard-line Khalqis and radical Islamists caused considerable consternation in Afghanistan. Tani and Hekmatyar were seen as determined to win power, regardless of ideological considerations. As a result of the coup, prominent Khalqis, including Asadullah Sarwari (q.v.) one-time chief of the Khalq intelligence agency, AGSA (q.v); Sayyid Muhammad Gulabzoi (q.v.), ambassador to Moscow; Niaz Muhammad Mohmand (q.v.); and Gen. Nazar Muhammad (q.v.) were dismissed. Najibullah's control of the air force and scrambling of the communications network enabled him to rout the rebels. Tanai made his appearance in the Hekmatyar camp, claiming to continue the campaign against Najibullah. As a sign of PDPA unity, Najibullah appointed two Khalqis, Muhammad Aslam Watanjar (q.v.) and Raz Muhammad Paktin (q.v.), as ministers of defense and interior.

TANG-I-GHARU (lat. 34-34' N, long. 69-30' E). A spectacular gorge through which pass the Kabul river and the road linking Kabul to Jalalabad. The gorge begins 5 miles below Pul-i- Charkhi, about seven miles east of Kabul, and extends for about ten miles to the vicinity of the village of Gogamanda. It is an alternate route to the difficult Lataband Pass (alt. 7,950 feet), and replaced it in 1963 when the new paved highway to Tor Kham at the Afghan border was completed. At the top of the gorge one can see five or six levels of highway winding within a short distance of three miles. The gorge narrows in places to 20 yards with cliffs on both sides rising almost perpendicularly.

TARAKI. A section of the Burhan branch of the Ghilzai tribe, estimated in the early nineteenth century at about 12,000 families. They inhabit Mukur and the country to the south.

TARAKI, NUR MUHAMMAD. Member of the Khalq faction of the PDPA and, after the Saur Revolt, president of the Revolutionary Council (q.v.) and prime minister of the Democratic Republic of Afghanistan. Taraki was born of a Ghilzai nomad family on July 15, 1917 in Ghazni province. After attending a village school in Nawa, Ghazni province, he took night courses in Bombay and college credit in Kabul. He worked as a clerk for Abdul Majid Zabuli (q.v.) at the Pashtun Trading Company in Kandahar and at its office in Bombay. Because of his knowledge of English he was able to obtain employment in various Afghan ministries and at Bakhtar News Agency. In the 1950s he became known as an author and journalist, and in 1953 he served for a few months as press attaché at the Afghan embassy in Washington. Subsequently he opened the "Nur Tanslation Bureau" in Kabul, which translated Dari and Pashto materials for various foreign missions in Kabul, including the American embassy.

His ideological transformation from social critic to Communist occurred in the early 1960s. Taraki convened the "founding congress" of the PDPA on January 1, 1965, which was attended by 30 persons. The members elected him secretary general in a split decision, some voting for his subsequent rival Babrak Karmal, who was elected secretary of the central committee. In April 1966, Taraki started publication of *Khalq* (q.v.), the party organ, which became also the name of his faction of the PDPA. In 1967 the party split into two factions over tactical and leadership disputes, until ten years later they reunited and attained power in a coup in April 1978 (See PEOPLE DEMOCRATIC PARTY OF AFGHANISTAN). After the Saur Revolt, Taraki became the "Great Leader" and a personality cult prepared the way to legitimize his rule as the "teacher and great guide" of the Communist movement. Leading Parchamis were purged from government positions and Taraki's Khalqis ruled until a new split developed among the Khalqis. Hafizullah Amin (q.v.) attacked his former teacher as unfit for leadership. The "red khalqis" of Taraki and "black khalqis" of Amin were pitted against each other and Hafizullah prevailed. On October 9, 1979, Taraki was secretly executed.

TARIN, FATH MUHAMMAD. Minister of repatriate affairs in the 1990 government of Prime Minister Khaliqyar. Born in 1934 in Kabul and educated in economics at Kabul University, he began a career in the ministry of mines and industries. In 1980 he was appointed deputy minister of light industries and foodstuffs and minister in 1988, as well as deputy minister of commerce. He is not a member of the PDPA.

TARNAK (lat. 31-26' N, long. 65-31' E). A river which rises near Muqur in Ghazni province and, flowing in a southwesterly direction, runs into the Dori river about 25 miles southwest of Kandahar.

TARZI, HAMIDULLAH. Minister of finance in Prime Minister Sharq's cabinet of 1988 and minister of civil aviation in May 1990. In 1991 he was nominated Afghan ambassador to Ankara, but did not assume his post. Born in 1932 in Kabul province and educated at Habibia School and in the United States, he began a career as an official in the ministry of commerce and served as commercial counselor in Peshawar, Pakistan. He became president of planning in 1968 and president of domestic trade in 1970. In 1975 he was appointed deputy minister of commerce. He is not a member of the PDPA.

TARZI, GHULAM MUHAMMAD (1830-1900). A calligrapher and poet who took the pen-name "Tarzi" (the stylist) and was the author of a large body of religious, mystic, and secular poetry. He was the son of Rahmdil Khan, a Muhammadzai from Kandahar. He received a yearly stipend from Amir Dost Muhammad (q.v.), but Amir Abdur Rahman (q.v.) in December 1881 forced him and his family into Indian exile. Tarzi traveled in 1885 to Baghdad and Istanbul and from there to Damascus, where he lived as a pensioner of the sultan/caliph, Abdul Hamid. Ghulam Muhammad had five daughters and six sons, one of whom, Mahmud Tarzi (q.v.), returned to Afghanistan after the death of his father and held high offices at the courts of Abdur Rahman's successors.

TARZI, MAHMUD. Prominent Afghan nationalist, "Father of Afghan Journalism," and high government official during the reigns of Amir Habibullah and King Amanullah. Born in Ghazni on August 23, 1865, the son of Ghulam Muhammad Tarzi (q.v.), he accompanied his father into exile and was educated in India and in Damascus under the supervision of his father. He returned to Kabul after the death of Amir Abdur Rahman and became editor of the *Seraj-ul-Akhbar* (q.v.). During the reign of King Amanullah, Tarzi served as foreign minister (1919-22) and headed the Afghan delegation at the peace conferences at Mussoorie (1920) and Kabul (1921). He was the first Afghan minister at Paris 1922-24, and again foreign minister 1924-27, and left Afghanistan with King Amanullah in January 1929. He was a great reformer, but did not agree with some of King Amanullah's innovations. One of his daughters was married to King Amanullah and another to Sardar Enayatullah. He died in Istanbul in 1933.

TASAWWUF See SUFISM.

TASHQURGHAN Now KHULM (lat. 36-42' N, long. 67-41' E). A town, now called Khulm, with 28,000 inhabitants which once was the principal market between Central Asia and Kabul. The town was founded on the site of an ancient town (destroyed as a result of Turco-Mongol invasions) in the early 19th century by Amir Kalich Ali Beg, Khan of Khulm, who built a citadel there and called it Tashqurghan (T. stone, or brick, fort). Ali Beg was able to expand his domains, creating the largest khanate in Afghan Turkestan. In 1850 Amir Dost Muhammad defeated the khan and brought Tashqurghan under the control of Kabul.

TATAR. An ethnic group of sunnis claiming to be of Mongol descent. They number about 60,000 and inhabit the northern part of Bamian and parts of Samangan provinces. Larger numbers of Tatars also live in Bukhara and Khiva in the Uzbek Soviet Republic. In the mid-nineteenth century their chief was Shah Pasand Khan. His son Dilawar Khan supported Amir Shir Ali (q.v., 1863-79) in the wars of the princes, but in the early 1880s Amir Abdur Rahman (q.v.), took the khanate under Kabul control.

TAWANA, SAYYID MUSA. A founder of the Islamist movement in Afghanistan. Born in Takhar province, he was educated at the Dar al-Ulum-i Shari'a (now Abu Hanifa) madrasa, Kabul University, and Cairo's Al-Azhar University. In the late 1950s he belonged to a small circle at Kabul University who perceived a "danger of apostasy among university students." The group designed a three-point program of action: 1) refute the claims of secularists on questions of Islam, 2) write and translate articles to propagate the teachings of Islamist scholars, and 3) study Communism and European history with a view of understanding the enemy. In 1961 he graduated from Kabul University and became lecturer at the faculty of theology of Kabul University until 1964, when he proceded to Cairo to study at Al-Azhar University. After graduating with the Ph.D. degree in 1971 he returned to Kabul and in 1972 was appointed a professor at the faculty of shari'a of Kabul University. At that time the "professors" founded the *jami'at-i Islami* with Rabbani (q.v.) as head and Sayyaf (q.v.) his deputy. Habiburrahman (q.v.) was secretary, and in charge of military affairs. Gulbuddin Hekmatyar (q.v.) was in a Kabul jail at the time. As a result of the Daud coup on July 17, 1973, the Islamist movement had to go underground. See ISLAMIST MOVEMENT IN AFGHANISTAN.

TAZI See AFGHAN HOUND.

THIRD ANGLO-AFGHAN WAR See ANGLO-AFGHAN WARS.

TIMURIDS See TIMUR-I-LANG.

TIMUR-I LANG Or **TAMERLANE** (1370-1405). "The Lame Timur" founded the Timurid dynasty and wreaked destruction on the towns he conquered, but made Samarkand into a city of splendor. He was a warrior, not an empire builder and could not hold his extensive territorial conquests. The "Lame Timur" was a Turk, born at Kesh, near Samarkand, who claimed Mongol descent and began as a raider for booty. Claiming to wage *jihad*, holy war, he fought Muslim rulers in Russia and India and subdued the Ottomans at the Battle of Ankara in 1404. He was preparing a campaign against China when he died in 1405. His son Shahrukh chose Herat as his capital and made it an important cultural center. Under Husain Baiqara (1468-1506), the last of the great Timurid rulers, Herat experienced a cultural renaissance, and artists, poets, and scholars enjoyed the sponsorship of the Timurid court. Architectural remains from the Timurid period include the Musalla (minarets) and the mausoleum of Gauhar Shad, the wife of Shahrukh. Timurid rule ended when the Uzbak Shaibanid dynasty took Herat in the early 16th century.

TIMUR SHAH (1773-93). One of Ahmad Shah's six surviving sons and governor of Herat at the time of the death of his father. He defeated his brother, Sulaiman Mirza, and quickly established himself as successor to the Afghan throne at Kandahar. To weaken the power of the Durrani chiefs he moved his capital to Kabul where he continued his father's policy of forging an alliance with the Barakzais, granting hereditary offices, and maintaining a strong army. He made alliances by marriage and further strengthened his power by creating an elite bodyguard of non-Pashtun soldiers. However, he was unable to create a centralized state. Afghan historians describe him as "humane and generous but ... more a scholar than a soldier." He appointed his sons Zaman, Humayun, Mahmud, Abbas, and Kohandil as governors of Afghan provinces, and upon his death in 1783 they started an internecine struggle for power that eventually cost the Sadozai rulers their throne. Timur Shah's tomb is located in Charbagh, Kabul, on the right bank of the Kabul river.

TIRAHI (TIRA'I). A small ethnic group which was moved by Timur-i Lang (q.v.) from the area of Tehran to the Tirahi plateau. Later expelled from Tirah, they settled in the Nangarhar valley, where they are engaged in agriculture. They were *shi'as* at one time but became sunnis and speak Pashto, although some may still know their original language. The Tirahis are divided into three sections: the Shabadwani, Sipai, and Lartoi. At the turn of the century they numbered about 3,000.

TOKHI. A section of the Ghilzai tribe. See GHILZAI.

TREATIES. See under individual treaties, AFGHAN FOREIGN RELATIONS and ANGLO-AFGHAN WARS.

TREATY OF KABUL See ANGLO-AFGHAN TREATY OF 1921.

TRIBES. See individual entries.

TRIBES, PASHTUNS. Pashtuns are tribally organized and derive their origin from an eponymic ancestor. Although they all speak Pasto, some may have been of Turkic or other ethnic background. Today, the Pashtuns are the dominant factor in Afghanistan and the North-West Frontier Province (NWFP) of Pakistan. Beyond these boundaries they can be found in considerable numbers in India and other neigboring countries.

The Pashtuns (Pathans) of the NWFP include the following tribes.

Afridis	Barbars	Bajauris (or Tarkanris)	
Bangash	Bannuchis	Batannis	
Bahramzais	Chamkannis	Daudzais	Daurs
Dilazaks	Gandapurs	Gaodarras	Gharbinas
Gigianis	Jajis	Khalils	Khasors
Khattaks	Khetrans	Kundis	Lohanis
Mahsuds	Makbals	Mangals	Marwats
Mishwanis	Mohmands	Mullagoris	Multanis
Muhammadzais	Niazis	Orakzais	Safis
Sam Ranizais	Shinwaris	Turis	Urmars
Ushtaranas	Utman Khel	Wazir (or Darwish Khel)	
Yusufzais	Zaimukhts		

Pashtuns in Baluchistan include the following:

Achakzais	Babis	Bearech	Ja'fars
Kakars	Kansis	Lunis	Mando Khel
Panis	Shiranis	Tarins	Zmarais

Pashtuns in Afghanistan include the following:

Durranis	Ghilzais	Khostwals	Jadrans
Safis	Shinwaris	Utman Khel	Yusufzais

as well as others present in the NWFP. (Ridgway, 1910)

For information on the major Pashtun tribes, see individual entries. Also see ETHNIC GROUPS for major non-Pashtun groups, and PASHTO, PASHTUN, AND PASHTUNISTAN.

TRIPARTITE AGREEMENT. An agreement signed on July 16, 1838 between Ranjit Singh (q.v.), ruler of the Sikh nation of the Punjab, Shah Shuja (q.v.), the exiled king of Afghanistan, and the British government. It stipulated relations between the future Afghan ruler and Ranjit Singh and allied the three powers in an attempt to restore Shah Shuja (q.v.) and the Sadozai dynasty to the Kabul throne. Ranjit Singh was not required to supply troops and wisely left the task of invading Afghanistan to the British "Army of the Indus." He was thus spared the British defeat in the first Anglo-Afghan war. See also AFGHAN FOREIGN RELATIONS, ANGLO-AFGHAN WARS, and SIMLA MANIFESTO.

TSARANDOY See SARANDOY.

TURI. A Pashtun tribe of the Ghurgusht branch. Babur Shah, founder of the Moghul dynasty of India (See BABUR), mentions the Turis as residing in 1506 in the Kurram valley, where they are found today. Kurram was part of Afghanistan until 1880 when the Turis revolted, coming under British "protection" in 1882. They are *shi'as* and disciples of one of four Sayyid families: the Tirah, Ahmadzai, Kirman, and Maura. In the present conflict between the mujahedin and the Kabul government, the Kurram valley is an important supply route of mujahedin operating in the Kabul area. This has resulted in friction between them and the local population of Turis.

TURKMANI, ABDUL RAUF. A Hazara intellectual and journalist who was imprisoned after the Saur Revolt and is said to have been killed during the Khalqi era. He was born in 1910 in the Turkman valley and attended secondary and military schools. He was the editor and publisher of *Payam-i Wejdan* and editor of *Payam-i Imruz* (q.v.) in 1966, and demanded minoritiy rights and accused the government of corruption.

TURKOMAN. A sunni Turkic people, estimated at from 125 to 400 thousand. They inhabit the northwestern part of Afghanistan, where the majority of them had fled after the Bolshevik Revolution. They contributed greatly to the Afghan economy as breeders of Qaraqul sheep and weavers of Turkoman carpets. The Marxist government has tried to win minority support and declared Turkmani one of the national languages, permitting the publication of newspapers and broadcasts in that language.

-U-

ULAMA. Doctors of Islamic sciences. The word comes from the Arabic word *'alim*, (pl. *ulama*) and denotes "one who possesses the quality of *'ilm*, knowledge, or learning, of the Islamic traditions and the resultant canon law and theology." Afghan rulers established a hierarchy of *ulama*, headed by the *khan-i-'ulum* (chief of the ulama) and including the *qazis* (judges), *muftis* (canon lawyers), and *mullas* (preachers) who, at the time of Amir Abdur Rahman, were members of his royal council, *darbar-i-'am*. They seldom enjoyed political power but were an influential factor in the mobilization of the masses against King Amanullah in 1929 and against the Marxist regime presently in control of the Kabul government. Also see individual entries of the above terms and ISLAMIC LAW.

ULFAT, GUL PACHA. One of the founders of *Wish Zalmayan* (q.v.), president of the Pashto Academy (1957, see AFGHAN ACADEMY), president of tribal affairs (1963-65), and popular Pashto poet. He was born in 1909 in Laghman province and educated in Islamic studies. In 1936 he became editor of daily newspaper *Anis* (q.v.), and subsequently served as director of *Ziray* (1938), *Himanat* (1940), *Kabul Magazine* (1942), and *Ittihad-i Mashriqi* (1947). He was member of the Loya Jirgas of 1956 and 1964 and of the 7th and 8th parliaments. He was a social critic, political writer and Pashtun nationalist. He died on December 20, 1977.

ULUMI, LT. GEN. NUR-UL-HAQ ('ULUMI NUR AL-HAQQ). President Najibullah's governor of Kandahar and commander of the second army corps. He is a member of the Parcham faction of the PDPA and is now a member of the central council of the Watan party.

UMMA. Name for the Islamic community; the pan-Islamic concept that all Mulims belong to one community, or Islamic nation.

UNITED STATES-AFGHAN RELATIONS. The United States was slow in establishing diplomatic relations with Afghanistan because of several factors: Afghanistan had achieved independence from Great Britain in the third Anglo-Afghan war, but Washington still considered the country within the British sphere of influence. Afghanistan was not attractive as a market for American industrial products nor as a source of vital raw materials. Americans knew little about the country and whatever the U.S. government wanted to know it learned from the British and they were not eager to have American competition in Afghanistan. Therefore, it is not surprising that Washington did not establish a legation at Kabul. The mission of Wali Muhammad (q.v.), which visited European capitals for the purpose of establishing diplomatic relations, arrived in Washington in July 1921 with high hopes. Faiz Muhammad, a member of the mission, later described the event as follows:

> After waiting for some weeks to present the letter from King Amanullah to the President of the United States the members of our delegation were very much humiliated to read in the newspapers that President Harding had entertained Princess Fatima [the Afghan "princess" was not known by any member of the mission] at luncheon.

Some days later we were received briefly and informally, presented our letter and received in reply one in which the President expressed regret at the death of the King's illustrious father [Amir Habibullah] and congratulated His Majesty on his ascension to the throne. It was all very disappointing and heart-breaking.

The Afghan government wanted to embark on a plan of development and modernization for which it needed the assistance of Western know-how. Both Britain and the Soviet Union were too close to permit a relationship of dependency. Kabul, therefore, hoped that the United States would become a "third power" which would balance the influences of Afghanistan's neighbors. Afghanistan offered incentives to American enterprises: In 1930-31 an American firm sold sixty-eight trucks for 121,000 dollars to the Afghan government, but Britain made this an expensive deal, insisting that the trucks be transported on the Indian railroad rather than proceeding on their own power. In the same year the U.S. consul at Karachi came to Kabul, but when asked why the United States was not ready to establish diplomatic relations with Afghanistan, he could not give a satisfactory reply. The speaker of parliament reproached him, saying "Americans had always said kind things about Afghanistan but, despite the fine opinion of the country, they refused to recognize a friendly state." In May 1935, W. H. Hornibrook arrived from Tehran to arrange for accreditation of U.S. diplomats stationed in India. The Afghans were ready to offer an oil concession to the United States. The Afghan foreign minister explained: "For obvious reasons we cannot give the concessions to the British and for the same reasons we cannot give it to the Russians.... We therefore look to your country to develop our oil resources." He added that this would require a permanent American legation in Kabul. An oil concession was signed and ratified in April 1937 with the Inland Oil Exploration Company, but the company cancelled the concession a year later "in view of the worsening of the international situation."

Finally, in 1942 the U.S. government established a permanent legation in Kabul because of geopolitical reasons. The German advance on Stalingrad threatened the Allied logistics link through western Iran. Eastern Iran or western Afghanistan were the only areas for an alternate route. An American presence in Kabul could help gain Afghan approval for construction of a railroad. Therefore, on June 6, 1942, Cornelius van Engert (q.v.) became the first resident minister. The German defeat at Stalingrad made it unnecessary to raise the question of a railroad project with Kabul.

In the post World War II era, the United States provided aid for the war-torn and impoverished world, and Afghanistan received loans in 1950 and 1954 to finance its Helmand Valley electrification and irrigation projects. The American Morrison-Knudsen Construction Company undertook the ambitious task, which consumed a considerable amount of Afghanistan's hard currency reserves and did not live up to expectations (see HELMAND VALLEY AUTHORITY. The beginning of the cold war further complicated American-Afghan relations.

The United States sought allies in its effort to contain Soviet expansionism and promised economic and military assistance to those states which were willing to join. The Afghan government was unable to obtain American guarantees of protection from Soviet aggression, but Pakistan did and became a member of the Baghdad Pact. The U.S. department of state made the decision to defend the Indian subcontinent at the Khaibar rather than at Afghanistan's northern boundary. This was bound to exacerbate relations with Pakistan (See PASHTUNISTAN) and prompted the Afghan goverment to pursue a policy of "positive neutrality," which eventually led to dependence on the Soviet Union. The American government was willing to help, but Washington was not willing to match Soviet aid. Between 1950 and 1971, the total of American loans and grants amounted to about $286 million as compared to $672 million from the Soviet Union. American policy was to foster cordial relations with Afghanistan, help expand its communications infrastructure, participate in certain sectors of education, and provide moral, but not military, support to strengthen Afghanistan's independence. In the late 1970s the U.S. department of state downgraded the American embassy in Kabul to the category of missions of countries of least importance to the United States and Afghanistan was tacitly left in the Soviet sphere of influence.

After the Saur Revolt, the United States recognized the Marxist government, but relations quickly deteriorated. The assassination of the American Ambassador, Adolf Dubs, in February 1979, in a botched rescue attempt from kidnapers by Kabul police, further worsened relations. The Soviet military intervention in December 1979, resulted in vital American support for the mujahedin, forcing the Soviet government to withdraw its forces by February 1989. Fearing a general massacre in Kabul and the quick defeat of the Kabul government, the United States closed its embassy for "security reasons" in January 1989 and prevailed on others to do likewise. But an Afghan charge d'affaires remained in Washington and, at the time of this writing, it appears that the United States will follow the Italian and French lead and send a representative to Kabul.

URTA TAGAI (LAT. 37-30' N, LONG. 69-30' E). A 160-square mile island in the Amu Daria, also called Yangi Qal'a and Darqad, which in the 1920s became an issue in Soviet-Afghan relations. See SOVIET-AFGHAN RELATIONS.

UZBAK (UZBEK). The largest Turkic-language group in Afghanistan, estimated to number about 1.3 million (the Uzbak Soviet Republic in Soviet Central Asia Union has a population of about 17.5 million, half of them Uzbaks). They inhabit northern Afghanistan from Fariab province in the west to Badakhshan province. The Uzbak trace their name to an eponymic ancestor or a major tribe which migrated from the area north of the Syr Daria to the area north of the Afghan border. In the 15th century the Uzbaks were clients of various Timurid princes, but soon struck out independently and by the early 16th century had captured Bukhara, Samarkand, and Khiva. They expelled Babur Shah (q.v.) from Ferghana, were defeated by Shah Isma'il of Persia in 1510, and carved out a khanate in Transoxania. Ahmad Shah Durrani gave Balkh to Haji Khan, Uzbak, to protect the border from raids, but after the latter's death the khanate became a source of dispute between the Afghans and the amir of Bukhara. In 1869, Amir Shir Ali placed the khanate under the administration of the governor of Balkh.

The Uzbaks are distinguished from other Turkic groups in their dress. They wear long striped *chapans* (kaftans - still popular in Afghanistan), small turbans, rather than the Turkoman sheep-skin caps, and boots of soft leather which fit tightly over wool stockings and reach up to the knees. They are largely sedentary agriculturalists. The Marxist government has tried to win their support and proclaimed Uzbak a national language, permitting the use of the language in education, the press, and the broadcasting media. Some Uzbak groups serve the Marxist government in Kabul as militia units in Pashtun areas.

-V-

VICTORIA LAKE See SAR-I-KOL.

VITKEVICH, CAPT. IVAN. A Russian agent, or adventurer, of Lithuanian descent who came to Kabul in December 1837 for the purpose of establishing commercial relations with Afghanistan. He had a letter from Count Simonich, the Russian ambassador to Tehran, and an unsigned letter purported to be from the Tsar. Alexander Burnes (q.v.) was also at Kabul on a similar assignment for the British-Indian government. Dost Muhammad wanted to regain Peshawar from Sikh control, but Burnes told him that he must surrender all claims to Peshawar and should make his peace with the Sikh ruler. Having gotten no help from the British, Amir Dost Muhammad negotiated with Vitkevich for Russian support. Vitkevich was later repudiated by the Russian government and, upon his return to St. Petersburg, committed suicide. The mission aroused fears in Britain that Dost Muhammad would ally himself with Russia and the decision was made to depose the Afghan ruler. See ANGLO-AFGHAN WARS, ALEXANDER BURNES, and DOST MUHAMMAD.

VON HENTIG See HENTIG-NIEDERMAYER EXPEDITION.

-W-

WAFADAR, PACHA GUL. A Khalqi member of the PDPA who participated in the 1973 coup, was appointed minister of frontier affairs (1973-74), and minister of civil aviation, 1988-89. He defected in December 1989 and, at a press conference organized by *Hizb-i Islami* of Hekmatyar (q.v.) in Peshawar, claimed he had been a Hizb member since 1980. He was arrested in 1985 when a bomb exploding in his place of business killed a Soviet soldier. After about 18 months in prison he was asked to serve in the Sharq administration until Najibullah dismissed the government in 1989. Born in 1943 in Jadran district of Paktia province and educated at military schools and in the Soviet Union, where he received an engineering degree. He was abroad for many years, serving as ambassador in Bulgaria (1974), Libya (1977), and India (1978-80).

WAHDAT. Name of a weekly newspaper in Dari/Pashto which was published and edited by the poet and calligrapher Khal Muhammad Khasta in 1966. It was the organ of *wahdat-i milli*, (National Unity Party) which was headed by the poet Khalilullah Khalili. The paper closed after six months because of financial difficulties. An issue, dated January 31, 1966 (11. Dalw 1344) published the party's manifesto. It demanded the rule of law, constitutionalism, nonalignment, struggle for human rights, and peaceful coexistence. It asked for agricultural development and Afghan cultural revival, the expansion of medical and educational facilities, and equal rights for women. An alliance of shi'a groups also adopted the name Wahdat (Unity), see MUJAHEDIN.

WAKHAN (LAT. 37-00' N, LONG. 73-00' E). The extreme northeastern district of Badakhshan province, extending from Ishkashim in the west to the borders of China in the east and separating Soviet territory from the Indo-Pakistani subcontinent. The Anglo-Russian Boundary Commission awarded this area in 1895-96 to Afghanistan to create a buffer between the two empires. Amir Abdur Rahman was reluctant to accept this gift, declaring he was not "going to stretch out a long arm along the Hindu Kush to have it shorn off." But eventually the Amir accepted the award when the gift was sweetened with a special annual subsidy of 50,000 rupees. The Wakhan is inhabited by some 6,000 Isma'ilis (Wakhis) and fewer than 2,000 sunni Qirghiz (q.v.). The latter emigrated to Turkey as a result of the Soviet intervention in Afghanistan. The area was ruled by an independent "mir" (from A., amir, prince) until 1882 when it came under the administrative control of the governor of Badakhshan. The Corridor consists of high valleys traversed by the Wakhan river which flows into the Ab-i-Panj, as the upper Amu Daria is called there. The two-humped Bactrian camel and yak are the major beasts of burden. In the years before the Saur Revolt the Wakhan Corridor attracted hunters for Marco Polo sheep and alpinists who explored its peaks. The inhabitants of the Wakhan Corridor are Uzbaks, and Wakhis. The Qirghiz herders lived in a symbiotic relationship with the agricultural Wakhis.

WAKMAN, MUHAMMAD AMIN. Chairman of the Afghan Millat (q.v.) party. Born in 1939 in Maidan and educated in Kabul and New Delhi, where he received the Ph.D. degree in international law and economics.

He was director of the protocol department of the ministry of information and culture and worked as radio announcer with Radio Afghanistan, All India Radio, and is presently employed with the Voice of America. Also see AFGHAN MILLAT.

WALI MUHAMMAD. Afghan foreign minister 1922-24, minister of war 1924-25, and regent during King Amanullah's journey abroad (1927-28). He was a descendant of the royal family of Darwaz and became custodian of Amir Habibullah's correspondence. He headed a mission to travel to Moscow and major European capitals to establish diplomatic relations. In July 1922 the mission arrived in the United States, but could not convince President Harding to establish relations with Afghanistan. After the downfall of King Amanullah, Muhammad Wali was imprisoned and, when Nadir Shah ascended the throne, he was sentenced to eight years imprisoment, but was executed with a number of supporters of King Amanullah in September 1933. Also see UNITED STATES-AFGHAN RELATIONS.

WARDAK. A community of Sayyids (q.v.) inhabiting a region which runs from the Hazara portion of the Ghazni province to the western part of the Logar valley. They are said to derive their name from an eponymic ancestor called Ward. In the late-19th century they numbered about 20,000 families.

WARDAK (lat. 34-15' N, long. 68-0' E). A province in east-central Afghanistan (formerly called Maidan) with an area of 3,745 square miles and a population of about 310,000 of whom about 23,000 live as refugees in Pakistan. The administrative center is the newly constructed town Maidanshahr (replacing Kot-i Ashro), located a few miles west of the Kabul-Kandahar highway. The province is mountainous, and crossed by the Kabul-Kandahar highway and the road west into the Hazarajat, and northwest to Bamian province. The inhabitants are Ghilzai and Durrani Pashtuns in the south and Hazara in the north and west. The province is 80 percent pasture land. About 60 percent of the farms comprise areas of less than five *jaribs* (one *jarib* = about 0.5 acre) The province has suffered considerably during the present war and has seen large-scale destruction of the infrastructure built during the 1970s.

WARDAK, ESMATI MA'SUMA See ESMATI.

WATAN. *Watan* (Homeland) is a biweekly, liberal newspaper in Persian, published by Mir Ghulam Muhammad Ghobar (q.v.) and Mir Muhammad Siddiq Farhang (q.v.) in 1951-52. It was closed by the government after the appearance of 48 issues.

WATAN, HIZB-I. "Homeland (or Fatherland) Party" is the new name of the PDPA since June 1990. See PEOPLES DEMOCRATIC PARTY OF AFGHANISTAN and Appendix.

WATANJAR, MUHAMMAD ASLAM. Minister of defense in Prime Minister Khaliqyar's government of May 1990. A member of the Khalq faction of the PDPA, he had a leading role in the coup of Muhammad Daud (1973) and the subsequent Saur Revolt (1978). In both events he rode the lead tank in the assault on the palace, and his tank was placed on a pedestal in the square facing the presidential palace in commemoration of the '78 coup. In April 1978 he and General Abdul Qadir headed the Revolutionary Council which formed the government until Nur Muhammad Taraki was installed as president. After the Saur Revolt he held the positions of minister of communication (April - June 1978), internal affairs (August 1978 - March 1979), defense (April - July 1979), interior (July - October 1979), defense (1987-88), and interior (1988-90). It is not clear why he was continuously transferred from one position to another, or why in spite of his achievements, he became a member of the PDPA politburo only in 1981. In September 1979 he was said to have been involved in a plot to remove Hafizullah Amin (q.v.) from power and fled to the protection of the Soviet embassy in Kabul until the Parcham takeover. After the revolt of Shahnawaz Tanai (q.v.) in March 1990, Dr. Najibullah appointed Watanjar minister of defense, the position previously held by Tanai. Watanjar was born in 1946 in Paktia province of an Andar Ghilzai family and was educated in military schools at Kabul and in the Soviet Union.

WAZIRI. The Waziris (also called Darwish Khel) are Ghurghusht Pashtuns claiming descent from Wazir. Their original home was in Birmal (now Paktika province) from where they gradually moved eastward in the 14th century and settled in the present Waziristan and across the border in Afghanistan. They are estimated to number about 250,000, most of them on the Pakistani side of the border. They are divided into two major branches: the Ahmadzai and Utmanzai. They supported Nadir Khan (the subsequent king) in his war against Habibullah Kalakani (q.v.) and, under the command of Marshal Shah Wali (q.v.) and their leader Allah Nawaz Khan, captured Kabul and the royal palace in October 1929.

WISH ZALMAYAN. A liberal political organization (Awakened Youth) founded in 1947 in Kandahar by writers and Pashtun nationalists. It included such individuals as Abdul Hai Aziz (q.v.), Gul Pacha Ulfat (q.v.), Shamsuddin Majruh (q.v.), Abdul Rauf Benawa (q.v.), Mir Ghulam Muhammad Ghobar (q.v.), Faiz Muhammad Angar (q.v.), and Nur Muhammad Taraki (q.v.). The organization wanted to reform Afghan society and aimed at the advancement of education, the eradication of corruption, the promotion of national welfare, understanding and respect among the people, and steadfastness in advancing toward their objectives.

It was one of the earliest political groups in Afghanistan and subsequently divided on the issue of Pashtun nationalism. The nationalists supported the Red Shirt movement of Khan Abdul Ghaffar Khan (q.v.).

WOLESI JIRGA. Literally "peoples' council," the name of the lower house (or House of the People) of parliament established by the Constitution of 1964. See CONSTITUTIONAL DEVELOPMENT.

-Y-

YAFTALI, MIRZA MUHAMMAD. Minister of trade (1930), commerce (1936), and finance (1956) and one of the prime movers in establishing the Ashami Company (later Bank-i Milli, q.v.). Born in Yaftal, a village in Badakhshan, he served as a page at the court of Amir Abdur Rahman (q.v.) and subsequently embarked on a diplomatic career. He was appointed Afghan minister in Moscow in 1921 and again in 1926. In 1924 he visited Europe and the United States to promote Afghan trade. In 1928 he served as deputy minister of foreign affairs. He died in 1960.

YAHYA KHEL See MUSAHEBAN.

YANGI QAL'A See URTA TAGAI.

YAQUBI, FAQIR MUHAMMAD. Member of the Parcham faction of the PDPA, serving as deputy minister of education (1980-81) and minister of education (1981-83). He was minister without portfolio in Prime Minister Hasan Sharq's government (1988), and adviser in 1990. Born in 1930, the son of Khan Muhammad (and brother of Ghulam Faruq Yaqubi, below) in Kabul province and educated in Kabul and the Soviet Union, where he obtained the Ph.D. degree in atomic physics. He taught at Najat School, Kabul University, and Kabul Polytechnic Institue and was appointed assistant dean at the faculty of sciences of Kabul University, and rector of the Kabul Polytechnic Institute. He is an academician of the Afghan Academy of Sciences.

YAQUBI, GEN. GHULAM FARUQ. Deputy President of State Security Services (KHAD, see AFGHAN SECURITY SERVICE), 1980-85. President, KHAD, succeeding Dr. Najibullah in December 1985. His position was upgraded to that of minister of state security (WAD), a position he held in the 1988 and 1990 governments. He became a member of the PDPA politburo in 1986 and is said to be an important ally of Najibullah. Born in 1938 in Kabul, the son of Khan Muhammad and educated at Najat school and the Kabul police academy and in West Germany, he began his career as a lecturer at the police academy in 1961. Subsequently he served as director of operations and general director of the criminal department of the ministry of interior.

YAQUB KHAN, AMIR MUHAMMAD. Born about 1849, the son of Amir Shir Ali (q.v.) and his governor of Herat. Yaqub Khan also coveted Kandahar and was greatly disturbed when in 1868 the amir gave his favorite son Abdullah Jan that post. In 1871 Yaqub Khan revolted and marched on Kabul but was forced to return·to Herat. Amir Shir Ali forgave Yaqub Khan and reappointed him governor of Herat. Yaqub Khan came to Kabul under a promise of safe conduct, which the amir did not keep, holding him in confinement until December 1878 when British troops invaded Afghanistan. Amir Shir Ali fled to northern Afghanistan and appointed Yaqub his regent and the latter proclaimed himself amir in February 1879, after he learned of the sudden death of his father. Hoping to save his throne, Yaqub concluded the Treaty of Gandomak (q.v.) with Britain and accepted a mission under Sir Louis Cavagnari (q.v.) at Kabul. When the latter was assassinated during an insurrection of troops, the British took control of government powers and Yaqub was forced to abdicate in October 1879. He went to India and lived there until his death in 1923. Also see ANGLO-AFGHAN WARS and GANDAMAK, TREATY OF.

YAR MUHAMMAD, WAZIR. Wazir, prime minister, of Prince Kamran (q.v., 1830-42) who ruled Herat as an independent principality. He is said to have been an able but cruel man who eventually became the virtual ruler of Herat. He ably withstood Persian attempts to capture Herat and led the defenses in two sieges in 1833 and 1837-38 in which the Russian General Berovski participated on the Persian side and Eldred Pottinger and Major Todd, British envoy to Herat, on the side of the defenders. Yar Muhammad had Prince Kamran assassinated in 1842 and embarked on an ambitious plan of conquest. He allied himself in marriage with Akbar Khan (q.v.), son of Amir Dost Muhammad (q.v.), and conquered the western Uzbak khanates of Afghan Turkestan. He died in 1851.

YAZDAN-BAKHSH, MIR. Born in 1790, the son of Mir Wali Beg, the chief of Behsud, Hazarajat. He expelled his older brother, Mir Mohammad Shah, who had become chief of Behsud after his father was assassinated by a minor chief. Mir Yazdan-bakhsh consolidated his power to become the undisputed chief of the Hazaras (1843-63). Amir Dost Mohammad Khan called him to Kabul and had him imprisoned. He escaped and fled to Bamian where he was assassinated. Also see HAZARA and HAZARAJAT.

YUNUS KHALES See KHALES, MUHAMMAD YUNUS.

YUSUF, DR. MUHAMMAD See MUHAMMAD YUSUF.

YUSUFZAI. A Pashtun tribe, originally setteld in Peshawar, which migrated to the Helmand valley and the Kabul region in the fifth century A.D., and in the 16th century returned to the northeastern corner of the Peshawar valley. They now inhabit the Pakistan districts of Peshawar, Mardan and

Swat. They then divided into two great branches: the Yusufzai and the Mandanr. They are agriculturists, usually dress in white clothes and shave their heads, leaving "a pair of lovelocks" at their temples. They have been romanticized as the "Pashtuns of the Pashtuns" among whom the Pashtunwali (q.v.) is still a living code of behavior. Khushhal Khan Khatak (q.v.), not himself a Ysufzai, extols their sense of honor, saying:
The nobles of the Afghans are the Yusufzai'is,
Hard in battlefield and hospitable at home,
All Pakhtuns possess the sense of honor (*nang*)
None, however, can vie with them.

-Z-

ZABIHULLAH, ABDUL QADIR. A mujahedin commander affiliated with Jam'iat who was a member of the Islamist youth organization (See ISLAMIST MOVEMENT) and operated successfully in the Mazar-i Sharif area. He was said to have been trained by Commander Mas'ud in Panjshir and subsequently cooperated with him. He was killed on December 14, 1984, when his jeep hit a land mine. Born in 1951 and educated in Mazar-i Sharif, he worked as a teacher and became a member of the Islamist movement. After the Saur revolt, he adopted the *nom de guerre* Zabihullah. He operated with Ahmad Shah Masud (q.v.) in the Panjshir valley and later moved to Mazar-i Sharif where he coordinated the activities of commanders and administered the territory under his control. After his death effective, large-scale resistance collapsed in the Mazar-i Sharif area.

ZABUL (lat. 32-0' N, long. 67-15' E). A province in south-central Afghanistan with an area of 6,590 square miles and a population of 181,000. The administrative center of the province is the town of Qalat, located about 87 miles northeast of Kandahar. The province is arid with almost perpetual winds and agriculture is limited to the valleys of the Tarnak and Arghastan rivers and a few areas which are irrigated by means of Kariz (q.v.). The province, however, abounds in almond trees, one of the major items of export. The Zabulis are noted as good horsemen and perform a game, called "tent pegging" (*naiza bazi*), in which they spear pegs planted in the ground. The population is largely Pashtun in the south and Hazara in the north. Also see QALAT.

ZABULI, ABDUL MAJID. The most successful Afghan capitalist and financier who founded the Ashami Company in 1933 which eventually developed into the Bank-i Milli (q.v.). He became minister of national economy in 1936 and established industries in Pul-i Khumri, Kunduz, and Kabul. He was instrumental in charting the course of Afghan economic development in cooperation with German commercial and industrial enterprises. Zabuli resigned in 1951 and went abroad. He was born in

1896 and educated in Herat and later at Tashkent. In 1917 he headed his father's export- import company in Herat, trading with Iran and Russia. In 1922 he moved his firm's office to Tashkent and from there to Moscow, to operate a textile mill under the Soviet "New Economic Policy." He moved to Germany in 1929 and devoted his activities to international investment. Invited by Nadir Shah to return to Afghanistan, he founded the Ashami Company in 1932 with 80 percent private and 20 percent government shares. He issued paper money and founded the Da Afghanistan Bank, Industrial Bank, and Bank-i-Milli branches in Berlin, London, Bombay, Karachi, Peshawar, and later in New York (Afghan-American Trading Company). Zabuli was seen as having political ambitions: he favored a laissez-faire economy and cooperation with Germany in Afghan economic development. Disagreements with Prime Minister Shah Mahmud Ghazi (q.v.) led to his resignation, but members of his family have continued to attend to family interests in Kabul. He retired and has been living in the United States since 1970.

ZADRAN See JADRAN.

ZAHIR, ABDUL See ABDUL ZAHIR.

ZAHIR SHAH, MUHAMMAD. King of Afghanistan, 1933-73. Born on October 15, 1914, the only surviving son of Nadir Shah (q.v.), he was educated at Kabul and in France. He was proclaimed king on November 8, 1933, within a few hours after his father's assassination and adopted the title *al-Mutawakkil Ala'llah, Pairaw-i Din-i Matin-i Islam*, (Confident in God, Follower of the Firm Religion of Islam). During the early period of his reign (1933-46), the young king reigned while his uncles Muhammad Hashim (q.v.) and Shah Mahmud Ghazi (q.v.) ruled, holding the powerful position of prime minister. His cousin, Muhammad Daud, succeeded as prime minister from 1953 until 1963, when Zahir Shah forced his resignation. In 1964 he promulgated a new constitution which excluded members of the royal family from certain government positions (see CONSTITUTIONAL DEVELOPMENT), provided for a bicameral parliament, free elections, a free press, and the formation of political parties. It ushered in a period of unprecedented political tolerance which was marred only by the intransigence of parliamentary representatives who could not establish a working coalition. The law on political parties was never ratified by the king, but parties were tolerated, although not legally permitted, and numerous groups published their manifestos in privately-published newspapers and periodicals. Members of parliament were elected as independents and not members of a party, but parliament was stymied with political infighting. Foreign aid from East and West kept flowing into the country, and Kabul experienced considerable growth. However, not all sectors of Afghan society benefitted from the economic development. Zahir Shah toured Afghanistan on several occasions and frequently traveled abroad. During one of his trips abroad, his cousin Muhammad Daud staged a coup and established a republican government with himself as president. Zahir Shah abdicated in August 1973 and has since lived in Italy. The impasse in the present war has led to demands by some that the ex-king return to serve as head of an interim government which would end the war and establish a representative government in Afghanistan. Zahir Shah's children include Princess Bilqis, 1932, wife of his cousin, General Abdul Wali; Muhammad Akbar, 1933-41; Ahmad Shah, 1934; Maryam, 1936; Muhammad Nadir, 1941; Shah Mahmud, 1946; Muhammad Daud Pashtunyar, 1949-80; and Mir Wais, 1957.

ZAKARIA See ZIKRIA.

ZAKAT. An alms-tax, one of the principal obligations in Islam. See ISLAM.

ZAKIM SHAH. Minister of commerce in Prime Minister Khaliqyar's government of May 1990. Born in 1944 in Khost and educated in Kabul, he became an official in the accounting department of the Kabul provincial government in 1969. He then moved to the treasury department of the ministry of finance and became director of the control section of Kabul customs in 1971. He became president of Kabul customs in 1979 and deputy minister of finance in 1985. He is not a member of the PDPA.

ZAMAN SHAH See SHAH ZAMAN.

ZAZAI, SARJANG. Minister of frontier affairs in Prime Minister Khaliqyar's government of May 1990. Born in 1927 in Ahmad Khel Zazai and educated in Kabul military schools and in India and Turkey. He was appointed chief of staff of Herat division in 1967 and commander of the 15th division in Kandahar. In 1975 he was commander of the 14th Ghazni division and subsequently served in other provinces until his retirement in 1978. Since 1985 he has served as minister without portfolio. He is not a member of the PDPA.

ZIAYI, ABDUL HAKIM. Minister of planning (1965-67), chief justice (*Qazi al-Quzat*), and head of the supreme court (1967), and a man known as a writer of sufi poetry. He was born in 1915 in Kabul, the son of Sardar Azizullah Qatil and grandson of Sardar Nasrullah Khan (q.v.), and educated in Kabul, Japan, and France. He served in the ministry of education prior to his appointment as minister of planning.

ZIAYI, MUHAMMAD ANWAR. Deputy minister of finance, 1963-66 and minister of finance, 1967-69. Educated at Najat School, he started his career in the Bank-i Milli.

ZIKRIA, FAIZ MUHAMMAD. Minister of education (1925-27 and 1949-50) and minister of foreign affairs (Nov. 1929-38), and known as a poet and writer. Born in 1892 in Kabul and educated at Habibia School, he was deputy of Muhammad Wali (q.v.), and traveled with him on a mission to Europe and the United States for the purpose of establishing diplomatic relations. Later he served as ambassador to Ankara (1938-48), London (1948-50), and Riyadh (1955). Retired in 1960 and went to United States, where he died in 1979.

ZIRAI (ZEARI), SALEH MUHAMMAD. A Khalqi and founding member of the PDPA who remained a member of the central committee until 1988. In July 1979 he was named by Amin minister of health. He objected to Hafizullah Amin's arbitrary distribution of land. In May 1980 Babrak Karmal appointed him to the politburo and secretary of the central committee. Najibullah appointed him to the council of ministers (1986) and chairman of the house of representatives (1988). He was implicated in the attempted coup of Shahnawaz Tanai (q.v.) and was expelled from the PDPA on March 8, 1990. According to reports he has been imprisoned for his part in the Tanai coup. Born in 1936 in Kandahar and educated at the faculty of medicine of Kabul University where he lead his class for seven years. In 1969 he was a candidate for parliament, but was arrested and jailed for six years.

ZIYARAT.   Tomb of a pir which has become a place of pilgrimage.

CHRONOLOGY

Ca. 2000-1000 B.C.	Move of the Arians from northern Afghanistan to northern India.
522-486	Darius I rules and Afghan territory becomes part of the Achaemenid empire.
330-327	Alexander the Great rules, Bactria (Balkh) becomes province of empire.
305	The Seleucids are defeated and Maurians establish rule.
ca. 250	Maurian kingdom under Asoka.
250-128	Graeco-Bactrian kingdom at Balkh.
ca. 50-250 A.D.	Afghanistan area is part of Kushanid empire.
ca. 225-600s	Sassanids establish control.
652-664	First Muslim-Arab conquests.
8th-10th cent.	Hindushahis rule Kabul and eastern part of Afghan territory.
871	Yaqub b. Laith, Saffarid, defeats Hindushahis.
997-ca. 1150	Ghaznavid rule.
1186	Ghorids succeed Ghaznavids.
1221-1222	Genghis Khan devastates Balkh, Bamian, and Herat.
1227-1350	Kurt dynasty in Balkh, Ghazni, and Sarakhs.
1370	Timur-i Lang crowned in Balkh.
1405-1506	Timurid rule in Herat and Balkh.

1504-1525	Babur invades; establishes capital in Kabul.
16th and 17th cent.	Safavids and Moghuls occupy Afghan territory.
1709-38	Ghilzais revolt against Safavid rule and establish a dynasty which also ruled Iran.
1747	Foundation of modern Afghanistan and rule by the Durrani dynasty. Ahmad Shah begins 26-year rule during which he united Afghan tribes under the Sadozai dynasty.
1761	Afghans defeat Maratha confederacy at Battle of Panipat, marking greatest extent of Ahmad Shah's empire which included Kashmir, the Panjab, and parts of Baluchistan.
1773	Timur Shah begins 20-year rule. Moves capital from Kandahar to Kabul. Campaigns in Sind and Bukhara.
1793	Zaman Shah begins six-year rule.
1798	Britain, fearing Afghan invasions of India, initiates policy of containment, enlisting Persia to keep Afghanistan in check.
1799	Zaman Shah deposed by Mahmud and goes into exile in India.
1803	Shah Shujah deposes Mahmud.
1805	Persian attempt to take Herat fails.
1807	At Tilsit, Alexander II and Napoleon plan joint Russian-French invasion of India through Persia.
1809	British envoy Mountstuart Elphinstone and Shah Shuja sign defensive alliance in first official contact between Afghanistan and a European power. Mahmud defeats Shah Shuja at Gandamak and rules until blinding of Fateh Khan, his Barakzai wazir, causes Barakzai revolt and Mahmud's downfall in 1818.
1816	Persian attempt to capture Herat fails.
1818	Civil war results in division of Afghanistan into virtually independent states until 1835.

1819	Ranjit Singh conquers Kashmir.
1826	Dost Muhammad, ruler of Ghazni, takes Kabul.
1834	Dost Muhammad defeats Shah Shujah and captures Kandahar.
1835	Dost Muhammad begins his first rule of Afghanistan. Persians attack and besiege Herat for three years but fail to the take city.
1837	Alexander Burnes arrives in Kabul on a diplomatic mission for British. Ivan Vitkewich (Witkiwicz), emissary from Russia, arrives in Kabul.
1838	British break relations with Dost Muhammad. Tripartite Treaty signed in July by Ranjit Singh, the British East India Company, and Shah Shujah to restore the latter to the Afghan throne.
1839	First Anglo-Afghan War begins.
1840	Dost Muhammad attempts to regain power, is defeated at Bamian, and goes into exile in British India.
1841	British envoys to Afghanistan assassinated: Alexander Burnes in November and William Macnaghten in December.
1842	British forces decimated on retreat from Kabul in January. British send punitive expedition led by Generals George Pollock and William Nott in August. British leave Afghanistan in October. Dost Muhammad restored to throne and rules for 21 years.
1855	Treaty of Peshawar reopens diplomatic relations between Britain and Afghanistan.
1856	Persians capture and hold Herat for a few months.
1857	Anglo-Afghan treaty signed in Peshawar in January provides subsidy for Dost Muhammad.
1863	Dost Muhammad dies. Shir Ali ascends Afghan throne. During next two years Shir Ali put down revolts by half-brothers, Azim and Afzal, and his brother, Muhammad Amin. Abdur Rahman and his uncle,

1863 (cont.)	Azim, attack Kabul, liberate Afzal, Abdur Rahman's father.
1866	Afzal becomes Amir. Shir Ali flees to Kandahar.
1867	Afzal dies.
1868	Azim becomes Amir.
1869	Shir Ali defeats Azim. Abdur Rahman goes into exile in Russia. British recognize Shir Ali as Amir but refuse to recognize his son, Abdullah Jan, as successor. Amballa Conference held between Amir Shir Ali and Lord Mayo, viceroy of India.
1872	In Granville-Gorchakoff Agreement Russia assures Britain that Afghanistan is outside Russia's sphere of influence. British commission marks Sistan boundary.
1873	Abdullah Jan named heir to Afghan throne. Shir Ali's oldest son, Yaqub Khan, revolts, flees to Herat. Russia takes Khiva.
1874	Yaqub Khan imprisoned in Kabul.
1876	British occupy Quetta.
1878	Russian mission under General Stolietoff arrives in Kabul in July. British representative, Major Louis Cavagnari, refused permission to proceed to Ali Masjid on Sept. 20 and 21. Earlier in September Shir Ali refused to allow British mission under Sir Neville B. Chamberlain to enter Afghanistan. Colonel Grodekoff arrives in Herat from Samarkand in November. Indian viceroy, Lord Lytton, denounces alliance with Dost Muhammad. Second Anglo-Afghan War begins as British armies cross border into Afghanistan on Nov. 22. Shir Ali flees.
1879	Shir Ali dies in February. Yaqub Khan ascends throne. Yaqub Khan signs Treaty of Gandamak with British in June, allows British agent to come to Kabul. British representative, Cavagnari, assassinated in Kabul in September; General Roberts occupies Dakka and enters Kabul with British troops.
1880	British recognize Abdur Rhaman as Amir. On July 27 Ayub Khan, governor of Herat, defeats General

1880 (cont.)	Burrows at Maiwand near Kandahar. General Roberts enters Kandahar in September.
1881	British leave Kandahar under control of Abdur Rahman in September.
1882	Muslim agent appointed to represent British in Kabul. Prince Lobanoff and Lord Granville discuss Gorchakoff's circular of 1873 during Anglo-Russian contacts.
1883	Russia occupies Tejend Oasis. Britain annexes Quetta district. Abdur Rahman occupies Shignan and Roshan. Britain grants Abdur Rahman subsidy of twelve lakhs (1,200,000) rupees.
1884	Britain and Russia open negotiations on northern boundary of Afghanistan. Sir Peter Lumsden leads British mission to Herat. British again start building Quetta railroad. Russians occupy Pul-i-Khatun.
1885	Russians occupy Zulfiqar and Aqrobat and take Panjdeh.
1886	British construct Bolan railway to Quetta. British boundary mission returns to India by way of Kabul in October.
1887	Russia occupies Karki. Britain and Russia make final settlement and demarcation of Afghan-Russian frontier. Ayub Khan escapes from Persia, but rebellion in Afghanistan fails and he surrenders at Mashhad and is exiled to India.
1888	British extend Quetta Railway to Kila Abdullah in January. In July Ishaq Khan, son of Azim, revolts in Turkestan, retreats to Samarkand.
1891	Abdur Rahman introduces oath of allegiance on the Koran among his councillors.
1892	Uprising of Hazaras suppressed.
1893	Afghanistan and Britain sign Durand Agreement on Nov. 12, which sets northern, eastern, and southern borders. British increase Amir Abdur Rahman's subsidy by six lakhs, and permit Afghanistan to import munitions. British occupy New Chaman as railway terminus.

1894	Illness prevents Abdur Rahman from accepting Queen Victoria's invitation to visit England.
1895	Abdur Rahman abolishes slavery in Afghanistan. Abdur Rahman accepts oaths of allegiance from whole state of Afghanistan. Abdur Rahman adopts title of *Zia ul-Millat wa ud-Din*. Sardar Nasrullah, second son of Abdur Rahman, visits England. Russia and Britain agree on Wakhan border.
1896	Kafiristan brought under Afghan control by Amir Abdur Rahman, renamed Nuristan.
1900	Russia presses for direct Afghan-Russian relations along northern Afghan border in memorandum of Feb. 6 to Britain.
1901	Abdur Rahman dies on Oct. 1. Habibullah proclaimed Amir on Oct. 3. Rules 18 years.
1902	British envoy, Sir Henry Dobbs, supervises reerection of boundary pillars on Afghan-Russian border during 1902 and 1903.
1903	A. H. McMahon leads British mission in demarcating Sistan boundary. Habibia College, first secular high school, opened in Kabul. British begin construction of Quetta-Nushki railroad.
1905	British agreements of 1880 and 1893 with Abdur Rahman confirmed by treaty with Amir Habibullah.
1906	Shah of Iran rejects McMahon arbitration award.
1907	Habibullah visits India in January. On Aug. 31, Britain and Russia sign convention concerning spheres of influence in Afghanistan, Persia, and Tibet.
1909	Plot on Amir Habibullah's life fails.
1910	First telephone line in Afghanistan built between Kabul and Jalalabad.
1911	Mahmud Tarzi begins publishing the newspaper *Seraj al-Akhbar*.

1914	General Muhammad Nadir Khan named commander-in-chief of the Afghan Army. Habibullah declares Afghanistan's neutrality in World War I.
1915	Niedermayer-Hentig mission from Germany arrives in Kabul in September and remains nine months.
1918	Kabul Museum opened.
1919	Feb. 20. Amir Habibullah assassinated in Laghman. Nasrullah Khan named Amir in Jalalabad.
	Feb. 25. Sardar Amanullah proclaimed Amir in Kabul.
	Feb. 28. Sardar Nasrullah arrested.
	Mar. 3. King Amanullah suggests new Anglo-Afghan agreement to viceroy of India.
	May 3. Third Anglo-Afghan War begins.
	May 21. General Nadir Khan crosses Indo-Afghan boundary, marches on Thal.
	May 28. Wali Muhammad Khan arrives in Tashkent on way to Moscow and Europe as Amanullah's envoy.
	Jun. 3. Afghanistan and Britain agree to ceasefire.
	Aug. 8. Preliminary Anglo-Afghan treaty signed at Rawalpindi peace conference.
	Sep. Soviet envoy arrives in Kabul.
	Oct. 10. Muhammad Wali Khan arrives in Moscow.
1920	Apr. 17. Mussoorie Conference opens. Mahmud Tarzi represents Afghanistan and Henry Dobbs, Britain.
	Jul. 18. Mussoorie Conference ends.
1921	Amir of Bukhara seeks asylum in Afghanistan.
	Jan. 20. Kabul conference between Afghanistan and Britain opens.
	Feb. 28. Treaty of friendship signed by Afghanistan and the Soviet Union.
	Mar. 1. Treaty of friendship signed by Afghanistan and Turkey.
	May 30. Fundamental law of government of Afghanistan goes into force.
	Jun. 3. Treaty of friendship signed by Afghanistan and Italy.
	Jun. 22. Treaty of friendship signed by Afghanistan and Persia.
	Dec. 2. Kabul Conference ends. Britain recognizes Afghanistan as independent in internal and external relations. Diplomatic relations established between the two states.

1922	Apr. 28. Treaty establishes diplomatic and commercial relations between France and Afghanistan. Sep. 9. Agreement gives France rights to conduct archaeological excavations in Afghanistan.
1923	Jan. Istiqlal high school founded in Kabul. Apr. 10. First Consititution adopted. Jun. 5. British-Afghan trade convention signed. Sep. French legation opened in Afghanistan. Oct. Criminal code adopted. Nov. Statute governing marriage issued. Dec. Statute on civil servants confirmed. Dec. German legation opened in Afghanistan.
1924	Najat high school founded. Jan. First hospital for women and children opened in Kabul. May. Uprising of tribes in Khost.
1925	Jan. Khost rebellion defeated.
1926	Afghani introduced as new monetary unit. Ten afghanis equal eleven Kabuli *ropia*. Mar. 3. Treaty of friendship signed by Afghanistan and Germany. Jun. 7. Amanullah adopts title of King. Aug. 15. Soviet Union agrees to cede Urta Tagai islands in Amu River to Afghanistan. Aug. 31. Treaty of neutrality and mutual nonaggression signed by Afghanistan and Soviet Union.
1927	*Anis* founded as fortnightly, later it becomes a major national daily newspaper. Nov. 27. Treaty of neutrality and mutual nonaggression signed by Afghanistan and Persia. Dec. King Amanullah leaves for visit to India, Egypt, Iran, and Europe.
1928	May 25. Treaty of friendship and collaboration signed by Afghanistan and Turkey. Jul. King Amanullah returns to Afghanistan. Jul. to Sep. Amanullah introduces reforms in dress. Nov. Uprising of Shinwari near Jalalabad. Dec. Habibullah Kalakani leads uprising in Kohistan.
1929	*Islah* newspaper founded. Jan. 14. Amanullah renounces throne. His brother, Enayatullah, abdicates after three days.

1929 (cont.)	Jan. 18. Habibullah Kalakani proclaimed Amir. Oct. 14 Kabul seized by Nadir Khan's troops. Oct.17. Nadir Khan proclaimed King. Nov. 3. Habibullah Kalakani caught and shot.

1930   May. Nadir Shah confirms validity of 1921 and 1923 Anglo-Afghan Agreements and other international treaties.
Sep. 20. Nadir Shah confirms statute governing elections of members of National Assembly.

1931   Jun. 24. New treaty of neutrality and mutual nonaggression signed by Afghanistan and Soviet Union.
Jul. Literary Society founded in Kabul.
Jul. Nadir Shah opens National Assembly session.
Oct. 31. New Constitution confirmed by Nadir Shah.

1932   Medical school founded and other schools closed by Habibullah Kalakani reopened.
May 5. Treaty of friendship signed by Afghanistan and Saudi Arabia.
Aug. 24. Statute setting up new administrative divisions issued. Five major and four minor provinces formed.
Oct. Uprising begins in Khost.
Nov. 8. Ghulam Nabi executed on charge of complicity in Dari Khel Ghilzai revolt.

1933   Road over Shibar Pass to north completed.
Jun. 6. Muhammad Aziz, Afghan minister to Germany, assassinated in Berlin.
Nov. 8. Nadir Shah assassinated. His son, Muhammad Zahir, becomes King, and brother of Nadir Shah, Muhammad Hashim prime minister. The cabinet is composed of the following:

Shah Mahmud	Minister of War
Faiz Muhammad	Foreign Affairs
Muhammad Gul Khan	Interior
Fazl Ahmad Mujaddidi	Justice
Mirza Muhammad Yaftali	Finance
Ahmad Ali Sulaiman	Education
Mirza Muhammad Yaftali	Commerce
Allah Nawaz	Public Works
Muhammad Akbar	Health
Rahimullah	PTT

1934   Feb. 16. Zahir Shah orders general election for National Assembly.

1934 (cont.)	Mar. State begins to control purchase and export of karakul skins. Bank-i Milli formed. Aug. 21. United States formally recognizes Afghanistan. Sep. 25. Afghanistan joins League of Nations.
1935	Apr.-May. W.H. Hornibrook accredited as nonresident minister to Kabul. May. Turkey arbitrates Afghanistan's boundary dispute with Persia. Jun. 8. National Assembly session opened by Zahir Shah. Sep. Mohmand uprising. Nov. Japanese legation established in Afghanistan.
1936	Pashto proclaimed national language of Afghanistan. Mar. Treaty on commerce and noninterference signed by Afghanistan and Soviet Union. Mar. 26. Treaty of friendship signed by Afghanistan and United States.
1937	Lufthansa starts weekly service between Berlin and Kabul; first regular air link between Afghanistan and Europe. Jul. 7. Treaty of Saadabad signed by Afghanistan, Iran, Iraq, and Turkey.
1938	May. Afghan Air Force expanded by purchase of planes from Italy and Britain. Officers sent to Britain, Soviet Union, and Italy for training. Arms bought from Britain and Czechoslovakia.
1939	Feb. 11. Afghan government plans to spend Afs. 8 million (1.7 mil. British pounds) for industrial development. Cotton raising to be encouraged and textile company founded. Sep. 3. Beginning of World War II and Afghan armed forces mobilized as precautionary measure.
1940	Jan. 12. All men over age 17 obliged to do national service. Special taxes imposed to pay for arms, build radio station. Radio Kabul gets 20 kilowatt medium wave transmitter. May. Joint stock company formed to handle ginning, spinning, and weaving of cotton. Sugar beet raising to be encouraged. Jul. 29. Trade agreement by Afghanistan and Soviet Union signed.

1940 (cont.)
Aug. 17. Zahir Shah declares Afghanistan's neutrality in World War II in statement to National Assembly.

1941
Jul. 28. Afghanistan reaffirms its neutrality in World War II.
Oct. 19. Afghanistan agrees to expel German and Italian residents at demand of Britain and the Soviet Union.

1942
Apr. 27. Cornelius van Engert, consul-general in Beirut, named resident U.S. minister to Afghanistan.
Nov. 5. Afghanistan reaffirms neutrality in World War II.

1943
May 16. Afghan consulate opened in New York.
Jun. 5. Abdul Husain Aziz, first Afghan minister to United States, presents credentials.
Dec. 28. Saadabad pact reported automatically renewed after five years.

1944
Mar. 5. Treaty of friendship signed by Afghanistan and China.

1946
Kabul University established by combining already existing faculties, such as medicine and law.
Jan. 22. King Zahir orders election of deputies for session of National Assembly to meet April 21.
May 9. Muhammad Hashem Khan resigns as prime minister, citing poor health as reason. Mahmud Khan, minister of defense, asked to form new government:

Ali Muhammad	Foreign Affairs
Muhammad Daud	War (Defense)
Ghulam Faruq Osman	Interior
Mir Ata Muhammad	Justice
Mir Muhd. Haidar Husaini	Finance
Najibullah Torwayana	Education
Abdul Majid Zabuli	National Economy
Muhammad Kabir	Public Works
Ahmad Ali Sulaiman	Health
Abdullah Malikyar	Information
Gholam Muhd. Sherzad	Mines
Muhammad Atiq Rafiq	Agriculture
Sayyid Qasim Reshtia	Press

Jun. 13. Boundary treaty signed with Soviet Union. Soviet Union gets Kushka River water rights.
Nov. 9. United Nations General Assembly approves entry of Afghanistan.

1946 (cont.)   Nov. 19. Abdul Husain Aziz, Afghanistan's first representative to United Nations, takes seat.

1947   Apr. 24. Afghan delegation arrives in Tashkent to start demarcation of Afghan-Soviet border.

Jun. 13. Afghanistan sends note to British and Indian governments saying that inhabitants of region between Afghan-Indian border and Indus River are Afghans and must decide themselves whether to join Afghanistan, Pakistan, or India or become independent.

Jul. 3. Britain replies it holds to Treaty of 1921 by which boundary was recognized by both nations and asks Afghanistan to abstain from any act of intervention on northwest frontier at time of transfer of powers to Indian government.

Jul. 10. Afghanistan reiterates views on Pashtuns in second note to Britain.

Jul. 26. Prime Minister Mahmud arrives in London.

Aug. 3. Prime Minister Mahmud arrives in New York City.

Sep. 18. Iran says diversion of Helmand waters in Afghanistan causes crop failures in Sistan.

Sep. 30. Afghanistan casts only vote against admitting Pakistan to United Nations on grounds that Pashtuns have not had a fair plebiscite.

1948   Apr. 1. Muhammad Naim named Afghan ambassador to United States.

Apr. 23. Sir Giles Squire named British ambassador to Afghanistan.

May 6. Faiz Muhammad named Afghan ambassador to Britain.

Jun. 5. United States legation elevated to status of embassy. Ely E. Palmer presents credentials as first U.S. ambassador.

Jun. 16. Pakistan arrests Abdul Ghaffar Khan and other *Khuda-i Khetmatgar* leaders. Afghanistan begins press and radio campaign for independent Pashtunistan.

Sep. 29. Afghan-Soviet mission completes demarcation of border. Agreement signed fixing revised boundary.

1949   Mar. 24. Foreign Ministry says statement of Pakistani governor general that tribal territory is integral part of Pakistan is contrary to pledges of Jinnah in 1948.

Apr. 2. Charge d'affaires in Karachi recalled after Pakistani bombing in Waziristan.

Apr. 20. Louis G. Dryfus named U.S. ambassador to Afghanistan.

1949 (cont.)

Jun. 4. Afghanistan restricts movement of vehicles along border with Pakistan.

Jun. 12. Pakistani plane bombs Moghalgai (inside Afghan territory), killing 23.

Jun. 20. Alfred Gardener named British ambassador to Afghanistan.

Jun. 30. Afghan National Assembly opens 7th Session, known as "Liberal Assembly."

Jul. 11. Pakistani foreign minister says Pakistan will discuss economic cooperation with Afghanistan, but rejects Afganistan's claims to tribal territory.

Jul. 26. Afghan National Assembly repudiates treaties with Britain regarding tribal territory.

1950

Jan. 4. Treaty of peace and friendship signed by Afghanistan and India.

Jan. 13. Afghanistan recognizes Chinese People's Republic.

Jan. 26. Sultan Ahmad presents credentials as Afghan ambassador to Soviet Union.

Mar. 8. Zahir Shah begins visit to Europe.

May 26. Recall of Pakistan embassy staff member for violating Afghan laws, requested by Afghanistan.

Jun. 22. United Nations technical assistance mission arrives to advise on development projects.

Jul. 11. Agreement signed by Afghanistan and UNICEF for $100,000 program to lower infant mortality rate.

Jul. 18. Four-year trade agreement signed by Afghanistan and Soviet Union.

Oct. 14. New cabinet announced by Prime Minister Shah Mahmud:

Muhammad Daud	Defense
Ali Muhammad	Foreign Affairs
Abdul Ahad Malikyar	Interior
Muhammad Nauroz	Finance
Mir Sayed Kasim	Justice
Abdul Majid	Education
Mir Muhammad Haider	National Economy
Ghulam Faruq	Public Health
Muhammad Akram	Public Works
Muhammad Naim Ziai	Mines

Oct. Emigration of Afghan Jews to Israel authorized by Afghan government.

Oct. 24. Afghanistan denies Pakistan allegations that Afghan tribesmen and soldiers violated frontier Sept. 30.

1951

Feb. 9. Agreement for technical assistance under Point Four program signed by Afghanistan and United States.

Mar. 19. George R. Merrell appointed U.S. ambassador to Afghanistan.

Apr. 25. Prime Minister Shah Mahmud arrives in United States.

May 28. United Nations assists in drilling exploratory oil wells in north.

1952

Jan. 15. United States suspends economic and technical aid to Afghanistan until bilateral agreement under Mutual Security Act signed.

Sep. 23. Soviet note expressing concern over activities of United Nations technical assistance experts in areas near Afghan-Soviet border rejected by Afghan government.

1953

Jan. 8. United States extends loan of $1.5 million for emergency purchase of wheat and flour from United States.

Mar. 18. Sultan Muhammad named foreign minister to succeed Ali Muhammad who remains deputy prime minister.

Sep. 6. Shah Mahmud resigns as prime minister, citing poor health. Zahir Shah asks cousin, Muhammad Daud, the then defense and interior minister, to form new cabinet.

Sep. 20. Prime Minister Daud announces cabinet members:

Ali Muhammad	Deputy Prime Minister
Muhammad Arif	Defense
Muhammad Naim	Foreign Affairs
Abdul Malik	Acting Finance
Abdul Hakim	Public Works
Abdul Majid	Education
Ghulam Faruq	Public Health
Muhammad Yusuf	Mines
Shamsuddin Majruh	Tribal Affairs
Mir Muhammad Yusuf	Agriculture
Salahuddin Saljuqi	Press

Oct. 26. Muhammad Hashem, prime minister from 1929 to 1946 and King's uncle, dies in Kabul.

Nov. United States Export-Import Bank makes loan of $18.5 million for development of Helmand Valley.

Dec. 30. Prime Minister Daud describes proposed U.S. military aid to Pakistan as a "grave danger to security and peace of Afghanistan."

1954

Jan. 27. Soviet Union makes loan of $3.5 million for construction of two grain mills and two silos. Soviet technicians to help carry out projects.

Feb. 8. Muhammad Atiq Rafiq named Afghan ambassador to Pakistan.

Feb. 8. Abdul Husain Aziz named Afghan ambassador to India.

Apr. 20. Afghanistan becomes member of United Nations Economic Commission for Asia and the Far East.

Sep. 17. Foreign Minister Naim arrives in Karachi to continue talks begun in Kabul on improving relations between Afghanistan and Pakistan.

Nov. 7. Foreign Minister Naim says Pashtunistan issue is not question of territorial adjustment but of giving Pashtuns an opportunity to express their wishes.

1955

Jan. 14. Former Prime Minister Shah Mahmud meets Pakistan prime minister.

Jan. 19. Afghanistan and the Chinese People's Republic establish diplomatic relations at embassy level.

Jan. 25. Legislation strengthening armed forces approved by upper house of parliament.

Feb. 15. Cement factory bought from Czechoslovakia.

Feb. 25. Japanese company agrees to invest in porcelain industry in Kunduz.

Mar. 2. Fine arts college opened under A.G. Breshna.

Mar. 29. Prime Minister Daud warns Pakistan of "grave consequences" if Pashtun areas of the Northwest Frontier Province are included in unified West Pakistan.

Mar. 30. Demonstrators march on Pakistani embassy and ambassador's residence in Kabul.

Mar. 31. Demonstrators march on Pakistani consulate in Kandahar.

Apr. 1. Demonstrators march on Pakistani consulate in Jalalabad. Afghan consulate in Peshawar attacked.

Apr. 4. Britain, Turkey, and United States protest attack on Pakistan embassy in Kabul.

Apr. 12. Pakistan rejects Afghan replies to its protests, evacuates families of diplomats and nationals, and closes Jalalabad consulate.

Apr. 18. Foreign Minister Naim goes to Bandung Conference.

Apr. 29. Col. Gamal Abdul Nasser, prime minister of Egypt, visits Afghanistan.

Afghanistan says it is willing to apologize, pay compensation for damage, and make amends for insult to Pakistani flag if similar amends are made for insult to its flag.

May 1. Pakistan demands closing of all Afghan consulates in Pakistan and says it will close its consulates in Afghanistan.

May 4. Afghanistan mobilizes troops.

May 13. Afghanistan and Pakistan accept Saudi Arabian offer of mediation.

Jun. 21. Five-year agreement signed with Soviet Union allowing goods of each nation free transit across territory of other.

Jun. 28. Saudi Arabian mediator announces his proposals have been rejected.

Jul. 5. Thin Kuo Yu, ambassador to Afghanistan from Chinese People's Republic, presents credentials.

Jul. 14. Afghanistan tells Pakistan it will be held responsible for any loss or damage to goods held up in transit to Kabul.

Jul. 14. Afghanistan becomes member of International Monetary Fund and International Bank.

Jul. 28. State of emergency ended; Afghan army demobilized.

Aug. 14. Postal agreement signed by Afghanistan and Soviet Union.

Aug. 17. India agrees to export four Dakota planes to Afghanistan for internal service.

Sep. 9. Foreign Minister Naim and Pakistan ambassador negotiate agreement to stop hostile propaganda.

Sep. 13. Pakistan flag raised over Pakistani embassy in Kabul.

Sep. 15. Afghan flag raised over consulate in Peshawar.

Oct. 11. Afghan leaders request meeting with Pakistani leaders on condition one-unit act can be postponed. Pakistan says postponement impossible.

Oct. 17. Afghanistan recalls ambassador from Karachi.

Oct. 18. Pakistan recalls ambassador from Kabul.

Nov. 8. Afghanistan protests further restrictions by Pakistan on transit of goods to Afghanistan.

Nov. 20. During five-day session, Loya Jirgah gives its approval to resolutions calling for plebiscite to decide future of Pashtun area disputed with Pakistan, recommending government find means to reestablish balance of power upset by Pakistan's decision to accept arms from the United States, and refusing to recognize Pashtunistan as part of Pakistan.

1955 (cont.)

Dec. 6. Defense Minister Muhammad Arif resigns.

Dec. 15-18. Soviet Prime Minister Bulganin and Soviet Communist Party Secretary Khrushchev make official visit to Kabul.

Dec. 16. Soviet Union backs Afghanistan in Pashtunistan dispute.

Dec. 18. Three agreements signed by Afghanistan and Soviet Union: a loan of $100 million, a protocol extending 1931 treaty of neutrality and nonagression, a statement of foreign policy matters. Foreign Minister Naim says agreements do not weaken Afghan determination to remain neutral.

Dec. 21. United States confirms it has offered to mediate Pashtunistan dispute between Afghanistan and Pakistan.

1956

Jan. 8. Afghan consul in Quetta recalled at request of Pakistan. Pakistan military attaché requested to leave Afghanistan.

Jan. 24. Soviet economic delegation begins talks with Afghan government on use of $100 million loan.

The following cabinet changes were announced:

Abdul Hakim	Interior
Sayyid Abdullah	Acting Justice
Abdul Zahir	Acting Public Health
Muhammad Hashem	Foreign Affairs Deputy

Jan. 30. Soviet Union presents Ilyushin 14 to Zahir Shah.

Feb. 18. Technical cooperation agreement signed by Afghanistan and the United States for 1956.

Mar. 1. Technical assistance agreement signed by Afghanistan and the Soviet Union for building of hydroelectric plants, highway through Hindu Kush, air fields, motor repair shop, and reservoirs.

Mar. 6. SEATO powers declare region up to Durand line is Pakistani territory and within treaty area.

Mar. 21. Afghanistan formally protests SEATO decision to uphold Durand line as Afghan-Pakistani border.

Mar. 26. United States International Cooperation Administration announces grant of $997,000 to Teachers College of Columbia University to set up English language program for Afghan secondary schools and train English teachers.

Mar. 31. Gift of 15 buses and equipment for 100-bed hospital to Kabul municipality from Soviet Union arrives.

Apr. 4-18. Afghan military mission visits Czechoslovakia.

1956 (cont.)

May 7. Regular air service available to Europe through Karachi after air agreement signed by Afghanistan and Pakistan.

Jun. 27. Agreement for $14 million to develop Afghan civil aviation signed by Afghanistan and United States.

Jul. 26. Soviet Union agrees to carry out Nangarhar irrigation project.

Aug. 7-11. Pakistan President Iskander Mirza visits Kabul.

Aug. 25. Prime Minister Daud announces military arms agreements with Czechoslovakia and Soviet Union.

Sep. 12. Pan American to supervise pilot and ground crew training of Ariana Afghan Airlines. A $2.5 million contract to be part of $14 million program announced earlier which also includes $5.5 million for Kandahar airport.

Sep. 24. Air service to Iran inaugurated.

Sep. 27. First installment of arms from Soviet Union and Czechoslovakia arrives.

Oct. 17-30. Prime Minister Daud visits Soviet Union.

Oct. 28. Afghan Air Force receives 11 jet planes from Soviet Union.

Nov. 5. Afghans call attention of United Nations to Israeli-British-French attack on Suez as violation of Charter.

Nov. 10. Gen. Muhammad Omar named Afghan ambassador to India.

Nov. 16. Afghanistan offers troops for United Nations police force in Suez.

Nov. 24. Prime Minister Daud discusses Pashtunistan question with Pakistani leaders during visit to Karachi.

1957

Jan. 8. Trade protocol signed with Soviet Union.

Jan. 19-23. Chou En-lai, prime minister of Chinese People's Republic, visits Afghanistan.

Jan. 27. M.C. Gillett named British ambassador to Afghanistan.

Feb. 10. Radio Moscow inaugurates Pashto program.

Mar. 31 - Apr. 3. United States Special Ambassador to the Middle East James P. Richards visits Kabul. Joint Afghan-U.S. statement says Afghanistan welcomes U.S. President Eisenhower's program of economic aid to Middle East.

Apr. 14 - May 19. Prime Minister Daud visits Turkey, Czechoslovakia, Poland, Austria, and Egypt.

Apr. 14-29. Foreign Minister Naim visits Turkey and Pakistan.

1957 (cont.)   Apr. 27. Agreement for increased aid from Czechoslovakia signed by Afghanistan.
Jun. 8-11. Pakistani Prime Minister Suhrawardy visits Kabul. Afghanistan and Pakistan agree to restore diplomatic relations.
Jun. 30. United States makes loan of $5,750,000 for Helmand Valley Authority and $2,860,000 for building roads and training personnel.
Jul. 17-31. Communique says Soviet Union will aid Afghanistan in prospecting for oil, that a special commission to regulate boundary questions will be created, and that an agreement was reached regarding use of waterways crossing the two countries.
Jul. 28. Trade agreement signed by Afghanistan and Chinese People's Republic.
Aug. 10. Ghulam Muhammad Sherzad, Afghan ambassador to France, named commerce minister.
Aug. 31. Foreign Minister Naim says Afghanistan to receive about $25 million in military assistance under arms agreement signed with Soviet Union in 1956.
Oct. 22. Prime Minister Daud begins visit to Chinese People's Republic.
Dec. 21. Andrei Gromyko, Soviet foreign minister, meets Afghan mission in Moscow to negotiate new frontier agreement.

1958   Jan. 8. Soviet Union agrees to survey oil deposits in Afghanistan.
Jan. 18. Treaty regulating Afghan-Soviet border signed by Afghanistan and Soviet Union.
Feb. 1-5. Zahir Shah visits Pakistan.
Feb. 11-26. Zahir Shah arrives in India for two-week visit.
Jun. 26. Cultural agreement signed by Afghanistan and United States.
Protocol on utilization of Amu Darya signed by Afghanistan and Soviet Union.
Jun. 30. Prime Minister Daud begins U.S. visit.
United States agrees to help Afghanistan improve highway from Spin Boldak to Kabul and makes $7,708,000 grant to Pakistan to improve its transport lines with Afghanistan.
Jul. 17. Agreement on transport of goods by road signed by Afghanistan and Pakistan.
Sep. 11. Czechoslovak firm to install telephone exchange in Kandahar.
Oct. 1-5. Marshal Voroshilov, president of the Supreme Soviet of the Soviet Union, visits Afghanistan.

1958 (cont.)   Nov. 18. Foreign Investment Law promulgated.
                      Dec. 7. Government puts Afs. 2 and Afs. 5 coins put in
                      circulation.

1959   Jan. 1-6. Foreign Minister Naim visits Soviet Union.
                      Jan. 12. United States agrees to ship 50,000 tons of
                      wheat to Afghanistan.
                      Jan. 20. Henry A. Byroade named U.S. ambassador to
                      Afghanistan.
                      Feb. 5-13. Prime Minister Daud visits India.
                      Mar. 9. Prime Minister Daud calls Baghdad Pact
                      aggravation of international tension.
                      Apr. 23. Afghanistan and Soviet Union sign protocol on
                      exchange of goods.
                      May 18-22. Prime Minister Daud visits Soviet Union.
                      May 28. Afghanistan and Soviet Union sign agreement
                      on building of 750 km. Kandahar-Herat-Kushka highway.
                      Jul. 15. Afghan military mission visits Turkey and United
                      Arab Republic.
                      Aug. 23. Soviet Union agrees to provide assistance to
                      complete Nangarhar irrigation project.
                      Aug. 31. Afghan women appear unveiled in public at
                      Jashen celebration.
                      Sep. 5. Foreign Minister Naim begins visit to Chinese
                      People's Republic.
                      Sep. 14. Indian Prime Minister Nehru visits Afghanistan.
                      Afghan women appear without veils at dinner for Nehru.
                      Henceforth veil no longer obligatory.
                      Oct. 28. Afghan-Soviet Friendship Society founded.
                      Dec. 1. Afghanistan and Soviet Union to begin joint
                      survey of Amu Daria for construction of dam to provide
                      electricity and water for irrigation.
                      Dec. 9. U.S. President Eisenhower spends six hours in
                      Kabul. Assures Afghanistan of continued economic
                      support.
                      Dec. 21. Police and army units suppress rioting in
                      Kandahar. No official figure of casualties given. Radio
                      Kabul blames on element trying to evade payment of
                      overdue taxes. Other reports say religious leaders
                      oppose government measures of allowing women to
                      remove veil and accepting Soviet assistance.

1960   Jan. 19. Afghanistan and Soviet Union sign agreement
                      for construction of irrigation and power project on Kabul
                      River.
                      Mar. 2-5. Soviet Prime Minister Khrushchev visits Kabul.
                      Inspects Soviet aid projects, signs cultural cooperation
                      agreement, assures Afghanistan support on Pashtun question.

1960 (cont.)

Mar. 6. Pakistan calls Soviet support of Afghanistan on Pashtun question interference in Pakistan's internal affairs.

Soviet Union announces gift of 50,000 tons of wheat to Afghanistan.

Mar. 7. Prime Minister Daud says Pakistan is putting out propaganda against reforms in Afghanistan such as the emancipation of women. Says Afghan monarchy has decided to give Afghans complete freedom to choose form of government and to organize political parties.

Apr. 3. Construction work begins on Kandahar-Herat-Kushka highway.

Apr. 26. Former King Amanullah dies in Switzerland.

May 6. Jagan Nath Dhamija named Indian ambassador to Afghanistan.

May 13. Prime Minister Daud meets Soviet Prime Minister Khrushchev while in Moscow for medical treatment.

May 18. Foreign Minister Naim protests to Pakistan and United States the violation of Afghan airspace by U.S. U-2 plane.

Jul. 2. Jangalak auto repair shops opened. Built with Soviet aid.

Jul. 15. Soviet prospecting team announces discovery of petroleum and natural gas deposits in northern Afghanistan.

Aug. 4. Czechoslovakia announces 100,000 pounds sterling technical assistance grant to Afghanistan.

Aug. 10. Two-year Afghan-Soviet barter agreement signed.

Aug. 13. Two Pakistani aircraft violate Afghan airspace, land at Kandahar. Pakistan says it was error. Planes and pilots returned to Pakistan September 17.

Aug. 18. Darunta Canal opened. Built with Soviet assistance.

Aug. 21-26. Chen Yi, foreign minister of Chinese People's Republic, visits Afghanistan.

Aug. 26. Treaty of friendship and nonaggression signed by Afghanistan and Chinese People's Republic. Commercial and payments agreement renewed.

Dec. 3. Agreements on trade and transit signed with Iran during visit of Iranian Prime Minister to Kabul.

1961

Feb. 15. Agreement signed by Afghanistan and India to increase trade.

Apr. 5. Prime Minister Daud confers with Soviet Prime Minister Khrushchev in Moscow on return from Rome where Daud underwent a spinal operation. *Pravda* ar-

1961 (cont.)

ticle says Pashtun situation is not a matter of indifference to Soviet Union.

Apr. 18. Cultural agreement signed by Afghanistan and Federal Republic of Germany.

May 19. Afghanistan denies Pakistani reports that Afghan soldiers are taking part in border fighting.

Jun. 6. Prime Minister Daud says Pakistan has savagely bombarded Afghan populations with aid of arms furnished by United States and has confined more than 1,200 leaders of Pashtunistan in Peshawar in past five days. Denies that Afghanistan has pushed Pashtun tribes to revolt.

Jun. 8. King Zahir opens National Assembly session with speech stressing economic development and self-determination for Pashtunistan. Dr. Abdul Zahir named president of Assembly.

Jun. 15. Pakistan protests acts of provocation and aggression in note to Afghan government.

Jun. 22. Pakistan says nomads will no longer be allowed to enter Pakistan without valid passports, visas, and international health certificates.

Jun. 23. Pakistan says friendlier atmosphere should exist between Afghanistan and Pakistan before any summit meeting held.

Jun. 26. Prime Minister Daud confers with British Foreign Secretary Home and is received by Queen Elizabeth during visit to London.

Jun. 28. Foreign Minister Naim tells news conference that Pashtun self-determination is only problem in Afghan- Pakistani relations which requires negotiations.

Jul. 23. Muhammad Hashem Maiwandwal, ambassador to the United States, expresses his government's grave concern over Pakistan's use of American arms against Pashtun tribes during meeting with President Kennedy.

Aug. 23. Pakistan announces it is closing Afghan consulates and trade offices in Pakistan and is considering prohibiting transit facilities given to Afghanistan.

Aug. 30. In reply to Pakistani note of August 23, Afghanistan says it considers decision to close consulates an inimical act and threatens to break diplomatic relations.

Prime Minister Daud leaves for Belgrade Conference of Nonaligned Nations.

Sep. 3. Afghanistan seals border. Transfer of merchandise suspended between Afghanistan and Pakistan.

1961 (cont.)

Sep. 6. Afghanistan breaks diplomatic relations with Pakistan.

Sep. 12. Islamic Congress of Jerusalem appeals to Afghanistan and Pakistan to resolve their differences.

Sep. 16-20. Foreign Minister Naim visits Soviet Union.

Sep. 18. Pakistan accepts Iranian offer of mediation in Pashtunistan dispute.

Sep. 19. Saudi Arabia agrees to look after Pakistani interest in Afghanistan.

Sep. 21. United Arab Republic agrees to look after Afghan interest in Pakistan.

Sep. 27. Foreign Minister Naim says Afghanistan will not allow its transit trade to pass through Pakistan unless its trade offices and consulates in Pakistan are reopened.

Sep. 29. Pakistani President Ayub Khan rejects possiblity of reopening Afghan consulates and trade offices, says they were used for subversive activities.

Oct. 4. U.S. President Kennedy sends messages to Zahir Shah and Pakistani President Ayub Khan suggesting the United States might make proposals to help improve relations.

Oct. 11. Soviet Army delegation arrives in Kabul for 11-day visit.

Oct. 16. Afghan-Soviet technical and economic cooperation agreement signed.

Oct. 24. Soviet Deputy Minister of Public Works arrives in Kabul to inspect projects carried out with Soviet assistance.

Nov. 2-8. Livingston Merchant, special representative of U.S. President Kennedy, visits Afghanistan and Pakistan. Finds no solution to Pashtunistan dispute.

Nov. 19. Supplementary transit agreement, providing expansion of facilities for Afghan foreign trade, signed with Soviet Union.

1962

Jan. 23. Four-year agreement signed with Soviet Union to develop Afghan meteorological services.

Jan. 24. John M. Steeves named U.S. ambassador to Afghanistan.

Jan. 29. Afghanistan opens border with Pakistan for eight weeks to allow entry of U.S. aid goods.

Apr. 14. Prime Minister Daud announces Second Five Year Plan. Calls for spending Afs. 31.3 billion for economic development.

Apr. 20. Five-year transit agreement signed by Iran and Afghanistan.

May 6. Pul-i Khumri power station opened. Built with Soviet assistance.

1962 (cont.)   July 1. Pakistan accepts Shah of Iran's offer to mediate its dispute with Afghanistan.

July 12. Afghanistan accepts Shah of Iran's offer to mediate its dispute with Pakistan.

July 27-31. Formal talks held in Kabul between Shah of Iran and Zahir Shah and in Rawalpindi between the Shah and President Ayub Khan in effort to settle Afghan-Pakistani dispute.

Aug. 6. During meeting in Quetta, Pakistani President Ayub Khan suggests a confederation of Afghanistan, Iran, and Pakistan.

Aug. 6-15. Zahir Shah makes visit to Soviet Union.

Oct. 24. Agreement signed by Afghanistan with Federal Republic of Germany for loan of DM 200 million to finance construction of a power station and a sewage network, improve drinking water, and develop industry.

1963   Feb. 5. Cabinet approves establishment of nation's second university--Nangarhar University, to be started in Jalalabad with a medical school.

Feb. 12. United States decides to ship all its foreign aid goods to Afghanistan via Iran because of the continuing dispute between Afghanistan and Pakistan.

Feb. 25. Trade and assistance agreement signed by Afghanistan and Soviet Union.

Mar. 10. Resignation of Prime Minister Daud announced.

Mar. 14. King Zahir Shah asks Muhammad Yusuf, former minister of mines and industries, to form new government.

Prime Minister Yusuf's first cabinet includes:

Ali Ahmad Popal	Deputy Prime Minister and Education
Abdullah Malikyar	Deputy Prime Minister and Finance
Sayyid Abdullah	Interior
Gen. Khan Muhammad	Defense
Shamsuddin Majruh	Justice
Gul Pacha Ulfat	Tribal Affairs
Abdul Hai Aziz	Planning
Abdul Rahim	Health
Sayyid Qasim Reshtia	Press

Prime Minister Yusuf to serve as own foreign minister.

1963 (cont.)

Mar. 25. Prime Minister Muhammad Yusuf says in an interview with a representative from a press agency in the Federal Republic of Germany that it was King Zahir Shah himself who decided that the government would no longer be composed of members of the royal family and that the Constitution promulgated 32 years ago would be modified and the question of formation of political parties considered.

Mar. 28. Constitutional Review Committee named. Headed by Minister of Justice Majruh.

Apr. 18. At press conference Prime Minister Yusuf says introducing democracy and improving economic conditions are major aims of the government.

He estimates that the United States has furnished about $252 million and the Soviet Union an equivalent amount plus arms.

Apr. 26. United States grants loan of $2,635,000 for purchase of a DC-6 and two convairs for Ariana Afghan Airlines. Purchase will bring Ariana's fleet to nine planes.

Apr. 29. Cultural cooperation agreement signed by Afghanistan and Soviet Union.

May 11-15. Indian President Radhakrishnan visits Afghanistan.

May 25. Afghan and Pakistani representatives begin meetings in Tehran to resolve dispute over Pashtunistan.

May 28. Shah of Iran announces that Afghanistan and Pakistan have agreed to reestablish diplomatic and commercial relations.

May 29. Joint Afghan-Pakistani communique confirms reestablishment of relations.

Jun. 14. Prime Minister Yusuf says at press conference that United States was asked to contribute $60 million to Second Plan, has promised $16 million.

Jul. 18. Afghan delegation, led by Dr. Abdul Zahir, president of the National Assembly, visits United States. Dr. Zahir tells press conference that Afghanistan is planning a new form of government with distinct separation of legislative, executive, and judicial powers.

Jul. 20. Afghan consuls reopen consulates in Peshawar and Quetta. Communication reestablished on Afghan-Pakistani border.

Jul. 25. First trucks cross Afghan-Pakistani border in 22 months. Ariana Afghan Airlines resumes flights halted at same time.

Aug. 12. Afghanistan and Pakistan exchange ambassadors. Muhammad Hashem Maiwandwal named

1963 (cont.)   Afghan ambassador to Pakistan and Lt. Gen. Muhammad
                      Yousuf named Pakistani ambassador to Afghanistan.
                      Aug. 15. Shah of Iran says confederation of Afghanistan,
                      Iran, and Pakistan is good idea but cites many obstacles.
                      Sep. 2-19. Zahir Shah and Queen Homaira visit United
                      States.
                      Sep 6. United States grants $125,000 to Afghanistan for
                      surveys of several industrial projects.
                      Afghanistan and Soviet Union sign agreement for
                      construction of atomic reactor in Afghanistan and
                      training of specialists in peaceful use of atomic energy.
                      Oct. 12-17. Soviet President Leonid Brezhnev visits
                      Afghanistan; lays cornerstone for new polytechnic
                      institute in Kabul.
                      Oct. 16. Agreement signed with Soviet Union for
                      technical assistance in extraction and exploitation of
                      natural gas in northern Afghanistan.
                      Nov. 8. United States makes loan of $2 million to
                      Afghanistan for trucks, tires, and spare parts.
                      Dec. 2. Border treaty signed by Afghanistan and
                      Chinese People's Republic.

1964   Feb. 29. Consultative Constitutional Commission,
                      headed by Abdul Zahir, begins sessions which last
                      through May 14.
                      May 31. Zahir Shah opens new Aliabad campus of
                      Kabul University, built with United States assistance.
                      Jun. 29-Jul. 14. Afghan military delegation visits Soviet
                      Union.
                      Jul. 1. During one-day stay in Kabul, Pakistani President
                      Ayub Khan discusses ways to improve Afghan-Pakistani
                      relations with King Zahir Shah and Prime Minister
                      Yusuf.
                      Jul. 4-5. Anastas Mikoyan, deputy prime minister of
                      Soviet Union, visits Kabul.
                      Jul. 8. Dr. Muhammad Anas, ambassador to India,
                      named minister of education, replacing Ali Ahmad Popal
                      who becomes ambassador to Federal Republic of
                      Germany. Sayyid Qasim Reshtia named minister of
                      finance, replacing Abdullah Malikyar who becomes
                      ambassador to Britain.
                      Jul. 13. Soviet Union makes loan of $25.2 million for
                      Pul-i Khumri--Mazar-i-Sharif--Shiberghan highway.
                      Jul. 21. Zahir Shah sets Loya Jirgah session for
                      September 9. Its 450 members will include member of
                      National Assembly, Cabinet, High Judicial Council, and
                      Constitutional Commission, 173 specially elected
                      representatives, and 27 members appointed by King.

1964 (cont.)   Jul. 26. Prime Minister Yusuf cautions students against engaging in political activity.

Jul. 27. Cabinet approves new Constitution.

Aug. 4.   Proposed content of new Constitution announced in press. It allows freedom of speech and press and formation of political parties, calls for two-house parliament and independent judiciary, and bars members of royal family from serving as prime minister, cabinet member, chief justice, or parliament members. King appoints prime minister and commands armed forces.

Sep. 3. Zahir Shah and Soviet Deputy Prime Minister Alexei Kosygin open Kabul-Doshi highway over Salang Pass. Built with Soviet assistance.

Sep. 6. Delegation returns from demarcating 90 km. border with Chinese People's Republic.

Sep 9-19.   Loya Jirgah debates and approves Constitution after adding that members of royal family cannot become members of political parties nor renounce their titles to participate in politics.

Sep. 21. Federal Republic of Germany loans DM 400,000 for dental and maternity clinics in Afghanistan.

Sep. 22.   Reception, given by embassy of Chinese People's Republic, marks founding of Afghan-Chinese Friendship Society.

Oct. 1. Zahir Shah endorses new Constitution. National Assembly dissolved. Transitional government to govern for a year.

Oct. 21. Siemens Company of the Federal Republic of Germany signs contract to install 8,000 line telephone exchange for Kabul which will bring total number of lines to 13,000.

Oct. 27. Soviet Union agrees to loan $6.2 million to build polytechnic institute in Kabul.

Oct. 29-Nov. 12. Zahir Shah, accompanied by Queen Homaira, makes first visit to Chinese People's Republic by any Afghan head of state. Communique says the two nations have agreed to develop economic and cultural relations and expand technical cooperation.

Nov. 18. Discovery of first Greek city to be found in Afghanistan announced. French archaeological team says city at confluence of Kokcha and Amu Rivers was abandoned in 130 B.C. and never reoccupied. Site now known as Ai Khanum.

Nov. 22-29. Walter Scheel, minister for economic cooperation in Federal Republic of Germany, visits Afghanistan, assures Afghanistan of expanding economic assistance particularly on Paktia regional project and

1964 (cont.)   urges protocol to improve atmosphere for foreign
                      investment.
                      Dec. 19. Muhammad Hashem Maiwandwal, ambassador
                      to Pakistan, named minister of press and information.

1965   Jan. 1. Founding of the PDPA.
                      Jan. 12. United States agrees to loan $7.7 million for
                      construction of 121 km. Herat-Islam Kala highway.
                      Jan. 18. Soviet Union agrees to loan Afghanistan $11.1
                      million over three years for import of consumer goods.
                      Jan. 20. United Nations Special Fund makes grant of
                      $7,178,200 for soil and water surveys, Hazarajat highway
                      survey, telecommunication and teacher training schools.
                      Jan. 22. Water supply network to serve 110,000 of
                      Kabul's residents completed with Japanese assistance.
                      Feb. 6. Nur Ahmad Etemadi named Afghan ambassador
                      to Pakistan.
                      Feb. 15. Protocol on exchange of goods and prices for
                      1965 signed by Afghanistan and Soviet Union. Increase
                      of 20 percent expected in reciprocal goods deliveries.
                      Feb. 24. Gen. Muhammad Arif named Afghan
                      ambassador to Soviet Union.
                      Feb. 18-28. Prime Minister Yousuf holds talks with
                      Indian Prime Minister Shastri during visit to India.
                      Mar. 2. New five-year trade transit agreement, replacing
                      1958 agreement, signed by Afghanistan and Pakistan.
                      U.S. Ambassador-at-large Averell Harriman meets Zahir
                      Shah and Prime Minister Yusuf during stop in Kabul.
                      Mar. 11. Zahir Shah and Soviet Prime Minister Dmitri
                      Polyansky open Nangarhar irrigation and power project,
                      built with Soviet assistance.
                      Mar. 22-25. Chen Yi, deputy prime minister and foreign
                      minister of Chinese People's Republic, confers with
                      Zahir Shah and Prime Minister Yusuf during a three-day
                      visit. Boundary protocol, cultural agreement, and
                      economic and technical cooperation agreement signed.
                      Apr. 5. High schools start requiring entrance exams to
                      give all students equal chance, avoid overcrowding, and
                      keep educational standards high.
                      Apr. 18-20. Cultural agreement signed by Afghanistan
                      and Britain during visit of Lord Walston, British
                      parliamentary under secretary of state for foreign
                      affairs.
                      Apr. 18. World Bank agrees to finance foreign exchange
                      cost of $350,000 to survey Kunduz and Khanabad basins
                      for possible irrigation and agriculture projects.

1965 (cont.)

Apr. 21-30. Prime Minister Yusuf makes official visit to Soviet Union. Gets assurance of Soviet help with Third Plan.

Apr. 28. Kunduz airport completed. Built with U.S. assistance.

May 11. New electoral law, providing for universal, direct vote by secret ballot for all Afghan men and women over 20, goes into effect.

May 23. Ariana Airlines begins weekly flight to Tashkent, its first to Soviet Union.

Jun. 5. Mazar-i Sharif airport completed. Built with U.S. assistance.

Jun. 6. First of three regional appellate courts established in Kabul. Others to be in Mazar-i Sharif and Kandahar.

Jun. 22. Jangalak smelts its first iron ore mined in Afghanistan.

Jul. 1. Land survey and statistics law goes into effect.

Jul. 7. King Zahir Shah announces plan to rebuild old city of Kabul.

Jul. 15. United States agrees to help increase wheat production and provide up to 150,000 tons of wheat; make $2 million credit for machinery purchase available; make long-term loan to build Kajaki power plant; provide credits up to $800,000 to import diesel generators; increase project planning in Helman Valley to 20,000 acres a year, and make $5 million long-term loan to construction unit of Helmand Valley Authority.

Jul. 18. Prime Minister Yusuf lays cornerstone for Jangalak technicum for 700 students being built with Soviet assistance.

Jul. 20. Cadastral survey of Kabul province begins. Direct telephone link between Kabul, Rawalpindi, and Lahore inaugurated.

Jul. 24. Soviet Union agrees to build 97 km. pipeline from Shiberghan gas fields to Soviet border and 88 km. line from fields to fertilizer and power plants in Balkh province.

Jul. 28. Soviet Union agrees to extend payment on loans to Afghanistan by 30 years and provide teachers for Polytechnic Institute.

Jul. 29. Federal Republic of Germany agrees to make loans.

Aug. 3-14. Zahir Shah and Queen Homaira visit Soviet Union. Afghanistan and Soviet Union agree to extend treaty on neutrality and mutual nonagression of 1931 for ten years.

Aug. 8. First census of Kabul finds population of 435,203.

Aug. 26-Sep. 28. Election of parliament members held. Over 1,000 run for 216 seats in Wolesi Jirgah (House of the People)and 100 for 28 elective seats in Meshrano Jirgah (House of Elders). All run as independents.

Sep. 9. New press law goes into effect allowing Afghan citizens freedom of expression while safeguarding the fundamental values of Islam and the principles embodied in the Constitution.

Oct. 12. Dr. Abdul Zahir elected president of Wolesi Jirgah. Zahir Shah names Abdul Hadi Dawai president of Meshrano Jirgah.

Oct. 13. Zahir Shah's appointees to Meshrano Jirgah announced.

Prime Minister Yusuf presents report of interim government and offers resignation. King asks him to form new government.

Oct. 14. Parliament officially opened by King Zahir Shah.

Oct. 19.   Wolesi Jirgah decides proposed cabinet members should submit lists of property they hold before vote of confidence is taken.

Oct. 24. Prime Minister Yusuf's presentation of his cabinet to Wolesi Jirgah postponed when spectators crowd into deputies' seats and refuse to leave.

Oct. 25. Wolesi Jirgah decides 191-6 to hold vote of confidence in secret session.

Student demonstrations are dispersed by force by police and army; three persons are killed. Schools are closed and public meetings banned.

Wolesi Jirgah approves Prime Minister Yusuf's cabinet. Vote reported to be 198 in favor and 15 abstaining. Ministers are:

Sayyid Shamsuddin Majruh	Deputy Prime Minister and Foreign Affairs
Gen. Khan Muhammad	Defense
Muhammad Husain Masa	Interior
Abdullah Yaftali	Finance
Muhammad Anas	Education
Mir Huhammad Akbar Reza	Agriculture
Ghulam Dastagir Azizi	Public Works
Muhammad Hashem Maiwandwal	Press, Information
Nur Ali	Commerce
Abdul Samad Hamid	Planning
Abdul Majid	Public Health
Muhammad Haidar	Communications

Justice, Mines and Industries, and Tribal Affairs left to be filled later.

1965 (cont.)

Oct. 27. King Zahir Shah receives cabinet.

Oct. 29. In wake of demonstrations, Prime Minister Yusuf resigns, giving poor health as reason. King Zahir Shah asks Muhammad Hashem Maiwandwal to form cabinet.

Nov. 2. Prime Minister Maiwandwal presents cabinet to Wolesi Jirgah and gets vote of confidence 190 to 7 with 3 abstaining and 16 absent. Entire proceedings broadcast over Radio Afghanistan. Cabinet members are:

Nur Ahmad Etemadi	Foreign Affairs
Gen. Khan Muhammad	Defense
Abdul Satar Shalizi	Interior
Abdullah Yaftali	Finance
Abdul Hakim Tabibi	Justice
Mir Muhammad Akbar Reza	Agriculture
Ahmadullah	Public Works
Nur Ali	Commerce
Muhammad Osman Anwari	Public Health
Abdul Samad Salim	Mines and Industries
Muhammad Haider	Communications

Maiwandwal is to act as his own minister of education and press and information. Planning and tribal affairs to be filled later.

Nov. 4. Prime Minister Maiwandwal makes unexpected appearance at condolence ceremony on Kabul University campus for those killed during Oct. 25, demonstrations. Brings King's message of sympathy and promises to consider student demands.

Toryalai Etemadi elected president of Kabul University by University Senate.

Nov. 6. Ministry of interior announces three people died during demonstrations on October 25.

Nov. 7. List of property belonging to ministers debated and accepted by Wolesi Jirgah members.

Nov. 27. Kabul University senate refuses to accept student demands for a lower passing grade and postponement of exams.

Dec. 1. Prime Minister Maiwandwal announces five cabinet appointments:

Muhammad Osman Anwari	Education
Miss Kobra Nurzai	Public Health
Muhammad Osman Sidki	Press, Information
Abdul Hakim Ziayi	Planning
Muhammad Khalid Roshan	Tribal Affairs

Dec. 13. Kabul University's college of science closed because of continued disturbances.

1965 (cont.)

Dec. 14. Ministry of interior forbids public gatherings after two days of demonstrations.

Dec. 16. Seven U.S. senators meet Zahir Shah and Prime Minster Maiwandwal during visit to Kabul.

1966

Jan. 1-2. President Ayub Khan of Pakistan makes stop in Kabul on way to Tashkent talks.

Jan. 14-15. Soviet Prime Minister Alexei Kosygin stops in Kabul for talks on way from Delhi to Moscow.

Jan. 17. Kabul University's college of education graduates its first 58 students.

Jan. 31. *Wahdat* publishes first edition. The Dari and Pashto weekly edited by Khal Muhammad Khasta is the first privately owned newspaper published in Kabul in 14 years.

Feb. 1-10. Prime Minister Maiwandwal visits Soviet Union.

Feb. 10. Ghulam Muhammad Sulaiman named Afghan ambassador to Pakistan.

Feb. 11. *Payam-i Imruz*, a twice weekly Dari newspaper published by Ghulam Nabi Khater, first issued.

Feb. 15. Dr. Muhammad Asif Sohail named Afghan ambassador to Chinese People's Republic.

Feb. 23. Nasir Zia named Afghan ambassador to India.

Mar. 2. New Kabul University constitution approved by cabinet.

Mar. 15. Khalilullah Khalili named Afghan ambassador to Saudi Arabia.

Apr. 4-9. Liu Shao-Chi, president of Chinese People's Republic, makes official visit to Kabul.

Apr. 5. *Afghan Millat*, a Pashto newspaper owned by Ghulam Muhammad Farhad, starts publication.

Apr. 11. *Khalq*, a Pashto and Dari newspaper published by Nur Muhammad Taraki, puts out first issue.

Apr. 13. Wolesi Jirgah begins consideration of political parties draft law.

May 4. After debate on *Khalq*, Meshrano Jirgah passes resolution saying any publication against values of Islam should be halted.

May 22. Wolesi Jirgah passes resolution, asking government to take action against *Khalq* for not following values of constitution.

May 23. Government bans distribution of *Khalq* under Art. 48 of the press law.

May 25. *Payam-i Imruz* newspaper stops publishing on instructions from ministry of information and culture, which says according to the press law, it cannot publish again until it has an editor. Previous editor resigned.

1966 (cont.)
May 31. Sayyid Shamsuddin Majruh named Afghan ambassador to UAR.

Jun. 20. Prime Minster Maiwandwal names Foreign Minister Etemadi and Interior Minister Shalizi first and second deputy prime ministers respectively. They are to continue to serve their ministries as well.

Jul. 19. Wolesi Jirgah approves political parties draft law.

Aug. 17. Prime Minister Maiwandwal appoints Muhammad Haider minister of justice and Abdul Karim Hakimi minister of communications.

Aug. 20. Supreme judiciary committee set up as foundation of future supreme court.

Aug. 24. Prime Minister Maiwandwal gives speech on eve of *Jashen* on Radio Afghanistan in which he explains his philosophy of progressive democracy.

Aug. 28. Former Prime Minister Yusuf named Afghan ambassador to Federal Republic of Germany.

Sep. 20. Abdul Rahman Pazhwak, Afghan representative to the United Nations, elected president of the UN general assembly.

1967
Jan. 25. Prime Minister Maiwandwal shuffles cabinet, names Abdullah Yaftali minister without portfolio, Abdul Karim Hakimi minister of finance, and Muhammad Hussein Masa minister of interior.

Feb. 12. Abdullah Malikyar named Afghan ambassador to United States. Abdul Majid named Afghan ambassador to Britain.

Mar. 25-Apr. 9. Prime Minister Maiwandwal visits United States.

Apr. 2. Abdul Hakim Tabibi named ambassador to Japan.

May 10. Protocol on export of natural gas signed by Afghanistan and Soviet Union. Afghanistan expected to earn over $320 million in next 18 years years from export of gas which is to reach 3 bil. cu.m. a year by 1971.

May 30-Jun. 2. Nikolai Podgorny, chairman of Presidium of Supreme Soviet of Soviet Union, visits Afghanistan.

Jun. 13. Abdul Rauf Binawa named minister of information and culture. Muhammad Osman Sidki named secretary general in Foreign Ministry.

Jul. 27. Prime Minister Maiwandwal appoints Abdullah Yaftali minister of planning, Dr. Muhammad Anas minister without portfolio, and Muhammad Ehsan Rostamel minister of justice.

Aug. 20. Direct telephone link between Kabul and Herat completed.

1967 (cont.)

Oct. 11. Prime Minister Maiwandwal resigns because of poor health. King Zahir Shah names Abdullah Yaftali acting prime minister.

Oct. 15. Zahir Shah inaugurates supreme court. Names four justices, Maulawi Abdul Basir, Dr. Mir Najmuddin Ansari, Obaidullah Safi, and Ghulam Ali Karimi, and chief justice, Dr. Abdul Hakim Ziayi.

Nov. 1. Zahir Shah asks Nur Ahmad Etemadi to form new government.

Nov. 13. Etemadi submits cabinet to Wolesi Jirgah.

Ali Ahmad Popal	First Depty. P. M. and Education
Abdullah Yaftali	Second Depty. P.M.
Gen. Khan Muhammad	Defense
Muhd. Omar Wardak	Interior
Muhammad Asghar	Justice
Muhammad Anwar Ziayi	Finance
Nur Ali	Commerce
Muhd. Husain Masa	Public Works
Muhammad Anas	Information, Culture
Muhammad Azim Gran	Communications
Miss Kubra Nurzai	Public Health
Abdul Samad Salim	Mines and Industries
Mir Muhd. Akbar Reza	Agriculture, Irrigation
Abdul Samad Hamid	Planning
Abdul Wahid Sorabi	Without Portfolio
Said Masud Pohanyar	Tribal Affairs

Nov. 15. Prime Minister Etemadi gets vote of confidence 173 to 7 with 6 abstentions after three-day debate in which 183 deputies spoke. Entire proceedings broadcast over radio. Etemadi pledges to work against bribery and corruption.

1968

Jan. 25. Education commission organized to decide national education policy for Afghanistan.

Jan. 31. Soviet Prime Minister Kosygin stops in Kabul to discuss economic questions.

Feb. 4. Chakhansur province renamed Nimruz, name given to area in Pahlavi literature.

Feb. 20. Afghan Polytechnic Institute, built with Soviet assistance, completes first year of instruction. Has 224 students in first class.

1968 (cont.)	Apr. 21. Indian Airlines introduces weekly jet airline service between Delhi and Kabul. Apr. 22. Shiberghan gas pipelines officially opened by Second Deputy Prime Minister Yaftali and Skachkov, president of Soviet Union's Council of Ministers Committee of External Affairs.
1969	May 25. U.S. Secretary of State Rogers paid a brief visit to Kabul for talks with government leaders. Jun. 10. Indian Prime Minister Indira Gandhi ended a five day official visit. Jun. 22. Afghan government ordered closing of all primary and secondary schools in Kabul, after a wave of student unrest and a student boycott of the Kabul University. Jul. 17. A Soviet military delegation led by Marshal of the Soviet Union Ivan Bagramyan began a visit. Nov. 17. New cabinet announced, as follows:

Nur Ahmed Etemadi	Prime Minister
Abdulla Yaftali	First Deputy
Abdul Qayyum	Second Deputy and Education
Khan Muhammed	Defense
M. Bashir Lodin	Interior
Abdul Wahid Sorabi	Planning
Abdul Satar Sirat	Justice
Muhammed Akbar Omar	Commerce
Muhammed Aman	Finance
Mahmud Habibi	Information and Culture
Muhammed Azim Gran	Communication
Ibrahim Majid Seraj	Public Health
Amanullah Mansuri	Mines and Industry
Abdul Hakim	Agriculture and Irrigation

The Ministers without Portfolio are Shafiqa Ziayi and Ghulam Ali Ayin.
Dec. 25. A Soviet military delegation led by Defense Minister Grechko arrived for an official visit.

1970	Jan. 21. The USSR signed a protocol for the export of 2.5 billion cubic meters of Afghan natural gas in 1970. Jan. 26. Defense Minister Khan Mohammed began an official visit to the US.
1971	May 17. It was announced that the government of Premier Nur Ahmad Etemadi resigned. King Zahir Shah

1971 (cont.)   accepted the resigntion and requested the premier stay
in office until a new government could be formed.
Jun. 8. Former ambassador to Italy, Abdul Zahir, was
asked to form a new Cabinet.

Dr. Abdul Zahir	Prime Minister
Dr. Abdul Samad Hamid	First Deputy
Gen. Khan Muhammad	Defense
Muhammad Musa Shafiq	Foreign
Amanullah Mansuri	Interior
Muhd. Anwar Arghandiwal	Justice
Dr. Ghulam Haidar Dawar	Finance
Hamidullah Enayat Seraj	Education
Muhd. Aref Ghausi	Commerce
Khwazak Khan	Public Works
Muhd. Ibrahim Abbasi	Information, Culture
Eng. Nasratullah Malikyar	Communications
Dr. Ibrahim Majid Seraj	Public Health
Eng. Muhd. Yaqub Lali	Mines & Industries
Abdul Hakim	Agric. & Irrig.
Dr. Abdul Wahid Sorabi	Planning
Mrs. Shafiqa Ziayee	Without Portf.
Dr. Abdul Wakil	Without Protf.
Abdul Satar Sirat	Without Portf.
Dr. Abdul Samad Hamid	Tribal Affairs

Jun. 13. Mohammad Zahir Shah ended a ten day visit
to the USSR with a joint communique reaffirming their
mutual allegiance to the principles of peaceful
coexistence.
Jul. 26. The National Assembly gave Abdul Zahir a vote
of confidence after a 17-day debate, and he took office
along with his Cabinet.
Aug. 22. Afghanistan is suffering the worst drought in its
recorded history.

1972   Jan. 3. The USSR signed an agreement for expanding
natural gas refining and collection centers in the north.
Jan. 11. Pakistan President Zulfikar Ali Bhutto arrived
in Kabul for official talks.
Apr. 3. Indian Foreign Affairs Minister Swaran Singh left
after a three-day visit and talks on economic aid and
cooperation.
Apr. 15. It was announced that Minister of Education
Enayat Seraj resigned for "health reasons."
May 16.   Kabul Radio broadcast a demand for
Pashtunistan's independence from Pakistan.
Jul. 21. U.S. special envoy John Connally told the
government that the U.S. could not make any further
commitment of aid.

1972 (cont.)   Aug. 25. A natural gas discovery at Jarquduq was estimated to be the second largest in the country.

Sep. 25. Premier Abdul Zahir tendered his resignation but it was refused by the King.

Dec. 5. Muhammad Zahir Shah accepted the resignation of Premier Abdul Zahir who agreed to remain in office until a new premier could be appointed.

Dec. 9. Musa Shafiq was appointed to form a new government.

Dec. 11. A new Cabinet was announced:

Muhammad Musa Shafiq	Premier and Foreign Affairs
Khan Muhammad	Defense
Nematullah Pazhwak	Interior
Muhammad Khan Jalallar	Finance
Khwazak Zalmai	Public Health
Sabahuddin Kushkaki	Information
Nasratullah Malikyar	Communications
Ghulam Dastagir Azizi	Industry
Abdul Wakil	Agriculture
Abdul Wahed Sorabi	Planning

1973   Jan. 17. It was announced that diplomatic relations would be established with East Germany.

Mar. 13. Iranian Prime Minister Amir Abbas Hoveyda and Prime Minister Muhammad Musa Shafiq of Afghanistan signed a formal settlement of the Helmand River dispute.

Apr. 21. A royal decree was issued setting general parliamentary election dates.

May 11. The border with Pakistan was ordered closed for two weeks for "administrative reasons."

Jul. 8. Zahir Shah arrives in Italy for a vacation.

Jul. 17. Sardar Muhammad Daud deposed his cousin, the king, and proclaimed a republic.

Jul. 18. Muhammd Daud proclaimed president and defense minister.

Jul. 19. The Soviet Union and India extend diplomatic recognition of the new government.

Jul. 27. President Daud abrogated the Constitution of 1964 and dissolved parliament.

Aug. 2. New cabinet announced:

Muhammad Daud	Premier, Defense and Foreign Affairs
Muhammad Hasan Sharq	Deputy Premier
Abdul Majid	Justice
Abdulillah	Finance
Faiz Muhammad	Interior

1973 (cont.)

Ne'matullah Pazhwak	Education
Pacha Gul	Frontier Affairs
Abdul Qayyum	Industry and Mines
Abdul Hamid	Communications
Nazar Muhd. Sikander	Health
Abdul Rahim Nawin	Information and Culture
Ghulam Jilani Bakhtari	Agriculture

Aug. 24. Deposed King, Muhammad Zahir, announced his abdication.
Sep. 23. It was announced that a plot to overthrow the government was discovered and a number of senior army officers arrested. Pakistan was accused of supporting the group.
Oct. 30. Indian Foreign Minister Swaran Singh arrived for an official visit.

1974

Feb. 16. A trade agreement was signed with Iran.
Apr. 5. It was reported that a new trade and payments agreement between Afghanistan and the Soviet Union was concluded after a visit to Moscow by Minister of Trade, Muhammad Khan Jalallar.
Jul. 7. A trade protocol was signed with India.
Jul. 19. Soviet assistance in the development of the Jarquduq natural gas field and in oil exploration was reported.
Jul. 24. Iran and Afghanistan signed a protocol for cooperation in a large scale development program in the "joint region of the Helmand River."
Nov. 1. U.S. Secretary of State Henry Kissinger arrived and met with Premier Muhammad Daud.

1975

Feb. 26. The government issued a statement protesting the U.S. decision to lift the arms ban on Pakistan.
Mar. 13. President Mohammad Daud concluded an official visit to India.
May 1. The government announced the nationalization of all banks and banking affairs.
Jul. 11. Deputy Foreign Minister Wahid Abdallah flew to Saudi Arabia to attend the Islamic Foreign Ministers Conference.
Jul. 28. Afghan security forces captured a terrorist group in Panjshir which was allegedly armed by Pakistan.
Oct. 17. Iran signed an agreement to provide aid and technical assistance to construct a raiload system and Kabul airport and to build a meat processing plant.

1975 (cont.)   Nov. 21. The following new cabinet was appointed in
                      October:

Muhammad Daud	President, Premier, Defense and Foreign Affairs
Muhammad Hasan Sharq	First Deputy Premier
Sayyid Abdulillah	Second Deputy Premier and Finance
Abdul Qadir	Interior
Abdul Tawab Asefi	Mines and Industry
Azizullah Wasefi	Agriculture
Abdul Karim Atayi	Communications
Ali Ahmad Khurram	Planning
Nazar Muhammad Sikandar	Public Health
Abdul Majid	Justice
Abdul Rahim Nawin	Information
Faiz Muhammad	Frontier Affairs

Dec. 2. Afghanistan denied Pakistani charges that it had
mobilized troops along its border with Pakistan.

1976   Jan. 2. An agreement was concluded with the Soviet
                      Union for the development of the Jarquduq gas fields
                      and the provision of gas production and processing
                      facilities.
                      Apr. 23. The League of Red Cross Societies said that
                      about 100,000 people in Afghanistan had been left
                      homeless by earthquakes, torrential rains, and floods.
                      Jun. 7. Pakistani President Zulfikar Ali Bhutto began a
                      visit to Afghanistan.
                      Jun. 8. Pakistani President Bhutto met with President
                      Mohammad Daud.
                      Jul. 4. Indian Premier Indira Ghandi arrived in Kabul
                      for a three-day visit.
                      Aug. 8. US Secretary of State Henry Kissinger met with
                      President Daud in Kabul.
                      Dec. 9. According to reports, more than 50 people had
                      been arrested and accused of a plot to overthrow the gov-
                      ernment.

1977   Jan. 30. President Muhammad Daud convened the
                      Loyah Jirgah, or Grand Assembly, to approve the draft
                      of a new constitution.
                      Feb. 14. The new constitution was approved by the
                      Loyah Jirgah.
                      Feb. 15. Muhammad Daud was sworn in and the Loyah
                      Jirgah was dissolved.
                      Feb. 24. President Muhammad Daud promulgated a new
                      constitution.

1977 (cont.)

Feb. 26. President Daud disbanded the cabinet and the central revolutionary committee.

Mar. 13. The Afghan government announced formation ot the following new government:

Ghulam Haidar Rasuli	National Defense
Sayyid Abdulillah	Finance
Abdul Majid	State
Wafiyullah Sami'i	Justice
Abdul Qadir	Interior
Ghulam Siddiq Muhibi	Higher Education
Ibrahim Majid Seraj	Education
Muhd. Khan Jalallar	Commerce
Azizullah Wasefi	Agriculture
Abdul Tawab Asefi	Mines and Industry
Ghausuddin Fayeq	Public Works
Abdul Rahim Navin	Information and Culture
Ali Ahmad Khurram	Planning
Abdul Karim Atayi	Communications
Abdullah Omar	Public Health
Juma Muhammad Muhammadi	Water and Power
Abdul Qayyum	Border Affairs
Wahid Abdullah	Deputy Minister of Foreign Affairs

Mar. 19. The members of the new government were sworn in.

Mar. 23. A Soviet trade delegation began a trip to Afghanistan to hold talks on bilateral trade.

Mar. 29. An agreement had been reached in Kabul to resume air links between Pakistan and Afghanistan.

Jun. 22. Pakistani Premier Zulfikar Ali Bhutto arrived in Kabul for talks with President Muhammad Daud.

Jul. 29. Afghanistan and the USSR concluded a six year consumer goods agreement in Kabul.

Oct. 11. Pakistani Chief Martial Law Administrator Mohammad Zia-ul-Haq met with President Daud at the Presidential Palace.

Nov. 7. President Daud appointed the following to the central council:

Abdul Majid	State
Ghulam Haidar Rasuli	National Defense
Sayyid Abdulillah	Finance
Abdul Qayyum	Border Affairs

Nov. 16. Minister of Planning Ali Ahmad Khurram was assassinated in Kabul.

1978

Feb. 19. Sayyid Abdulillah was appointed vice president.

1978 (cont.)   Feb. 21. President Mohammad Daud left Kabul for Belgrade on an official visit to Yugoslavia.

Feb. 24. A trial of 25 people accused of plotting to assassinate President Daud had begun in Kabul.

Mar. 4. President Daud met with Indian Premier Morarji Desai in New Delhi.

Apr. 17. Mir Akbar Khaibar, one of the founders of the PDPA, was assassinated in Kabul.

Apr. 27. Members of the PDPA gained power in a coup led by insurgents in the armed forces. The military revolutionary council formed a new government.

Apr. 29. The government radio reported that Defense Minister Ghulam Haidar Rasuli, Interior Minister Abdul Qadir Nuristani, and Vice President Sayyid Abdulillah had been killed in the coup along with President Daud and his brother Muhammad Naim.

Apr. 30. A "Revolutionary Council" was proclaimed. Nur Muhammad Taraki was named president and premier of the Democratic Republic of Afghanistan.

The Revolutionary Council selected the following ministers:

Babrak Karmal	Deputy Premier
Hafizullah Amin	Deputy Premier and Foreign Minister
Muhammad Aslam Watanjar	Deputy Premier and Communications
Abdul Qadir	National Defense
Shah Wali	Public Health
Nur Ahmad Nur	Interior
Dastagir Panjshiri	Education
Sultan Ali Keshtmand	Planning
Sulaiman Layeq	Radio and Television
Saleh Muhammad Zirai	Agriculture
Abdul Karim Misaq	Finance
M. Hasan Bareq-Shafi'i	Information and Culture
Abdul Hakim Shara'i	Justice and Attorney General
Anahita Ratebzad	Social Affairs
Abdul Quddus Ghorbandi	Commerce
Muhammad Ismail Danesh	Mines and Industries
Muhammad Rafi'i	Public Works
Muhammad Mansur Hashimi	Water and Power
Mahmud Suma	Higher Education
Nizamuddin Tahzib	Tribal Affairs

May 1. Shah Muhammad Dost and Abdul Hadi Mokamel were named deputy ministers of foreign affairs.

1978 (cont.)

May 6. Premier Taraki said Afghanistan was "nonaligned and independent."

May 18. Foreign Minister Hafizullah Amin left Kabul for Havana for a meeting of nonaligned countries.

Jul. 5. Kabul Radio said that Interior Minister Nur Ahmad Nur had been named ambassador to Washington and that Vice President and Deputy Premier Babrak Karmal had been named ambassador to Czechoslovakia.

Aug. 17. The central committee of the People's Democratic Party decided that President of the Revolutionary Council Nur Mohammad Taraki would assume the duties of minister of defense.

Aug. 18. Kabul Radio announced that a plot to overthrow the government had been foiled and Defense Minister Abdul Qadir had been arrested for his role in the plot.

Aug. 23. The politburo of the PDPA ordered the arrest of Planning Minister Sultan Ali Keshtmand and Public Works Minister Muhammad Rafi'i for their parts in the conspiracy.

Aug. 28. The following appointments were announced:

Dastagir Panjshiri	Public Works
Abdul Rashid Jalili	Education
Sahebjan Sahrayi	Border Affairs

Sep. 9. Pakistani Chief Martial Law Administrator Mohammad Zia-ul-Haq met with Chairman of the Revolutionary Council Taraki at Paghman, near Kabul.

Sep. 17. The government announced it was breaking diplomatic relations with South Korea.

Sep. 19. Indian External Affairs Minister Atal Bihari Vajpayee met with Taraki in Kabul.

Sep. 22. Taraki dismissed six ambassadors who had been appointed in July. All were members of the Parcham section of the PDPA.

Oct. 19. Afghanistan adopted a red flag as its new national emblem.

Dec. 3. President Nur Mohammad Taraki arrived in Moscow for talks with Soviet leaders.

Dec. 5. Afghanistan and the Soviet Union signed a 20 year treaty of friendship and cooperation in Moscow.

1979

Jan. 28. Guerrillas were fighting government troops in the eastern provinces bordering Pakistan.

Feb. 14. U.S. Ambassador to Afghanistan Adolph Dubs was taken hostage by terrorists in Kabul. Afghan forces rushed the building in which he was being held and he was slain.

1979 (cont.)   The U.S. protested against the use of force by the Afghan
government to free the U.S. ambassador.
Feb. 19. Foreign Minister Hafizullah Amin rejected a
U.S. protest over the incident leading to the slaying of
the U.S. ambassador as "completely baseless."
Feb. 22. U.S. President Jimmy Carter ordered U.S. aid
to Afghanistan to be reduced.
Mar. 16.   Revolt and uprising in Herat with the
participation of the military garrison. Thousands were
said to have been killed in recapture of town by
government troops.
Mar. 23. A U.S. spokesman said the U.S. expected that
the "principle of noninterference " in Afghanistan would
be respected by all parties in the area "including the
Soviet Union."
Mar. 27. Foreign Minister Amin was named premier.
Apr. 1. The new Afghan government was announced:

Hafizullah Amin	Premier and Foreign Affairs
Shah Wali	Deputy Premier and Health
Saleh Mohammad Zirai	Agriculture
Dastagir Panjshiri	Public Works
Abdul Karim Misaq	Finance
Mahmud Suma	Higher Education
Aslam Watanjar	Defense
Abdul Rashid Jalili	Education
Abdul Hakim Shara'i	Justice and Attorney General
Mahmud Hashemi	Water and Power
Khial M. Katawazi	Information and Culture
Muhammad Ismail Danesh	Mines and Industries
Abdul Quddus Ghorbandi	Commerce
Hasan Bareq-Shafi'i	Transport
Sahibjan Sahra'i	Frontier Affairs

Apr. 8.   Soviet Vice Minister of Defense Akeksey
Yepishev met with President Nur Mohammad Taraki in
Kabul.
Apr. 30.   Taraki said Pakistani President Muhammad
Zia-ul-Haq was "involved" with attacks on border
positions in eastern Afghanistan.
Jun. 13. Afghanistan accused Pakistan of involvement in
a rebellion against the Afghan government.
Jun. 23.   Kabul Radio reported that anti-government
demonstrators (Hazaras) in Kabul had been "annihilated
and arrested" during the day.

1979 (cont.)   July. 28. The cabinet was reshuffled:

Hafizullah Amin	Premier and Vice President of the Revolutionary Council
Shah Wali	Depty. P.M. and Foreign Affairs
Muhammad Gulabzoi	Posts and Telecom-Telecommunications
Muhammad Aslam Watanjar	Interior
Abdul Rashid Jalili	Agriculture
Muhammad Siddiq Alemyar	Planning
Saleh Muhammad Zirai	Public Health
Muhammad Salim Masudi	Education
Abdul Qudus Ghorbandi	Commerce
Muhd. Hasan Bareq-Shafi'i	Transport
Dastagir Panjshiri	Public Works
Abdul Hakim Shara'i Jauzjani	Justice
Khiyal Muhammad Katawazi	Information and Culture
Sherjan Mazduryar	Border Affairs
Mahmud Suma	Higher Education
Muhammad Ismail Danesh	Industry and Mines
Abdul Karim Misaq	Finance
Mansur Hashemi	Water and Electricity

Aug. 5. Heavy fighting broke out in Kabul between loyal troops and a rebellious army unit at the Bala Hissar Fort. The rebellion was crushed and a curfew was imposed on the city.

Aug. 19. Premier Hafizullah Amin said there were "no more than 1,600 Soviet advisers" in Afghanistan.

Sep. 15. Kabul radio reported that Interior Minister Aslam Watanjar and Frontier Affairs Minister Sherjan Mazuryar had been removed from their posts.

It was reported that gunfire and explosions had occurred in Kabul following the announcement of the cabinet dismissals.

Sep. 16. Kabul Radio reported that President Taraki had asked to be relieved of his government positions because of "bad health and nervous weakness."

Premier Amin assumed the additional post of president. The Afghan government announced the following cabinet appointments:

Faqir Muhd. Faqir	Interior
Sahibjan Sahra'i	Frontier Affairs

Sep. 23. President Amin said that former President Taraki was "alive but definitely sick."

1979 (cont.)   Oct. 8.   Kabul announced that President Amin had
commuted death sentences of former Defense Minister
Abdul Qadir and former Planning Minister Sultan Ali
Keshtmand to 15 years imprisonment.
Rebel tribesmen said they had cut the road leading from
Kabul to Gardez during fighting with government troops.
Oct. 9.   Kabul radio announced that Taraki had died.
President Amin publishes a list of 12,000 killed by Taraki
regime.
Oct. 14.   Heavy fighting took place at Rishkur barracks
southwest of Kabul.
Oct. 16.   It was reported that the government had
crushed an army mutiny near Kabul.
Nov. 9. It was reported that several ambush attacks had
been launched on government tropps near Kabul, killing
200 persons.
Dec. 21.   U.S. officials said that the Soviet Union had
moved 3 army divisions to the border with Afghanistan
and had sent about 1,500 combat soldiers to an air base
near Kabul.
Dec. 26.   A U.S. government spokesman said that in the
past 24 hours there has been "a large-scale Soviet airlift"
to Kabul, raising Soviet military involvement in Afghanistan to "a new threshhold."
Dec. 27.   Fighting broke out in Kabul and President
Hafizullah Amin was overthrown and executed. Former
Deputy Premier Babrak Karmal assumed the post of
president.
It was reported that Soviet tropps had taken part in the
fighting in Kabul.
Dec. 28.   President Karmal said the Soviet Union had
agreed to supply Afghanistan "urgent political, moral and
economic aid, including military aid."
U.S. President Jimmy Carter called the Soviet military
intervention "a grave threat to the peace" and a "blatant
violation of accepted rules of international behavior."
A Cabinet was formed as follows:

Babrak Karmal	Premier, Chairman, Revolutionary Council, Secretary General, Central Committee
Asadullah Sarwari	Deputy Premier
Sultan Ali Keshtmand	Deputy Premier and Planning
Muhammad Rafi'i	National Defense
Sayyid Muhd. Gulabzoi	Interior
Shah Muhammad Dost	Foreign Minister
Anahita Ratebzad	Education

1979 (cont.)   Abdul Wakil   Finance
                    Sherjan Mazduryar   Transport
                    Faiz Muhammad   Borders and Tribes
                    Muhammad Khan Jallalar   Trade

1980   Jan. 1. Afghanistan said it had invited Soviet troops into
                    the country "in view of the present aggressive actions of
                    the enemies of Afghanistan."
                    Jan. 2. Karmal addressed government leaders near
                    Kabul and called on the Afghan people to "come together
                    and support our glorious revolution."
                    Jan. 5. The Security Council opened debate on
                    Afghanistan.
                    Jan. 7. The Soviet Union vetoed a UN resolution that
                    called for the immediate withdrawal of "all foreign troops
                    in Afghanistan." The vote was 13 to 2 in favor of the
                    resolution.
                    Jan. 9. The Security Council voted by 12 by 2 with 1
                    abstention for for a resolution to move the issue of
                    Afghanistan to the General Assembly.
                    Jan. 10. The Afghan cabinet was expanded:
                    Muhammad Aslam Watanjar   Communications
                    Abdul Majid Sarbiland   Information   and
                                                   Culture
                    Abdul Rashid Arian   Justice
                    Muhammad Ismail Danesh   Mines and Industries
                    Raz Muhammad Paktin   Water and Power
                    Guldad   Higher Education
                    Nazar Muhammad   Public Works
                    Muhammad Ibrahim Azim   Public Health
                    Fazl Rahim Mohmand   Agriculture and Land
                                                   Reform
                    Jan. 14. The General Assembly voted by 104 to 18 with
                    18 abstentions for a resolution which "strongly deplored"
                    the "recent armed intervention" in Afghanistan and called
                    for the "total withdrawal of foreign troops" from the
                    country.
                    Jan. 27. A conference of Islamic Foreign Ministers
                    opened in Islamabad to consider the situation in
                    Afghanistan.
                    Jan. 29. The conference in Islamabad adopted a
                    resolution which condemned "the Soviet military
                    aggression against the Afghan people."
                    Feb. 13. Egyptian Defense Minister Kamal Hasan 'Ali
                    said that Egypt was providing assistance to Afghan rebels
                    and was "training some of them."
                    Feb. 14. The UN Human Rights Commission voted by
                    27 to 8 with 6 abstentions to condemn the Soviet's 1980

1980 (cont.)   intervention in Afghanistan as "an aggression against human rights."

Feb. 15. The New York Times cited "White House officials" as saying the U.S. had begun an operation to supply light infantry weapons to Afghan insurgent groups.

Feb. 19. Foreign Ministers of the European Economic Community (EEC) proposed that Afghanistan be declared a neutral country under international guarantees if the Soviet Union would withdraw its troops.

Feb. 22. Soviet President Leonid Brezhnev said that the Soviet Union would withdraw its troops from Afghanistan "as soon as all forms of outside interference" were "fully terminated."

Demonstrations and rioting against the government and the Soviet Union took place in Kabul.

Feb. 25. Shops remained closed in Kabul.

Feb. 26. It was reported that mass arrests had been made in Kabul during the day.

Feb. 28. Almost all shopkeepers opened for business in Kabul. It was reported that striking civil servants had returned to work.

Mar. 3. The *Hizb-i Islami* of Hekmatyar, one of six Afghan insurgent groups negotiating an alliance, said it had withdrawn from the alliance.

Mar. 7. Soviet soldiers appeared on the streets of Kabul. Soviet fighter planes and helicopter gunships flew over the city.

Mar. 10. Justice Minister Abdurrashid Arian said that forty-two associates of former President Hafizullah Amin were being held for trial.

Mar. 12. It was announced that the following ministers had been appointed:

Muhammad Khan Jalallar   Commerce
Fazl Rahim Mohmand   Agriculture

Mar. 13. Foreign Minister Shah Muhammed Dost arrived in Moscow on a "friendly visit."

May 18. Indian Foreign Secretary R.D. Satha met with President Babrak Karmal in Kabul.

May 22. A Conference of Islamic Foreign Ministers, meeting in Islamabad, adopted a resolution which demanded the "immediate, total and unconditional withdrawal of all Soviet troops from Afghanistan" and decided to establish a committee that would open "appropriate consultations" to seek a solution to the crisis in Afghanistan.

May 24. Demonstrators protesting the Soviet presence in Afghanistan marched in Kabul.

1980 (cont.)

Jun. 8. Kabul Radio announced that 10 supporters and aides of slain former President Hafizullah Amin had been executed.

Jun. 14. Kabul news service reported that former Communications Minister Muhammad Zarif, former Frontier Affairs Minister Sahibjan Sahra'i, and former Planning Minister Muhammad Siddiq Alemyar had been executed.

Jul. 2. The Soviet Communist Party newspaper *Pravda* said that for a political settlement of the situation in Afghanistan to take place, armed incursions by the "mercenaries of the imperialist and reactionary forces from the territory of neighboring states" must first be ended.

Aug. 16. Kabul radio reported that Justice Minister Abdurrashid Arian had been named to the additional post of deputy premier.

Sep. 14. Frontier Affairs Minister Faiz Mohammad was killed earlier in the week while trying to enlist the support of Afghan tribes.

Oct. 15-Nov. 5. President Karmal and other high officials left Kabul on a visit to the Soviet Union.

Nov. 13. President Karmal said that those who were not working for the good of the party would be expelled "even if they had been heroes in the past."

Nov. 20. The UN General Assembly voted by 111 to 22 with 12 abstentions for a resolution which called for the "unconditional" pullout of "foreign troops" from Afghanistan.

Nov. 21. Foreign Affairs Minister Shah Muhammad Dost said the UN resolution was "a flagrant interference in Afghanistan's internal affairs."

Dec. 25. Egyptian President Anwar al-Sadat said that he had "sent weapons" and would "send more weapons" to Afghan insurgents.

Dec. 27. Deposed King Muhammad Zahir said in exile that he prayed to God "to aid the Afghan people in its heroic struggle and its legitimate war for independence."

1981

Feb. 18. President Babrak Karmal arrived in Moscow for talks with Soviet leaders.

Mar. 9. U.S. President Ronald Reagan said that if Afghan "freedom fighters" who were fighting Soviet forces asked for weapons, it would be something "to be considered."

Apr. 7. Saudi Arabia announced it was severing diplomatic relations with "the current illegal regime" in Afghanistan.

1981 (cont.)

May 9. Pakistani officials estimated the number of Afghan refugees in Pakistan at 2 million.

May 11. Sultan Ali Keshtmand becomes prime minister.

Jun. 11. President of the Revolutionary Council Babrak Karmal turned the post of premier over to Sultan Ali Keshtmand and removed Abdul Rashid Arian as deputy premier.

Jun. 13. The Revolutionary Council elected as its vice presidents Nur Ahmad Nur and Abdul Rashid Arian.

Jul. 12. Member of the National Committee of the National Fatherland Front, Gen. Fateh Muhammad was killed by rebels.

Jul. 22. Diplomatic sources in Kabul reported heavy fighting between the rebels and Soviet forces in Paghman, 16 miles from the capital.

Aug. 6. Foreign Minister Shah Muhammad Dost met with UN representative Javier Perez de Cuellar.

Aug. 12. Kabul radio announced changes in the land distribution program that lifted restrictions on acreage held by religious and tribal leaders.

Aug. 22. Five Afghan resistance groups formed an alliance and created a 50-member advisory council.

Sep. 9. Foreign Minister Dost met with Prime Minister Indira Ghandi in New Delhi.

Sep. 22. Egyptian President Anwar al-Sadat said in a U.S. television interview that the U.S. had been buying old Soviet-made arms from Egypt and sending them to rebels fighting Soviet forces in Afghanistan. U.S. officials had no comment.

Nov. 18. By a vote of 116-23 with 12 abstentions the UN General Assembly voted for the third time that the Soviet Union must withdraw its troops from Afghanistan.

Dec. 15. President Babrak Karmal began a visit to Moscow.

1982

Jan. 6. In Washington, military analysts said Soviet troops in Afghanistan had grown to 110-120,000.

Feb. 20. The Afghan Government rejected the appointment of Archer K. Blood, designated U.S. Charge d'Affaires to Kabul. In response, the U.S. state department imposed travel restrictions on Afghan diplomats in Washington.

May 16. A two-day PDPA conference ended in Kabul with the 841 delegates endorsing resolutions aimed at purging dissidents and continuing a program of land reform.

Apr. 1. The revolutionary council presidium announced

1982 (cont.)

new appointments:
Khalil Ahmad Abawi, Vice Chairman and Council of Ministers; Muhammad Yasin Sadiqi, Director, Local Organizations Committee and Director, Council of Ministers; Mehrabuddin Paktiawal, Director, Central Bank.

The UN World Food Program announced an additional $18.5m in food aid to Afghan refugees in Pakistan.

Jun. 8. Soviet and Afghan troops regained control of the key Panjshir Valley in a major offensive against rebel forces.

Jun. 16. In Geneva the foreign ministers of Pakistan and Afghanistan met separately with UN negotiators in the first round of talks aimed at ending the Soviet presence in Afghanistan.

Aug. 2. The Afghan government ammended the conscription law, lengthening the term of service.

Aug. 28. President Karmal approved four appointments changes:

Abdul Ghaffar Lakanwal	Agriculture and Land Reform
Abdul Samad Qayyumi	Local Government
Fazl Rahim Mohmand	Central Statistics
Najibullah Masud	Secretary of the Council Ministers.

Sept. 12. Minister of Education Guldad and Minister of Information and Culture Abdul Majid Sarbiland were removed from their posts but retained their positions as deputy prime ministers.

1983

Jan. 19. UN Deputy Secretary General Diego Cordovez began a peace mission to Geneva, Tehran, Islamabad, and Kabul to resolve the Afghan crisis.

Feb. 16. The UN Human Rights Commission voted 29-7 with five abstentions for an immediate Soviet withdrawal from Afghanistan.

Jun. 15. The foreign ministers of Afghanistan and Pakistan arrived in Geneva for a third series of talks on the withdrawal of foreign troops.

Jun. 24. UN sponsored talks on Soviet troop withdrawal ended in Geneva without progress.

Nov. 23. The UN General Assembly called for the immediate withdrawal of Soviet troops by a vote of 116-20 with 16 abstentions.

Dec. 27. The Afghan government said it would request the departure of 105,000 Soviet troops if it received international guarantees that all opposition would end.

1984

Jan. 24. President Karmal had replaced his three top military advisers. Chief of Staff Gen. Baba Jan was replaced by Lt. Gen. Nazar Mohammad, Deputy Defense Minister Maj. Gen. Khalilullah by Maj. Gen. Muhammad Nabi Azami, and Chief of Operations Gen. Nuristani by Maj. Gen. Ghulam Qadir Miakhel.

Mar. 21. A bomb exploded in a Kabul mosque, killing four people and injuring seven.

Apr. 11. The Kabul government ordered the expulsion of Third Secretary Richard S. Vandiver of the U.S. embassy in Kabul on charges of espionage. The U.S. denied the charge.

May 14. The National Olympic Committee announced Afghanistan would boycott the 1984 Summer Olympics in Los Angeles.

May 17. U.S. Vice President George Bush visited the Khaiber Pass, where he condemned the Soviet invasion and expressed support for the Afghan resistance.

Jul. 7. Radio Kabul announced nomination of Muhammad Kabir as Minister of Finance.

Jul. 26. The U.S. House of Representatives appropriations committee approved $50 million in covert aid to Afghan mujahedin, according to intelligence sources.

Aug. 27. The foreign ministers of Afghanistan and Pakistan met separately in Geneva with a UN intermediary in talks on a political settlement to the Afghan war.

Aug. 30. The third round of talks between Afghanistan and Pakistan adjourned in Geneva with no sign of progress.

Aug. 31. A bomb explosion occurred at the Kabul airport.

Nov. 4. Nine people were executed for the August 31 bomb explosion at Kabul airport.

Dec. 3. Radio Kabul reported that President Karmal had appointed Army Chief of Staff Brig. Gen. Nazar Muhammad to replace Lt. Gen. Abdul Qadir as defense minister.

1985

Jan. 18. The U.S. announced it would increase its aid to Afghan mujahedin in 1985 to approximately $280 million. Saudi Arabia, Israel, and China were also reportedly assisting the rebels.

Jan. 26. The Afghan mujahedin leader, Khan Gul, was sentenced to death in Paktia province.

Jan. 29. Zabihullah, a leader of the *Jam'iat-i Islami*, was killed when his jeep hit a mine.

1985 (cont.)

Mar. 3. According to reports from Iran, four shi'a mujahedin groups merged: the *Sazman-i Nasr*, the *Pasdaran* (Guards), the Islamic Mouvement of Afghanistan, and the United Front of the Islamic Revolution.

Apr. 8. Maulawi Abdul Wali was appointed minister of Islamic affairs.

Apr. 23. President Karmal opened a grand tribal assembly (Loya Jirga) in Kabul in an effort to gain popular support in the government's war against the mujahedin.

May 10. Leaders of three of the main mujahedin groups in Peshawar denounced the attempt by Abd al-Rabb Sayyaf to appoint himself for another term as head of the seven-member Alliance of Afghan Mujahedin.

Jun. 17. U.S. and Soviet officials met in Washington to discuss the war in Afghanistan.

Jun. 19. UN-sponsored "proximity talks" began in Geneva between Afghan and Pakistani governments regarding the war in Afghanistan.

Jun. 24. Afghan-Pakistani talks ended in Geneva, and were described as "intense and fruitful."

Aug. 29. UN-sponsored indirect talks on Afghanistan between Pakistani and Afghan officials opened in Geneva.

Oct. 23. Afghan Foreign Minister Shah Muhammad Dost said Afghanistan could not reach agreement on the withdrawal of Soviet troops unless Pakistan enters direct negotiations.

Nov. 2. Afghan troops ringed the US embassy in Kabul in an effort to force the release of a Soviet soldier who walked into the embassy Oct. 31, reportedly seeking help to return to the USSR.

Nov. 13. By a vote of 122 to 19, the UN General Assembly adopted a Pakistani resolution calling for the immediate withdrawal of Soviet troops from Afghanistan.

Nov. 22. Three senior members of the PDPA were removed from the politburo: Maj Gen. Abdul Qadir, Ghulam Dastagir Panjshiri, and Ismail Danesh.

Nov. 30. Sayyid Muhammad Nasim Maihanparast was appointed deputy chairman of the council of ministers.

Dec. 6. Radio Kabul announced that Ghulam Faruq Yaqubi had been named director of the KHAD, Afghanistan's secret police.

Dec. 13. The State Department notified the UN that the U.S. was ready to act as guarantor of a peace settlement in Afghanistan that would involve a Soviet troop withdrawal and an end to U.S. aid to the mujahedin.

1985 (cont.)   Dec. 19. In Geneva, Afghanistan and Pakistan suspended their latest round of peace talks to study new UN proposals for a timetable for Soviet withdrawal.

Dec. 26. The DRA council of ministers made the following new appointments:

Sayyid Amanuddin Amin	Vice Chairman of the Council of Ministers
Sarjan Khan Zazay	Tribal and Nationalities Affairs
Abdul Wahid Sorabi	Social and Cultural Affairs
Abdul Ghafur Baher	Islamic Affairs
Fazl Haq Khaliqyar	Economic Affairs

1986   Jan. 11. President Babrak Karmal rejected the U.S. offer to serve as guarantor of a peace settlement.

Feb. 4. Guerrilla activity near Kandahar had reportedly declined in recent days after former rebel leader Asmatullah Achakzai Muslim and his militia decided to back the Kabul government.

Feb. 20. The Revolutionary Council Presidium appointed a 74- member commission to draft a constitution.

Mar. 17. The Foreign Ministry rejected a UN report on human rights violations in Afghanistan as "a collection of groundless slanders and accusations."

Mar. 20. Pakistan lodged a "strong protest" over Afghan attacks on a border post and refugee camp in Khurram Agency which killed six people on March 16 and 18.

Apr. 2. The U.S. reportedly agreed to supply hundreds of Stinger missiles to Afghan mujahedin.

Apr. 6. Kabul Radio said that rebels detonated a car bomb in Kabul that wounded 22 people.

May 4. Babrak Karmal resigned as secretary general of the PDPA because of "ill health," according to Kabul Radio. He was replaced by Najibullah, former head of KHAD, the secret police. Babrak retained the post of chairman of the Revolutionary Council and a seat in the seven-member politburo.

May 5. The seventh round of peace talks between the foreign ministers of Afghanistan and Pakistan opened at UN headquarters in Geneva.

May 15. Najibullah announced a collective leadership including himself as party leader, Babrak as head of the Revolutionary Council Presidium, and Prime Minister Sultan Ali Keshtmand.

May 19. The seventh round of UN-sponsored indirect talks Afghanistan and Pakistan resumed in Geneva.

May 28. Najibullah announced that a bicameral parliament would be established "within a few months," on the basis of "free and democratic elections."

Jun. 16. President Reagan met with Afghan mujahedin in Washington and promised an "unshakable commitment" to their cause.

Jun. 17. Mujahedin leaders Gulbuddin Hekmatyar and Rasul Sayyaf criticized the four other Peshawar leaders for the Washington visit.

1987   Feb. 18. Prime Minister Sultan Ali Keshtmand arrived in Moscow for talks.

Feb. 23. Pakistan's Foreign Minister Yaqub Khan met with Soviet Foreign Minister Shevardnadze in Moscow to discuss Afghanistan.

Feb. 25. The tenth round of negotiations aimed at ending the war in Afghanistan opened in Geneva.

Mar. 24. Agriculture Minister Abdul Ghaffar Lakanwal and Public Health Minister Nabi Kamyar were replaced by Ghulam Faruq and Sher Bahadur.

Jul. 20. Afghan leader Najibullah met with Soviet leader Mikkhail Gorbachev.

Aug. 11. Felix Ermacora, the UN special human rights investigator, was allowed to visit three Afghan prisons and interview political prisoners.

Oct. 10. Najibullah authorized the purchase of weapons from mujahedin who put down their arms.

Oct. 13. Yunus Khales, leader of the *Hizb-i Islami*, denied reports that his commanders had sold Stinger missiles to Iranian Pasdaran.

Oct. 18. Maulawi Yunus Khales was elected spokesman of the seven-party mujahedin alliance.

Oct. 24. Shi'a groups headquartered in Iran announced a new coalition of mujahedin groups headquartered in Iran.

Oct. 30 The Revolutionary Council announced the appointment of Muhammad Ishaq Kawa as minister of mines and industries and Najibullah Masir as minister of light industry and foodstuffs.

Nov. 10. Kabul radio announced that the Revolutionary Council Presidium endorsed a decree providing for the formation and registration of political parties.

Nov. 22 Col. Muhammad Rasi was appointed minister of technical and vocational education.

Nov. 24 Three new members were appointed to the Council of Ministers: Muhammad Aziz as deputy chairman of the council, Abdul Wahid Sorabi as minister

1987 (cont.)   of higher and vocational education, and Muhammad
                                Akbar Shormach as minister of nationalities affairs.
                                Lt. Gen. Muhammad Nabi Azimi, first deputy of defense,
                                was reported to have committed suicide after an offensive
                                he led ended in failure.
                                Nov. 29. A Loya Jirga had been called to approve a new
                                constitution.
                                Nov. 30.   The Loya Jirga confirmed Najibullah as
                                president under the new "Islamized" constitution.
                                Dec. 6.   Mujahedin leader Yunus Khales said the
                                seven-party Alliance would not accept communist
                                participation in any future Afghan government.
                                Dec. 10. UN envoy Diego Cordovez was reported having
                                opened negotiations between exiled King Muhammad
                                Zahir and mujahedin leaders regarding forming a
                                transitional coalition government.

1988   Jan. 4. Soviet Foreign Minister Shevardnadze arrived for
                                an "official working visit."
                                Jan. 6.   In an interview with Afghan News Agency,
                                Shevardnadze said the Soviet Union hoped to be out of
                                Afghanistan by the end of 1988 regardless of the type of
                                rule established there.   He, however, linked troop
                                withdrawal to the cessation of U.S. aid to the mujahedin.
                                Jan. 12.   Pakistani President Zia-ul-Haq and Prime
                                Minister Muhammad Khan Junejo said in separate
                                interviews that members of the pro-Moscow government
                                must be allowed to participate in any future government
                                as a condition for the withdrawal of Soviet troops from
                                the country.
                                Jan. 17.   Mujahedin leader Yunus Khalis rejected
                                statements by Pakistani leaders that the mujahedin would
                                have to "coexist with remnants of a communist regime."
                                Jan. 20. At a press conference Najibullah stated that his
                                government would be committed to nonalignment,
                                following the withdrawal of Soviet forces and that Kabul
                                was willing to accept aid from any country willing to give
                                it.
                                Jan. 22. In Jalalabad at least 17 people were killed when
                                two bombs exploded at the public funeral of Khan Abd
                                al-Ghaffar Khan, who died on Jan. 20.
                                Feb. 8. Soviet leader Mikkhail Gorbachev said Soviet
                                troops would begin pulling out of Afghanistan on May 15
                                if a settlement could be reached by mid-March.
                                Feb. 10. Reagan administration officials said a U.S.
                                commitment was made in 1985 to end military aid to the
                                mujahedin at the start of Soviet withdrawal.   This
                                commitment was made by a state department official

1988 (cont.)   without the knowledge of the president. The official U.S. position is that the cutoff of aid would occur 60 days after a peace settlement and concur with a simultaneous withdrawal.

Feb. 11. Sayyid Bahauddin Majruh, head of the Afghan Information Office in Peshawar, was assassinated in Peshawar city.

Feb. 23.   The mujahedin alliance announced the formation of an interim government.

Mar. 4. The Reagan administration said it would not halt aid to the mujahedin until Moscow stopped its supply to the Afghan government.

Mar. 14. Gulbudin Hekmatyar was reported appointed spokesman of the mujahedin alliance.

Mar. 17. *Bakhtar* reported that Mines and Industries Minister Najibullah Masir was appointed deputy prime minister in charge of the administration of the northern provinces.

Mar. 23. Nikolai Egorchev (?) was reported to have replaced Pavel Mojayev as Soviet ambassador to Afghanistan after Mojayev suffered a heart attack.

Mar. 24. U.S. officials reported that Pakistan withdrew its demand that an interim government be formed to oversee the Soviet withdrawal.

Mar. 26.   The Reagan administration was reported ending its supply of Stinger missiles to the mujahedin in anticipation of a Geneva settlement.

Mar. 29.   President Najibullah promised opposition groups 54 of the 229 lower house seats and 18 out of 62 in the senate if they would participate in the coming parliamentary elections.

Mar. 30. The mujahedin rejected President Najibullah's offer to form a coalition government.

Apr. 3.   The Kabul government created Sar-i Pol province and appointed Gharib Husain as governor. The new province is part of the Hazarajat.

Apr. 9.   A mujahedin leader said that the mujahedin "would not be bound by the outcome of the Geneva agreements."

Apr. 14. Afghanistan, Pakistan, the Soviet Union, and the United States signed the Geneva accords. Under the agreement the Soviet Union would withdraw its troops within nine months. The United States and the Soviet Union would be the guarantors of the agreement, which also provided for the return of Afghan refugees and a halt to military aid by both sides.

Apr. 21. President Najibullah said that 1.55 million voted in the Afghan elections.

Apr. 25. A UN "implementation assistance group," headed by the Finnish Maj. Gen. Rauli Helminen, arrived in Islamabad to monitor the Geneva accord.

Minister of Defense Maj. Gen. Muhammad Rafi'i was promoted to lieutenant general as was Armed Forces Chief of Staff Shanawaz Tanai. Minister of Communications Muhammad Aslam Watanjar was promoted to major general.

Apr. 28. President Najibullah said that Soviet military advisors would remain after the Soviet troop withdrawal.

May 4. President Najibullah arrived in New Delhi for three days of talks.

May 8. The Kabul government announced the names of those elected to the lower house in the April national assembly elections.

May 9. The government announced the names of senators elected in April.

May 11. The United Nations appointed Sadruddin Agha Khan as coordinator for relief and resettlement in Afghanistan.

May 12. The government announced the appointment of 23 provincial governors.

May 15. The Soviet Union began withdrawing troops from Afghanistan.

May 19. Afghan army Maj. Gen. Fazil Ahmad Samadi defected to the mujahedin.

May 25. The Soviet Union announced the following casualties in the Afghan war: 13,310 dead, 35,478 wounded, and 311 missing.

May 26. Muhammad Hasan Sharq was appointed prime minister, replacing Sultan Ali Keshtmand who became secretary of the PDPA central committee.

May 27. Sayyid Muzafaruddin Shah was elected temporary president of the House of Representatives.

May 31. A State Department official said U.S. aid to the mujahedin to continue because the Soviet Union planned to leave $1 billion worth of equipment in Afghanistan.

Jun. 3. The National Assembly approved the appointment of four vice presidents by presidential decree:

Abdul Hatef, Defense Minister Muhammad Rafi'i,

Deputy Prime Minister Abdul Hamid Mohtat, and

Minister of Higher and Vocational Education Abdul Wahid Sorabi.

Jun. 7. President Najibullah addressed the UN General Assembly, complaining that Pakistan continued to violate the Geneva accords.

1988 (cont.)

Jun. 9. President Najibullah said, according to the Bakhtar news agency, that 243,900 soldiers and civilians had died in ten years of war.

Jun. 15. Pir Sayyid Ahmad Gailani, Head of the National Islamic Front, became spokesman of the seven-member mujahedin alliance.

Jun. 16. President Najibullah announced the formation of a new government:

Muhammad Hasan Sharq	Prime Minister
Abdul Wakil	Foreign Affairs
Sayyid Muhammad Gulabzoi	Internal Affairs
Ghulam Faruq Yaqubi	State Security
Hamidullah Tarzi	Finance
Muhammad Bashir Baghlani	Justice
Shah Muhammad Dost	UN Representative
Muhammad Aslam Watanjar	Communications
Muhammad Khan Jalalar	Commerce
Abdul Ghafur	Returnees Affairs
Sulaiman Layeq	Tribal Affairs
Sultan Husain	Planning
Muhammed Asef Zaher	Rural Develop.
Muhammad Ghofran	Agric. and Land Reform
Abdul Fatah Najm	Public Health
Ghulam Rasul	Education
Nur Ahmad Baritz	Higher Education
Muhd. Ishaq Kawa	Mines and Industries
Muhammad Aziz	Transportation
Nazar Muhammad	Construction
Pacha Gul Wafadar	Civil Aviation
Dost Muhammd Fazl	Light industries and Foodstuffs
Raz Muhammad Paktin	Water and Power

Without Portfolio: Nematullah Pazhwak, Ghulam Faruq Yaqubi, Fazl Haq Khaliqyar, Shah Muhammad Dost, Sarjang Khan Jaji.

Jun. 9. Ahmad Bashir Ruigar was appointed minister of culture and information.

Jul. 18. Sebghatullah Mujaddidi's National Front for the Liberation of Afghanistan joined Sayyid Ahmad Gailani's National Islamic Front of Afghanistan in expressing support for UN envoy Diego Cordovez's peace plan to establish a neutral government.

Jul. 21. President Najibullah approved the creation of Nuristan province.

Jul. 23. President Najibullah approved the formation of a political organization called the Self-Sacrificing Afghan

1988 (cont.)   People's Solidarity Movement (*Nahzat-i Hambastagi-yi Mardom-i Afghanistan Fedaiyan*).

Jul. 27. The Kabul government announced the permission for formation of a new party, the Union of God's Helpers (*Ittehadia-ye Ansarullah*).

Aug. 1. The Constitution Council was set up to examine the constitutionality of laws and compliance of treaties and laws.

Aug. 8. Soviet troops began the withdrawal from Kabul.

Aug. 17. Lt. Gen. Shahnawaz Tanai was appointed defense minister and Maj. Gen. Muhammad Asef Delawar was appointed chief of the armed forces general staff.

Aug. 29. Abdul Ahad Mohmand and two Soviet cosmonauts lifted off in their Soyuz TM-6 spacecraft for a six-day voyage that threatened to strand them in outer space.

Sept. 25. Edmund McWilliams, Jr. was appointed special U.S. envoy to the mujahedin.

Oct. 5. Maulawi Zahir, a commander of Burhanuddin Rabbani's was killed in Nejrab by Hekmatyar's forces.

Oct. 13. Yuli Vorontsov, Soviet first deputy foreign minister, was appointed Ambassador to Kabul.

Oct. 17. Burhanuddin Rabbani, head of the *Jam'iat-i Islami*, became spokesman of the seven-member mujahedin alliance.

Oct. 19. Saleh Muhammad Ziray and Abdul Zuhur Razmjo were dismissed from politburo membership.

The ministry of tribal affairs was renamed ministry of border affairs.

Oct. 21. Diego Cordovez, UN special representative for Afghanistan, called on ex-King Muhammad Zahir to assist in establishing a national reconciliation government. Cordovez also called for the participation of Abdul Samad Hamed, former deputy prime minister; Abdul Satar Sirat, former justice minister; and Abdul Wakil, former agriculture minister.

Oct. 26. Herat Governor Khaliqyar was also appointed governor of Badghis and Ghor provinces.

Nov. 2. The Kabul government made the following new appointments:

Nizamuddin Tahzib	Chief Justice
Abdul Karim Shadan	Special Court of National Security

Nov. 8. Kabul Radio reported Soviet acceptance of Sayyid Muhd. Gulabzoi's appointment as Afghanistan's ambassador to the Soviet Union.

1988 (cont.)

Nov. 16. The appointment of Muhammad Aslam Watanjar as interior minister has been approved.

Nov. 17. Deputy Foreign Minister Abdul Ghafur Lakanwal and Sayyid Kamaluddin, deputy director in the foreign ministry were reported to have defected.

Nov. 28. Muhammad Gul, a KHAD brigadier general and cousin of Najibullah, was reported to have defected.

Dec. 3. Alliance leaders, headed by Burhanuddin Rabbani, met in Ta'if, Saudi Arabia, for talks with Soviet Deputy Minister Vorontsov.

Dec. 19. Mir Azmuddin was approved as minister of communications, and Khalilullah was approved as transportation minister.

Dec. 25. Soviet Deputy Vorontsov met with ex-King Muhammad Zahir in Rome (at the request of Moscow).

1989

Jan. 1. The newspaper *Haqiqat-i Saur Inqilab* (Truth of the April Revolution) appeared for the first time under the new name *Payam*.

Jan. 2. Sebghatullah Mujaddidi succeeded Rabbani as spokesman of the alliance.

Jan. 13. Soviet Foreign Minister Eduard Shevardnadze arrived in Kabul.

Jan. 18. Sebghatullah Mujaddidi returned from Iran where he unsuccessfully tried to invite the shi'a mujahedin groups to join an interim government.

Jan. 21. West Germany's diplomatic staff left Kabul.

Jan. 25. The United States decided to close its embassy.

Jan. 26. A mujahedin delegation, headed by Gulbuddin Hekmatyar, met with Iranian Foreign Minister Ali Akbar Velayati in Tehran.

Jan. 27. Britain, France, Japan, and Italy announced their decision to withdraw their diplomats from Kabul.

Jan. 28. Soviet Defense Minister Dimitri Yazov ended two days of talks with President Najibullah. He said Moscow would "not abandon its friends."

Jan. 29. President Najibullah approved the appointment of Sayyid Sharafuddin Sharaf as attorney general.

Jan. 30. The United States formally closed its embassy.

Feb. 2. President Najibullah denounced the closing of Western embassies as "psychological war."

In Peshawar some 500 Afghans demonstrated for the return of ex-King Muhammad Zahir.

Feb. 7. A mujahedin commander said that the "Pakistanis are pushing us now to do an all-out attack on Jalalabad," but the mujahedin wanted to wait to prevent a bloodbath.

1989 (cont.)   Feb. 13.   President Bush signed a National Security
                    Directive pledging continued financial and military
                    support.
                    Feb. 14.   The last Soviet soldier left Kabul airport.
                    Feb. 15.   The United States rejected a Soviet call for an
                    end to arms shipments to Afghanistan.
                    Feb. 18.   President Najibullah appointed new cabinet
                    members:

Burhanuddin Ghiasi	Commerce
Sher Jan Mazduryar	Civil Aviation
Abdul Baher	Light Industry and Foodstuffs
Ismail Danesh	Higher and Vocational Training
Sayyid Amin Zara	Public Health
Sayyid Akram	Returnee's Affairs
Abdul Ghafur Baher	Islamic Affairs and Endowments
Nur Ahmad Barits	Min. Without Portfolio

The government declared a nationwide state of emergency.

Muhammad Nabi Muhammadi became spokesman of the mujahedin alliance.

Feb. 20.   Prime Minister Sharq resigned.

Feb. 21.   Sultan Ali Keshtmand was appointed chairman of the executive committee of the council of ministers.

Feb. 23.   Mujahedin leaders elected Abdul Rabb Sayyaf as acting prime minister and Sibghatullah Mujaddidi as acting president of the interim government. The portfolios were distributed as follows:

Muhammad Nabi Muhammadi	Defense
Muhammad Shah Fazli (Harakat)	Scientific Research
Maulawi Islamuddin (Harakat)	Agriculture
Gulbuddin Hekmatyar (Hizb-K)	Foreign Affs.
Ali Ansari (Hizb-H)	Frontier Affs.
Qazi Najiullah (Hizb-H)	Justice
Yunus Khales (Hizb-K)	Interior
Haji Din Muhammad (Hizb-K)	National Security
Maulawi Abdul Razzaq (Hizb-K)	Religious Affairs
Burhanuddin Rabbani (Jami'at)	Reconstruction
Najibullah Lafa'i (Jami'at)	Islamic Guidance
Ishan Jan (Jami'at)	Mining and Industries
Ahmad Shah (Ittihad)	Communications

Sayyid Nadir Khurram (Jabha)   Health
Pir Sayyid Gailani challenged the legitimacy of the government.

Mar. 5. The mujahedin launched an offensive against Jalalabad.

Mar. 16. Afghan Army Chief of Staff Lt. Gen. Asef Delawar was reported in Jalalabad supervising its defense.

Mar. 20. Mujahedin attempt to capture Jalalabad failed.

Mar. 24. An 85-truck government convoy broke through to Jalalabad.

Mar. 27. President Najibullah offered mujahedin commanders autonomy if they ended the war. A council of 35 commanders rejected the offer.

Apr. 6. U.S. Secretary of State James Baker III recommended Peter Thomsen as special envoy to the mujahedin with the rank of ambassador.

Apr. 12. The mujahedin cabinet began a three-day session in Afghan territory.

Apr. 24. Afghan Foreign Minister Abdul Wakil accused Pakistan of aggression.

Yuri Gankovsky, researcher at Institute of Oriental Studies, stated that Soviet troops had a direct role in 1979 coup.

May 6. Valentin I. Varennikov, Soviet deputy minister of defense, ended a four-day visit to Kabul.

May 9. Sayyid Ahmad Gailani challenged the legitimacy of the interim government.

May 16. KHAD chief Abdul Rahman is said to have defected to Yunis Khalis mujahedin group.

May 17. Government troops reopened Jalalabad-Kabul road.

May 18. President Najibullah invited mujahedin leaders and commanders to take part in the Loya Jirga.

May 21. President Najibullah offered regional autonomy to mujahedin commanders if they agreed to stop fighting.

May 24. A convoy of Soviet-made tanks and artillery arrived in Kabul.

Jun. 24. President Najibullah appointed Mahmud Baryalai as first deputy prime minister.

Jul. 5. Government troops recaptured Tor Kham.

Jul. 19. President Najibullah replaced Education Minister Ismail Danesh with Mehr Muhammad Azizi.

Units of Burhanuddin Rabbani and Muhd. Nabi Muhammadi were fighting over turf in Helmand province.

Jul. 24. Defense Minister Shahnawaz Tanai under house arrest.

Jul. 26. Najmuddin Kawiani, head of foreign relations committee of the national assembly and politburo member, reported secret peace talks with the "opposition."

Jul. 29. Nur Ahmad Nur was appointed ambassador and permanent representative to the United Nations.

Aug. 1. Defense Minister Tanai reported to be implicated in coup attempt.

Aug. 3. Some 700 members of *Harakat-i-Islami* under Ibrahim Beg joined "national reconciliation process."

Aug. 7. Haji Abdul Latif, 76-year-old commander with National Islamic Front, died from poisoning.

Aug. 8. Two bodyguards of Abdul Latif who confessed to killing him were executed.

Aug. 10. Government denied it was behind poisoning of Abdul Latif.

Aug. 11. Abdul Rabb Sayyaf, prime minister, rejected Gulbuddin Hekmatyar's suggestion that the rebels should take control by backing an army coup.

Aug. 14. Government spokesman Muhammad Nabi Amani said 183 civilians killed in Kabul by rockets in one week.

Aug. 20. Maj. Gen. Muhammad Faruq Zarif, head of Najib's security force, announced his defection.

Aug. 25. *Jam'iat-i Islami* Commander Mas'ud accused *Hizb-i Islami* of collusion with Kabul government.

Aug. 29. Fighters of Sayyaf and Muhammadi battle over control of a bridge in Helmand province that produced lucrative tax and toll revenues.

Aug. 30. Gulbuddin Hekmatyar's *Hizb-i Islami* withdrew from the mujahedin alliance.

Oct. 11. Muhammad Asghar becomes president of the 15-member National Salvation Society, which was formed to seek a peaceful solution to the war.

Oct. 17. Boris Nikolayevich Pastukhov, Soviet ambassador, presented his credentials.

Nov. 7. Lt. Gen. Ali Akbar killed in fighting in Kandahar.

Nov. 14. Mujahedin launched a three-pronged attack on Jalalabad which was repulsed.

Nov. 21. President Najibullah extended the state of emergency for another six months.

Nov. 30. Mujahedin leaders Burhanuddin Rabbani and Gulbuddin Hekmatyar announced a cease-fire and exchange of prisoners and captured land.

Dec. 2.   The Kabul government arrested 127 people suspected of plotting a coup.

Brig. Gen. Ghulam Haidar was killed in fighting at Jalalabad.

Dec. 21.   Jam'iat executed four members of Hizb, including Sayyid Jamal, who had ambushed Jam'iat commanders.

Dec. 26.   Government released head of defense ministry's communications department and a senior general who was among 127 arrested on Dec. 2.

Dec. 31.   President Najibullah called for PDPA to change its name.

1990

Jan. 2.   Muhammad Qasim Jamadar, research director of the ministry of higher education defected. Pacha Gul Wafadar, former aviation minister, was also said to have defected.

Jan. 9.   France confirmed that it planned to reopen its Kabul embassy.

Jan. 24.   President Najibullah said that he would step down if his government was defeated in UN-supervised elections.

Feb. 2.   Some 10,000 refugees demonstrated in favor of the return of Zahir Shah in Quetta.

Feb. 12.   Farid Ahmad Mazdak was appointed acting chairman of the National Front's central council, replacing Abdur Rahim Hatif.

Mar. 5.   Trials began of some 124 Afghans arrested in December and charged with plotting a coup.

Mar. 6.   Defense Minister Shahnawaz Tanai launched a coup against President Najibullah.

Mar. 7.   Gulbuddin Hekmatyar said his forces were supporting the Tanai coup.   Other mujahedin groups refused to support the Tanai coup.

Mar. 9.   Government troops recaptured the Bagram air base.

Mar. 18.   The PDPA plenum expelled twenty-four members for "treachery" against the party and country.

Apr. 6.   Two generals and 11 other people were killed at a ceremony when a mujahedin group who promised to surrender opened fire on Government troops. Fazl Haq Khaliqyar, governor of Herat, was wounded.

Apr. 14.   The Kabul government accused the United Nations of failing to monitor alleged violations of the Geneva accords.

May 21.   Prime Minister Khaliqyar presents his new cabinet:

1990 (cont.)

Mahmud Baryalai	First Deputy Prime Minister
Abdul Wahid Sorabi	Deputy Prime Minister
Ne'matullah Pazhwak	Deputy Prime Minister
Abdul Qayyum Nurzai	Deputy Prime Minister
Sarwar Mangal	Deputy Prime Minister
Mahbubullah Kushani	Deputy Prime Minister
Nur Ahmad Barits	Adviser
Faqir Muhammad Yaqubi	Adviser
Shah Wali	Adviser
Sayyid Akram Peigir	Adviser
Muhd. Aslam Watanjar	Defense
Raz Muhammad Paktin	Interior
Abdul Wakil	Foreign Affairs
Muhammad Hakim	Finance
Abdul Wahid Sorabi	Planning
Mas'uma Esmati Wardak	Education and Training
Anwar Shams	Higher and Vocational Education
Faqir Muhammad Nikzad	Construction
Zakim Shah	Commerce
Bashir Ruigar	Information and Cultur
Mehr Muhammad Ejazi	Health
Sayyid Nasim Alawi	Comunications
Anwar Dost	Light Industry and Foodstuffs
Muhd. Siddiq Sailani	Islamic Affairs
Khalilullah	Transport
Hamidullah Tarzi	Civil Aviation
Hayatullah Azizi	Reconstruction and Rural Development
Ghulam Faruq Yaqubi	State Security
Sarjang Zazai	Border Affairs
Muhammad Ghufran	Agriculture and Land Reform
Ghulam Muhyiuddin Shahbaz	Minister of Central Statistics
Saleha Faruq Etemadi	Social Affairs
Fath Muhammad Tarin	Repatriation
Abdul Samad Saleh	Mines and Industries
Ghulam Muhyiuddin Daris	Justice
Abdul Ghafur Rahim	Water and Power

May 28. Kabul government convenes a Loya Jirga in preparation for amending the constitution.
Jun. 11. Agreement of economic cooperation signed between the Kabul government and India.
Jun. 16. Nine shi'a mujahedin parties unite in the *Hizb-i Wahdat*, Party of Unity.

Jun. 17. French embassy is reopened in Kabul.

Jun. 22. Conference of mujahedin commanders in Paktia province.

Jun. 27. Opening of the second party congress which reelects Dr. Najibullah and changes the name of the party to "Homeland Party" (*Hizb-i Watan*).

Jun. 30. Meeting of former prominent government officials at the invitation of President Mujaddidi. Members invited include:

Muhammad Yusuf, prime minister
Abdul Samad Hamed, minister
Rawan Farhadi, minister and diplomat
Sabbahuddin Kushkaki, minister and writer
Abdul Hakim Tabibi, minister and diplomat
Nangyalai Tarzi, diplomat
Humayun Asefi, diplomat
Agha Jan Barakzai
Sayyid Ishaq Gailani, mujahedin leader
Sayyid Makhdum Rahin, poet and writer
Abdul Ahad Karzai, parliament member
Abdul Hai Tokhi (Tukhay)
Abdur Rahman Ulfat, agric. adviser
Ihsanullah Mayar
Sayyid Asadullah Nuktadan
Abdul Aziz Firogh
Abdul Qadir Nurzai
Wali Ahmad Sherzai
Enayatullah Iblagh
Ishaq Akhlaqi
Muhammad Akram, scholar and diplomat
Muhammad Anwar Sherzai
Siddiq Rashid Saljuqi
Muhammad Gulab Nangarhari, minister and poet
Muhammad Hashim Mujaddidi, educator and senator
Muhammad Yahya Nauruz, general
Members of the *shi'a Whadat* alliance of mujahedin groups based in Iran also participated.

Jul. 9. Nizamuddin Tahzib, a Parchami, is relieved from his post as chief justice of the supreme court.

Jul. 18. Italian embassy reopened in Kabul.

Jul. 25. Beginning of UN-assisted repatriation of refugees from Pakistan.

Jul. 29-Aug. 25. Najibullah visited the Soviet Union; Abdur Rahim Hatef is acting president.

Aug. 3. Columbia establishes diplomatic relations with Afghanistan.

Aug. 29. Najibullah leaves for official visit to Delhi.

1990 (cont.)   Sep. 3. Najibullah participates in UN conference at
                      Paris, pays courtesy visit to French minister of foreign
                      affaires.
                      Sep. 4. Jamiat and Hizb (H) clash in vicinity of Kabul
                      in which 16 mujahedin fighters were killed.
                      Sep. 5. Kabul government removed unruly militias from
                      the city.
                      Sep. 11. Najibullah decrees legalization of political
                      parties.
                      Sep. 30. Alliance of democratic parties of the left
                      dissolves itself.
                      Oct. 1. Mr. Mujaddidi returns from a three-week visit to
                      Badakhshan and Parwan.
                      Oct. 3. Kabul government established diplomatic rela-
                      tions with Ecuador and Namibia.
                      Oct. 5. Tirin Kot, administrative center of Oruzgan
                      province, captured by mujahedin forces.
                      Oct. 15. Mas'ud, the Jamiat commander, visits
                      Islamabad where he meets the Pakistani head of state
                      and Gulbuddin Hekmatyar.
                      Oct. 25. The U.S. congress reduces its aid to the Afghan
                      resistance.
                      Nov. 19. President Najibullah arrived in Switzerland for
                      discussions with Afghan personalities.
                      Dec. 10. Afghanistan and Venezuela establish diplomatic
                      relations.

1991   Jan. 9. Afghan General Hashim was captured by the
                      resistance and executed.
                      Jan. 22. Esmat Muslim, chief of the pro-government
                      militia, died.
                      Jan. 23. Prof. Rabbani opens embassy of the resistance
                      in Khartum.
                      Feb. 5. Floods cause considerable damage in soutwestern
                      Afghanistan.
                      Feb. 7. President Najibullah appointed new ministers:
                      Ghulam Muhyiuddin Shahbaz   Planning
                      Muhammad Nazir Shahadi   Statistics
                      Wadir Safi   Civil Aviation and Tourism
                      Feb. 8. Afghan resistance sends 300 mujahedin to Saudi
                      Arabia in war with Iraq. Sayyaf and Hekmatyar protest.
                      Mar. 31. Khost captured by mujahedin forces headed
                      by Commander Haqani (q.v.), 2,200 prisoners taken and
                      seven generals (including Col. Gen. Muhammad Zahir
                      Solamal - deputy minister of defense, Maj. Gen. Ghulam
                      Mustafa - chief of political affairs of the armed forces,
                      Maj. Gen. Muhammad Qasim, commander of artillery
                      special guards, Maj. Muhammad Azam - an air force

1991 (cont.)   commander, Lt. Gen. Gul Aqa - commander of the Khost division, and Lt. Gen. Shirin - commander of the Khost militia units). Kabul government declares a "Day of 1991 Mourning" on April 2nd.

Apr. 6. Muhammad Nurzad elected Mayor of Kabul to replace Abdul Karim Misaq who defected and moved to Germany.

Apr. 10. Vice President Sultan Ali Keshtmand was dismissed.

Apr. 16. President Najibullah offers a new amnesty to all Afghans living abroad who accept to return to Afghanistan.

Apr. 20. Explosion at Jamilurrahman's Asadabad (Wahabi) headquarter in Kunar province results in some 500 killed and 700 wounded. According to eyewitness accounts, the explosion occurred at the Dawa (formerly Asadabad Hotel and a number of Arabs and 63 Pakistanis were among the killed. Some sources suspect a car bomb for the explosion, whereas the "Wahabis" claim it was the result of a SCUD missile attack.

Apr. 22. Afghan Foreign Minister Abdul Wakil sets out on a trip to Moscow and New York.

Apr. 26. Representatives of the Pakistan military intelligence sevice (ISI) meet in Geneva with representatives of the Kabul government.

May 4. Yunus Khales, leader of the *Hizb-i Islami*, resigned from the Afghan Interim Government.

May 21. Javier Pérez de Cuéllar, United Nations secretary general, issued a five-point proposal for a political settlement in Afghanistan.

June 20. Babrak Karmal returned to Afghanistan from exile in the Soviet Union.

BIBLIOGRAPHY

The sources presented in the following sections are a representative selection of books and articles, with special emphasis on materials in English. Because French and German scholars have been pioneering in certain fields (archaeology and the sciences) a number of sources in French and German were also listed.

The reader who desires a comprehensive survey may refer to the blibliographies listed below, especially the more up-to-date one by Keith McLachlan and William Whittaker (1983). An excellent, though dated, bibliography is the two volume *Bibliographie der Afghanistan-Literatur* (1968 and 1969) which also lists sources in Dari and Pashto. The most recent bibliographical compilation is the work by Muhammad Akram (1990) which is available on microfiche at the Bibliotheca Afghanica in Liestal, Switzerland.

Scholars may obtain access to the research libraries of the Bibliotheca Afghanica, founded by Paul Bucherer-Dietsche, which is probably the most comprehensive depository of Afghanistan materials in Western languages. The Afghanistan Archiv of the Institut fuer Entwicklungsforschung und Entwicklungspolitik of the Ruhr University of Bochum has a considerable amount of material in the fields of economics and the sciences. It is headed by Professor E-A von Renesse. Probably the best library for Dari/Pashto sources in the United States is at the Center for Afghanistan Studies, at Omaha, Nebraska, headed by Thomas E. Gouttierre.

The most important sources for archival materials are the National Archives of India at New Delhi, India, and the India Office Records and Library of the Commonwealth Office in London, England. German foreign ministry archives exist on microfilm from about 1867 to 1945. Catalogs of files and microfilms of the German foreign ministry archives are available in the United States at major university libraries. Microfilm copies of German sources may be obtained from the United States National Archives in Washington, DC. The Washington archives also have American consular reports, and studies by various American agencies. Most foreign political archives are closed for a period of 25 years; but with special permission a scholar may obtain access to closed materials.

CONTENTS

1. GENERAL

Bibliographies

Akram, Muhammad. *Bibliographie analytique de l'Afghanistan*. Paris: Centre de Documentation Universitaire, 1947. This has been updated to 1990 and is available on microfiche from the Bibliotheca Afghanica, Liestal, Switzerland.

Beaureceuil, Serge de. "Manuscrits d'Afghanistan," vol 3: *Melange de l'Institut Dominicain d'Etudes Orientales*. Cairo, 3, 1956. Pp. 75-206.

____. "Les Publications de la Societe d'Histoire d'Afghanistan," *Melange de l'Institut Dominicain d'Etudes Orientales*. Cairo, 7, 1963. Pp. 236-240.

Deutsches Orient Institut. *Bibliographie der Afghanistan Literatur, 1945-1967.* Vol 1: *Literatur in europaeischen Sprachen.* Vol 2: *Literature in orientalischen Sprachen.* Institut fuer Entwicklungsforschung und Entwicklungspolitik der Ruhr-Universitaet Bochum, Hamburg und Bochum, 1969.

Jones, S. *An Annotated Bibliography of Nuristan (Kafiristan) and the Kalash Kafirs of Chitral: Selected Documents from the Secret and Political Records, 1885-1900.* Videnskabernes Selskab, Kobenhavn, 43/1, 1969.

Mayel-Harawi, Ghulam Reza. *Fehrest-i Kutub-i Matbu'-i Afghanistan az Sal-i 1330 ila 1344.* Government Press, Kabul, 1965.

McLachlan, Keith & William Whittaker. *A Bibliography of Afghanistan.* Menas Press, Cambridge, England, 1983.

North, R. *The Literature on the North-West Frontier.* Peshawar, 1947.

Ovesen, J. "An Annotated Bibliography of Sources Relating to the Pashai People of Afghanistan," *Afghanistan.* 32/1, 1979. Pp. 87-98.

Pickett, L.C., Mayar, and Saleh. *Bibliography of Materials Dealing with Agriculture in Afghanistan.* Kabul University, Kabul, 1968.

319

Pourhadi, Ibrahim V. *Persian and Afghan Newspapers in the Library of Congress, 1871-1978*. Library of Congress, Washington, DC, 1979.

Rosenbaum, H. "Das Afghanistan Archiv des Instituts fuer Entwicklungs-forschung und Entwicklungspolitik der Ruhr-Universitaet Bochum," *Afghanistan Journal*. 2/4. Bochum, 1975. P. 151.

Stwoda, M. Ibrahim and Ahmad Ziya Mudarresi. *Hutakian: Ketabshenasi-yi Tausifi*. (Bibliography of the Hotakis) Government Press, Kabul, 1357/1978.

United Nations. *Afghanistan, a Selected and Partially Annotated Bibliography*. UNICEF, Kabul, 1972.

Wilber, Donald N. *Annotated Bibliography of Afghanistan*. Human Relations Area Files, New Haven, 1968.

Witherell, Julian W. *Afghanistan: An American Perspective* (A guide to U.S. Official Documents and Government-Sponsored Publications). Washington, DC, 1986.

Archival Works

Aitchison, C. U. *Treaties Engagements and Sanads*. Vol. 13: *Persia and Afghanistan*. Calcutta, 1933.

Baluchistan Intelligence Bureau. *Notes on the Tribes of Afghan Descent in Baluchistan*. Government of India. Quetta, 1937.

Bruce, C. E. *The Tribes of Waziristan*. India Office, London, 1929.

Defense Mapping Agency. *Gazetteer of Afghanistan*. Washington, DC. 1983.

Dundas, A. D. F. *Precis on Afghan Affairs, 1927-1936*. Government of India, New Delhi, 1938.

General Staff, India. *A Dictionary of the Pathan Tribes on the North-West Frontier of India*. Calcutta, 1910.

____. *Brief Gazetteer of the Most Important and Useful Place Names in the Waziristan District*. Dera Ismail Khan, 1935. (Official use only.)

____. *Handbook of Kandahar Province, 1933*. Simla, 1933. (Secret.)

____. *Routes in Afghanistan, South-East*. Calcutta, 1937.

Hayat Khan, Muhammad. *Afghanistan and its Inhabitants*. Transl. by Henry Priestley, Indian Public Opinion Press, Lahore, Pakistan, 1874.

Johnson, H. H. *Notes on Mahsuds*. India Office, London, 1934.

Maconachie, R. R. *Precis on Afghan Affairs, 1919-1927*. Government of India, Simla, 1928.

Maitland, P. J. *A Note on the Movements of Turkoman Tribes*. Government of India, Simla, 1888.

Ridgway, Major R. T. I. *Handbooks for the Indian Army: Pathans*. Government of India, Calcutta, 1910.

Robinson, J. A. *Notes on Nomad Tribes of Eastern Afghanistan*. Government of India, Peshawar, 1934. (Confidential.)

Wheeler, J. Talboys. *Memorandum on Afghanistan Affairs, from A. D. 1700*. Calcutta, 1896.

Wynne, LePoer. *Narrative of Recent Events in Afghanistan from the Recovery of Candahar to the Conclusion of the Rebellion of Yacoob Khan*. Government of India, Simla, 1871. (Secret.)

Dictionaries and Grammars

Arayanpur-Kashani, Abbas. *The Concise English-Persian Dictionary*. Amir Kabir, Tehran, 1977.

____. *The Concise Persian-English Dictionary*. Amir Kabir, Tehran, 1976.

____. *The New Unabridged English-Persian Dictionary*. 6 vols. Amir Kabir, Tehran 1963.

Badakhshi, Shah Abdullah. *A Dictionary of Some Languages and Dialects of Afghanistan*. Government Press, Kabul, 1960.

Farhadi, A. G. Rawan. *The Spoken Dari of Afghanistan*. Peace Corps, Kabul, 1975.

Gilbertson, George W. *The Pakkhto Idiom: A Dictionary*. 2 vols. Austin & Sons, Hertford, England, 1932.

Haim, S. *The Larger English-Persian Dictionary*. 2 vols. Beroukhim, Tehran, 1959, 1960.

____. *New Persian-English Dictionary*. 2 vols. Beroukhim, Tehran, 1960, 1962.

Lorentz, M. *Lehrbuch des Pashto/Afghanisch.* Leipzig, 1979.

Penzl, Herbert. *A Grammar of Pashto.* ACLS, Washington, DC, 1955.

_____. *A Reader of Pashto.* University of Michigan, Ann Arbor, 1962.

Phillot, D.C. *Higher Persian Grammar.* Baptist Mission Press, Calcutta, 1919.

Pushto Academy. *English-Pushtu Dictionary.* Kabul, 1975.

Raverty, H. G. *Dictionary of the Pukhto, Pushto, Language of the Afghans.* Indus Publication, Karachi, 1980.

Steingass, F. *A Comprehensive Persian-English Dictionary.* Routledge & Kegan Paul, London, 1957.

Yearbooks

Afghanistan Almanac. A yearbook, published in Dari and Pashto by the Afghan government from 1311/1932 under the title *Salnama-yi Majalla-yi Kabul* until 1940 and then called in Pashto *Da Kabul Kalanai* and finally *Da Afghanistan Kalanai.*

Baryalai, Mahmud. *Republic of Afghanistan Annual.* Government Press, Kabul 1978.

_____. *Democratic Republic of Afghanistan Annual: Saur 7, 1358.* Government Press, Kabul, 1979.

Danishyar, Abdul Aziz. *Afghanistan Republic Annual, 1975.* Government Press, Kabul, 1975.

_____. *Afghanistan Republic Annual, 1976.* Government Press, Kabul, 1976.

_____. *Afghanistan Republic Annual, 1977.* Government Press, Kabul, 1977.

Khalil, Sayyid. *The Kabul Times Annual, 1970.* Government Press, Kabul, 1970.

Rahimi, Nur M. *The Kabul Times Annual, 1967.* Government Press, Kabul, 1967.

Yusufzai, G. R. *Democratic Republic of Afghanistan Annual.* Government Press, Kabul, 1980.

Guides and Description

Abdul Rahim, Munshi. *Journey to Badakhshan, 1879-80.* Government of India, n.d.

Ali, Muhammad. *A New Guide to Afghanistan.* Afghan Historical Society, Kabul, 1958.

Dupree, Nancy Hatch. *Bamian.* Afghan Tourist Organization, Kabul, 1967.

____. *Herat: A Pictorial Guide.* Afghan Tourist Organization, Kabul, 1966.

____. *An Historical Guide to Kabul.* Afghan Tourist Organization, Kabul, 1977.

____. *The Road to Balkh, Kabul, Koh-i-Daman, Salang, Pul-i- Khumri, Surkh Kotal, Samangan, Tashkurghan, Mazar-i-Sharif, Qunduz.* Kabul, 1967.

Fodor, Les Guides Modernes. *Afghanistan.* Edition Vilo, Paris, 1972.

Gharghasht, Muhammad Naser. *Rahnama-yi Kabul.* (A Guide to Kabul) Government Press, Kabul, 1345/1966.

Kabul Times Publishing Agency. *Afghanistan at a Glance.* Kabul, 1967.

Klimburg, Max. *Afghanistan.* Austria Edition, Wien, 1966.

Kohzad, Ahmad Ali. *Bala Hesar-i Kabul.* Government Press, Kabul, 1340/1961.

Kraus, Willy. *Afghanistan.* Horst Erdmann Verlag, Tuebingen, Germany, 1972.

Kushkaki, Maulawi Burhanuddin. *Rahnama-yi Qataghan wa Badakhshan.* Ministry of War, Kabul, 1302/1923. Translated from Dari into French by Marguerite Reut under the title *Qataghan et Badakhshan.* Sorbonne, Paris, 1979.

Michaud, Roland and Sabrina. *Afghanistan.* Vendome Press, Paris, 1980.

ORBIS. *Afghanistan Yesterday and Today.* Prague, 1982.

Poulton, Michelle and Robin. *Que Sais-je? L'Afghanistan.* Presses Universitaires de France, Paris, 1981.

United States. Government Printing Office. *Afghanistan: A Country Study.* Washington, DC, 1986.

Wolfe, Nancy Hatch (Dupree).   *The Valley of Bamian*. Afghan Tourist
    Organization, Kabul, 1963.

Journals

Afghan Information Centre. Ed. Sayyid B. Majruh. Peshawar, Pakistan.

Afghan News. Published by Jam'iat Islami Afghanistan. Peshawar, Pakistan.

Afghanistan Forum. New York, by Mary Ann Siegfried and Leonard
    Oppenheim.

Afghanistan Journal. Akademische Druck-u. Verlagsanstalt. Graz, Austria.

Afghanistan Tribune. Afghanisches Nachrichtenmagazin in Deutscher Sprache.
    Aachen, Germany.

A'ina-yi Afghanistan (Afghanistan Mirror). Published by Sayed Khalilollah
    Hashemeyan, Montclair, Calif.

American Universities Field Staff Reports. Louis Dupree. New York.

Central Asia: Journal of Area Study Centre. University of Peshawar, Pakistan.

EFIS Afghans. Published by the Bureau International Afghanistan (BIA).
    Paris, France.

The Firmest Bond. Islamic Unity Magazine. Publisher and Editor-in-Chief,
    Dr. Abdul Hakim Tabibi. Geneva, Switzerland.

Les Nouvelles d'Afghanistan. Published by the Amitie Franco-Afghane
    (AFRANE). Paris, France.

Writers Union of Free Afghanistan (WUFA). 'Editor-in-Chief, Rasul A. Amin.
    Peshawar, Pakistan.

2. CULTURAL

Archaeology and Prehistory

Allchin, F. R. and N. Hammond. *The Archaeology of Afghanistan from the
    Earliest Times to the Timurid Period*. Academic Press, London, New York,
    San Francisco. 1978.

Barthoux, J. *Les Fouille de Hadda: Figures et Figurines.* G. Van Oest, Paris and Brussels. 1930.

Bernard, P. "Ai Khanum on the Oxus: a Hellenistic City in Central Asia," *Proceedings of the British Academy.* London, 1967.

_____. "La Campagne de Fouilles de 1970 a Ai Khanoun (Afghanistan)," *Comptes Rendus de l'Academie des Inscriptions et Belles Lettres.* Paris, 1971.

Berre, M. Le, D. Schlumberger and B. Dagens. "Monuments Pre-Islamiques d'Afghanistan," *Memoires de la Delegation Archeologique Francaise en Afghanistan.* 19, 1964.

Bombaci, A. "Ghazni," *East and West.* 8, 1957. Pp. 247-260.

Courtois, J. C. "Summary of the History of Archaeological Research in Afghanistan," *Afghanistan.* 16/2, 1961. Pp. 18-29.

Dor, R. "Lithoglyphes du Wakhan et du Pamir," *Afghanistan Journal.* 3/4, 1976. Pp. 122-129.

Dupree, L. "An Archaeological Survey of N. Afghanistan," *Afghanistan.* 15/3, 1960. Pp. 13-15.

_____. "Results of a Survey for Palaeolithic Sites in Dasht-i-Nawur," *Afghanistan.* 29/2, 1976. Pp. 55-63.

Fischer, K. "Archaeological Field Surveys in Afghan Seistan, 1960-1970," Hammond, *South Asian Archaeology.* 1973. Pp. 131-155.

Foucher, A. "The French Archaeological Delegation in Afghanistan Oct. 1922-Nov. 1925," *Comptes Rendus de l'Academie des Inscriptions.* 1927. Pp. 117-123.

Franz, H. G. "Der Buddhistishe Stupa in Afghanistan, Urspruenge und Entwicklung," *Afghanistan Journal.* 4/4, 1977, Pp. 131-143 and 5/1, 1978. Pp. 26-38.

_____. "Erste Monographie zur Archaeologie Afghanistans," *Afghanistan Journal.* 6/4, 1979. Pp. 109-116.

Fussman, G. "Daniel Schlumberger, 1904-1972," *Bulletin de l'Ecole Francaise d'Extreme-Orient.* 60, 1973. Pp. 411-422.

_____. *Monuments Buddhiques de la Region de Caboul.* Boccard, Paris, 1976.

Ghirshman, R. "Die Franzosische Archaeologische Forschung in Iran und Afghanistan, 1940-1952," *Saeculum, Jahrbuch fuer Universal-Geschichte*. 4/1, 1952.

Grenet, F., J. Lee and R. Pinder-Wilson. "Les Monuments Anciens du Gorzivan (Afghanistan du Nord-Ouest)," *Afghanistan Quarterly*. 33/3, 1980. Pp. 17-51.

Grousset, R. "Un Savant Francais: Joseph Hackin," *Revue de Paris*. 52/1, 1945. Pp. 78-85, and *Afghanistan*. 5/4, 1950. Pp. 1-12.

Hackin, J. "The Recent Work of the French Archaeological Mission at Bamiyan," *Indian Art and Letters*. 8/1, 1934. Pp. 36-42.

____. "Recherches Archeologiques en Afghanistan," *Revue de l'Art Anciente Moderne*. 1937. Pp. 302-304.

____. *Diverses Recherches Archeologiques en Afghanistan (1933-1940)*. Paris, Presses Universitaire de France, 1959.

Jackson, A. V. W. "The Tomb of the Moghul Emperor Babar in Afghanistan," *Proceedings of the American Philosophical Society*. 68/3, 1929. 195-207.

Jettmar, K. "Bronze Axes from the Karakoram," *Proceedings of the American Philosophical Society*. 105/1, 1961. Pp. 98-104.

Knobloch, E. "Survey of Archaeology and Architecture in Afghanistan," *Afghanistan Journal*. 8/1, 1981. Pp. 3-20.

Kohzad, A. A. "Archaeology in Afghanistan," *Afghanistan*. 1956.

Masson, C. "Notes on the Antiquities of Bamian," *Journal of the Asiatic Society of Bengal*. 1836. P. 707.

Moline, J. "The Minaret of Jam," *Kunst des Orients*. 9, 1973-1974. Pp. 131-148.

Motamedi, A. A. "Hada After the last Seasons of Excavation at Tepe Hotor," *Afghanistan*. 32/3, 1979. Pp. 49-55.

Pugachenkova, G. A. "A l'Etude des Monuments Timurides d'Afghanistan," *Afghanistan*. 23/3, 1970. Pp. 24-49.

Schlumberger, D. "The Archaeological Exploration of Afghanistan," *Afghanistan*. 2/4, 1947. Pp. 1-22.

____. "Surkh Kotal and the Ancient History of Afghanistan," *Afghan Information Bureau*. London, 1960.

Trousdale, W. "The Homeland of Rustam," *Afghanistan*. 29/2, 1976. Pp. 64-71.

Architecture

Anand, M. R. "The Development of Islamic Architecture in Afghanistan," *Marg*. 24/1, 1970. Pp. 17-46.

Bechhoefer, W. B. "Serai Lakon: Traditional Housing in the Old City of Kabul," *Afghanistan Journal*. 3/1, 1976. Pp. 3-15.

____. "Architectural Education in Afghanistan," *Afghanistan Journal*. 4/4, 1977. Pp. 147-148.

Fischer, K. "Interrelations of Islamic Architecture in Afghanistan. The Remains of Afghan Seistan," *Marg*. 24/1, 1970. Pp. 47-56.

Frye, R. N. "Observations on Architecture in Afghanistan," *Gazette des Beaux-arts*. 6/29, 1946. Pp. 129-138.

____. "Notes on the History of Architecture in Afghanistan," *Ars Islamica*. 11-12, 1946. Pp. 200-202.

Hallet, S. I. and R. Samizay. *Traditional Architecture of Afghanistan*. Garland, STPM Press, New York, 1980.

Stark, F. *The Minaret of Djam: an Excursion in Afghanistan*. London, 1970.

Linguistics and Literature

Ali, M. "Khushhal Khan Khattak, the Soldier Poet," *Afghanistan*. 17/3, 1962. Pp. 1-6.

____. "Maulana Jalal-du-Din Balkhi, the Great Sufi Poet and Profound Philosopher," *Afghanistan*. 18/1, 1963. Pp. 1-12.

Barret, P. and J. Ahmad. *A Collection of Afghan Legends*. Ed. Press, Kabul, 1970.

Beaureceuil, Serge de. "Abdullah Ansari, a Profile," *Afghanistan*. 29/1, 1976. Pp. 88-90.

____. "Studying Ansari of Herat," *Afghanistan*. 29/1, 1976. Pp. 91-97.

Benava, A. R. "Les Poetesses de l'Aryana," *Afghanistan*. 9/3, 1954. Pp. 49-55.

Breshna, A. G. "Haji Mirwais Khan, an Historical Play," *Afghanistan*. 23/2, 1970. Pp. 59-81.

Dupree, L. "Ajmal Khattak, Revolutionary Pushtun Poet," *American Universities Field Staff Reports*. 20/9, 1976. P. 13.

Dvorjankov, N. A. "The Development of Pushtu as the National and Literary Language of Afghanistan," *Central Asian Review*. 14/3, 1966. Pp. 210-220.

Farhadi, A. G. R. "The Meaning of Love According to Mawlana Jalaluddin of Balkh," *Afghanistan*. 29/1, 1976. Pp. 1-7.

Fussman, G. *Atlas Linguistique des Parlers Dardes et Kafirs*. Ecole Francaise d'Extreme- Orient, Paris, 2 vols. 1972.

Habibi, A. H. "Pashto Literature at a Glance," *Afghanistan*. 20/4, 1968. Pp. 51-64; 21/1, 1968. Pp. 53-57.

Lorimer, D. L. R. *The Phonology of the Bakhtiari, Badakhshani and Madaglashti Dialects of Modern Persian, with vocabularies*. Royal Asiatic Society, 1922.

Morgenstierne, G. "The Language of Afghanistan," *Afghanistan*. 20/3, 1967. Pp. 81-90.

Weiers, M. "Die Sprache der Hazara und der Mongolen von Afghanistan in Lexikostatischer Sicht," *Afghanistan Journal*. 2/3, 1975. 98-102.

3. ECONOMIC

General

Asian Development Bank. *Economic Report on Afghanistan*. Kabul, 1973.

Asiel, M. A. and G. Schmitt-Rink. *Aussenhandel und 'Terms of Trade' Afghanistans 1961-1975*. Studienverlag, Bochum, 1979.

Balland, D. "Une Nouvelle Generation d'Industries en Afghanistan. Contribution a l'Etude de l'Industrialisation du Tiers-monde," *Bulletin de la Societe Languedocienne de Geographie*. 7/1, 1973.

Buescher, H. and N. Assad and H. Berger. "Betriebswirschaftiche Probleme in Afghanischen Industrieunternehmen," *Afghanische Studien*. Anton Hain, 17, 1977.

Dorner, K. *Entwicklung und Entwicklungpolitik in Afghanistan.* Bochum, Germany, 1967.

Ekker, M. H. *Economic Aspects of Development in Afghanistan.* UN, 1952.

Fry, M. J. *Kabul and Kandahar Money Bazaars: their Role in Afghanistan Foreign Trade.* Kabul, USAID, 1973.

____. *The Afghan Economy: Money, Finance and the Critical Constraints to Economic Development.* E. J. Brill, Leiden, Netherlands, 1974.

____. *The Afghan Economy: Money, Finance and the Critical Constraints to Economic Development.* Kabul, USAID, 1973.

____. *The Financial Institutions of Afghanistan: Description and Analysis.* Kabul, USAID, 1973.

Guha, "Economic Development of Afghanistan, 1929-1961," *International Studies.* 6, 1965. Pp. 421-439.

____. "The Rise of Capitalistic Enterprises in Afghanistan, 1929-45," *Indian Economic and Social History Review.* 1, 1963. Pp. 145-176.

Hapgood, D. *Policies for Promoting Agricultural Development. Report of a Conference on Productivity and Innovation in Agriculture in the Underdeveloped Countries.* MIT, Cambridge, 1964.

Jensch, W. *Die Afghanischen Entwicklungsplane vom Ersten bis zum Dritten Plan.* Verlag Anton Hain, Meisenheim, Germany, 1973.

Kamrany, N. M. *Peaceful Competion in Afghanistan: American and Soviet Models for Economic Aid.* Communication Service Corp., Washington, DC, 1969.

Kanun, M. H. "The System of Taxation of Afghanistan in the Nineteenth Century," *Afghanistan.* 30/3, 1977. Pp. 1-26.

McChesney, R. D. "The Economic Reforms of Amir Abdur Rahman Khan," *Afghanistan.* 21/3, 1968. Pp. 11-34.

Monsawi, G. *Wirtschaftspolitische Chronik.* Köln, Germany, 1980.

Noorzoy, M. Siddieq. "Planning and Growth in Afghanistan," *World Development.* 4/9, 1976. Pp. 761-773.

____. "Alternative Economic Systems for Afghanistan," *International Journal of Middle East Studies.* 15, 1983.

Paul, A. "Constraints on Afghanistan's Economic Development and Prospects for the Future," *Asia*. 29, 1973. Pp. 1-15.

Picard, P. *A Chief Social and Economic Survey of the Central Provinces*. Ministry of Agriculture, Kabul, 1968.

Stilz, D. *Entwicklung und Struktur der Afghanisschen Industrie*. Verlag Anton Hain, Meisenheim, Germany, 1974.

United States Agency for International Development. *Afghanistan - Financial Development Committee Reports 1973*. Kabul, 1973.

Agriculture

Allen, R. H. *Agricultural Development in Afghanistan*. Nathan Associates, Kabul, 1965.

Amin, H. *Agricultural Geography of Afghanistan*. Kabul University, Kabul, 1974.

Arez, G. J. *The Pattern of Agriculture in Afghanistan*. Kabul University, Kabul, n.d.

Burns, R. H. *Helmand Valley and Research Programs*. Wyoming Team, Kabul, 1957.

Coleman, J. C. *Afghanistan: Helmand-Argandab Valley Project Executive Management*. USAID, Bost, Afghanistan, 1967.

Democratic Republic of Afghanistan. *The Democratic Land Reforms in Afghanistan: Full Action to Uproot Feudalism*. Kabul, n.d.

Gul, A. et al. *An Agronomic Survey in Six Eastern Provinces of Afghanistan*. Kabul, 1966.

International Cooperation Administration, et al. *Development of Afghan Agriculture*. Kabul, ICA, 1960.

Janata, A. "Landwirtschaftliche Struktur Afghanistan," *Bustan*. 3, 1963. Pp. 36-48.

Lateef, N. V. *Characteristics and Problems of Agriculture in Afghanistan*. Background Country Study, No. 5, Rome, 1957.

Lewis, R. H. *General Description of Afghanistan and Its Agriculture*. USAID, Kabul, n.d.

Ministry of Agriculture and Irrigation (Afghanistan). *First Five Year Plan of Ministry of Agriculture.* Kabul, 1957.

____. *Summary of Five Year Plan of Ministry of Agriculture, 1961-1966.* Kabul, 1961.

Ministry of Planning (Afghanistan). *Afghan Agriculture in Figures.* Kabul, 1978.

Schah-Zeidi, M. "Die Afghanische Agrarverfassung," *Bustan.* 8/3, 1967. Pp. 36-48.

Senzai, M. O. and R. K. Harlan. *Agri-facts: Report on Economic Survey of Agriculture in Nangarhar Province.* Kabul University, Kabul, 1965.

Stevens, I. M. and K. Tarzi. *Economics of Agricultural Production in Helmand Valley, Afghanistan.* U.S. Department of Interior, Bureau of Reclamation, Denver, 1965.

Stiller, F. K. "Die Landwirtschaft Afghanistans," *Der Diplomlandwirt.* 4, 1954. P. 76.

Mining and Minerals

"Afghanistan," *World Oil.* 157/3, 1967. Pp. 188-189.

"Afghanistan," *World Petroleum Report.* 1973, 1974, 1975.

Aurah, A. L. and A. Q. Majeed. "Case History of the Khwaja Gogerdak and Yatim Tagh Gas Fields of Northern Afghanistan," *3rd ECAFE Symposium on the Development of Petrol Resources in Asia and the Far East.* 3/43, 1965.

"(Barite Reserves in) Afghanistan," *World Minerals.* 29/8, 1976.

Bouladon J. and A. F. de Lapparent. "The Hajigak Iron Ore Deposit. Afghanistan Stratigraphic Position, Geological Environment and Paragenesis (Lower Paleozoic)," *Miner Deposita.* 10/1, 1975. Pp. 13-25.

Bruckl, K. "Die Minerallagerstaetten von Ost-Afghanistan; Versuch Einer Gliederung Nach Genetischen Gesichtspunkten," *Neues Jahrbuch fuer Mineralogie, Abhandlungen.* 72/1, 1936. Pp. 1-97.

Clapp, F. G. "Explorations in Iran and Afghanistan," *Oil Weekly.* 92/12, 1939. Pp. 71-72.

Fuchs, G. and A. Matura, O. Schermann. "Preliminary Report on Geological and Mineral Investigations in Nurestan, Afghanistan," *Verhandlungen der Geologischen Bundesanstalt*. 1, 1974. Pp. 9-23.

Furon, R. "Les Resources Minieres de l'Afghanistan," *Revue Scientifique*. 1924.

Hendrikson, K. H. *Industrial Survey, 1966/67 - 1969/70*. Ministry of Mines and Industries, Kabul, 1971.

Kinney, G. T. (Ed.) "Survey Finds Gas Prospects Good in N. Afghanistan," *Oil and Gas Journal*. 75/15, 1977. P. 40.

Kulke, H. "Die Lapislazuli-Lagerstaette Sare Sang (Badakhshan). Geologie, Entstehung, Kulturgeschichte und Bergbau," *Afghanistan Journal*. 3, 1976. 43-56.

Mazina, B. G. *Mineral Resources of Iran and Afghanistan*. Moscow, 1949.

McLean, P. "Time of Development of Processes of Oil-Gas Formation in Mesozoic and Paleogene Sediments of the Afghano-Tadzhik Oil-gas Region," *Petroleum Geology*. 12/7, 1975. 362-363.

Rossovskiy, L. N. and V. M. Chmyrev. "Distribution Patterns of Rare-Metal Pegmatites in the Hindu Kush (Afghanistan)," *International Geological Review*. 19/5, 1977. Pp. 511-520.

Rossovskiy, L. N., V. M. Chmyrev, and A.S. Salakh. "New Fields and Belts of Rare-Metal Pegmatites in the Hindu Kush (Eastern Afghanistan)," *International Geological Review*. 18, 1976. Pp. 1339-1342.

Shroder, John F. Jr. *The USSR and Afghanistan Mineral Resources*. Omaha, n.d.

Smith, G. I. *Potash and Other Evaporite Resources of Afghanistan*. U.S. Geological Survey, Washington DC, 75/89, 1975.

Weber, G. "Afghanistan (Petroleum Production Statistics)," *International Petroleum Encyclopaedia*. 10, 1977.

Williams, L. "Afghanistan Coal (Development)," *Mining Magazine*. London, 136/6, 1977. P. 509.

Woods, C. W. "Inland Exploration Co. Acquires all Afghanistan for Oil Search: Five Provinces to be Chosen Eventually. An Outline of the Concession Terms," *Petrol Times*. 38/967, July 24, 1937. Pp. 78-79 and 121-122.

Water

Auden, J. B. and A. E. Pallister. "Survey of Land and Water Resources," *Afghanistan.* 2/1 and 2/2, 1965.

Bruns, W. *Analysis of Water.* Kabul University, Kabul, 1950.

Field, N. C. "The Amu Darya: a Study in Resource Geography," *Geographical Review.* 44, 1954. 528-542.

Helmand River Delta Commission. *Report of the Helmand River Delta Commission; Afghanistan and Iran.* 1951.

Jentsch, C. "Die Kareze in Afghanistan," *Erdkunde.* 24/2, 1970. 112-120.

Proctor and Redfern International Ltd. *Water Supply, Sewage Drainage and Solid Waste Systems for Greater Kabul.* 3 vols. World Health Organization, Kabul. N.d.

Rathjens, C. "Das Hilmend-Projekt in Afghanistan," *Petermanns Geographische Mitteilungen.* 100, 1956.

Rawlinson, H. C. "Monograph on the Oxus," *Journal of the Royal Geographical Society.* 42, 1872.

World Health Organization. *Water Quality in Afghanistan.* WHO, 1972.

4. HISTORIC AND POLITICAL

Early Period to End of the Monarchy

Abdul Ghani, *A Brief Political History of Afghanistan.* Najaf Publishers, Lahore, Pakistan, 1989. Edited by Abdul Jaleel Nafji.

Adamec, Ludwig W. *Afghanistan 1900-1923: A Diplomatic History.* University of California Press, Berkeley, 1967.

____. *Afghanistan's Foreign Affairs to the Mid-Twentieth Century: Relations with the USSR, Germany, and Britain.* University of Arizona Press, Tucson, 1974.

____. *Biographical Dictionary of Contemporary Afghanistan.* ADEVA, Graz, Austria, 1987.

____. *Historical and Political Who's Who of Afghanistan.* ADEVA, Graz, Austria, 1975.

Alder, G. J. *British India's Northern Frontier 1865-95: A Study in Imperial Policy.* London, 1963.

Ali, Mohammed. *Afghanistan (The Mohammadzai Period). A Political History of the Country Since the Beginning of the Nineteenth Century with emphasis on its Foreign Relations.* Punjab Educational Press, Pakistan, 1959.

____. "The Battle of Maiwand," *Afghanistan.* 10/2, 1955. Pp. 26-38.

____. *A Cultural History of Afghanistan.* Punjab Educational Press, Lahore, Pakistan, 1964.

Anwar Khan, M. *England, Russia and Central Asia: a Study in Diplomacy, 1857-1878.* Peshawar, Pakistan, 1963.

Bennigsen, Alexandre. "Mullahs, Mujahidin and Soviet Muslims," *Problems of Communism.* 33, 1984.

Beveridge, A. S. *The Babar Nama.* Brill, Leyden, Netherlands, 1905.

Bosworth, C. E. *The Gaznavids: Their Empire in Afghanistan and Eastern Iran, 994-1040.* Edinburgh, 1963.

Broxup, Marie. "Afghanistan: The Last Thirty Years." A special issue of CEREDAF Conference papers, in *Central Asian Survey.* 1988.

Buescher, H. "Demokratisierung und Ansaetze zur Parteienbildung in Afghanistan," *Vierteljahresberichte.* 3942, 1970. Pp. 1-32.

Bunbury, N. L. *A Brief History of the Hazara Pioneers.* London, 1949.

Caroe, Olaf. *The Pathans, 550 BC - AD 1957.* Macmillan, London, 1958.

Castagne, Joseph A. "Notes sur la Politique Exterieure de l'Afghanistan Depuis 1919." *Revue du Monde Musulman.* 48, Paris, 1921, Pp. 1-75.

Curzon, G. N. *Russian in Central Asia in 1889, and the Anglo-Russian Question.* London, 1889.

Dupree, Louis. *Afghanistan.* Princeton University Press, Princeton, 1980.

Dupree, Louis and Linette Albert eds. *Afghanistan in the 1970s.* Praeger, New York, 1974.

Edwardes, Michael. *Playing the Great Game*. Hamish Hamilton, London, 1975.

Elliot, H. M. and Dowson, J. *History of Ghazni*. Calcutta, 1953.

Elphinstone, Mountstuart. *An Account of the Kingdom of Caubul, and its Dependencies in Persia, Tartary and India*. Longman, London, 1815.

Emadi, Hafizullah. *State, Revolution, and Superpowers in Afghanistan*. New York, 1990.

Ferrier, J. P. *History of the Afghans*. London, 1858.

Fletcher, Arnold. C. *Afghanistan: Highway of Conquest*. Cornell University Press, Ithaca, New York, 1965.

Fraser-Tytler, W. Kerr. *Afghanistan: A Study of Political Developments in Central and Southern Asia*. Oxford University Press, London, 1953.

Ghaus, Abdul Samad. *The Fall of Afghanistan*. Pergamon-Brassey, Washington, DC, 1988.

Ghobar, G. *Afghanistan dar Masir-i Tarikh*. Government Press, Kabul, 1968.

Grassmuck, George and Ludwig W. Adamec. *Afghanistan: Some New Approaches*. University of Michigan, Ann Arbor, 1969.

Gray, J. A. *My Residence at the Court of the Amir*. London, 1901.

Gregorian, Vartan. *The Emergence of Modern Afghanistan: Politics of Reform and Modernization, 1880-1946*. Stanford University Press, California, 1969.

Grevemeyer, Jan-Heeren. *Afghanistan*. Berlin, 1986.

____. "Bericht ueber die Afghanische Historiographie," in K. Rathjens, *Neue Forschungen in Afghanistan*. Opladen, 1981.

____. *Herrschaft, Raub und Gegenseitigkeit: Die Politische Geschichte Badakhschans*. Otto Harrassowitz, Wiesbaden, 1982.

Griffiths, John C. *Afghanistan*. Pall Mall Press, London, 1967.

Habberton, W. *Anglo-Russian Relations Concerning Afghanistan*. University of Illinois, Urbana, 1937.

Habibullah, Amir. *My Life from Brigand to King*. Sampsom Low, Marston & Co., London, n.d.

Harrison, Selig S. *In Afghanistan's Shadow: Baluch Nationalism and Soviet Temptations.* Carnegie Endowment for International Peace, Washington, DC, 1981.

Hauner, M. "The Soviet Threat to Afghanistan and India, 1938-40," *Modern Asian Studies.* 15/2, 1981. Pp. 287-309.

Heathcote, T. A. *The Afghan Wars, 1839-1919.* Osprey, London, 1980.

Jansson, Erland. *India, Pakistan or Pakhtunistan?* Almqvist, Uppsala, Sweden, 1981.

Kakar, M. Hasan. *Government and Society in Afghanistan: The Reign of Amir Abd al-Rahman Khan, 1880-1901.* University of Texas Press, Austin, 1979.

———. *Afghanistan: A Study in Internal Political Developments, 1880-1896.* Punjab Educational Press, Lahore, 1971.

Kaye, J. *History of the War in Afghanistan.* W.H. Allen, London, 3 vols. 1890.

Khan, Sultan Mahomed. *The Life of Abdur Rahman: Amir of Afghanistan.* John Murray, London, 1901.

Lal, M. M. *Life of Amir Dost Mohammad Khan of Kabul.* Oxford University Press, Oxford, 1979.

Lockhart, L. *The Fall of the Safavi Dynasty and the Afghan Occupation of Persia.* Cambridge University Press, Cambridge, 1958.

Maxwell, Leigh. *My God-Maiwand!* London, 1979.

McChesney, R. D. *Waqf in Central Asia: Four Hundred Years in the History of a Muslim Shrine, 1480-1889.* Princeton University Press, 1991.

McMunn, G. *Afghanistan from Darius to Amanullah.* G. Bell & Sons, London, 1929 and 1977.

Miller, Charles. *Khyber: British India's North West Frontier.* MacDonald & James, London, 1977.

Molesworth, George Noble. *Afghanistan 1919: an Account of Operations in the Third Afghan War.* Asia Publishing House, London, 1962.

Nawid, Senzil. "King Amanullah and the Afghan Ulama: Religious Response to Reform, 1919-1929." Ph.D. Disser. University of Arizona, 1978.

Nazaim, M. *The Life and Times of Sultan Mahmud of Ghazna*. London, 1931.

Newell, Richard S. *The Politics of Afghanistan*. Ithaca, Cornell University Press, 1972.

Pazhwak, Abdur Rahman. *Afghanistan (Ancient Aryana)*. Key Press, Hove, England, 1954.

____. *Pakhtunistan*. N.p., New Delhi, 1955.

Pennel, Theodore L. *Among the Wild Tribes of the Afghan Frontier*. Oxford University Press, London, 1927.

Poladi, Hassan. *The Hazaras*. N. p. 1989.

Poullada, Leon B. *Reform and Rebellion in Afghanistan, 1919-1929*. Cornell University Press, Ithaca, 1973.

Poulton, M. and R. Poulton. *L'Afghanistan*. Presses Universitaires de France, Paris, 1981.

Rubinstein, Alan Z. *Soviet Policy Toward Turkey, Iran and Afghanistan*. Praeger Special Studies, New York, 1982.

Sale, F. *A Journal of the Disasters in Afghanistan, 1841-1842*. John Murray, London, 1843.

Schinasi, M. *Afghanistan at the Beginning of the Twentieth Century. Nationalism and Journalism in Afghanistan. A Study of Seraj ul-Akhbar (1911-1918)*. Instituto Universario Orientali, Naples, 1979.

Shah, Iqbal Ali. *Afghanistan of the Afghans*. The Diamond Press, London, 1928.

Singh, G. *Ahmad Shah Durrani, Father of Modern Afghanistan*. Asia Publishing House, Bombay, 1959.

Singhal, D. P. *India and Afghanistan 1876-1907. A Study in Diplomatic Relations*. University of Queensland Press, Melbourne, 1963.

Stewart, Rhea Talley. *Fire in Afghanistan, 1914-1929*. Doubleday, New York, 1973.

Sykes, Sir P. *A History of Afghanistan*. AMS Press, New York, 1940.

Tabibi, Abdul Hakim. *Afghanistan: A Nation in Love With Freedom*. Igram Press, Cedar Rapids, 1985.

338

Tarn, W. W. *The Greeks in Bactria and India*. Cambridge University Press, Cambridge, 1951.

Trousdale, William. *War in Afghanistan, 1879-80*. Wayne State University Press, Detroit, 1985.

Van Dyk, Jere. *In Afghanistan: An American Odyssey*. New York, 1983.

Viollis, Andree. *Tourmente sur l'Afghanistan*. 1930.

Wheeler, S. *The Amir Abdur Rahman*. London, 1895.

Wilber, Donald N., ed. *Afghanistan*. New Haven, 1956.

Yapp, Malcolm E. *Strategies of British India: Britain, Iran, and Afghanistan, 1798-1850*. Oxford, 1980.

The Afghan Republic and War

Adamec, Ludwig. W. *Biographical Dictionary of Contemporary Afghanistan*. ADEVA, Graz, Austria, 1987.

Amstutz, J. Bruce. *Afghanistan: The First Five Years of Soviet Occupation*. Washington, DC, 1986.

Arnold, Anthony. *Afghanistan: The Soviet Invasion in Perspective*. Hoover Institution Press, Stanford, 1981.

——. *Afghanistan's Two-Party Communism: Parcham and Khalq*. Hoover Institution Press, Stanford, 1983.

Ashraf, Abdur Rahman. *Muhammad Zahir Shah: Payam-ha, Musahebe-ha, wa Bayanayi-ha Ishan dar Dehat-i Jehad*. (Muhammad Zahir Shah: His Messages, Interviews, Statements in the Decade of the Jehad), Bonn 1990.

Bennigsen, Alexandre and Marie Broxup. *The Islamic Threat to the Soviet State*. New York, 1983.

Bennigsen, Alexandre et al. *Afghanistan: Dix Annees Terribles, 1977-1987*. Paris, n.d.

Bernstein, Carl. "Arms for Afghanistan," *The New Republic*. 18 July 1981. Pp. 8-10.

Bonosky, Phillip. *Washington's Secret War Against Afghanistan*. New York, 1985.

Bradsher, Henry S. *Afghanistan and the Soviet Union*. Duke University Press, Durham, 1983.

____. "Afghanistan," *The Washington Quarterly*. 1984.

Brigot, Andre and Olivier Roy. *The War in Afghanistan*. New York, 1988.

Broxup, J. M. "The Soviets in Afghanistan: The Anatomy of a Takeover," *Central Asian Survey*. 1983.

Bucherer-Dietschi, Paul. *Afghanistan: Vom Koenigreich zur Sovietischen Invasion*. Liestal, 1985.

Centlivres, Pierre et al. *Afghanistan: La Colonisation Impossible*. Paris, 1984.

Central Asian Survey. *Children in War*. Geneva, n.d.

Chaliand, Gerard. *Report from Afghanistan*. Viking Press, New York, 1982.

Collins, Joseph J. *The Soviet Invasion of Afghanistan: A Study of the Use of Force in Soviet Foreign Policy*. Lexington, 1985.

____. "The Soviet Invasion of Afghanistan: Methods, Motives and Ramifications," *Naval War College Review*. 1980.

____. "Soviet Military Performance in Afghanistan: A Preliminary Assessment," *Comparative Strategy*. 1983.

Democratic Republic of Afghanistan. *Babrak Karmal's Speeches*. Kabul, 1980.

____. *Documents and Records of the National Conference of the People's Democratic Party of Afghanistan*. Kabul, 1982.

____. *Excerpts of Interviews and Speeches Delivered by Babrak Karmal*. Kabul, 1981.

____. *White Book: Foreign Policy Documents of the Democratic Republic of Afghanistan*. Kabul, 1981.

Deutsches Orient-Institut. *Afghanistan Seit dem Sturz der Monarchie*. Hamburg, 1981.

Dupree, Louis. "Afghanistan under the Khalq," *Problems of Communism*. 28, August 1979.

____. "The Democratic Republic of Afghanistan, 1979," *American Universities Field Staff Reports*. Asia, 32 1979. Pp. 11.

____. "Red Flag over Hindu Kush, Part I: Leftist Movements in Afghanistan," *American Universities Field Staff Reports.* Asia 44, 1979.

____. "Red Flag over Hindu Kush, Part II: The Accidental Coup, or Taraki in Blunderland," *American Universities Field Staff Reports.* Asia, 45, 1979.

____. "Red Flag over the Hindu Kush, Part III: Rhetoric and Reforms, or Promises!" *American Universities Field Staff Reports.* Asia 23, 1980.

____. "Red Flag over the Hinduskush, Part IV: Foreign Policy and Economy," *American Universities Field Staff Reports.* Asia, 27, 1980.

____. "Red Flag over the Hindu Kush, Part V and VI: Repressions, or Security Through Terror Purges," *American Universities Field Staff Reports.* Asia 28, 1980.

Duran, Khalid. *Islam und Politischer Extremismus.* Deutsches Orient Institut, Hamburg, 1985.

Es'haq, Mohammed. *Situation in the North of Afghanistan, 1987.* Peshawar, Pakistan, n.d.

Gall, Sandy. *Behind Russian Lines: An Afghan Journal.* The Bodley Head, London, 1983.

Gibbs, David. "Does the USSR Have a Grand Strategy? Reinterpreting the Invasion of Afghanistan," *Journal of Peace Research.* 21/4, Oslo, 1987.

____. "The Peasant as Counterrevolutionary: The Rural Origins of the Afghan Insurgency," *Studies in Comparative International Development.* 21/1, New Jersey, 1986.

Girardet, Edward R. *Afghanistan: The Soviet War.* New York, 1985.

Gille, Etienne and Sylvie Heslot. *Letters d'Afghanistan de Serge de Beaurecueil.* CEREDAF, Paris, n.d.

Goldman, Minton F. "Soviet Military Intervention in Afghanistan: Roots and Causes," *Polity.* Spring 1984.

Greussing, Kurt and Jan-Heeren Grevemeyer et al. *Revolution in Iran und Afghanistan.* Frankfurt am Main, 1980.

Grevemeyer, Jan-Heeren. "Religion, Ethnizitaet und Nationalismus im Afghanischen Widerstand," *Leviathan.* 13/1, 1985.

Guptas, Bhabani Sen. *Afghanistan.* London, 1986.

Halliday, Fred. "Afghanistan: A Revolution Consumes Itself," *The Nation*. 229, November 1979.

____. "The Revolution in Afghanistan," *New Left Review*. 112, 1978.

____. "War in Afghanistan," *New Left Review*. 119, 1980.

Harrison, Selig S. "Rough Plan Emerging for Afghan Peace," *Washington Quarterly*. 3, Summer 1980.

Hammond, Thomas T. *Red Flag over Afghanistan: The Communist Coup, the Soviet Invasion, and the Consequences*. Westview Press, Boulder, 1984.

Hauner, Milan and Robert L. Canfield. *Afghanistan and the Soviet Union*. Boulder, 1989.

Hyman, Anthony. *Afghanistan under Soviet Occupation*. St. Martin's Press, New York, 1982.

Kakar, Hasan. "The Fall of the Afghan Monarchy in 1973," *International Journal of Middle Eastern Studies*. 9/2, 1978. Pp. 195-224.

Kaplan, Robert D. *Soldiers of God: With the Mujahidin in Afghanistan*. Boston, 1990.

Khalilzad, Zalmay. "Soviet-Occupied Afghanistan," *Problems of Communism*. 29/6, 1980. Pp. 23-40.

Khurasani, Hamid. *Facts and Fiction: Human Rights in the Democratic Republic of Afghanistan*. Kabul, 1986.

Klass, Rosanne T. *Afghanistan: The Great Game Revisited*. Freedom House, New York, 1987.

Laber, Jeri and Barnett R. Rubin. *A Nation is Dying*. Evanstone, 1988.

Magnus, Ralph H. Ed. *Afghanistan Alternatives: Issues, Options, and Policies*. New Brunswick, 1985.

Majrooh, S. B. and S. M. Y. Elmi. *The Sovietization of Afghanistan*. Peshawar, n.d.

Male, Beverley. *Revolutionary Afghanistan: A Reappraisal*. St. Martin's Press, New York, 1982.

Malhuret, Claude. "Report from Afghanistan," *Foreign Affairs*. Winter 1983-1984.

Maprayil, Cyriac. *The Soviets and Afghanistan.* Cosmic Press, London, 1982.

Misra, K. P. *Afghanistan in Crisis.* Vikas Publishing House, New Delhi, 1980.

Monks, Alfred L. *The Soviet Invasion in Afghanistan.* American Enterprise Institute, Washington, DC, 1981.

Moorcraft, Paul L. "Bloody Standoff in Afghanistan," *Army.* April 1985.

Muhammad Daud, Sardar. *The Republic of Afghanistan: Statements, Messages, and Press Interviews of the National Leader and the Founder of the Republic.* Kabul, 1973.

Naby, Eden. "The Changing Role of Islam as a Unifying Force in Afghanistan," in Ali Banuazizi, *The State, Religion, and Ethnic Politics.* New York, 1986.

Nayar, Kuldip. *Report on Afghanistan.* Allied Publishers, New Delhi, 1980.

Newell, Nancy Peabody and Richard S. *The Struggle for Afghanistan.* Cornell University Press, Ithaca, 1981.

Nikolayev, Lev. *Afghanistan: Between the Past and the Future.* Moscow, 1986.

Picolyer. "Caravans on Moonless Nights: How the CIA Supports and Supplies the Anti-Soviet Guerrillas," *Time.* 11 June 1984.

Reshtia, Sayed Qassem. *The Price of Liberty: The Tragedy of Afghanistan.* Rome, 1984.

Roy, Olivier. *Islam and Resisance in Afghanistan.* Cambridge University Press, Cambridge, 1986.

Rubin, Barnett R. "The Fragmentation of Afghanistan," in *Foreign Affairs.* Winter, 1989-90.

Ryan, Nigel. *A Hitch or Two in Afghanistan: A Journey Behind Russian Lines.* London, 1983.

Saikal, Amin. "The Afghanistan Crisis: A Negotiated Settlement?" *The World Today.* November 1984.

Saikal, Amin and William Maley. *The Soviet Withdrawal from Afghanistan.* Cambridge University Press, Melbourne, 1989.

Samimy, S. M. *Hintergruende der Sovietischen Invasion in Afghanistan.* Bochum, Germany, 1981.

Shahrani, M. Nazif and Robert L. Canfield. Eds. *Revolutions and Rebellions in Afghanistan*. Institute of International Studies, University of California, Berkeley, 1984.

Shansab, Nasir. "The Struggle for Afghanistan," *Combat on Communist Territory*. Lake Bluff, Virginia, 1985.

Simons, Lewis M. "Standoff in Afghanistan," *The New Republic*. 187. August 1982.

"Special Issue on Afghanistan," *World Affairs*. 145/3, 1982-83.

Stahel, Albert A., Herrliberg and Paul Bucherer. *Afghanistan, 1984/85: Besetzung und Widerstand*. Liestal, Switzerland, 1985.

____. *Afghanistan, 1985/86: Besetzung und Kriegfuehrung der UdSSR*. Liestal, Switzerland, 1986

____. *Afghanistan, 1986/87: Internationale Strategische Lage und Sovietisierung Afghanistans*. Liestal, Switzerland, 1987.

____. *Afghanistan: 5 Jahre Widerstand und Kleinkrieg*. Liestal, Switzerland, n.d.

Vertzberger, Yaacov. "Afghanistan in China's Policy." *Problems of Communism*. 31 June 1982.

Vogel, Claudia and Michael Sagurna. *Der Freiheitskrieg in Afghanistan*. Bonn, 1984.

Wiegandt, Winfried F. *Afghanistan: Nicht aus Heiterem Himmel*. Zurich, 1980.

Zeray, Muhammad Saleh. "Afghanistan: the Beginning of a New Era," *World Marxist Review*. 22 January 1979.

5. JURIDICAL

Laws and Constitutions

Afghanistan. "The Flag Law in Afghanistan," *Afghanistan*. 27/1, 1974. Pp. 1-8.

Asia Society. *The Constitution of the Republic of Afghanistan*. Afghanistan Council, New York, 1977.

____. "Afghanistan: laws, statutes, etc., English Translation of some of the New Laws Promulgated by the Republic of Afghanistan," Afghanistan Council. 1975.

Beck, Sebastian. "Das Afghanische Strafgesetzbuch vom Jahre 1924 mit dem Zusatz vom Jahre 1925," *Die Welt des Islam*. 2/1-2, Berlin, 1928.

____. "Afghanistan: Das Hoechste Gericht," In Julius Magnus, *Die Hoechsten Gerichte der Welt*. Leipzig, 1929.

Brunner, Christopher. "New Afghan Laws Regarding Agriculture," *Afghanistan Council*, Occasional Paper 12, 1977.

Dari, Gholam M. *Huquq-i Famil dar Afghanistan.* (Family Law in Afghanistan) Kabul, 1971.

Dupree, Louis. "Constitutional Development and Cultural Change," *American Universities Field Staff Reports, Afghanistan*, 9/1-10. 1965.

Franklin Book Programs. *Draft of the New Constitution of Afghanistan.* Kabul, 1964.

Hager, P. "Compiled Translations of the Laws of Afghanistan," *United Nations Development Programme*. Kabul, 1975.

Haqqani, Abdul Karim. *Rahnama-yi Mu'amilat.* (Guide on Transactions) Kabul, 1348/1969.

Huququi, Walid A. *Judicial Organization in Afghanistan.* Kabul, 1971.

Kabul Times Publishing Company. *Law on Basic Administration.* Kabul, n.d.

Kamali, Muhammad H. *Law in Afghanistan.* Leiden, Netherlands, 1985.

Karimi, Ahmadullah. "The Constitution of Afghanistan," *Afghanistan*. 1/1, 1946.

Khan, Sultan Mahomed. *The Constitutions and Laws of Afghanistan.* London, 1900.

Libesny, Herbert J. "Judicial Systems in the Near and Middle East: Evolutionary Development and Islamic Revival," *The Middle East Journal*. 37/2, 1983.

Massoun, Gholam Sakhi. "Der Voelkerrechtliche Status von Afghanistan," Disser. Hamburg, 1960.

Parker, G. L. "Central Bank Law," (Preliminary Draft) Nathan Associates. Kabul, 1967.

Royal Government of Afghanistan, Ministry of Commerce. *Foreign and Domestic Private Investment Law*. Kabul, 1965.

United States Agency of International Development. *Commercial Law of Afghanistan*. USAID, Kabul, 1955.

United States Department of Labor. *Labor Law and Practice in Afghanistan*. Bureau of Labor Statistics, Washington, DC, 1969.

Weinbaum, Marvin G. "The Legislator as Intermediary: Integration of the Center and Periphery in Afghanistan," In Albert F. Eldridge, (Ed.) *Legislatures in Plural   Societies: The Search for Cohesion in National Development*. Durham, NC, 1977.

____. "Legal Elites in Afghan Society," *IJMES*. 12/1, 1980. Pp. 39-51.

Wilber, Donald N. "Commentary on the Constitution of Afghanistan of 1st October 1964," *Middle East Journal*. Spring, 1965.

Wiseman, H. Victor.   "The New Constitution of Afghanistan: Some Observations," *Parliamentary Affairs*. 18/4, 1965. Pp. 434-441.

Zhwand, Samiuddin. "The Judiciary," *The Kabul Times Annual*, 1967. Kabul, 1967.

6. SCIENTIFIC

Flora and Fauna

Aitchinson, J. F. T. "The Botany of the Afghan Delimitation Commission," *Transactions of the Linnean Society*. London, 1888.

Akhtar, S. A. "Ab-Istadeh, a Breeding-place of the Flamingo in Afghanistan," *Journal of the Bombay Natural History Society*. 47/2, 1947. Pp. 308-315.

Annandale, N. "Report on the Aquatic Fauna of Seistan," *Record of the Indian Museum*. Calcutta, 18, 1919-21. Pp. 1-24.

Balthazar, V. "Neue Spheciden aus Afghanistan (Opuscula Hymenopteralogica)," *Mitteilungen der Munchner Entomologischen Gesellschaft*. 47, 1957. Pp. 186-200.

Breckle, S. W. and W. Frey. "Die Vegetationsstufen in Zentralen Hindukusch," *Afghanistan Journal.* 1/3, 1974. Pp. 75-80.

_____, S. W. and W. Frey. "Afghanistanische Drogen und Ihre Stammpflanzen, 1. Seissholz," *Afghanistan Journal.* 6/3, 1979. Pp. 87-91.

_____, S. W. and W. Frey. "Botanical Literature of Afghanistan," *Edinburgh Royal Botanical Garden Notes.* 29/3, 1969. Pp. 357-372.

_____, S. W. and W. Frey. "Botanical Literature of Afghanistan: Supplement 1," *Edinburgh Royal Botanical Garden Notes.* 33/3, 1975. Pp. 503-521.

Cumming, J. W. N. "Birds of Seistan, Being a list of the Birds shot or seen in Seistan by the Arbitration Commission, 1903-1905," *Journal of the Bombay Natural History Society.* 1905. Pp. 686-699.

Dupree, L. "Note in the Distribution of the Indian Crested Porcupine," *Afghanistan Journal of Mammalogy.* 37/2, 1956. Pp. 299-300.

Eshghy, N. and M. K. Nushine. "Insecticide Resistance of Anopheles Culicifacies in the Province of Helmand, Southwest Afghanistan, 1976," *Mosquito News.* 38/1, 1978. Pp. 97-101.

Gaedike, R. "Austrian Entomological Expedition to Iran and Afghanistan, Contributions to the Lepidoptera Fauna," *Annalen de Naturhistorischen Musueums in Wien.* 72, 1968. Pp. 529-533.

Hassanyar, A. S. "Environmental Problems in Afghanistan," *Geographical Review of Afghanistan.* 12/2, 1973. Pp. 1, 9-17.

Hassinger, J. D. "A Survey of the Mammals of Afghanistan," *Feldiana Zoology.* 60, 1973. P. 195.

Hoogstraal, H. "Biological Patterns in the Afghanistan Tick Fauna," *Proceedings of the 3rd International Congress of Acarology.* Prague, 1971. Pp. 511-514.

Kitamura, S. *Flora in Afghanistan, Results of the Kyoto University Scientific Expedition to the Karakorum and Hindu Kush, 1955.* Kyoto University Press, Kyoto, 1960.

_____. *Plants of West Pakistan and Afghanistan, Committee of the Kyoto University Scientific Expedition to the Karakorum and Hindu Kush.* Kyoto University Press, Kyoto, 1964.

Kullmann, E. "The Mammals of Afghanistan," *Science Quarterly Journal.* 3, 1965. P. 20.

Leviton, A. E. "Report on a Collection of Reptiles from Afghanistan," *Proceedings of the California Academy of Sciences.* 29/12, 1959. Pp. 445-463.

Linchevsky, I. A. and A. V. Prozorovski. "The Basic Principles of the Distribution of the Vegetation of Afghanistan," *New Bulletin.* 2, 1949. Pp. 179-214.

Meyer-Oehme, D. "Die Saugetiere Afghanistans 3. Chiroptera," *Science Quarterly Journal.* 1965.

Millett, E. R. "Annual Reports, Regional Insect Control Project, Afghanistan," *USAID/USDA/ARS.* Kabul, 1960.

____. "Annual Reports, Summary of Insect Conditions in Afghanistan," *USAID.* Kabul, 1961.

____. "Insect Pests Identified from Afghanistan," *USDA and USNM Taxonomists.* Kabul, 1961.

Papp, L. "New Species and Records of Sphaeroceridae (Diptera) from Afghanistan," *Acta Zoologica.* 24/1-2, 1978. Pp. 149-168.

Rathjens, C. "Klimatische Jahreszeiten in Afghanistan," *Afghanistan Journal.* 1/1, 1974. Pp. 13-18.

____. "Vegetation and Flora of the Central Hindu Kush, Afghanistan," *Geographische Zeitschrift.* 69/2, 1981. P. 159.

Schneider, P. "Honigbienen und ihre Zucht in Afghanistan," *Afghanistan Journal.* 3, 1976. Pp. 101-104.

Vaurie, C. "A Revision of the Bird Family Dicruridae: Afghanistan," *American Museum of Natural History.* 93/4, 1949. Pp. 199-342.

Wendelbo, P. and J. Hedge. *Studies in the Flora of Afghanistan.* Arbok University, Bergen, Norway, 18, 1963. P. 56.

Geography

Adamec, Ludwig W. *Historical and Political Gazetteer of Afghanistan.* 6 vols. ADEVA, Graz, 1972-1985.

Ali, Muhammad. "Afghanistan's Mountains," *Afghanistan.* 8/1, 1953. Pp. 47-52.

____. *Guide to Afghanistan.* Northern Pakistan Publishing Co., Lahore, 1938.

Amin, Hamidullah and Gordon B. Schiltz. *A Geography of Afghanistan.* Center for Afghanistan Studies, Omaha, 1976.

Arez, G. J. "Geography of Afghanistan," *Kabul Times Annual.* 1970. Pp. 19-28.

____. "The Urban Structure of Kabul," *Geographical Review of Afghanistan.* 12/3, 1973. Pp. 1-19.

Balland, D. "Reflexions d'un Geograph sur une Decennie de Recherches Francaises en Afghanistan (1968-1978)," *Mission Scientifique, Afghanistan Bulletin.* 8, 1979. Pp. 3-21.

____. "Le Coton en Afghanistan: Essay d'Analyse Geographique et economique d'une Culture Industrielle dans une Pay Sous-Industrialise," *Revue Geographique de l'Est.* 13/1-2, 1973. Pp. 17-75.

Bellew, Henry W. *Journal of a Political Mission to Afghanistan, in 1857.* Smith, Elder & Co. London, 1862.

Brandenburg, D. *Herat: Eine Timuridische Hauptstadt.* ADEVA, Graz, Austria, 1977.

Burnes, A. *Kabool: Being a Personal Narrative of a Journey to, and Residence in that City, in the year 1836,7,8.* London, 1842; and ADEVA, Graz, Austria, 1975.

Dehmel, R. "Neue Stauseen in Afghanistan," *Geographische Rundschau.* 1953.

Diemberger, A. "Begsteiger Erschliessen den Hindukush," *Jahrbuch des Deutschen Alpenvereins*, 90, 1965.

Douglas, W. O. "West from the Khyber-Pass," *National Geographical Magazine.* 114, 1958.

Dupree, Louis. "Aq Kupruk: A Town in North Afghanistan," Part I: "The People and their Cultural Patterns." Part II: "The Political Structure and Commercial Patterns," *Universities Field Staff, South Asia Series.* X/9-10, 1966.

English, P. "The Traditional City of Herat, Afghanistan," Brown, L. C., *From Madina to Metropolis.* Princeton University Press, Princeton, NJ, 1973.

Fairchild, Inc. "Making of Afghanistan," *Afghanistan.* 3, 1960.

Field, Neil, C. "The Amu Daria: A Study in Resource Geography," *Geographical Review.* 44, 1954. Pp. 528-542.

Fischer, K. "Zur Lage von Kandahar an Landverbindungen zwischen Iran und Indien," *Bonner Jahrbuecher*. 167, 1967. Pp. 129-232.

Fischer, L. "Afghanistan eine Geographisch-Medizinische Landeskunde," *Medizinische Laenderkunde*. Springer Verlag, Berlin 1968.

Geokart. *National Atlas of the Democratic Republic of Afghanistan*. Warsaw, 1985.

Ghoubar, M. "Les Provinces Orientales de l'Afghanistan," *Afghanistan*. 2, 1947.

Glicken, Milton. "Making a Map of Afghanistan," *Photogrammetric Engineering*. 26/5, 1960.

Groetzbach, Erwin. *Afghanistan*. Darmstadt, Germany, 1990.

_____. *Aktuelle Probleme der Regionalentwicklung und Stadtgeographie Afghanistans*. Verlag Anton Hain, Meisenheim, Germany, 1976.

_____. "Kulturgeographische Wandel in Nordost-Afghanistan seit dem 19.Jahrhundert," *Afghanische Studien*. Verlag Anton Hain, Meisenheim, Germany, 4, 1974.

_____, *Staedte und Basare in Afghanistan*. Wiesbaden, Germany, 1979.

Gysel, Alfred. "Afghanistan-Klima und Landschaft," *Mitteilungen der Naturerforschenden Gesellschaft in Bern*. 9, 1952. Pp. 36-37.

Hahn, Helmut. "Geography in the Frame of the Social Sciences," *The Geographical Review of Afghanistan*. 1/2, 1962. Pp. 38-40.

_____. "Die Stadt Kabul (Afghanistan) und ihr Umland," I. "Gestaltwandel einer Orientalischen Stadt," and II. "Sozialstrukstur und Wirtschafliche Lage der Agrarbevoelkerung im Stadtumland," *Bonner Geographische Abhandlung*. Bonn, 1964, 1965.

Hasse, D. "Hindukusch: Allgemeiner Uberblick sowie Vorschlag fuer eine Begrenzung und Gliederung," *Osterreichische Alpenzeitung*. 83, 1965.

Humlum, J. *La Geographie de l'Afghanistan*. Scandianvian University Books, Kopenhagen-Stockholm-Oslo- Helsinki, 1959.

Jentsch, Ch. "Das Nomadentum in Afghanistan," *Afghanische Studien*. Verlag Anton Hain, Meisenheim, Germany, 9, 1973.

Kohzad, Ahmad Ali. "Nimruz ou le Bassin Inferieur de l'Hilmend," *Afghanistan*. 8/4, 1953.

Kohzad, Mohammad Nabi. "Kabul," *Afghanistan* 8/4-14/1, 1958-59. Pp 1-15.

Kushkaki, Burhanuddin. *Kataghan o Badakhsan*. French transl. Marguerite Reut, Edition du Centre National de la Recherche Scientifique, Paris, 1979.

Masson, Ch. *Narrative of Various Journeys in Balochistan, Afghanistan, and the Panjab*. London, 1842; ADEVA, Graz, Austria, 1975

Mattai, James. "A Geographical Introduction to Herat Province," *Kabul University*, Kabul, 1966.

Michaud, R. and S. Michaud. "Winter Caravan to the Roof of the World," *National Geographic Magazine*. April, 1972. Pp. 435-465.

____. *Caravans to Tartary*. Editions du Chene, Paris, 1978.

Michel, Aloys A. "The Kabul, Kunduz, and Helmand Valleys and the National Economy of Afghanistan," *National Academy of Sciences*. Washington, DC, 1959.

Niedermayer, O. V. *Afghanistan*. K. W. Hiersmann, Leipzig, 1924.

Rathjens, Carl. "Afghanistan," *Die Weltwirtschaft*. 2, 1957. Pp. 59-60.

____. "Der Afghanische Hindukusch," *Jahrbuch des Deutschen Alpenvereins*. 80, 1955.

____. "Erschliessung des Hindukusch," *Mitteilungen des Deutschen Alpenvereins*. 17, 1965. Pp. 8-10.

____. "Kabul die Hauptstadt Afghanistan," *Leben und Umwelt*. 13, 1957. Pp. 73-82.

____. "Landschaft und Mensch im Hindukusch," *The Geographical Review of Afghanistan*. 2, 1963. Pp. 1-12.

Reshtya, Sayed Qasim. "L'Afghanistan du Point de Vue Geographique," *Afghanistan*. 2/1, 1947. Pp. 16-22.

____. "The Rivers of Afghanistan," *Afghanistan*. 2/2 1943, Pp. 8-14.

Schurmann, H. F. *The Mongols of Western Afghanistan: An Ethnography of the Mongols and Related People of Afghanistan*. University of California, Berkeley, 1957.

Snoy, Peter. "Nuristan und Mungan," *Tribu*. 14, 1965. Pp. 101-148.

Szabo, Albert and Thomas J. Barfield. *Afghanistan: An Atlas of Indigenous Domestic Architecture*. Austin, 1991.

Thesiger, Wilfred. "A Journey in Nuristan," *Geographical Journal*. 123, 1957. Pp. 457-464.

Wiebe, D. "Die Raeumliche Gestalt der Alstadt von Kandahar: Ein Kulturgeographischer Beitrag zum Problem der Partiellen Modernisierung," *Afghanistan Journal*. 4, 1976. Pp. 132-146.

Geology

Afghanistan Geological Survey. *South Afghanistan, Sedimentary Basin Structure*. 1963. Pp. 198-200.

Clapp, F. G. "Geology of Afghanistan," *Bulletin of the Geological Society of America*. 50/12, 1939. P. 1904.

Desto, A. *Geology of Central Badakhshan, North East Afghanistan and Surrounding Countries*. Leiden, Netherlands, 1975.

Fuchs, G. and A. Matura. "The Geology of the Nilaw Area in Central Nurestan, Afghanistan," *Jahrbuch der Geologischen Bundesanst*. 119/2, 1976. Pp. 97-128.

Griesbach, C. L. "Afghan Field-Notes," *Records of the Geological Survey of India*. 18/1, 1885. Pp. 57-64.

____. "Geologische Notizen aus Afghanistan," *Verhandlungen der K.K. Geologischen Reichsanstalt*. 28, 1885. Pp. 314-315.

Hayden, H. H. "The Geology of Northern Afghanistan," *Memoirs of the Geological Survey of India*. 29/1, 1911.

Hunger, J. P. *Geological Survey in Afghanistan*. Kabul, 1964.

Lapparent, A. F. de. "La Montagne du Fer d'Hajigek en Afghanistan Central," *Afghanistan Journal*. 2/1, 1975. Pp. 8-11.

Popal, S. A. *Geologie von Afghanistan*. Ariana 1955.

Reed, F. R. C. "Upper Carboniferous Fossils from Afghanistan," *Palaeontologia Indica*. 1931. Pp. 1-39.

Schwab, M. *Establishment of a Geological Survey Department in Afghanistan*. UN Report, New York, 1955.

Wolfart, R. and H. Wittekindt. *Geologie von Afghanistan*. Berlin, 14, 1980.

Geomorphology

Balland, V. and J. Lang. "Les Rapports Geomorphologique Quarternaises et
    Actuels du Bassin de Banyan et de Ses Bordures Montagneuses," *Revue
    de Geographie Physique et de Geologie Dynamique*. 16/3, 1974. Pp. 327-
    350.

Burnes, A. "On the Reg-Ruwan or Moving Sand, a Singular Phenomenon of
    Sound Near Cabul," *Journal of the Asiatic Society of Bengal*. 7, 1838.
    Pp. 324-325.

Taniwal, Z. "La Region de Band-i-Amir: Etude de Geographie Physique,"
    Afghanistan. 31/4, 1979. Pp. 29-60.

Meteorology

British Embassy. *Weather Records for Kabul, 1942 through 1953*. Kabul, 1953.

Matthai, J. *Climate Statistics for Afghanistan*. Faculty of Education, Kabul
    University, Kabul, 1966.

Rathjens, C. "Hohe Tagessummen des Niederschlags in Afghanistan,"
    Afghanistan Journal. 5/1, 1978. 22-25.

Sivall, T. R. "The Problems of Meteorology in Afghanistan," *Geographical
    Review of Afghanistan*. 1/2, 1962. Pp. 16-21.

Stenz, E. "Precipitation, Evaporation and Aridity in Afghanistan," *Acta
    Geophysica Polonica*. 5, 1957. Pp. 245-266.

7. SOCIAL

Ethnography

Ali, Muhammad. *Manners and Customs of Afghans*. Punjab Education Press,
    Lahore, 1958.

Anderson, Jon. W. and Richard. F. Strand. "Ethnic Processes and Intergroup
    Relations in Contemporary Afghanistan," *The Afghanistan Council of the
    Asia Society*. 1978.

Bacon,E.E. "The Inquiry into the History of the Hazara Mongols of Afghanistan," *Southwestern Journal of Anthropology.* 7, 1951. Pp. 230-247.

Bellew, H. W. *A General Report on the Yusufzeis.* Lahore, India, 1864.

_____. *An Enquiry Into the Ethnography of Afghanistan Prepared for and Presented to the Ninth International Congress of Orientalists.* London, 1891; and ADEVA, Graz 1973.

Broguetti, Michele. *The Current Situation in Hazarajat.* Oxford, England, 1982.

Burnes, A. "On the Siah-posh Kafirs, With Specimens of their Language and Costume," *Journal of the Asiatic Society of Bengal.* 7, 1838. Pp. 325-333.

Centlivres, P. "La Contribution Francaise et Suisse a l'Ethnographie de l'Afghanistan Depuis la Seconde Guerre Mondial," *Central Asiatic Journal.* 16, 1972. Pp. 181-193.

Charpentier, C. J. *Bazaar-e Tashqurghan: Ethnographical Studies in an AfghanTraditional Bazaar.* Uppsala, Sweden, 1972.

Clifford, M. L. *The Land and People of Afghanistan.* Lippincott, 1973.

Dianous, H. J. de. "Hazaras and Mongols en Afghanistan," *Orient.* 19, 1961. Pp. 71-98.

Dupree, L. "Nuristan: (The Land of Light) seen darkly," *American Universities Field Staff Reports.* 15/16, 1971.

Edelberg, L. and S. Jones. *Nuristan.* ADEVA, Graz, Austria, 1979.

Ferdinand, K. "Ethnographical Notes on Chahar Aimaq, Hazara and Moghol," *Acta Orientalia.* 28/3-4, 1964. Pp. 175-203.

Fischel, W. J. "The Rediscovery of the Medieval Jewish Community at Firuzkuh in Central Afghanistan," *Journal of the American OrientalSociety.* 85, 1965.

Janata, A. "Die Afghanischen Sammlungen des Museums fuer Voelkerkunde in Wien," *Afghanistan Journal.* 1/1, 1974. Pp. 5-12.

_____. *Schmuck in Afghanistan.* ADEVA, Graz, Austria, 1980.

Kohzad, A. A. "The Panjsher," *Afghanistan.* 3/4, 1948. Pp. 17-29.

Orywal, Erwin. *Die Ethnischen Gruppen Afghanistans.* Ludwig Reichert Verlag, Wiesbaden, 1986.

Rao, A. "Qui Sont les Jat d'Afghanistan," *Afghanistan Journal*. 8/2, 1981. Pp. 55-65.

Raverty, H. G. "Indian, Afghan and Pathan Tribes," *Asiatic Quarterly Review*. 7, 1894.

____. "Kafiristan and the Kafiri Tribes," *Calcutta Review*. 1896.

Robertson, G. S. *The Kafirs of the Hindu Kush*. London, 1896; and Oxford University Press, London and New York, 1974.

Schurmann, H. F. *The Mongols of Western Afghanistan: an Ethnography of the Mongols and Related Peoples of Afghanistan*. University of California Press, Berkeley, 1957.

Shahrani, M. N. M. *The Kirghiz and Wakhi of Afghanistan: Adaptation to Closed Frontiers*. University of Washington Press, Seattle and London, 1979.

Wadud, A. *The Story of Swat*. Peshawar, Pakistan, 1963.

Anthropology

Anderson, Jon. "Tribe and Community Among the Ghilzai Pashtun. Preliminary Notes on Ethnographic Distribution and Variation in Eastern Afghanistan," *Anthropos*. 70, 1975. Pp. 575-601.

Barfield, T. J. *The Central Asian Arabs of Afghanistan*. University of Texas Press, Austin, 1981.

Bauer, W. P. and A. Janata. "Kosmetik, Schmuck und Symbolik in Afghanistan," *Archiv fuer Volkerkunde*. 28, 1975. Pp. 1-43.

Canfield, R. *Factions and Conversion: Study on the Hazara*. France, 1969.

____. "Hazara Integration into the Afghan Nation, some Changing Relations between Hazaras and Afghan Officials," *Asia Society*. New York, 1973.

Jones S. *An Outline of the Political Organization of the Kam Kafirs*. University of Edinburgh, Edinburgh, 1965.

____. *Men of Influence in Nuristan: a Study of Social Control and Dispute Settlement in Waigal Valley, Afghanistan*. Seminar Press, London, 1974.

Katz, David J. "Kafir to Afghan." UCLA Disser. Los Angeles, 1982.

Lentz, W. *Zeitrechnung in Nuristan und am Pamir.* ADEVA, Graz, Austria, 1978.

Spain, J. W. *The Way of the Pathans.* Hale, London, 1962.

Zadran, A. S. "Kinship, Family and Kinship Terminology," *Afghanistan Quarterly.* 33/2, 1960. Pp. 45-68.

Demography

American Universities Field Staff. *Population: Perspective 1973.* Freeman, Cooper & Co., California, 1973.

Amerkhail, N. "Family Planning in Afghanistan," *Population Review.* 1961.

Asia Society, Afghanistan Council. *Demographic Research in Afghanistan: a National Survey of the Settled Population.* New York, 1977.

Blanc, J. C. *L'Afghanistan et Ses Populations.* Presses Universitaires de France, Paris, 1976.

Dupree, L. "Population Review 1970: Afghanistan," *American Universities Field Staff Reports.* 15/1, 1971. P. 20.

Government of Afghanistan and United States Agency for International Development. *National Demographic and Family Guidance Survey of the Settled Population of Afghanistan.* 3 vols. New York and USAID, 1975. *A Provisional Gazetteer of Afghanistan.* 3 vols. Central Statistics Office, Kabul, 1975.

Hendrick P. *Infant and Early Childhood Mortality Survey: Protocol for Prospective Study in Kabul.* Ministry of Public Health, Kabul, 1973.

Institute of Social Studies. *Methodology of Population Censuses and Practical Problems in Afghanistan.* The Hague, 1970.

Langley, G. *Population: Family Planning.* Kabul, USAID, 1972.

Puffer, R. R. *Patterns of Mortality in Childhood. Report of the Inter-American Investigation of Mortality in Childhood.* Pan American Health Organization, Washington, 1973.

Trussel, J. and E. Brown. "A Close Look at the Demography of Afghanistan," *Demography.* 16/1, 1979. 137-156.

Education

Dupree, L. "The Afghan-American Education Commission," *American Universities Field Staff Reports*. 18/2, 1973.

____. "The Afghan-American Education Commission," *American Universities Field Staff Reports*. 18/2, 1974.

____. "Afghan Studies: an Overview , with Notes on Research, Institutional Activity and Bibliography," *American Universities Field Staff Reports*. 20/4, 1976.

Harris, F. *Public School Education in Afghanistan*. U.S. Operations Mission to Afghanistan, Kabul, n.d.

Hoelgaard, S. *Plan for Operation for Improvement of Primary Education in Afghanistan*. Kabul, UNICEF, 1974.

Martin, R. T. *Kabul University, its Role in Education, Research, and Public Service in Afghanistan*. University of Illinois, Kabul, 1959.

Ministry of Education (Afghanistan). *Education in Afghanistan During the Last Fifty Years*. Kabul, 1968.

____. *Education Statistics, Afghanistan: 1969, '70, '71, '72*. Kabul, 1969-72.

Natik, G. N. *Engineering Education in Afghanistan*. Kabul University, Kabul, 1972.

Ordyniec, J. *Women's Education in Afghanistan: Mission Oct.1967-March 1970*. UNESCO, 1970.

Rahel, S. *Monograph on Cultural Policy in Afghanistan*. UNESCO, Paris, 1975.

Rishtya, Sayyid Q. "Education in Afghanistan," *Afghanistan*. 1/1, 1946. Pp. 20-25.

Health

Care Medico. *Report on Afghanistan Nutrition Study Project*. AID, Kabul, 1970.

Clarke, J. A. K. *Nutritional Status in the Hazarajat*. Medical Assistance Program, Kabul, 1970.

Fischer, L. *Afghanistan: Eine Geographischmedizinische Landeskunde.*
Springer Verlag, Berlin, 1968.

____. "Volksmedizin in Afghanistan," *Afghanistan Journal.* 1/3, 1974. Pp. 15-
64.

Gobar, A. H. "Drug Abuse in Afghanistan," *Bulletin on Narcotics.* 28/2, 1976.
Pp. 1-11.

Helfenbein, S. and M. Higgins. *Afghanistan Nutrition Study Project.* Care
Medico, Final Report, n.d. Kabul.

O'Connor, R. W. *Managing Health Systems in Developing Areas: Experiences
from Afghanistan.* Lexington, 1980.

Prowi, T. T. *Foods and Nutrition in Afghanistan.* Kabul University, Kabul,
1962.

United States Agency for International Development. *A Health Survey of
Afghanistan.* Kabul, 1963.

Wakeham, P. *Annual Report of the Medical Assistance Program, Afghanistan
Project.* Kabul, 1972-1973.

Refugees

Steul, Willi and Wolfgang G. Beitz. *Hilfe Fuer Afghanistan.* Bonn 1981.

United Nations High Commissioner for Refugees, UNHCR Background
Reports: *Ghazni Province*, 1990; *Wardak Province*, 1990;
Laghman Province, 1989; *Logar Province*, 1989;
Kandahar Province, 1989; *Kunar Province*, 1989;
Paktia Province, 1989; *Paktika Province*, 1989.

Religion

Barry, M. "Afghanistan, Terre d'Islam," *Les Temps Modernes.* 408-409, 1980.
Pp. 29-52.

Canfield, R. L. *Faction and Conversion in a Plural Society: Religious
Alignments in the Hindu Kush.* Museum of Anthropology, University of
Michigan, Ann Arbor, 1973.

____. *Factions and Conversion: Study on the Hazara.* France, 1969.

____. *Suffering as a Religious Imperative in Afghanistan.* 9th International Congress of Anthropological and Ethnological Sciences, 1973.

Dupree, L. "Afghanistan, Islam in Politics: a Symposium," *Moslem World.* 56, 1966. Pp. 269-276.

____. "The Afghans Honor a Muslim Saint: Reprise," *American Universities Field Staff Reports.* 20/7, 1976. P. 12.

____. "Militant Islam and Traditional Warfare in Islamic South Asia," *American Universities Field Staff Reports.* 21, 1980. P. 12.

____. "Saint Cults in Afghanistan," *American Universities Field Staff Reports.* 20/1, 1976. P. 26.

Einzmann, H. "Religious Folk Tradition in Afghanistan, Pilgrimage and Veneration of Saints," *Islam in Southern Asia.* Heidelberg University, 1975. Pp. 61-63.

Farhadi, A. G. R. "Ibn Sina und Sufism," *Afghanistan Quarterly.* 33/2, 1980. Pp. 1-8.

Ghani, Ashraf. "Islam and State-building in a Tribal Society, Afghanistan 1880-1901," *Modern Asian Studies.* 12, 1978. Pp. 269-284.

____. "Disputes in a Court of Shariaa, Kunar Valley, Afghanistan, 1885-1890." *IJMES*, 15. 1983.

Ghobar, M. "Le Role de l'Afghanistan Dans la Civilisation Islamique," *Afghanistan.* 1/1, 1946. Pp. 27-34.

Jettmar, K. *Die Religionen des Hindukusch.* Kohlhammer, Stuttgart, 1975.

Kohzad, A. A. "L'Afghanistan au Point de Vue de la Religion," *Afghanistan.* 8/3, 1953. Pp. 1-17.

Majrouh, S. B. "The Message of a Sufi for the Modern World," *Afghanistan.* 29/3, 1976. Pp. 38-55.

Schimmel, A. "The Meaning of Prayer in Mawlana Jalaloddin Balkha's Work," *Afghanistan.* 23/3, 1974. Pp. 33-45.

Tabibi, A. H. "The great Mystics of Afghanistan," *Afghanistan.* 30/2, 1977. Pp. 25-39.

____. *Sufism in Afghanistan.* Kabul, 1977.

Utas, B. "Notes on Afghanistan. Sufi Orders and Khanaqahs," *Afghanistan Journal*. 7/2, 1980. Pp. 60-67.

_____. "Scholars, Saints and Sufis in Modern Afghanistan," *The Tragedy of Afghanistan*, eds. Bo Hultdt, Erland Jansson et al. London, 1988.

Wiebe, D. "Die Heutigen Kultstaetten in Afghanistan un Ihre Inwertsetzung fuer den Fremdenverkehr," *Afghanistan Journal*. 7/3, 1980. Pp. 97-108.

Wilber, D. N. "The Structure and Position of Islam in Afghanistan," *Middle East Journal*. 6/1, 1952. Pp. 41-48.

Sociology

Ahmed, A. S. *Social and Economic Change in Tribal Areas.* Oxford University Press, Karachi, 1977.

Anderson, J. "There are no Khans Anymore: Economic Development and Social Change in Tribal Afghanistan," *Middle East Journal*. 32/2, 1978. Pp. 167-183.

Boesen, I. W. "Women, Honour and Love: Some Aspects of the Pashtun Woman's Life in Eastern Afghanistan," *Afghanistan Journal*. 7/2, 1980. Pp. 50-59.

Buescher, H. *Die Industriearbeiter in Afghanistan: eine Studie zur Gesellschaftpolitischen Problematik Sozial Schwacher Bevolkerungsschichten in Entwicklungslaendern.* Verlag Anton Hain, Meisenheim, Germany, 1969.

Dupree, L. "Religion, Technology and Evolution: a Case Study of a Muslim Community," *Journal of Social Research*. 4, 1961. Pp. 341-354.

_____. "The Green and the Black: Social and Economic Aspects of a Coal Mine in Afghanistan," *American Universities Field Staff Reports*. 7/5, 1963. P. 30.

_____. "Tribalism, Religionism and National Oligarchy," *Expectant Peoples*. Ed. K. Silbert, New York, 1963. Pp. 41-76.

Ghani, A. "Continuity and Change in the Function of Pashtun Intellectuals," *Afghanistan*. 30/2, 1977. Pp. 40-53.

Jarring, G. "An Uzbek on his Native Town and its Circumstances," *Ethnos*. 4, 1939. Pp. 73-80.

Knabe, E. *Frauenemanzipation in Afghanistan.* Ein Empirischer Beitrag zur Untuchung von Soziokulturellem Wandel und Sozio-Kultureller Bestandigkeit. Verlag Anton Hain, Meisenheim, Germany, 1977.

Mormann, H. and E. Ploger. *Buskaschi in Afghanistan.* Bucher, Lucern and Frankfurt, 1978.

Sarwari, M. S. *Afghanistan Zwischen Tradition und Modernisierung.* H. Lang, Bern and Frankfurt, 1974.

Shalinsky, A. *Central Asian Emigres in Afghanistan: Problems of Religious and Ethnic Identity.* Afghanistan Council, Asia Society, New York, 19, 1979.

Strand, R. F. "The Changing Herding Economy of the Kom Nuristani," *Afghanistan Journal.* 2/4, 1975. Pp. 123-134.

Swinson, A. *North-West Frontier: People and Events, 1839-1947.* Hutchinson, London, 1967.

Nomads

Besters, H. H. and K. H. Kraus. "Nomadismus als Entwicklungproblem," *Bochumer Symposium.* Bielefeld, 1969.

Centlivres, P. and M. Centlivres-Demont. "Chemins d'Ete, Chemins d'Hiver Entre Darwaz et Qataghan," *Afghanistan Journal.* 4/4, 1977. Pp. 155-163.

Dakshieyger, G. F. *Settlement and Traditional Social Institutions of the Former Nomads (on the Example of the Kazakh People),* 9th International Congress of Anthropological and Ethnological Sciences, 1973.

Ferdinand, K. *Aspects of the Relations Between Nomads and Settled Populations in Afghanistan.* Seventh International Congress of Anthropological and Ethnological Studies, Moscow, 1964.

____. *Nomad Expansion in Central Afghanistan: A Sketch of Some Modern Trends.* Aarhus, 1962. Also *Folk.* 4, 1962. Pp. 123-159.

____. "Nomadism in Afghanistan with an Appendix on Milk Products," *Viehwirtschaft und Hirt Kultur.* Ed. L. Forder, Budapest, 1969. Pp. 127-160.

____. "Ost-Afghanischer Nomadismusein Beitrag zur Anpassungsfahigkeit der Nomaden," *Nomadismus als Entwicklungsproblem.* 1969. Pp. 107-128.

Glatzer, B. *Nomaden von Gharjistan: Aspekte der Wirtschaftlichen, Sozialen und Politischen Organisation Nomadischer Durrani- Paschtunen in Nordwestafghanistan.* F. Steiner, Wiesbaden, 1977.

Jentsch, C. *Das Nomadentum in Afghanistan.* Verlag Anton Hain, Meisenheim, 1973.

____. "Structural Changes of Nomadism in Afghanistan," *Geographical Review of Afghanistan.* 7/2, 1969. Pp. 8-13.

____. "Die Wirtschaftlichen und Politischen Aspekte des Nomadentums in Zentralasien. Besonders die Jungste Entwicklung Afghanistan," *National Schweizerische UNESCO - Kommission.* (Eds.), Seminar Uber das Nomadentum in Zentralasien (Afghanistan, Iran, USSR), Schlussbericht Bern, 1976. Pp. 45-57.

Kraus, R. W. H. "Siedlungsprojekte in der Provinz Helmand (Afghanistan) unter Besonderer Berucksichtigung Gesiedelter Nomaden," *Vierteljahresberichte.* 46, 1971. Pp. 419-432.

Majruh, S. B. "Aktuelle Fragen des Nomadismus in Afghanistan," *Nomadismus als Entwicklungsproblem.* 1969. Pp. 155-160.

Pedersen, G. "Socio-economic Change Among a Group of East Afghan Nomads," *Afghanistan Journal.* 8/4, 1981. Pp. 115-122.

Renesse, E. A. von and H. C. G. Sponeck. "Nomadismus in Afghanistan als soziookonomisches Problem," *Nomadismus als Entwicklungsproblem.* 1969. Pp. 161-170.

____. "Nomadism in Afghanistan," *Nomadismus als Entwicklungsproblem.* 1969. Pp. 173-182.

Robinson, J. A. *Notes on Nomad Tribes of Eastern Afghanistan.* Nisa Traders, Quetta, Pakistan, 1978.

Shahrani, M. N. M. *Kirghiz Pastoral Nomads of the Afghan Pamirs: A Study in Ecological and Intra-Cultural Adaptation.* Seattle, 1976.

Singer, A. "Problems of Pastoralism in the Afghan Pamirs," *Asian Affairs.* 63, 1976. Pp. 156-160.

Strand, R. F. "The Changing Herding Economy of the Kom Nuristani," *Afghanistan Journal.* 2/4, 1975. Pp. 123-134.

Tapper, N. "Pashtun Nomad Women in Afghanistan," *Asian Affairs.* 64/2, Pp. 163-170.

APPENDIX

WATAN PARTY

President of Watan and the ROA   Najibullah

Executive Body Vice Presidents

Sulaiman Layeq
Farid Ahmad Mazdak
Najmuddin Kawyani
Nazar Muhammad

Members

Raz Muhammad Paktin
Sultan Ali Keshtmand
Abdul Wakil
Ghulam Faruq Yaqubi
Muhammad Aslam Watanjar
Muhammad Rafi'i
Mahmud Baryalai
Nur Ahmad Nur

Central Council,
    Executive Body

Sayyid Akram Peigir
Abdul Quddus Ghorbandi

Members

Adina Sangin	Khalil Kargar
Ahmad Nabi	Khial Muhammad Katawazi
Asadullah Habib	Dastagir
Asadullah Payam	Sultanjan Shafa
Auraq Dehqan	Sarfaraz Monand
Ahmad Bashir Ruigar	Sarwar Mangal
Babrak Karmal	Sadat Gul Ahangar
Burhanuddin Ghiasi	Sayyid Basir Manawi
Taza Khan Weyal	Sayyid Nasim Maihanparast
Jamila Palwasha	Sayyid Tahir Shah Paikargar
Jangul Karkar	Sayyid Azam Sa'id
Habib Mangal	Sayyid Hamidullah Rogh
Hisamuddin Hisam	Shah Muhammad Dost
Hashmatullah Kaihani	Shah Wali
Khudaidad	Shafiqullah Toda'i
Basharmal	Shir Agha Srishk
Khwaja Zamiruddin	Shir Bahadur

Shaikh Muhammad Bawar
Shirjan Mazduryar
Abdul Baqi
Abdul Razzaq Asmar
Abdul Rahim
Abdullah Bahar
Abdullah Spangar
Abdul Wahid Farahi
Abdul Majid Sarbiland
Abdul Haq Ulumi
Abdul Hamid Mohtat
Abdul Rahim Pahlawan
Abdul Rashid Waziri
Ata Muhammad Sarkanai
Abdul Rauf Begi
Abdul Satar Mokamel
Abdul Satar Razim
Abdul Satar Purdili
Abdul Shokur Khushachin
Abdul Wasi Kargar
Abdul Qayyum Nurzai
Abdul Qayyum Qawim
Abdul Fayaz Mehrayin
Abdul Ghani Hadafmand
Abdul Ratah
Abdul Samad Azhar
Abdul Samad Poya
Abdul Zuhur Razmju
Abdul Karim Misaq
Abdul Mobayen Mobin
Abdul Rashid Dostum
Ghulam Sarwar Yurish
Ghulam Faruq
Ghulam Qadir Miakhel
Ghulam Mustafa
Fazl Ahmad Toghyan
Faqir Muhammad Wadan
Fahim Ada
Faizullah Zaki
Faizullah Albarz
Gul Muhammad Kushan
Guldost Sangar Khel
Manukai Mangal
Muhammad Ismail Danesh
Muhammad Afzal Lodin
Muhammad Ihsan Wasil
Muhammad Asif Nabard
Muhammad Asif Delawar

Muhammad Anwar Isar
Muhammad Israel Rasi
Muhammad Anwar Hasil
Muhammad Ishaq Tokhi
Muhammad Ibrahim
Muhammad Ibrahim Kawush
Muhammd Bashir Layeq
Muhammad Juma Asak
Muhammad Hasan Bareq-Shafi'i
Muhammad Paiman
Muhammad Husain Halali
Muhammad Hakim Mangal
Muhammad Hakim Malyar
Muhammad Hasan Sepahi
Muhammad Khan Sepahi
Muhammad Daud Razmyar
Muhammad Sharif
Muhammad Siddiq Kawhun
Muhammad Muafaq
Muhammad Zahir Tanin
Muhammad Zahir Hatam
Muhammad Zahir Sulamal
Muhammad Arif Sakhra
Muhammad Azim Zurmati
Muhammad Alim
Muhammd Ewaz Nabizada
Muhammad Qasim
Muhammad Kasim Malwan
Muhammad Nabi Azimi
Muhammad Wali
Gen. Muhammad Wali
Muhammad Yasin
Muhammad Yunus
Miftahuddin Safi
Mir Afghan Bawari
Mir Abdul Karim Baha
Mir Abdullah
Lt. Col. Muhd. Mustafa
Muhammad Masum Sarbaz
Momin
Nurullah
Najibullah Ajand
Nurulhaq Ulumi
Nizamuddin Tahzib
Nafas Jahid
Nematullah
Yar Muhammad

Alternate Members

Ibrahim Ahmadzai
Ahmad Ali
Asadullah Keshtmand
Imamuddin
Amir Muhammad
Babrak Shinwari
Baqir Farin
Barat Dihqan
Soraya
Janbaz
Jura Beg Danishmal
Habib Shah
Hazratullah Hamgar
Hamidullah Siddiqi
Khuda-i Nur Bawar
Khalil Zalmai
Dad Ali Nairo
Daud Kawyan
Rahmatullah Hamdard
Ruhafza Kargar
Ramazan
Ramazan Kohistani
Rajab
Sayim
Sakhi Marjan
Sayyid Amir Shah Zara
Shah Mahmud Paiwastun
Salahuddin
Abdul Ahad Mohmand
Abdul Baqi
Abdul Basir Ranjbar
Abdul Jamil Nuristani
Abdul Hai Muram
Abdul Khaliq
Abdul Sam'i Ghafari
Abdul Kabir Ranjbar
Abdul Samad Qayyumi
Abdul Karim
Abdul Mutalib
Abdul Wahab Raz
Ali Asghar Paiman
Ghulam Sakhi Kargar
Ghulam Faruq Pasdar
Ghulam Mustafa
Fazl Ahmad

Faqir Muhammd Faqir
Muhammad Aslam
Muhammd Shirin Afzali
Muqim Paikar
Muhammad Hashim
Meraj
Mir Abdullah
Nabi Shurida
Nazir Ahmad Maihanpur
Najiba Arash
Najibullah Fayez
Wali Muhd. Rukhshani
Wais Muhd. Dehmal
Yazi Qilich

Supervisory Board of Watan

President
Sayyid Basir Manawi

First Vice Pres.
Abdul Ahad

Vice President
Abdul Samad

Members

Ahmadullah Poya
Bibi Shirin
Prit Paul Singh
Jamal
Hayatullah Emal
Khudai Nazar Sarmuchar
Salam Dehqan
Sohaila Siddiq
Saleh Muhammad Piruz
Zia Dastur
Abdul
Abdul Rahman
Abdul Sabur Nabard
Abdul Aziz Saghari
Abdul Qadir

Ali Gul Pawand
Qutbuddin Sharafmal
Lajward Kargar
Muhd. Daud Mazyar
Muhammad Salim Jarmal
Muhd. Husain Karwan
Muhammad Sadiq
Muhammd Azim Rahi
Muhammad Gul
Muhammad Isa Rasid
Mahram Ali
Mastura Emal
Najib Arya
Yunus Akbari

Membership as of July 1990.

PRINCIPAL MUHAMMADZAI FAMILIES

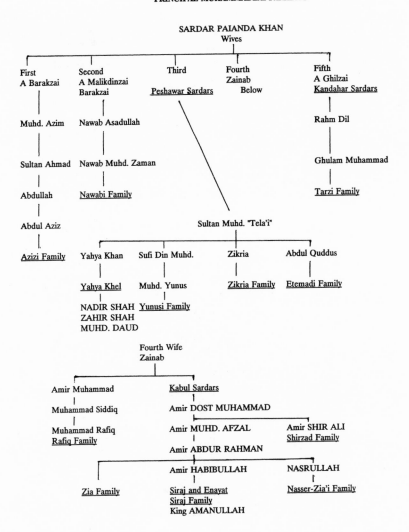

SARDAR PAIANDA KHAN
Wives

| First
A Barakzai | Second
A Malikdinzai
Barakzai | Third
Peshawar Sardars | Fourth
Zainab
Below | Fifth
A Ghilzai
Kandahar Sardars |

Muhd. Azim   Nawab Asadullah   Rahm Dil

Sultan Ahmad   Nawab Muhd. Zaman   Ghulam Muhammad

Abdullah   Nawabi Family   Tarzi Family

Abdul Aziz

Azizi Family

Sultan Muhd. "Tela'i"

| Yahya Khan | Sufi Din Muhd. | Zikria | Abdul Quddus |

Yahya Khel   Muhd. Yunus   Zikria Family   Etemadi Family

NADIR SHAH   Yunusi Family
ZAHIR SHAH
MUHD. DAUD

Fourth Wife
Zainab

Amir Muhammad   Kabul Sardars

Muhammad Siddiq   Amir DOST MUHAMMAD

Muhammad Rafiq   Amir MUHD. AFZAL   Amir SHIR ALI
Rafiq Family   Shirzad Family

                     Amir ABDUR RAHMAN

                     Amir HABIBULLAH   NASRULLAH

Zia Family   Siraj and Enayat   Nasser-Zia'i Family
                     Siraj Family
                     King AMANULLAH

TRIBAL TABLE OF GHILZAIS

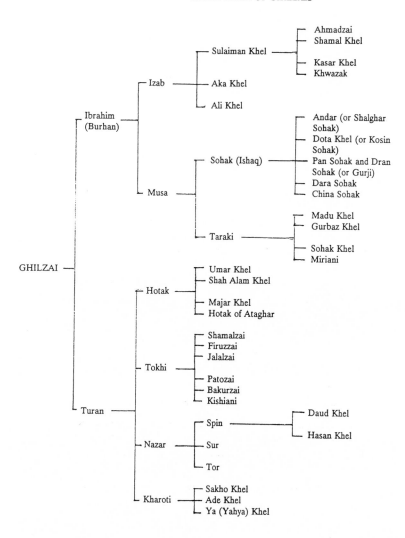

(Robinson, 1934)

HAZARAS

Clan		Division	Settlement
1.	Jaghuri	Musa Oki Baba Pashi Kalandar Shardakh Nidam Pate Daud Anguri Muhammad Khwaja Ajubini Ata Marka Bak Chaksayi	Near Ghazni
2.	Oruzgani	Dechepo Sultan Ahmad Nukroz Shira Bainto Beruz Chulkur Mianshi Shaikha (Shaikh Ali?) Chora Kimsi	North of Ghazni
3.	Dezinghi	Dai Kundi Dai Mirdad Dechopat (Dai Chopan?) Daizangi	North of Kabul & near Herat
4.	Behsud	Darwish Ali Bul Hasan Daulat Pai Jirgai	North of Kabul
5.	Polada	Polad (Fulad?) Oruzgan Daira	Between Dezinghi & Behsud & Jaghori
6.	Daya		
7.	Zauli		(Ridgeway, 1910)

HAZARAS

Besud

1. Daulat Bai
2. Darwish Ali
3. Isam (or Yasam) Timur
4. Mizah
5. Nauruz
6. Kaptasum
7. Bul Hasan
8. Burjigai
9. Jirghai
10. Ramuz
11. Damardah

Dai Zangi

1. Bacha Ghulam
2. Neka
3. Yangur
4. Sehpai
5. Takana

Dai Kundi

1. Daulat Beg
2. Jami
3. Urdu Shah
4. Alak
5. Moshun
6. Baibogha
7. Jasha
8. Haidar Beg
9. Kaum-i Ali
10. Taristan
11. Saran
12. Khudi
13. Chaush
14. Mamaka
15. Mir Hazar
16. Barat
17. Khushak
18. Sargin
19. Tajiks

Independent Hazara

1. Jirghai Usi Muhammad
2. Dayah
3. Zaoli
4. Faoladi (Fuladi)
5. Sultan Ahmad
6. Uruzgan
7. Kalandar
8. Kolian
9. Dai Chopan (or Khatai, or Babali)
10. Dai Zangi

Jaghatu	1.	Aludani
	2.	Islam
	3.	Kataghan
	4.	Shakha
	5.	Kimlut
	6.	Ilias
	7.	Biat
	8.	Khwaja Miri
	9.	Kari Suf
	10.	Aishghi
	11.	Farash
	12.	Laghri
	13.	Karghani
	14.	Ahmada
	15.	Mixed
Jaghuri	1.	Izdari
	2.	Hajibini
	3.	Geri (Geru)
	4.	Maska
	5.	Kalandar
	6.	Sherdagh
	7.	Pashe
	8.	Mir
Shaikh Ali	1.	Karam Ali
	2.	Dai Kalan
	3.	Naiman
	4.	Karluk (Kalluk)
	5.	Ali Jam
	6.	Babar
	7.	Nekpai
Darghan Hazara	1.	Shekha
	2.	Shakh
	3.	Gudi
	4.	Khida
	5.	Karkadam
	6.	Ahingaran
	7.	Thakarachi
	8.	Khwaja Jama

(According to P. J. Maitland in 1888.)

372

GAILANI (GILANI) FAMILY

The Gailani clan of Qadiri pirs was established in Afghanistan with Sayyid
Hasan Gailani, the son of Sayyid Ali Gailani, son of Salman Gailani,
descendant of Shaikh Abdul Qadir Gailani, a descendant of Imam Hasan,
son of Imam Ali, son of Abi Talib.

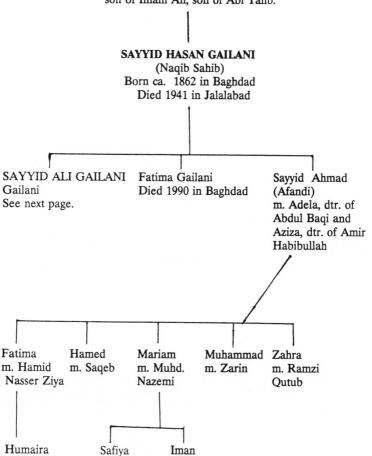

SAYYID HASAN GAILANI
(Naqib Sahib)
Born ca. 1862 in Baghdad
Died 1941 in Jalalabad

SAYYID ALI GAILANI   Fatima Gailani   Sayyid Ahmad
Gailani   Died 1990 in Baghdad   (Afandi)
See next page.   m. Adela, dtr. of
                                        Abdul Baqi and
                                        Aziza, dtr. of Amir
                                        Habibullah

Fatima   Hamed   Mariam   Muhammad Zahra
m. Hamid m. Saqeb m. Muhd. m. Zarin m. Ramzi
Nasser Ziya   Nazemi   Qutub

Humaira   Safiya   Iman

Gailani - Table 1

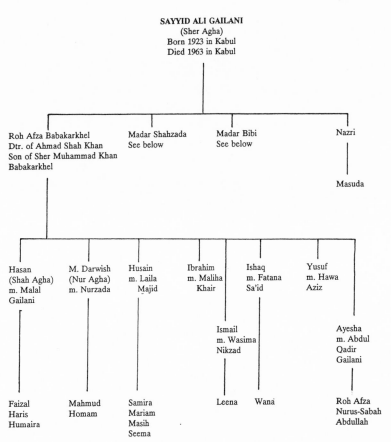

SAYYID ALI GAILANI
(Sher Agha)
Born 1923 in Kabul
Died 1963 in Kabul

Gailani - Table 2

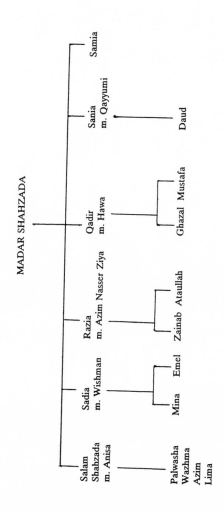

MADAR SHAHZADA

Salam Shahzada m. Anisa — Sadia m. Wishman — Razia m. Azim Nasser Ziya — Qadir m. Hawa — Sania m. Qayyumi — Samia

Palwasha Wazhma Azim Lima

Mina Emel

Zainab Ataullah

Ghazal Mustafa

Daud

Gailani - Table 3